# Stitching Magic

Coral Moss and Wendy Sysouphat

First edition, 2020

ISBN 978-0-6487265-1-7

NATIONAL LIBRARY OF AUSTRALIA

A catalogue record for this book is available from the National Library of Australia

For any enquiries or comments, please contact:

**Wendy Sysouphat**
E: wendy_sysouphat@internode.on.net
W: www.wendysysouphatgallery.com

For Inspiration and Creativity

# Contents

## Stitches, designs, and project ideas 39

# Welcome to the amazing world of stitching!

Be captivated by the exquisite charm of embroidery and join us in this exciting endeavour!

## With stitching you can:

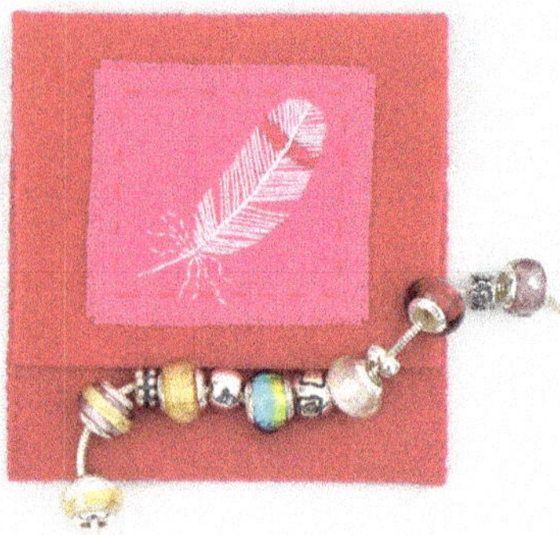

**Feature a patch**
*Fluttering Feather Jewel Purse*

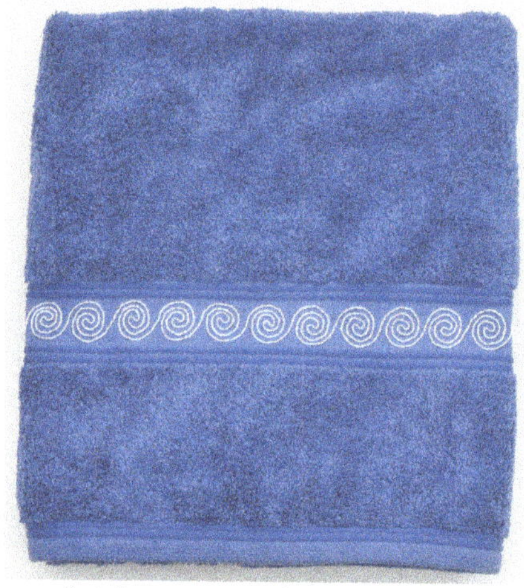

**Add some unique details**
*Seaspray Bath Towel*

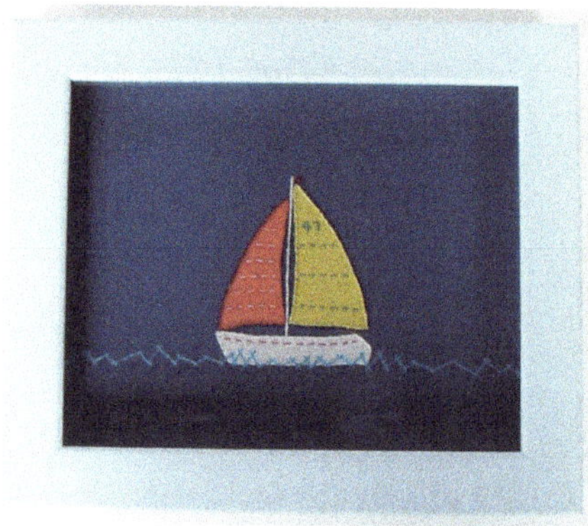

**Create an artwork**
*Sail Away Framed Picture*

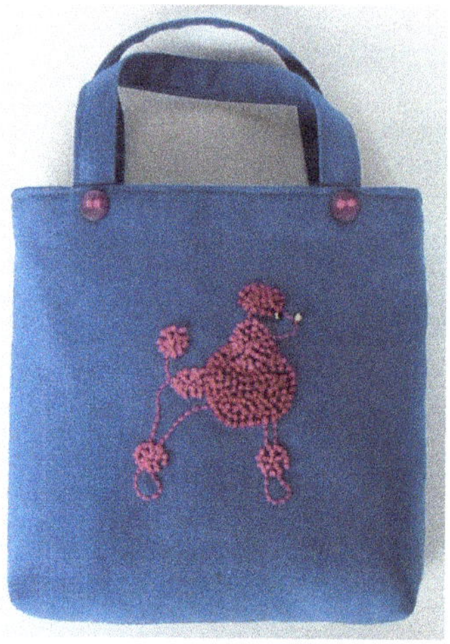

**Make an attractive bag**
*Pompom Poodle Handbag*

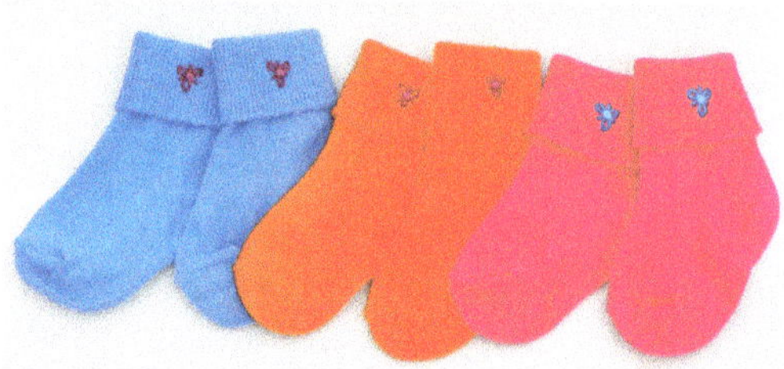

**Give exceptional gifts**
*Flower Socks*

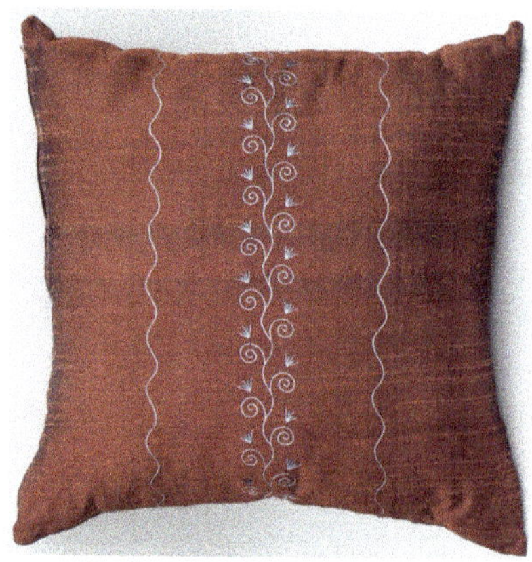

**Relax with a cushion**
*Moonlit Forest Cushion Cover*

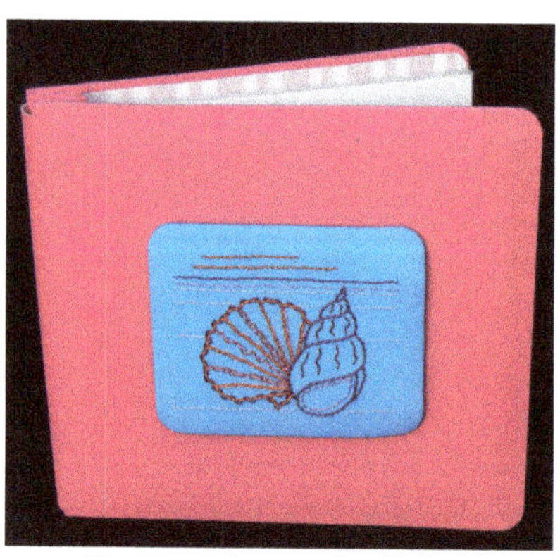

**Remember a holiday**
*Sunset Beach Album Cover*

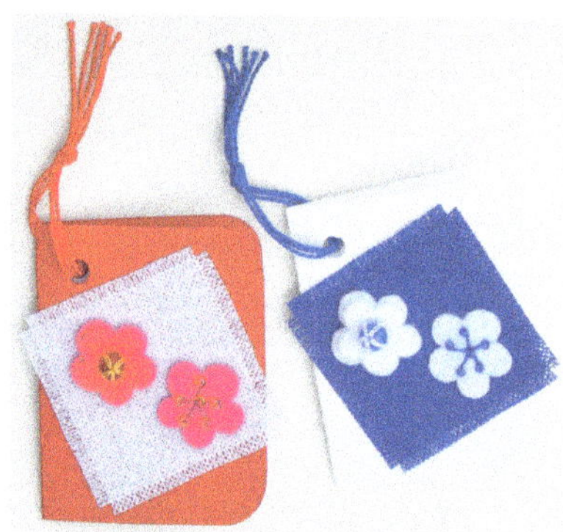

**Send special messages**
*Rose Essence Gift Cards*

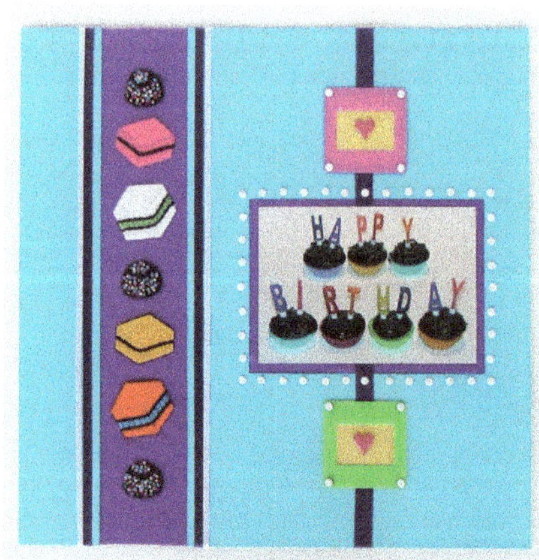


**Add charm to a scrapbooked page**
*Liquorice Allsorts Scrapbooking Decoration*

# About this book

Stitching is a wonderfully varied and versatile creative art, with spectacular qualities of design, colour, texture, and detail. This book presents a selection of easy stitches that are worked by hand. It explains how to use them to create an immense range of stitched works. The book has been designed for maximum enjoyment and stress-free ease of use for people with a variety of skill levels in embroidery. It is suitable for the absolute beginner learning to stitch for the very first time, right through to experienced embroiderers who may like to add some refreshing new ideas to their repertoires.

*Stitching Magic* is an information book, an instruction manual, and a resource for design ideas, helpful advice, and hints. It has been created as a multi-purpose approach to learning the art of embroidery. Readers may simply look through the pages until they find a design that appeals to them, and then the complete instructions for stitching that item can easily be followed. The text will refer the reader to help elsewhere in the book as required. Alternatively, readers can use this book as a comprehensive embroidery text book that can be systematically worked through from beginning to end as a structured, easy-to-follow course.

An original, fresh new approach to learning the gentle and expressive art of hand embroidery is here at last!

## Useful information

In this section of the book, the reader is introduced to useful information about fabrics, threads, needles and other items, and about how to use patterns and transfer them to the fabric, how to back the fabric, how to flatten a stitched work once it is completed, and how to prepare a stitched work for framing.

## The stitches and techniques

This book features the following stitches and techniques: straight stitch, running stitch, back stitch, stem stitch, herringbone stitch, blanket stitch, fly stitch, chain stitch, French knot, couching, appliqué, and beading, including several variations and alternative methods. These have been carefully selected for their versatility and their ability to give delightfully effective results.

Each stitch chapter begins with information about the stitch, supported by a stitched sampler. Following each sampler, there are complete step-by-step illustrated instructions for working each stitch and its variations, both right-handed and left-handed.

## The designs

In each of the stitch chapters, there are six designs that showcase the featured stitch or technique. A full size pattern and complete instructions are both provided for working every design. The text will refer you to help elsewhere in the book as required for any other stitches used in each design. All of the designs in this book are of a similar size.

## Design categories

There are essentially six categories of designs: animals, flowers, foods, vehicles and built items, hearts and natural phenomena, and lastly gardens and forests. There is one of each of these for every stitch, with the result that there are twelve animals, twelve flowers, twelve food items, and so on. A stitcher could choose to work sets of designs, for example children's clothing or cushion covers featuring all of the animals or all of the flowers, or perhaps a set of pictures featuring all of the foods, vehicles, or gardens.

## Individual style

As with any other art form, embroidery is a pursuit within which each person can develop their own unique style. The designs in this book will look impressive whether they are stitched ultra-neatly or with a more sketchy, free approach. Relax and stitch however you wish. Hand embroidery displays a natural variation, giving each stitcher's work particular appeal and character!

The book emphasizes each stitcher's individuality. You may choose to work the embroideries simply as shown in the book, or you may decide to branch out into alternative choices with respect to the designs and project ideas as well as the stitching style.

## The project ideas

Each design is accompanied by a project idea that demonstrates how the design could be worked on an item such as a cushion cover or a T-shirt, or on fabric that is then constructed into a work such as a handbag, a wall hanging, or a sachet. In addition, the designs have been created in such a way that many of them can be worked interchangeably on the other projects throughout the book.

## The colours

The variety of designs and project ideas throughout the book illustrate how colours can be used effectively in a range of ways. Experimentation with alternative colour schemes is encouraged as this can greatly expand the creative possibilities of embroidery.

## The index

An index is provided at the back of the book for easy reference.

# Useful information

# Designs

## Using the designs

The designs in this book can be worked on squares of fabric, for example to be presented in picture frames, or as part of a quilt, or they can be worked into the project ideas that accompany each of them. As the designs are all approximately the same size, many of them can be used interchangeably on any of the projects throughout the book. Many of the designs are made up of smaller elements that can be isolated and stitched separately or grouped in different ways.

The following options can be considered:

**Same design on different projects**
The same design could be worked on a variety of projects.

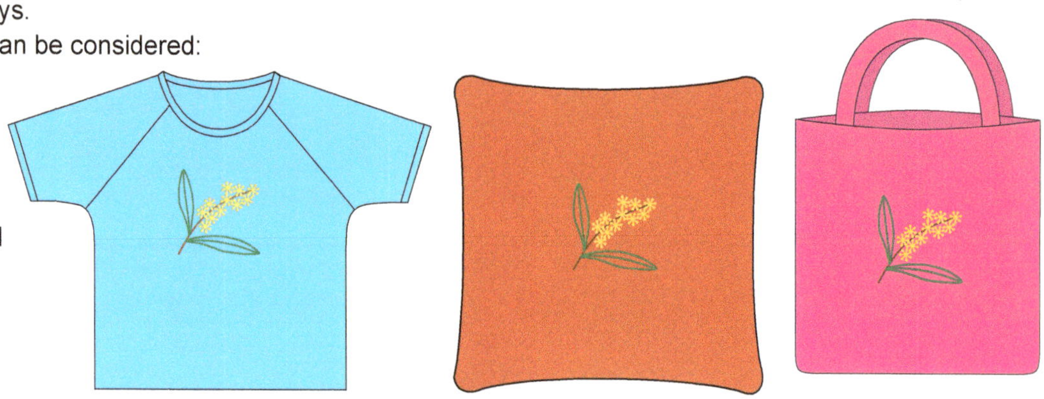

**Combining designs on one project**
Designs from a similar subject category could be worked together on one project, such as the many animals featured on the quilt shown in the first example. Small elements could be selected from more than one design and worked together, as on the two cushions shown in the second example.

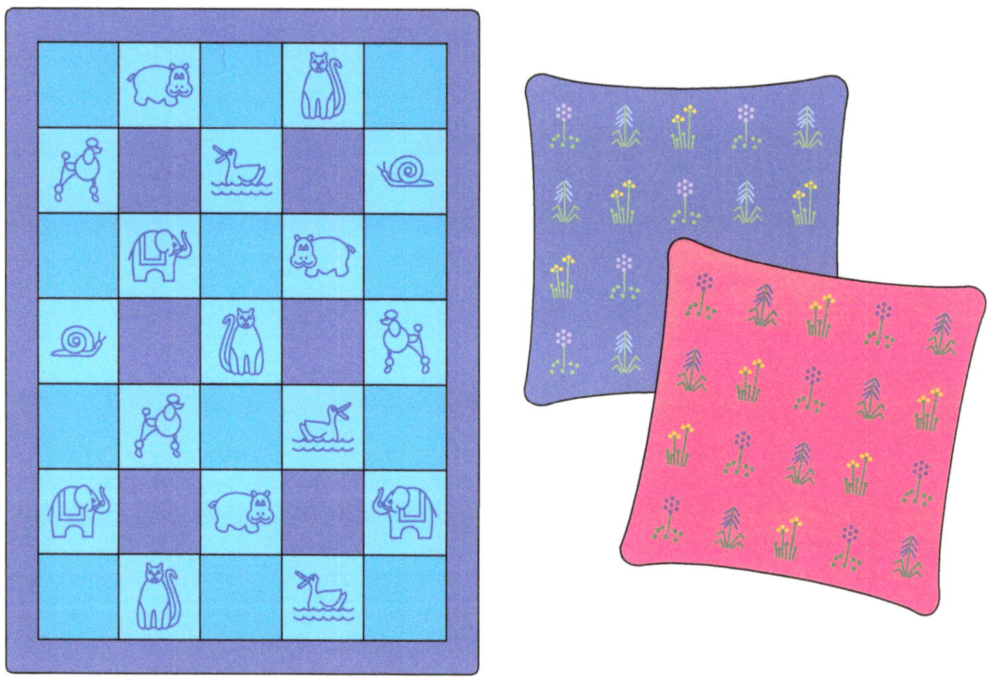

**Themed series of projects**
A themed series could be worked using a number of designs selected from one subject category, for example the food items shown here.

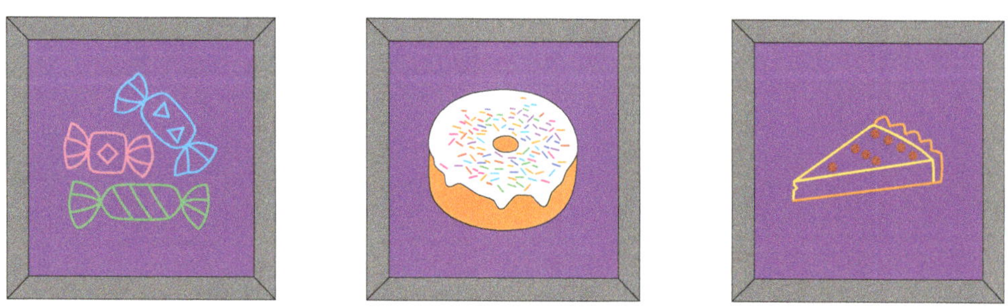

**Placing a design**
By changing the placement of a design, an entirely different effect can be achieved. A design can be placed centrally, as shown in the first example, or off-centre, as shown in the second. A design can also be repeated and scattered randomly, as shown in the third example.

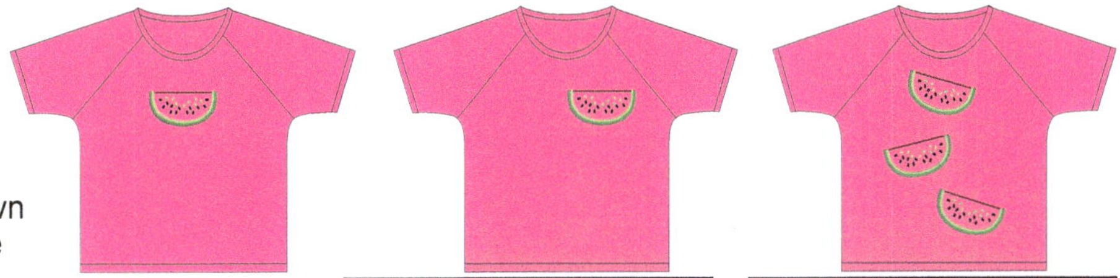

**Changing the size**
In the first example the design has been worked in its original size. The second example shows the design worked at a larger and a smaller scale. When worked at a larger scale, the design becomes more dramatic and when worked at a smaller scale, it becomes more delicate.

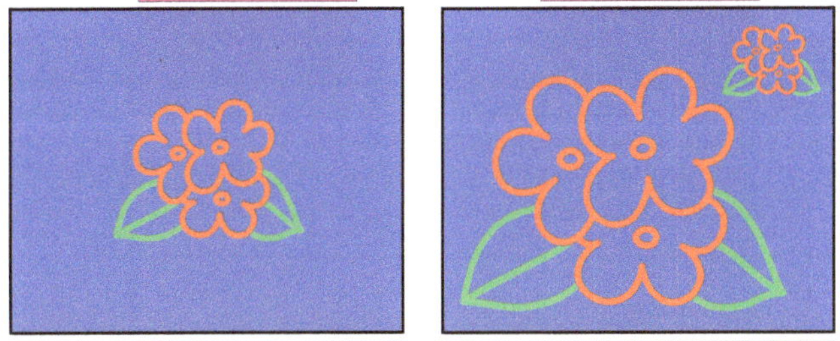

**Mirroring a design**
A design may be more suitable if it faces in the opposite direction. The original design, shown in the first example, can be reversed. The original design and the mirrored design are shown in the second example.

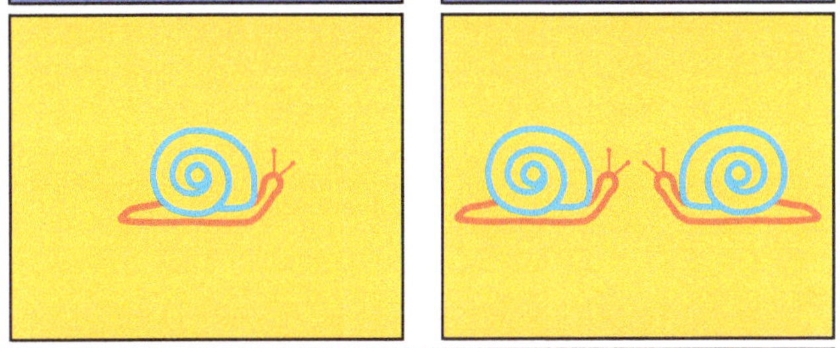

**Design repeated in a row**
A design can create a different impact when worked in a row. The original design, shown on the left, can be repeated as a row, as shown on the right.

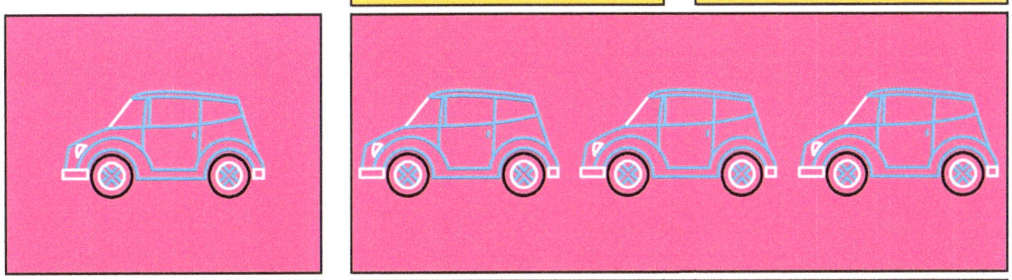

**Design repeated continuously in a row**
Some designs, such as this one on the left, have been created so that they join when repeated, as shown on the right. The joined designs flow continuously along the row. This can be worked as a border or a strip.

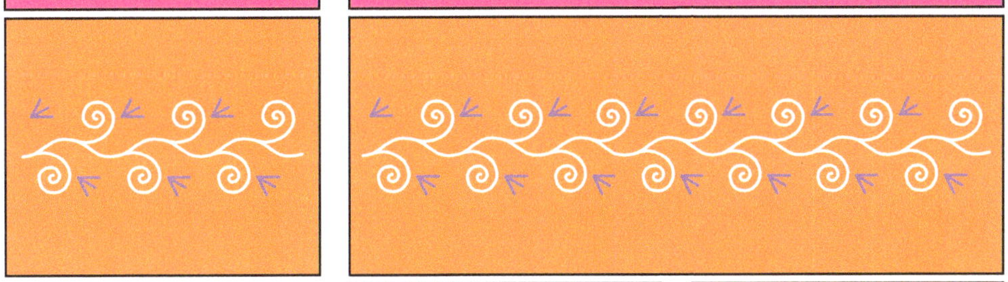

**Isolating an element**
A single element can be isolated from a design, such as this plant that is indicated by the dashed line. It can then be worked separately, as shown on the right.

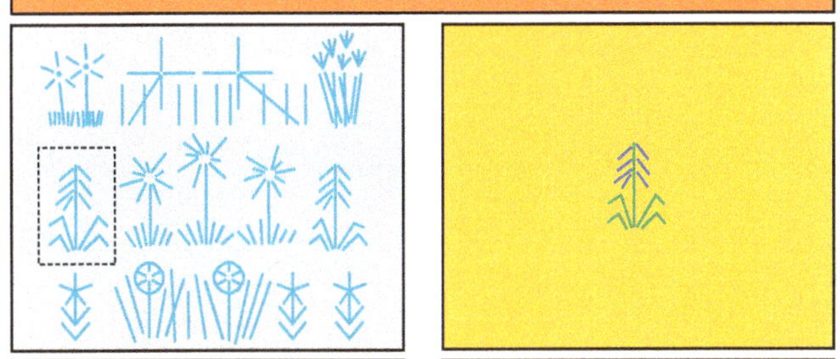

**Isolated element in a row or scattered**
From the garden design above, an isolated element can be worked in a row, as shown in the first example. The second example shows the same isolated element, this time scattered.

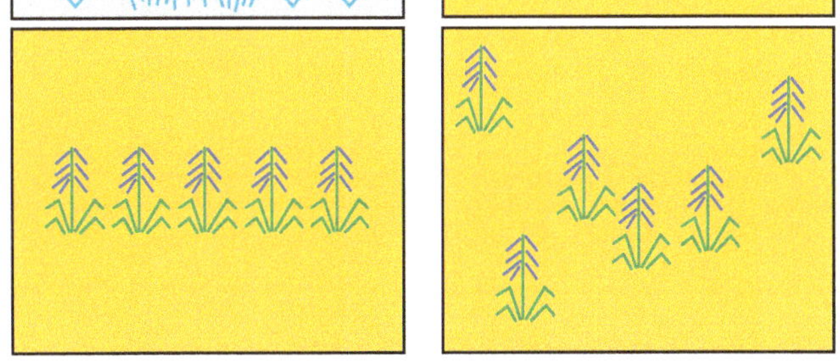

# Colours

## Varying the colours

The designs in this book feature different combinations of a range of bright colours. They can be stitched in the colours as suggested, or the colours can be interchanged. Alternatively, you can experiment with entirely new colour schemes.

Different combinations of fabric and thread colour can greatly affect the overall appearance of a work. When selecting colours, it often helps to drape some lengths of thread across pieces of fabric to see which combinations of colours look best together.

Be aware that not everyone sees colours in exactly the same way, and preferences for colours and colour schemes are very much an individual choice.

The following information may be helpful when selecting new colour schemes.

## Understanding colour

Inspiration for colours and combinations can be found everywhere. As an excellent resource, an artist's colour wheel, which illustrates the colours in a sequence, can be useful when selecting a colour scheme. For example, colours that are opposite each other on the colour wheel can be highly contrasting and dramatic when used in an artwork. Colours next to each other on the colour wheel can produce a more subtle colour scheme.

Within each colour there can also be a great deal of variation. Any colour may be of light, medium, or dark shades. It may also be bright or subdued, shiny or dull. Metallic colours such as gold and silver have a highly reflective appearance, adding another dimension.

The selection of different combinations of colours can create works that range widely in mood, for example some combinations are warm while others are cool, some are lively while others are peaceful.

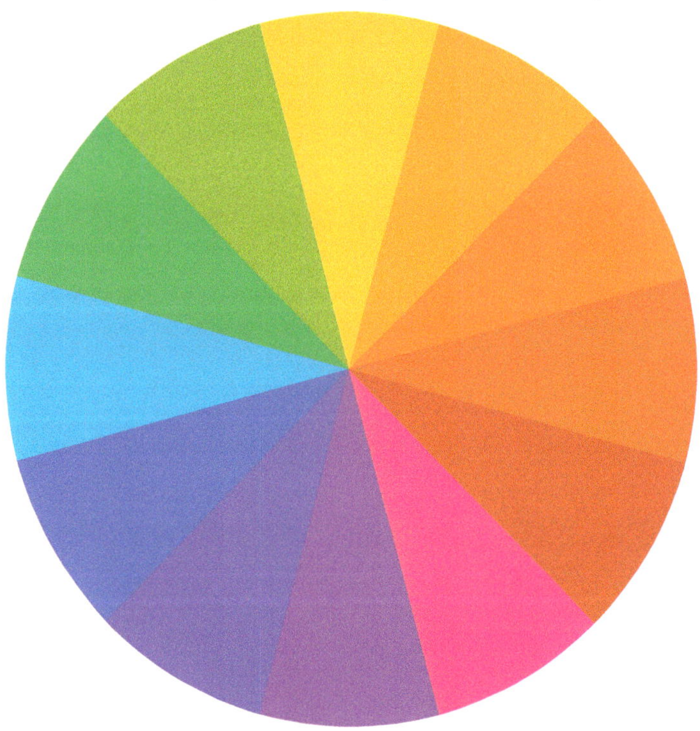

**An artist's colour wheel**

**Highly and less contrasting colours**
Colours on opposite sides of the colour wheel contrast highly, creating a vibrant colour scheme, as shown in the first example. Colours closer to each other on the colour wheel create a less contrasting, more subtle colour scheme as shown in the second.

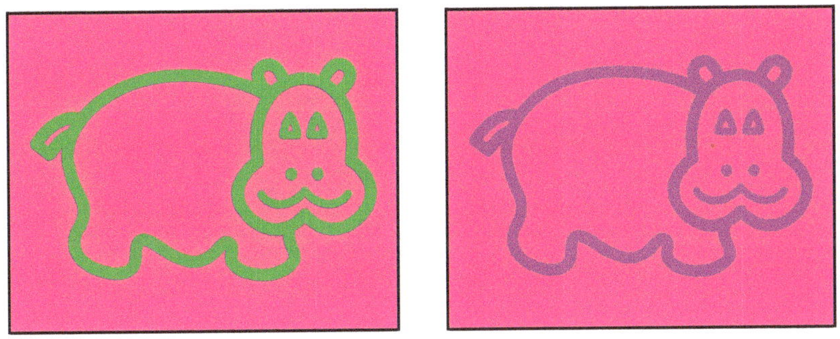

**Proportions of colours**
In the first example, a large shape on a background creates a bold, powerful work with a lot of drama. In the second, the same shape at a smaller scale, with a larger proportion of the background, creates a different look. The small shape becomes a focal point.

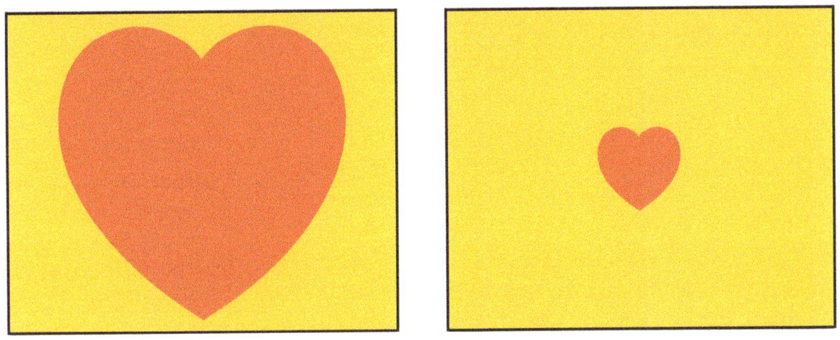

**Reversing colours**
The colours of the first design have been reversed for the second, creating a different effect.

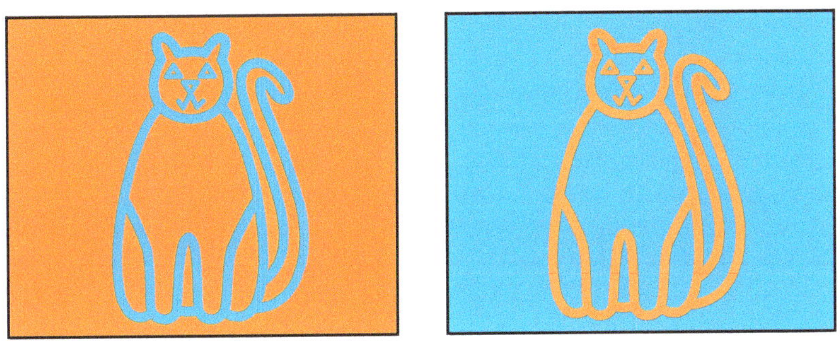

**Shades of one colour**
The first example shows a design featuring two shades of one colour. The second shows a more complex colour scheme, using four shades of one colour, creating more depth.

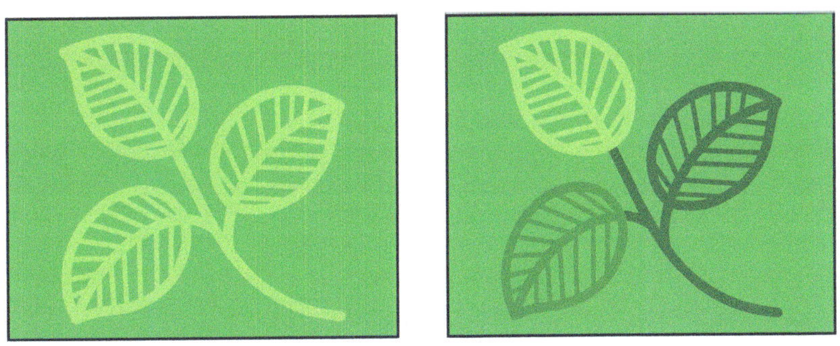

**Multi-coloured or white**
As shown in the first example, the parts of a multi-coloured design will show up differently depending on the background selected. In the second example, a design worked entirely in white on a dark background will show up dramatically.

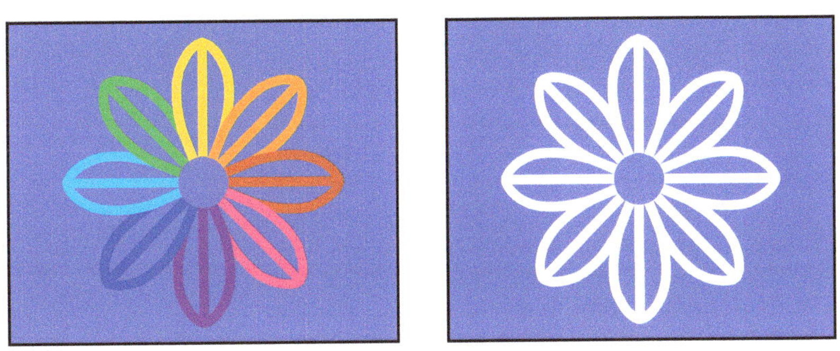

# Fabric

## Choosing the fabric

Choosing the most suitable fabric for a stitched work is important. It should complement the stitched design, but not overshadow it. Some textured and patterned fabrics may be quite dominant when used as a background, whereas plain fabrics may allow the stitching to be more easily seen.

Fabrics differ in type and thickness of fibres, as well as in weave, colour, and handling and wearing qualities. For a stitched work, the fabric needs to be of a weight that will support the stitches without it being pulled out of shape. If the fabric is very thick or tightly woven, it may be difficult to pass a threaded needle through it. If the fabric is very loosely woven, the stitches may sink into the fabric and therefore be difficult to see, or the stitches may distort the fabric.

When choosing the colour of the fabric, consider whether the colours in the design should contrast with the fabric or be more similar. The effects created can vary widely.

Fabrics range from those that have two very different surfaces, through to those that appear the same on both sides. For example, some fabrics differ greatly in colour and texture on their two surfaces while others do not. When creating a stitched work on fabric, be aware of which surface you will be using as the visible side, or front of the work, which is referred to as the right side of the fabric. The other surface is therefore the unseen side, or back of the fabric, which is referred to as the wrong side of the fabric.

### Fabrics for the designs and projects

The brightly coloured fabrics used for the designs in this book are medium weight cotton, in a plain weave. They are easy to handle, wash well, and have very little surface texture, allowing the design to be the major focus.

The projects use various fabrics including cotton, both woven and knitted, as well as towelling, felt fabric, and synthetic fabrics such as polar fleece and linen-look.

When choosing fabric for a project, make sure that it is suited to the use of the item. Consider how the project will be cared for. For example, some fabrics do not wash well and are therefore not recommended for an item that will require frequent laundering. If the finished work will be laundered, it is recommended to wash and dry the fabric or item before stitching. This will help to limit fabric shrinkage and colour running that may otherwise occur.

## Pressing the fabric

Press out any wrinkles and creases in the fabric before beginning, as this will give an even, smooth surface on which to work. If possible, test the temperature of the iron on a scrap of the same fabric first.

Many fabrics have a right and a wrong side. When pressing, it is best to press the fabric on the wrong side, protecting it by covering it with either a commercially available pressing cloth or a piece of pale coloured cotton cloth.

To press with a pressing cloth, place the fabric, right side facing down, onto the ironing board. Cover with the pressing cloth. Set the iron to the correct temperature for the fabric and press using an even pressure and steady movement.

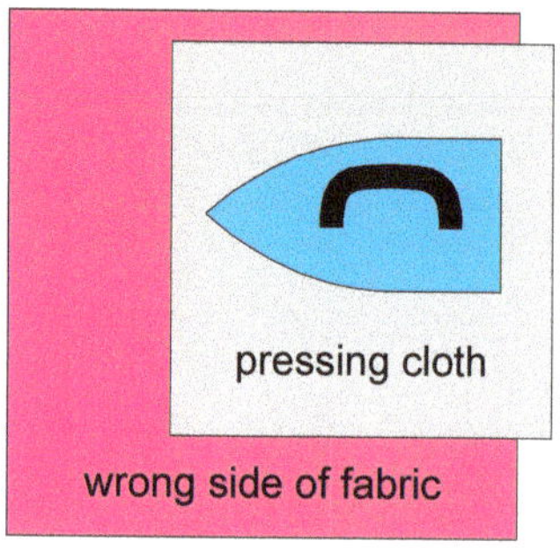


When pressing, dampening the fabric by spraying a fine mist of water onto the wrong side may help to remove any creases. Alternatively, wet the pressing cloth before placing it onto the fabric. If the fabric has been washed, it is easier to press while the fabric is still only partly dry.

## Cutting out the fabric

A design may be stitched directly onto a ready-made item such as a bath towel, a T-shirt, or a baby's bib, in which case there is no need to cut out a background fabric. However, the design may alternatively be stitched on a piece of background fabric that is cut to a manageable size. The size will depend on how the design is to be presented when the stitching is completed. Usually, extra fabric needs to be allowed beyond the design area.

Any of the designs in this book can be worked on a square piece of fabric. By allowing extra fabric beyond the design on all sides, the stitched square can be, for example, presented as a framed picture, used as a patch on clothing, or incorporated into a quilt. The same design worked on a larger piece of fabric can, for example, be made into a bag. The amount of extra fabric to allow beyond the design area will be different in each case.

### Grain of the fabric

Unless otherwise instructed, cut out the required fabric piece accurately following the vertical and horizontal threads (warp and weft) of the fabric.
This is referred to as cutting following the grain of the fabric.

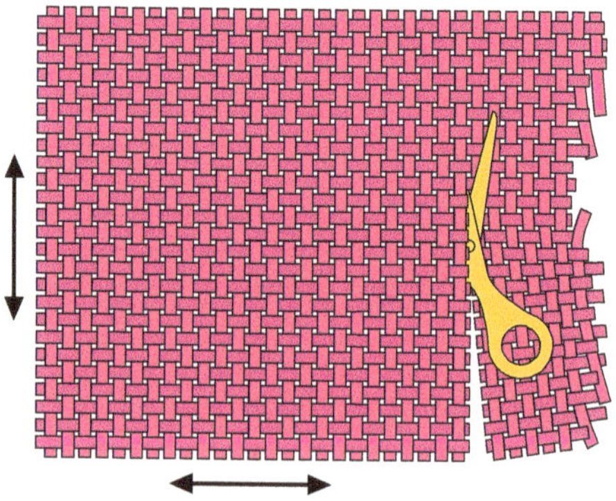

## Backing the fabric

Backing the fabric, or applying a backing, means attaching a second layer of fabric, or a layer of interfacing, onto the wrong side of the background fabric before the embroidery begins. This is not always necessary, but it can be helpful if the background fabric is delicate, loosely woven, or thin, and the stitching could possibly distort it, or the carried threads could show through from the wrong side. Backing can also be useful when working a design on a stretchy item such as a T-shirt, as the layer will stabilize the design area, preventing it from going out of shape. Backing will also provide a good surface, on the back of the work, on which to begin and end off the stitching.

### Choosing the backing

The choice of backing can vary, and depends on the chosen background fabric. The backing can be an extra layer of the same fabric, a layer of a different fabric, or a layer of interfacing. Interfacing is available in a variety of weights and colours, either woven or non-woven. Some types are iron-on, also known as fusible interfacing. Aim for the backing to be of a similar weight and darkness to the fabric, so that it does not affect the appearance of the fabric on the right side. If using fabric for the backing layer, wash it before use in the same way as the fabric to be backed, as they may otherwise shrink at different rates when laundering later.

### Attaching the backing

In most cases, cut the backing to the same size as the background fabric. However, on a garment, cut the backing a little larger than the area to be stitched, and any excess backing is trimmed away once the stitching is finished. If using backing that is not iron-on, attach it to the wrong side of the fabric with tacking stitches. Depending on the method used to transfer the pattern onto the fabric, this backing can be attached before transferring the pattern, or after transferring. When using iron-on interfacing as a backing, it is best to attach the backing before transferring the pattern because the heat of the iron may permanently set pattern marks made by water erasable fabric markers, transfer paper, and some chalk-based pencils. Considering the transfer method to be used, attach the backing in one of the following ways.

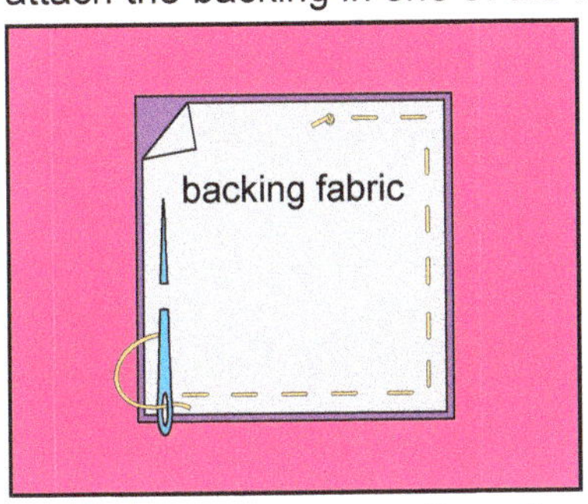


**Method 1: Tack a small work**
Aligning grains of the fabrics, place backing onto wrong side of fabric. Keeping layers flat, tack together around all sides.

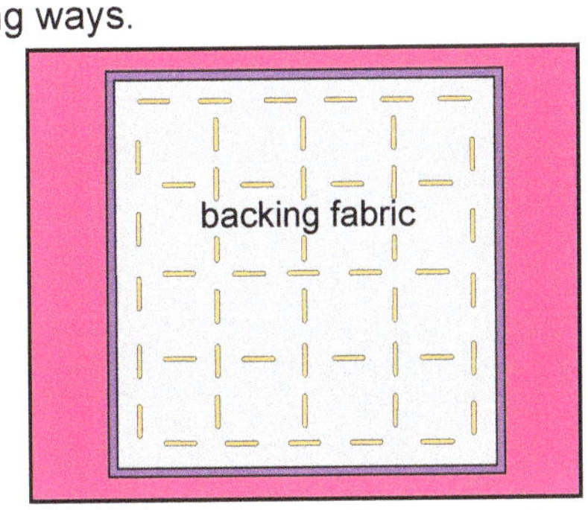


**Method 2: Tack a large work**
Aligning grains, place backing onto wrong side of fabric. Keeping layers flat, tack together in a grid formation.

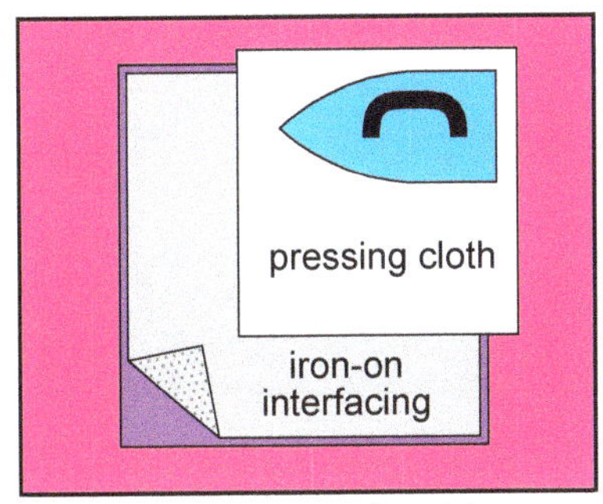


**Method 3: Iron-on backing**
Place iron-on interfacing, glue side down, onto wrong side of fabric. Cover with a pressing cloth. Press to fuse with a hot iron.

## Prevent fraying of the fabric edges

After the fabric has been cut to size and any backing has been attached, sew the edges as follows to prevent them fraying while the embroidery is being worked. The first two methods are suitable for most fabrics, while the third method is suited to fabrics that are not too bulky.

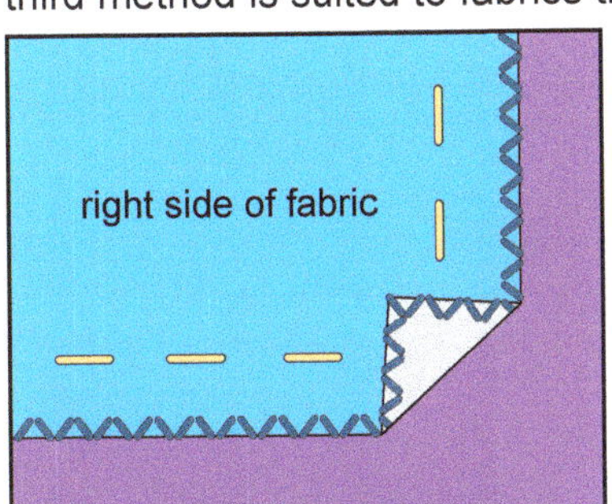


**Method 1: Zigzag stitching**
Using a zigzag stitch on the machine, stitch around all four sides through the fabric and the backing.

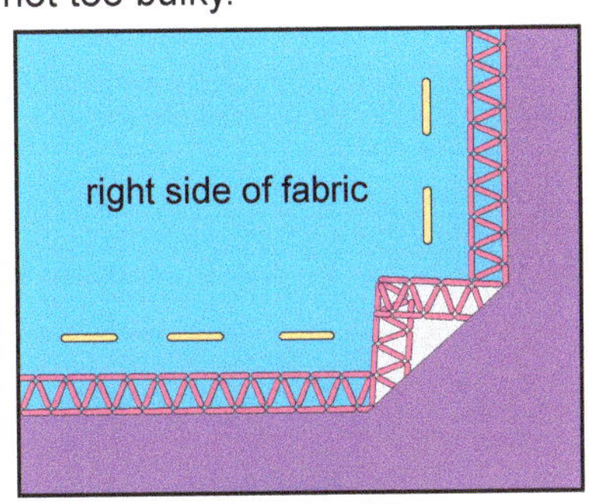


**Method 2: Overlocking**
Using an overlock machine, stitch around all four sides through the fabric and the backing.

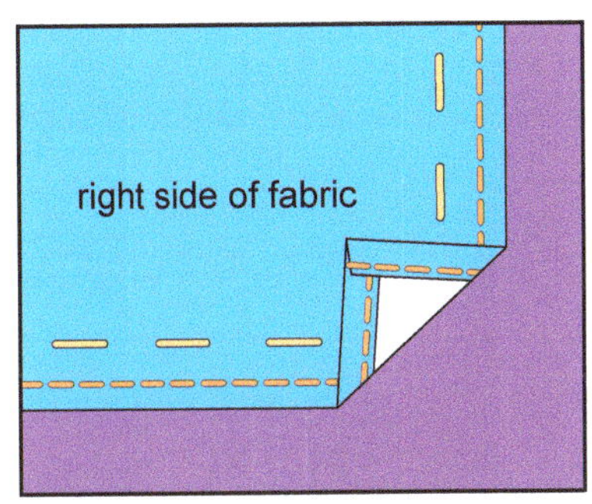


**Method 3: Turning under**
Turn under a small hem to the wrong side. Using a straight stitch on the machine, stitch through all layers.

# Threads

## Choosing the threads

Exploring the vast range of exciting threads available can be very exciting.
Threads vary in type, appearance, thickness, lustre, colour, handling, and wearing qualities. Selecting threads for an embroidery is an important and enjoyable part of the creative process.

### Threads for the designs and projects

In this book the designs and projects are worked using the following types of thread. They have been chosen for visual impact, suitability for working the stitches, for ease of use, and for durability:

***Stranded cotton***
This slightly shiny thread is made up of six strands twisted loosely together. All six strands can be used in the needle for work requiring a thick thread, while the strands can be separated and fewer used for finer work.
Stranded cotton is also available as variegated thread, where the colour changes along its length. This gives an interesting effect of colour variation within a design.

***Stranded silk***
This thread, which is made up of strands twisted loosely together, has a sheen that gives the finished work a luxurious appearance.
Stranded silk can be used in a similar way to stranded cotton.

***Stranded rayon***
This thread is made up of six strands twisted loosely together. All six strands can be used in the needle for work requiring a thick thread, while the strands can be separated and fewer used for finer work.
Stranded rayon threads have a brilliant shine, but they may tangle more easily and become worn more quickly than some other types of thread. To minimise this, it is best to use shorter than normal lengths of thread. As rayon thread is springy and can easily work loose, begin and end off the thread securely.

***Perlé cotton***
This tightly twisted thread is slightly shiny. Unlike stranded thread it is always used as a whole thread, without separating any strands. Perlé cotton is available in various thicknesses, the smaller the number, the thicker the thread. In this book, the designs use No. 5 perlé cotton, which is a medium thickness thread.

***Perlé metallic***
Perlé metallic thread, which is made up of 8 ply, can be used as a whole thread, or it can be carefully separated into 4 ply or fewer ply for finer work. This synthetic thread adds shimmer and sparkle, but it may become worn more quickly than some other types of thread. This is overcome by using shorter than normal lengths of thread.

***Fine 2 ply wool yarn***
This fine wool yarn adds a fluffy texture. Each strand, made up of 2 ply, is used as a whole thread, without separating the ply.

### Experiment with threads

As an alternative to following the design and project ideas instructions for thread choices, feel free to experiment with different types and colours of threads to achieve new effects. For special shaded and variegated effects, try stitching with more than one colour or type of thread mixed in the needle.

## Preparing the threads

### Rinsing threads

As many threads are not colourfast, it is recommended that they be carefully rinsed in cold water and thoroughly dried before beginning to stitch. If not, the colour may bleed into the fabric if the work is laundered later.

### Labelling threads

For the purpose of this book, the threads can be identified by coding them with an alphabet letter according to the shopping list given in the instructions for each design. This can be done by attaching a coded label to each skein of thread.

### Length of thread

Threads can become dull, thin, and worn by being repeatedly passed through the fabric during stitching. This problem can be overcome by using lengths of approximately 50cm (20"). Use even shorter lengths for more fragile threads.

### Separating strands and recombining

When using several strands of thread, separate the strands and then recombine them. The combined strands will lie more neatly and give a better coverage on the fabric.

# Preparing the threads

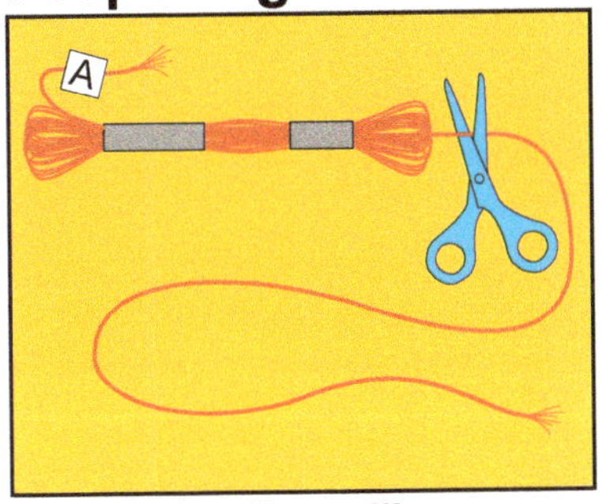


**Stranded cotton, silk, or rayon**
**1** Attach alphabet label to the skein for identification. Cut lengths of thread. Rinse and dry thoroughly.

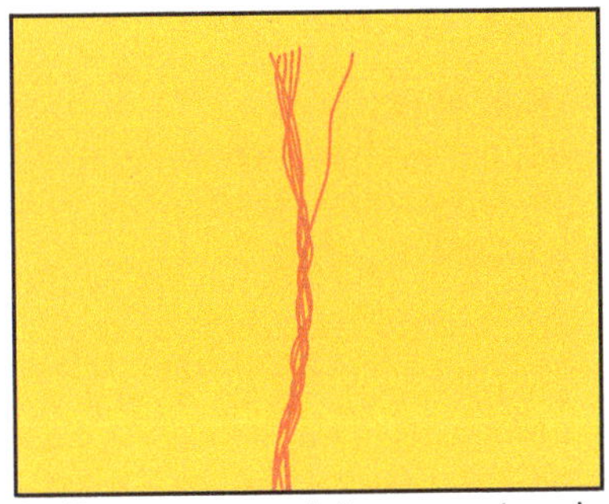

**2** From one end, tease out a single strand so it is separated from the other five strands.

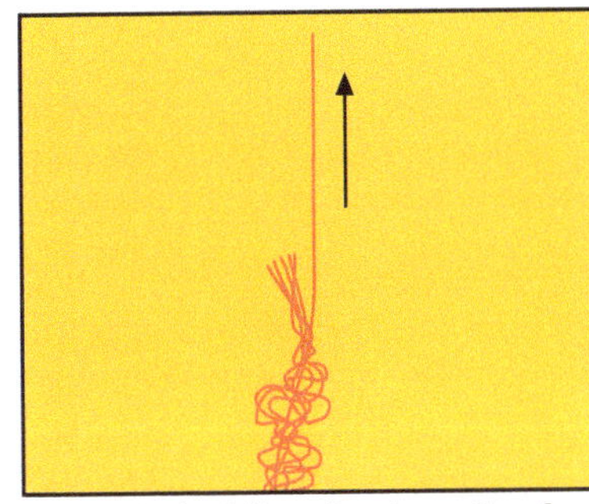

**3** While holding the length of thread, pull the single strand up. The other five strands will bunch up. Pull the strand out.

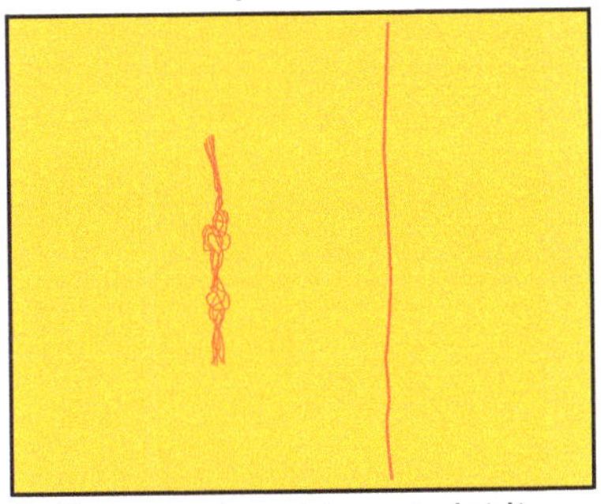

**4** Dangle strand to untwist it. Straighten out the other five strands. Continue pulling out the required number of strands in the same way.

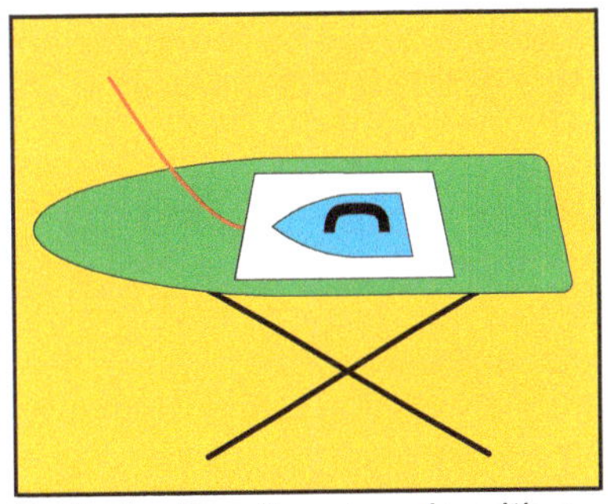

**5** Protecting the strands with a pressing cloth, straighten each by drawing it out from under an iron set to the correct temperature.

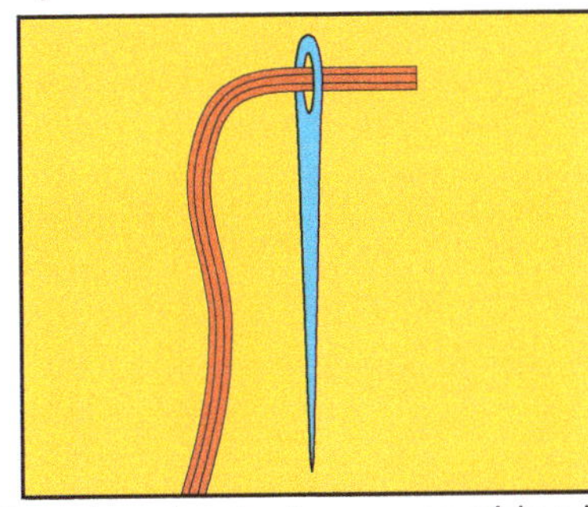

**6** Use strands singly or recombine by lying them down side by side. Thread into needle. Recombining helps the strands to lie parallel when stitching.

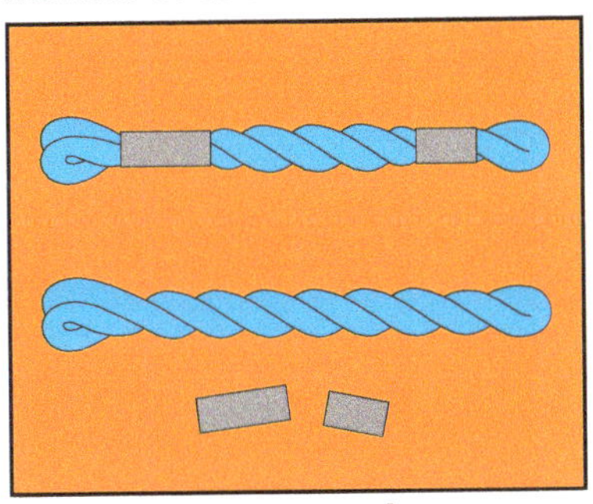

**Perlé cotton or wool yarn**
**1** Perlé cotton thread or wool yarn is often purchased as a twisted skein. Remove the labels.

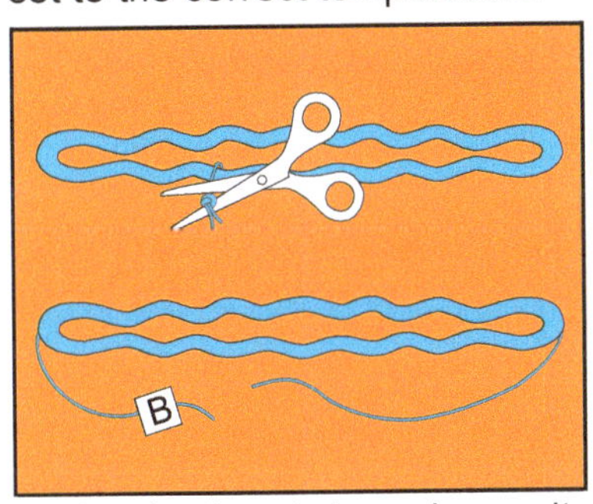


**2** Untwist the skein and open it into a circle. The ends are usually knotted together. Snip off the knot and attach an alphabet label.

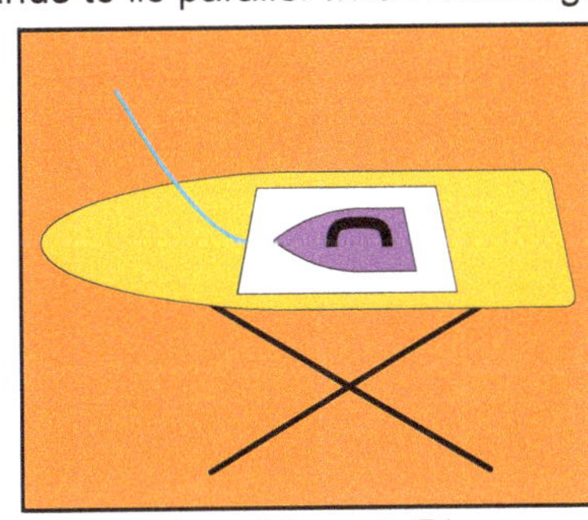

**3** Cut lengths of thread. Rinse and dry. Can use wool yarn once dry. For perlé cotton, protect with a cloth, then draw out under iron to flatten.

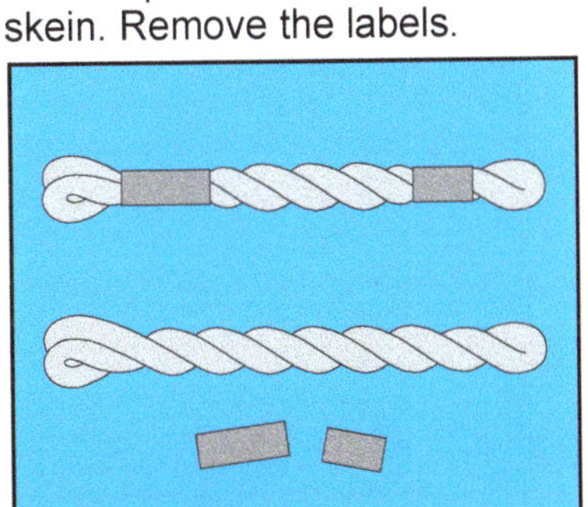

**Perlé metallic**
**1** This thread is often purchased as a twisted skein. Remove labels.

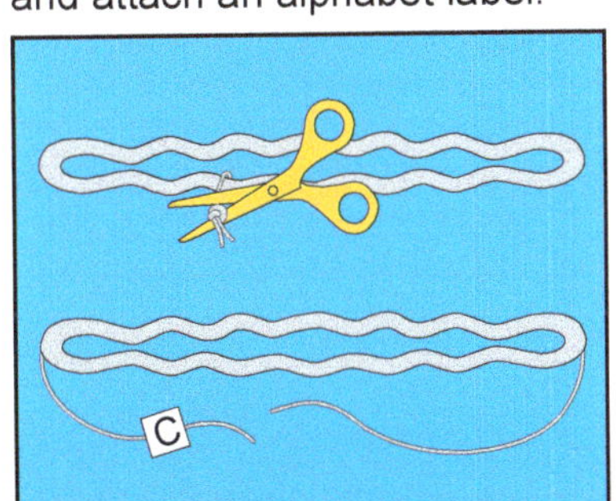


**2** Untwist skein and open out. The ends may be knotted together. Snip off knot and attach a label. Cut required lengths.

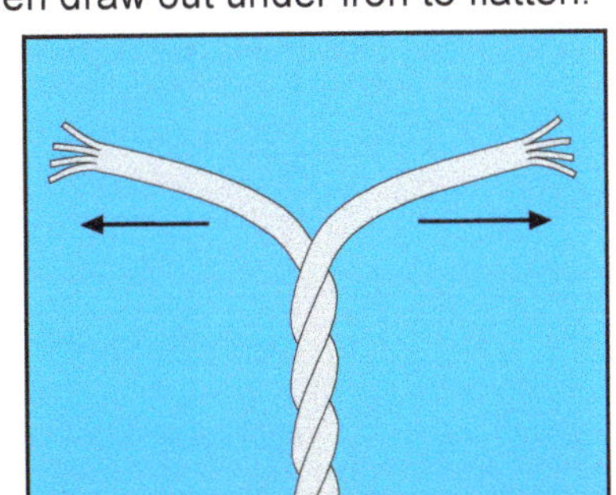

**3** To divide 8 ply into halves, allow to hang freely. Slowly pull halves, untwisting. For fewer ply, repeat.

# Needles

## Choosing needles

When selecting a needle for hand stitching, it is helpful to choose one that is a suitable shape and size for the type of fabric, thread, and stitches to be worked.

Needles are available in many shapes and sizes. They are named according to the length and width of the eye and shaft, and the sharpness of the tip. They are also graded by a number. The higher the number on the packet, the smaller the needle.

In most cases, aim for a needle with a shaft that is the same thickness as the thread. This ensures that the thread will fill the hole in the fabric created by the needle. Also, choose a needle with an eye that is large enough to thread easily, but not so large that the thread keeps falling out of the needle as you work.

## Needles to work the designs

To work the designs in this book you will require only the following needles:

- No. 3 embroidery/crewel needle
- No. 7 embroidery/crewel needle
- No. 22 tapestry needle

The embroidery/crewel needles have pointed ends and large, long eyes. They are general-purpose needles, suitable for working on plain weave fabric using one to several strands of thread. The larger needle (No. 3) is suitable for thick threads such as No. 5 perlé cotton, wool yarn, or five or six strands of stranded cotton, silk, or rayon thread. The smaller needle (No. 7) is suitable for one to four strands of stranded cotton, silk, or rayon thread.

The tapestry needle has a blunt, rounded end. In this book it is used when lacing and whipping previously worked stitches as the blunt end prevents the splitting of the threads of the previous stitches.

# Other items

In addition to fabrics, threads, and needles, the following items may be useful. Many of them are not essential.

**Fabric scissors**
Large scissors used for cutting fabric, interfacing, and wadding, and for trimming seams.

**Embroidery scissors**
Small sharp-pointed scissors used for cutting threads and small fabric shapes. Choose a pair that will cut right to the tip of the blades.

**Paper scissors**
For cutting paper, tracing paper, paper-backed fusible webbing, card, and cardboard.

**Pins**
Used to hold fabrics in place temporarily, and sometimes used to mark the position for placing a pattern on the fabric.

**Tape measure and ruler**
Marked with measurements, these are used for determining the dimensions of your work accurately.

**Tracing paper**
Paper that you can see through for tracing, available in various weights. Trace the patterns from the pages of this book onto medium weight tracing paper using an HB pencil.

**HB pencil**
Can be used to trace the patterns from the pages of this book onto tracing paper, or to mark a pattern onto fabric. Pencil lines on fabric are often permanent, so pencil may only be suitable to use if the stitches will cover all of the pattern marks.

**Water erasable fabric marker**
Used for marking the pattern onto fabric. Some types work better than others, so try a few different brands. Will wash out by rinsing the work in cold water when the stitching is complete. Suitable to use if the stitches will not completely cover the pattern marks.

**Chalk-based pencil**
Used for marking the pattern onto fabric. Some can be removed by brushing, while others will wash out by rinsing the work in cold water when the stitching is complete. Suitable to use if the stitches will not completely cover the pattern marks.

**Fine permanent pen**
Used for marking the pattern onto fabric. Will not wash out in water. Suitable to use if the stitches will cover all of the pattern marks.

**Light box**
Used to shine light through a traced pattern plus a layer of fabric so that the pattern lines show through. Lines can then be traced onto the fabric. Alternatively, use a sunlit window, or a glass table and lamp.

**Transfer paper, including erasable**
Paper that is used for transferring patterns onto fabric, available in many colours. Some types work better than others, so try a variety of brands. The most suitable of these papers produce fine lines that do not disappear from the fabric while you are stitching, but can be removed by rinsing the work in cold water when the stitching is done.

**Stylus or empty ballpoint pen**
Used to draw over the pattern lines when transferring a pattern onto fabric with transfer paper.

**Interfacing**
A layer that can be used as a backing for a fabric, to give extra thickness and support. It can be woven or non-woven. It is available in various thicknesses and colours. Interfacing can be attached to the fabric by tacking. If the interfacing is iron-on, it will have glue on one side and is attached to the fabric using a hot iron.

**Paper-backed fusible webbing**
Also known as iron-on adhesive webbing, it consists of a thin web of glue, backed with a layer of paper. It is used in appliqué to fuse two layers of fabric together with an iron. It is available as a roll or in squares. Note that some fusible webbing available is for 'non-stitch' appliqué. It has very heavy duty glue and is not suitable for the projects in this book because it is difficult or impossible to stitch through.

**Pressing cloth**
Used between the iron and the fabric or thread to prevent damage when pressing.

**Hoops and frames**
Useful for holding fabric taut while working some types of stitching. They are not essential for working the designs in this book. The use of these is entirely your own choice.

**Blocking board, corkboard, or cork tile** Used for pinning out a completed stitched work in order to straighten and flatten it.

**Sewing machine**
Useful for sewing the edges of fabrics to prevent fraying and for any projects requiring construction, such as bags.

**Fibre filling**
Soft fibres used for filling items such as pincushions.

**Wadding**
A spongy layer of synthetic or other fibres used to pad a stitched work.

**Paper, card, and cardboard**
Available in an immense range of colours, textures, and weights. We recommend using archival paper, card, and cardboard for projects as they resist disintegration.

**Steel ruler, craft knife, and cutting mat** Used for cutting paper, cardboard, and foam core board or similar.

**Sticky tapes/adhesive tapes**
Available in many forms and may be single or double-sided, temporary or permanent. We recommend using archival sticky tapes for projects as they resist disintegration.

**Glues**
Many types are available. We recommend using archival glues for projects as they resist disintegration.

**Foam core board or similar**
Used as a firm, flat base over which to stretch and lace a stitched work. We recommend using archival foam core board or similar for projects.

**Notebook**
Useful for jotting down ideas for future stitched projects.

# Patterns

A full size pattern is provided for each of the designs featured in this book.
The pattern is a simplified drawing of the design, usually represented with lines or dots. It is usually transferred to the fabric to indicate the placement of the stitches to be worked.
Patterns vary in their complexity. They can be quite detailed, where every element of the design is represented, or they can be simply a few guidelines, in which case the design is worked by referring to the photo, and judging the position of the stitches by eye.

It may be difficult to transfer some of the details onto the fabric, for example if the pattern has been reduced in size, or if textured fabric is used. It may not be necessary to transfer the pattern to the fabric at all, particularly if the design is very simple. In these cases, transfer the major pattern marks only, or no marks at all, and simply use the photo and the pattern as a visual guide to shapes and placement while working the stitches.

### Pattern key

Accompanying each pattern in this book, there is a pattern key giving an explanation of the symbols used on the pattern. The centre of the pattern and its orientation is indicated. This centre symbol is not transferred to the fabric. Sometimes, the order for working the design elements, the starting point, the stitches used, and the position for the stitches and their direction are shown. Where numbers appear on the pattern, there is usually no need to transfer the numbers onto the fabric.

## Preparing the pattern

For each design in this book, the pattern can be used unchanged, or it can be altered in a variety of ways to create a new design.

The first step is to trace the pattern from the book onto medium weight tracing paper using an HB pencil. The traced pattern can then be adapted in a number of ways.

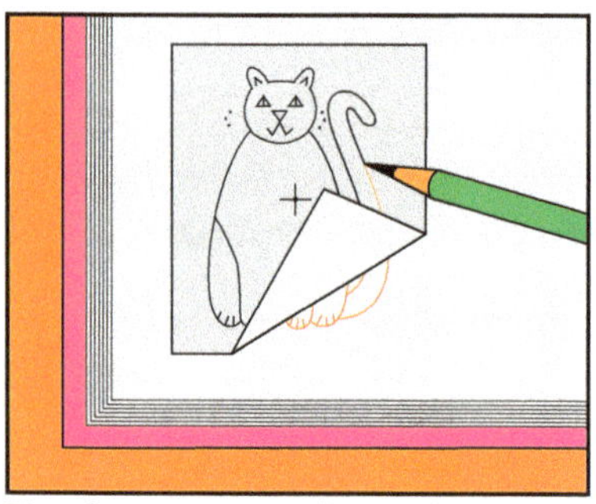

**Tracing pattern from the book**
Using an HB pencil trace the pattern, including the centre symbol, accurately onto medium weight tracing paper.

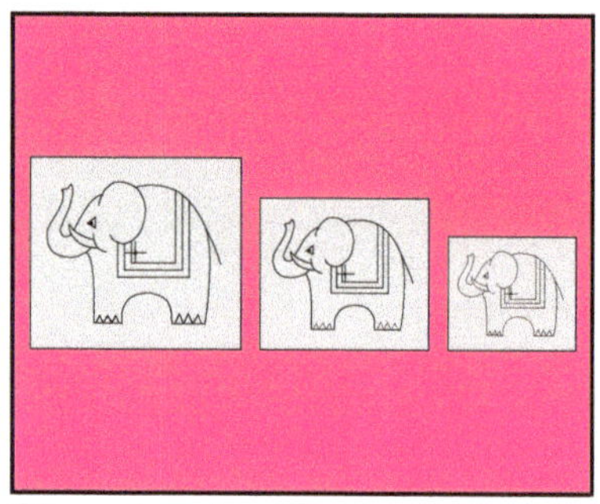

**Changing the size**
The pattern can be made larger or smaller. When stitching, change thickness of thread and size of stitches to suit the scale.

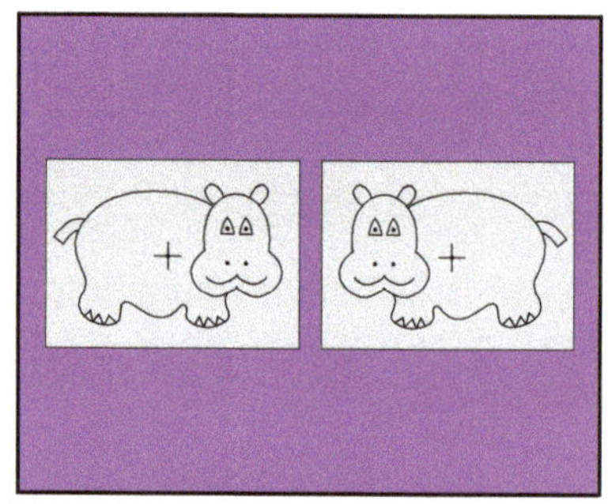

**How to mirror the pattern**
The pattern can be reversed. Turn original tracing over and tape to a window. Trace the pattern onto a second piece of tracing paper.

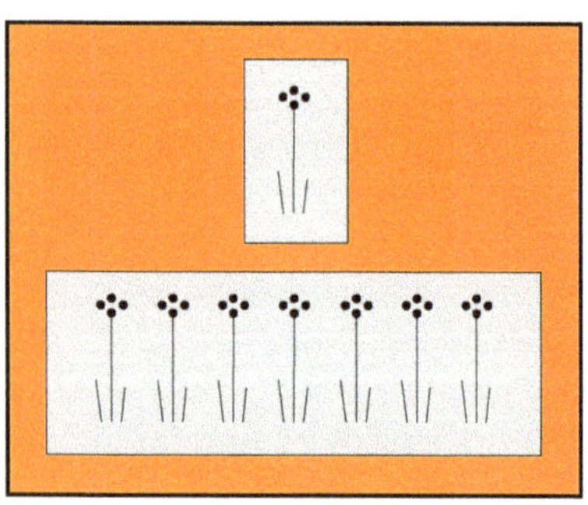

**Single element of the pattern**
Part of a more complex design can be selected and worked as a single element, or repeated in a line creating a decorative row.

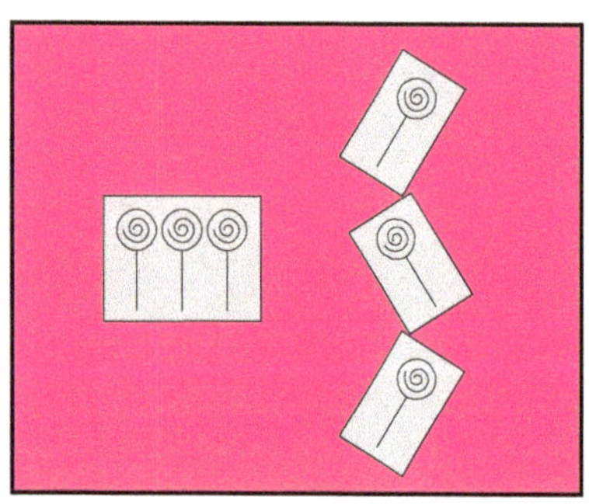

**Rotating the pattern**
The pattern can be oriented at an angle that is different from the original. In this example, separate elements are rotated.

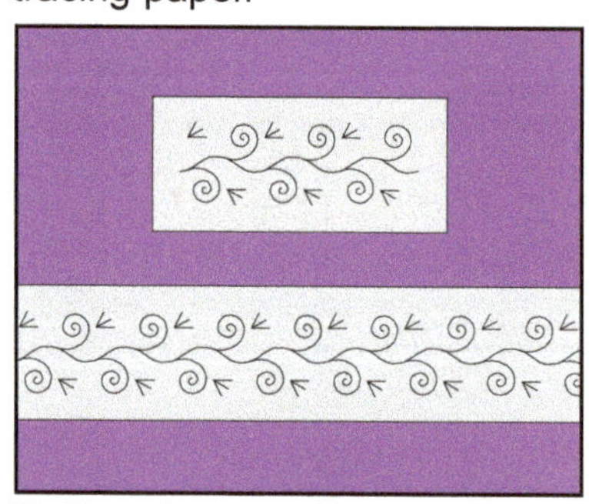

**Pattern in a continuous row**
Some patterns are designed to form a continuous row by being repeated so that the pattern lines flow continuously.

## Placing the pattern

When working the designs on a square piece of fabric, place the pattern so that it is centred and aligned squarely unless otherwise instructed. Each of the patterns includes a symbol consisting of a circle representing the centre of the design, and crossed lines indicating the orientation of the design, both vertically and horizontally. When transferring the pattern onto the fabric, this symbol helps in placing the pattern centrally, as well as following the grain of the fabric. There is no need to transfer the symbol onto the fabric.

When applying a design onto a project such as an item of clothing, to help in deciding the placement of the pattern, move the tracing around until it is visually appealing. It may look best centred, or off to one side. Give consideration to the practicality of the position and how the stitched design will look when the garment is worn, as some parts may be hidden under the arms or be too high at the neckline. If scattering several designs, move each tracing until the overall effect is balanced. Mark the positions with pins or tacking and then transfer the patterns using a suitable method.

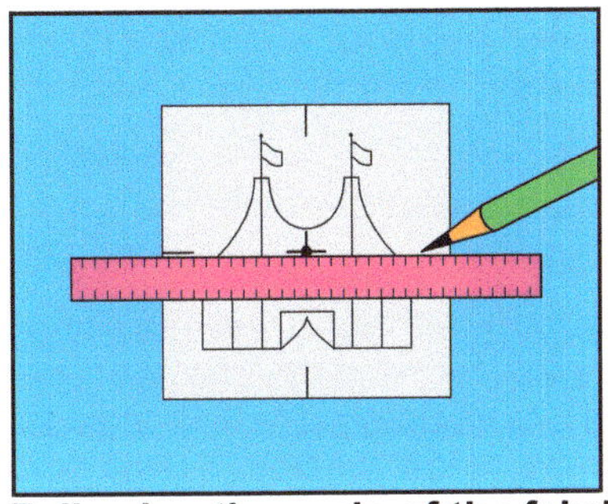

**Following the grain of the fabric**
**1** On the tracing, place a ruler on the vertical line of the centre symbol. Rule lines on edges of tracing. Repeat for horizontal line.

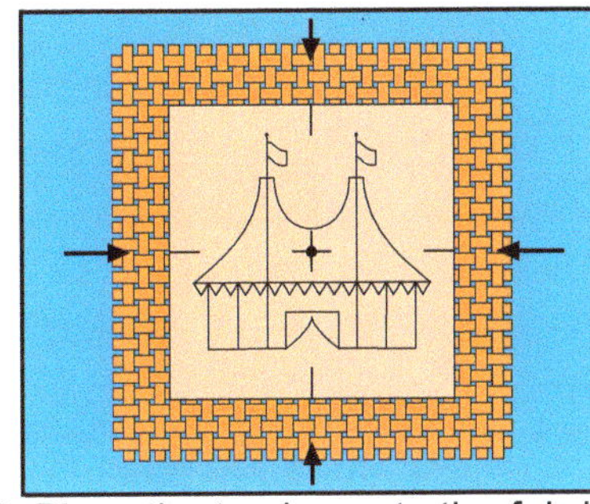

**2** Place the tracing onto the fabric with the ruled lines parallel to the grain (warp and weft) of the fabric. Transfer the pattern using a suitable method.

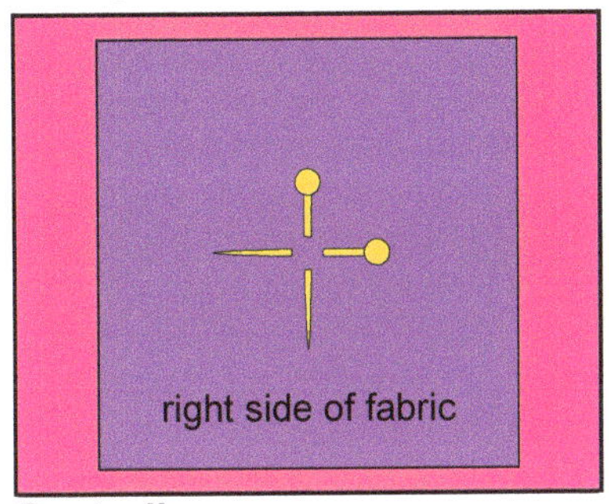


**Centrally on a square**
**1** Find the centre of the square piece of fabric and mark it with pins placed in a cross.

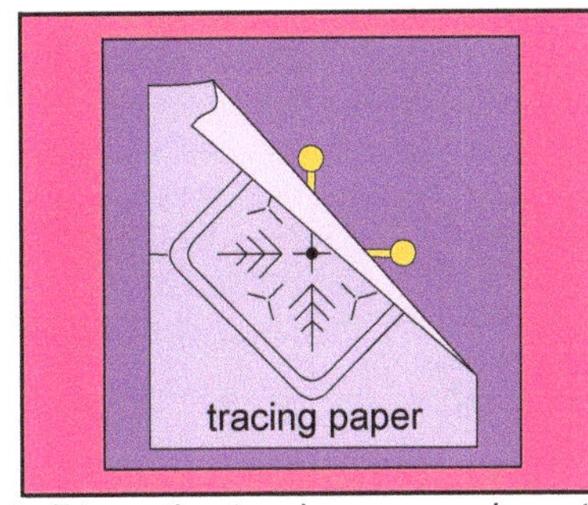


**2** Place the tracing squarely onto the fabric, with the marked centre matching the pins. Transfer the pattern using a suitable method.

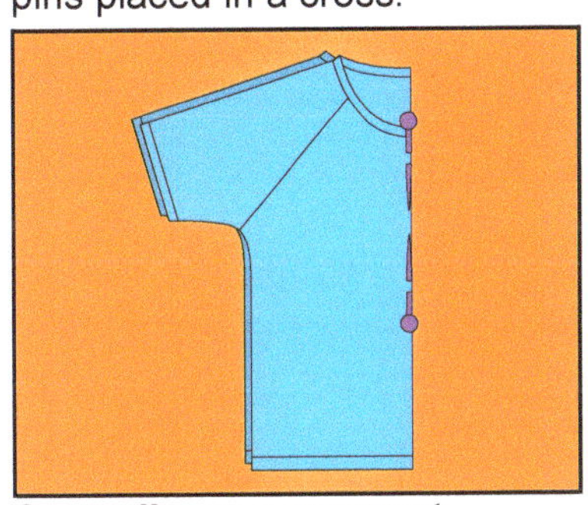

**Centrally on a garment**
**1** Fold the garment in half and mark the centre fold line with pins.

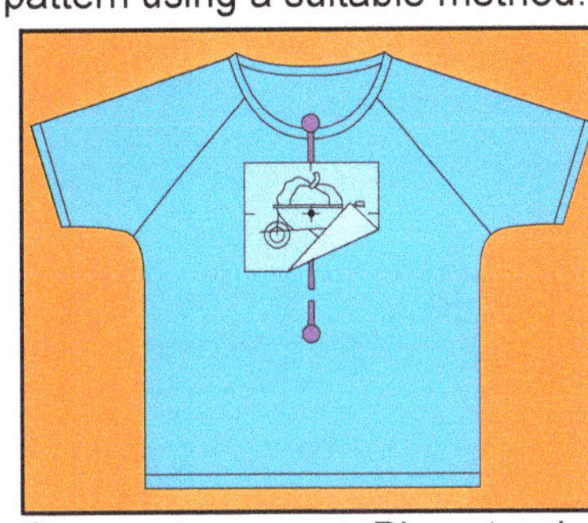

**2** Open out garment. Place tracing centred over pins, in position. Mark position, then transfer pattern.

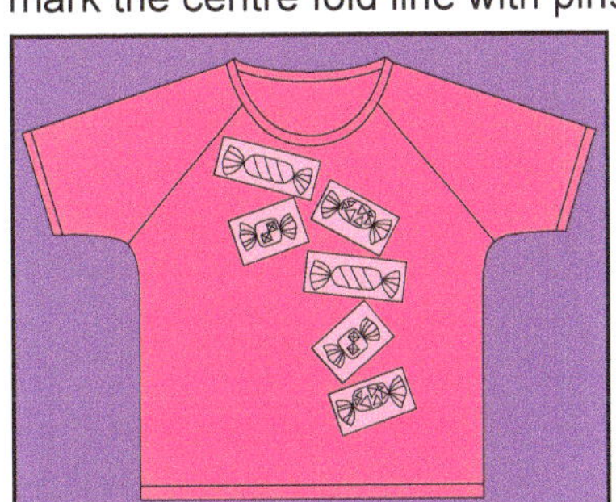

**Placing multiple patterns**
Arrange separate tracings in place. Mark positions, then transfer the patterns.

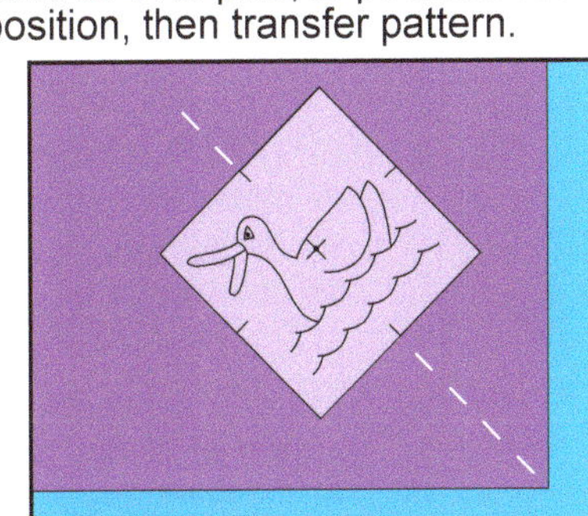

**Diagonally on a corner**
Place the tracing so that the vertical line on the centre symbol is oriented at 45 degrees to the corner.

# Transferring the pattern onto the fabric

Simple designs or elements of a design, such as a single flower, can often be stitched freehand, without the need to mark the fabric at all. Looking at the photo and referring to the pattern as a visual guide when working the stitches may be all that is required. For most of the designs, however, the pattern may need to be transferred onto the fabric as a marked guide to the placement of the stitches. The amount of detail transferred to the fabric will vary depending on such factors as the design complexity and the fabric used.

## Fabric markers

For some designs and fabrics, the pattern can simply be drawn or traced onto the fabric with a sharp HB pencil, which may be permanent on some fabrics, or a fine permanent pen. Alternatively, the pattern can be transferred with removable marks using a water erasable fabric marker, a chalk-based pencil, or transfer paper. When the stitching is complete these marks can be removed, in some cases by gently brushing and in other cases by rinsing the work in cold water. Some types work better than others, so try a few different brands. Always follow the manufacturer's instructions and be aware that some water erasable fabric markers and transfer papers are permanently set into the fabric if heat is applied. For this reason, if using iron-on interfacing as a backing, it needs to be attached to the wrong side of the fabric before transferring the pattern. Do not press the fabric again until the stitching is complete and the pattern marks have been removed. Ideally, the pattern marks need to be easily seen on the fabric, so choose a fabric marker in a contrasting or obviously different colour.

## Methods of transfer

As well as the variety of tools available, there are several different ways by which to transfer the pattern onto the fabric. The three methods recommended for the designs and projects in this book are easy to manage. They are as follows:

- Transferring the pattern by tracing
- Transferring the pattern using transfer paper
- Transferring the pattern using the pierce and dot method

Instructions for the methods are given on the next few pages.

If possible, test the chosen method on a scrap of the same fabric before using it on the actual piece.

## Choosing the fabric marker and method

When choosing the correct fabric marker and method to use, take into account the following points:

Consider the weight and colour of the fabric. It may be thin, or of a pale colour. In this case, transferring the pattern by tracing with the aid of a sunlit window or using a light box is a good choice. However, the fabric may be thick, or of a dark colour, in which case it may be difficult to see the pattern lines through the fabric, so tracing is not an option. Using either transfer paper or the pierce and dot method would be a good choice.

Pay attention to the texture of the fabric. Some fabrics, such as towelling, have an uneven surface or a raised pile, in which case drawing a line can be difficult and marking with dots might be a better choice.

Decide whether the fabric needs a backing applied. The type of backing and the order in which it is attached will determine the method of transferring the pattern to the fabric. Some fabrics are not washable, so in this case use a method of transferring the pattern that does not require the later removal of the pattern marks by rinsing the fabric in water.

Consider that some stitches completely cover the pattern lines, while others do not. For those that do not, use either a removable transfer method, or use small dots that can be covered, instead of lines.

# Transferring the pattern by tracing

This method can be used on fabrics that will allow the traced pattern on tracing paper to show through the fabric with the aid of a light source such as a sunlit window or a light box. Alternatively, a glass tabletop and lamp can be used. A sharp HB pencil or a fine permanent pen, or a removable marker such as a water erasable fabric marker or a chalk-based pencil, can be used to mark the fabric, depending on whether the stitches will cover the marks or not.

When the design has been stitched it may be necessary to remove any traces of the fabric marker not covered by the stitches. Always follow the manufacturer's instructions regarding fabric markers.

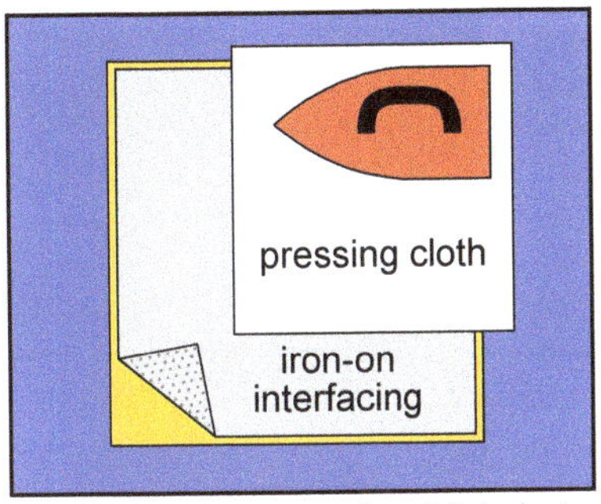


**1** Wash, press, and cut fabric to size. If using iron-on interfacing for backing, attach it before transferring pattern, as heat may set pattern marks.

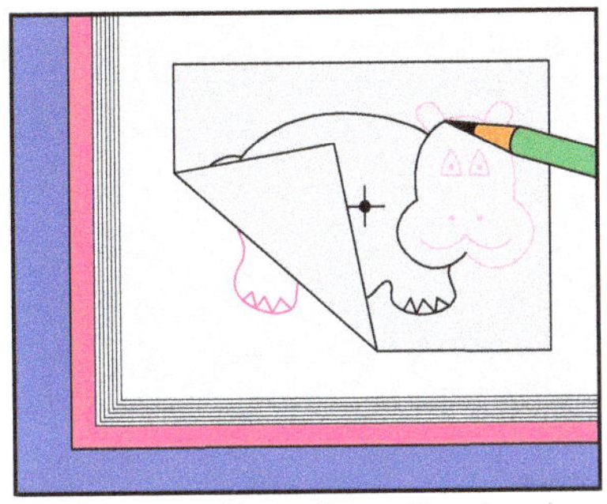

**2** Trace pattern from the book onto medium weight tracing paper using an HB pencil. Include the symbol indicating the centre of the pattern.

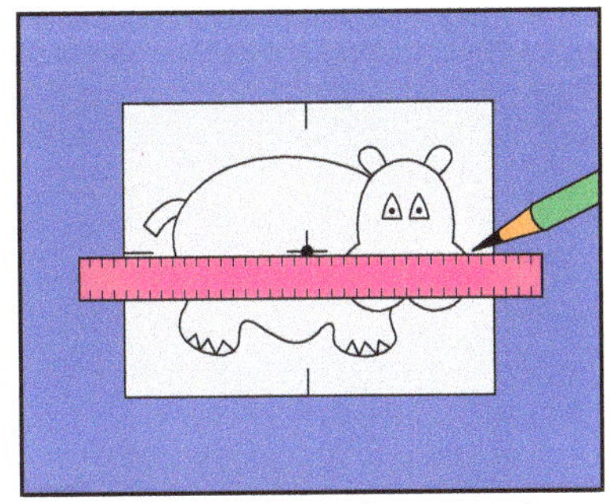

**3** On the tracing, place a ruler along the vertical line of the centre symbol. Rule lines on the outer edges of the tracing. Repeat for the horizontal line.

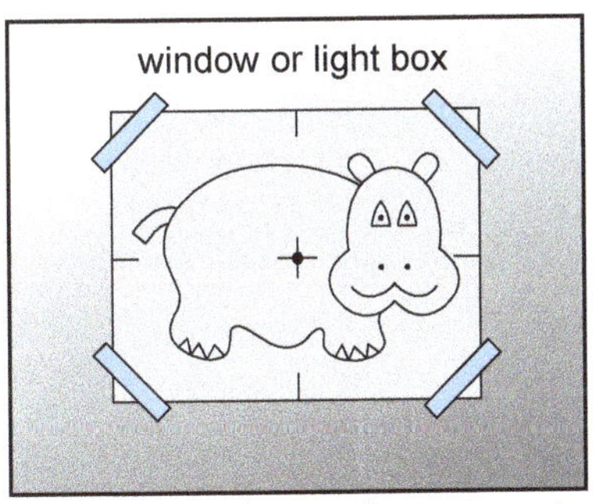


**4** Orienting the tracing squarely, tape the tracing to a sunlit window or a light box.

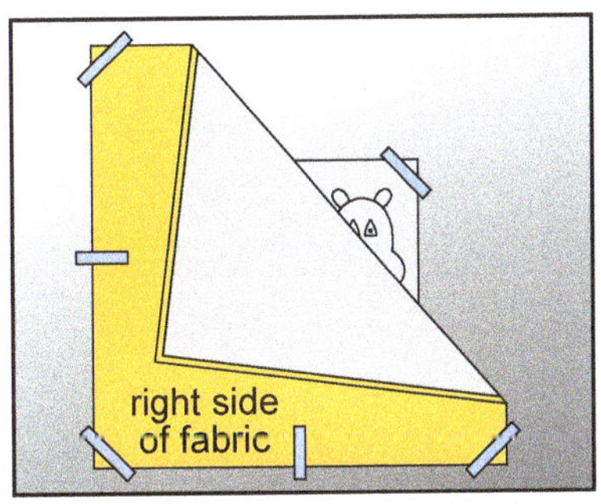


**5** Place the fabric over tracing with the right side facing you. Orient it squarely and match its centre to the marked centre on the pattern. Tape in place.

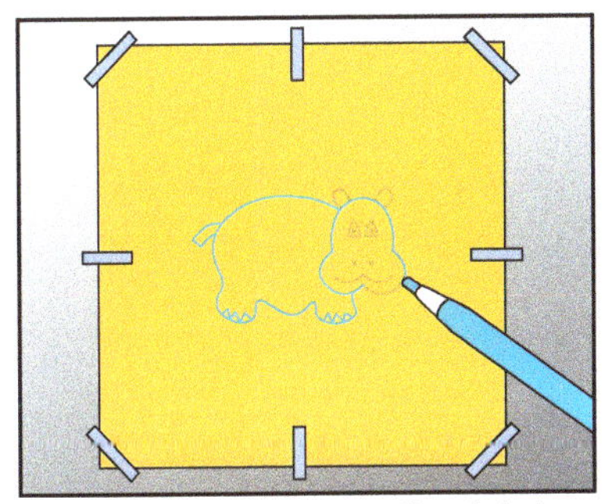

**6** Trace pattern onto the fabric using an HB pencil, a pen, a water erasable fabric marker, or a chalk-based pencil, but no need to trace the centre symbol and ruled lines.

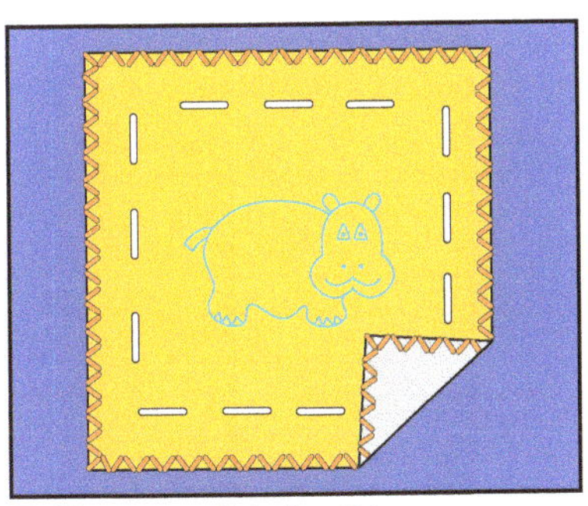

**7** Remove fabric. If iron-on interfacing has not been used, tack backing fabric to wrong side. Sew the fabric edges to prevent fraying.

## Hints

**If tracing is not visible**

If the tracing is not visible through the fabric, remove the fabric and redraw over the pattern lines on the tracing with a darker pencil to make the lines more obvious. Reposition the fabric and continue transferring the pattern.

**No need to transfer the centre symbol or numbers**

When transferring the pattern onto the fabric, there is no need to transfer the centre symbol or any numbers that are present on the pattern.

# Transferring the pattern using transfer paper

This method is recommended for fabrics that have a smooth surface and are densely woven, heavy in weight, or are a dark colour. For these fabrics tracing is not an option because the pattern lines cannot be seen easily through the fabric.

Transfer paper has a water erasable waxy coating on one side. The coating transfers as marks onto the fabric when pressure is applied to the reverse side of the paper with a stylus or an empty ballpoint pen. There are a wide variety of colours available, so choose one that will contrast with the fabric so that the marks show up easily.

When the design has been stitched it may be necessary to remove any traces of the transfer paper marks not covered by the stitches. Always follow the manufacturer's instructions when using transfer paper.

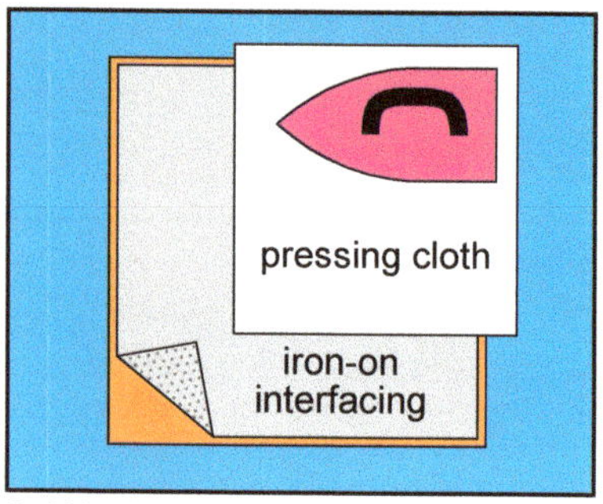


**1** Wash, press, and cut fabric to size. If using iron-on interfacing for backing, attach it before transferring the pattern, as heat may set transfer paper marks.

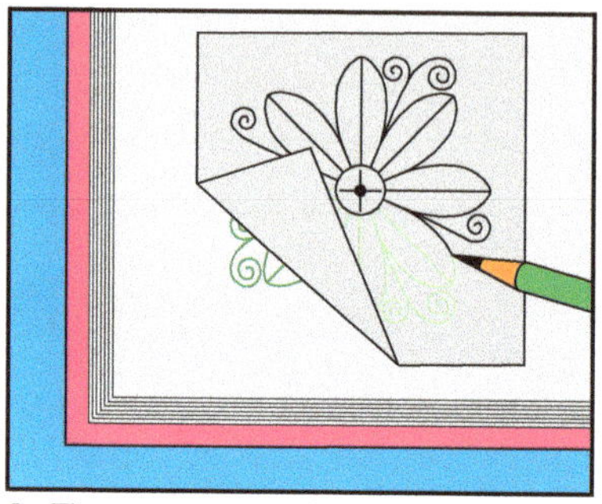

**2** Trace pattern from the book onto medium weight tracing paper using an HB pencil. Include the symbol indicating the centre of the pattern.

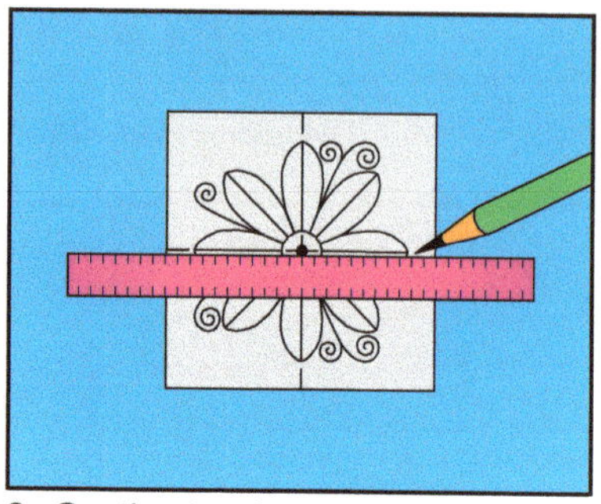

**3** On the tracing, place a ruler along the vertical line of the centre symbol. Rule lines on the outer edges of the tracing. Repeat for the horizontal line.

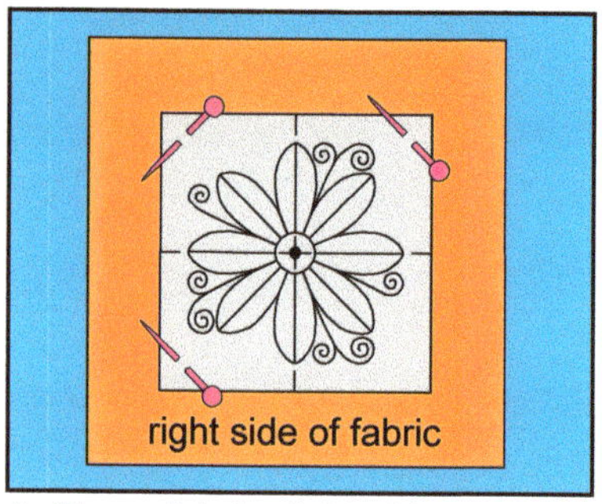


**4** Place fabric right side up on a flat surface. Place tracing squarely onto fabric, matching its centre to the centre of the fabric. Pin together at three corners.

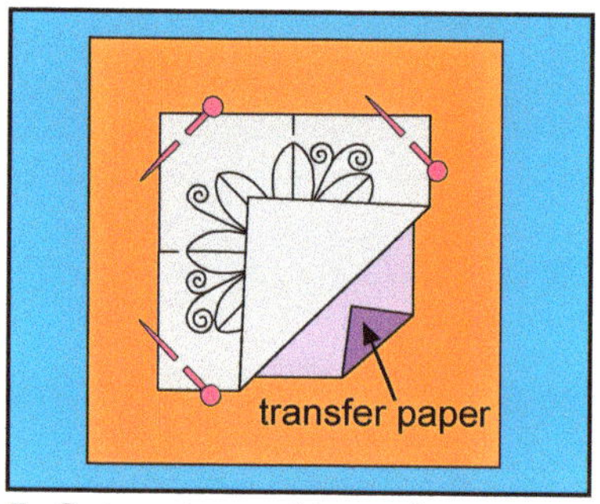


**5** Cut a piece of transfer paper a little larger than the size of the pattern. Slip the paper between the fabric and the tracing with the coated side facing down.

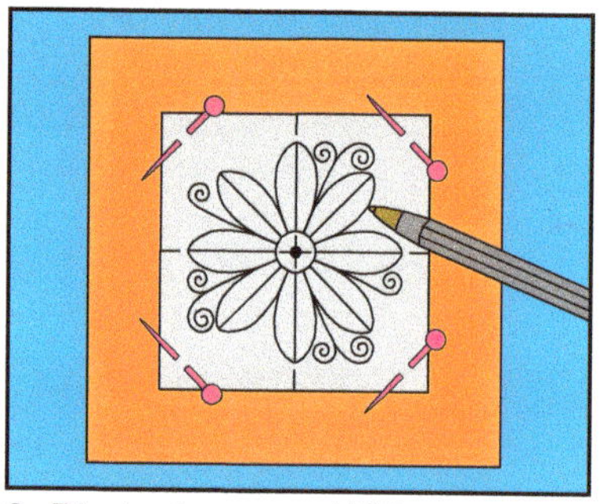

**6** Pin last corner. With stylus or empty pen, draw over pattern lines. Lift a corner to check that marks are visible. If not, redraw. No need to transfer centre symbol and ruled lines.

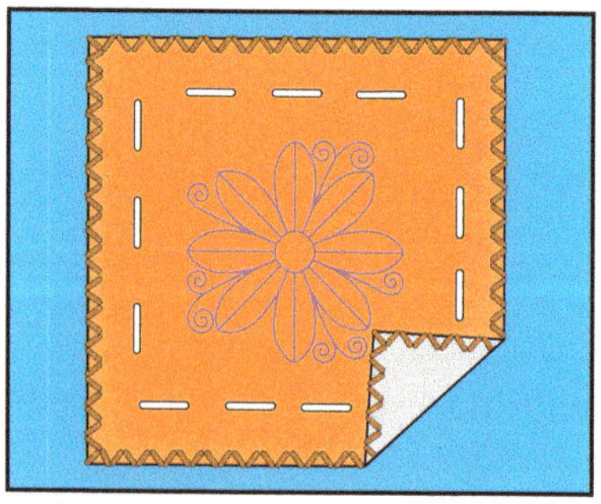

**7** Remove tracing and transfer paper from fabric. If iron-on interfacing has not been used, tack backing fabric to wrong side. Sew the fabric edges to prevent fraying.

## Hints

### Stylus or empty ballpoint pen

When drawing with a stylus or an empty ballpoint pen, do not use too much pressure, as it is likely to puncture the tracing or transfer paper and may then damage the fabric.

### No need to transfer the centre symbol or numbers

When transferring the pattern onto the fabric, there is no need to transfer the centre symbol or any numbers that are present on the pattern.

## Transferring the pattern using the pierce and dot method

This method is recommended for any fabric on which it is difficult to draw a line. This may be because it has a raised or fluffy surface, such as towelling, felt, and polar fleece. It is also recommended for heavy or dark coloured fabrics for which tracing is not an option.

The pierce and dot method involves piercing holes through the tracing paper along the traced pattern lines and then marking the fabric through the holes with a fabric marker. This method allows for the tracing to be re-used several times when working with multiples of the design.

A sharp HB pencil or a fine permanent pen, or a removable marker such as a water erasable fabric marker or a chalk-based pencil, can be used to mark the fabric, depending on whether the stitches will cover the marks or not.

When the design has been stitched it may be necessary to remove any traces of the fabric marker not covered by the stitches. Always follow the manufacturer's instructions when using any type of fabric marker.

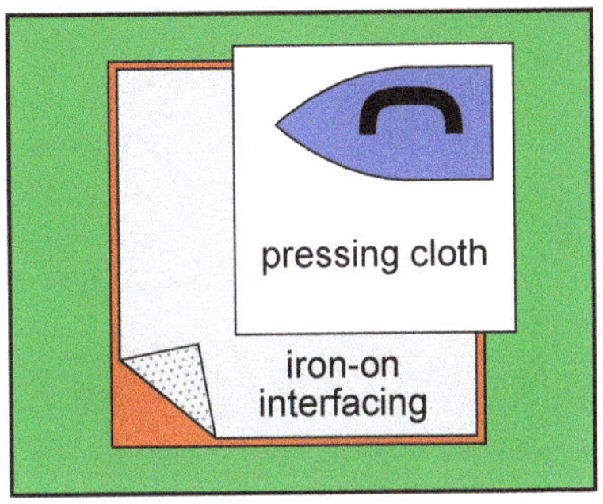


**1** Wash, press, and cut fabric to size. If using iron-on interfacing for backing, attach it before transferring the pattern, as heat may set pattern marks.

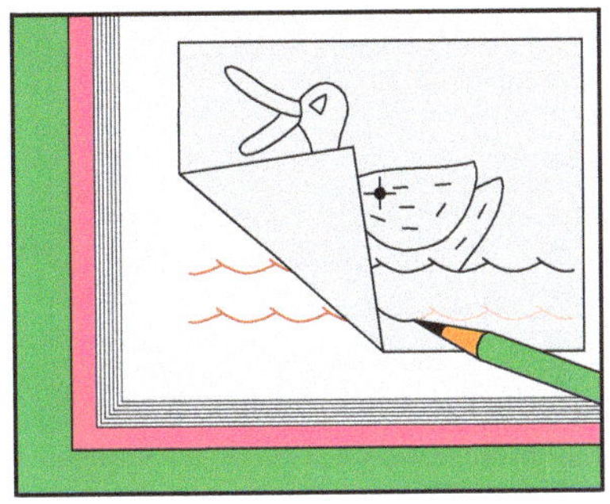

**2** Trace pattern from the book onto medium weight tracing paper using an HB pencil. Include the symbol indicating the centre of the pattern.

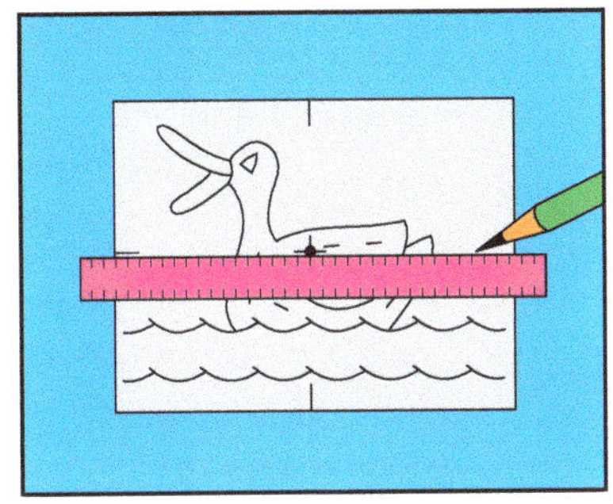

**3** On the tracing, place a ruler along the vertical line of the centre symbol. Rule lines on the outer edges of the tracing. Repeat for the horizontal line.

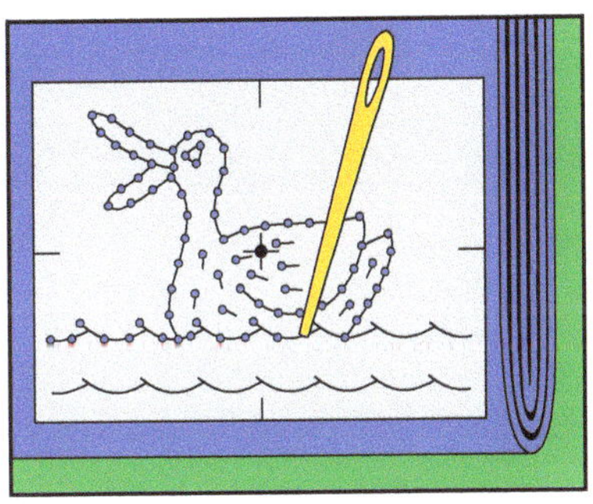

**4** Place tracing on a pad of folded fabric. With a large needle, pierce holes through tracing at regular intervals along pattern lines, but no need to pierce the centre symbol.

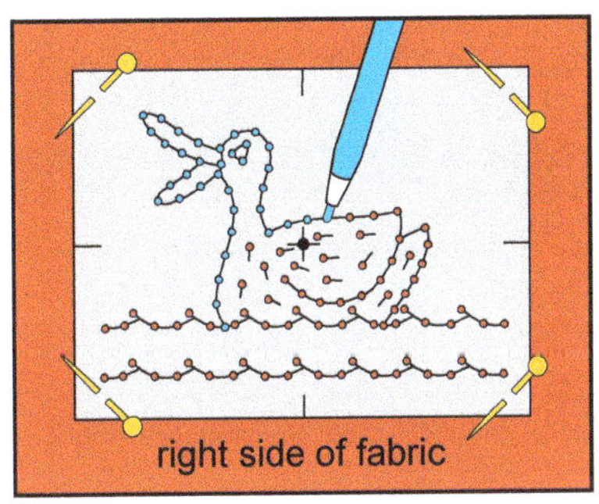


**5** Place fabric right side up. Pin tracing squarely onto fabric, matching centres. With fabric marker, mark dots onto fabric through pierced holes.

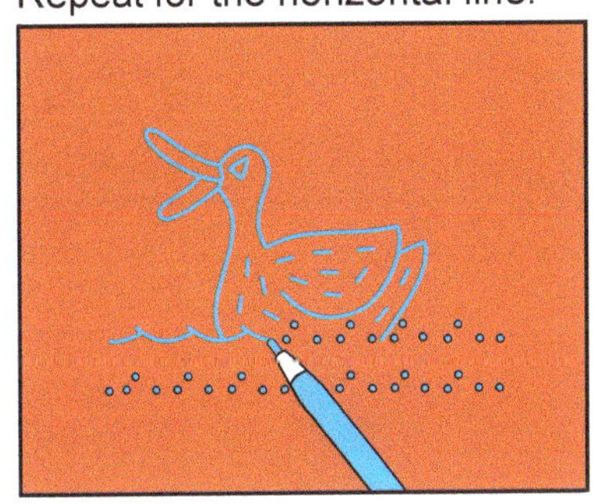

**6** Remove the tracing from the fabric. If possible and useful, join the dots to create continuous pattern lines on the fabric. Use the pattern as a guide.

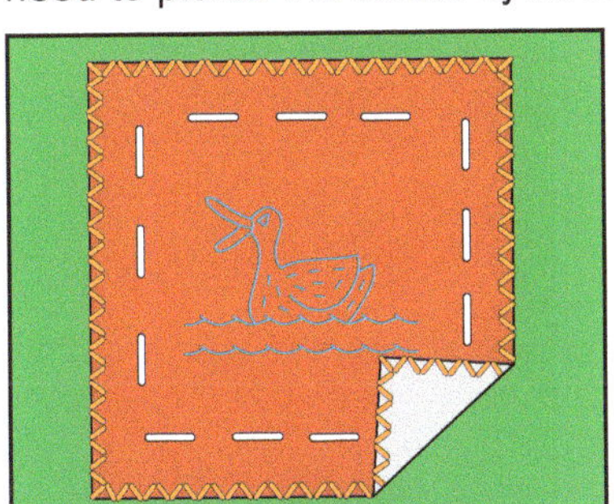

**7** If iron-on interfacing has not been used, tack the backing fabric to the wrong side. Sew the fabric edges to prevent fraying.

## Hints

### Dots can indicate length of stitches

For patterns using stitches such as running stitch and back stitch, the holes in the tracing can be pierced the same distance apart as the length required for the stitches. When stitching, use the dots to indicate the beginning and end of each stitch.

### No need to transfer the centre symbol or numbers

When transferring the pattern onto the fabric, there is no need to transfer the centre symbol or any numbers that are present on the pattern.

# Stitching

**Using the stitches**
It is important to develop an understanding of the wide range of effects that can be created with each stitch. For example, stitches that are frequently used for outlining shapes may be equally effective for filling areas or for use as tiny highlights.

**Developing a style**
Stitching is a creative activity, so feel free to develop your own individual style. It is like many other art forms in that you can work as neatly and accurately as you wish to, or you can work more freely, with a more sketchy technique.

**Direction of stitching**
You can stitch in whichever direction feels comfortable to you. People vary a great deal in this. If it feels at all awkward or uncomfortable to be stitching in a certain direction, try holding the fabric differently or try working in a different direction.

**Order of stitching**
Our instructions recommend the order in which the elements of the design are best worked.
As a general guide when stitching a design, work the flatter stitches first and the more dimensional stitches like French knots last. This helps to avoid your working thread catching on the previously worked stitches.
If elements of a design overlap, work those that are at the back before those that are at the front. For example, a stem should be worked first if it is behind a flower, as it is difficult to stitch behind previously worked stitches.
If you decide to stitch multiples of a design, for example a row of one animal repeated many times, it may be easiest to work all of the body outlines first, then all of the eyes next, and so on, rather than working one complete animal before starting the next. In this way, the repeated animals will be more consistent in style, and also you are using only one thread type at a time.

**Right-handed and left-handed instructions**
As right-handed or left-handed people work the stitches differently, step-by-step instructions for working every stitch in this book, as well as for beginning to stitch, working the stitches by skimming or stabbing, and for ending off the stitching, are provided for both.

# Threading a needle

Some threads are more difficult than others to pass through the eye of the needle. This is often because the thread end has unravelled or several strands have become separated and are therefore too large to easily push through the eye. Threads that are textured, such as wool that is fluffy and springy, can also cause problems by spreading out when being passed through the eye.

To thread a needle easily, try one of the methods shown here.

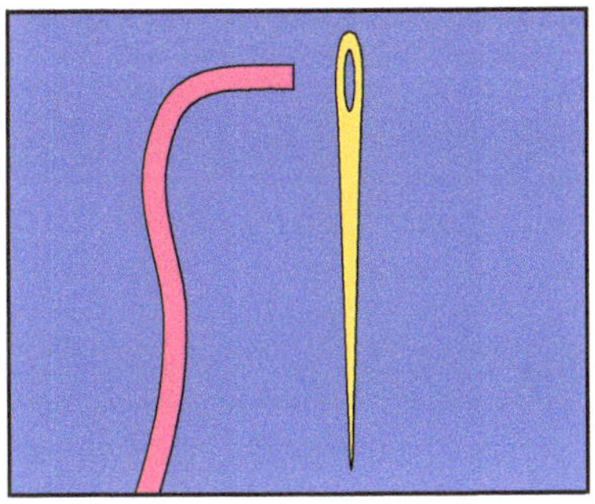

**Method 1: Cut**
**1** Cut the thread so that it has a tidy end. This can be straight across or cut at an angle.

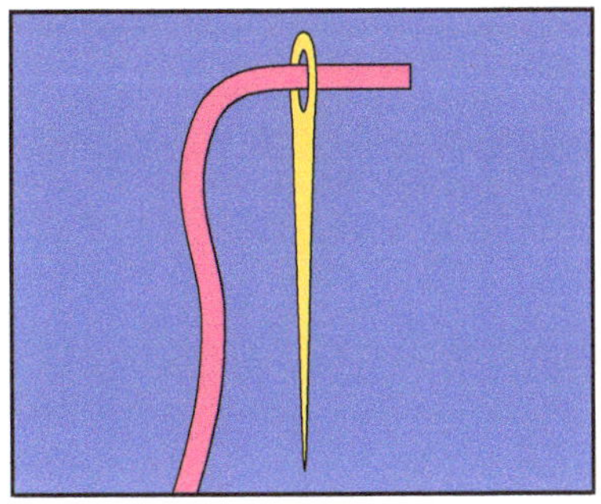

**2** Pass the cut end of the thread through the eye of the needle. Allow a small length of thread to extend beyond the eye.

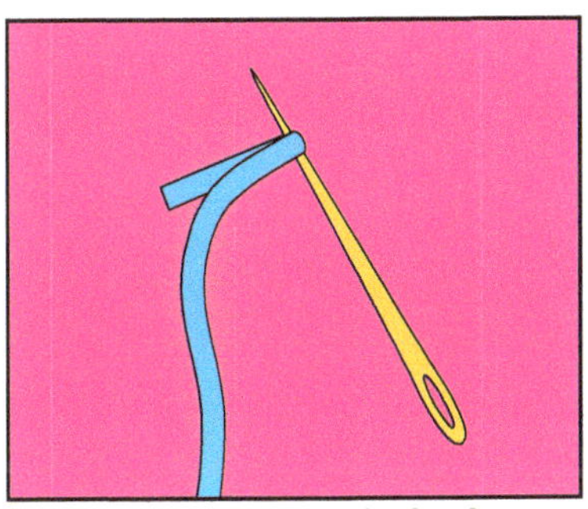

**Method 2: Fold and pinch**
**1** Fold the end of the thread over the point of the needle and pinch the folded thread tightly. Slide the needle out.

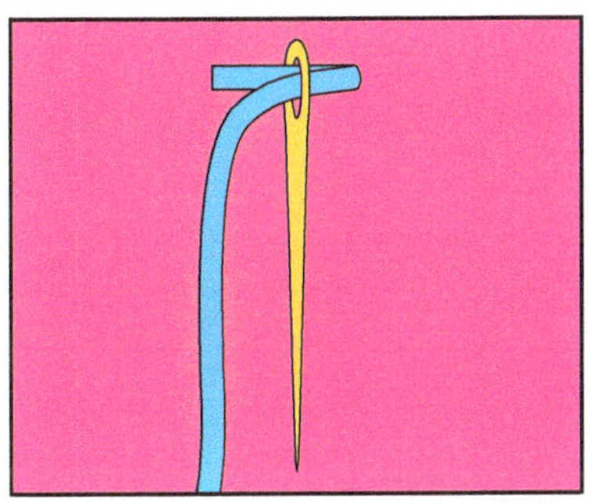

**2** Turn the needle upright. Still pinching the folded thread, pass this through the eye.

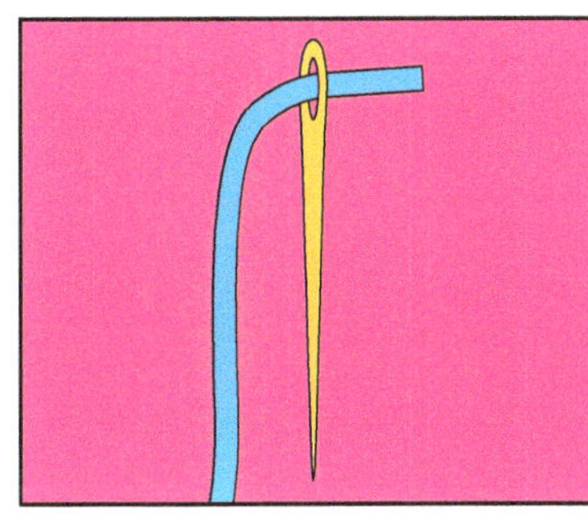

**3** Pull the folded end completely through. Allow a small length of thread to extend beyond the eye.

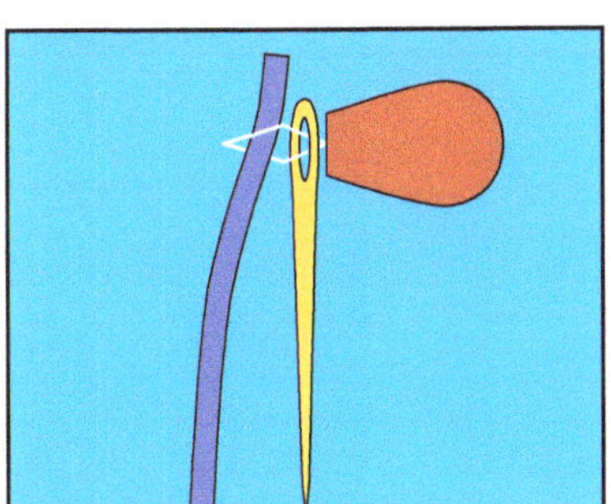

**Method 3: Needle threader**
**1** Push the wire loop of the needle threader through the eye in the needle. Pass the end of the thread through the loop.

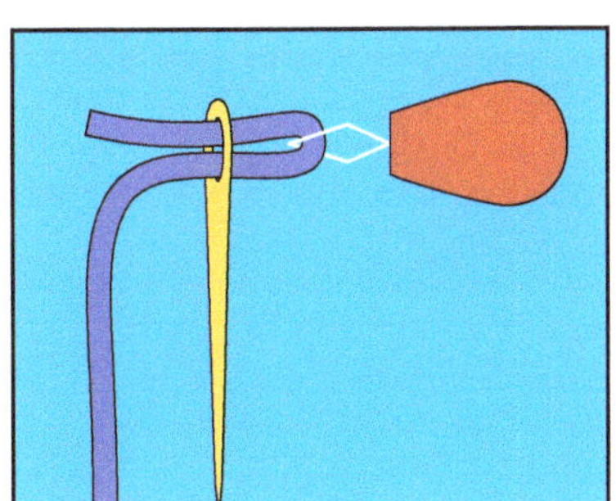

**2** Pull the wire loop and the thread through the eye of the needle.

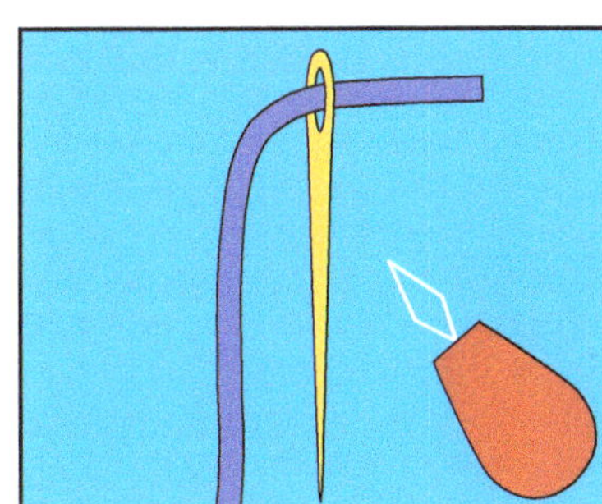

**3** Remove the needle threader from the thread. Allow a small length of thread to extend beyond the eye.

## Beginning to stitch

When beginning to stitch, the thread must be securely attached to the fabric so that the stitches do not later work loose. This can be achieved by various methods. Depending on the fabric, thread, and stitches that are used, one method may be better than the others, so you may need to experiment.

**Beginning with a knot**

Beginning with a knot is the most basic way of securing the thread, however problems can be encountered with this method. If a knot is too small, it may pull straight through the fabric. If the knot is too large, it may cause unnecessary bulk on the back of the work. If the needle catches the knot as you stitch, the needle may drag the knot away from its original position, distorting the first few stitches worked.

**Beginning with a waste knot**

A good alternative is to use a waste knot, so called because the knot is used to hold the thread end temporarily and then is cut off later, once several stitches have been worked. The thread end that remains is then secured by weaving it into the back of the stitches. A waste knot is also called an away knot because it is positioned at a distance away from the first stitch to be worked. Place the waste knot outside the design area, or in an area that will be covered with stitching later. Sufficient thread length should be allowed between the knot and the first stitch so the thread can be secured once the waste knot is cut off. You can begin with a knot, or a waste knot, whether the fabric has been backed with an extra layer or not.

**Beginning with tiny stitches**

Another method is to work two or three tiny stitches into the back of the work, without the need for a knot. This method is particularly easy to use with fabric that has been backed. If used with fabric that has not been backed, then work the tiny stitches in a position that will be covered with stitching later.

**Beginning by weaving**

Once some stitching has been worked, a new thread can be secured by weaving through the back of previously worked stitches. This method is suitable to use with or without backing the fabric first. It is easier to weave through the back of a row of dense stitches such as back stitch or chain stitch, than it is through the back of sparse stitches.

## Beginning to stitch: right-handed

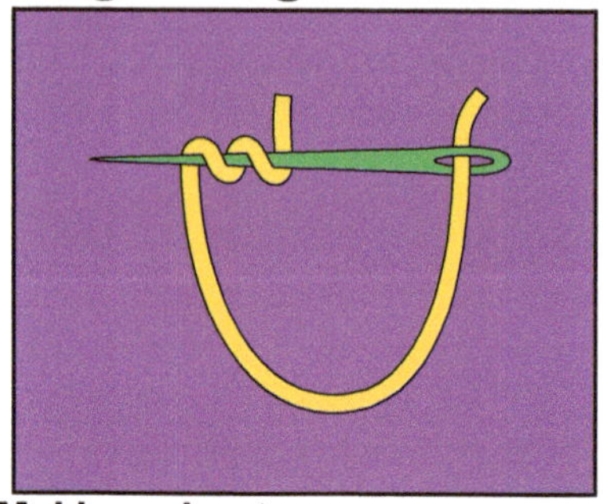

**Making a knot**

**1** Thread needle. Hold free end of thread behind needle. Wrap thread two to four times around needle.

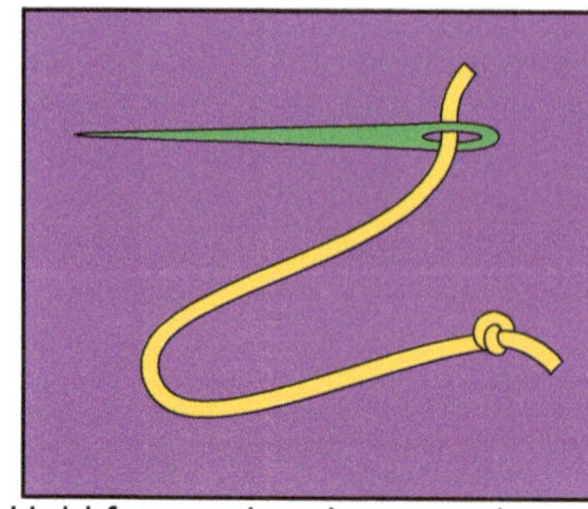

**2** Hold free end and wrapped needle and then pull needle and thread all the way through the wraps. A knot will form close to the end.

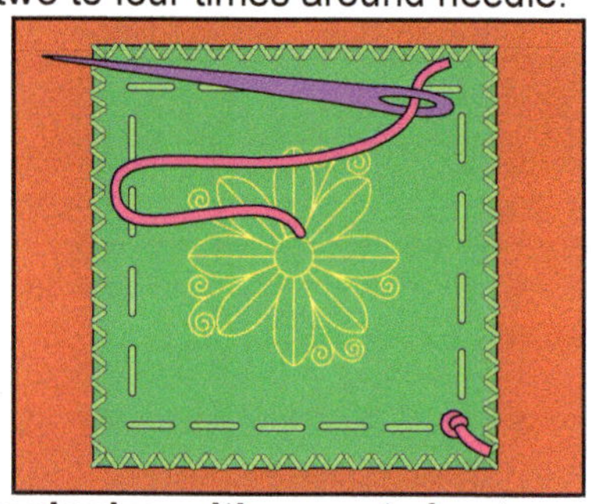

**Beginning with a waste knot**

**1** Knot thread. Take thread from front to back of work, away from design. Bring to front at position of first stitch.

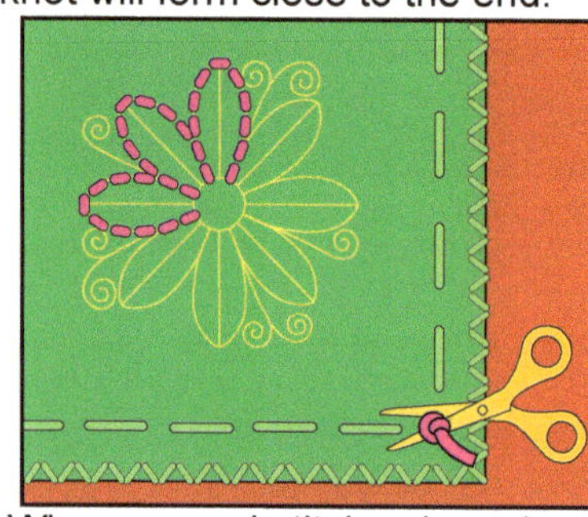

**2** When several stitches have been worked, cut off waste knot. On wrong side of work, end off by weaving the thread tail into the back of stitches.

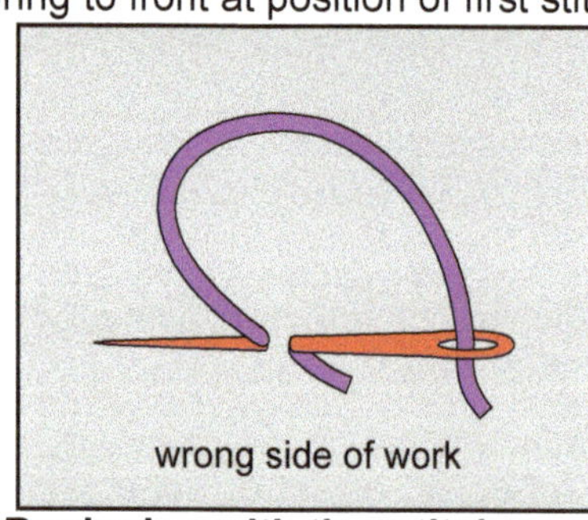


**Beginning with tiny stitches**

**1** Work a stitch in backing only, or where stitching will cover later. Leave small tail. Work second stitch through the same two holes.

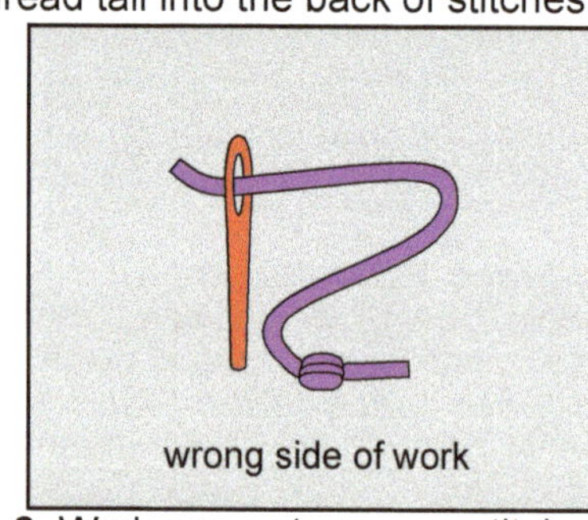


**2** Work one or two more stitches through the same two holes. If necessary, repeat until thread is secure. Take needle to front to begin stitching.

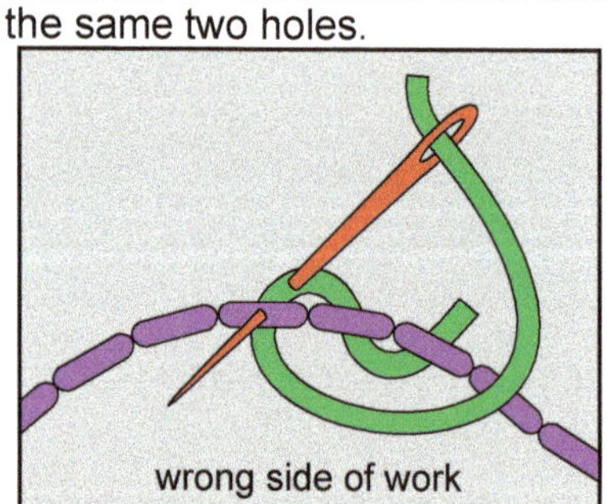


**Beginning by weaving**

**1** Weave new thread through back of previous stitches. Take needle through weaving thread and a stitch.

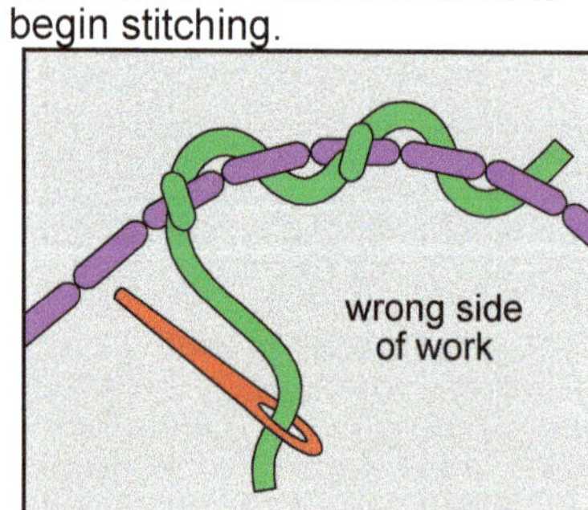


**2** Pull through and repeat until thread is secure. Take the needle to the front of the work at the position of first stitch to be worked.

# Beginning to stitch: left-handed

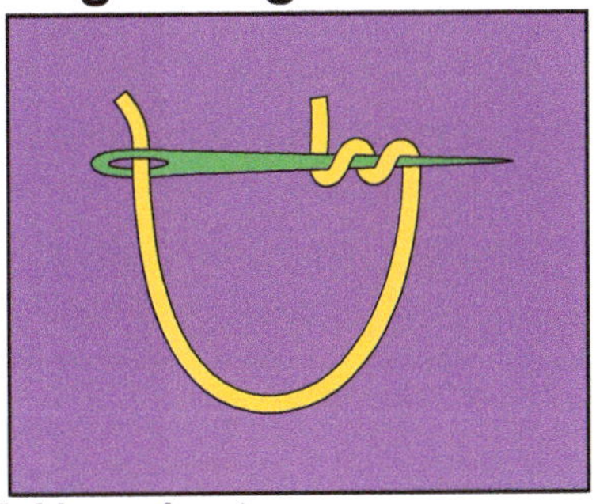

**Making a knot**
**1** Thread needle. Hold free end of thread behind needle. Wrap thread two to four times around needle.

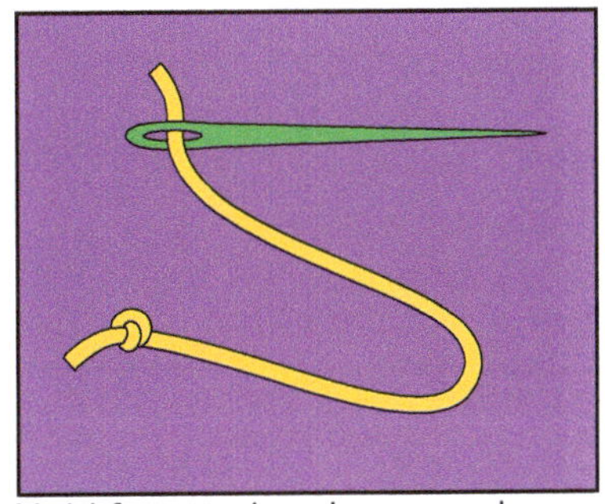

**2** Hold free end and wrapped needle and then pull needle and thread all the way through the wraps. A knot will form close to the end.

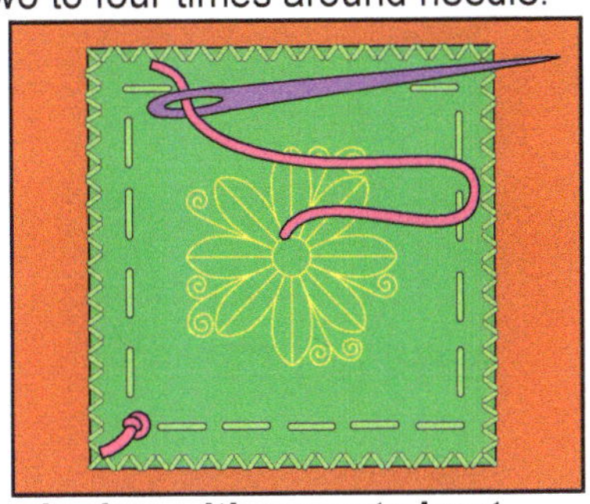

**Beginning with a waste knot**
**1** Knot thread. Take thread from front to back of work, away from design. Bring to front at position of first stitch.

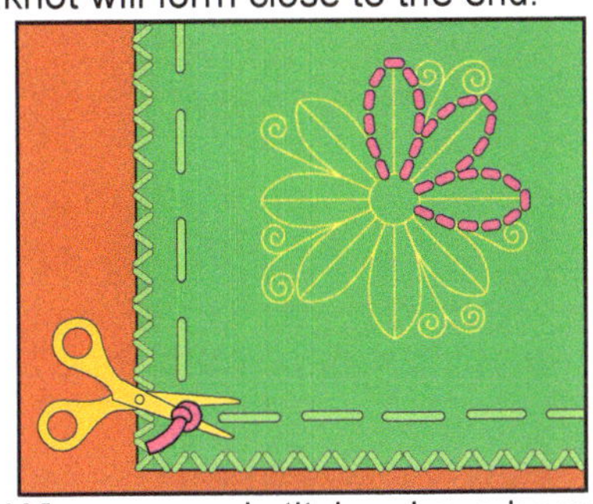

**2** When several stitches have been worked, cut off waste knot. On wrong side of work, end off by weaving the thread tail into the back of stitches.

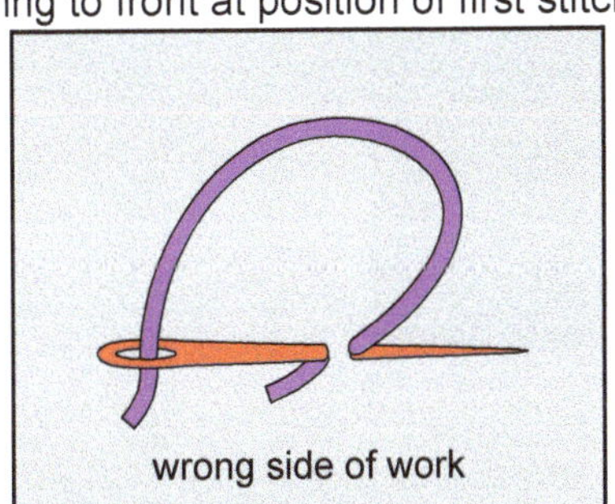


**Beginning with tiny stitches**
**1** Work a stitch in backing only, or where stitching will cover later. Leave small tail. Work second stitch through the same two holes.

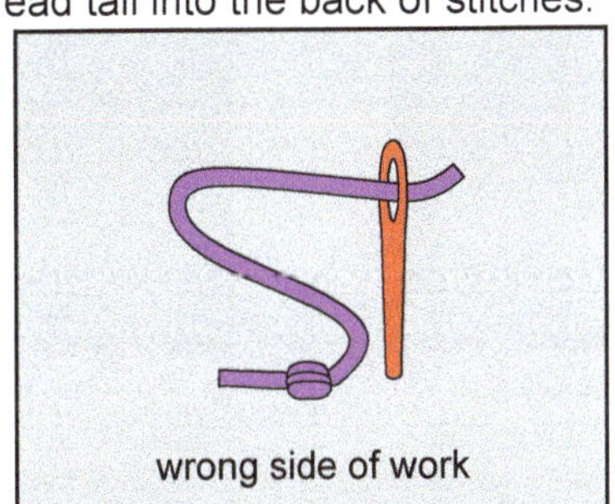


**2** Work one or two more stitches through the same two holes. If necessary, repeat until thread is secure. Take needle to front to begin stitching.

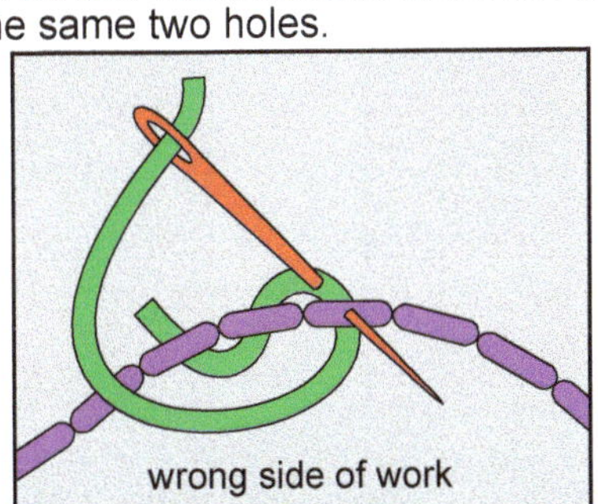


**Beginning by weaving**
**1** Weave new thread through back of previous stitches. Take needle through weaving thread and a stitch.

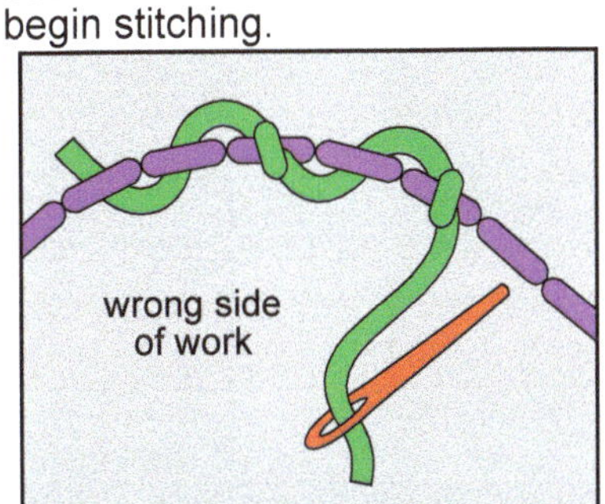


**2** Pull through and repeat until thread is secure. Take the needle to the front of the work at the position of first stitch to be worked.

## Working the stitches by skimming or stabbing

Stitches can often be worked in one movement, called skimming. In other cases, stitches can be worked in two separate movements, called stabbing.

Whether to skim or to stab the stitches depends on many factors. These include the actual stitch to be worked, the thickness of the fabric, whether or not the fabric is held taut in a hoop or a frame, and personal choice as to which is most comfortable and easiest.

The examples shown here all feature running stitch.

## Stitching by skimming or stabbing: right-handed

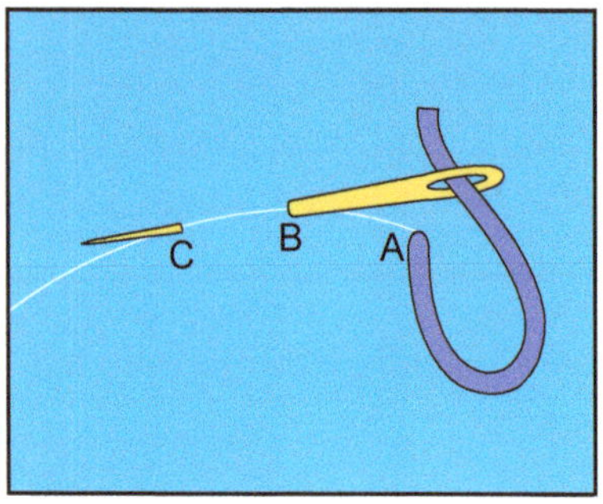


**Skimming**
**1** Come up at A. In one movement, take the needle through the fabric at B and emerge at C.

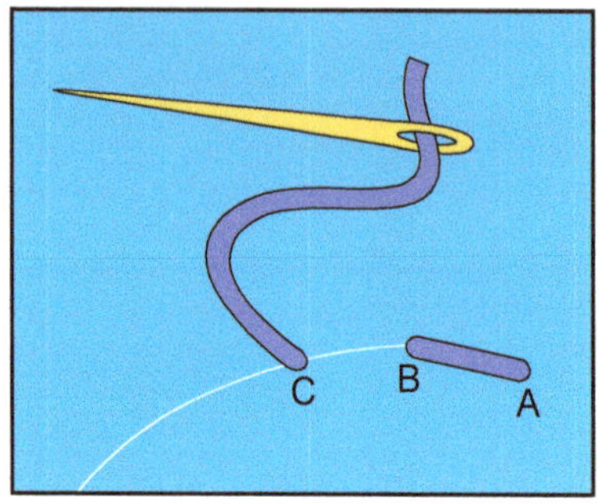


**2** Pull the thread through to form the stitch and to be ready to begin the next stitch.

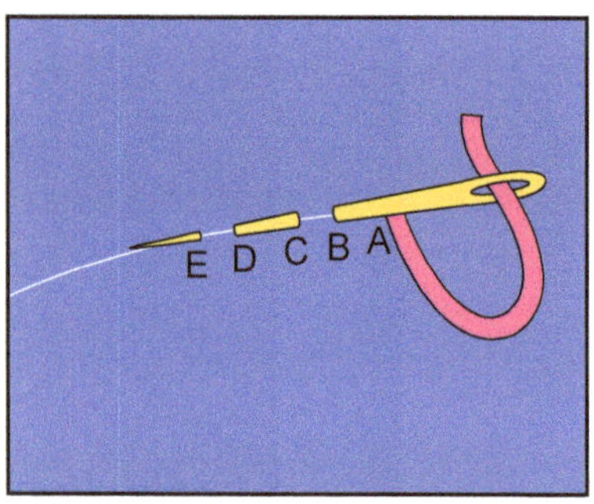


**Skimming several stitches**
**1** Come up at A. Skim needle through the fabric at B, C, D and E, noting that more stitches than this can be skimmed.

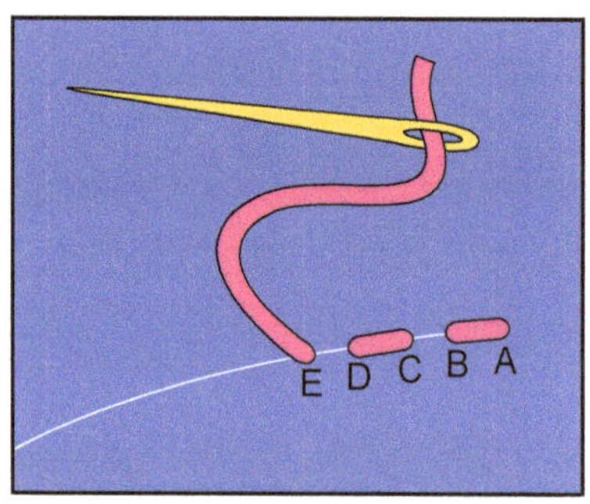


**2** Pull the thread through to form the stitches and to be ready to work the next group of stitches.

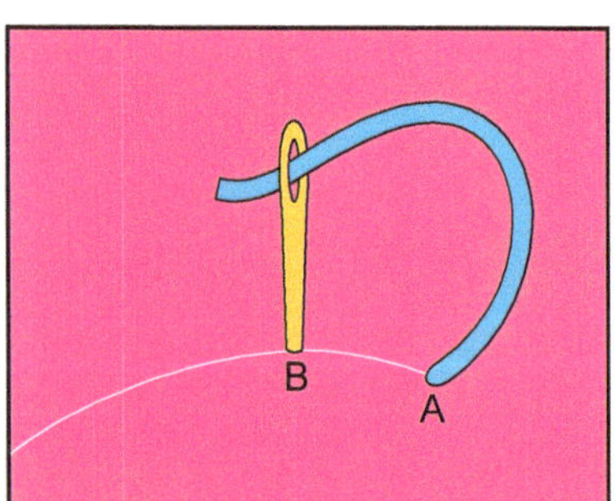


**Stabbing**
**1** Come up at A. Stab the needle through to the back of the fabric at B.

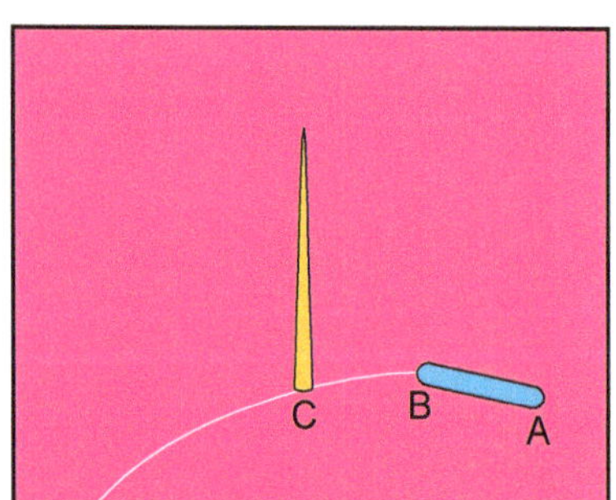


**2** Pull the thread through to the back, forming the stitch. Stab the needle to the front of the fabric at C.

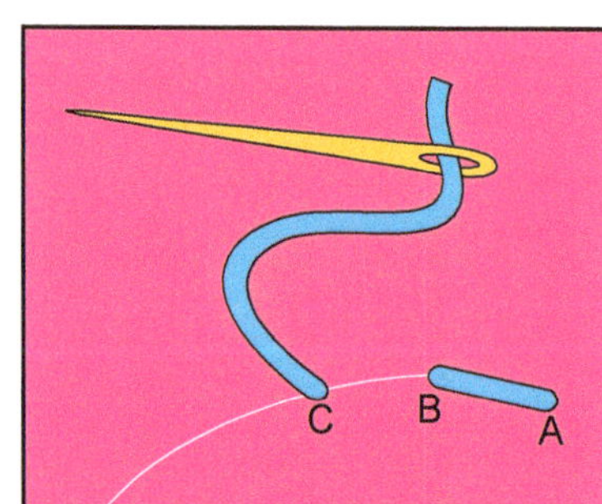


**3** Pull the thread through to the front, ready to begin the next stitch.

## Stitching by skimming or stabbing: left-handed

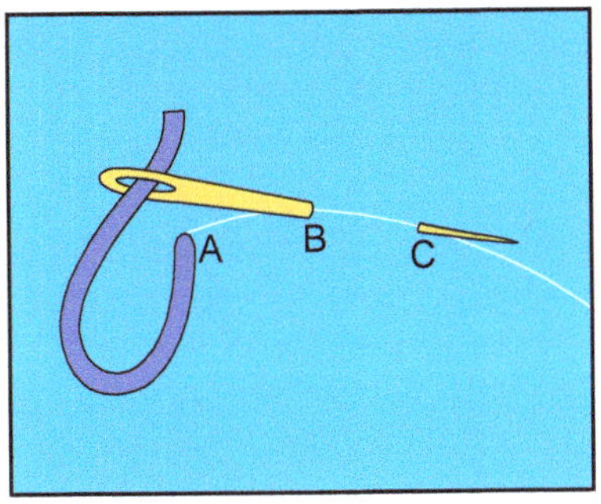


**Skimming**
**1** Come up at A. In one movement, take the needle through the fabric at B and emerge at C.

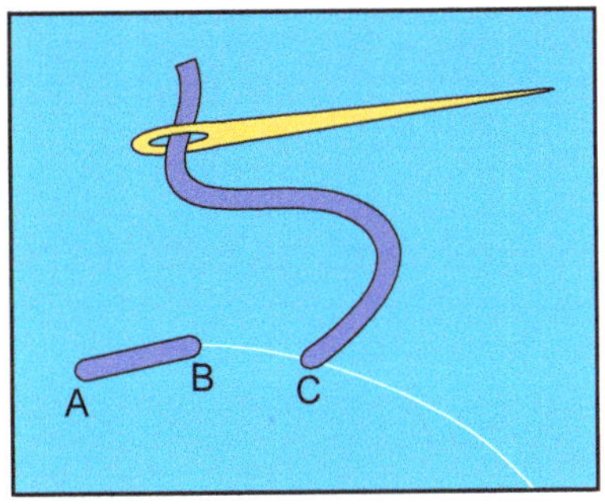


**2** Pull the thread through to form the stitch and to be ready to begin the next stitch.

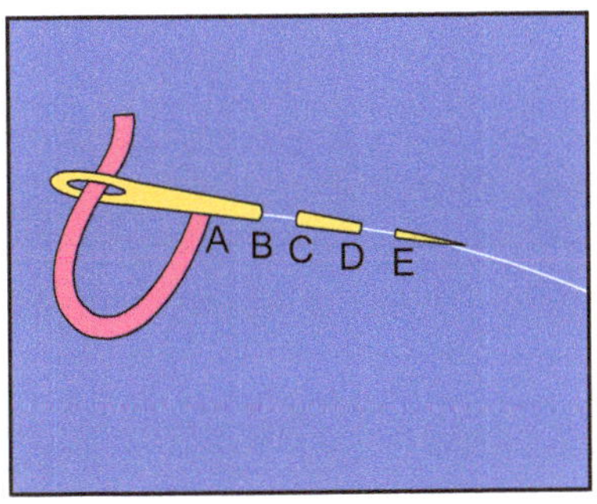


**Skimming several stitches**
**1** Come up at A. Skim needle through the fabric at B, C, D and E, noting that more stitches than this can be skimmed.

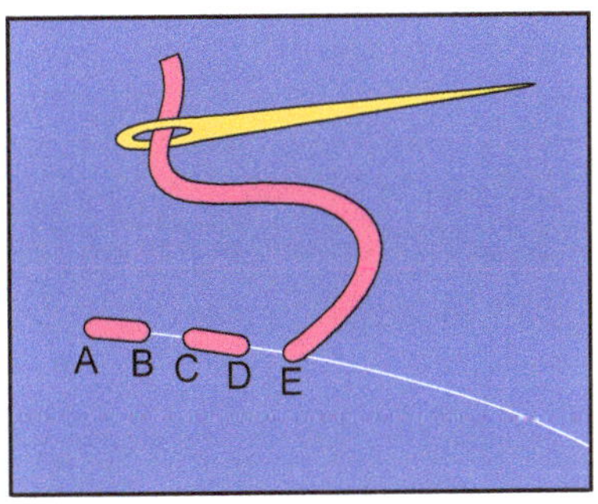


**2** Pull the thread through to form the stitches and to be ready to work the next group of stitches.

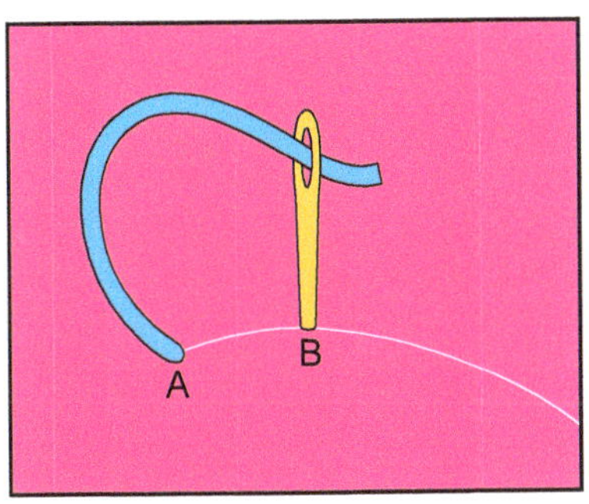


**Stabbing**
**1** Come up at A. Stab the needle through to the back of the fabric at B.

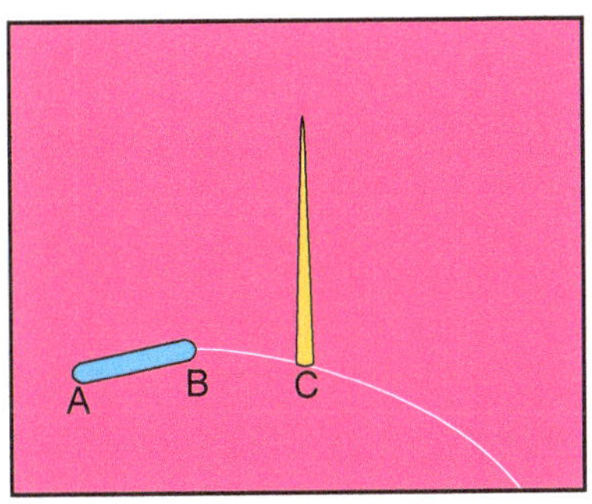


**2** Pull the thread through to the back, forming the stitch. Stab the needle to the front of the fabric at C.

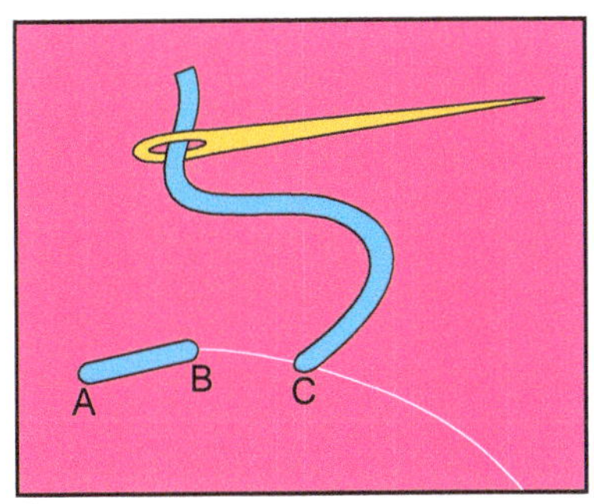


**3** Pull the thread through to the front, ready to begin the next stitch.

# Hints for working the stitches

### Stitches covering pattern lines

Some stitches, such as back stitch and stem stitch, completely cover the marked pattern lines. Others, such as running stitch, do not.
Chain stitch may or may not cover the marked lines, depending on the type and thickness of the thread used and the size of the stitches. Consider this when deciding which method to use for transferring the pattern onto the fabric as some transfer methods are permanent.

### Stitch tension

How tightly or how loosely the stitches are worked is called stitch tension. If the tension of the stitches is too tight, the stitches will be strained and the fabric will not lie flat. If the tension of the stitches is too loose, the stitches may not form properly. Check the tension as you work each stitch as it is easier to fix a problem when it occurs rather than to fix it later. When working with more than one strand of thread, aim to keep the tension the same on all the strands. If stitching on fabrics that have a raised surface, such as towelling, polar fleece, or felt, do not pull the thread too tightly or the stitches may sink into the fabric.

### Untwisting the thread

As you stitch, the thread may become over-twisted, resulting in tangles or knots. This is easily overcome by regularly allowing the needle and thread to dangle freely from the fabric.

### Parking the needle

To leave the work for a short time between stitching sessions, secure the needle near the edge of the fabric, away from the design area. If the needle is left in the middle of the work, the stitches or the fabric may be damaged, and if the needle is not secured, it is easily lost. If storing an unfinished project for a long period of time, it may be best not to leave the needle in the work at all.

### Rotating the fabric

In order to stitch around a curve, a corner, or the outline of a shape, it is usually necessary to rotate the fabric as you work.

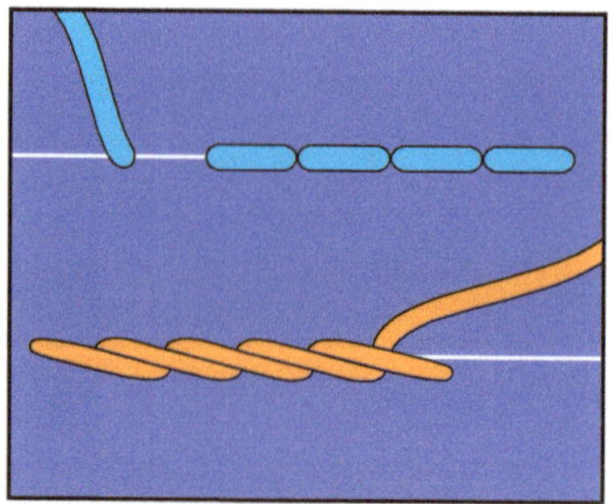

**Covering pattern lines**
Back stitch, in upper row, and stem stitch, in lower row, cover the pattern lines completely.

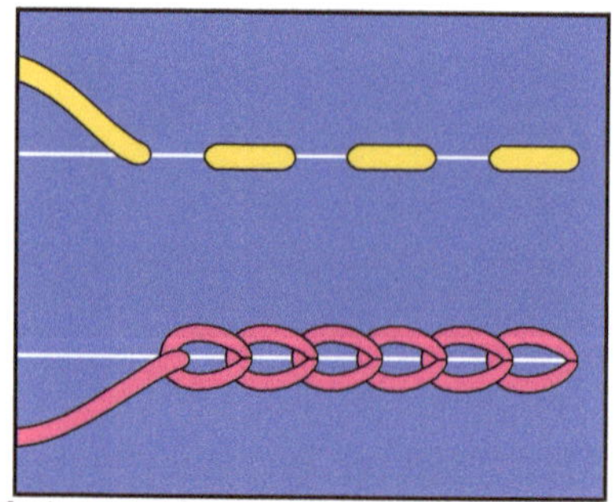

**Not covering pattern lines**
Running stitch, in upper row, and chain stitch, in lower row, do not cover the pattern lines completely.

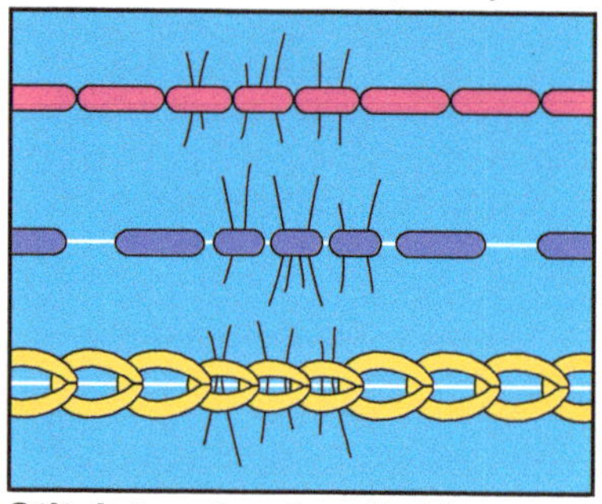

**Stitch tension too tight**
Working with the tension too tight results in puckered fabric. The examples shown are back stitch, running stitch, and chain stitch.

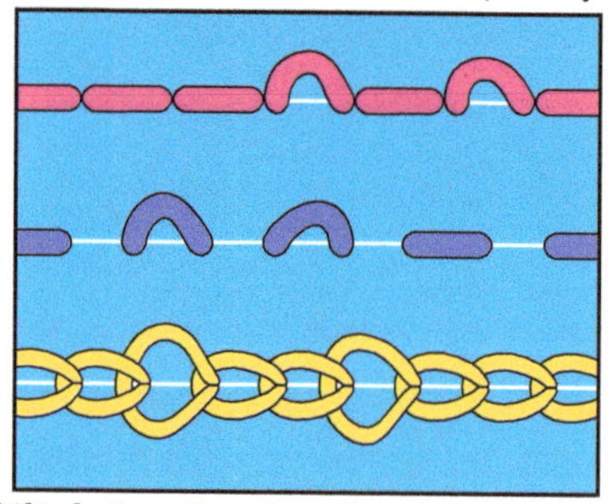

**Stitch tension too loose**
Working with the tension too loose produces distorted stitches. The examples shown are back stitch, running stitch, and chain stitch.

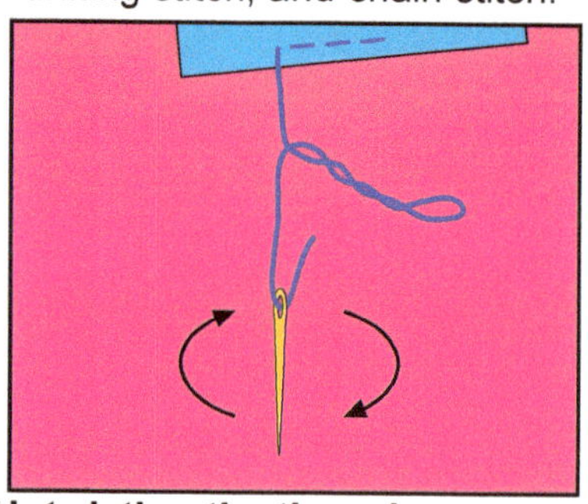

**Untwisting the thread**
Regularly allow the needle and thread to dangle freely in order to unwind any extra twists that may have formed in the thread.

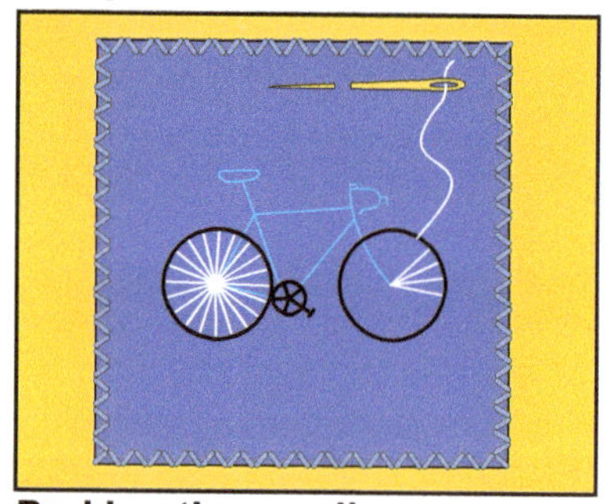

**Parking the needle**
To leave the work for a short time, park the needle near the edge of the fabric, well outside the design area.

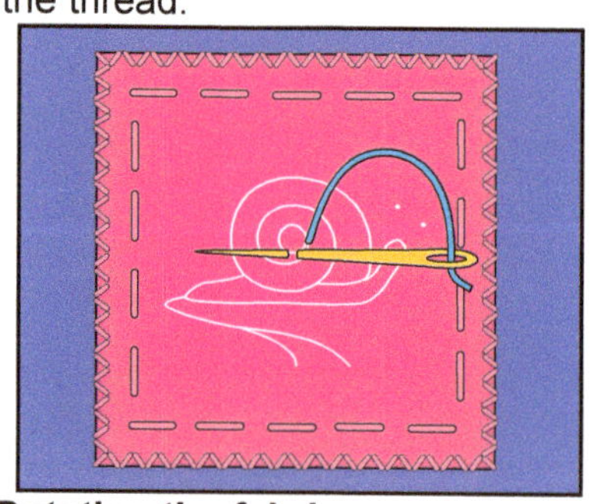

**Rotating the fabric**
**1** To stitch around a marked shape, begin stitching in a direction that is comfortable.

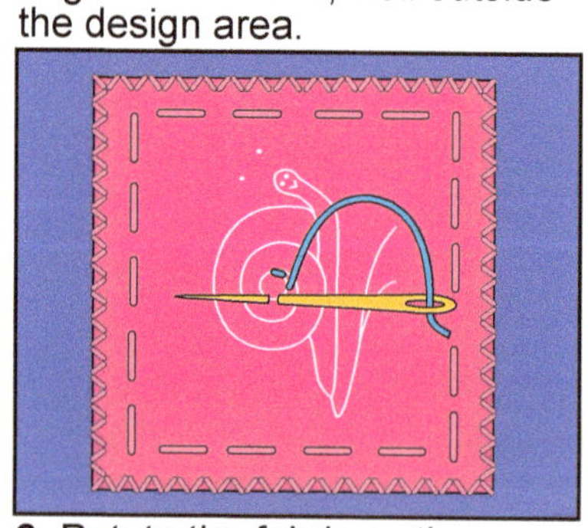

**2** Rotate the fabric as the stitching progresses around the marked shape.

# More hints for working the stitches

### Carrying the thread

Continuing with the same thread from one row or area of stitching across to the next is called carrying the thread. There are a few factors to consider when deciding whether to carry a thread on the back of the work or to end it off and then begin the next area with a new thread. Carried threads may be visible through some fabrics, or they may form ridges. If a design is worked on items such as clothing or towels, exposed carried threads may catch on things and the stitches on the right side may therefore be damaged.

### Fitting stitches along a row

To work a row of stitches of even length, towards the end of the row, visually judge whether the last few stitches will fit exactly. If not, consider whether either a few slightly smaller stitches or perhaps a few slightly larger stitches will fit better into the space available. This will avoid ending with the last stitch of a very uneven size.

### Stitches that meet

When working stitches that meet, work through the same hole in the fabric as the previously worked stitch, or stitches, but avoid splitting the thread of any stitches with the needle.

### Unpicking

If a stitch or an area of stitching is not correct, it may need to be unpicked. It is often worth taking the time to unpick a mistake rather than have it spoil the work. When unpicking, make sure that the stitches that are correct are not damaged during the process.

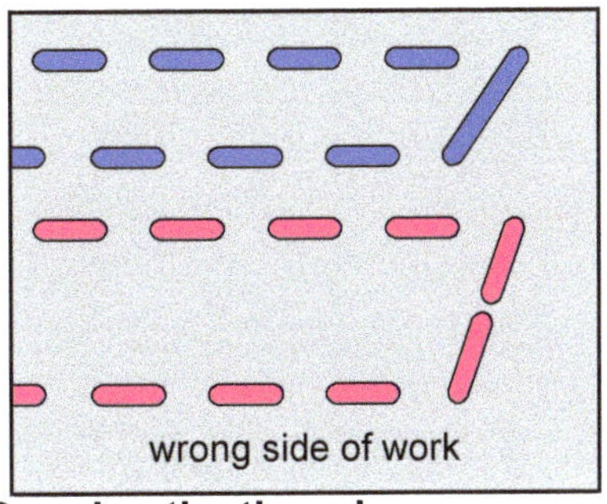


**Carrying the thread**
**1** Carry thread to next stitched line (blue). If work is backed, you can carry thread by stitching through the backing fabric only between stitched lines (pink).

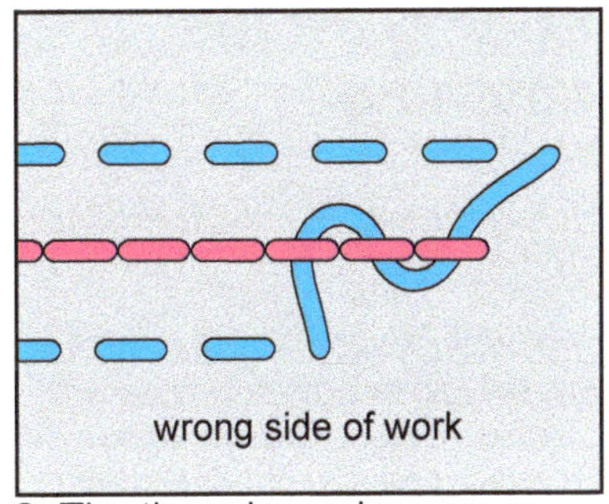


**2** The thread may be woven through the back of previously worked stitches to move from one area to another, whether backing is used or not.

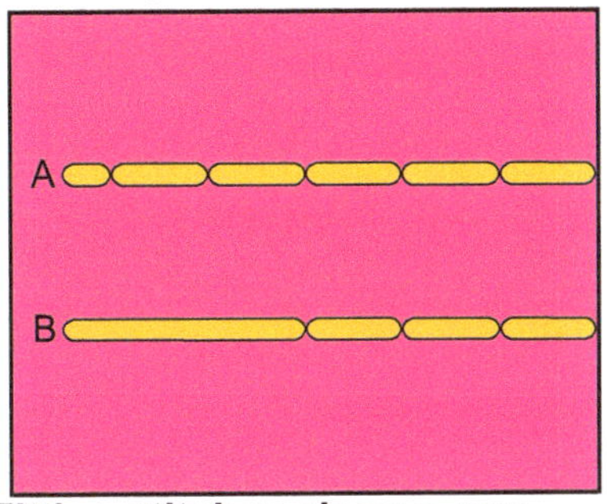


**Fitting stitches along a row**
**1** In A, the row ends with a tiny stitch. In B, the row ends with a large stitch. Other options are shown at right.

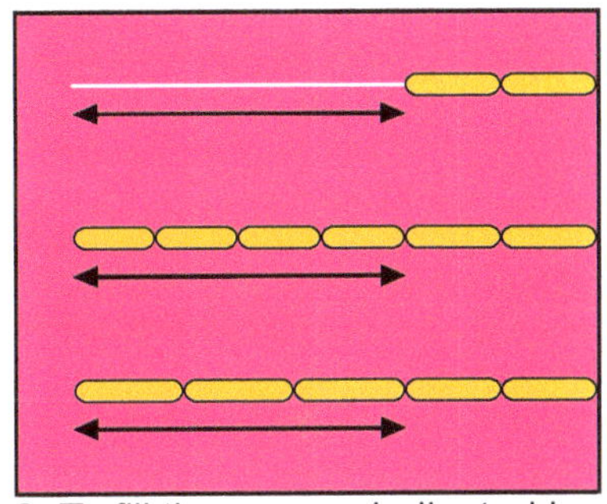

**2** To fill the spaces indicated by the arrows, you could work four slightly smaller stitches, or three slightly larger stitches.

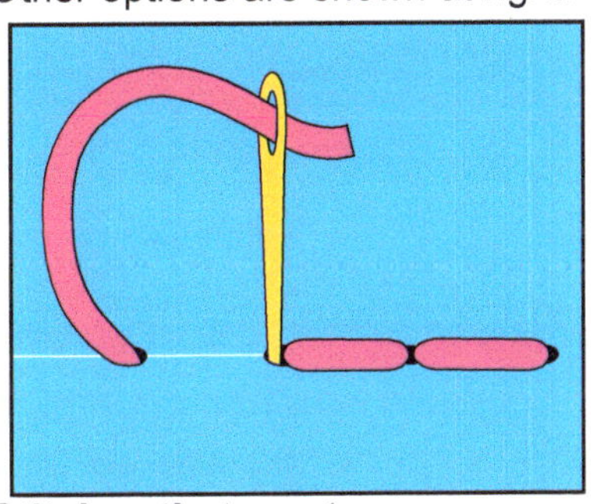

**Stitches that meet**
**1** In a row of back stitch, the stitches meet end to end and share the same hole in the fabric where they touch.

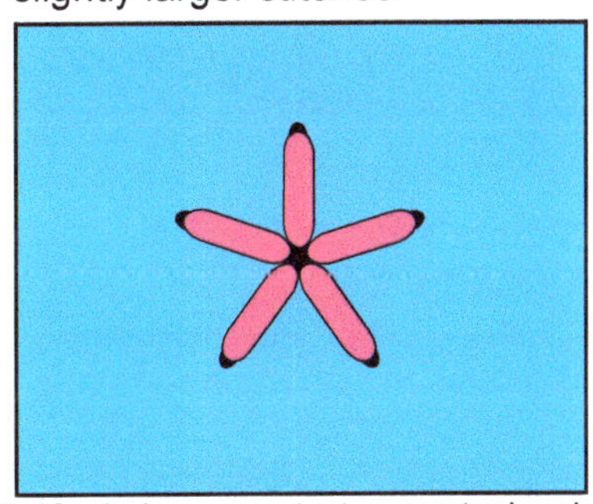

**2** If stitches meet at a central point, work each stitch from the outside towards centre. The stitches share the same hole in the centre.

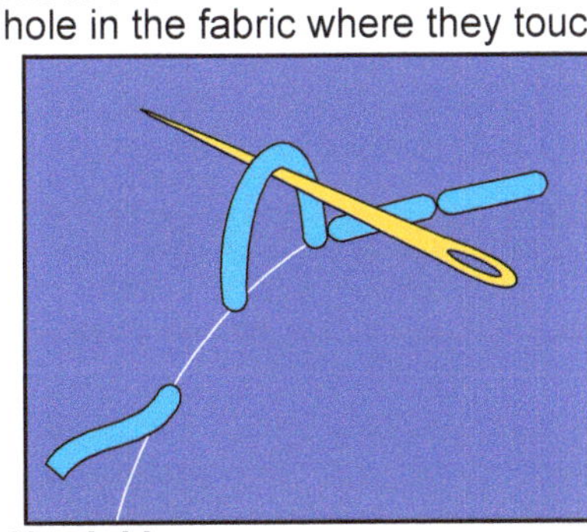

**Unpicking**
**1** If a stitch is worked incorrectly, unthread needle. Use the needle to loosen the stitch and unpick it. Rethread needle and continue.

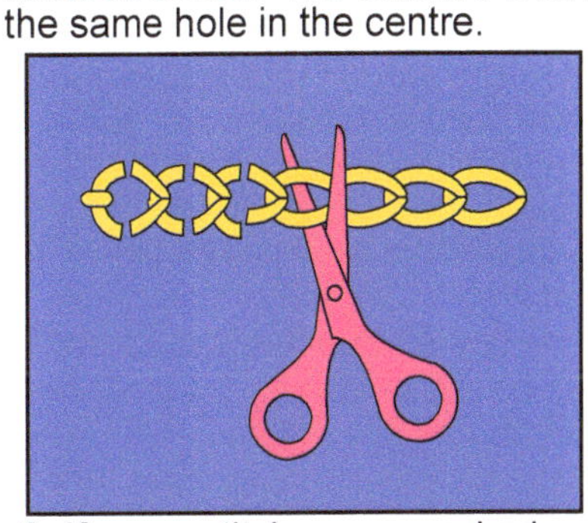

**2** If many stitches are worked incorrectly, carefully cut through them and then remove the cut threads. Work the stitches again with a new length of thread.

# Ending off the stitching

When you have reached the end of a row of stitching, or when your thread is becoming too short to continue stitching, the process of securing the end of the thread is called ending off.
In most cases, it is important that the ending off is not visible on the front of the work.
Be careful that the ending off does not distort the stitches, especially the last stitch that was worked, which will often be a little loose at first.

Rayon or metallic threads may need to be ended off extra securely because they can be springy and have a tendency to undo very easily. End them off by working either many tiny stitches or by weaving a few more times than you would normally do with other threads.

### Length of thread

Always leave enough thread length to end off, as it can be difficult to manage if the thread is too short.

### Methods for ending off

There are a number of methods used to end off the thread on the back of the fabric so that it will not become loose. The method chosen depends on whether the fabric is backed or not, the actual stitches worked, and the type of thread used.
Two easy methods for ending off are shown on these pages. Both are suitable to use whether the fabric has been backed or not.
If you are ending off with tiny stitches on fabric that has not been backed, make sure that the tiny stitches are worked in such a way that they will not be visible on the front.

## Ending off: right-handed

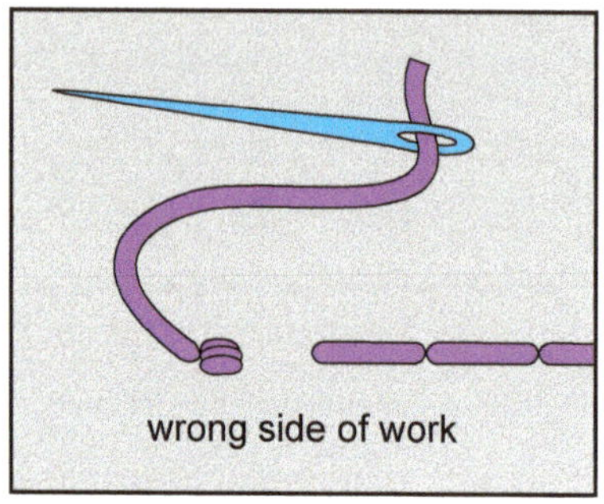


**With tiny stitches**
**1** On the back, work two or more tiny stitches through the same two holes in the backing, or in the unbacked fabric.

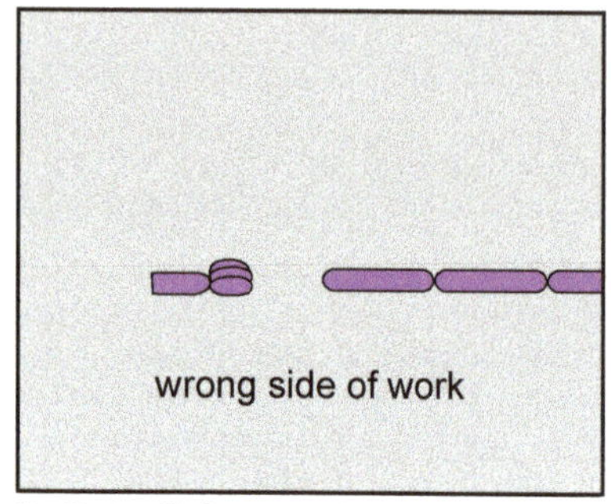


**2** Cut off the surplus thread, leaving a small tail.

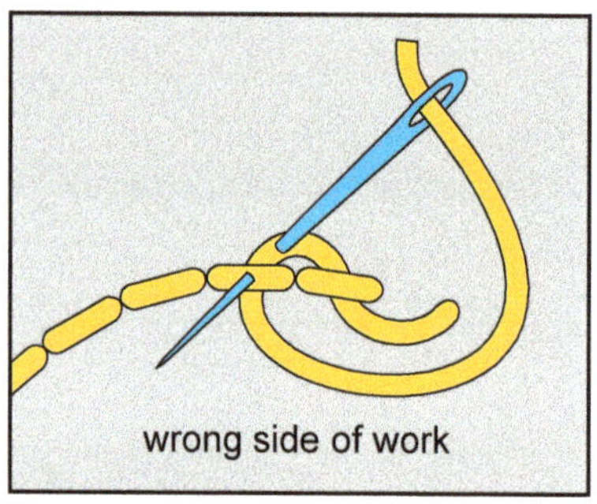


**By weaving**
**1** Weave the thread through the back of the stitches. Take the needle through the weaving thread and the back of a stitch.

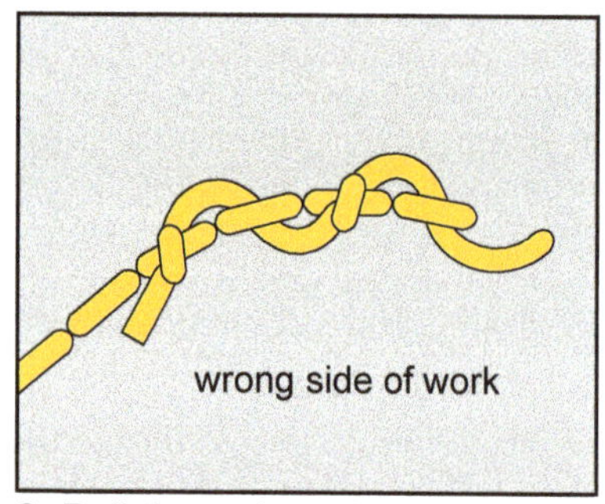


**2** Pull through and repeat until the thread is secure. Cut off the surplus thread, leaving a small tail.

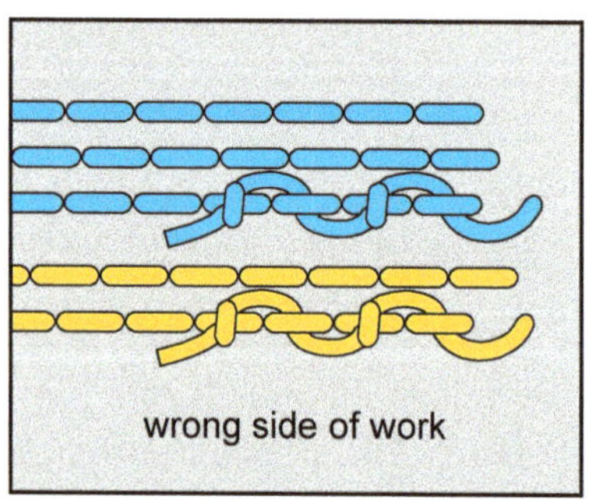


**Behind same colour of thread**
If possible, aim to end off each thread on the back of the work behind stitches of the same colour.

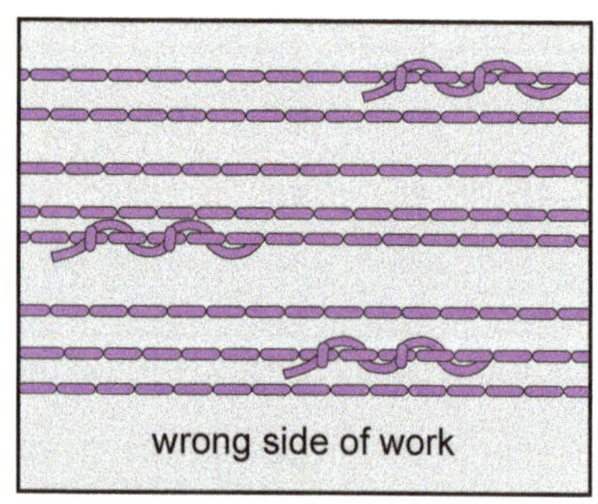


**Avoiding bulk**
If possible, end off the threads behind different parts of the design, so that the bulk of thread is not all in one area.

# Ending off: left-handed

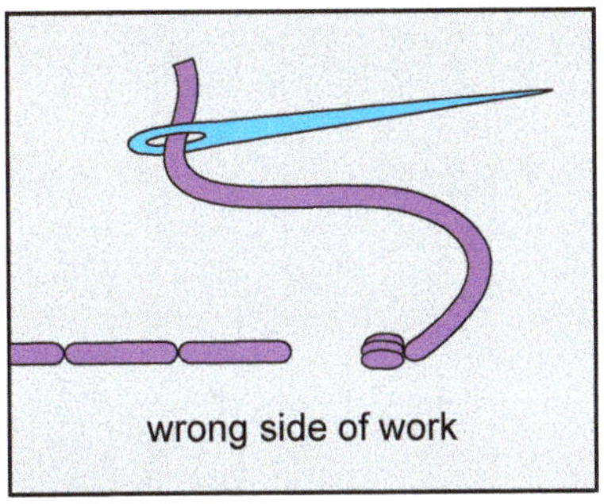


**With tiny stitches**
**1** On the back, work two or more tiny stitches through the same two holes in the backing, or in the unbacked fabric.

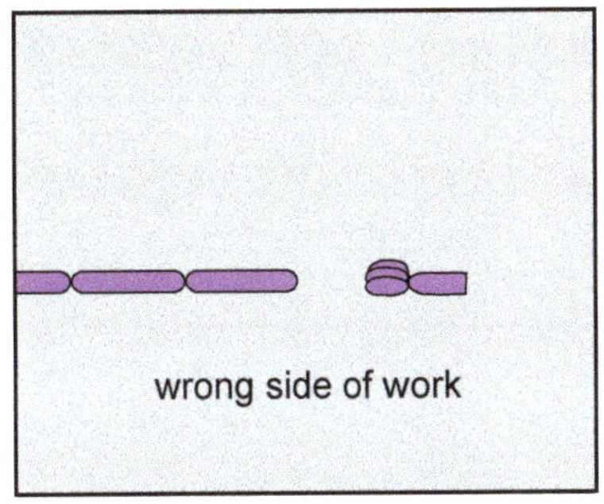


**2** Cut off the surplus thread, leaving a small tail.

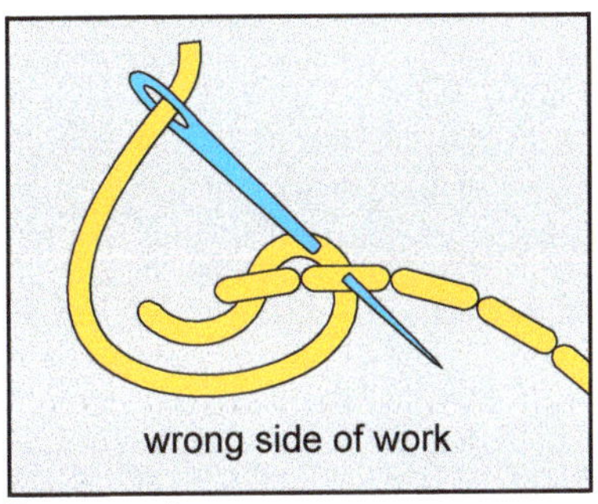


**By weaving**
**1** Weave the thread through the back of the stitches. Take the needle through the weaving thread and the back of a stitch.

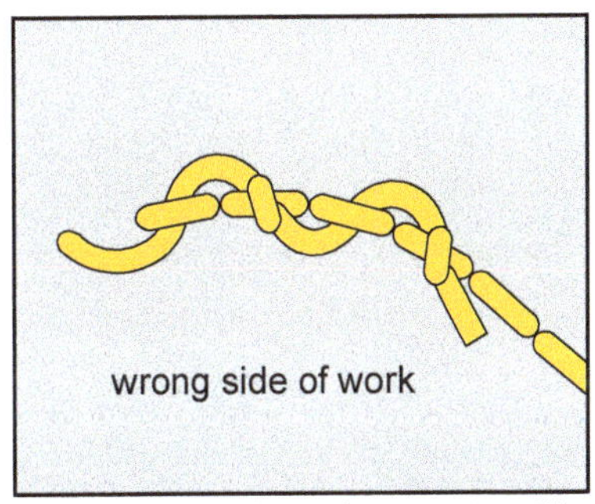


**2** Pull through and repeat until the thread is secure. Cut off the surplus thread, leaving a small tail.

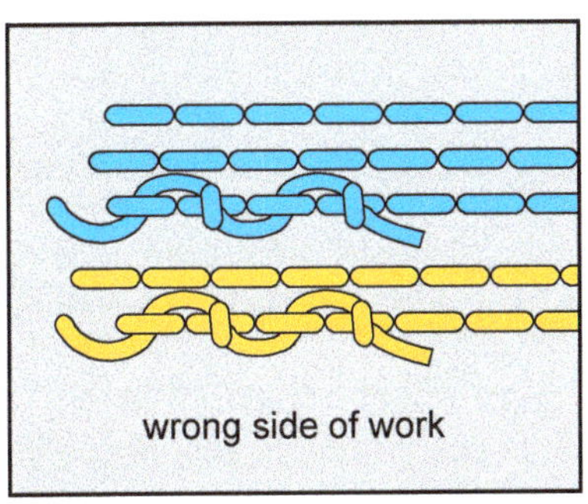


**Behind same colour of thread**
If possible, aim to end off each thread on the back of the work behind stitches of the same colour.

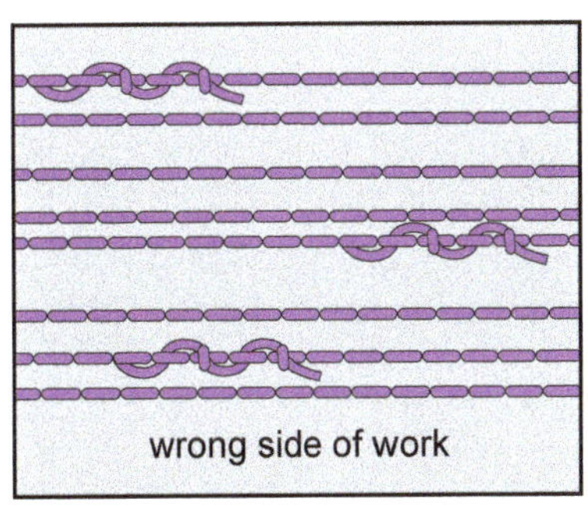


**Avoiding bulk**
If possible, end off the threads behind different parts of the design, so that the bulk of thread is not all in one area.

# Finishing

Finishing involves the final stages needed to transform a stitched work into a completed project.

## Removing tacking and pattern markings

When the stitching is complete, carefully remove any tacking stitches remaining in the work. Depending on the type of stitches or threads used to work the design, there may be some pattern markings still visible on the fabric, which will need to be removed before the fabric can be pressed. If a method of transfer that will brush off has been used, gently brush the marks until they are removed. If any type of water erasable fabric marker has been used, completely immerse the fabric in cold water to dissolve the pattern marks. Lift the fabric out of the water, without wringing, and place it out flat on a towel. Making sure that the fabric has not been pulled out of shape, leave it to partially dry on the towel.

## Straightening and flattening the stitched work

Even if the fabric has not been distorted by the stitches forming the design, there may still be some creases in the area surrounding the design. These can be pressed out with an iron. Use water from a spray bottle to dampen the fabric if necessary, or, if it has been rinsed, then press while it is still partly dry. Protect the fabric from damage due to the heat of the iron by using a pressing cloth. Be careful when pressing near the stitched area, as pressing may damage the stitches.

If the fabric has been distorted by the stitches, it will need to be stretched back to shape by pinning it out tightly onto a blocking board, corkboard, cork tile, or similar, that has been covered with a layer or two of white cloth or a sheet of plastic. This process is most effective if the stitched fabric is damp, either by being dampened with water from a spray bottle, or from having been rinsed. The white cloth or sheet of plastic on the board or cork will prevent any colour from the board or cork from damaging the stitched work.

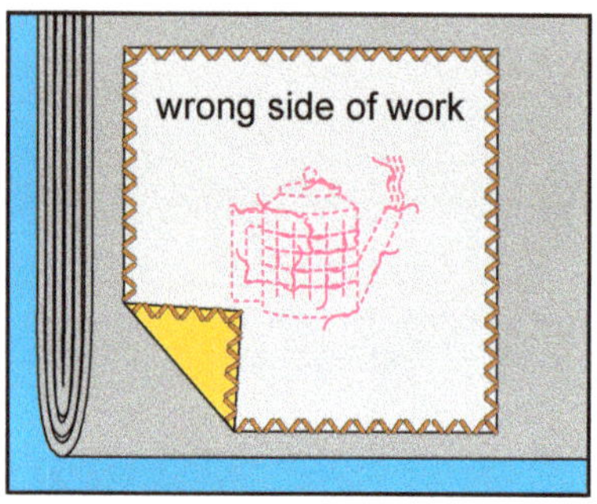


**Pressing**
**1** Place work, right side facing down, onto a padded surface such as a folded white cotton sheet placed on an ironing board.

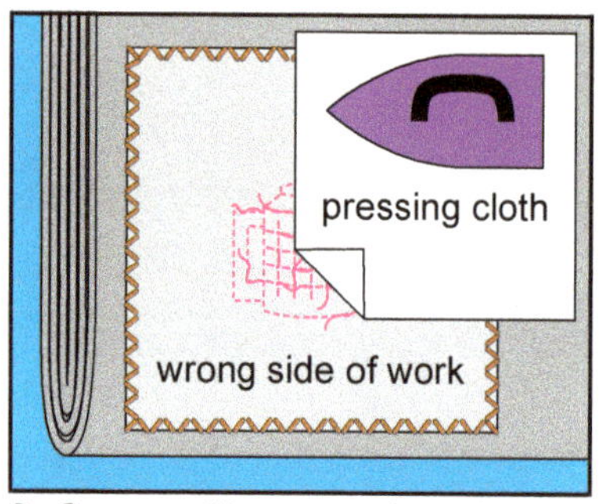


**2** Cover with a pressing cloth. Set iron to correct temperature. Press fabric surrounding design with an even pressure and steady movement.

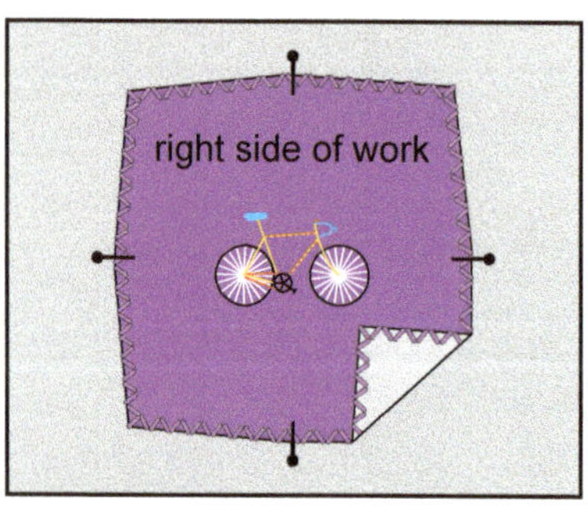


**Pinning out**
**1** Place one or two layers of white fabric or a sheet of plastic onto blocking board, corkboard, cork tile, or similar. Place dampened work right side up onto this. Stretch the fabric and pin at the centres of the sides.

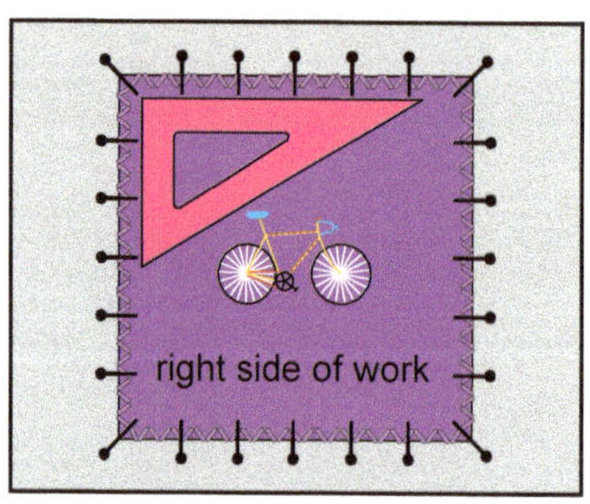


**2** Working outwards to corners, stretch the fabric and add pins at regular intervals along each side. Use a set square to check that the fabric is square.

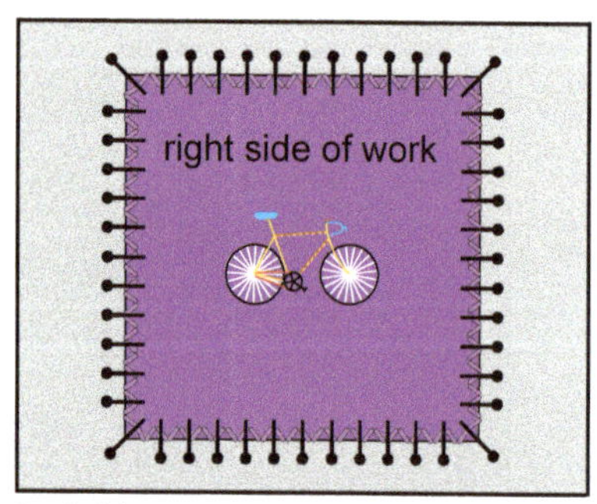


**3** Add more pins in the spaces, adjusting the tightness of the fabric as necessary. Allow the fabric to dry completely overnight before removing it from the board.

## Lacing the stitched work over board

A stitched design can be stretched and laced over a padded piece of archival foam core board or similar to keep it flat and give it a firm base. The work can then either be placed in a frame, or could be applied as decoration onto the front of an album cover.

Prepare the archival foam core board or similar by cutting it to the required size. Cut a piece of wadding the same size as the foam core board. The wadding acts as a layer of padding. Trim away any excess fabric and backing from the stitched work so that it is approximately one third larger than the foam core board on all sides.

If you will be framing the stitched work yourself, choose the frame before lacing the work over board. The dimensions of the frame determine the measurements for cutting the archival foam core board or similar and the wadding. Make sure that the frame has a deep enough recess to allow for the thickness of the laced work.

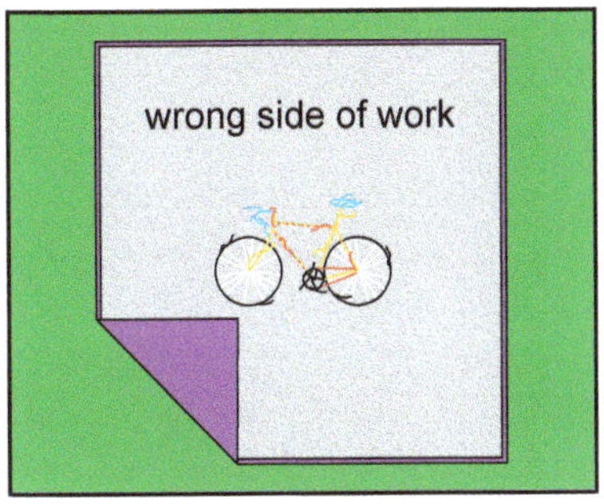


**Lacing over board**
**1** Place the work right side facing down on a flat surface.

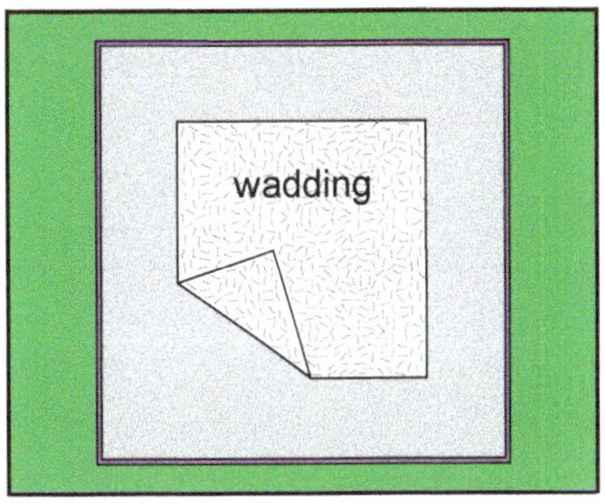


**2** Place the wadding centrally onto the back of the stitched design.

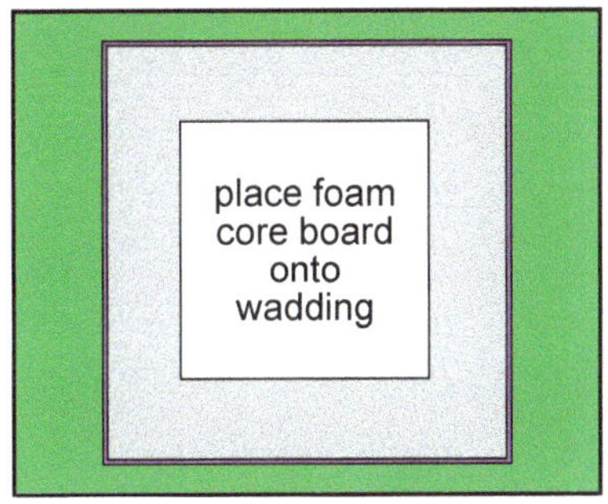


**3** Place the foam core board centrally onto the wadding.

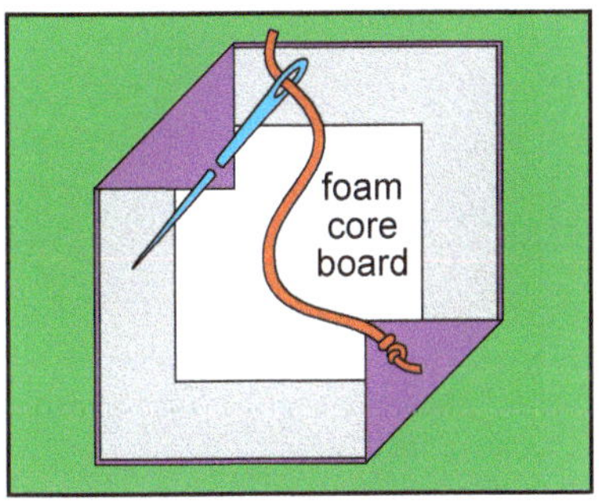


**4** Secure strong thread such as linen or crochet cotton at one corner of the fabric. Take needle through the diagonally opposite fabric corner.

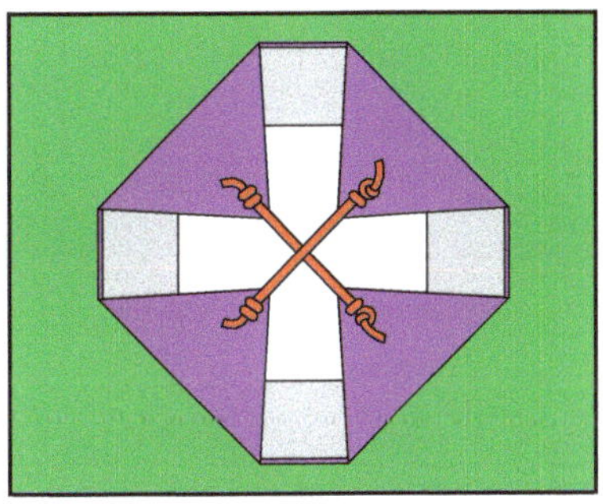

**5** Pull the thread tight and end off securely. Repeat for the remaining two corners. Check that the design is still centred in the correct position.

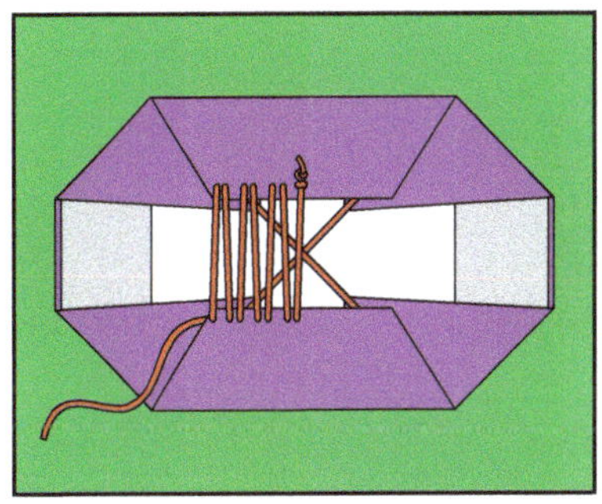

**6** Secure a new thread firmly at the centre of one side, then stitch to and fro to lace opposite sides together. Leave the thread hanging at the end.

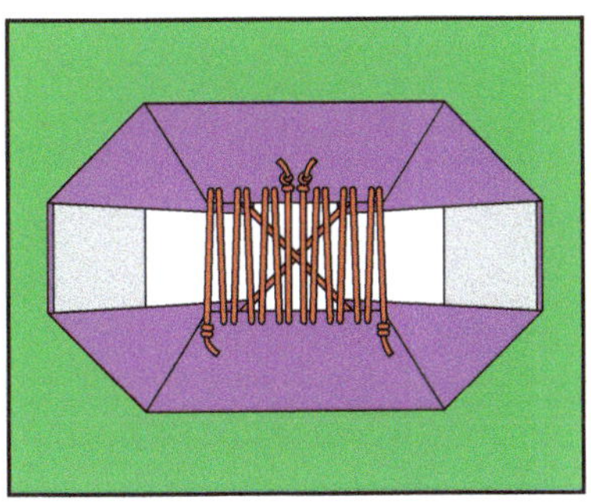

**7** Repeat for the second half. Working out from the centre each time, tighten the threads. Rethread the needle and end off securely.

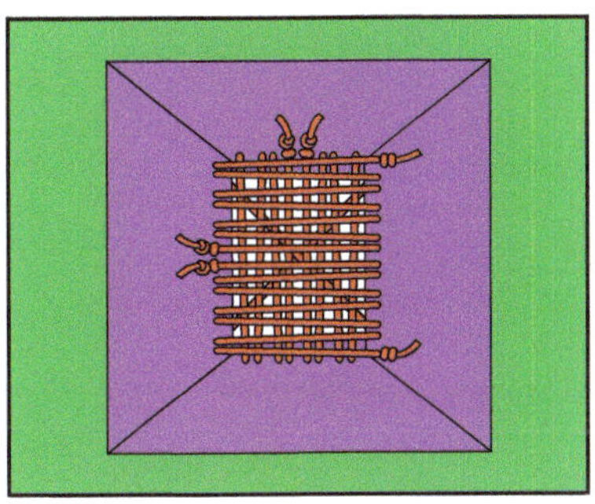

**8** Repeat for the remaining two sides of fabric.

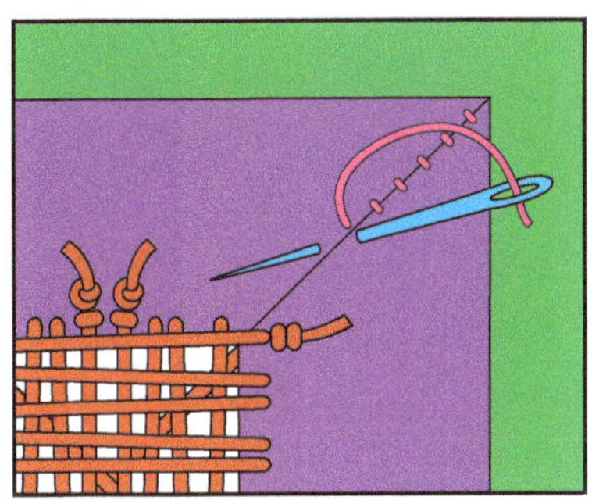

**9** Using machine sewing thread, hand stitch the folds of fabric together at each corner, forming mitred corners.

# Stitches, designs, and project ideas

# Straight stitch
## and variations

Straight stitch, one of the simplest of all the stitches, is useful in a wide variety of applications. It can be worked as the only stitch featured in a design, or it can be used in combination with other stitches.

Straight stitches can be of any length, worked in any direction. A single straight stitch can be worked on its own, or groups of them can be stitched in regular arrangements or scattered randomly. Arranged in any way, groups of them can be used to fill a shape, creating a wide variety of textures.

Straight stitches can be worked so that they overlap, meet, radiate, or so that they form crosses, angular shapes, or flower shapes. For a more textured effect, two or more straight stitches can be worked through the same two holes in the fabric.

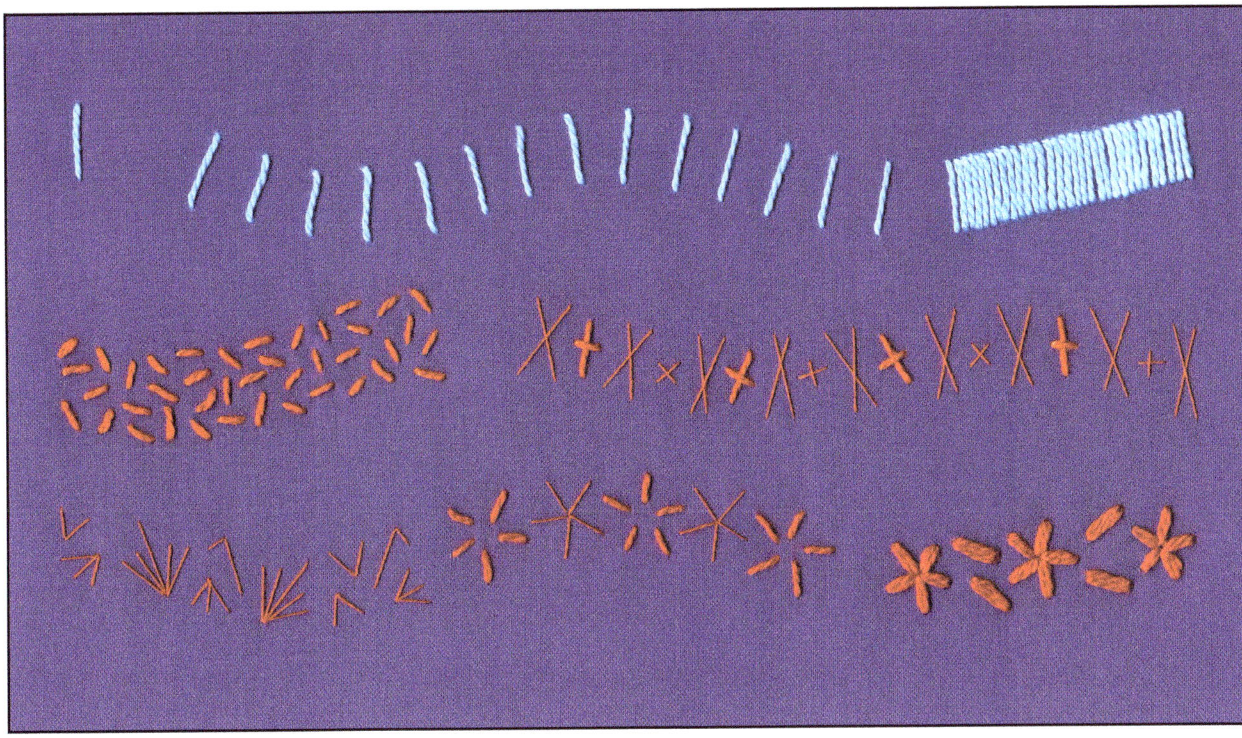

## Straight stitch and variations sampler

Single straight stitch

Spaced row of straight stitches

Close row of straight stitches

Scattered small straight stitches

Straight stitches that cross

Straight stitches that meet at one point

Straight stitches that radiate

Two straight stitches worked through same two holes

# Straight stitch and variations

## Hints

Straight stitch can be worked by skimming the needle in and out of the fabric before pulling the thread through. Alternatively, it can be worked in two stabbing movements, by taking the needle and thread up through the fabric, and then taking the needle and thread down through the fabric.

Do not work straight stitches with the tension of the thread too tight or the fabric will not lie flat.

When working two or more straight stitches through the same hole in the fabric, or through the same two holes, avoid splitting the threads of the previously worked stitches as you take the needle through. The stitches will then lie more neatly.

If stitching a large number of straight stitches that radiate from a central point, work the stitches one after the other in order around the centre. The stitches will then lie evenly and also the bulk on the back of the work will be minimised.

When radiating straight stitches meet, if possible begin each stitch at its outer end and complete it at the central meeting point. This way the needle is taken down at the meeting point each time, making it easier to avoid splitting the threads of the previously worked stitches.

Two or more straight stitches worked through the same two holes in the fabric, using one or two strands of thread, can create extra texture without the need to thread many strands into the needle. Keep on adding straight stitches until the required texture is achieved. This avoids the problem of having too many strands of thread to end off on the back of the work. Also with this method, the position of each additional stitch can be precisely controlled.

## Straight stitch and variations: right-handed

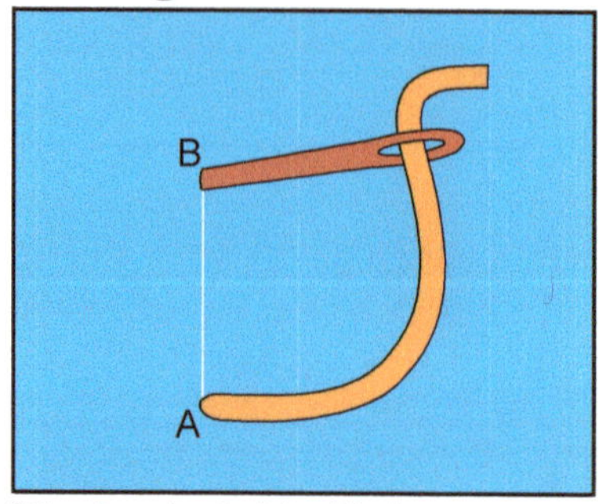


**Single straight stitch**
**1** Come up at A. Take the needle down at B.

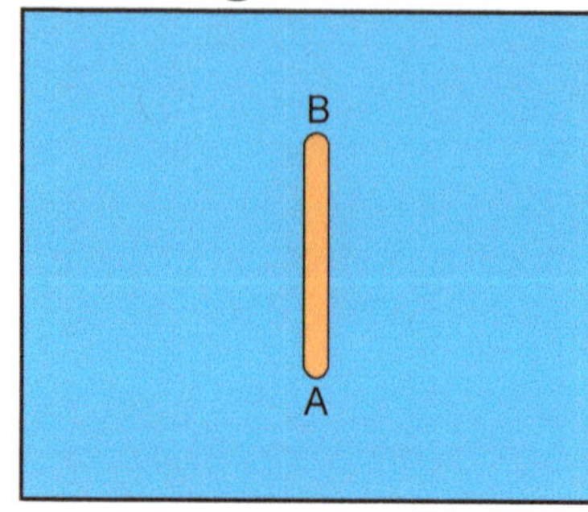


**2** Pull the thread through, forming the stitch.

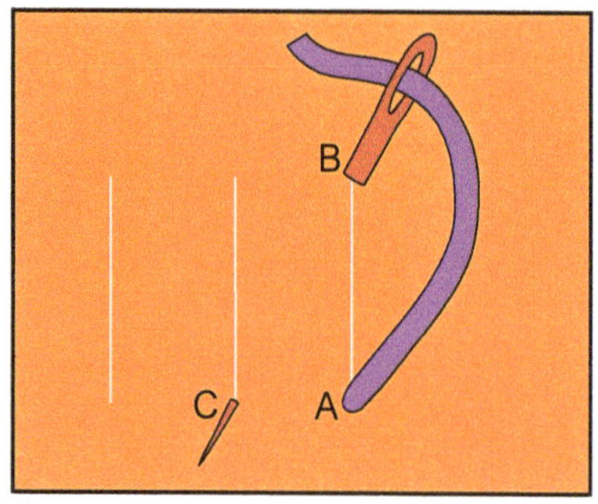


**Spaced row**
**1** Come up at A. Take the needle down at B and emerge at C.

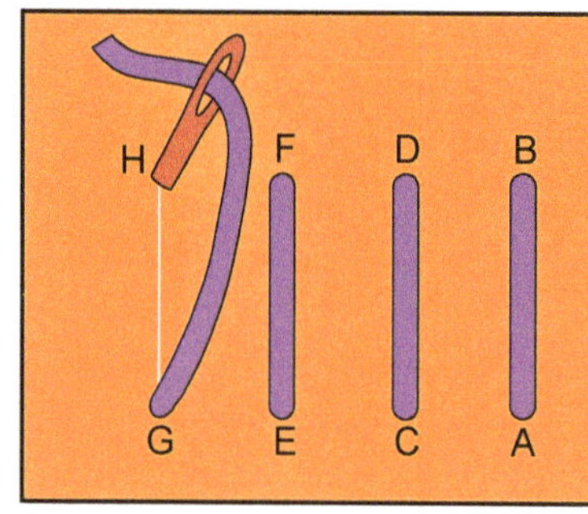


**2** Pull the thread through, forming the stitch. Continue along the row.

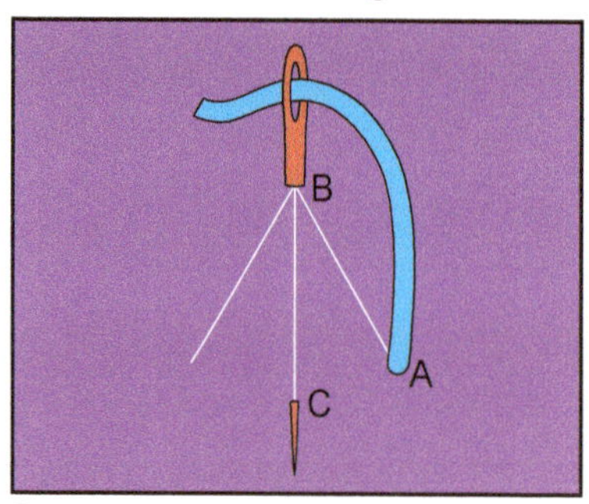


**Stitches that meet**
**1** Come up at A. Take the needle down at B and emerge at C.

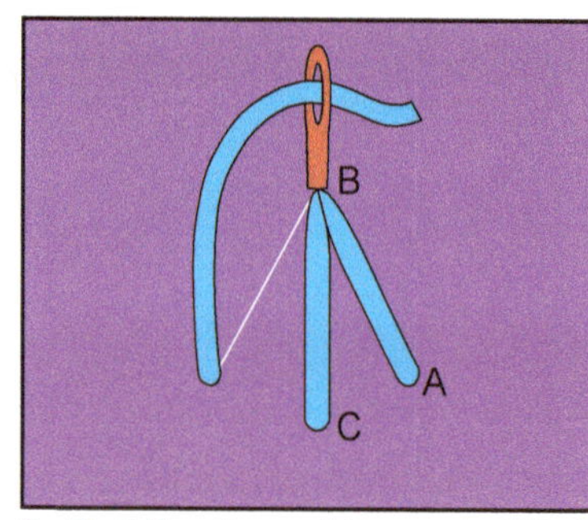


**2** Pull the thread through. Work the remaining stitches down through the same hole in the fabric at B.

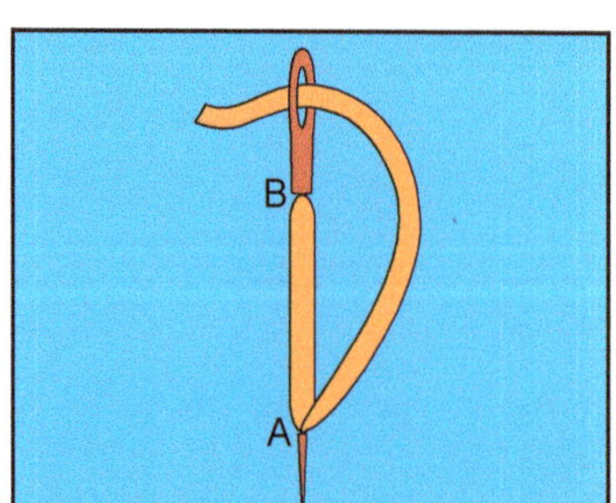


**Stitches using same two holes**
**1** Come up at A and down at B. Work a second stitch through the holes at A and B. Make it lie beside the first stitch.

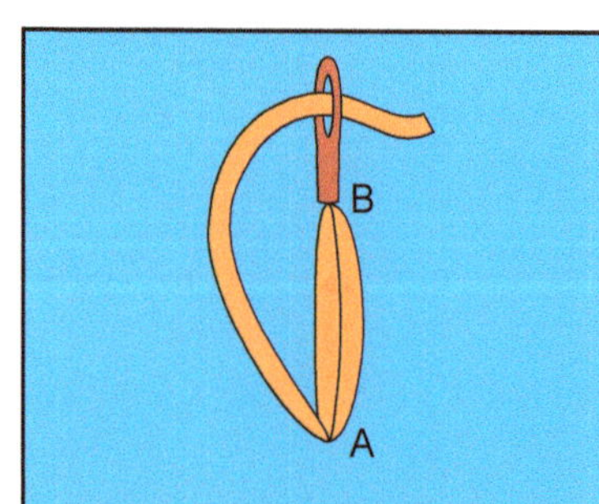


**2** Work any additional stitches through the same holes in the fabric at A and B. Make them lie evenly.

# Straight stitch and variations: left-handed

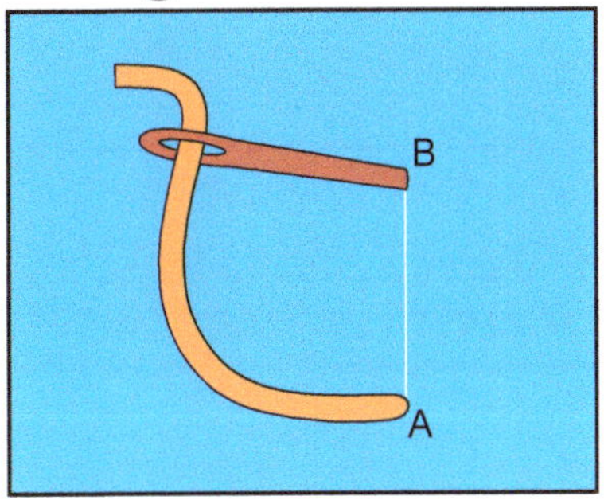


**Single straight stitch**
**1** Come up at A. Take the needle down at B.

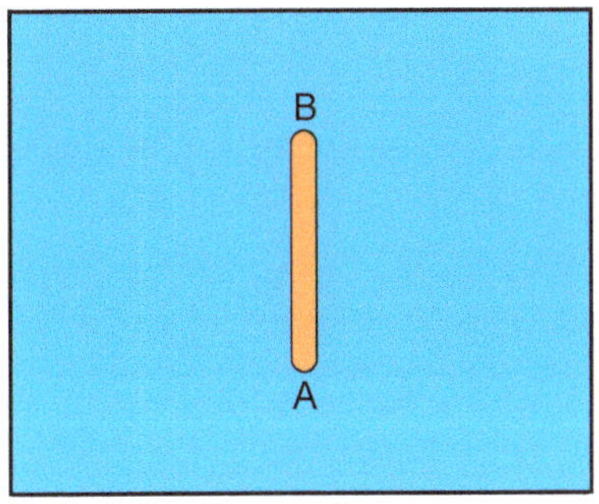


**2** Pull the thread through, forming the stitch.

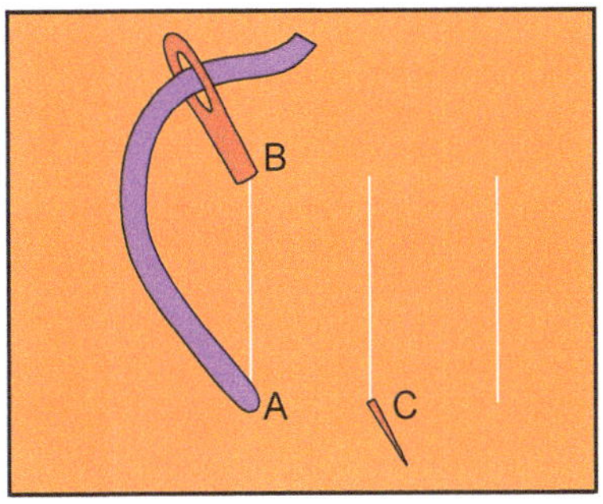


**Spaced row**
**1** Come up at A. Take the needle down at B and emerge at C.

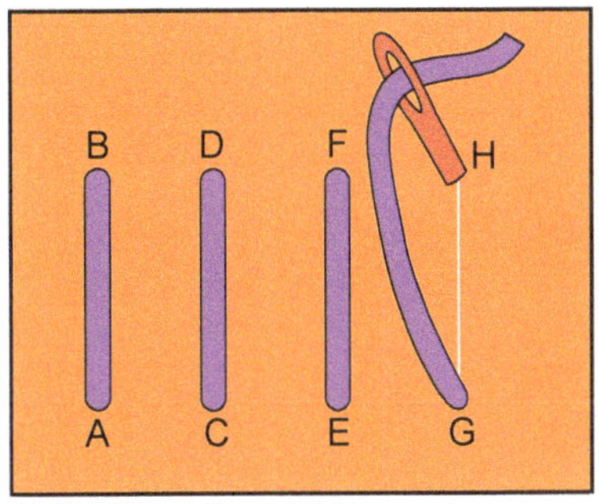


**2** Pull the thread through, forming the stitch. Continue along the row.

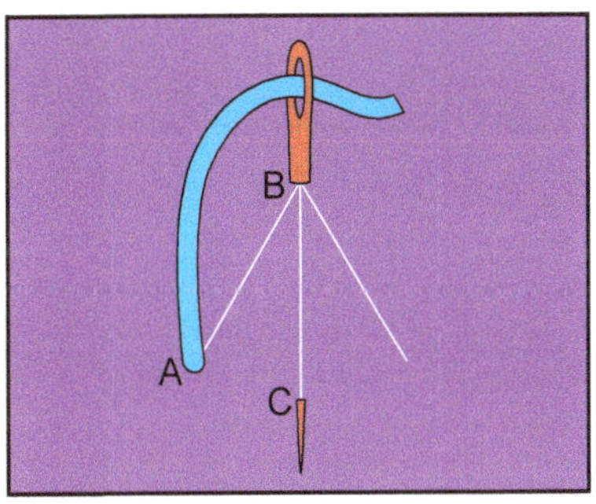


**Stitches that meet**
**1** Come up at A. Take the needle down at B and emerge at C.

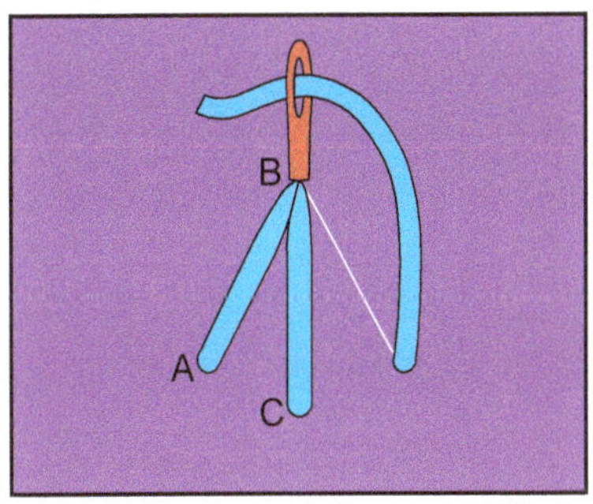


**2** Pull the thread through. Work the remaining stitches down through the same hole in the fabric at B.

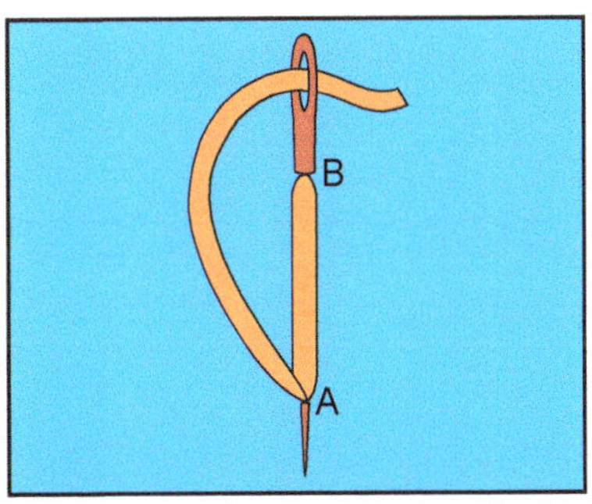


**Stitches using same two holes**
**1** Come up at A and down at B. Work a second stitch through the holes at A and B. Make it lie beside the first stitch.

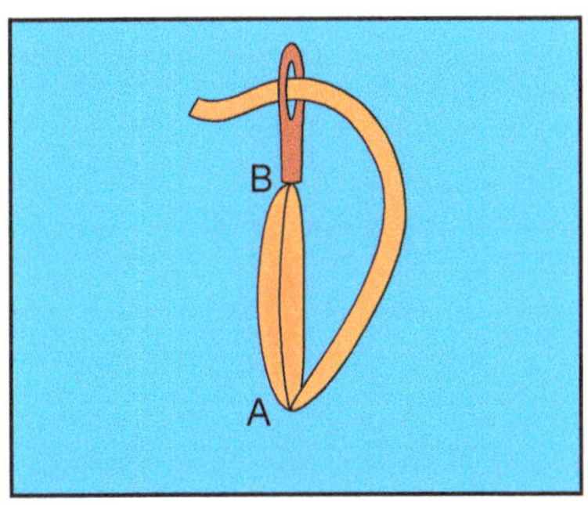


**2** Work any additional stitches through the same holes in the fabric at A and B. Make them lie evenly.

# Straight stitch
## and variations

# Designs and project ideas

## The designs

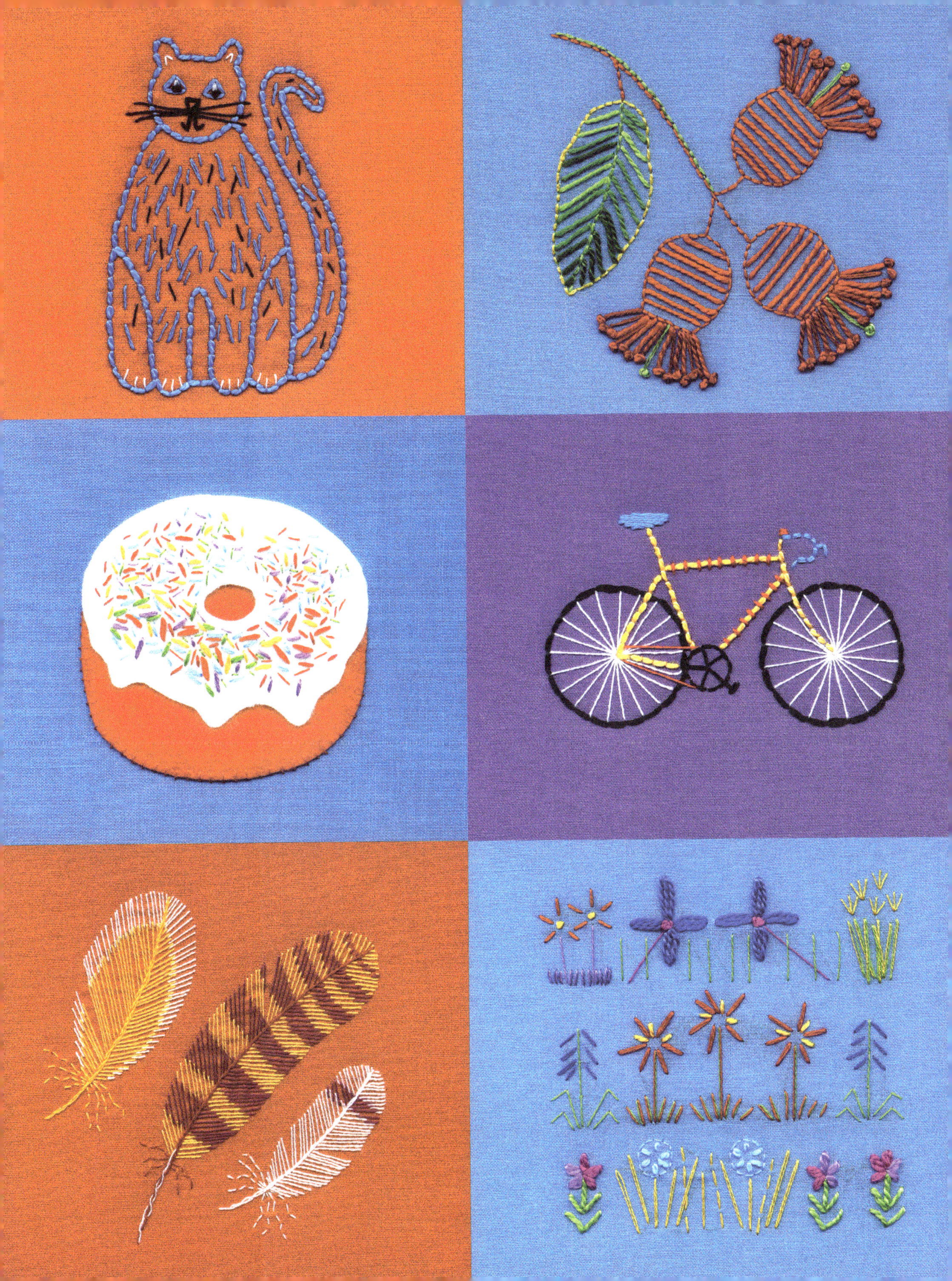

# Curious Cat

The curious cat sat for hours wondering where the mouse had gone!

## The design

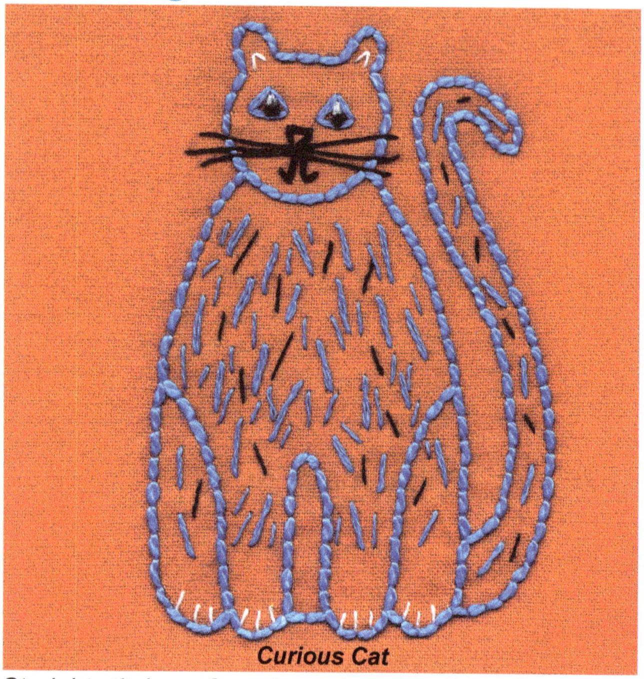

*Curious Cat*

Straight stitches of varying colour, length, and thickness are used to depict the fur, whiskers, inner ears, and claws of this cat. Back stitch and French knot are also included in this easy design.

To work *Curious Cat* as shown above, use the instructions on this page. To feature this design on a scarf, see the project idea on the following page.

## The pattern

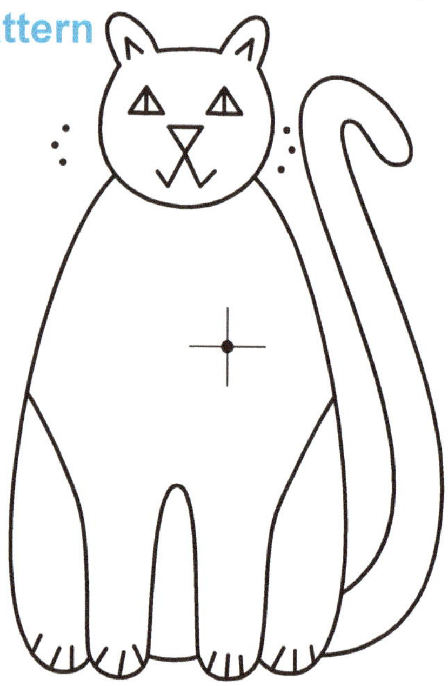

**Key:** **Centre of design** **Begin whiskers here**

## Shopping list

- Orange cotton fabric for background: 25cm (10") square
- Fabric or interfacing for backing: 25cm (10") square
- Stranded cotton thread: (A) black (B) dark aqua (C) white
- No. 5 perlé cotton thread: (D) dark aqua
- Tracing paper and other items for transferring the pattern onto the fabric

## Let's begin

Read page 15 for backing the fabric, and pages 22-25 for transferring the pattern onto the fabric, then select and use suitable methods for your fabric. For the orange fabric shown here, the pattern was transferred centrally onto the fabric by tracing with an HB pencil and then the backing fabric was tacked to the wrong side.

## Stitch!

For help, see pages 40-43 for straight stitch, 76-79 for back stitch, and pages 184-187 for French knot.

1 Outline the head, body, legs, and tail in back stitch (1 strand D).
2 Using the photo as a guide, stitch the aqua fur on the body, legs, and tail with randomly placed straight stitches (1 or 2 strands B), then add the black fur with straight stitches in the same way (1 strand A).
3 Outline the eyes in back stitch (2 strands B).
4 Stitch the whites of the eyes (Diagram 1), each with three straight stitches worked through the same two holes in the fabric (1 strand C).
5 Stitch the inner ears and the claws with straight stitch (1 strand C).
6 Add each pupil (Diagram 2) with a two wrap French knot (2 strands A).
7 Work the nose and then the mouth in back stitch (2 strands A).
8 Beginning at the marked dots and ending at the base of the nose, add the whiskers with long straight stitches (1 strand A).

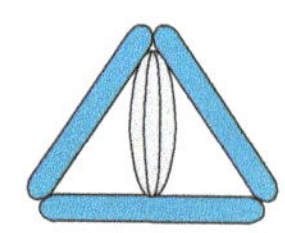

**Diagram 1**

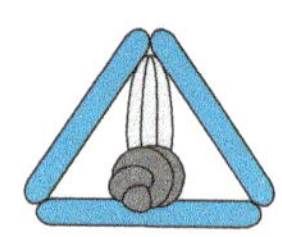

**Diagram 2**

## Let's finish

Take out the tacking. Press or pin out the work. See page 36 for pressing and for pinning out.

## Hint

**Stitching the cat's fur**

When working straight stitch for the fur of *Curious Cat*, keep an even, but not tight, tension.

# Curious Cat Winter Scarf

Be cosy this winter with a decorated scarf.

## The project

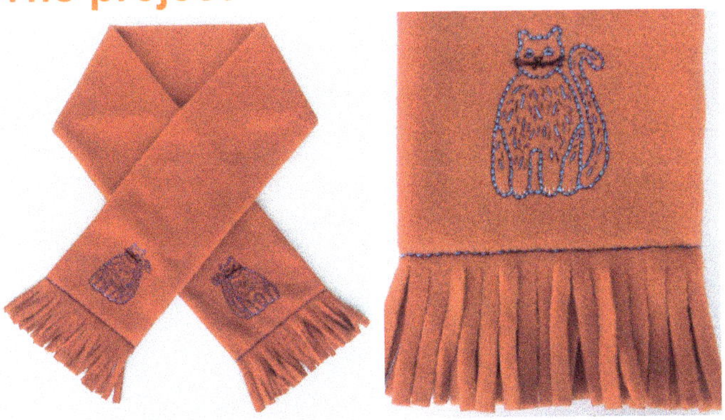

***Curious Cat Winter Scarf* and Detail**

For this project idea, *Curious Cat* is worked on each end of a piece of polar fleece fabric that is then made up into a double-layered scarf.

The finished size of this scarf is 17cm x 135cm (7" x 53").

The design could be worked on a purchased scarf, but note that the back of the stitching would be visible if the scarf was only a single layer of fabric.

## Shopping list

- Orange polar fleece fabric: 36cm x 135cm wide (14 1/4" x 53")
- Threads as listed for the original design on the page opposite
- Machine sewing thread: orange
- Medium weight tracing paper and other items for transferring the pattern onto the fabric

## Let's begin

See the page opposite for the *Curious Cat* pattern.

Trace the pattern, including the centre symbol but omitting the face and feet details, onto tracing paper. Make a second tracing that is a mirror image of the first. See page 20 for how to mirror the pattern.

Place each tracing over a pad of folded fabric and pierce holes through the tracing at regular intervals along the outline for the cat using a large needle.

Place the polar fleece fabric right side facing up. Find the placement for the pattern by measuring 14.5cm (5 3/4") up from one short end and 9.5cm (3 3/4") in from one long side. Mark the junction with pins.

Repeat at the other end, again measuring in from the same long side (Diagram 1).

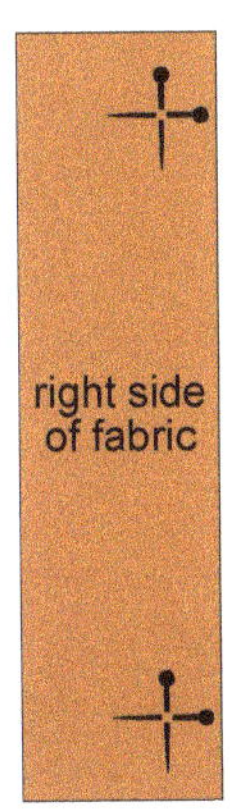


**Diagram 1**

Place the first tracing squarely onto one end of the polar fleece with its marked centre aligned with the pins (Diagram 2). Using a water erasable fabric marker, draw dots onto the fabric through the holes in the tracing paper to transfer the outline, then remove the tracing. See page 25 for transferring the pattern using the pierce and dot method.

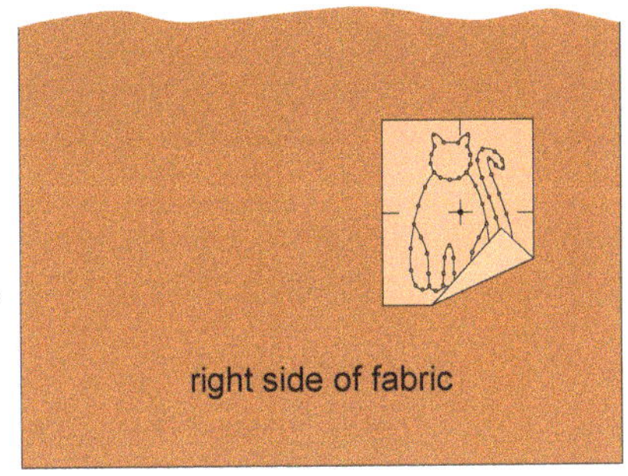


**Diagram 2**

Using the mirrored tracing, transfer the outline to the other end in the same way.

## Stitch!

Following steps 1-8 of the stitch instructions opposite, work both cats in the same way as the original design. Refer to the photo and the pattern for the face and feet details, as they have not been transferred.

## Let's finish

Rinse the work in cold water to remove the water erasable fabric marker. Allow to dry. On the wrong side of each end, rule a line 7cm (2 3/4") up from the short edge using a chalk-based pencil. Beginning at the raw edge and finishing at the ruled line, rule lines 1cm (3/8") apart across the width of the fabric. Cut along these lines to make a fringe. On each end of the scarf, cut away the first and last strip of the fringe (Diagram 3).

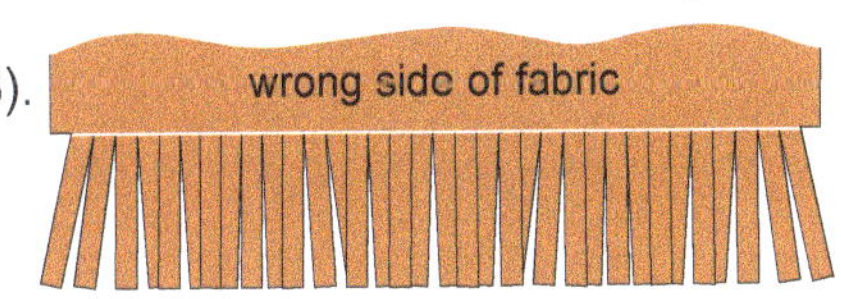


**Diagram 3**

With right sides together, fold the fabric in half along the length. Using a 1cm (3/8") seam allowance, machine stitch the layers together down the long side (Diagram 4).Turn the scarf through to the right side and position the seam so that it lies along one long edge.

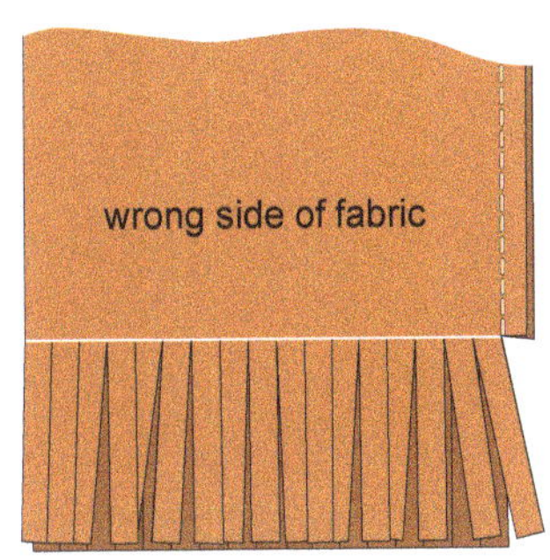


**Diagram 4**

At each end, tack the layers together just below the cat. With the chalk-based pencil, rule a line just above the top of the fringe.

With the dark aqua thread (D), and using a stabbing movement, work a row of back stitch along each line through the two layers to hold them together. On the reverse side, whip the wrong side of the back stitches with the same thread. See pages 96 and 97 for help.

# Red Flowering Gum

The red flowering gum, with its bright flowers, is one of Australia's favourite trees.

## The design

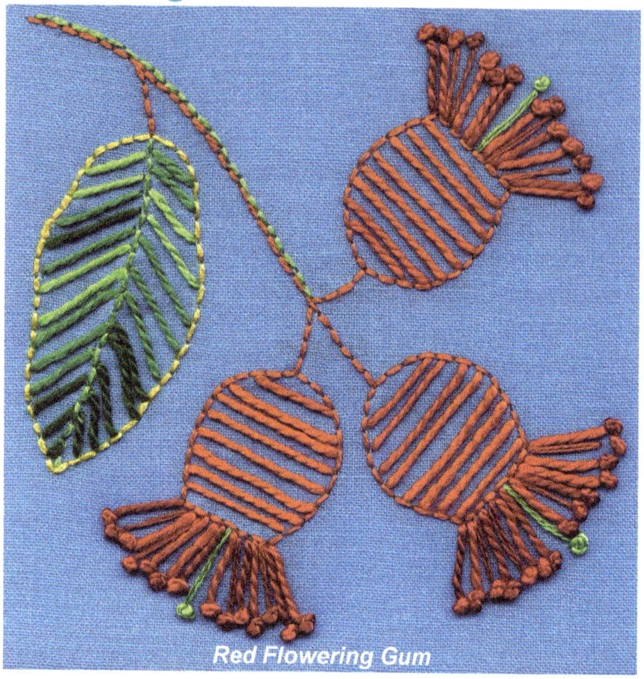

*Red Flowering Gum*

This quick and easy design features straight stitch, back stitch, and French knot.

Follow the instructions on this page to work the design exactly as shown here on an aqua background. See the project idea on the facing page to apply the design onto the front of an album.

## The pattern

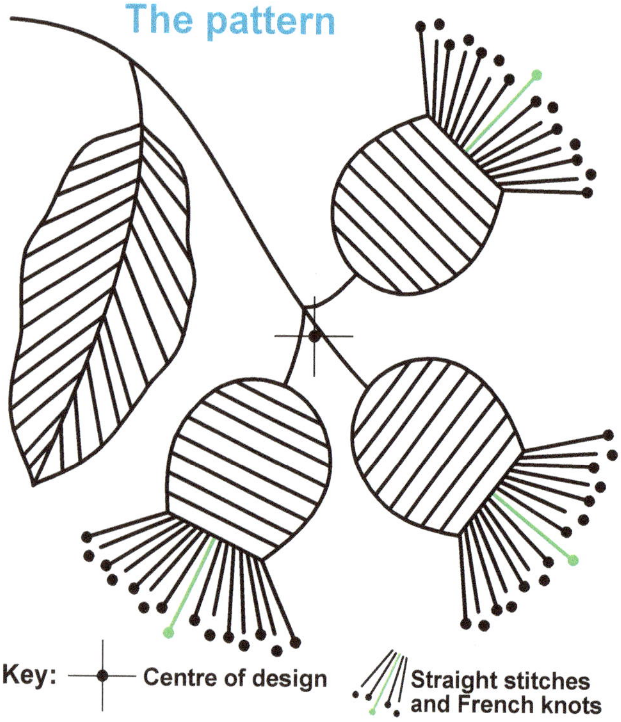


## Shopping list

- Aqua cotton fabric for background: 25cm (10") square
- Fabric or interfacing for backing: 25cm (10") square
- Stranded cotton thread:
  (A) light green (B) medium yellow
  (C) medium orange (D) dark red (E) medium red
- No. 5 perlé cotton thread:
  (F) dark green (G) medium green (H) light green
  (I) medium orange (J) dark red (K) medium red
- Tracing paper and other items for transferring the pattern onto the fabric

## Let's begin

Read page 15 for backing the fabric, and pages 22-25 for transferring the pattern onto the fabric, then select and use suitable methods for your fabric. For the aqua fabric shown here, the pattern was transferred centrally onto the fabric by tracing with a water erasable fabric marker and then the backing fabric was tacked to the wrong side.

## Stitch!

For help, see pages 40-43 for straight stitch, 76-79 for back stitch, and pages 184-187 for French knot. As the straight stitches in this design are quite long, make sure they are not pulled too tightly. Use the photo as a guide when placing the green on the main stem, and the colours for the leaf side veins, the gumnuts (flower bases), and the stamens in shades of red.

1. Work the stems in back stitch (2 strands C). With the same thread, outline the gumnuts in back stitch.
2. Work the leaf outline in back stitch (2 strands B).
3. Stitch along the upper side of the main stem in back stitch (2 strands A). With the same thread, stitch the leaf central vein in back stitch.
4. Add the leaf side veins in straight stitch (1 strand F, G, or H).
5. Stitch across each gumnut using straight stitch (1 strand I or K).
6. Work one straight stitch (2 strands A) at the central marked line at the end of each gumnut. This is indicated in green on the pattern. Add a one wrap French knot at the marked dot (1 strand H).
7. For the stamens, work straight stitches in shades of red at the remaining marked lines (2 strands D or E, or 1 strand J or K). Every flower should have some of each colour in each thickness. Add one wrap French knots at the marked dots (1 strand J or K).

## Let's finish

Take out the tacking. Rinse work in cold water to remove the fabric marker. When partly dry, press or pin out the work. See page 36 for pressing and for pinning out.

# Red Flowering Gum Album Cover

Let's decorate an album cover with some Australian flora.

## The project

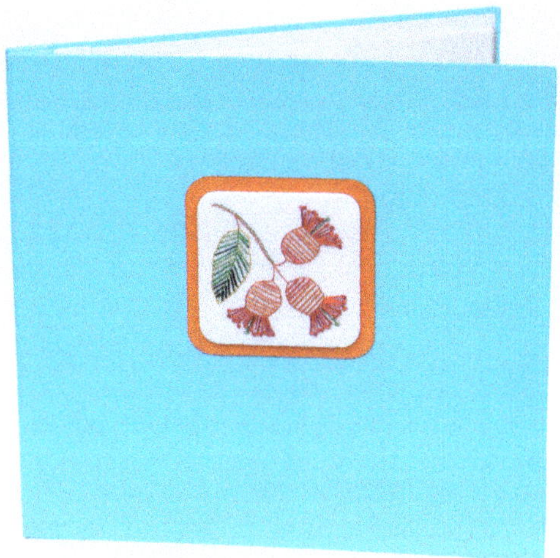

*Red Flowering Gum Album Cover*

*Red Flowering Gum* is stitched in the original thread colours on a white background for this project. The work is then laced over cardboard and attached to the front of an album.
The album shown here is 32.5cm x 33.5cm wide (12 3/4" x 13 1/4") in size.

## Shopping list

- Aqua album
- White linen-look fabric for background: 25cm (10") square
- Fabric or interfacing for backing: 25cm (10") square
- Threads as listed for the original design on the page opposite
- Machine sewing thread for gathering
- Strong thread for lacing
- Tracing paper and other items for transferring the pattern onto the fabric
- Thin wadding: 10cm (4") square
- White cardboard: 10cm (4") square
- Orange card: 12cm (4 3/4") square
- Archival double-sided sticky tape or glue

## Let's begin

See the page opposite for the pattern.
Transfer the pattern centrally onto the white fabric by tracing with a water erasable fabric marker or by using transfer paper. See pages 22-25 for transferring the pattern onto the fabric. Tack the backing to the wrong side of the fabric. See page 15 for backing the fabric.

**Detail of**
***Red Flowering Gum Album Cover***

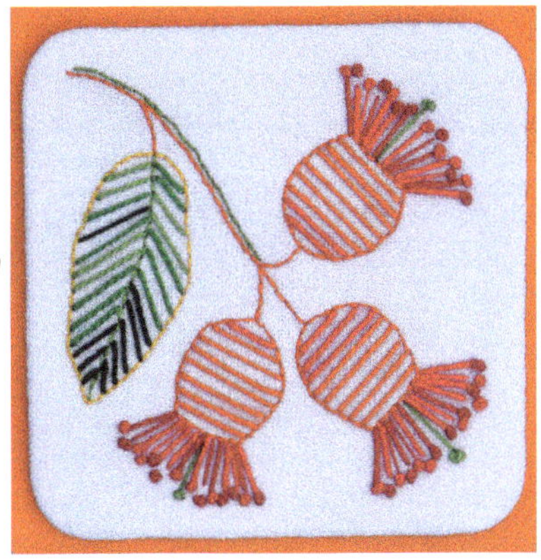

## Stitch!

Work the design following steps 1-7 of the stitch instructions on the facing page.

## Let's finish

Rinse the work in cold water to remove the pattern markings. When partly dry, press or pin out the work. See page 36 for pressing and for pinning out.
Trim the corners of the white fabric and the backing, and also the corners of the white cardboard and the wadding, so that they are rounded.
Using machine sewing thread, and leaving both ends of the thread dangling, work a row of running stitch around the edge of the backing and the fabric together. See pages 58-61 for running stitch. Take out any remaining tacking. Place the wadding and then the cardboard centrally onto the wrong side of the stitched work (Diagram 1).
Pull the two thread ends to gather the fabric over the padded cardboard, then tie them in a knot. Trim the excess thread.

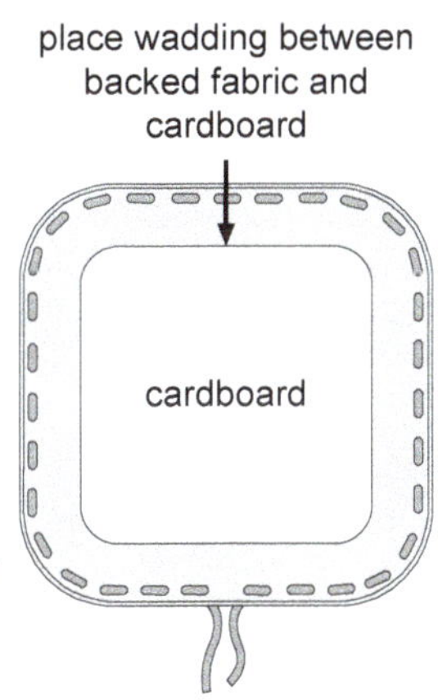


**Diagram 1**

Lace the work tightly. As a guide, see page 37 for lacing. Using archival double-sided sticky tape or glue, adhere the laced side of the work onto the orange card. Attach this onto the album front.

## Hints

**Use other designs on an album cover**
Many of the designs in this book would be suitable to feature on the front of an album.

**Themed series**
*Red Flowering Gum* could be stitched as a pair to *Golden Wattle* on page 192 which also depicts a much-loved Australian plant.

# Delicious Doughnut

Please join us for coffee and a doughnut!

## The design

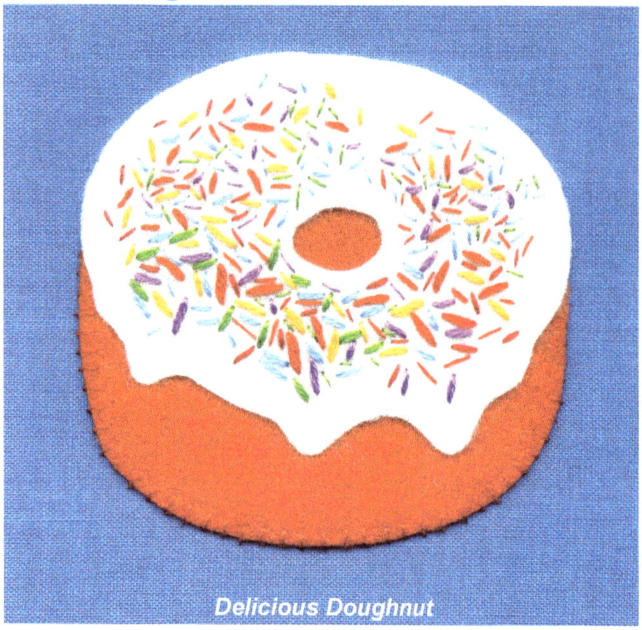

*Delicious Doughnut*

In this design, a felt fabric shape depicting a doughnut is attached to the background fabric with straight stitches worked around its edge. The white felt for the icing is attached with multi-coloured straight stitches randomly scattered to create sprinkles. Felt is easy to work with, as the cut edges do not fray.

Use the instructions on this page to work the design exactly as shown here on an aqua background. To present the design as a trio of framed pictures, see the project idea on the following page.

## The pattern

**Note: Trace each felt shape separately**

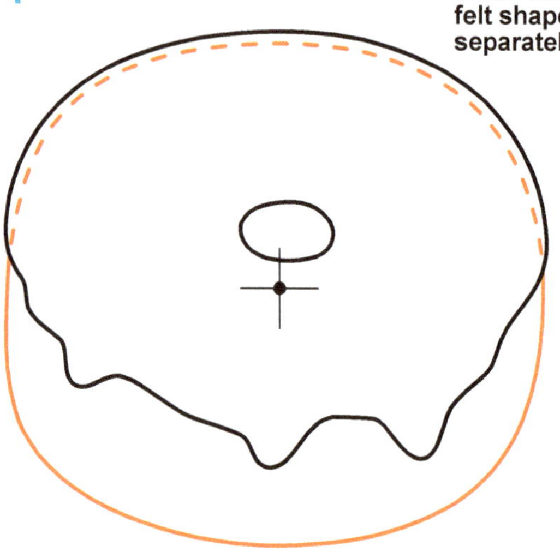

**Key:** **Centre of design** **Upper edge of orange shape**

## Shopping list

- Aqua cotton fabric for background: 25cm (10") square
- Fabric or interfacing for backing: 25cm (10") square
- Orange and white felt fabric for the shapes: 10cm (4") square of each colour
- Stranded cotton thread:
  (A) medium violet (B) medium aqua (C) light green
  (D) medium yellow (E) medium orange (F) medium red
- Tracing paper and other items for preparing the felt shapes

## Let's begin

For this design the pattern is not transferred onto the background fabric.

Attach the backing fabric to the wrong side of the background fabric. See page 15 for backing the fabric.

Following the orange line on the pattern, trace the doughnut shape onto tracing paper. Pin the tracing to the orange felt. Cut out the felt shape, and then remove the tracing. Place the orange felt shape over the pattern. Using a chalk-based pencil, mark the felt with a dot at each junction where the doughnut and icing cross over. Using the black line on the pattern, cut out the icing, including the hole, from the white felt in the same way as the orange felt. Mark the white felt at the junctions, this time with pins.

## Stitch!

For help, see pages 40-43 for straight stitch.

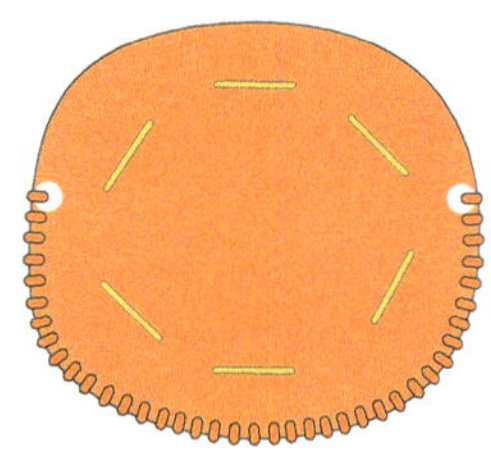

**Diagram 1**

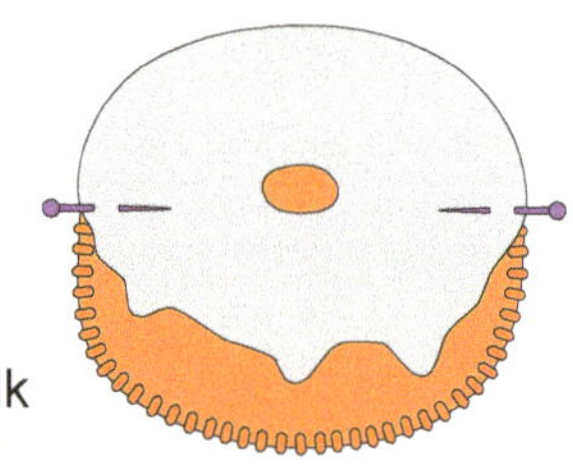

**Diagram 2**

1. Place the orange felt shape centrally onto the background fabric. Pin and tack in place.
2. Beginning and ending at the chalk dots (Diagram 1), work a row of small straight stitches along the lower edge of the doughnut shape (1 strand E). Remove the tacking.
3. Place the white icing shape onto the doughnut shape, matching the pins with the chalk dots (Diagram 2). Pin and tack the icing in place. Remove pins.
4. On the icing, stitch the sprinkles with randomly placed straight stitches worked through both layers of felt and the background fabric (1, 2, or 3 strands A, B, C, D, E, or F). Make the stitches in the foreground longer and closer together than those in the background.

## Let's finish

Take out the tacking. Press the background fabric only. It is not recommended to dampen the felt. See page 36 for pressing.

# Delicious Doughnut Framed Pictures

Have a party creating these pictures.

## The project

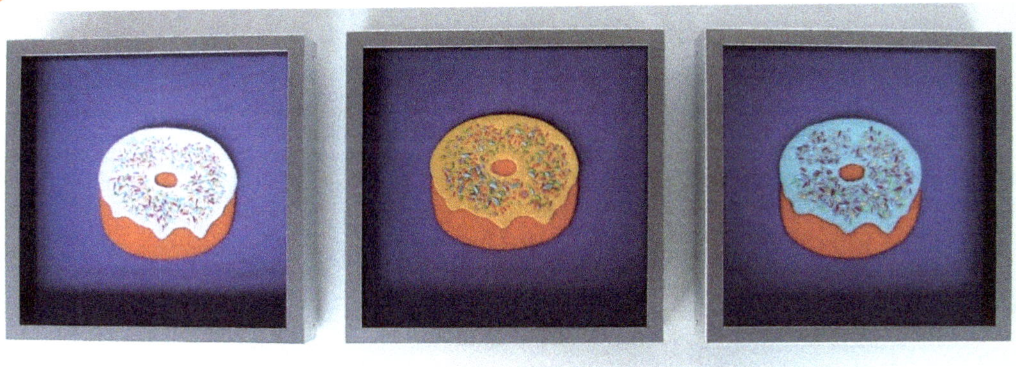

*Delicious Doughnut Framed Pictures*

The three doughnuts presented in individual picture frames are all worked in the same way as the original design. The colour for the background fabric of each has been changed to violet. White, yellow, and aqua felt fabrics have been used for the icing shapes.
The measurements given in the shopping list on this page are suitable for square picture frames with window dimensions of 13cm (5") square. If your picture frames have different dimensions, you will need to adjust the shopping list measurements accordingly. The dimensions of the wadding and foam core board, or similar, are determined by the size of the backing board of the frame you select.

## Shopping lists

***White doughnut picture***

- Silver picture frame: 13cm (5") square window
- Violet cotton fabric for background: 23cm (9") square
- Fabric or interfacing for backing: 23cm (9") square
- Orange and white felt fabric for the shapes as listed for the original design on the page opposite
- Threads as listed for the original design on the page opposite
- Strong thread for lacing
- Tracing paper and other items for preparing the felt shapes
- Thin wadding
- Foam core board, or similar

***Yellow doughnut picture***

- As for the white doughnut picture, but substitute yellow felt fabric for the white felt fabric

***Aqua doughnut picture***

- As for the white doughnut picture, but substitute aqua felt fabric for the white felt fabric.

## Let's begin

See the page opposite for the pattern.
Attach the backing fabric to each of the violet fabric pieces and prepare the felt shapes following the instructions given in this section on the previous page.

## Stitch!

Attach the felt shapes to each of the violet fabric pieces and stitch all three doughnuts following steps 1-4 of the stitch instructions on the previous page.

## Let's finish

Take out the tacking. Press the background fabric only. It is not recommended to dampen the felt. See page 36 for pressing.
Pad, lace, and frame the works. See page 37 for lacing. Alternatively, take them to a professional framer who specializes in framing textiles.

## Hint

**Change the colours**

You could be adventurous and try other colour combinations.

**Change the stitch**

As a variation, the sprinkles on the icing could be changed to hundreds and thousands by working French knots instead of the straight stitches.

# The Racing Bike

Feel the excitement as the race begins!

## The design

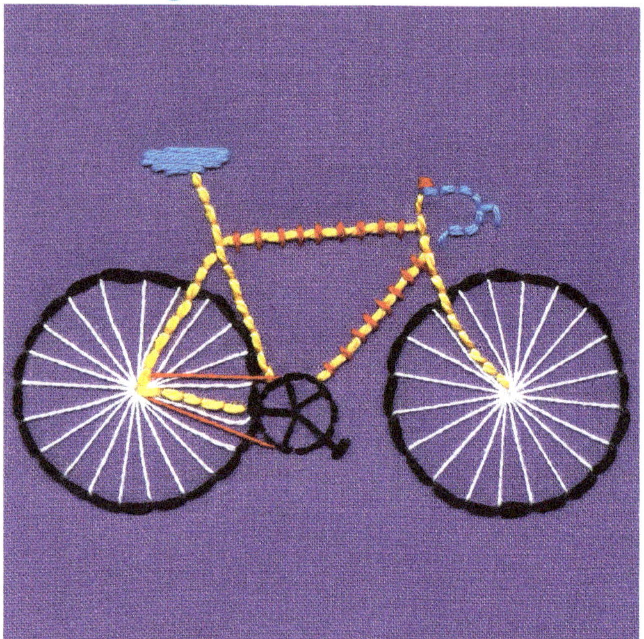

*The Racing Bike*

In this design, long straight stitches are used as the spokes on the wheels and for the bike chain. Shorter straight stitches and back stitch complete the design. The bike is detailed, but the stitches are easy to work. Use the instructions on this page to work the design exactly as shown here on a violet background. To apply the design, see the project idea on the following page where it is worked as a patch that is then attached to a baseball cap.

## The pattern

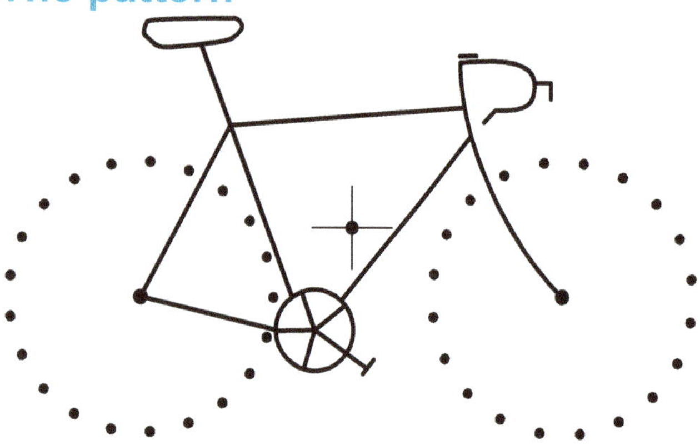

**Key:** **Centre of design** **Placement of back stitches for tyres**

## Hint

**Using a hoop**

The straight stitches used for the spokes of the wheels may be easier to work if the fabric is placed in a hoop.

## Shopping list

- Violet cotton fabric for background: 25cm (10") square
- Fabric or interfacing for backing: 25cm (10") square
- Stranded cotton thread: (A) black (B) dark aqua (C) medium red (D) white
- No. 5 perlé cotton thread: (E) medium yellow
- Tracing paper and other items for transferring the pattern onto the fabric

## Let's begin

Read page 15 for backing the fabric, and pages 22-25 for transferring the pattern onto the fabric, then select and use suitable methods for your fabric. For the violet fabric shown here, the pattern was transferred centrally onto the fabric by tracing with a water erasable fabric marker and then the backing fabric was tacked to the wrong side.

## Stitch!

For help, see pages 40-43 for straight stitch and pages 76-79 for back stitch.

1 Following the marked dots for stitch length, stitch the tyres in back stitch (4 strands A).

2 Work the outline for the cog in back stitch (2 strands A). Using the same thread, add the internal lines with straight stitch, then stitch the pedal with three straight stitches worked through the same two holes in the fabric (Diagram 1).

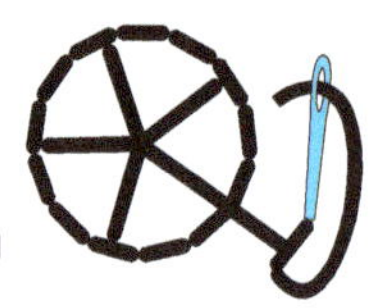

**Diagram 1**

3 Starting at the tyre each time, work long straight stitches for the wheel spokes, spacing them the length of the back stitches apart (1 strand D).

4 Stitch the frame and the front and back forks in back stitch (1 strand E). Using the photo as a guide, work small straight stitches (2 strands C) over the yellow back stitches for the stripes on the frame (Diagram 2).

5 Stitch the handle bar and brake lever in back stitch (3 strands B). Add the seat with a stack of straight stitches worked horizontally (3 strands B).

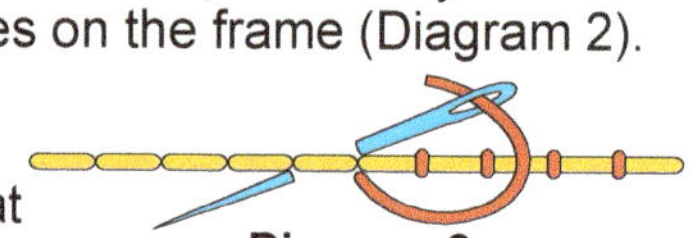

**Diagram 2**

6 Using the photo as a guide, add the chain with two long straight stitches (1 strand C).

7 Stitch the speedometer on the handle bars with three straight stitches worked horizontally and closely together (1 strand C).

## Let's finish

Take out the tacking. Rinse the work in cold water to remove the fabric marker. When partly dry, press or pin out the work. See page 36 for pressing and pinning out.

# The Racing Bike Baseball Cap

Be part of the team – add a patch.

## The project

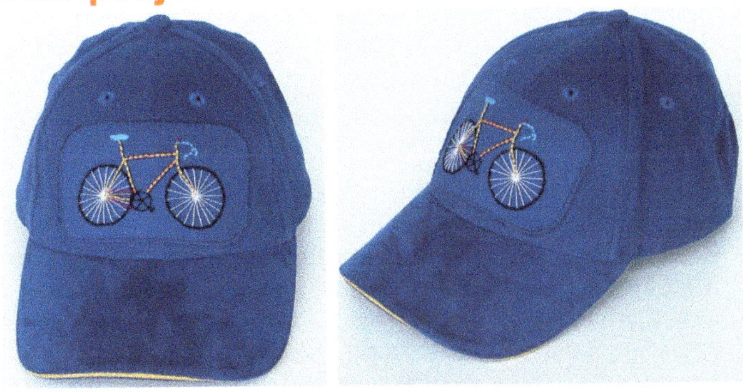

***The Racing Bike Baseball Cap***

For this project, the design is worked on fabric that is made into a patch. This is then attached to a purchased baseball cap. When choosing the colour of the fabric for the patch, match the colour to the cap so the emphasis is on the design and not on the patch itself. To avoid any excess dye running from the cap onto the fabric or threads of the patch when it is laundered, it is recommended to wash the cap before attaching the patch.

## Shopping list

- Blue baseball cap
- Blue cotton fabric for the patch:
  13cm x 18cm wide (5" x 7")
- Medium weight iron-on interfacing:
  13cm x 18cm wide (5" x 7")
- Threads as listed for the original design on the page opposite
- Machine sewing thread: blue
- Tracing paper and other items for transferring the pattern onto the fabric
- Cardboard:
  13cm x 18cm wide (5" x 7")

## Let's begin

See the page opposite for the pattern.
Following the instructions on page 15 for backing the fabric, attach the interfacing onto the wrong side of the blue fabric. This will stabilize the area where the design is to be stitched and will also make the patch easier to handle when attaching it to the cap.
Transfer the pattern centrally onto the right side of the blue fabric using transfer paper. See page 24 for transferring the pattern using transfer paper.

## Stitch!

Work the bike following steps 1-7 of the stitch instructions on the page opposite.

## Let's finish

Rinse the work in cold water to remove the pattern markings. When partly dry, press or pin out the work. See page 36 for pressing and for pinning out.
From the cardboard, make a template that has a centrally placed cut-out window measuring 7cm x 12cm wide (2 3/4" x 4 3/4") with rounded corners (Diagram 1).

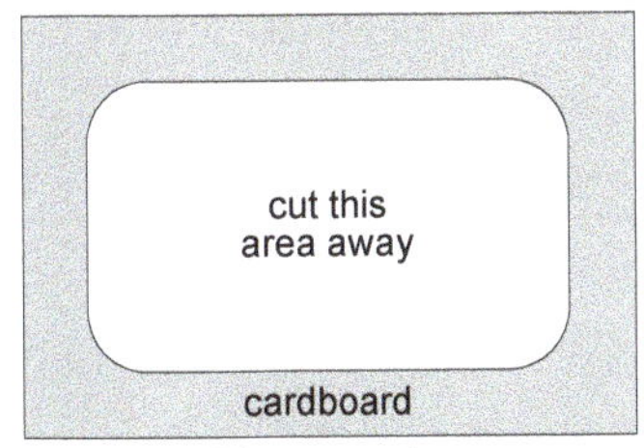


**Diagram 1**

Place this template so that the window is positioned centrally over the stitched bike.
Trace around the window with a chalk-based pencil. Using a close zigzag stitch on the machine, and with blue machine sewing thread, stitch around the patch over the marked line.
Carefully cut away the excess fabric close to the zigzag stitching (Diagram 2).

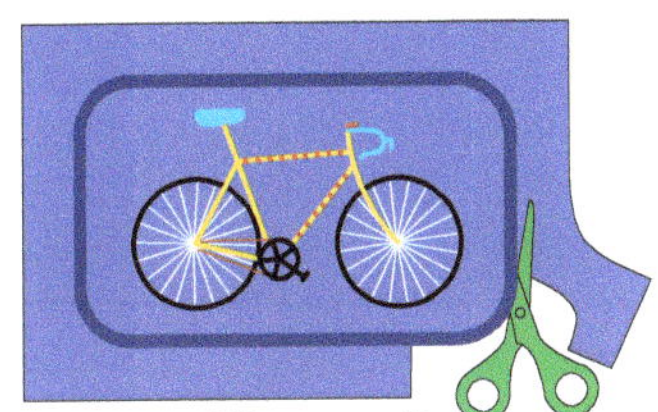

**Diagram 2**

Position the patch onto the centre front of the cap and tack it firmly in place. Using the machine sewing thread, sew the patch to the cap with small hand stitches placed over the zigzag stitches.

## Hint

**Work the design as a framed picture**
This bike would be fun to display as a framed picture, perhaps alongside a framed version of *The Penny-farthing Bicycle* on page 142.

**Another project idea**
*The Racing Bike* would also look good featured on a sports bag.

# Fluttering Feathers

The infinite variety of colours and patterns on feathers is truly amazing.

## The design

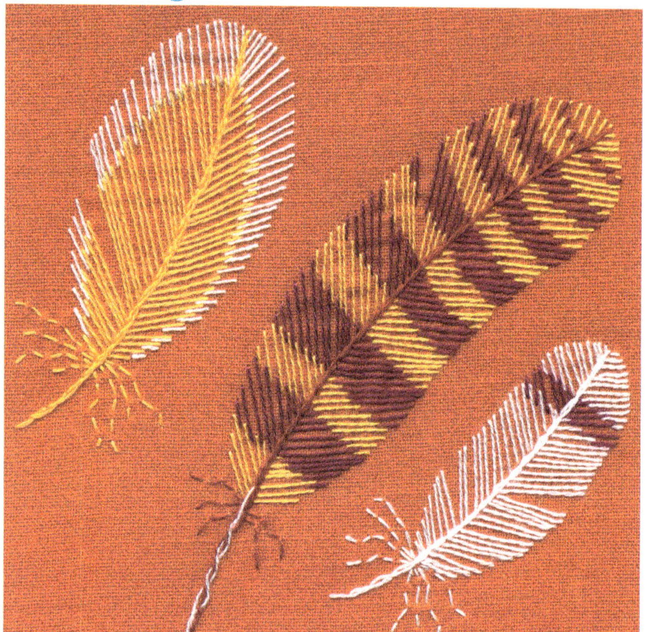

*Fluttering Feathers*

The areas of colour on these feathers are worked in straight stitch. Running stitch and stem stitch are also used. The feathers are quite intricate and take some time to work, but they are actually quite easy.
To work the design as shown on orange fabric, follow the instructions here. See opposite for how to work one feather from the design on a petite jewel purse.

## The pattern

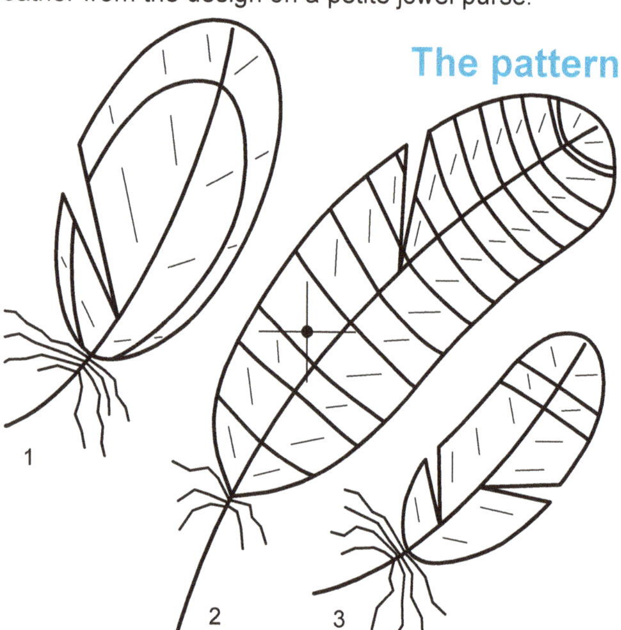


**Key:** Centre of design | Direction of straight stitches

## Shopping list

- Orange cotton fabric for background: 25cm (10") square
- Fabric or interfacing for backing: 25cm (10") square
- Stranded cotton thread: (A) medium yellow (B) dark red (C) dark magenta (D) white
- Tracing paper and other items for transferring the pattern onto the fabric

## Let's begin

Read page 15 for backing the fabric, and pages 22-25 for transferring the pattern onto the fabric, then select and use suitable methods for your fabric. For the orange fabric shown here, the pattern and the extra lines that indicate the direction of the straight stitches were transferred onto the fabric by tracing with a water erasable fabric marker. The backing fabric was then tacked to the wrong side.

## Stitch!

For help, see pages 40-43 for straight stitch, 58-61 for running stitch, and pages 94-97 for stem stitch.

**Feather 1**

1 Stitch the yellow area in straight stitch (1 strand A), working from the pattern line towards the central rib (see Diagram 1).
2 Stitch the white area in straight stitch (1 strand D) by bringing the needle up at the feather edge and taking it down between the ends of two yellow stitches (Diagram 1).
3 Work running stitch for the down. Add the central rib in stem stitch (1 strand A).

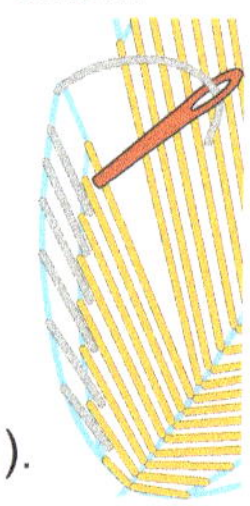

**Diagram 1**

**Feather 2**

1 Stitch the lowest yellow band in straight stitch (1 strand A), working from the pattern lines towards the central rib.
2 Stitch the lowest magenta band in straight stitch (1 strand C) as shown (Diagram 2).
3 Continue working bands of the two colours.
4 Work running stitch for the down (1 strand B).
5 Add the lower part of the central rib in stem stitch (1 strand B mixed in the needle with 1 strand D), then complete the rib in stem stitch (1 strand B).

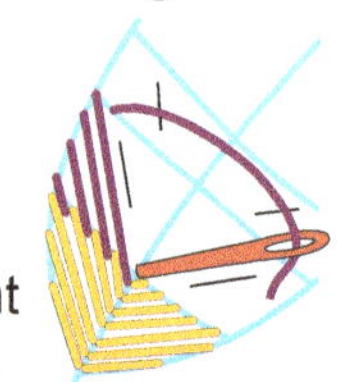

**Diagram 2**

**Feather 3**

1 Stitch the lower white area in straight stitch (1 strand D), working from the pattern lines towards the central rib.
2 Stitch the magenta band in straight stitch (1 strand C) in a similar way to the magenta band of **Feather 2** above.
3 Work the upper white area in straight stitch (1 strand D).
4 Work running stitch for the down, then add the central rib in stem stitch (1 strand D).

## Let's finish

Take out the tacking. Rinse the work in cold water to remove the water erasable fabric marker. When partly dry, press or pin out the work. See page 36 for pressing and for pinning out.

# Fluttering Feather Jewel Purse

Give a feathery touch to a jewel purse.

## The project

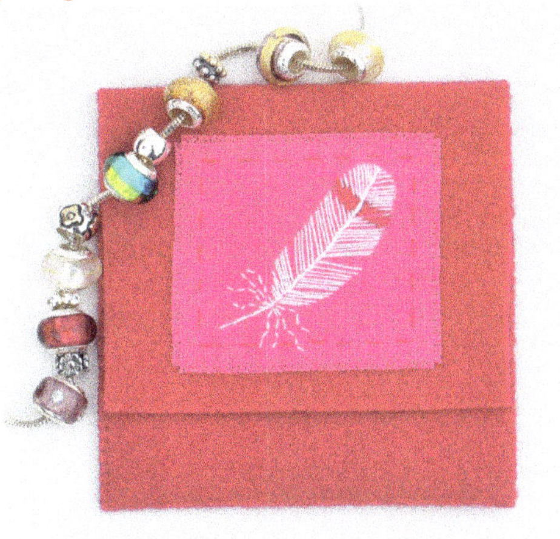

***Fluttering Feather Jewel Purse***

This project features the smallest feather, **Feather 3**, from *Fluttering Feathers*. It is worked on a piece of pink fabric that is then applied as a patch onto a very simply constructed felt purse.
The finished size of this purse is 10cm (4") square.

## Shopping list

- Pink linen-look fabric for the patch: 14cm (5 1/2") square
- Lightweight iron-on interfacing for backing: 4.5cm x 5cm wide (1 3/4" x 2")
- Dark magenta felt fabric for the purse: 28cm x 10cm wide (11" x 4")
- Stranded cotton thread: (C) dark magenta (D) white
- Machine sewing thread: dark magenta
- Tracing paper and other items for transferring the pattern onto the fabric
- Self-adhesive hook and loop dot

## Let's begin

See the page opposite for the pattern.
Attach the iron-on interfacing centrally onto the wrong side of the pink fabric, noting that the fabric extends beyond the backing on all sides. See page 15 for backing the fabric. Transfer the pattern for **Feather 3** centrally onto the right side of the pink fabric by tracing with a water erasable fabric marker or by using transfer paper. See pages 22-25 for transferring the pattern onto the fabric.

## Stitch!

Stitch the feather following steps 1-4 of the stitch instructions for **Feather 3** on the page opposite.

## Let's finish

Rinse the work in cold water to remove the pattern markings. When partly dry, press the work. See page 36 for pressing.

### *Making the patch*

Place the stitched work with the wrong side facing up. Following the pink fabric threads, trim away the excess fabric from around the work, leaving 5mm (1/4") extending outside the edge of the interfacing to make a rectangular patch.
Pull two or three fabric threads away from all four sides to create a frayed edge, but stop fraying just before reaching the edge of the interfacing.

### *Making the purse*

With the felt fabric, create a square purse by folding up 10cm (4") from one end. Using the machine sewing thread, hand stitch the layers together along each side with small stitches (Diagram 1).
Fold down the purse flap.
Centre the pink patch on the flap and attach it with running stitch worked through both the patch and the flap using stranded cotton (1 strand C). See pages 58-61 for running stitch. Attach the self-adhesive hook and loop dot under the flap as a closure for the purse.

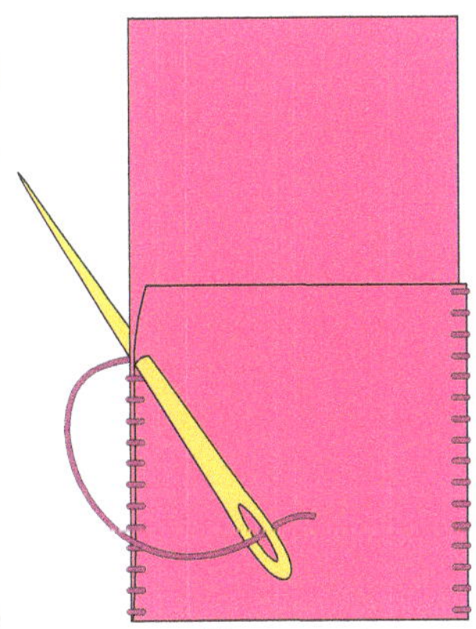

**Diagram 1**

## Hints

**Use other designs on jewel purses**
Small elements from many of the designs in this book can be worked on a jewel purse.

**Card making, scrapbooking, journalling, or decorating tags**
A frayed edge patch as created for this project, featuring any of the designs in this book, or small selected elements from them, can be used to embellish handmade greeting cards, scrapbooking or journal pages, or to decorate tags.

# Rainbow Garden

There's a rainbow of vivid colours in this garden.

## The design

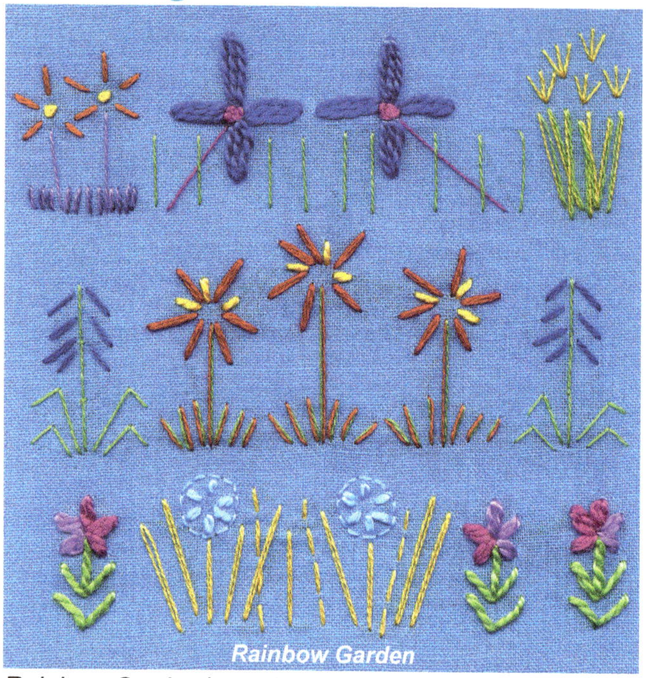


*Rainbow Garden* is worked mostly in straight stitch. This very easy design also features running stitch, back stitch, and French knot.

Follow the instructions on this page to work the design as shown here on an aqua background. See the next page to stitch one selected element from the design as a framed picture.

## The pattern

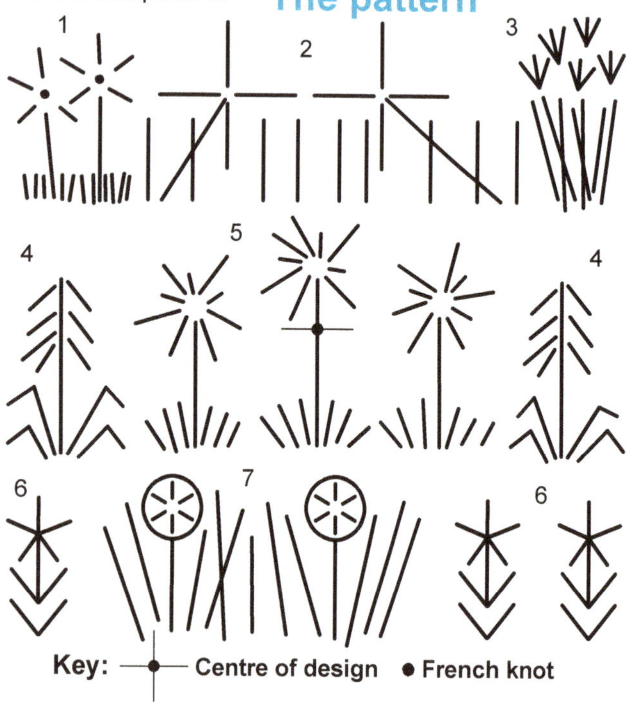


## Shopping list

- Aqua cotton fabric for background: 25cm (10") square
- Fabric or interfacing for backing: 25cm (10") square
- Stranded cotton thread:
  (A) medium violet (B) medium blue (C) medium aqua
  (D) light green (E) medium yellow (F) medium orange
  (G) medium red (H) medium magenta
- No. 5 perlé cotton thread:
  (I) medium violet (J) medium blue (K) medium aqua
  (L) light green (M) medium yellow (N) medium magenta
- Tracing paper and other items for transferring the pattern onto the fabric

## Let's begin

Read page 15 for backing the fabric, and pages 22-25 for transferring the pattern onto the fabric, then select and use suitable methods for your fabric. For the aqua fabric shown here, the pattern was transferred centrally onto the fabric by tracing with a water erasable fabric marker and then the backing fabric was tacked to the wrong side.

## Stitch!

For help, see pages 40-43 for straight stitch, 58-61 for running stitch, 76-79 for back stitch, and pages 184-187 for French knot.

**Flower 1** Stitch the petals in straight stitch (2 strands F). Add a two wrap French knot at each centre (2 strands E). Work stems (1 strand A) and leaves (1 strand A mixed in the needle with 1 strand B) in straight stitch.

**Flower 2** Stitch each petal with three straight stitches worked through the same two holes (1 strand J). Add a one wrap French knot at each centre (1 strand N). Work the stems in straight stitch (1 strand H). Add the leaves in straight stitch (1 strand D).

**Flower 3** Stitch each flower with three straight stitches (1 strand E). Work the stems and leaves in straight stitch (1 strand D mixed in the needle with 1 strand E).

**Flower 4** Stitch each leaf with two straight stitches (1 strand D). Work each stem with one long straight stitch held in place with two tiny straight stitches worked across it (1 strand D), then flowers in straight stitch (2 strands B).

**Flower 5** Work the long petals in straight stitch (3 strands G). Add the short petals in straight stitch (1 strand M). Work the stems and leaves in straight stitch (1 strand D mixed in the needle with 1 strand F).

**Flower 6** Stitch each petal with two straight stitches worked through the same two holes (1 strand I or N). Add stem and leaves in straight stitch (1 strand L).

**Flower 7** Work the flower outlines in back stitch (1 strand C). Stitch the petals in straight stitch (1 strand K). Work three leaves in running stitch, the stems and remaining leaves in straight stitch (2 strands E).

## Let's finish

Take out tacking. Rinse the work in cold water to remove the fabric marker. When partly dry, press or pin out the work. See page 36 for pressing and for pinning out.

# Blue Flowers Framed Picture

Select your favourite flowers for this picture.

## The project

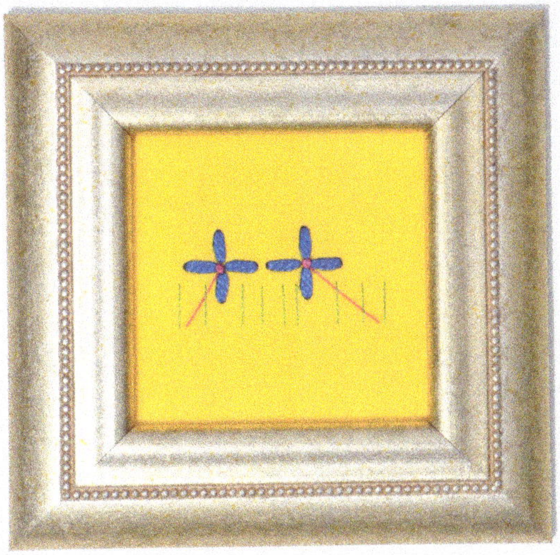

***Blue Flowers Framed Picture***

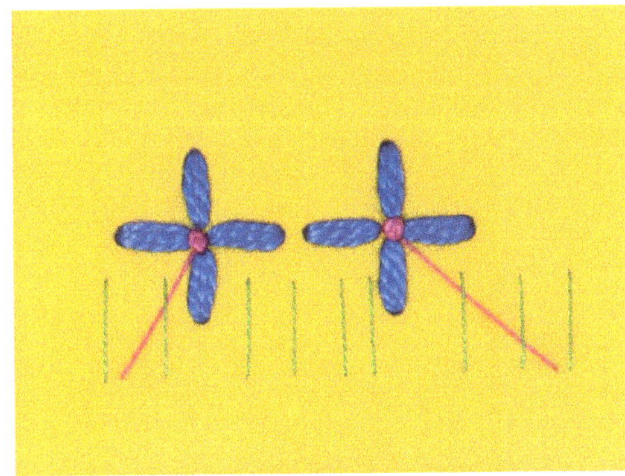

**Detail of**
***Blue Flowers Framed Picture***

This quick and easy project features one element selected from *Rainbow Garden*. **Flower 2** is worked in its original threads on an alternative coloured background. The measurements given in the shopping list on this page are suitable for a picture frame with a window dimension of 8cm (3") square. If your picture frame has different dimensions, you will need to adjust the shopping list measurements accordingly. The dimensions of the wadding and foam core board, or similar, are determined by the size of the backing board of the frame you select.

## Shopping list

- Light gold picture frame: 8cm (3") square window
- Yellow cotton fabric for background: 18cm (7") square
- Fabric or interfacing for backing: 18cm (7") square
- Threads (D), (H), (J), and (N) as listed for the original design on the page opposite
- Strong thread for lacing
- Tracing paper and other items for transferring the pattern onto the fabric
- Thin wadding
- Foam core board, or similar

## Let's begin

See the page opposite for the pattern.
Transfer the pattern for **Flower 2** centrally onto the fabric by tracing with a water erasable fabric marker or by using transfer paper. See pages 22-25 for transferring the pattern onto the fabric.
Tack the piece of backing fabric to the wrong side of the yellow fabric. See page 15 for backing the fabric.

## Stitch!

Work the flower following the stitch instructions for the blue flower, **Flower 2**, on the previous page.

## Let's finish

Take out the tacking. Rinse the work in cold water to remove the pattern markings. When partly dry, press or pin out the work. See page 36 for pressing and for pinning out.
Pad, lace, and frame the work. See page 37 for lacing. Alternatively, take the work to a professional framer who specializes in framing textiles.

## Hints

**Work a single element**
Worked with just a few simple stitches, even a tiny flower isolated from a more complex design makes an artistic statement.

**Themed series**
All of the garden designs from this book, or flowers chosen from them, could be stitched as a garden or flower series. They could be worked on a quilt, on cushions, or they could be presented as framed pictures. See page 201 to see another framed picture that similarly features a single plant.

**Journalling, card and tag making, or scrapbooking**
Small pieces of fabric featuring one or a few small flowers, such as those in *Rainbow Garden*, can be used to decorate a journal, a handmade greeting card, tags, or a scrapbooking page.

# Running stitch
## and variations

Running stitch is created with multiple straight stitches worked in a row, forming a broken or dashed line. The stitches can be the same length as the spaces between them, or they can be smaller or larger than the spaces. This stitch can be worked regularly, with the stitch length and space relationship the same all along the row, or it can be worked irregularly, with the stitches or spaces varying along the row.

Running stitch can be used to work lines and outline shapes. As it is a dashed line, it has a more subtle and delicate appearance than many other stitches.
By working multiple rows of running stitch to create patterns, it can be very useful to fill a shape. Rows can be worked, for example, with the stitches at right angles to each other, or they can be lined up or placed randomly.
An interesting and well-defined line can be achieved by working a foundation row of running stitch that is then whipped, laced, or double laced. The whipping or lacing can be worked using the same thread as the running stitch row, or using a different thread.

Running stitch can be used in combination with other stitches, for example, with a French knot worked in every space.

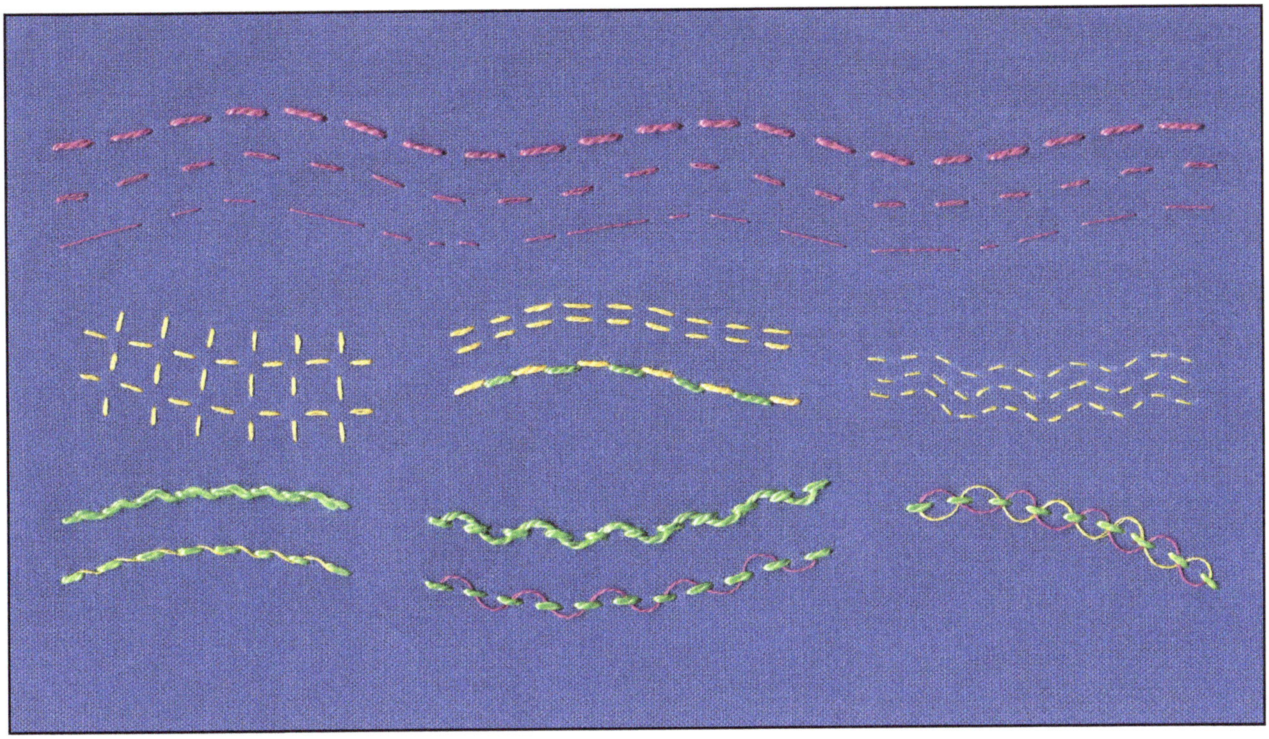

# Running stitch and variations sampler

Running stitch with small spaces
Running stitch with larger spaces
Running stitch with irregular stitches and spaces

Running stitch rows worked at right angles

Two rows of running stitch lined up
Two rows of running stitch offset

Running stitch rows worked in waves

Whipped running stitch
Whipped running stitch

Laced running stitch
Laced running stitch

Double laced running stitch

# Running stitch and variations

## Hints

Running stitch can be worked by skimming the needle in and out of the fabric one or more times before pulling the thread through. Alternatively, it can be worked in two stabbing movements, by taking the needle and thread up through the fabric, and then taking the needle and thread down through the fabric.

Do not work running stitch with the tension of the thread too tight or the fabric will gather up.

Towards the end of a row of running stitch, it may be necessary to vary the length of the last few stitches in order that they fit into the remaining space. A small amount of variation in the length of the last few stitches is better than the last stitch being more noticeably smaller or larger than the rest.

Use a tapestry needle for whipping or lacing running stitch. The rounded end allows this needle to pass under the running stitches without splitting the thread or piercing the fabric.

When whipping or lacing a row of running stitch, pull the thread through and settle the whipping or lacing loosely on each running stitch before moving on to the next stitch.

## Tacking

Tacking is simply a temporary row of running stitches generally used to hold fabric layers together until they are more firmly secured. It can also be used to mark the centre of the fabric in preparation for placing and transferring a pattern.

Tacking is worked in the same way as running stitch, although the stitches are often longer, and machine sewing thread is used. Choose a thread colour that is different from the colour of the background fabric, so that the tacking is easily seen when it is to be removed. Avoid using very dark threads on light coloured fabrics, however, as some threads give off colour that will remain on the fabric.

## Running stitch and variations: right-handed

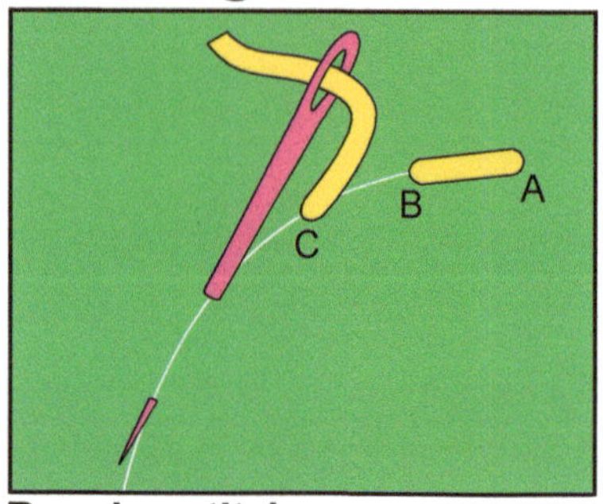


**Running stitch**
Come up at A. Take the needle down at B and emerge at C. Pull the thread through. Continue row.

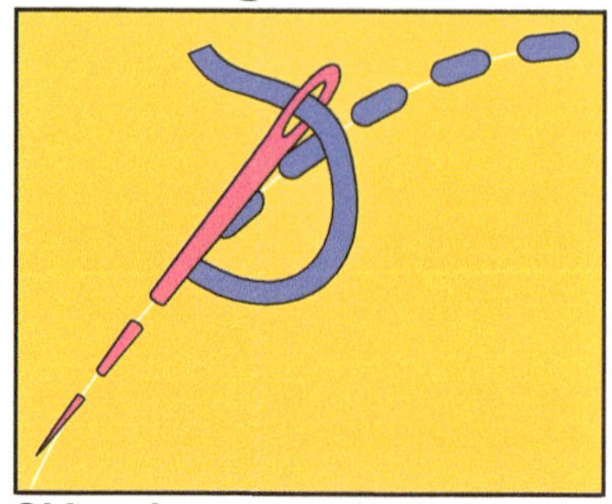

**Skimming several stitches**
Take the needle in and out of the fabric a few times before pulling the thread through.

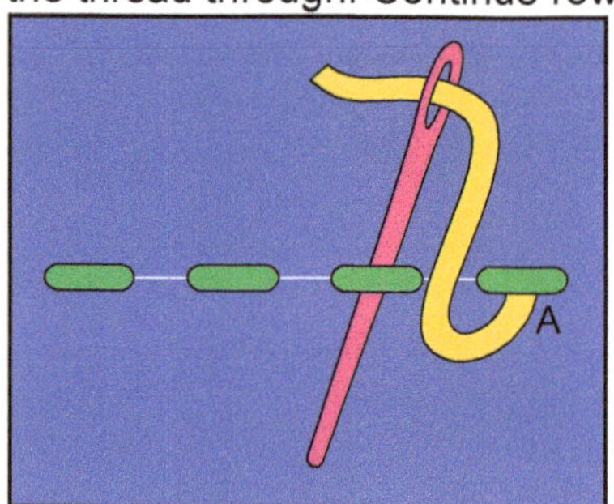


**Whipped running stitch**
**1** Work running stitch. Bring new thread up at A. Pass thread under second stitch, but do not pierce fabric.

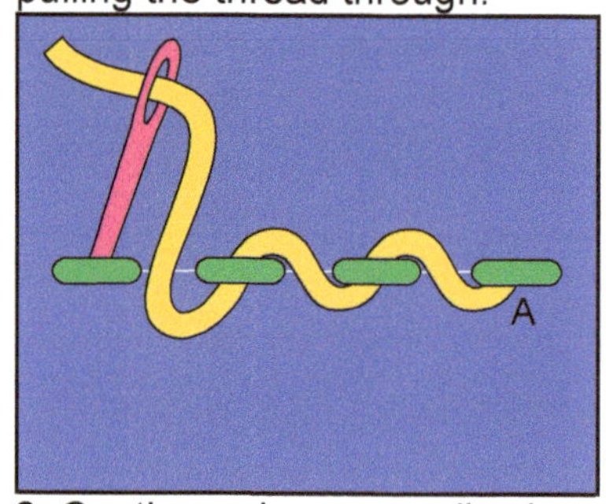


**2** Continue along row, allowing each whipping to settle in place. At the end, take the thread to the back and secure.

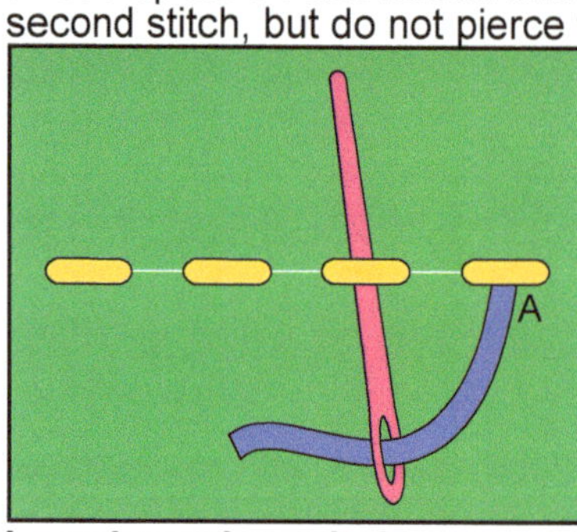


**Laced running stitch**
**1** Work running stitch. Bring new thread up at A. Pass thread under second stitch. Do not pierce fabric.

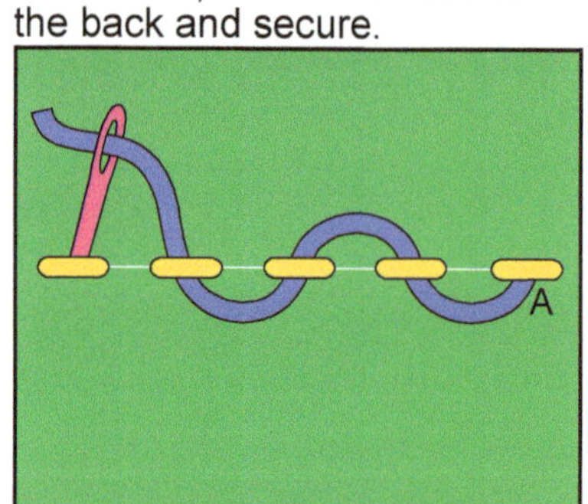


**2** Continue along row, alternating direction of the needle. Allow each lacing to settle loosely in place. At end, take thread to back and secure.

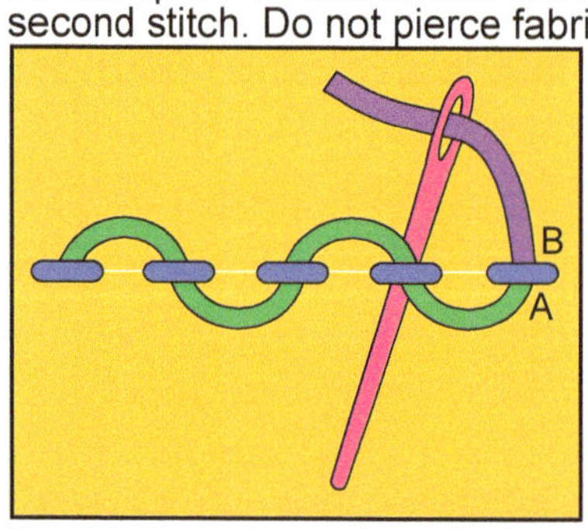


**Double laced running stitch**
**1** Work a row of laced running stitch. Bring new thread up at B. Pass it under second stitch and previous lacing in other direction.

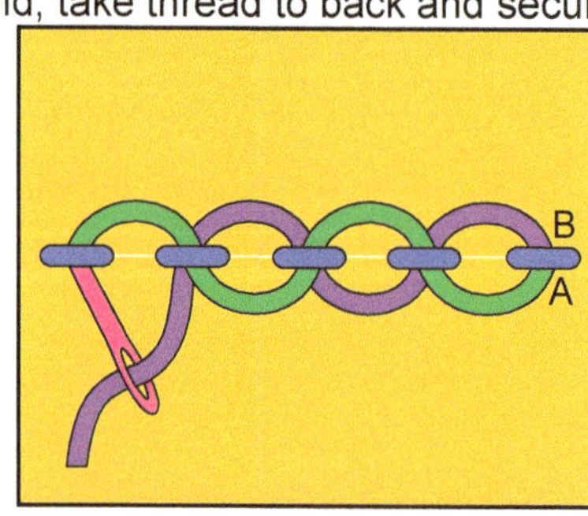


**2** Continue lacing along the row, alternating the direction of the needle. At the end, take the thread to the back and secure.

# Running stitch and variations: left-handed

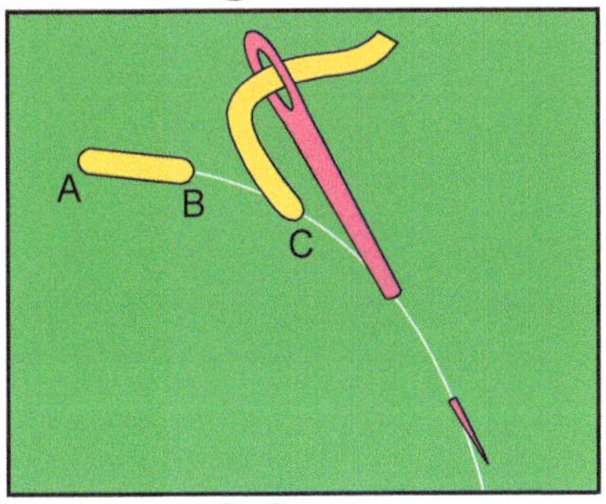


**Running stitch**
Come up at A. Take the needle down at B and emerge at C. Pull the thread through. Continue row.

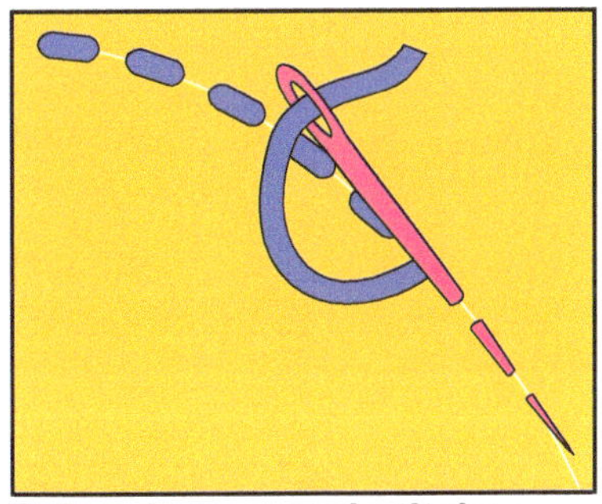

**Skimming several stitches**
Take the needle in and out of the fabric a few times before pulling the thread through.

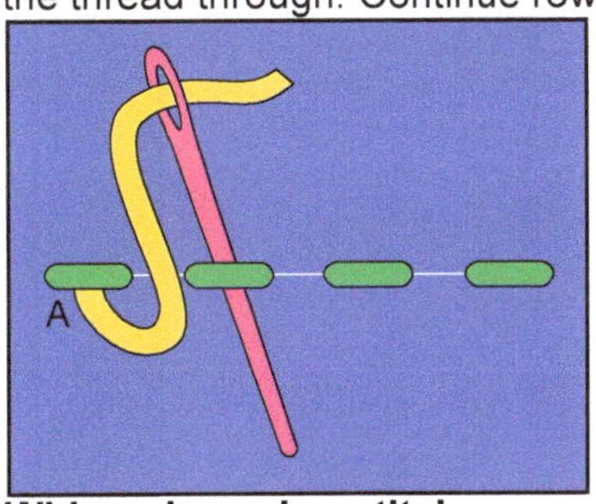


**Whipped running stitch**
**1** Work running stitch. Bring new thread up at A. Pass thread under second stitch, but do not pierce fabric.

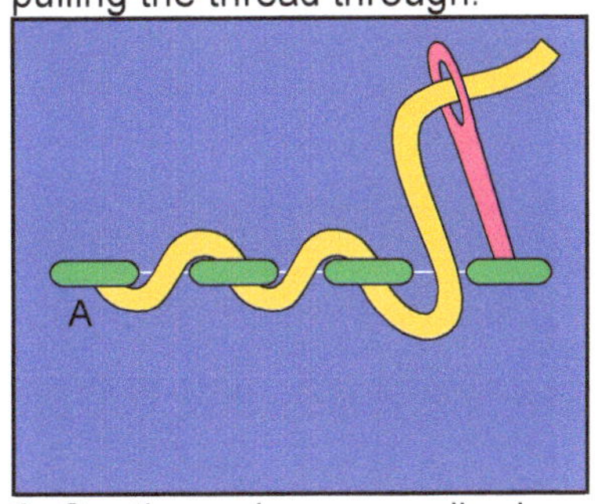


**2** Continue along row, allowing each whipping to settle in place. At the end, take the thread to the back and secure.

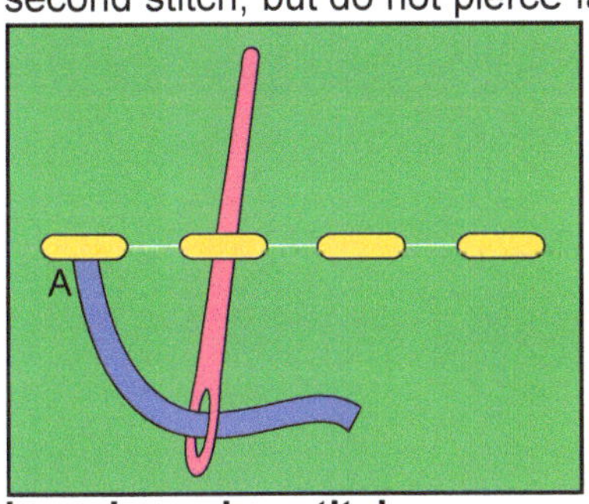


**Laced running stitch**
**1** Work running stitch. Bring new thread up at A. Pass thread under second stitch. Do not pierce fabric.

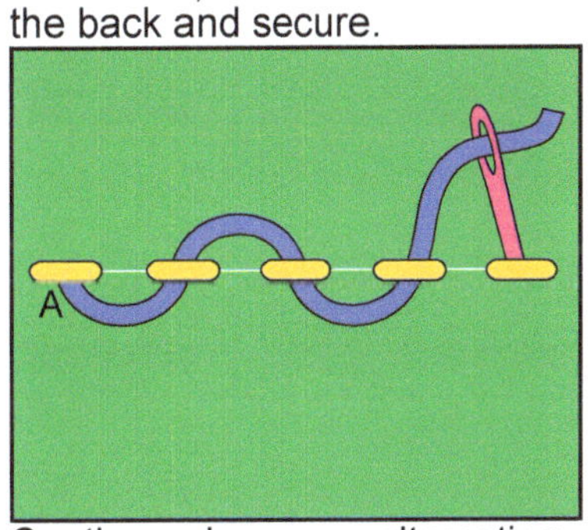


**2** Continue along row, alternating direction of the needle. Allow each lacing to settle loosely in place. At end, take thread to back and secure.

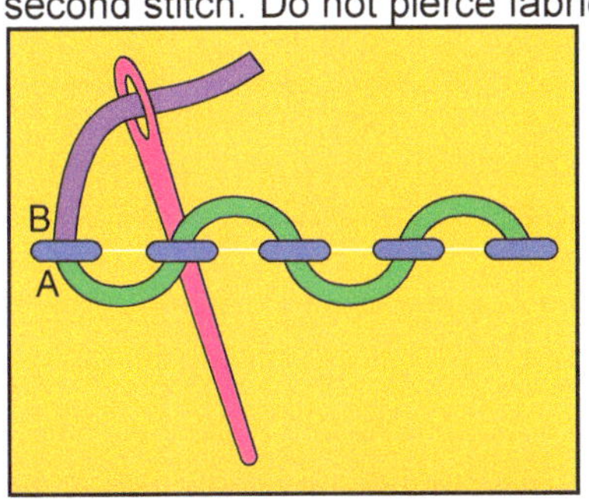


**Double laced running stitch**
**1** Work a row of laced running stitch. Bring new thread up at B. Pass it under second stitch and previous lacing in other direction.

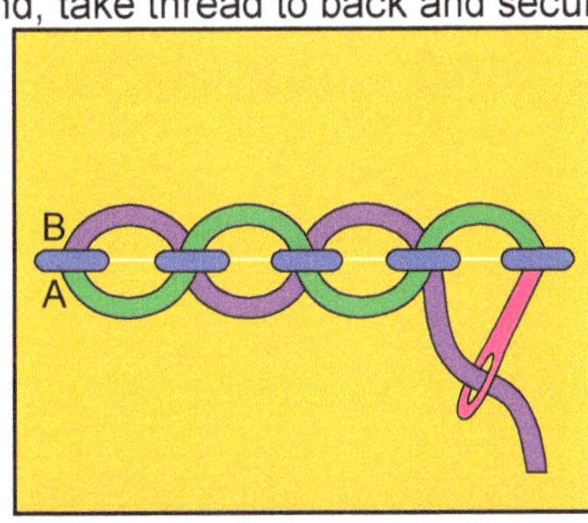


**2** Continue lacing along the row, alternating the direction of the needle. At the end, take the thread to the back and secure.

# Running stitch
## and variations

# Designs and project ideas

## The designs

Snail Trail

Fine Chocolates

Love Heart

Flower Magic

Tea for Two

Silver Forest

# Snail Trail

The snail, with its spiral-shaped shell, can move house whenever it wishes.

## The design

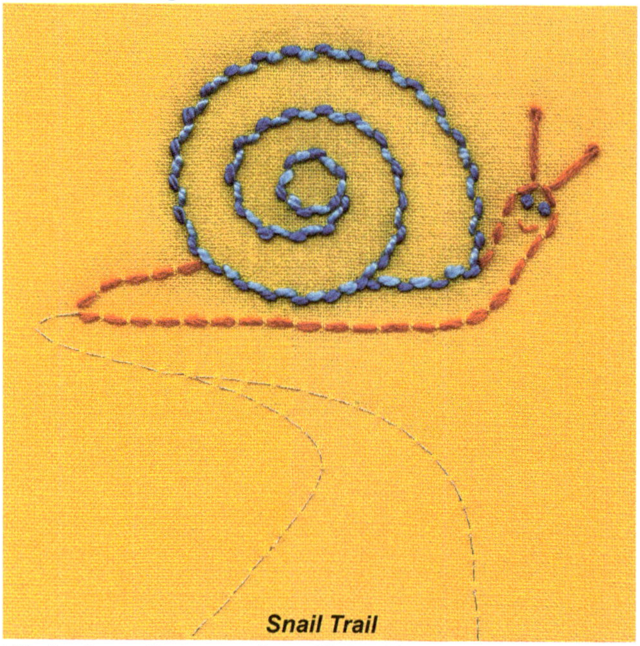

*Snail Trail*

Worked mostly in running stitch, this easy design also uses straight stitch, French knot, and pistil stitch. The design is worked using three types of thread, including metallic thread, which makes the snail's trail silvery. Use the instructions on this page to work the design as shown here on a yellow background. To apply the design, see the project idea on the next page where the snail is worked on four patches on a cushion cover.

## The pattern

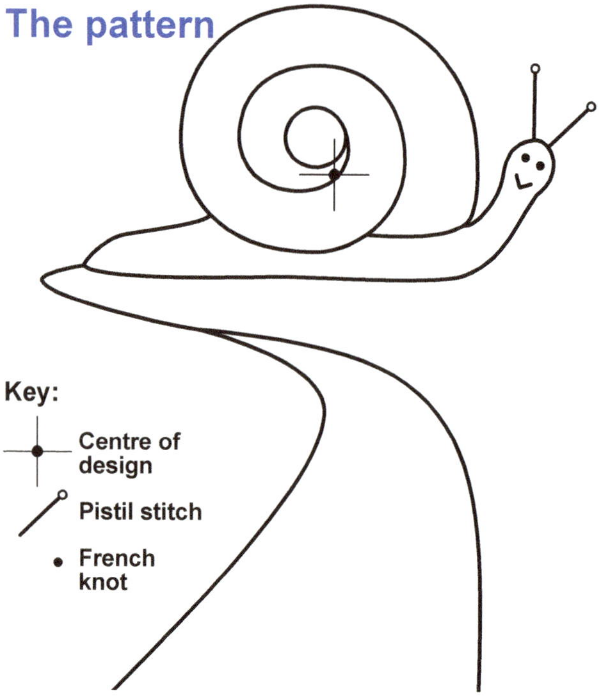


## Shopping list

- Yellow cotton fabric for background: 25cm (10") square
- Fabric or interfacing for backing: 25cm (10") square
- Stranded cotton thread:
  (A) dark aqua (B) medium orange
- No. 5 perlé cotton thread:
  (C) dark aqua (D) medium aqua
- No. 5 perlé metallic thread: (E) silver
- Tracing paper and other items for transferring the pattern onto the fabric

## Let's begin

Read page 15 for backing the fabric, and pages 22-25 for transferring the pattern onto the fabric, then select and use suitable methods for your fabric. For the yellow fabric shown here, the pattern was transferred centrally onto the fabric by tracing with a water erasable fabric marker and then the backing fabric was tacked to the wrong side.

## Stitch!

For help, see pages 40-43 for straight stitch, 58-61 for running stitch, 184-187 for French knot and pistil stitch, and page 17 for preparing perlé metallic thread.

1 Beginning at the centre of the shell, work around the spiral in running stitch (1 strand C). Make the stitches and the spaces between them equal in length (Diagram 1).

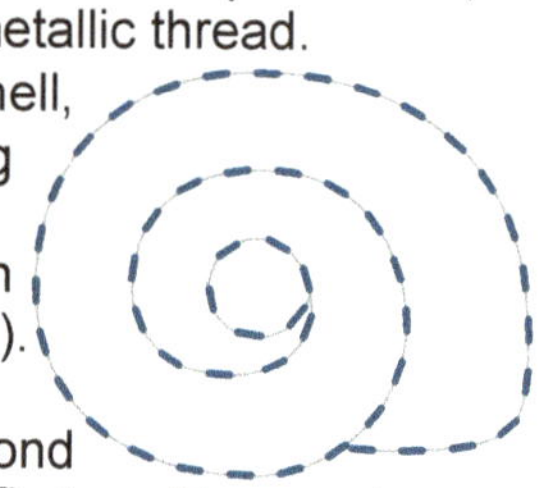

Diagram 1

2 Lining up the stitches with the spaces (Diagram 2), work a second row of running stitch beside the first row (1 strand D).

3 Stitch the body and head with running stitch, leaving tiny spaces between the stitches (3 strands B).

4 Work each of the antennae with a two wrap pistil stitch (3 strands B).

5 Add the mouth with two straight stitches worked through the same lower hole in the fabric (1 strand B).

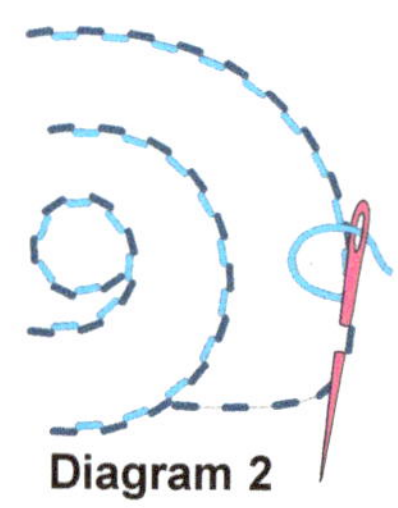

Diagram 2

6 Work a two wrap French knot for each eye (2 strands A).

7 Stitch the snail trail in running stitch leaving small spaces between the stitches (1 ply E).

## Let's finish

Take out the tacking. Rinse the work in cold water to remove the fabric marker. When partly dry, press or pin out the work. See page 36 for pressing and for pinning out.

## Hint

**Using perlé metallic thread**

When stitching the snail trail, separate the perlé metallic thread so that you use one ply only. Metallic thread can become damaged as it is repeatedly drawn through the fabric, so it is easiest to work with short lengths of thread.

# Snails Cushion Cover

Add colourful patches to a cushion cover.

## The project

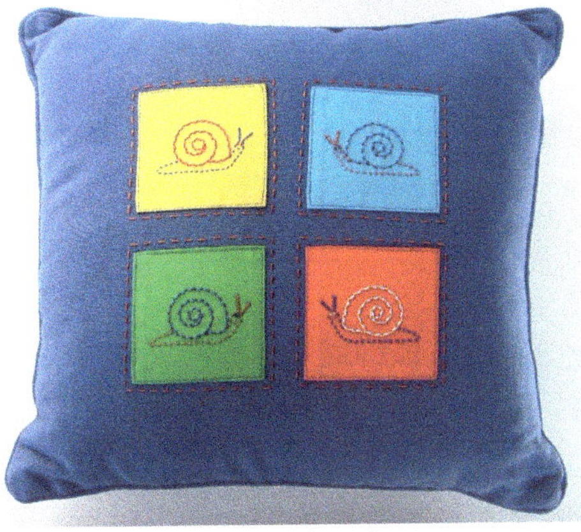

***Snails Cushion Cover***

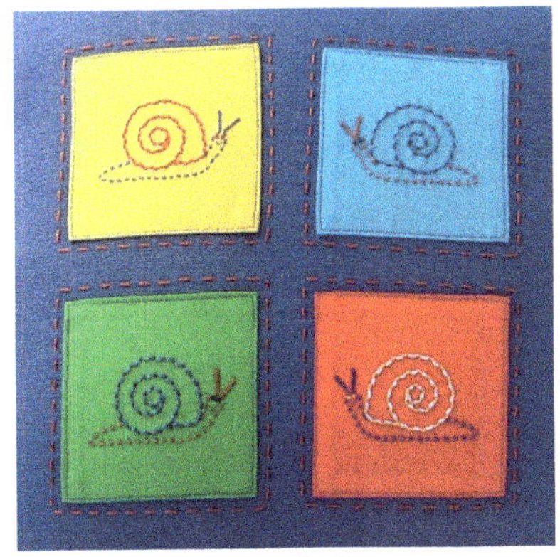

**Detail of *Snails Cushion Cover***

This purchased cushion cover is decorated with four colourful patches that have been stitched with snails using alternative coloured threads. For this project the trails have been omitted. For the yellow and green patches, the snails face the same direction as the original design, while on the aqua and red patches they are mirrored. The patches are attached to the cushion cover with machine stitching, and a row of running stitch is worked around each patch.
This cushion is 45cm (18") square.

## Shopping list

- Blue cushion cover and insert
- Cotton fabric in yellow, aqua, green, and red: 12cm (4 3/4") square of each colour
- Medium weight iron-on interfacing: four 10cm (4") squares
- No. 5 perlé cotton thread for the borders: medium orange
- Machine sewing thread: dark blue
- Tracing paper and other items for transferring the pattern onto the fabric
- Threads for the patches:

***Yellow patch***

- Stranded cotton thread:
  (A) dark red (B) medium blue
- No. 5 perlé cotton thread:
  (C) dark red (D) medium red

***Aqua and green patches***

- Stranded cotton thread:
  (A) dark blue (B) medium orange
- No. 5 perlé cotton thread:
  (C) dark blue (D) medium blue

***Red patch***

- Stranded cotton thread:
  (A) medium yellow (B) medium blue
- No. 5 perlé cotton thread:
  (C) medium yellow (D) white

## Let's begin

See the page opposite for the pattern.
Following the instructions on page 15 for backing the fabric, attach one of the squares of interfacing centrally onto the wrong side of each piece of fabric.
Fold under the edges of each square 1cm (3/8") on all sides, and tack around all four sides.
Transfer the pattern, omitting the snail trail, onto the centre of the yellow and green squares using transfer paper. Transfer a mirrored pattern onto the centre of the aqua and red squares in the same way. See page 20 for how to mirror the pattern, and page 24 for transferring the pattern using transfer paper.

## Stitch!

Work the snails on each square following steps 1-6 of the stitch instructions for the original design on the previous page, substituting the alternative threads.

## Let's finish

Rinse each square in cold water to remove the pattern markings. When almost dry, press. See page 36 for pressing.
Remove the cushion insert. Following the photo as a guide for placement, pin and tack the squares onto the front of the cushion cover. Leave a 3cm (1 1/4") space between the squares.
Using a straight stitch on the sewing machine, and with dark blue machine sewing thread, stitch around the squares just inside their edges to attach them to the front of the cushion cover. Take out all the tacking.
Using medium orange perlé cotton, work a square border on the cushion fabric 5mm (1/4") outside each patch in running stitch.
Place the cushion insert back inside the cover.

# Flower Magic

A delicate flower shimmers in the clear sunlight.

## The design

In *Flower Magic*, the petals and centre are worked in running stitch while the tendrils are worked in whipped running stitch. This easy design is worked in shiny stranded rayon threads and in stranded cotton. To work the design as shown above, follow the instructions on this page. See the next page for information on how to feature two different versions of this flower design on sachets for dried flowers.

## The pattern

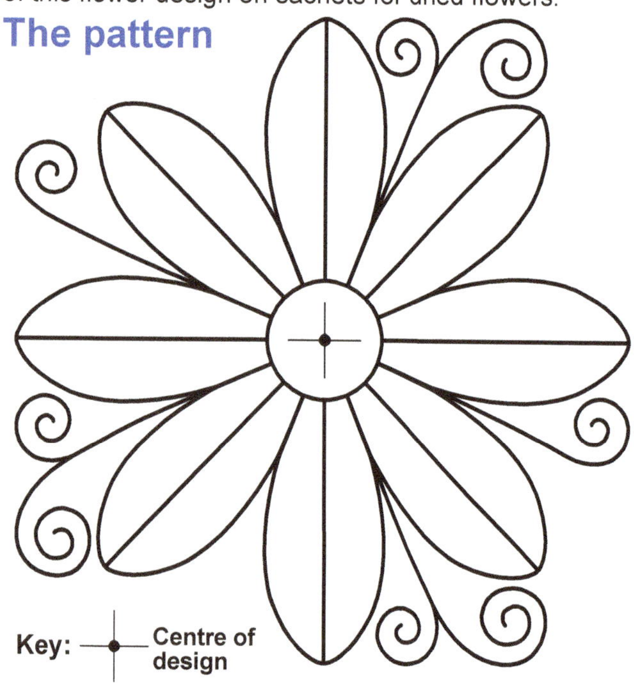


## Shopping list

- Green cotton fabric for background: 25cm (10") square
- Fabric or interfacing for backing: 25cm (10") square
- Stranded cotton thread: (A) dark magenta
- Stranded rayon thread: (B) light green (C) medium magenta (D) light magenta
- Tracing paper and other items for transferring the pattern onto the fabric

## Let's begin

Read page 15 for backing the fabric, and pages 22-25 for transferring the pattern onto the fabric, then select and use suitable methods for your fabric. For the green fabric shown here, the pattern was transferred centrally onto the fabric by tracing with a water erasable fabric marker and then the backing fabric was tacked to the wrong side.

## Stitch!

For help, see pages 58-61 for running stitch and whipped running stitch. All the running stitches in this design are small and are worked with tiny spaces between them.

1 Stitch the petal outlines in running stitch (1 strand A). Note that on each petal there is a running stitch worked across its end (Diagram 1).

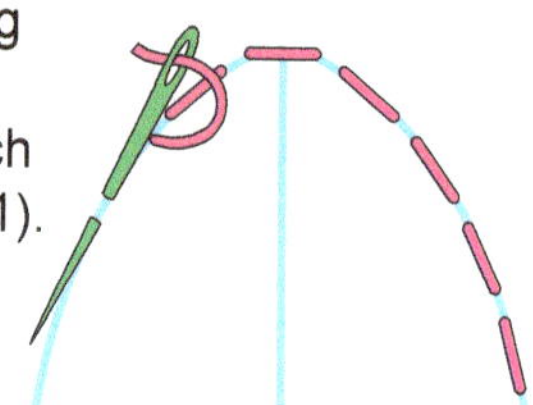

Diagram 1

2 Following the marked line, work the circle for the flower centre in running stitch (1 strand A).

3 Work a second circle of running stitch just inside the first (1 strand C mixed in the needle with 1 strand D).

4 Stitch the line on each petal in running stitch (1 strand C mixed in the needle with 1 strand D).

5 Stitch the tendrils in running stitch (2 strands B), then, using a tapestry needle, whip this running stitch (1 strand B).

## Let's finish

Take out the tacking. Rinse the work in cold water to remove the water erasable fabric marker. When partly dry, press or pin out the work. See page 36 for pressing and for pinning out.

## Hints

**Stitch tension**

Make sure the running stitches in this design are not pulled too tightly or the fabric will gather up.

**Using rayon thread**

Begin and end off the rayon thread extra securely on the back of the work as it is springy and can easily work loose.

# Flower Magic Sachets

Let's perfume a room with these floral sachets!

## The projects

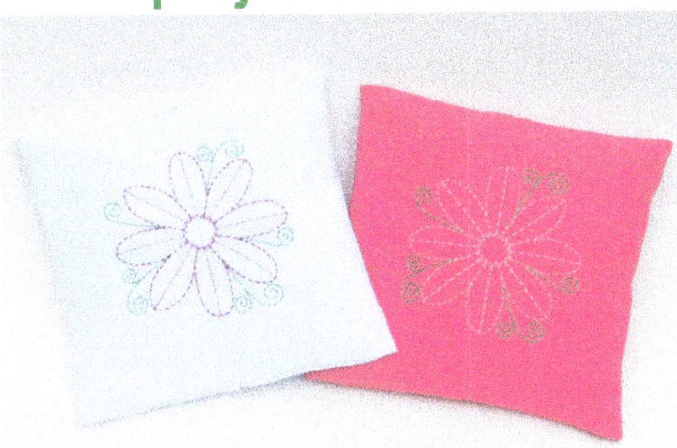

***Flower Magic Sachets***

*Flower Magic*, in alternative colour schemes, is featured on these easily constructed sachets.
The finished size of each sachet is 16cm (6") square.

## Shopping list

***White sachet***

- White linen-look fabric for the sachet: 18cm x 42cm wide (7" x 16 1/2")
- Fabric or interfacing for backing: 18cm x 39cm wide (7" x 15 1/4")
- White closely-woven cotton fabric for the insert: two 18cm (7") squares
- Threads as listed for the original design on the page opposite
- Machine sewing thread: white
- Tracing paper and other items for transferring the pattern onto the fabric
- Dried rose petals, rosebuds, or lavender flowers

***Pink sachet***

- Pink linen-look fabric for the sachet: 18cm x 42cm wide (7" x 16 1/2")
- Fabric or interfacing for backing: 18cm x 39cm wide (7" x 15 1/4")
- White closely-woven cotton fabric for the insert: two 18cm (7") squares
- Stranded cotton thread: white
- Stranded rayon thread: white and light green
- Machine sewing thread: pink and white
- Tracing paper and other items for transferring the pattern onto the fabric
- Dried rose petals, rosebuds, or lavender flowers

## Hint

**An alternative filling for the sachets**

You could fill the insert with cloves and small pieces of cinnamon stick.

## Let's begin

See the page opposite for the pattern.

***For either sachet*** With the right side of the linen-look fabric facing up, place pins 17.5cm (7") in from the left hand short side and half way between the two long sides (Diagram 1).

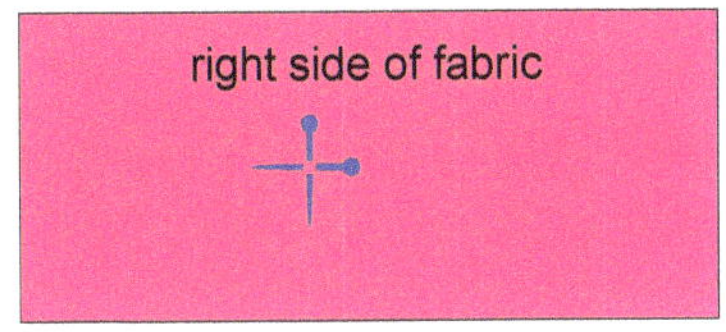


**Diagram 1**

Centering the pattern at the point marked by the pins, transfer the pattern by tracing with a water erasable fabric marker or by using transfer paper. See pages 22-25 for transferring the pattern. Tack the backing fabric centrally to the wrong side, noting that the linen-look fabric extends beyond the backing at each short end. See page 15 for backing the fabric.

## Stitch!

***For the white sachet*** Work the design following steps 1-5 of the stitch instructions on the page opposite.

***For the pink sachet*** Follow steps 1-5 of the stitch instructions on the page opposite, using the following:
Steps 1 and 2: white stranded cotton (1 strand)
Steps 3 and 4: white stranded rayon (2 strands)
Step 5: green stranded rayon (2 strands, then 1 strand)

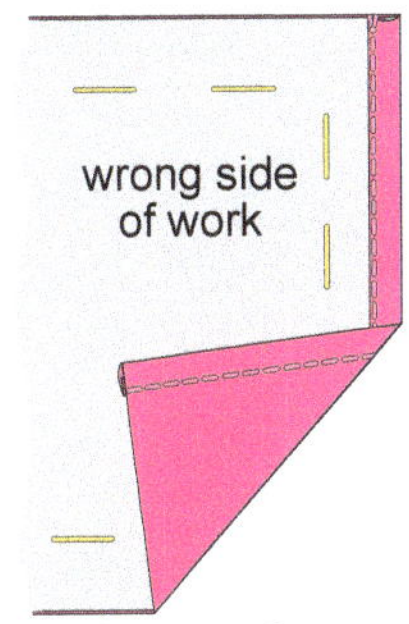


**Diagram 2**

## Let's finish

***Making the white or pink sachet*** Rinse the work in cold water to remove the pattern markings. When almost dry, press. See page 36 for pressing. On each short end, fold the raw edge 5mm (1/4") to the wrong side and press. Fold again 1cm (3/8") and press. Using matching machine sewing thread, machine stitch near the first fold through all layers (Diagram 2).

Place the work with the stitched design facing up. With right sides together, fold the hemmed end that is closest to the stitched design over for 8cm (3 1/4") and pin (Diagram 3).

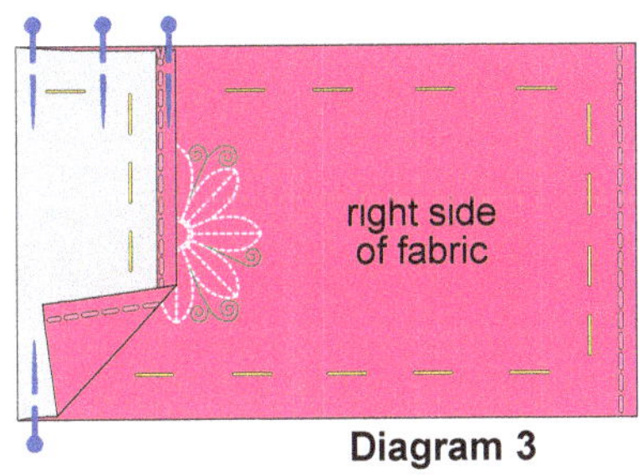


**Diagram 3**

Fold the remaining hemmed end over for 15cm (5 3/4"), overlapping the first end, and pin. Machine stitch through all layers 1cm (3/8") from the upper and lower edges. Take out the tacking and trim the corners (Diagram 4).

Turn the sachet through to the right side and press.

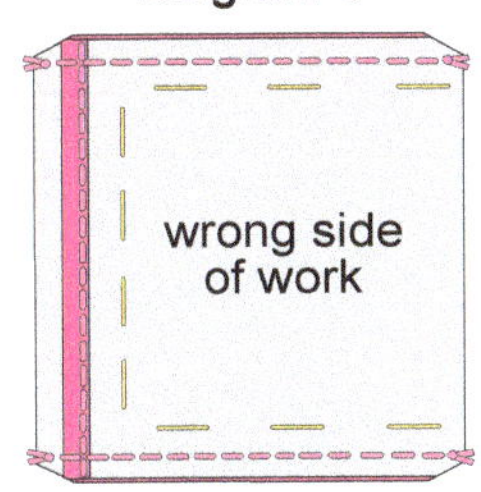


**Diagram 4**

***Making the insert*** Place the two squares of fabric right sides together and pin around the edge. Using white machine sewing thread and a 1cm (3/8") seam allowance, machine stitch around the square, leaving a 5cm (2") opening in the middle of one side. Ensure that 20cm (8") of machine thread length remains before cutting it. Knot the machine sewing threads and trim three of them, leaving one of the long ends. Trim the corners (Diagram 5).

Turn the insert to the right side through the opening and press. Fill with the dried filling. Using the long end of machine sewing thread, hand stitch the opening closed. Place the filled insert into the sachet.

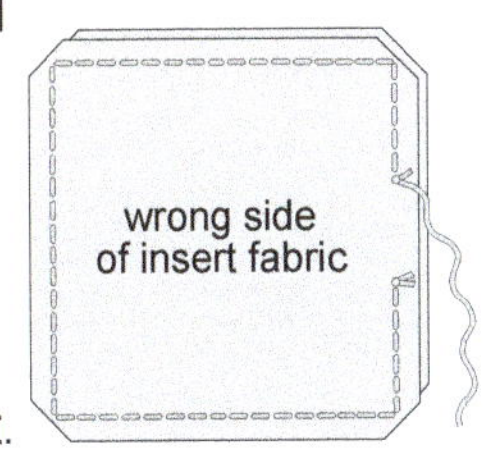


**Diagram 5**

# Fine Chocolates

Absolute bliss on a cold winter's night is a cosy fire, a good book, and a tasty selection of fine chocolates.

## The design

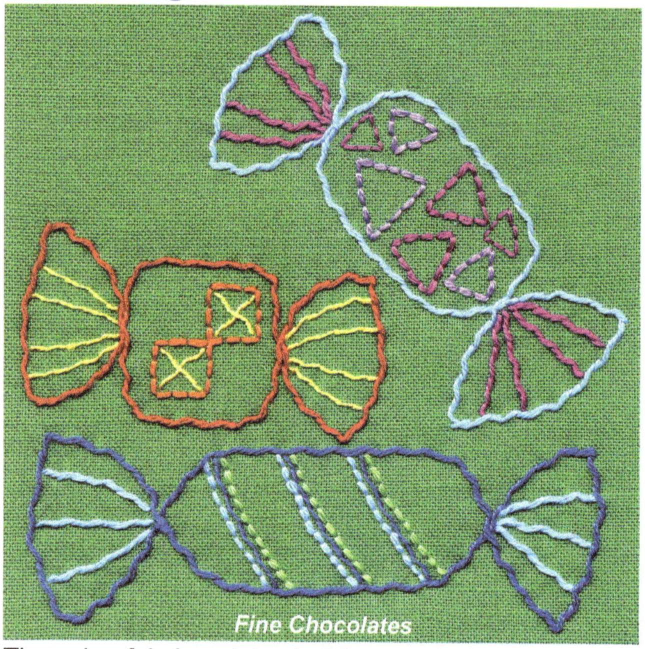


The colourful chocolates in this easy design are worked in running stitch that has been whipped to add definition. Further details are added in back stitch.
Use the instructions here to work the design on a green background. See the project on the following page where scattered chocolates are worked on a child's top.

## The pattern

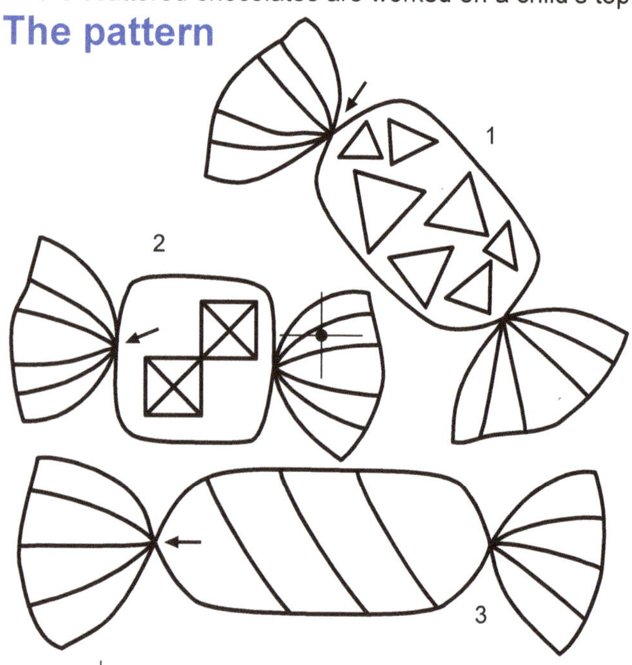


**Key:** Centre of design  **Begin running stitch and whipping here**

## Shopping list

- Green cotton fabric for background: 25cm (10") square
- Fabric or interfacing for backing: 25cm (10") square
- Stranded cotton thread:
  (A) medium violet (B) medium blue (C) medium aqua
  (D) light green (E) medium yellow (F) medium orange
  (G) medium red (H) medium magenta
- Tracing paper and other items for transferring the pattern onto the fabric

## Let's begin

Read page 15 for backing the fabric, and pages 22-25 for transferring the pattern onto the fabric, then select and use suitable methods for your fabric. For the green fabric shown here, the pattern was transferred centrally onto the fabric by tracing with a water erasable fabric marker and then the backing fabric was tacked to the wrong side.

## Stitch!

For help, see pages 58-61 for running stitch and whipped running stitch, and pages 76-79 for back stitch. Use a tapestry needle for all the whipping.

**Chocolate 1**

1. Starting at the arrow and stitching in a continuous line, work the outline of the chocolate in running stitch (2 strands C). Using the same thread and beginning at the same point, whip the running stitch.
2. Work the stripes on the wrapper ends in running stitch and then whip the stitches (2 strands H).
3. Stitch the triangles in back stitch (2 strands A or H for the large and medium, 1 strand H for the small).

**Chocolate 2**

1. As for Chocolate 1, work the outline of the chocolate in running stitch, then whip the running stitch (2 strands G).
2. Work the stripes on the wrapper ends in running stitch and then whip the running stitches (1 strand E).
3. Work the squares in back stitch (2 strands F).
4. Stitch the crosses in the squares in running stitch, then whip the running stitches (1 strand E).

**Chocolate 3**

1. As for Chocolate 1, work the outline of the chocolate in running stitch, then whip the running stitch (2 strands B).
2. Work the stripes on the wrapper ends in running stitch and then whip the running stitch (2 strands C).
3. Following the marked line, stitch each blue stripe in running stitch, then whip the running stitch (1 strand B).
4. Add a row of back stitch on the left of each stripe (2 strands C) and a row of back stitch on the right (2 strands D).

## Let's finish

Take out tacking. Rinse the work in cold water to remove the fabric marker. When partly dry, press or pin out the work. See page 36 for pressing and for pinning out.

# Fine Chocolates T-shirt

Add sweet decorations to a child's T-shirt.

## The project

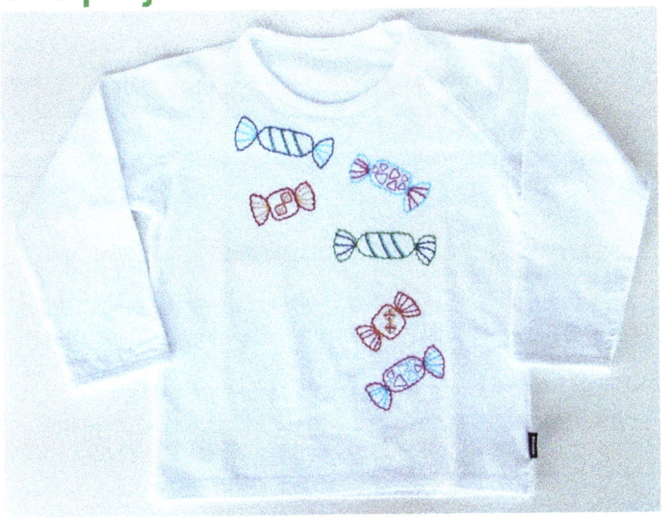

*Fine Chocolates T-shirt*

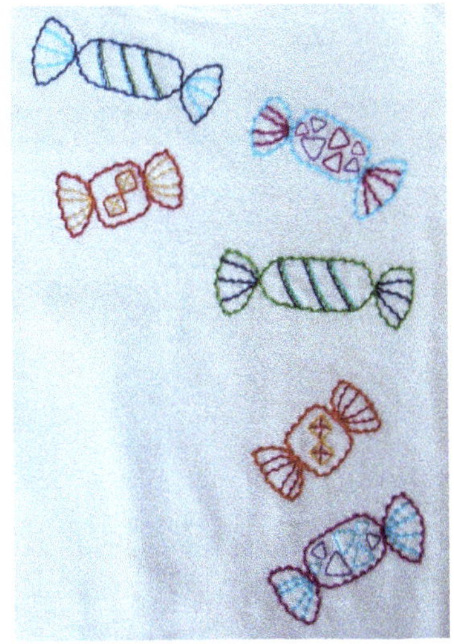

**Detail of *Fine Chocolates T-shirt***

Six chocolates scattered over the front of this garment have transformed a plain white top into a piece of wearable art. The upper three chocolates are worked in the same colours as the original design. The lower three chocolates use the same thread colours, but the colours within each chocolate have been swapped around.

## Shopping list

- White stretch knit top
- Lightweight iron-on interfacing: six pieces 5cm x 10cm wide (2" x 4")
- Threads as listed for the original design opposite
- Tracing paper and other items for transferring the pattern onto the garment

## Let's begin

See the page opposite for the pattern.

Using the pattern, and with a separate piece of tracing paper for each, make two tracings of each chocolate. Referring to the photo, the numbers on the pattern, and the diagram, position the tracings on the front of the garment. Rotate the tracings and move them around until you are happy with their placement (Diagram 1).

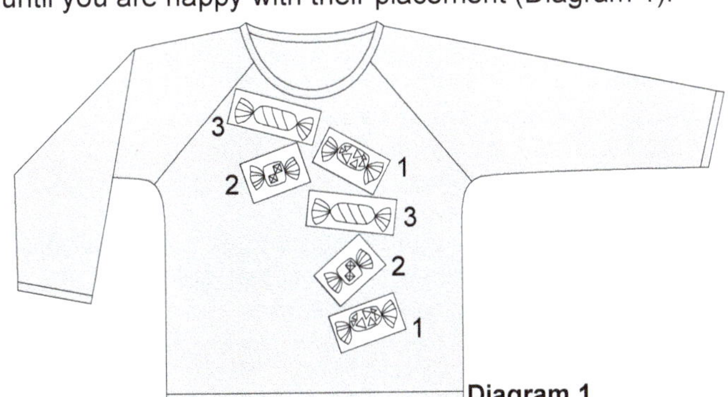


**Diagram 1**

Using tacking stitches in a light colour, record the position at which each chocolate is to be stitched. From here on, each chocolate is prepared and stitched before moving on to the next one. Begin with the chocolate that is closest to the neckline. Following the instructions on page 15 for backing the fabric, attach one piece of interfacing onto the wrong side of the front of the garment at the position for the chocolate. This will stabilize the area where the design is to be stitched.

Transfer the pattern onto the front of the garment by tracing with a water erasable fabric marker. See page 23 for transferring the pattern by tracing.

## Stitch!

Work this first chocolate using the same threads and following the stitch instructions for **Chocolate 3** on the previous page.

Continue in this way for each chocolate, working the next two chocolates following the stitch instructions and with the same colours as the original design. For the lower three chocolates, follow the stitch instructions and use the same colours as those in the original design, but swap the colours around within each chocolate.

## Let's finish

Take out the tacking and turn the T-shirt inside out. On the wrong side, peel back any excess interfacing from its outer edge and trim it back close to the stitches. Rinse the T-shirt in cold water to remove the pattern markings. When dry, turn it inside out and press it. See page 36 for pressing.

# Tea for Two

One teaspoonful of tea leaves for each person and one for the pot!

## The design

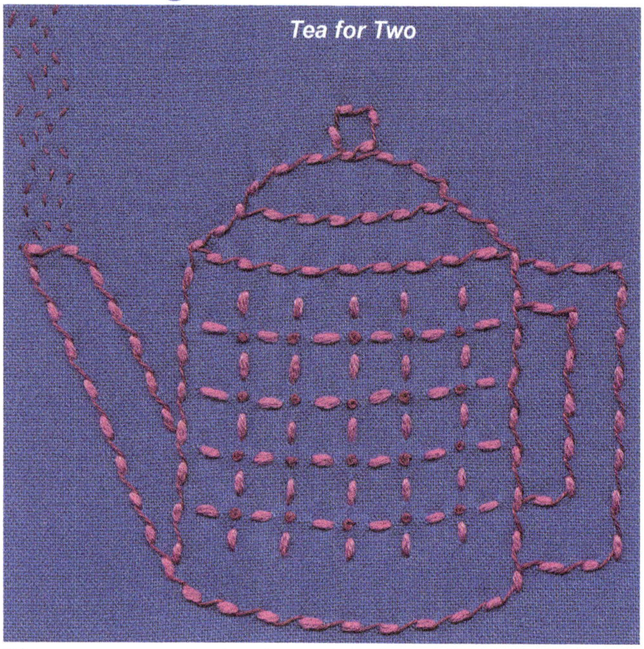


This very easy design is worked in running stitch, whipped running stitch, and French knot. The teapot is stitched using two shades of just one colour to create an interesting monochrome effect. Use the instructions on this page to work the design as above. To work the design on a set of tea towels, see the page opposite.

## The pattern

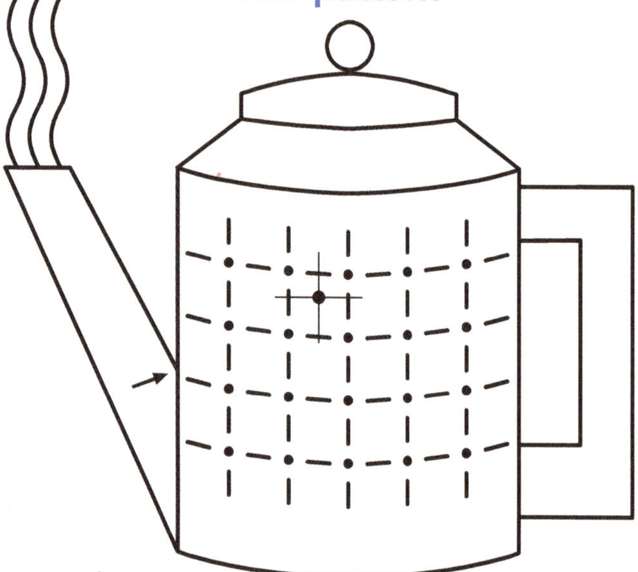

Key: Centre of design; Begin running stitch and whipping here; • French knot

## Shopping list

- Blue cotton fabric for background: 25cm (10") square
- Fabric or interfacing for backing: 25cm (10") square
- Stranded cotton thread: (A) dark magenta (B) medium magenta
- Tracing paper and other items for transferring the pattern onto the fabric

## Let's begin

Read page 15 for backing the fabric, and pages 22-25 for transferring the pattern onto the fabric, then select and use suitable methods for your fabric. For the blue fabric shown here, the pattern was transferred centrally onto the fabric by tracing with a water erasable fabric marker and then the backing fabric was tacked to the wrong side.

## Stitch!

For help, see pages 58-61 for running stitch and whipped running stitch, and pages 184-187 for French knot. Use a tapestry needle for all the whipping.

1 Beginning at the marked position, work the outline for the spout in running stitch, ready for whipping in step 2 (4 strands B). Continuing with this thread, work the pot, the lid, and the handle in the same way.
2 Following the same order, whip the running stitches (1 strand A).
3 Following the marked lines, stitch the petals for the flower decoration in running stitch. Work them as rows stitched horizontally, then vertically (4 strands B).
4 Work a two wrap French knot at the centre of each flower (1 strand A).
5 Beginning at the end of the spout, work three vertical rows of running stitch for the steam (1 strand A).

## Let's finish

Take out the tacking. Rinse the work in cold water to remove the water erasable fabric marker. When partly dry, press or pin out the work. See page 36 for pressing and for pinning out.

## Hint

**Using whipped running stitch**

When used as an outline, running stitch is often whipped. The whipping links the running stitches and makes the outline more defined.

In this design, one strand of thread has been used for the whipping the outline. For a thicker line, use a greater number of strands of thread.

# Tea Towels

Brighten up the kitchen with colourful tea towels.

## The project

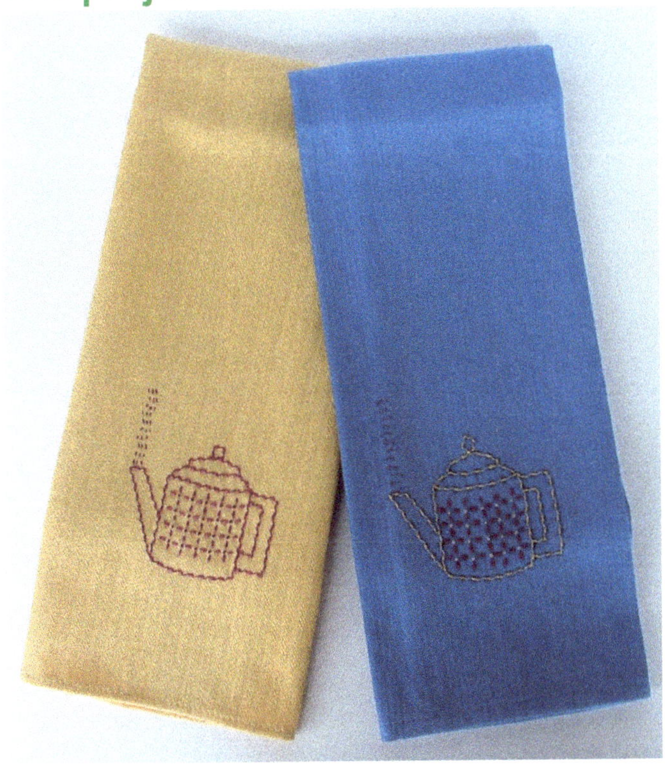

***Tea Towels***

Two purchased tea towels are decorated with the teapot. The yellow tea towel is worked in the same colours as the original design, while the colours on the blue tea towel have been changed to a different colour scheme.

## Shopping list

***Yellow tea towel***

- Yellow tea towel
- Threads as listed for the original design on the page opposite
- Tracing paper and other items for transferring the pattern onto the tea towel

***Blue tea towel***

- Blue tea towel
- Stranded cotton thread: medium yellow and medium red
- Tracing paper and other items for transferring the pattern onto the tea towel

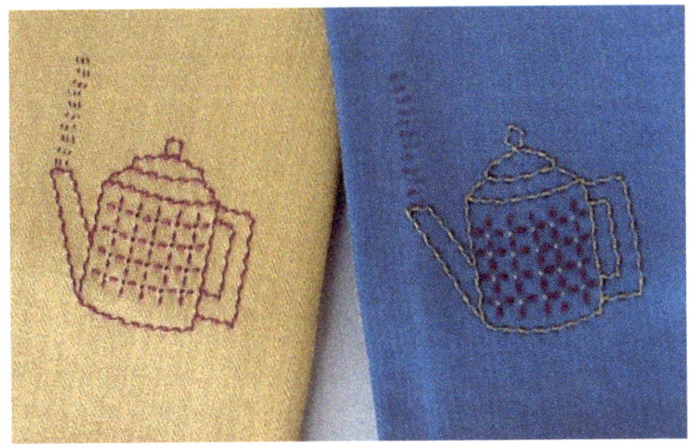

**Detail of**
***Tea Towels***

## Let's begin

See the page opposite for the *Tea for Two* pattern. Transfer the pattern onto the right side of each tea towel at the centre of the lower edge using transfer paper. See page 24 for transferring the pattern using transfer paper.

## Stitch!

***Yellow tea towel***

Work the teapot on the yellow tea towel following steps 1-5 of the stitch instructions on the previous page.

***Blue tea towel***

Work the teapot on the blue tea towel following steps 1-5 of the stitch instructions on the previous page, substituting the following colours:
Step 1: medium yellow (4 strands)
Step 2: medium yellow (1 strand)
Step 3: medium red (4 strands)
Step 4: medium yellow (1 strand)
Step 5: medium red (1 strand)

## Let's finish

Rinse the tea towels in cold water to remove the pattern markings. When almost dry, press. See page 36 for pressing.

## Hint

**Adapt the design**

You can reverse the design to make a pair of tea towels with images that are a mirror image of each other. See page 20 for how to mirror the pattern.

# Love Heart

A love heart with a delicate lacy border and a radiant flower.

## The design

*Love Heart*

This easy design features a double laced running stitch border. Running stitch, detached chain stitch, and French knot are used for the flower.

Follow the instructions on this page to work the design exactly as shown here on a yellow background. To display the design as a framed picture, see the project idea on the facing page.

## The pattern

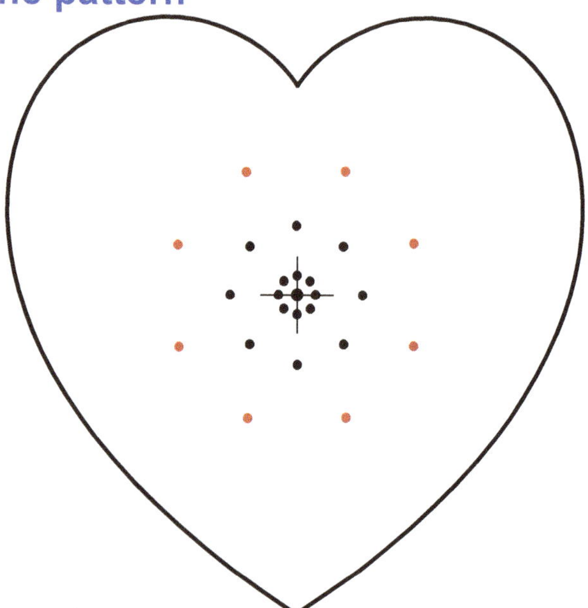

**Key:** **Centre of design** • **Begin running stitch here** • **Detached chain stitch petal**

## Shopping list

- Yellow cotton fabric for background: 25cm (10") square
- Fabric or interfacing for backing: 25cm (10") square
- Red felt fabric for the heart shape: 10cm (4") square
- Stranded cotton thread:
  (A) medium yellow (B) medium red (C) light red
- No. 5 perlé cotton thread:
  (D) medium yellow (E) medium red
- Tracing paper and other items for preparing the shape

## Let's begin

For this design, the pattern is not transferred onto the background fabric. Attach the backing fabric to the wrong side of the background fabric. See page 15 for backing the fabric. Trace the pattern onto tracing paper. Place the tracing over a pad of folded fabric and, using a large needle, pierce holes in the tracing at each dot. Pin the tracing to the red felt and cut out the heart shape along the pattern outline. Using a sharp HB pencil, draw dots onto the felt through the holes in the tracing to mark the placement for the flower. See page 25 for transferring the pattern using the pierce and dot method. Remove the tracing from the felt.

## Stitch!

For help, see pages 58-61 for running stitch and double laced running stitch, 166-169 for detached chain stitch, and pages 184-187 for French knot. Apart from the lacing, all stitches on the felt are worked through all layers using a stabbing movement. Please see hint opposite.

1 Pin and tack the heart shape onto the yellow fabric. Work the petals in detached chain stitch (1 strand D) following the marked dots (Diagram 1).

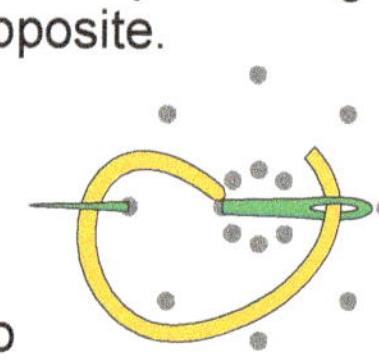

**Diagram 1**

2 Work three French knots, each with two wraps, in space at centre (1 strand D).

3 Beginning at the remaining marked dots, work the light red lines between petals in running stitch (2 strands C).

4 Keeping an even distance inside the felt edge and following the diagrams for the points (Diagrams 2 and 3), work a row of running stitch around the heart (1 strand D). This row is to be double laced later.

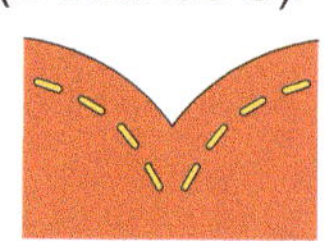

**Diagram 2**

5 Keeping an even distance outside the felt edge, work a row of running stitch around the heart on the background fabric (1 strand E). Work the stitches at the points in the same way as those on the felt. This row is to be double laced. Using a tapestry needle, lace both of the running stitch rows with yellow (1 strand A) and then in the other direction with red (1 strand B).

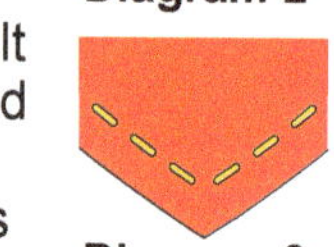

**Diagram 3**

## Let's finish

Take out tacking. Press or pin out work. Do not dampen the felt. See page 36 for pressing and for pinning out.

# Love Heart Framed Picture

Capture a heart with this framed picture!

## The project

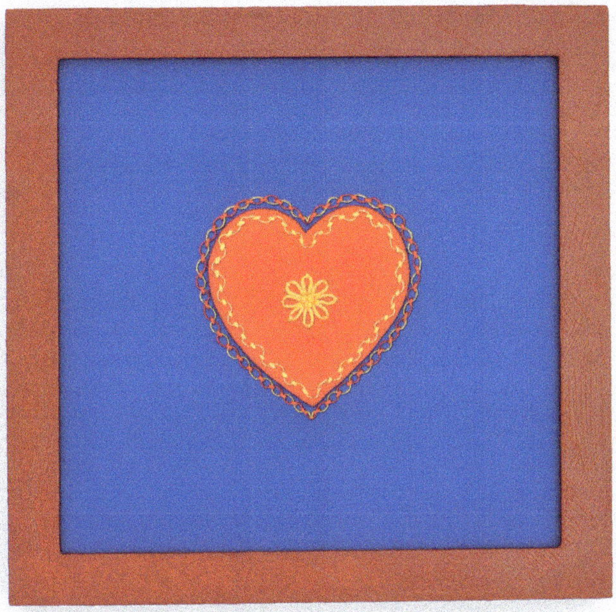

***Love Heart Framed Picture***

**Detail of**
***Love Heart Framed Picture***

*Love Heart* is stitched on an alternative coloured background and displayed in a square red frame. The frame that you choose can dramatically alter the overall appearance of the picture.

The measurements given in the shopping list on this page are suitable for a picture frame with a window dimension of 19cm (7 1/2") square. If your picture frame has different dimensions, you will need to adjust the shopping list measurements accordingly. The dimensions of the wadding and foam core board, or similar, are determined by the size of the backing board of the frame you select.

## Shopping list

- Red picture frame:
  19cm (7 1/2") square window
- Blue cotton fabric for background:
  36cm (14") square
- Fabric or interfacing for backing:
  36cm (14") square
- Red felt fabric for the heart shape:
  10cm (4") square
- Threads as listed for the original design on the page opposite
- Strong thread for lacing
- Tracing paper and other items for preparing the shape
- Thin wadding
- Foam core board, or similar

## Let's begin

See the page opposite for the pattern.

Attach the backing fabric to the blue fabric and prepare the felt shape following the instructions given in this section on the page opposite.

## Stitch!

Following steps 1-5 of the stitch instructions on the page opposite, attach the felt heart to the blue fabric and work the design.

## Let's finish

Take out the tacking. Press or pin out the work. It is not recommended to dampen the felt. See page 36 for pressing and for pinning out.

Pad, lace, and frame the work. See page 37 for lacing. Alternatively, take the work to a professional framer who specializes in framing textiles.

## Hints

**Stitch tension**

Work the anchors of the detached chain stitches in *Love Heart* loosely so that they do not disappear into the felt.

**Use a hoop if you'd like to**

The row of double laced running stitch that is worked on the background fabric may be easier to stitch if the work is placed in a hoop.

# Silver Forest

In the depths of the tranquil forest, water droplets on the leaves sparkle softly in the filtered sunlight.

## The design

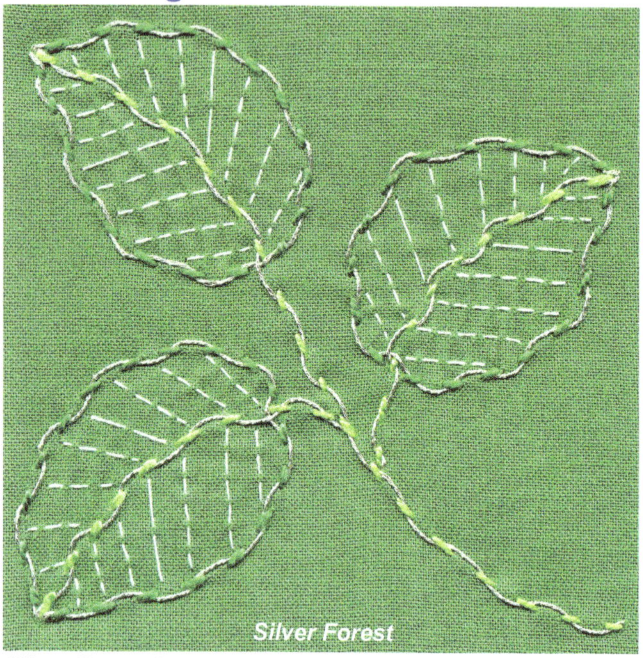


*Silver Forest* is worked in running stitch and laced running stitch. This simple design features an interesting combination of threads, including silver metallic thread for extra sparkle.

Follow the instructions on this page to work the design exactly as shown here on a green background.

To adapt the design for a decorated tag, see the project idea on the next page.

## The pattern

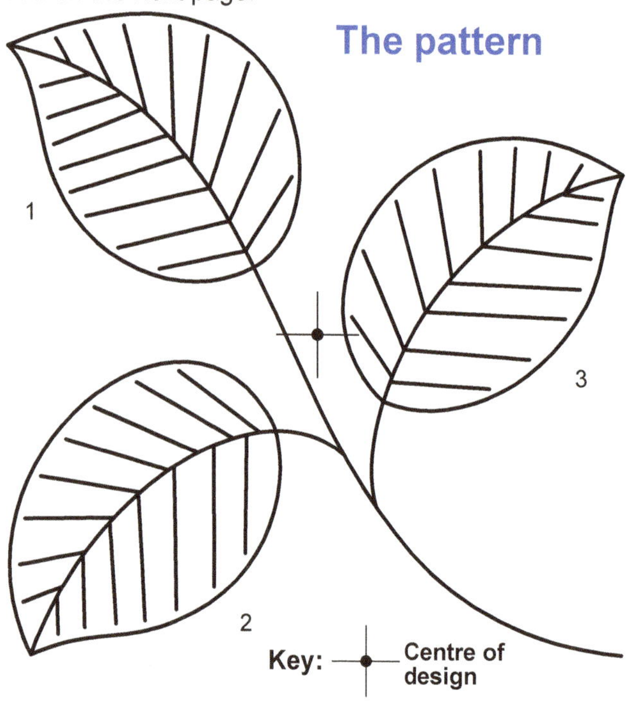


## Shopping list

- Green cotton fabric for background: 25cm (10") square
- Fabric or interfacing for backing: 25cm (10") square
- Stranded cotton thread: (A) white
- No. 5 perlé cotton thread:
  (B) medium green (C) light green
- No. 5 perlé metallic thread: (D) silver
- Tracing paper and other items for transferring the pattern onto the fabric

## Let's begin

Read page 15 for backing the fabric, and pages 22-25 for transferring the pattern onto the fabric, then select and use suitable methods for your fabric. For the green fabric shown here, the pattern was transferred centrally onto the fabric by tracing with a water erasable fabric marker and then the backing fabric was tacked to the wrong side.

## Stitch!

For help, see pages 58-61 for running stitch and laced running stitch. See also page 17 for preparing perlé metallic thread. Use a tapestry needle for all the lacing.

1. Stitch the leaf central veins and the stems in running stitch (1 strand C), and then stitch the leaf outlines in running stitch (1 strand B).
2. Beginning at the tip of leaf 1, lace the leaf outline (4 ply D). On reaching the tip again, take the thread to the back (Diagram 1). On the wrong side of the work, take the thread under the back of a previously worked stitch and then bring the thread to the front through the same hole at the leaf tip (Diagram 2).
3. Continuing with the same thread, lace from the leaf tip down the leaf central vein and to the end of the stem.
4. Repeat steps 2 and 3 for the remaining leaves, ending lacing where the leaf stems meet the main stem.
5. Keeping within the laced outline, stitch the leaf side veins in running stitch. Vary stitch lengths and have tiny spaces between stitches (1 strand A).

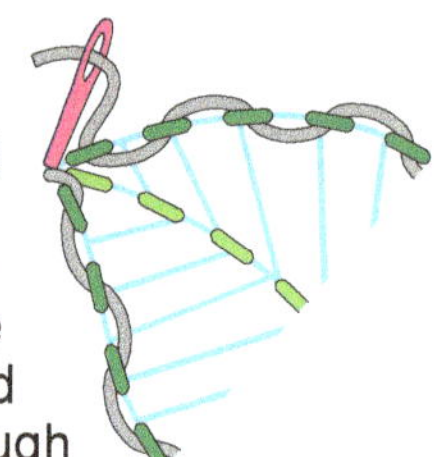

**Diagram 1**

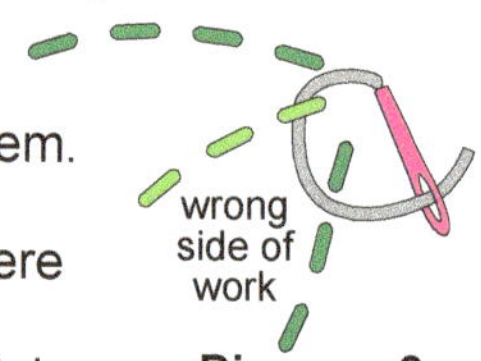


**Diagram 2**

## Let's finish

Take out the tacking. Rinse the work in cold water to remove the water erasable fabric marker. When partly dry, press or pin out the work. See page 36 for pressing and for pinning out.

## Hints

**Stitch tension**

Work the lacing loosely and evenly so that it is wavy.

**Using perlé metallic thread**

Begin and end off the metallic thread securely on the back of the work as it can easily work loose.

# Silver Leaf Tag

Add special charm with this leafy tag.

## The project

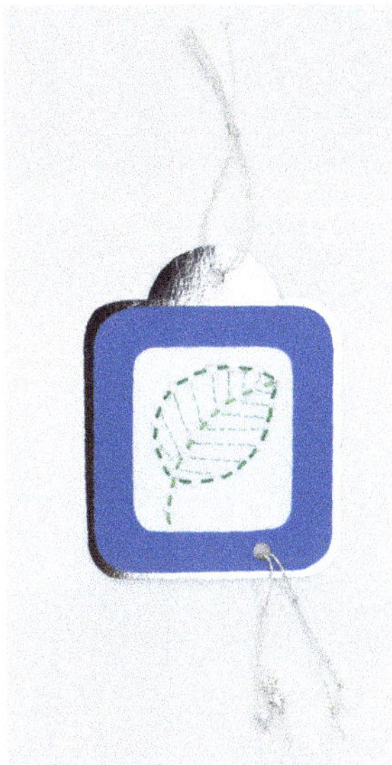

*Silver Leaf Tag*

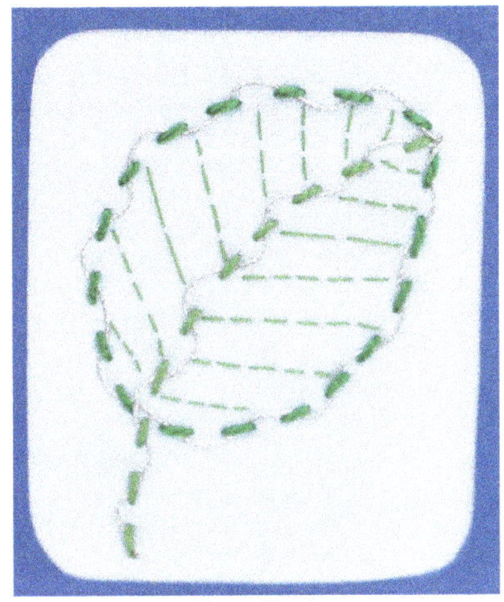

Detail of
*Silver Leaf Tag*

An infinite variety of tags, greeting cards, scrapbooking decorations, and journalling embellishments can be created from the designs in this book. A single leaf from *Silver Forest* is featured on this tag.
The size of this tag is 10cm x 8cm wide (4" x 3")

## Shopping list

- White cotton fabric for background: 15cm (6") square
- Medium weight iron-on interfacing for backing: 15cm (6") square
- Stranded cotton thread: (A) light green
- No. 5 perlé cotton thread:
  (B) medium green (C) light green
- No. 5 perlé metallic thread: (D) silver
- Tracing paper and other items for transferring the pattern onto the fabric
- Silver card: 10cm x 8cm wide (4" x 3")
- Blue card: 8cm x 7.5cm wide (3 1/4" x 2 3/4")
- Archival double-sided sticky tape
- 3 large round silver beads

## Let's begin

See the page opposite for the pattern.
Attach the iron-on interfacing onto the wrong side of the white fabric. See page 15 for backing the fabric.
Transfer the pattern for **Leaf 3** centrally onto the right side of the white fabric by tracing with a water erasable fabric marker or by using transfer paper. See pages 22-25 for transferring the pattern onto the fabric.

## Stitch!

Work the leaf following steps 1-3 and step 5 of the stitch instructions on the page opposite, using the alternative coloured thread for the leaf veins.

## Let's finish

Rinse the work in cold water to remove the water erasable fabric marker. When partly dry, press or pin out the work. See page 36 for pressing and for pinning out.
Using the photo as a guide, from the blue card cut a rectangular frame that has rounded corners and is slightly larger than the area of stitching. Trim the stitched work a little larger than the inside dimension of the frame. From the silver card, cut a tag shape a little larger than the frame. Using archival sticky tape, attach the frame centred over the stitched work. Attach the framed work to the front of the silver tag. Punch a hole centrally at the top of the tag. Thread two lengths of silver thread (D) through the hole and tie in a knot. Punch a hole through all layers at the lower right of the frame. Thread a length of the silver thread (D) through the hole and tie in a knot. Add one or two knots to each end separately and trim away any excess length.
Repeat, this time adding two beads and a knot to one end, and one bead and a knot to the other. Trim away any excess length (Diagram 1).

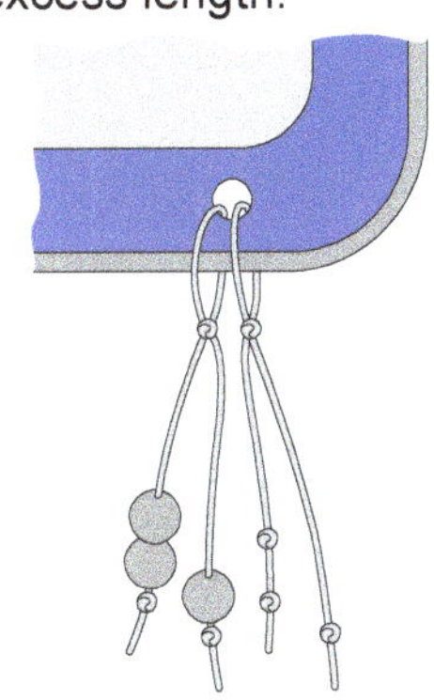

**Diagram 1**

## Hint

**Change the colours**
For autumn leaves, work this design in reds or oranges, laced with gold metallic thread.

# Back stitch

## and variations

Back stitch is one of the most commonly used stitches. It can be worked as the only stitch featured in a design, or it can be used in combination with other stitches. As back stitch creates a continuous row of stitches, it is well suited to working lines and outlining shapes, and it can be used to follow intricate pattern lines such as scallops or spirals. Back stitch can be worked with all the stitches equal in length along the row. Its appearance then resembles machine straight stitching. Alternatively, the stitches can vary in length along the row, giving a more irregular appearance.

A row of back stitch can be worked with spaces between the stitches. This is called spaced back stitch. Back stitch can also be worked as isolated stitches oriented in any direction. For a more decorative or textured effect, a row of back stitch can form a foundation that is then whipped, laced, or double laced. The whipping or lacing can be worked using the same thread as the back stitch row or using a different thread.

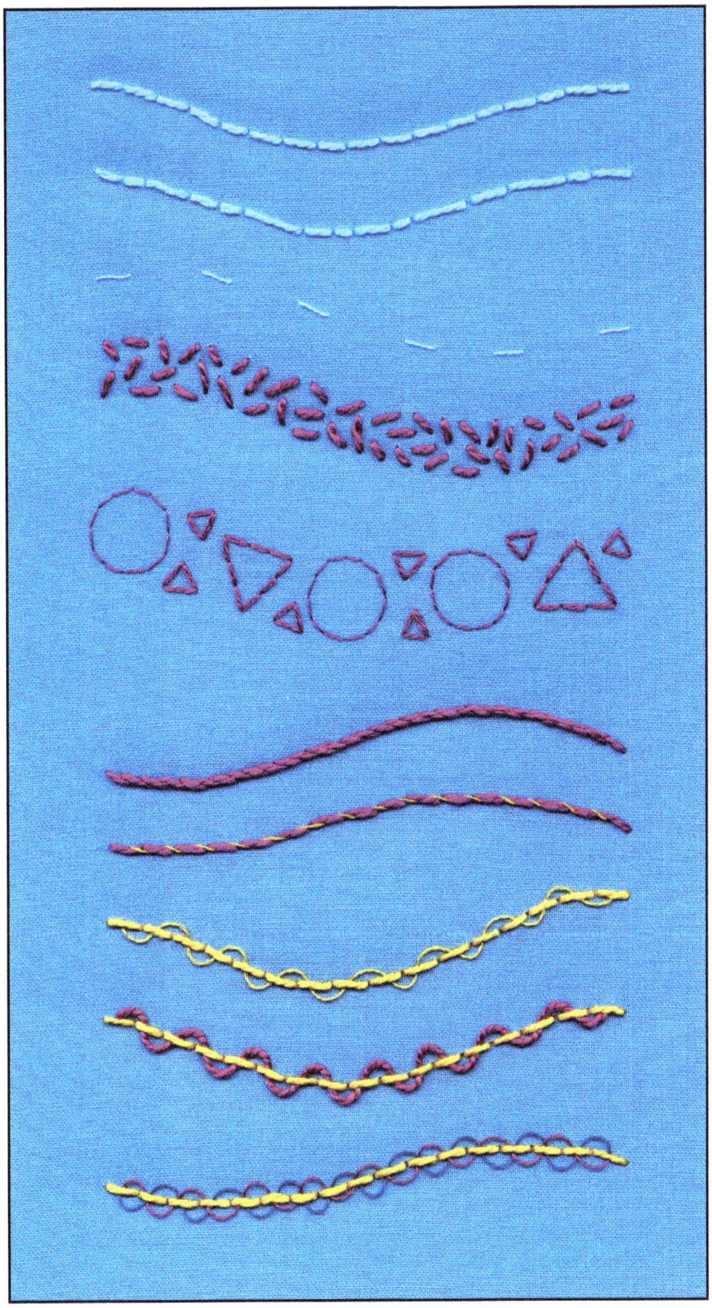


**Back stitch and variations sampler**

# Back stitch and variations

## Hints

Back stitch can be worked by skimming the needle in and out of the fabric before pulling the thread through. Alternatively, it can be worked in two stabbing movements, by taking the needle and thread up through the fabric, and then taking the needle and thread down through the fabric.

When working back stitch, take the needle through the same hole in the fabric as the previously worked stitch each time, but do not split the thread with the needle.

Make sure that the tension of the thread is not too tight or the fabric will not lie flat. This is especially important when working spaced back stitch and isolated back stitch because the carried thread on the back of the work can be quite long.

If working back stitch along a curve, use small stitches so that they lie smoothly along the curve, and corners do not form where the stitches meet.

Towards the end of a row of even back stitch, visually judge whether the last few stitches will fit exactly. If not, consider whether a few slightly smaller stitches or a few slightly larger stitches will fit better into the space available. This will avoid ending with the last stitch of a very uneven size.

Use a tapestry needle for whipping or lacing back stitch. The rounded end allows this needle to pass under the back stitches without splitting the thread or piercing the fabric.

When working laced or double laced back stitch, allow each lacing to settle loosely in place, giving a lacy effect.

## Back stitch and variations: right-handed

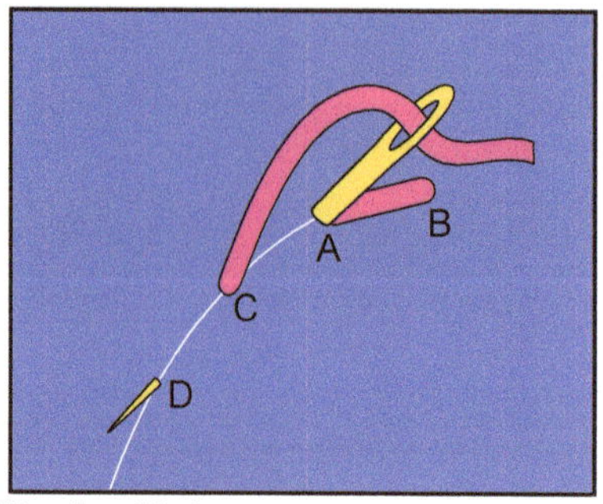


**Back stitch**
Come up at A, a stitch length from start. Take thread down at B and emerge at C. Pull through. Continue.

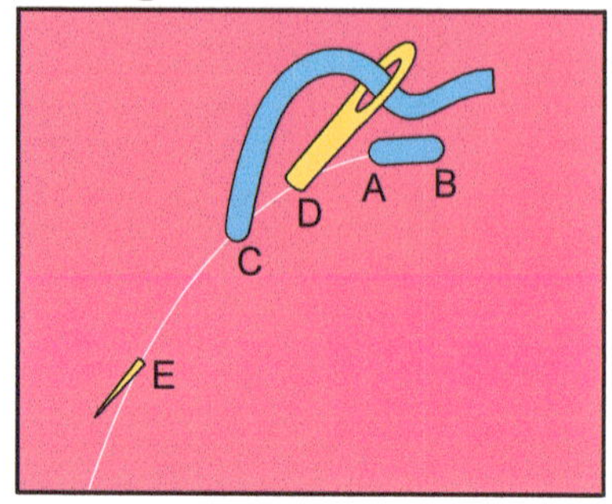


**Spaced back stitch** Come up at A, a stitch length from start. Take needle down at B and up at C. Pull through. Work D to E. Continue.

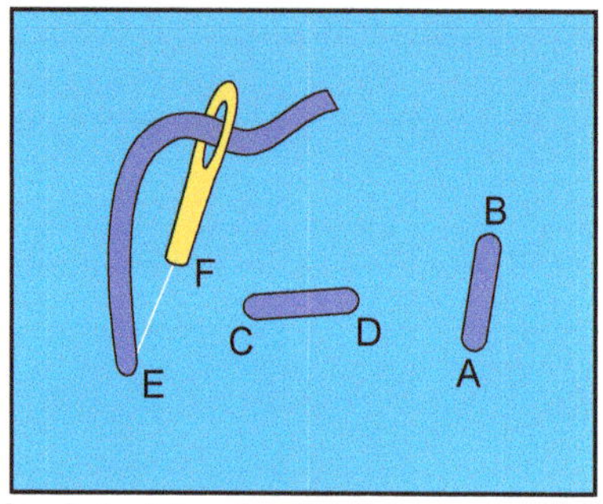


**Isolated back stitch**
Work the stitches in the order given, carrying the thread on the back. The stitches will be slightly raised.

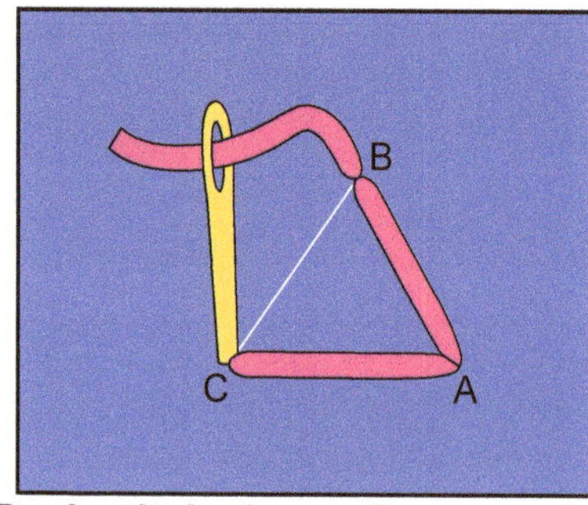


**Back stitch shape** Come up at A and down at B. Emerge at C. Pull through. Take thread down at A, emerge at B. Last stitch down at C.

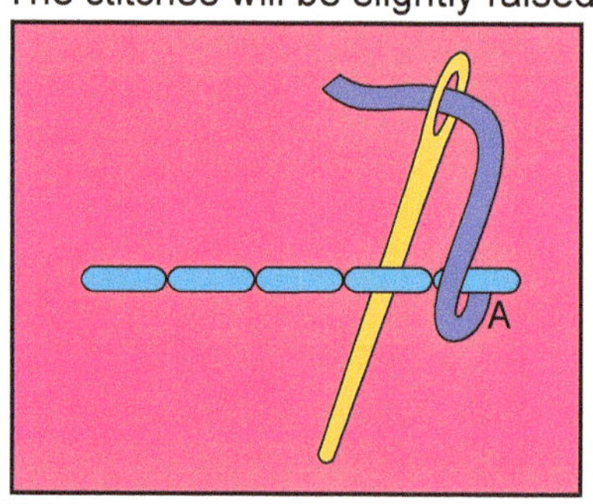


**Whipped back stitch**
**1** Work back stitch row. Bring new thread up at A. Pass the thread under the next stitch but do not pierce fabric.

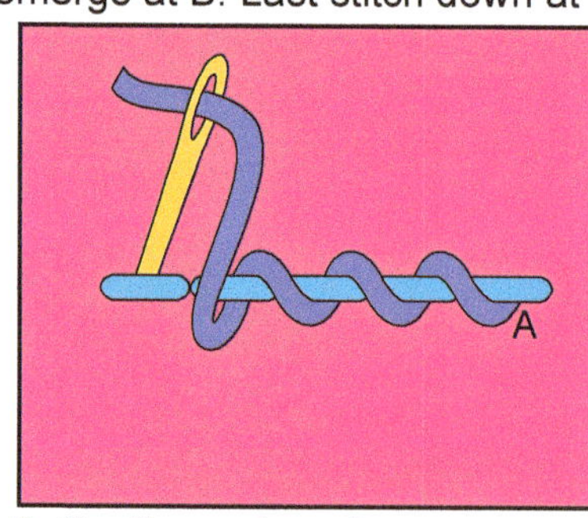


**2** Continue along the row, allowing each whipping to settle in place. At the end, take the thread to the back and secure.

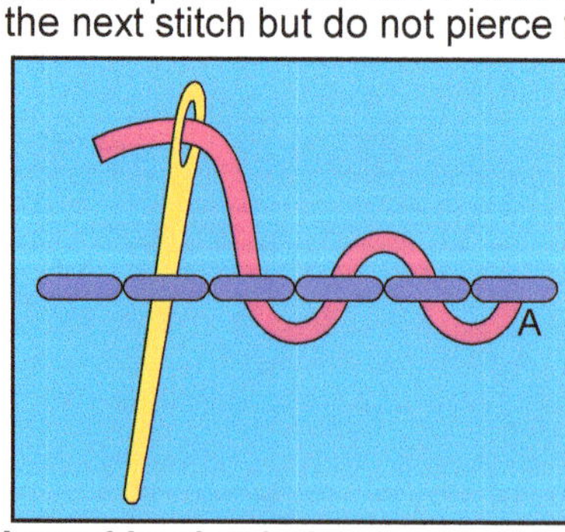


**Laced back stitch**
Work back stitch row. Bring new thread up at A. Pass thread under stitches. Do not pierce fabric.

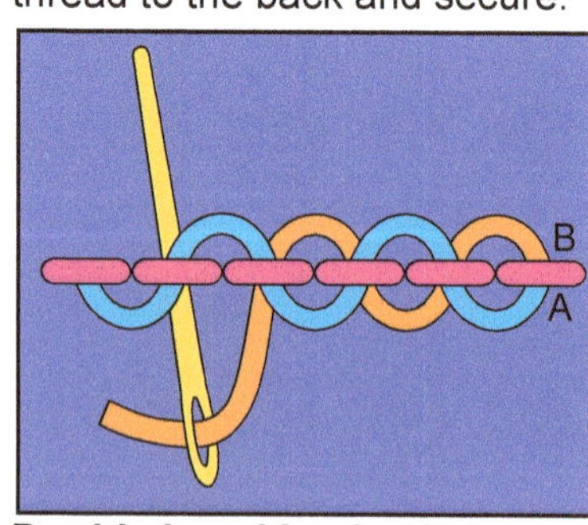


**Double laced back stitch**
Work laced back stitch row. Bring new thread up at B. Pass it under stitches and previous lacing.

# Back stitch and variations: left-handed

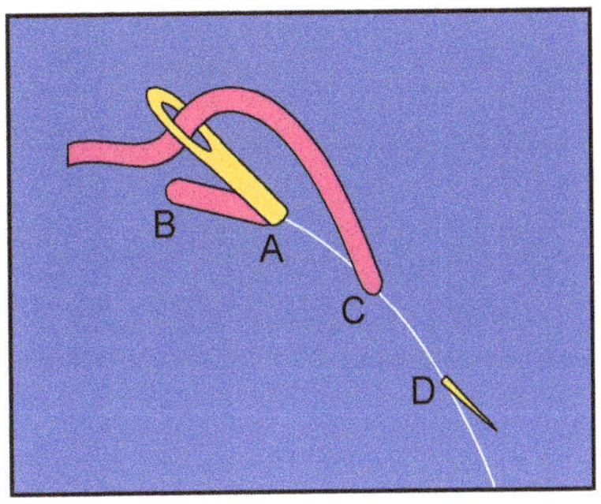


**Back stitch**
Come up at A, a stitch length from start. Take thread down at B and emerge at C. Pull through. Continue.

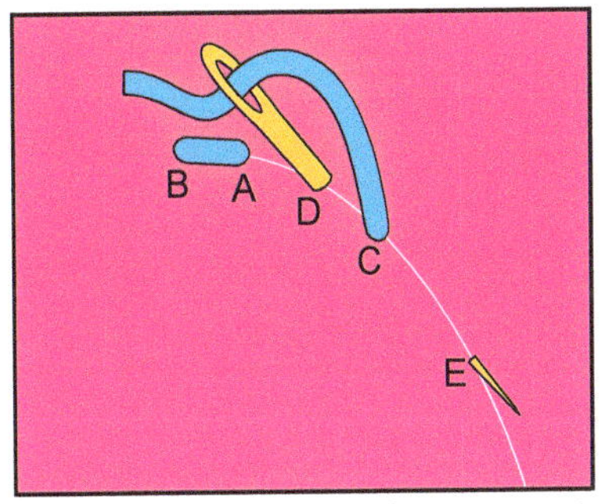


**Spaced back stitch** Come up at A, a stitch length from start. Take needle down at B and up at C. Pull through. Work D to E. Continue.

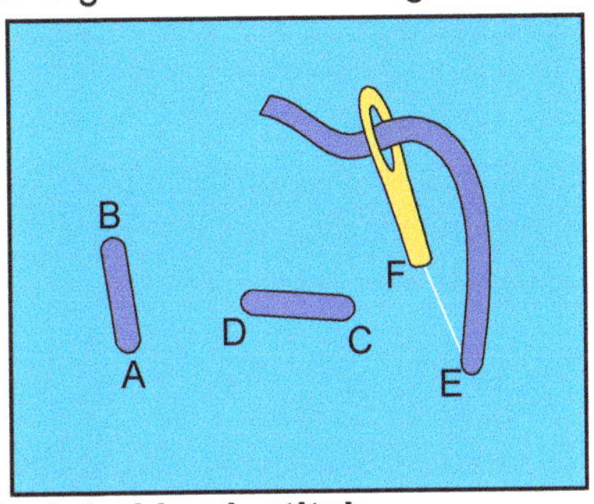


**Isolated back stitch**
Work the stitches in the order given, carrying the thread on the back. The stitches will be slightly raised.

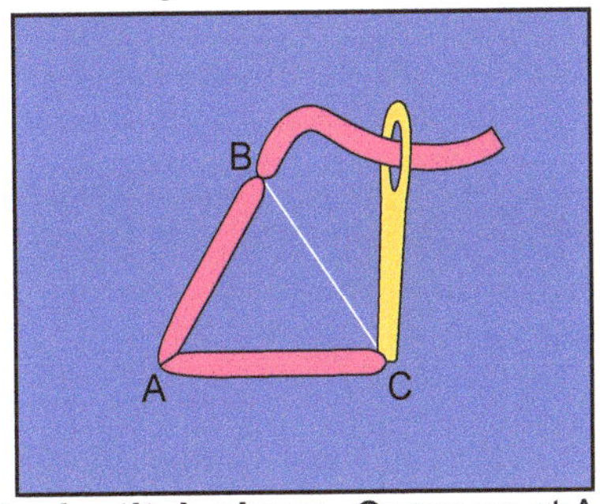


**Back stitch shape** Come up at A and down at B. Emerge at C. Pull through. Take thread down at A, emerge at B. Last stitch down at C.

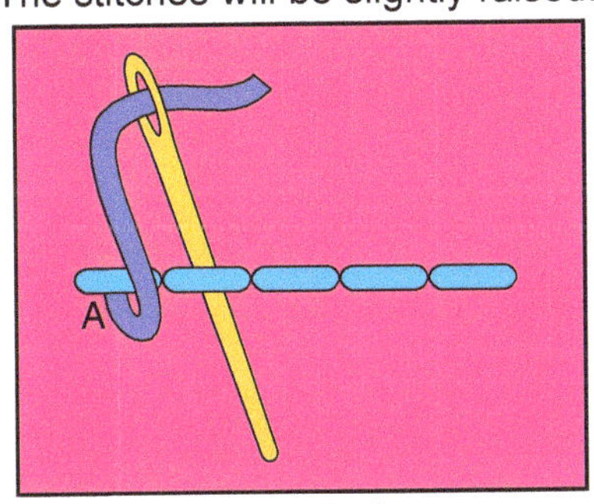


**Whipped back stitch**
**1** Work back stitch row. Bring new thread up at A. Pass the thread under the next stitch but do not pierce fabric.

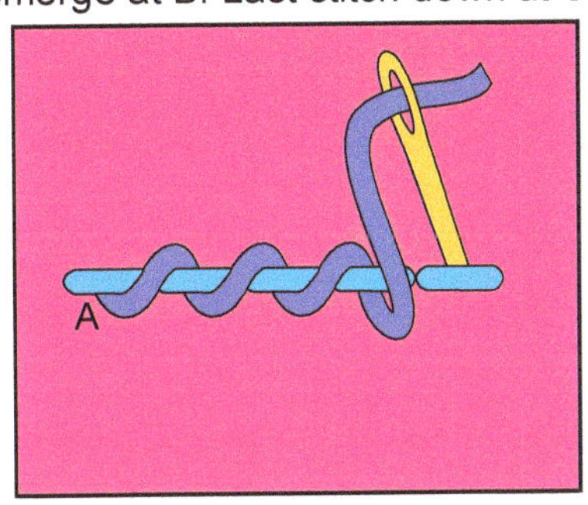


**2** Continue along the row, allowing each whipping to settle in place. At the end, take the thread to the back and secure.

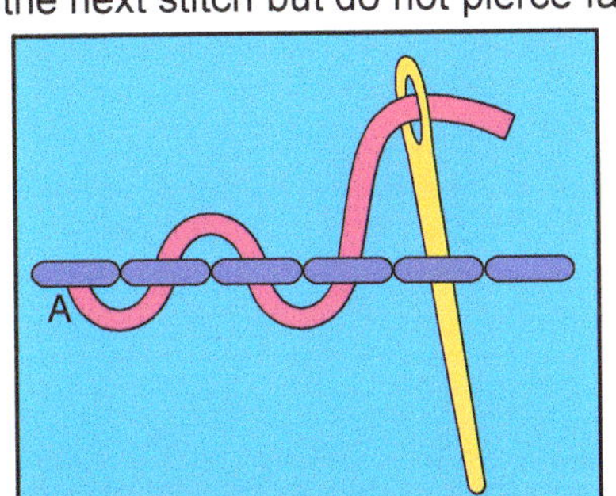


**Laced back stitch**
Work back stitch row. Bring new thread up at A. Pass thread under stitches. Do not pierce fabric.

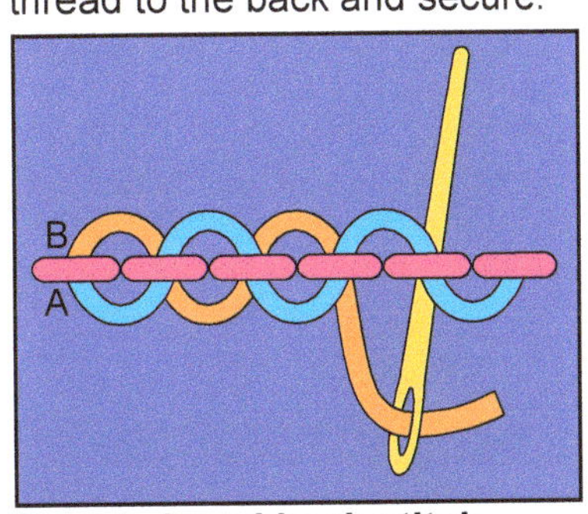


**Double laced back stitch**
Work laced back stitch row. Bring new thread up at B. Pass it under stitches and previous lacing.

# Back stitch
## and variations

# Designs and project ideas

## The designs

| | |
|---|---|
| Humphrey Hippo | Plum Blossom |
| Garden Fresh Carrots | First Prize Pumpkin |
| Sunset Beach | Enchanted Forest |

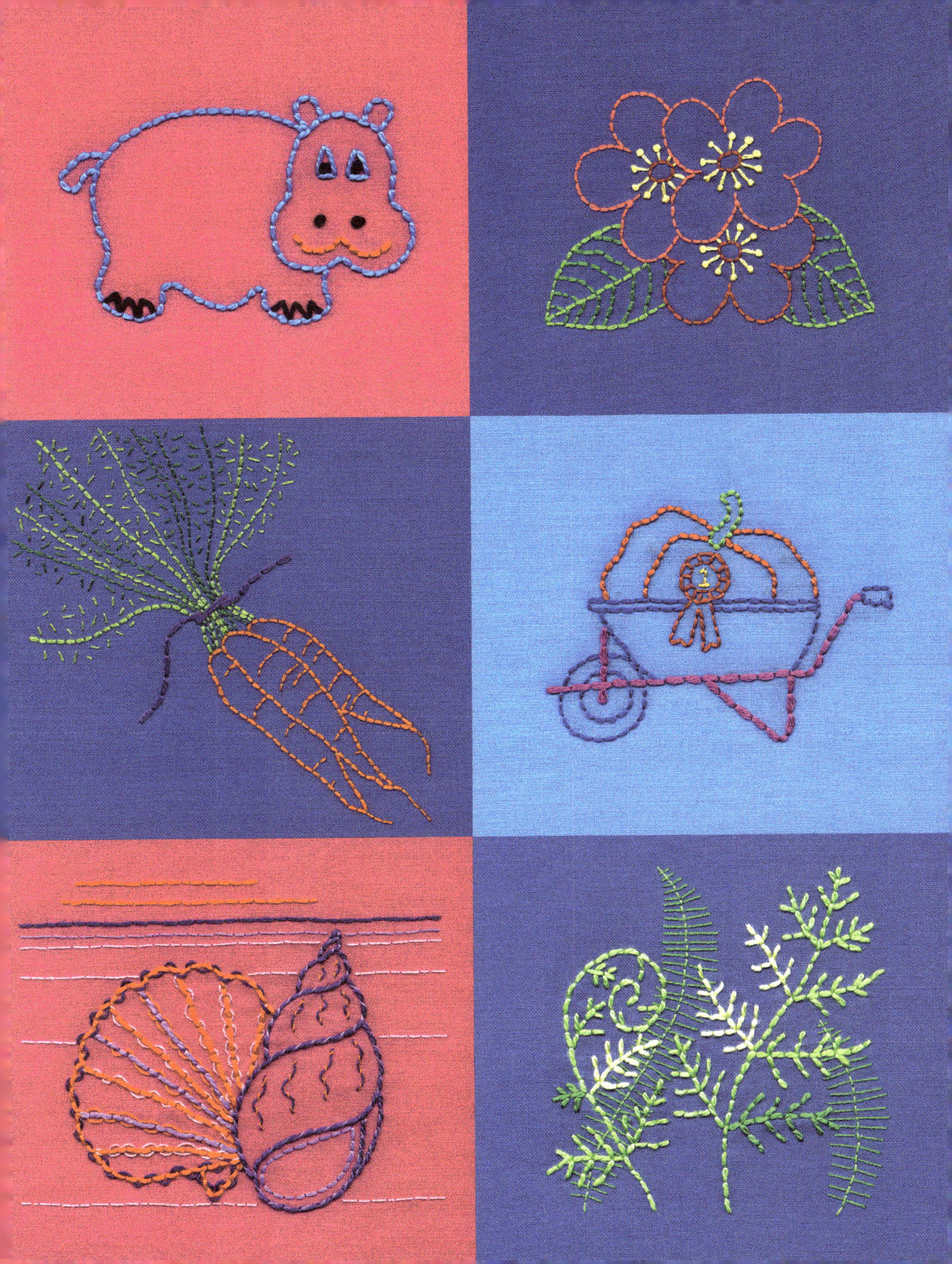

# Humphrey Hippo

This hippopotamus will gladden your heart!

## The design

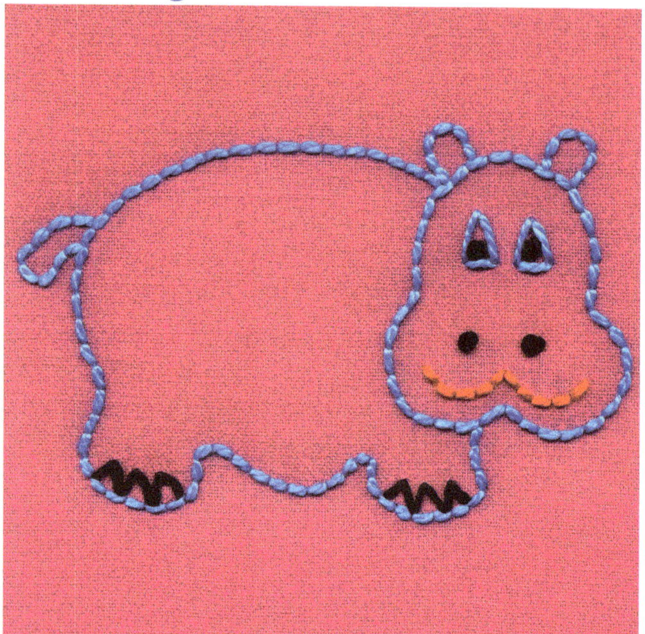

*Humphrey Hippo*

This design shows how effective a simple image can be when worked using just back stitch and French knot in a limited colour scheme. The design is very easy to work and is quick to complete.
Use the instructions on this page to work the design exactly as shown here on a pink background. To adapt the design for a project, see the idea on the following page, where *Humphrey Hippo* is featured on three bibs for a baby.

## The pattern

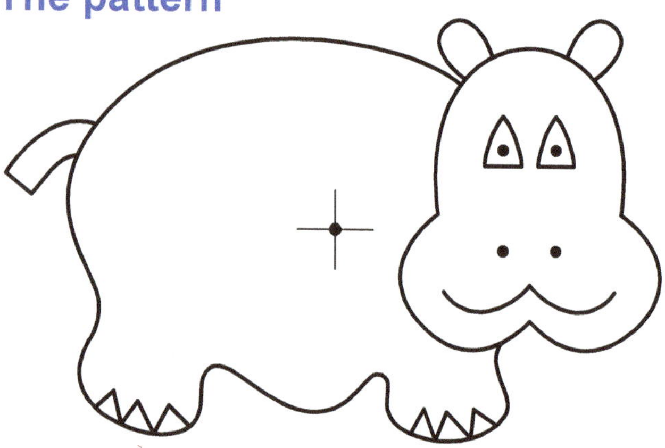

**Key:** ┼ **Centre of design** • **French knot**

## Shopping list

- Pink cotton fabric for background: 25cm (10") square
- Fabric or interfacing for backing: 25cm (10") square
- No. 5 perlé cotton thread: (A) black (B) dark aqua (C) medium red
- Tracing paper and other items for transferring the pattern onto the fabric

## Let's begin

Read page 15 for backing the fabric, and pages 22-25 for transferring the pattern onto the fabric, then select and use suitable methods for your fabric. For the pink fabric shown here, the pattern was transferred centrally onto the fabric by tracing with a water erasable fabric marker and then the backing fabric was tacked to the wrong side.

## Stitch!

For help, see pages 76-79 for back stitch and pages 184-187 for French knot.

1. Work the outline for the head and ears, then the body, tail, and legs in back stitch (1 strand B).
2. Work each eye outline in back stitch (1 strand B).
3. Stitch the mouth in back stitch (1 strand C).
4. Add a two wrap French knot inside each eye outline for the pupils (1 strand A).
5. Work the nostrils, each with a two wrap French knot. Weave the thread on the reverse side of the mouth when moving from the first nostril to the second (1 strand A).
6. Stitch the toes in back stitch (1 strand A).

## Let's finish

Take out the tacking. Rinse the work in cold water to remove the water erasable fabric marker. When partly dry, press or pin out the work. See page 36 for pressing and for pinning out.

## Hint

**Achieving evenness**

To achieve an even appearance for the outline of *Humphrey Hippo*, aim to keep the length of all the back stitches the same.

# Humphrey Hippo Bibs

Invite Humphrey to dinner – decorate a baby's bibs.

## The project

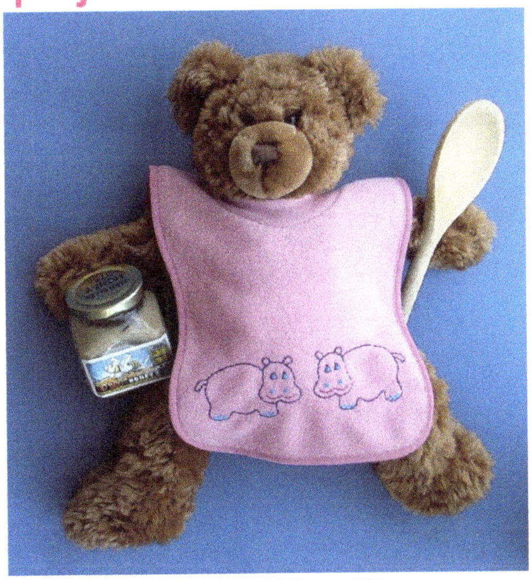

***Humphrey Hippo Bib***

*Humphrey Hippo* has a charming appeal, making it the perfect choice to decorate purchased plain towelling bibs. This trio shows how using different coloured and textured background fabric can change the overall appearance of a stitched design.

The white bib features the original design. The yellow bib is worked in an entirely different colour scheme and the design is mirrored. The pink bib uses a third colour scheme and features the design worked as a mirrored pair.

## Shopping list

***White bib***

- White towelling bib
- Threads as listed for the original design on the page opposite
- Tracing paper and other items for transferring the pattern onto the bib

***Yellow bib***

- Yellow towelling bib
- No. 5 perlé cotton thread:
  (A) dark violet (B) medium magenta
  (C) medium violet
- Tracing paper and other items for transferring the pattern onto the bib

***Pink bib***

- Pink towelling bib
- No. 5 perlé cotton thread:
  (A) dark aqua (B) dark violet (C) medium magenta
- Tracing paper and other items for transferring the pattern onto the bib

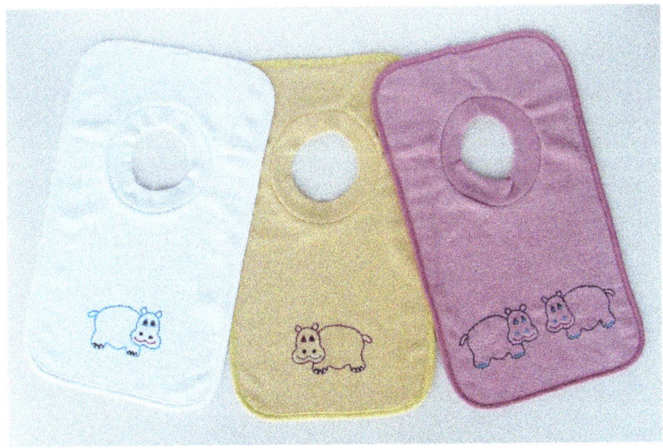

***Humphrey Hippo Bibs***

## Let's begin

See the page opposite for the *Humphrey Hippo* pattern. Using tracing paper, make an exact copy of the pattern for the white bib. Make a mirrored copy for the yellow bib. For the pink bib, make an exact copy and a mirrored copy. See page 20 for information on how to mirror the pattern.

Transfer the pattern onto the front of the bibs at chosen positions using the pierce and dot method with a water erasable fabric marker. See page 25 for transferring the pattern using the pierce and dot method.

## Stitch!

Work the white bib following steps 1-6 of the stitch instructions on the facing page.

Stitch the yellow or the pink bib in a similar way, using the alternative coloured threads.

## Let's finish

Rinse the bibs in cold water to remove the water erasable fabric marker. When almost dry, press the bibs lightly on the wrong side. See page 36 for pressing.

## Hints

**Stitch tension**

Work the back stitches with a slightly loose tension, so that the thread does not sink into the raised pile of the towelling fabric.

**Use other designs**

Many other designs from this book can also be worked on bibs. However, as bibs are washed frequently, do not choose a design that features felt, long or loopy stitches, or threads that will not stand up to repeated washing. Also, note that it is not safe to work designs that include beads on projects for babies and very small children.

# Plum Blossom

There is a lovely perfume in the air. The plum tree is blossoming.

## The design

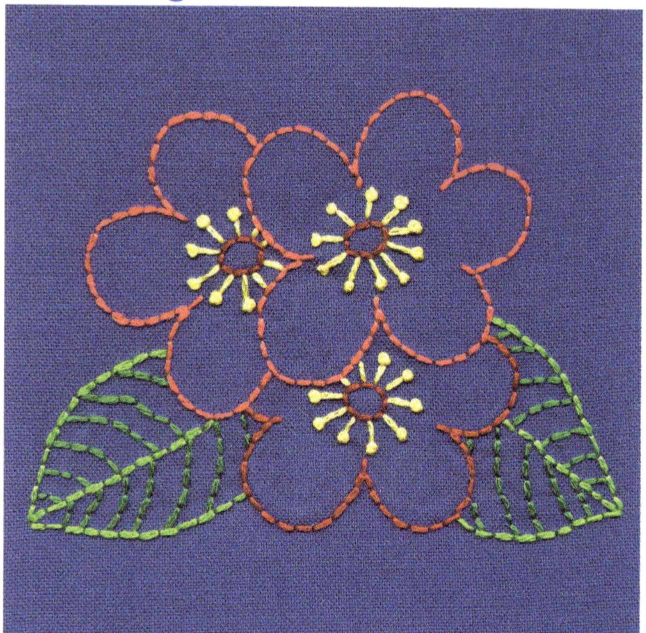

*Plum Blossom*

Back stitch is used for almost all of this very easy design, with the addition of straight stitches and French knots for the stamens. In this stylized design, the petals are simple curved lines and the flower centres and leaves are more detailed.

Follow the instructions on this page to work the design exactly as shown here on a blue background. To apply *Plum Blossom* to a cushion cover, see the project idea on the facing page.

## The pattern

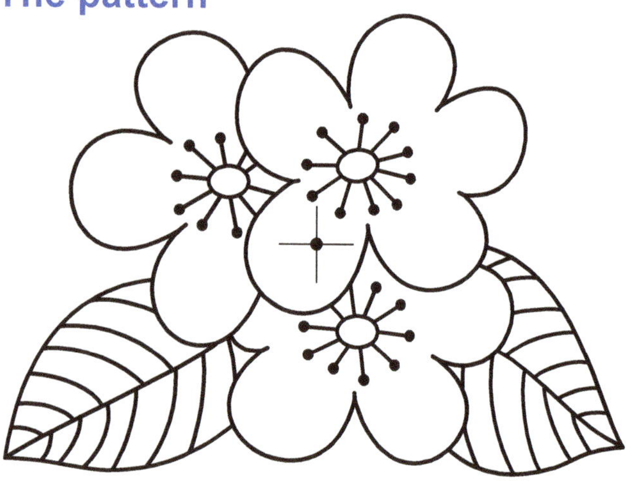

**Key:** Centre of design  Straight stitches and French knots

## Shopping list

- Blue cotton fabric for background: 25cm (10") square
- Fabric or interfacing for backing: 25cm (10") square
- Stranded cotton thread: (A) medium green (B) light green (C) light yellow (D) dark red (E) medium red (F) light red
- Tracing paper and other items for transferring the pattern onto the fabric

## Let's begin

Read page 15 for backing the fabric, and pages 22-25 for transferring the pattern onto the fabric, then select and use suitable methods for your fabric. For the blue fabric shown here, the pattern was transferred centrally onto the fabric by tracing with a chalk-based pencil and then the backing fabric was tacked to the wrong side.

## Stitch!

For help, see pages 40-43 for straight stitch, 76-79 for back stitch, and pages 184-187 for French knot.

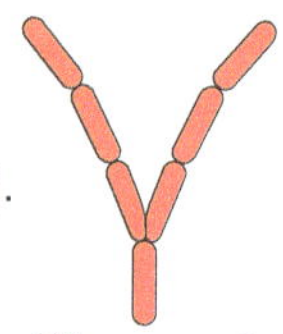

**Diagram 1**

1. Stitch the petal outlines of the two upper flowers in back stitch (2 strands F). At each valley between the petals, work the stitches in a Y shape (Diagram 1).
2. Work the petals of the lower flower in back stitch in the same way (2 strands E).
3. Add the red oval at the centre of each flower in back stitch (2 strands D).
4. Stitch the side veins of the leaves in back stitch (2 strands A).
5. Work the outline and central vein of each leaf in back stitch (2 strands B).
6. Stitch the stamens in straight stitch, working each stitch from its outer end towards the central red oval (2 strands C).
7. Complete the stamens by adding a two wrap French knot at the end of each straight stitch, except where the flowers overlap (2 strands C).

## Let's finish

Take out the tacking. Press or pin out the work. See page 36 for pressing and for pinning out.

## Hint

**Achieving evenness**

To achieve an overall even appearance for *Plum Blossom*, aim to keep the length of all the back stitches the same.

# Plum Blossom Cushion Cover

Let's stitch some spring blossom on a cushion!

## The project

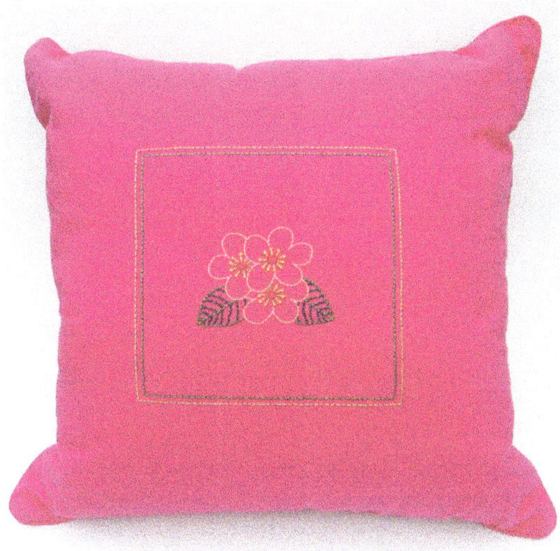

***Plum Blossom Cushion Cover***

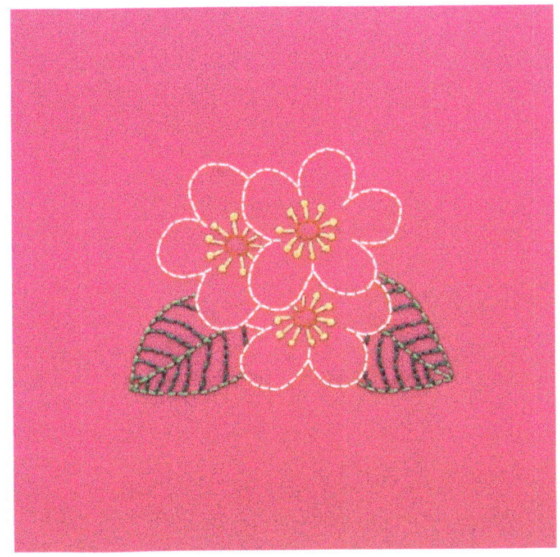

**Detail of *Plum Blossom Cushion Cover***

*Plum Blossom* is stitched with white flowers on a purchased pink cushion cover. Two back stitch squares are added around the flowers and leaves to give them a frame. This project demonstrates that a design can look quite different when worked in a different colour scheme and with a frame.
The size of this cushion is 43cm (17") square.

## Shopping list

- Pink cushion cover and insert
- Fabric or interfacing for backing: see the Let's begin instructions below for determining the dimensions
- Threads as listed for the original design on the page opposite, but with white stranded cotton for the petal outlines instead of the medium red and light red threads, (E) and (F)
- Tracing paper and other items for transferring the pattern onto the cushion cover

## Let's begin

See the page opposite for the pattern.
Remove the cushion insert. Transfer the pattern centrally onto the front of the cushion cover using transfer paper. See page 24 for transferring the pattern using transfer paper. Using a chalk-based pencil, draw two ruled squares onto the fabric as a frame around the design. Cut the piece of backing fabric a little larger than the ruled frame and tack it centrally to the wrong side of the front of the cushion cover. See page 15 for backing the fabric.

## Stitch!

Work the design following steps 1-7 of the stitch instructions on the page opposite, using 2 strands of the white thread for the petals. Work the stitched frame in back stitch, beginning with the green inner square (2 strands B), and then stitching the light yellow outer square (2 strands C).

## Let's finish

Take out the tacking. Turn the cushion cover inside out. Trim away any excess backing fabric close to the outer edge of the back stitch frame. Press the cushion cover. See page 36 for pressing. Turn through to the right side and place the insert back into the cover.

## Hints

**More project ideas**

This design, or simply a single flower from it, could be featured on many of the other projects in this book, such as a T-shirt or the front of an album.

**Change the colours**

*Plum Blossom* could be worked completely in black or white thread on any coloured background for dramatically different colour schemes.

# Garden Fresh Carrots

There are times when harvesting from the vegetable patch can be very rewarding!

## The design

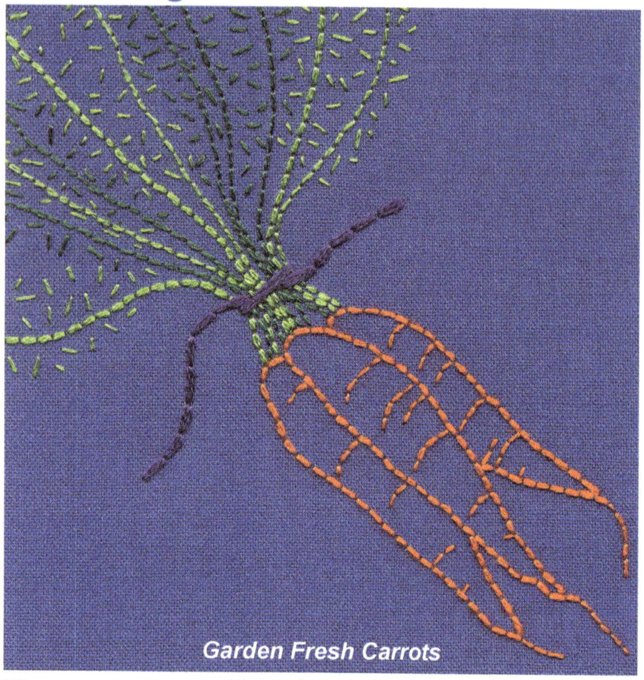

Garden Fresh Carrots

These carrots are stitched entirely in back stitch using silk threads. The interesting effects of thick and thin texture are achieved by varying the number of strands of thread.

Use the instructions on this page to work the design exactly as shown here. To apply the design to babywear, see the project ideas on the following page.

## The pattern

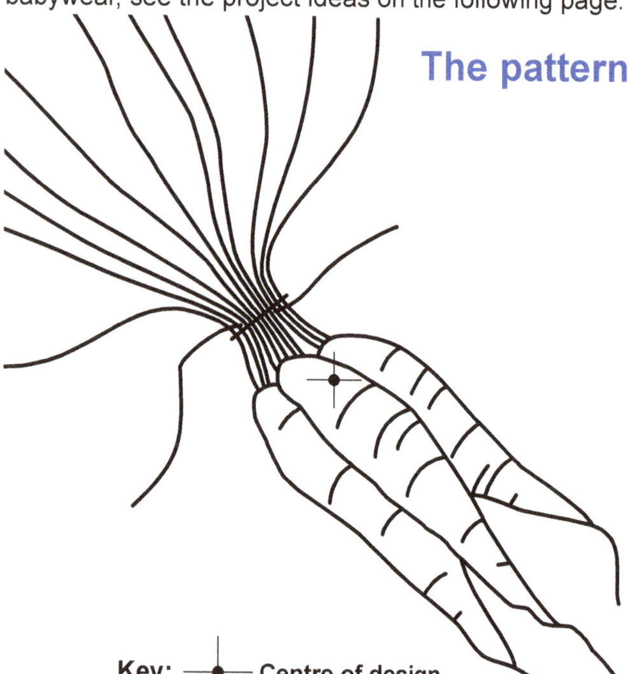

**Key:** Centre of design

## Shopping list

- Blue cotton fabric for background: 25cm (10") square
- Fabric or interfacing for backing: 25cm (10") square
- Stranded silk thread: (A) dark violet (B) dark green (C) light green (D) medium orange
- Tracing paper and other items for transferring the pattern onto the fabric

## Let's begin

Read page 15 for backing the fabric, and pages 22-25 for transferring the pattern onto the fabric, then select and use suitable methods for your fabric. For the blue fabric shown here, the pattern was transferred centrally onto the fabric by tracing with a chalk-based pencil and then the backing fabric was tacked to the wrong side.

## Stitch!

For help, see pages 76-79 for back stitch.

1 Work the outline, excluding the root tips, for the three carrots in back stitch (2 strands D).
2 Stitch the root tips and the internal lines on the carrots in back stitch (1 strand D). Weave the thread through the back of previously worked stitches as you move from one line to the next.
3 Using one strand for the thin foliage stems and two strands for the thick, work the light green stems in back stitch (1 or 2 strands C). Use the photo as a guide for placement.
4 Stitch the dark green stems in back stitch (1 strand B).
5 Placing the light green leaves along the light green stems and the dark green along the dark green stems, work the leaves using randomly placed isolated back stitches (1 strand B or C). Use the photo as a guide for placement.
6 Using long back stitches, stitch the string that is tying the bunch together (3 strands A). Work one long back stitch where the string covers the stems (Diagram 1).

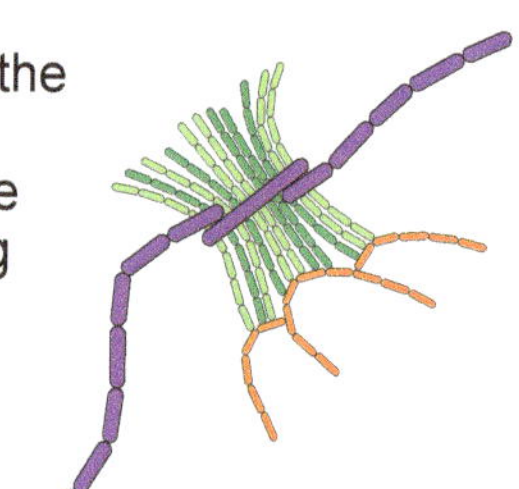

**Diagram 1**

## Let's finish

Take out the tacking. Press or pin out the work. See page 36 for pressing and for pinning out.

## Hint

**Realistic appearance**

To make the leaves look realistic, vary the angle of the stitches and place some of them in tighter groups than others.

# Garden Fresh Carrots Babywear

Brighten a baby's clothes with embroidered carrots!

## The projects

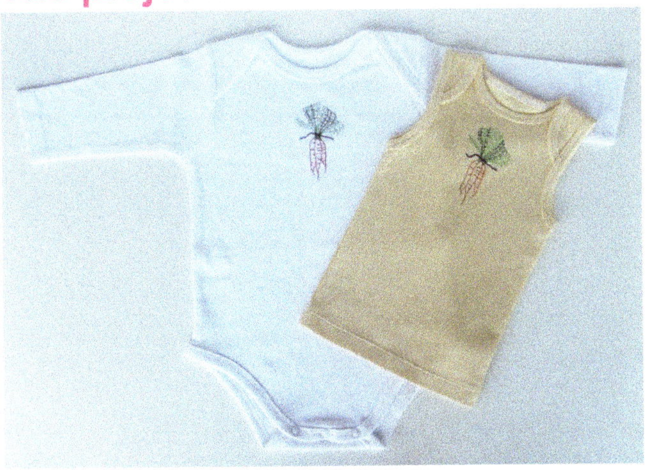

***Garden Fresh Carrots Babywear***

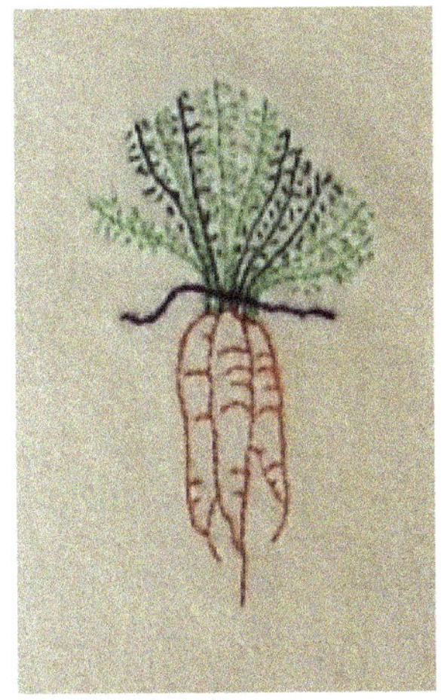

**Detail of**
***Garden Fresh Carrots Baby's Singlet***

These quick and easy projects use the design to decorate purchased stretch knit babywear. The design has been reduced in size, and the stitching is worked using stranded cotton threads, replacing the silk threads.
Use the following instructions to work the design on either garment.

## Shopping list

- White stretch knit baby suit or yellow stretch knit baby's singlet
- Lightweight iron-on interfacing for backing: 10cm x 7cm wide (4" x 3")
- Stranded cotton thread in the colours as listed for the original design on the page opposite
- Tracing paper and other items for transferring the pattern onto either garment

## Let's begin

See the page opposite for the pattern.
Prepare the pattern by reducing it to 60% of its original size. Trace the reduced pattern onto tracing paper. Noting that the carrots are rotated so that they are vertical, attach the piece of iron-on interfacing onto the wrong side of the front of the garment at the selected position. This will stabilize the area where the design is to be stitched. See page 21 for placing the pattern and page 15 for backing the fabric.
Transfer the pattern onto the front of the garment by tracing with a water erasable fabric marker or by using transfer paper. See pages 22-25 for transferring the pattern onto the fabric.

## Stitch!

Work the carrots following steps 1-6 of the stitch instructions for the original design on the facing page, replacing the silk threads with the stranded cotton threads. As the carrots have been reduced in size from the original design, use one strand of thread for the carrots and foliage and two strands of thread for the string.

## Let's finish

Turn the garment inside out. On the wrong side, peel back any excess interfacing from its outer edge and trim it back close to the stitches. Rinse the garment in cold water to remove the pattern markings. When dry, turn it inside out and press it. See page 36 for pressing.

## Hints

**Using stretch knit fabric**

Knit fabrics are designed to stretch, allowing ease of movement when worn. However, this stretching is usually not desirable on the area where the design is stitched. By attaching interfacing onto the wrong side of the fabric, the amount of stretch on the area to be worked is minimised and controlled. This makes the stitching much easier to manage.

**More project ideas**

It could be fun to decorate table linen or tea towels with *Garden Fresh Carrots*.

# First Prize Pumpkin

The crowd cheered loudly when the farmer wheeled in the enormous pumpkin.

## The design

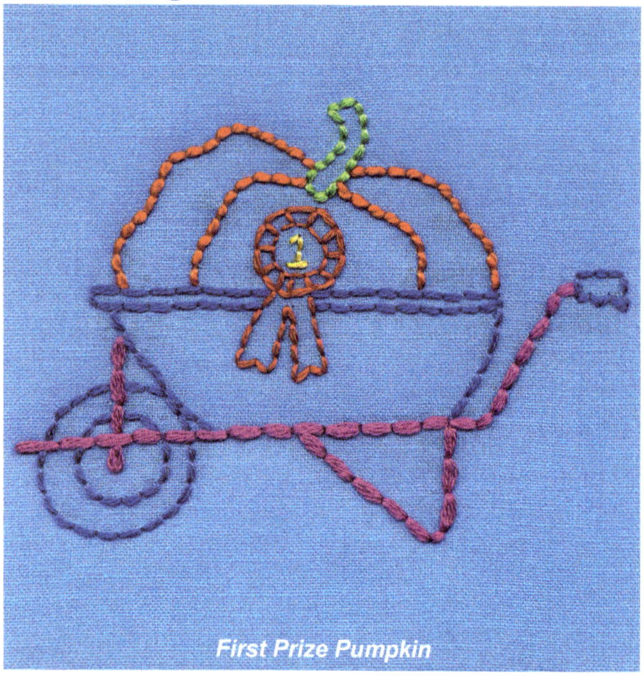

*First Prize Pumpkin*

This colourful design is worked completely in back stitch. The length of the stitches and the thickness of the threads vary with the many different colours used. Follow the instructions on this page to work the design exactly as shown here on an aqua background. To apply the design to a project, see the idea on the facing page where it is featured on a child's T-shirt.

## The pattern

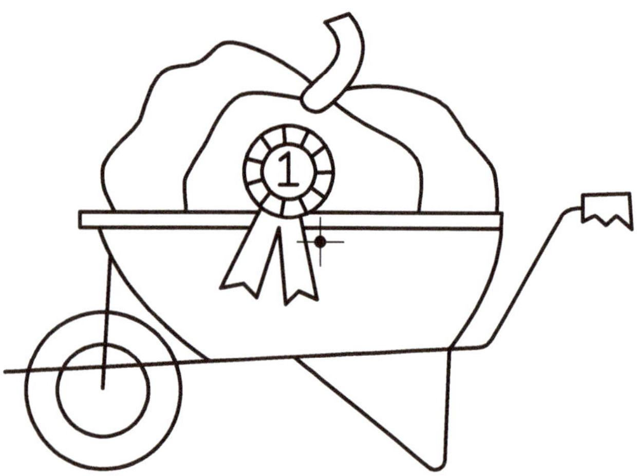


**Key:** ─┼─ **Centre of design**

## Shopping list

- Aqua cotton fabric for background: 25cm (10") square
- Fabric or interfacing for backing: 25cm (10") square
- Stranded cotton thread: (A) medium blue (B) light green (C) medium yellow (D) medium red (E) medium magenta
- No. 5 perlé cotton thread: (F) medium orange
- Tracing paper and other items for transferring the pattern onto the fabric

## Let's begin

Read page 15 for backing the fabric, and pages 22-25 for transferring the pattern onto the fabric, then select and use suitable methods for your fabric. For the aqua fabric shown here, the pattern was transferred centrally onto the fabric by tracing with an HB pencil and then the backing fabric was tacked to the wrong side.

## Stitch!

For help, see pages 76-79 for back stitch.

1 Work the sides and upper edge of the wheelbarrow tray in back stitch, keeping the rows parallel to each other along the upper edge (3 strands A).
2 Stitch the inner and outer circles for the wheel in back stitch (3 strands A).
3 Work the handle in back stitch (3 strands A).
4 Add the wheelbarrow frame with large back stitch (6 strands E).
5 Stitch the pumpkin in small back stitch (1 strand F).
6 Add the stalk in small back stitch (4 strands B).
7 Stitch the inner circle of the rosette in small back stitch (1 strand D). Using two strands of the same thread and beginning at the outer circle, follow the diagrams to add the pleated frill in small back stitch (Diagrams 1 and 2).
8 Stitch the rosette ribbons in small back stitch (2 strands D).
9 Add the number 1 at the centre of the rosette in small back stitch (2 strands C).

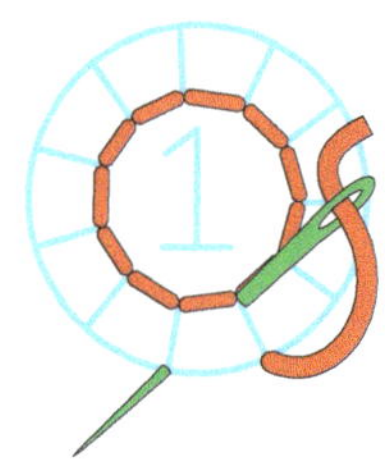


**Diagram 1**

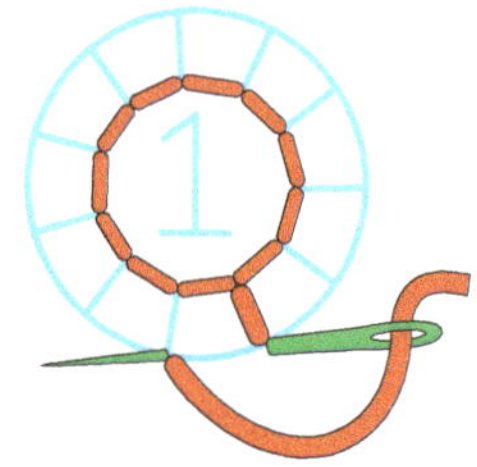


**Diagram 2**

## Let's finish

Take out the tacking. Press or pin out the work. See page 36 for pressing and for pinning out.

# First Prize Pumpkin T-shirt

Have fun decorating a T-shirt for a child.

## The project

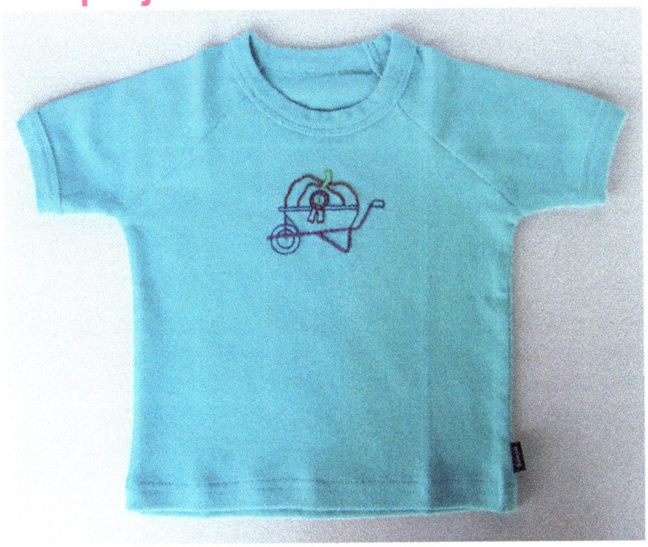

***First Prize Pumpkin T-shirt***

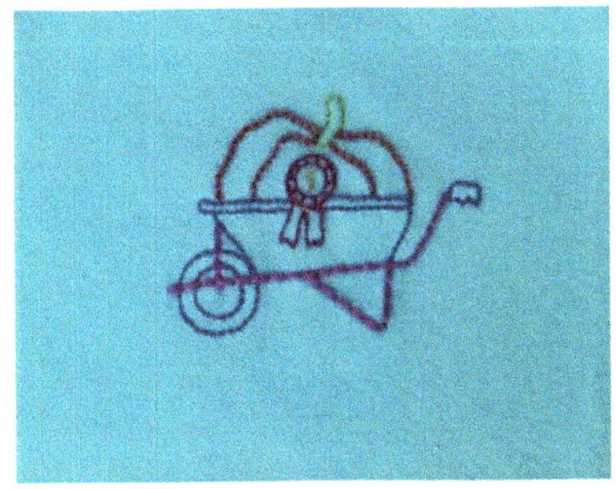

**Detail of**
***First Prize Pumpkin T-shirt***

Adding this design to a purchased T-shirt is a simple, yet effective, way to add colour and visual interest to an otherwise plain item of clothing.
This aqua stretch knit T-shirt features *First Prize Pumpkin* worked with exactly the same colours, threads, and stitching as the original design opposite.

## Shopping list

- Aqua stretch knit T-shirt
- Lightweight iron-on interfacing for backing: 9cm x 11cm wide (3 1/2" x 4 1/2")
- Threads as listed for the original design on the page opposite
- Tracing paper and other items for transferring the pattern onto the T-shirt

## Let's begin

See the page opposite for the *First Prize Pumpkin* pattern.
To help in deciding the placement of the design on the T-shirt, first trace the pattern onto tracing paper. Fold the garment in half and mark the centre front with pins (Diagram 1). Open out the garment and place the tracing, centred over the pins, an appropriate distance below the front neckline (Diagram 2).
Move the tracing up or down until it is in a visually appealing position. Note its position with pins.

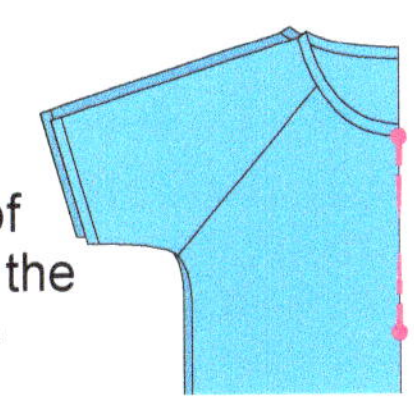

**Diagram 1**

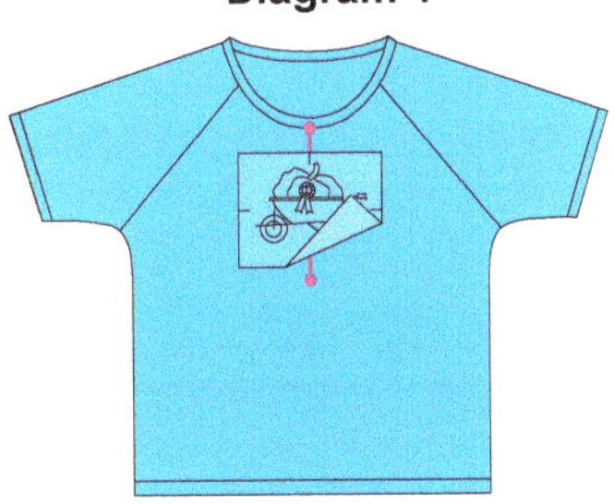

**Diagram 2**

Following the instructions on page 15 for backing the fabric, attach the piece of iron-on interfacing onto the wrong side of the front of the T-shirt at the selected position. This will stabilize the area where the design is to be stitched.
Transfer the pattern onto the front of the T-shirt by tracing with a water erasable fabric marker or by using transfer paper. See pages 22-25 for transferring the pattern onto the fabric.

## Stitch!

Work the design following steps 1-9 of the stitch instructions on the facing page.

## Let's finish

Turn the T-shirt inside out. On the wrong side, peel back any excess interfacing from its outer edge and trim it back close to the stitches. Rinse the T-shirt in cold water to remove the pattern markings. When dry, turn the T-shirt inside out and press it. See page 36 for pressing.

## Hints

**Change the colours**

For an individual look, you could purchase a different coloured T-shirt and change the thread colours.

**More project ideas**

This quick and easy design is also ideal to be used as decoration on other purchased clothing for children such as a singlet or on the pocket of a pair of jeans.

# Sunset Beach

In the light of the setting sun on a summer evening, the seashells glow with colour.

## The design

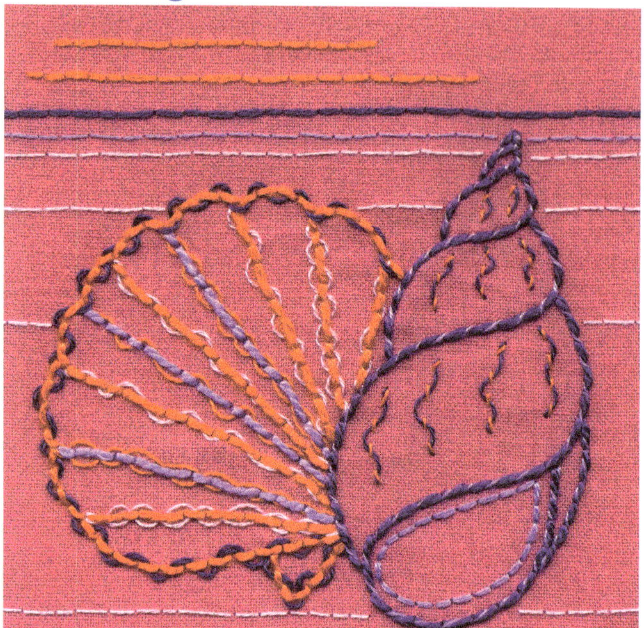

*Sunset Beach*

Back stitch in many forms is used to work this design, creating a variety of textures. Although the sea shells are quite detailed, they are easy to work.

Follow the instructions on this page to work the design as shown here. To feature *Sunset Beach* on the front of an album, see the project idea on the next page.

## The pattern

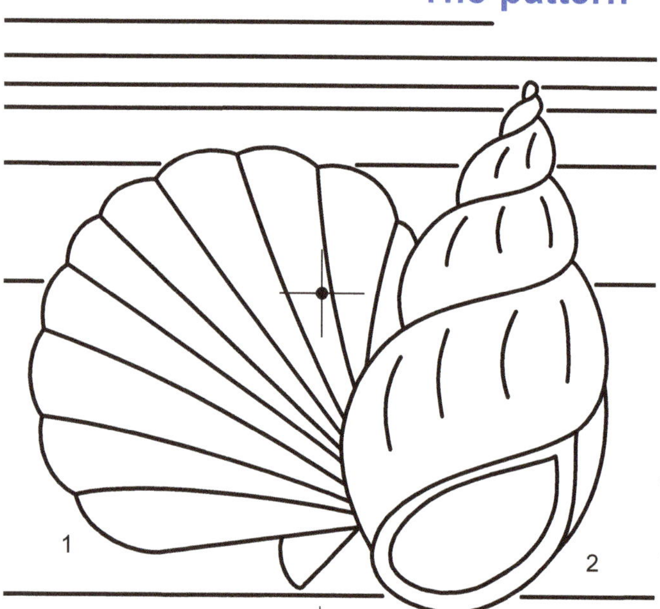


Key: Centre of design

## Shopping list

- Pink cotton fabric for background: 25cm (10") square
- Fabric or interfacing for backing: 25cm (10") square
- Stranded cotton thread:
  (A) dark violet (B) medium violet
  (C) light violet (D) medium orange
- No. 5 perlé cotton thread:
  (E) dark violet (F) medium violet (G) medium orange
- Tracing paper and other items for transferring the pattern onto the fabric

## Let's begin

Read page 15 for backing the fabric, and pages 22-25 for transferring the pattern onto the fabric, then select and use suitable methods for your fabric. For the pink fabric shown here, the pattern was transferred centrally onto the fabric by tracing with a water erasable fabric marker and then the backing fabric was tacked to the wrong side.

## Stitch!

For help, see pages 76-79 for back stitch, and for whipped, laced, and double laced back stitch.

Use a tapestry needle when working the whipping, lacing, and double lacing.

**Sunset, sea, and sand** When stitching the lines for the sunset, sea, and sand, work the stitches slightly wavering up and down. Leave spaces for the shells.

Work the background lines in uneven backstitch: two orange lines (2 strands D), the third line (2 strands A), then the fourth line (1 strand B). Finally stitch the remaining lines in uneven back stitch (1 strand C).

**Shell 1** Stitch the scalloped outline and the triangular base of the shell in back stitch, with stitches equal in length (1 strand G). Lace these back stitches (2 strands A). Referring to the photo for colour placement, add the orange ribs (1 strand G) and the violet ribs (1 strand F) in back stitch, worked with the stitches uneven in length. Lace or double lace the orange ribs (1 strand C) and the violet ribs (1 strand D).

**Shell 2** Stitch the shell outline, including the outer line around the opening, in back stitch, with stitches equal in length (1 strand E). Whip the shell outline and opening (1 strand B). Work the inner line around the shell opening in back stitch, with stitches equal in length (2 strands B).

On the shell, work the vertical orange markings in spaced back stitch (1 strand D). Lace the orange stitches (Diagram 1) with dark violet (1 strand A).

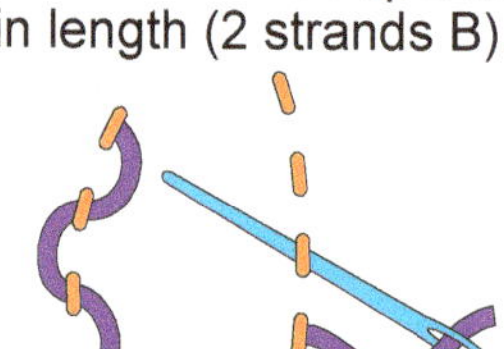

Diagram 1

## Let's finish

Take out the tacking. Rinse the work in cold water to remove the fabric marker Press or pin out the work. See page 36 for pressing and for pinning out.

# Sunset Beach Album Cover

Keep memories of a beach holiday in this album.

## The project

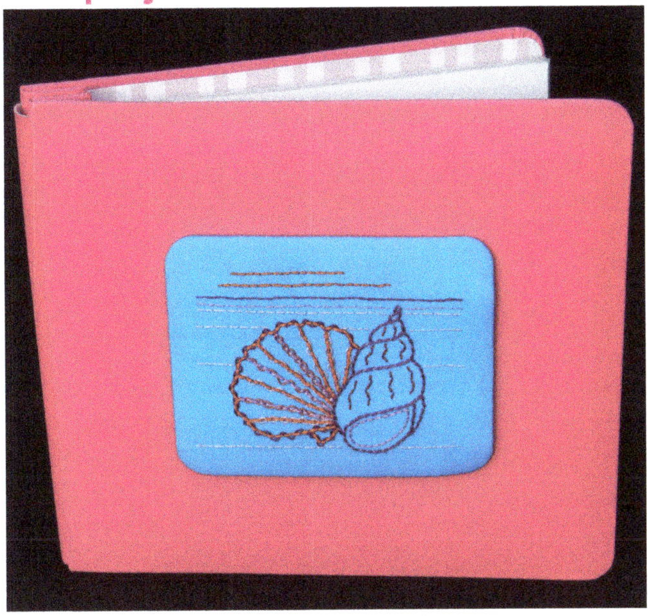

***Sunset Beach Album Cover***

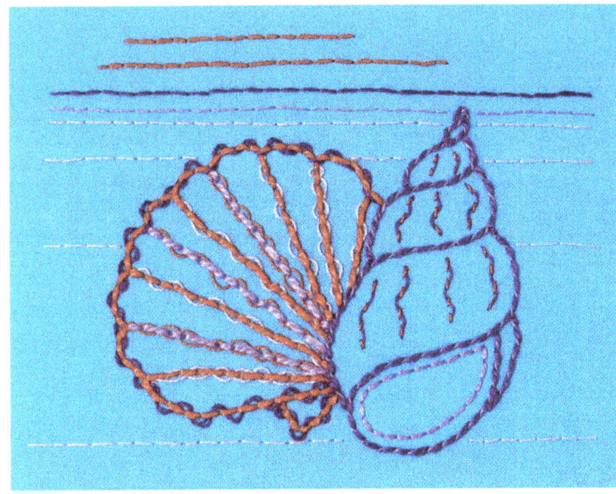

**Detail of**
***Sunset Beach Album Cover***

For this project, *Sunset Beach* is worked in the original thread colours on an alternative coloured background. The work is then laced over cardboard and attached to the front of an album.
This album is 22cm x 25cm wide (8 3/4" x 10") in size.

## Shopping list

- Pink album
- Aqua cotton fabric for background:
  18cm x 21cm wide (7" x 8 1/4")
- Fabric or interfacing for backing:
  18cm x 21cm wide (7" x 8 1/4")
- Threads as listed for the original design opposite
- Machine sewing thread for gathering
- Strong thread for lacing
- Tracing paper and other items for transferring the pattern onto the fabric
- Thin wadding: 11cm x 14cm wide (4 3/8" x 5 1/2")
- White cardboard: 11cm x 14cm wide (4 3/8" x 5 1/2")
- Archival double-sided sticky tape or glue

## Let's begin

See the page opposite for the *Sunset Beach* pattern. Transfer the pattern centrally onto the aqua fabric by tracing with a water erasable fabric marker or by using transfer paper. See pages 22-25 for transferring the pattern onto the fabric. Tack the backing to the wrong side of the fabric. See page 15 for backing the fabric.

## Stitch!

Work the design following the stitch instructions on the page opposite.

## Let's finish

Rinse the work in cold water to remove the pattern markings. When partly dry, press or pin out the work. See page 36 for pressing and for pinning out.
Trim the corners of the aqua fabric and the backing, and also the corners of the cardboard and the wadding, so that they are rounded.
Using machine sewing thread, and leaving both ends of the thread dangling, work a row of running stitch around the edge of the backing and the fabric together. See pages 58-61 for running stitch. Take out remaining tacking. Place the wadding and then the cardboard centrally onto the wrong side of the stitched work (Diagram 1). Pull the two thread ends to gather the fabric over the padded cardboard, then tie them in a knot. Trim the threads. Lace the work tightly. As a guide, see page 37 for lacing. Using archival double-sided sticky tape or glue, adhere the laced side of the work centrally onto the album front.

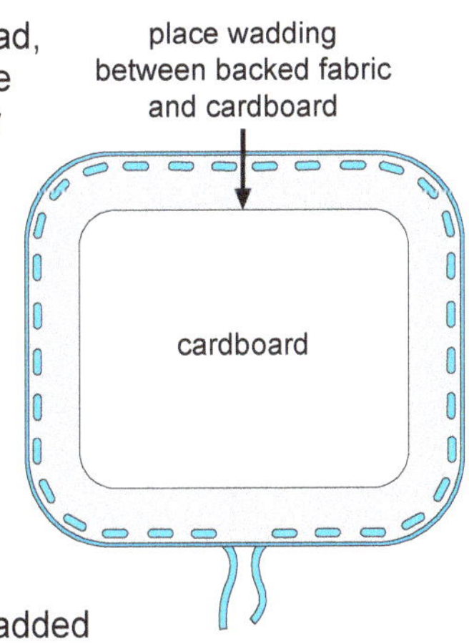


**Diagram 1**

## Hint

**Adapt the design**

Depending on the size and dimensions of your selected album, *Sunset Beach* can be worked on a wider rectangle of fabric with the stitched lines for the sunset, sea, and sand extending further on each side.

# Enchanted Forest

Ferns add a delicate enchantment to a forest walk.

## The design

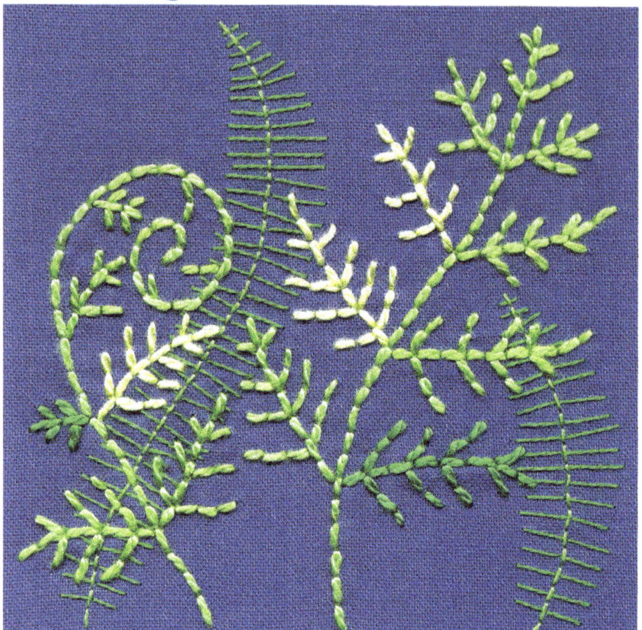

*Enchanted Forest*

*Enchanted Forest* is worked in back stitch and straight stitch. This design introduces the concept of stitching overlapping elements, which is easier than it looks. Follow the instructions on this page to work the design as shown here. See the next page, where a fern from this design is featured on a pincushion.

## The pattern

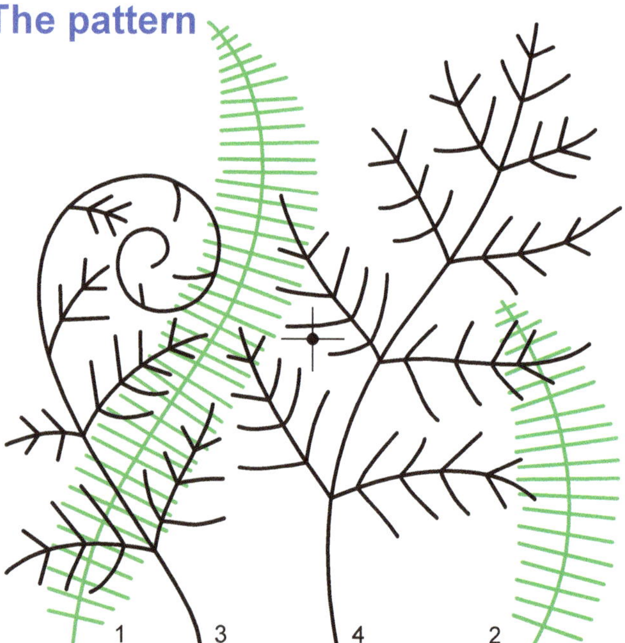


**Key:** ⌖ **Centre of design**

## Shopping list

- Blue cotton fabric for background: 25cm (10") square
- Fabric or interfacing for backing: 25cm (10") square
- Stranded cotton thread:
  (A) medium green (B) light green
- No. 5 perlé cotton thread:
  (C) medium green (D) light green (E) very light green
- Tracing paper and other items for transferring the pattern onto the fabric

## Let's begin

Read page 15 for backing the fabric, and pages 22-25 for transferring the pattern onto the fabric, then select and use suitable methods for your fabric. For the blue fabric shown here, the pattern was transferred centrally onto the fabric by tracing with a chalk-based pencil and then the backing fabric was tacked to the wrong side.

## Stitch!

For help, see pages 40-43 for straight stitch, and pages 76-79 for back stitch.

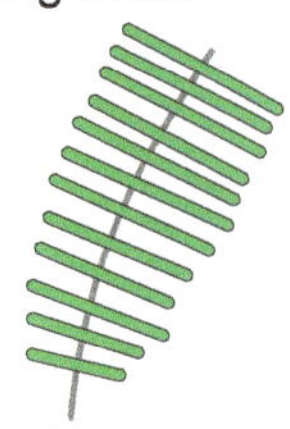

**Diagram 1**

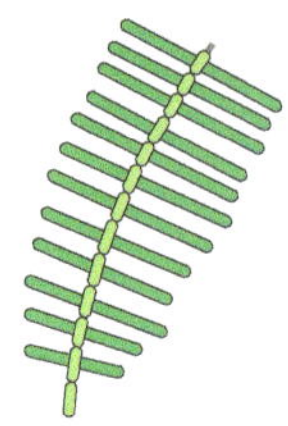

**Diagram 2**

**Ferns 1 and 2**

1. Stitch the leaflets of each fern in straight stitch (1 strand A). Make each stitch the whole width of the fern (Diagram 1).
2. For each fern, work a back stitch at the base of the stem (1 strand B). Continuing with the same thread, work back stitch all the way up the stem, with each back stitch holding a straight stitch in place at approximately its centre (Diagram 2).

**Ferns 3 and 4**

1. Beginning at the base of each fern, work the stem in back stitch (1 strand D).
2. Continuing with the same thread, and using the photo as a guide for colour placement, stitch the leaflets that are the same colour as the stem in back stitch. To move from one leaflet to the next, weave the thread along the stem on the back of the work.
3. Work the remaining leaflets in back stitch (1 strand C or E), using the photo as a guide for placing the colours.

## Let's finish

Take out the tacking. Press or pin out the work. See page 36 for pressing and for pinning out.

## Hint

**Overlapping elements**

When working designs with overlapping elements, firstly stitch the part that is behind, and secondly the part that is in front, as it is difficult to stitch behind areas that you have already worked.

**Shades of one colour**

Using three shades of green thread adds movement, depth, and the impression of dappled light on the ferns.

# Enchanted Forest Pincushion

Embellish a pincushion with lush greenery.

## The project

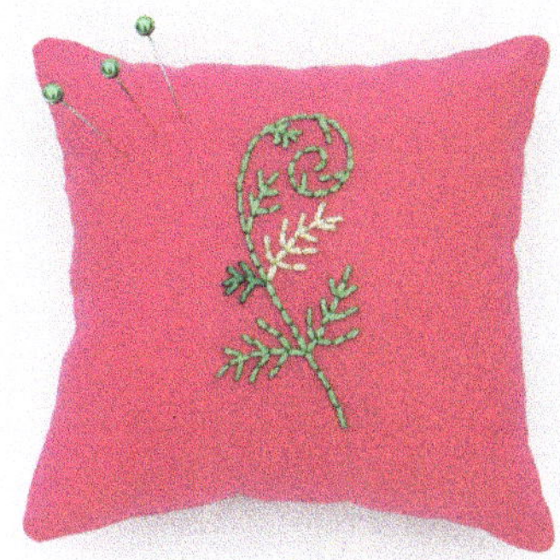

*Enchanted Forest Pincushion*

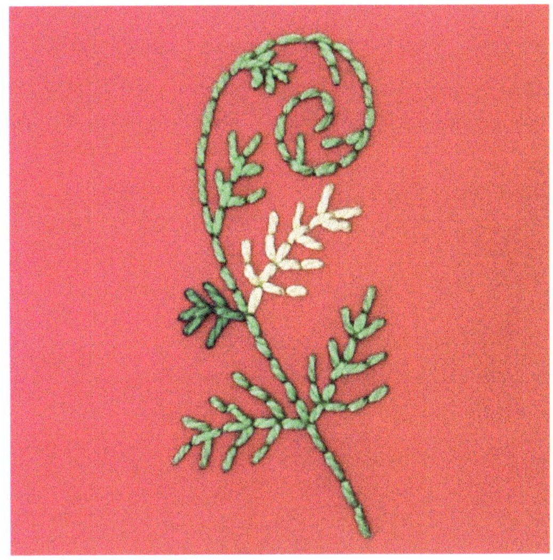

Detail of
*Enchanted Forest Pincushion*

One fern has been selected and featured on this easily constructed pincushion, illustrating that a single element from a design can be chosen and worked separately on a project.
The finished size of this pincushion is 12cm (4 3/4") square.

## Shopping list

- Pink cotton fabric for the pincushion: two 14cm (5 1/2") squares
- Fabric or interfacing for backing: 14cm (5 1/2") square
- Threads (C), (D), and (E) as listed for the original design on the page opposite
- Machine sewing thread: pink
- Tracing paper and other items for transferring the pattern onto the fabric
- Fibre filling

## Let's begin

See the page opposite for the *Enchanted Forest* pattern.
Transfer the pattern for **Fern 3** centrally onto the right side of one pink square by tracing with a water erasable fabric marker or by using transfer paper. See pages 22-25 for transferring the pattern onto the fabric.
Tack the backing fabric to the wrong side of the same pink fabric square. See page 15 for backing the fabric.

## Stitch!

Work the fern following the stitch instructions for **Fern 3** on the page opposite.

## Let's finish

Rinse the work in cold water to remove the pattern markings. When almost dry, press. See page 36 for pressing.
With right sides together, pin the stitched square onto the second pink square around the edge. Using pink machine sewing thread and a 1cm (3/8") seam allowance, machine stitch around the square, leaving a 5cm (2") opening in the middle of one side.
Ensure that 20cm (8") of machine thread length remains before cutting it. Knot the machine sewing threads and trim three of them, leaving one of the long ends. Take out the tacking. Trim the seam allowances and cut away the excess fabric at the corners (Diagram 1).

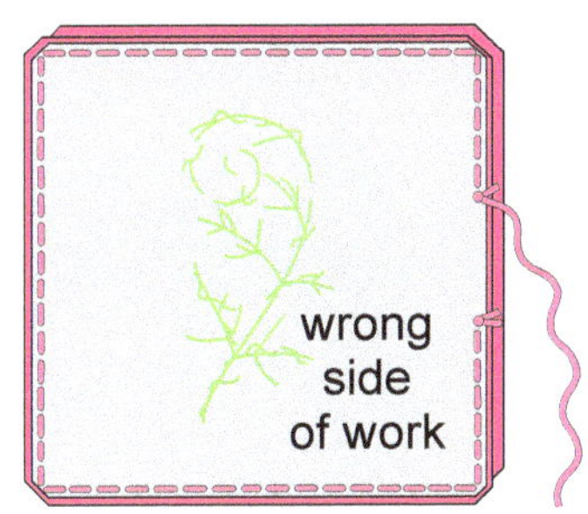


**Diagram 1**

Turn the pincushion to the right side through the opening and press. Fill the pincushion with fibre filling. Using the long end of pink machine sewing thread, hand stitch the opening closed.

# Stem stitch

## and variations

Stem stitch is worked as a row of overlapping stitches that slant in one direction, creating a corded or rope-like appearance. When the stitches are worked so that they slant in the opposite direction, it is sometimes called outline stitch.

Stem stitch is one of the most frequently used stitches for working lines and for outlining shapes. When worked in close rows, it is very suitable to fill an area. For a more decorative appearance, a row of stem stitch can form a foundation that is then whipped. The whipping can be worked using the same thread as the stem stitch row or using a different thread.

Stem stitch, when worked with less overlap between the stitches, is called spaced stem stitch. It gives a more open appearance and is useful for working sketchy lines.

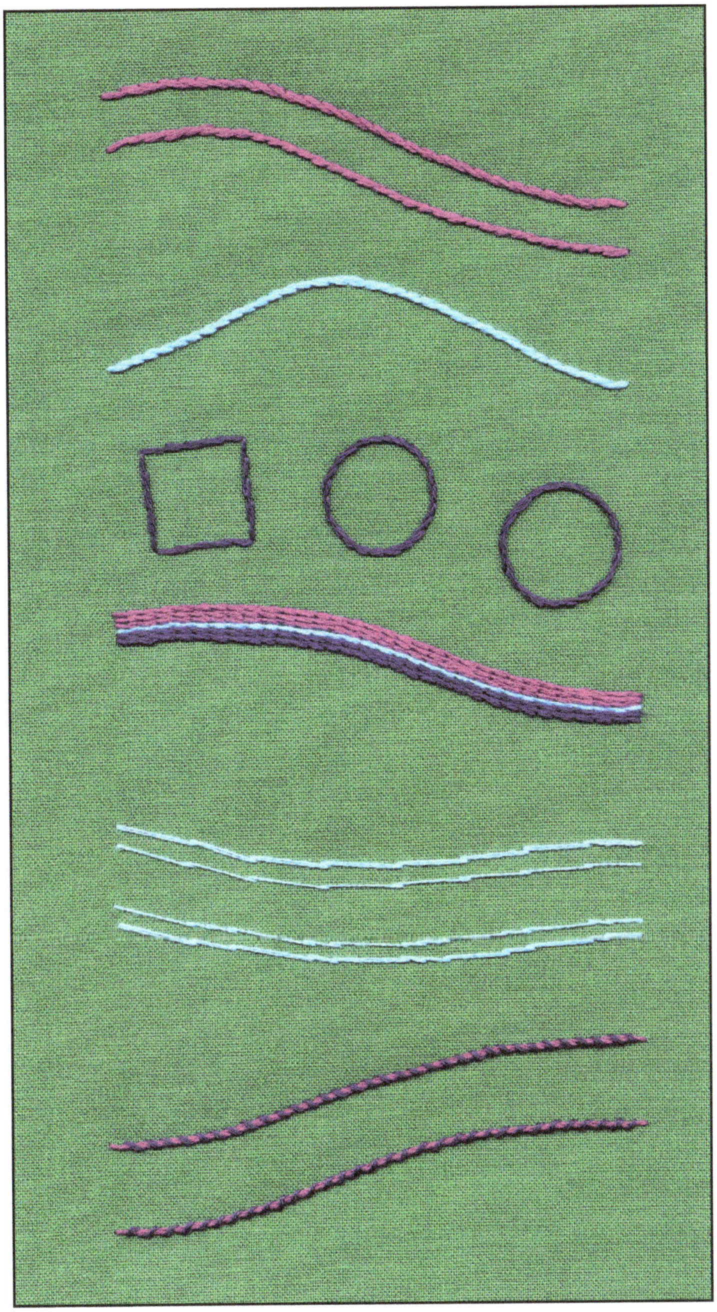


**Stem stitch and variations sampler**

# Stem stitch and variations

## Hints

Stem stitch is most commonly worked by skimming the needle in and out of the fabric before pulling the thread through. Notice that to form stitches slanting in either direction, the methods for right-handers are different from the methods for left-handers. The direction of the slant of the stitches is determined by holding the thread either below or above the needle.

When working stem stitch, bring the needle up through the same hole in the fabric as the previously worked stitch each time, but do not split the thread. Do not work stem stitch with the tension of the thread too tight or the fabric will not lie flat. If curving lines are featured in a design, use smaller stem stitches on the tightest curves. Use a tapestry needle for whipping stem stitch. The rounded end allows this needle to pass under the stem stitches without splitting the thread or piercing the fabric.

## Stem stitch and variations: right-handed

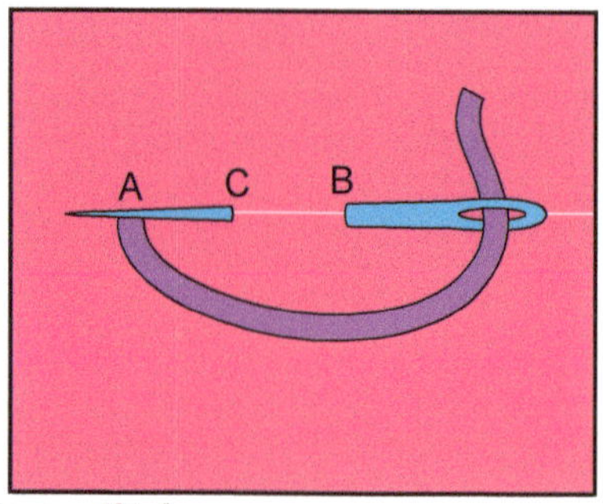


**Stem stitch**
**1** Come up at A at the start of the line. With the thread below the needle, take the needle down at B and emerge at C.

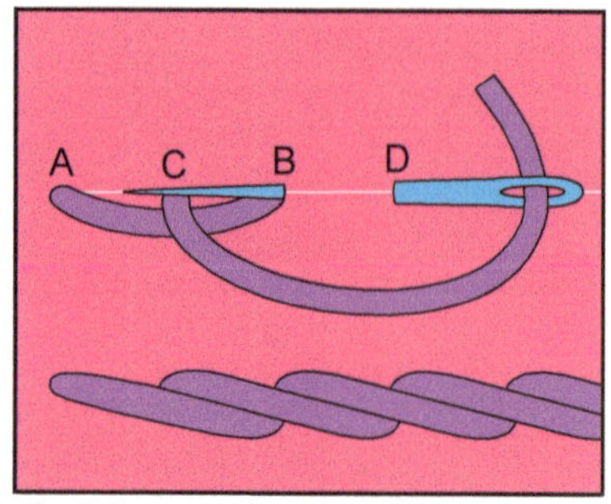


**2** Pull thread through. With the thread below, take the needle down at D and emerge at B. Pull thread through. Continue along line.

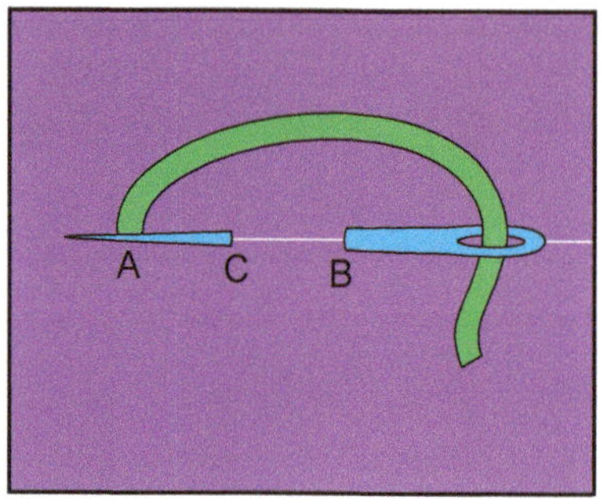


**Opposite slant**
**1** Come up at A at the start of the line. With the thread above the needle, take the needle down at B and emerge at C.

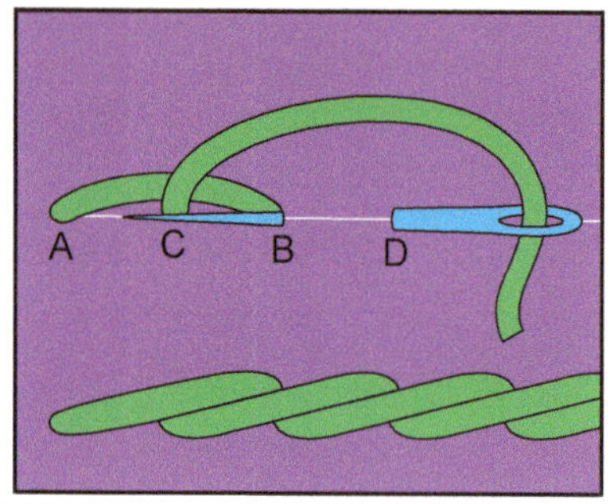


**2** Pull thread through. With the thread above, take the needle down at D and emerge at B. Pull thread through. Continue along line.

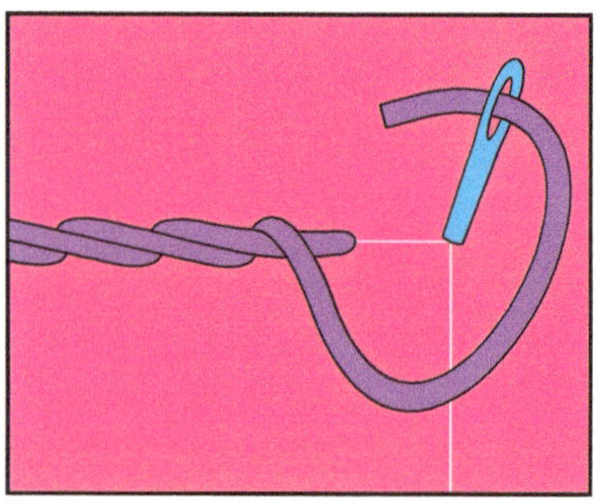

**Turning a corner**
**1** Work stem stitch along first side. At corner, take thread to back of work.

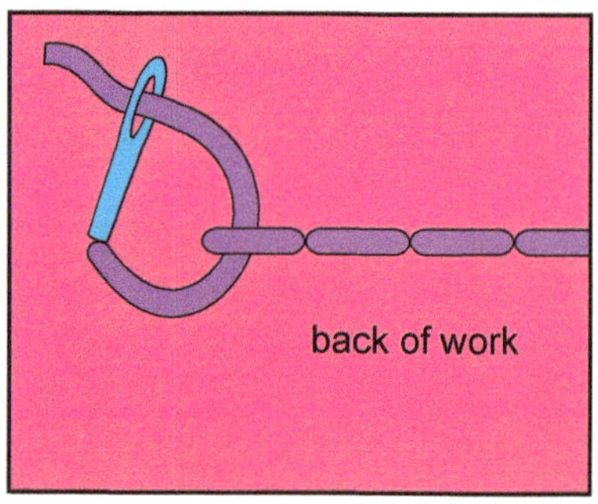


**2** Slide the needle under the last stitch on the back of the work. Return the needle to the front at the corner.

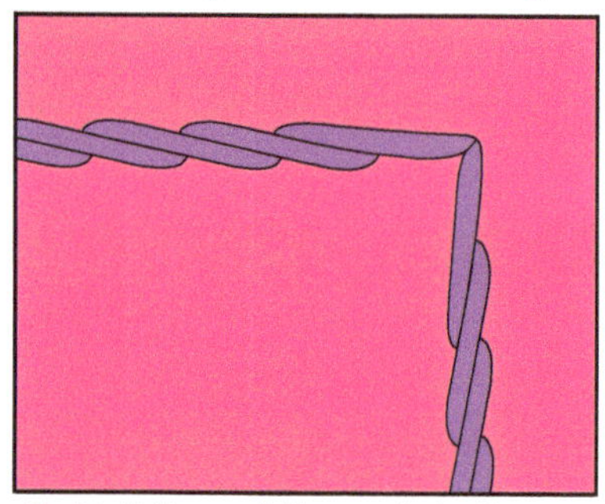

**3** Pull thread through to the front. Continue working stem stitch along the second side.

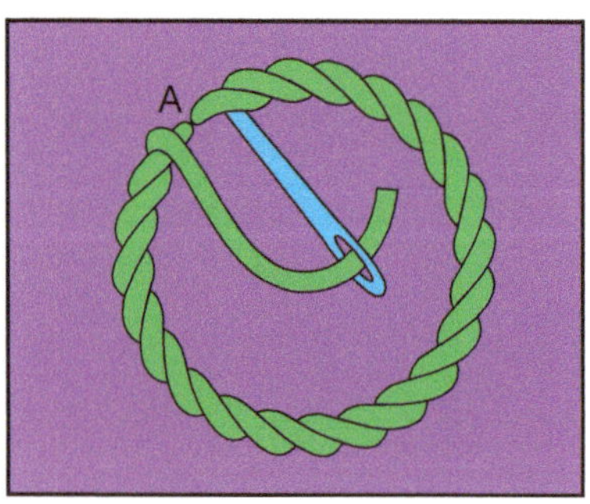


**Completing a shape** Beginning at A, stitch the shape clockwise. Work the last stitch so that it overlaps the stitches at the join.

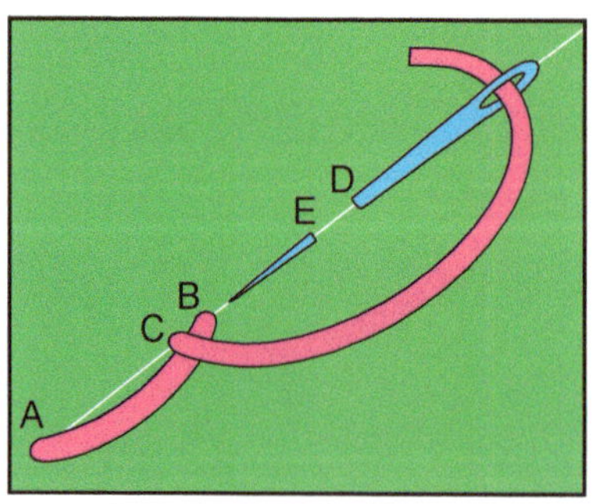


**Spaced stem stitch** Work a stitch A to B, emerge at C. Take needle down at D, emerge at E, noting space between B and E. Continue.

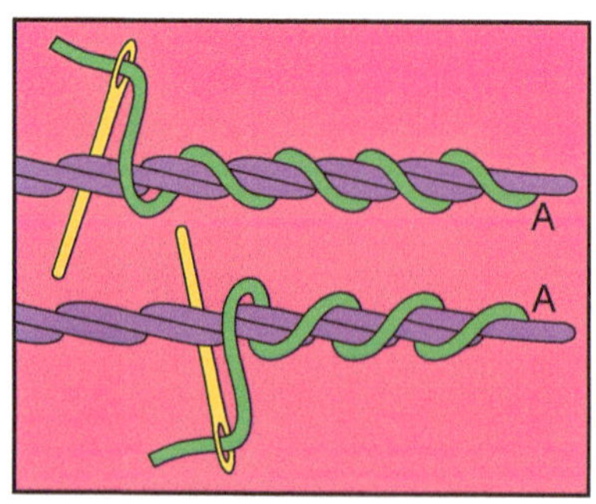


**Whipped stem stitch** Work stem stitch. Bring new thread up at A. Pass thread under overlap of stem stitches. Two directions are shown.

# Stem stitch and variations: left-handed

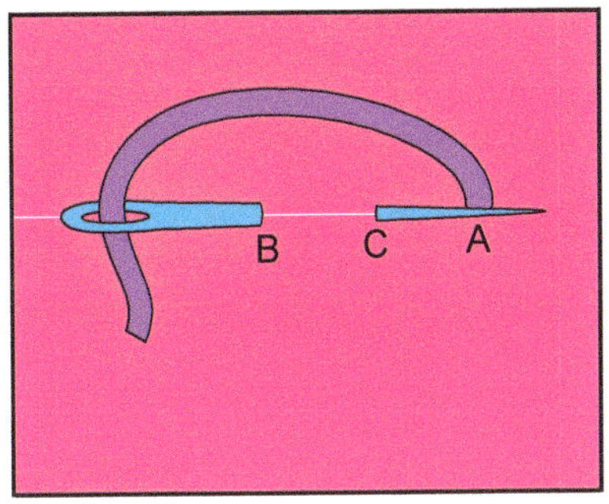


**Stem stitch**
**1** Come up at A at the start of the line. With the thread above the needle, take the needle down at B and emerge at C.

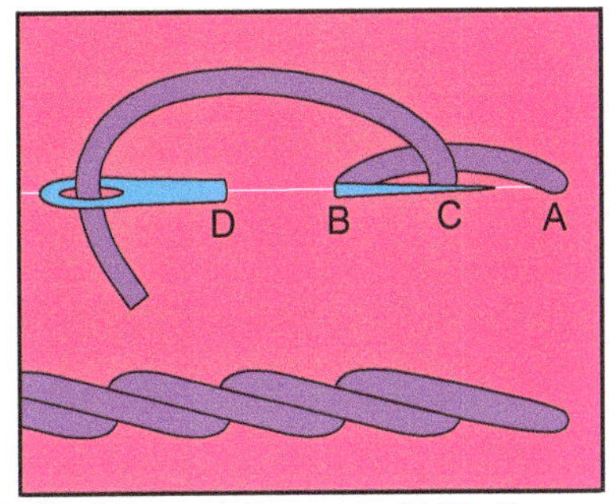


**2** Pull thread through. With the thread above, take the needle down at D and emerge at B. Pull thread through. Continue along line.

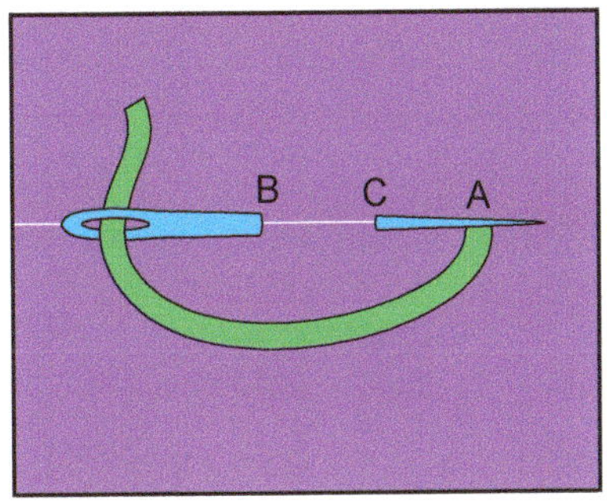


**Opposite slant**
**1** Come up at A at the start of the line. With the thread below the needle, take the needle down at B and emerge at C.

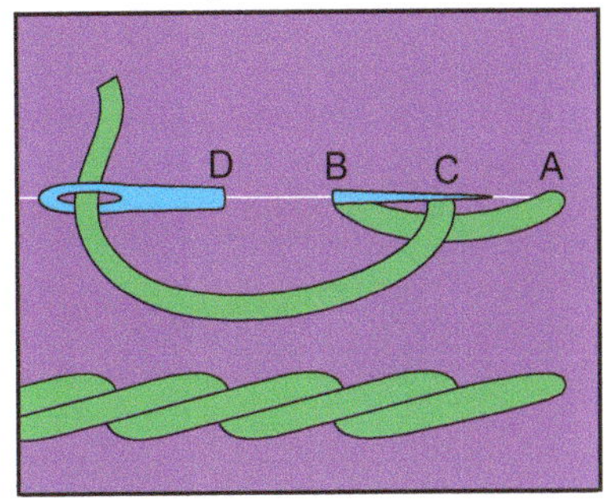


**2** Pull thread through. With the thread below, take the needle down at D and emerge at B. Pull thread through. Continue along line.

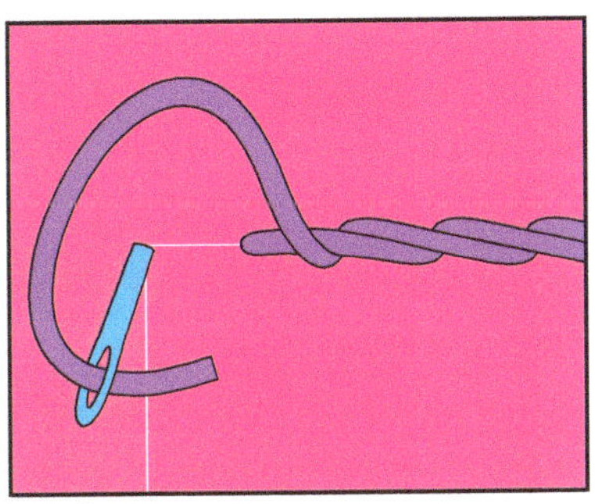

**Turning a corner**
**1** Work stem stitch along first side. At corner, take thread to back of work.

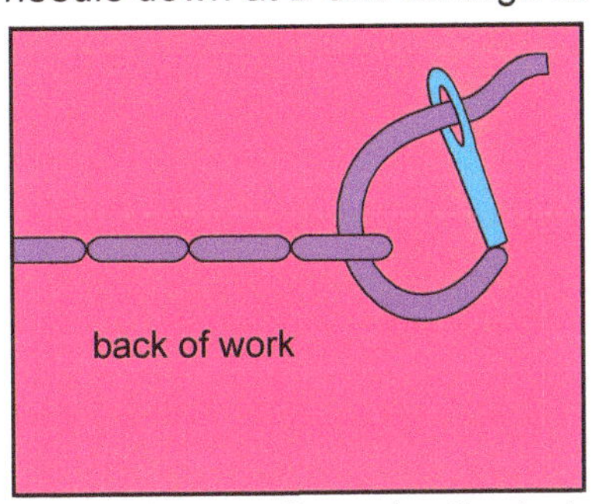


**2** Slide the needle under the last stitch on the back of the work. Return the needle to the front at the corner.

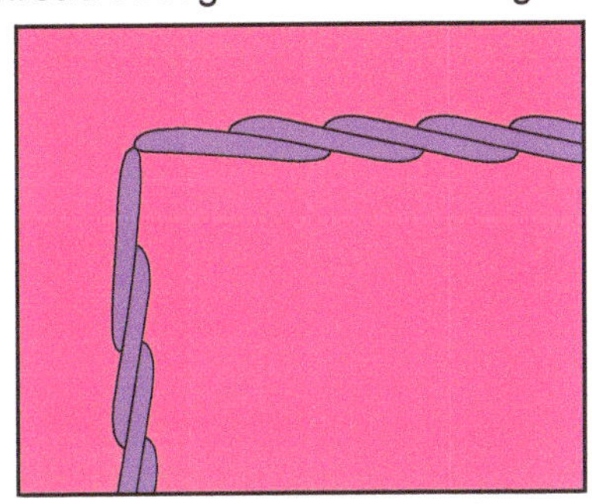

**3** Pull thread through to the front. Continue working stem stitch along the second side.

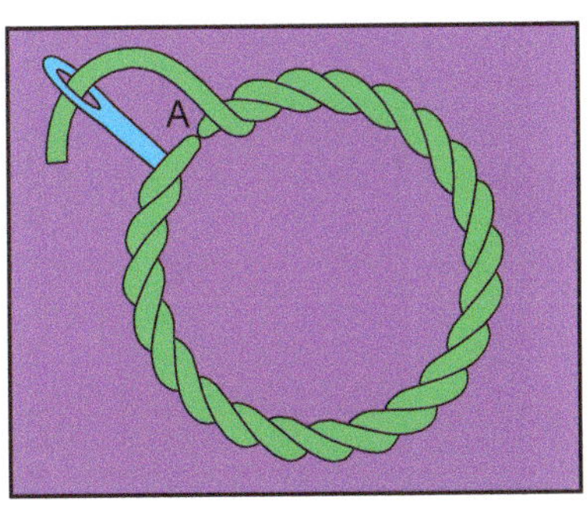


**Completing a shape** Beginning at A, stitch the shape anticlockwise. Work the last stitch so that it overlaps the stitches at the join.

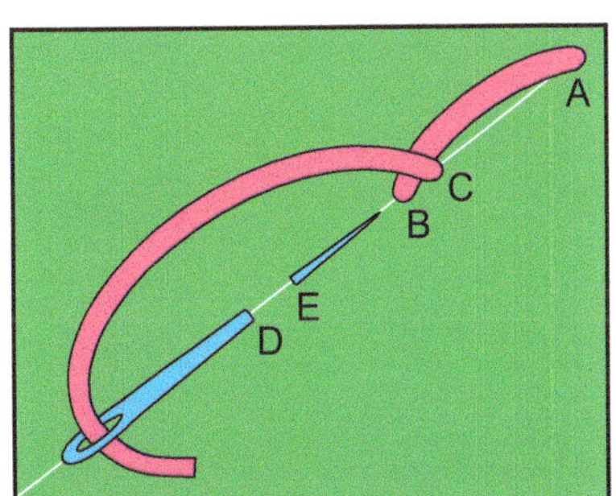


**Spaced stem stitch** Work a stitch A to B, emerge at C. Take needle down at D, emerge at E, noting space between B and E. Continue.

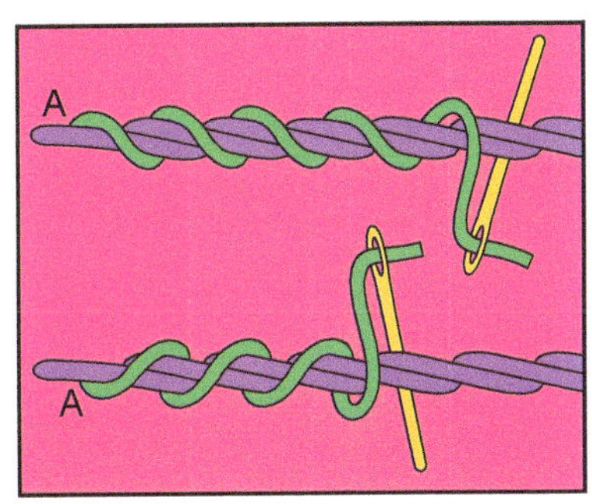


**Whipped stem stitch** Work stem stitch. Bring new thread up at A. Pass thread under overlap of stem stitches. Two directions are shown.

# Stem stitch
## and variations

# Designs and project ideas

## The designs

| | |
|---|---|
| Ellie Elephant | Lily of the Valley |
| Watery Watermelon | The Big Top |
| Sea Breeze | Starlit Garden |

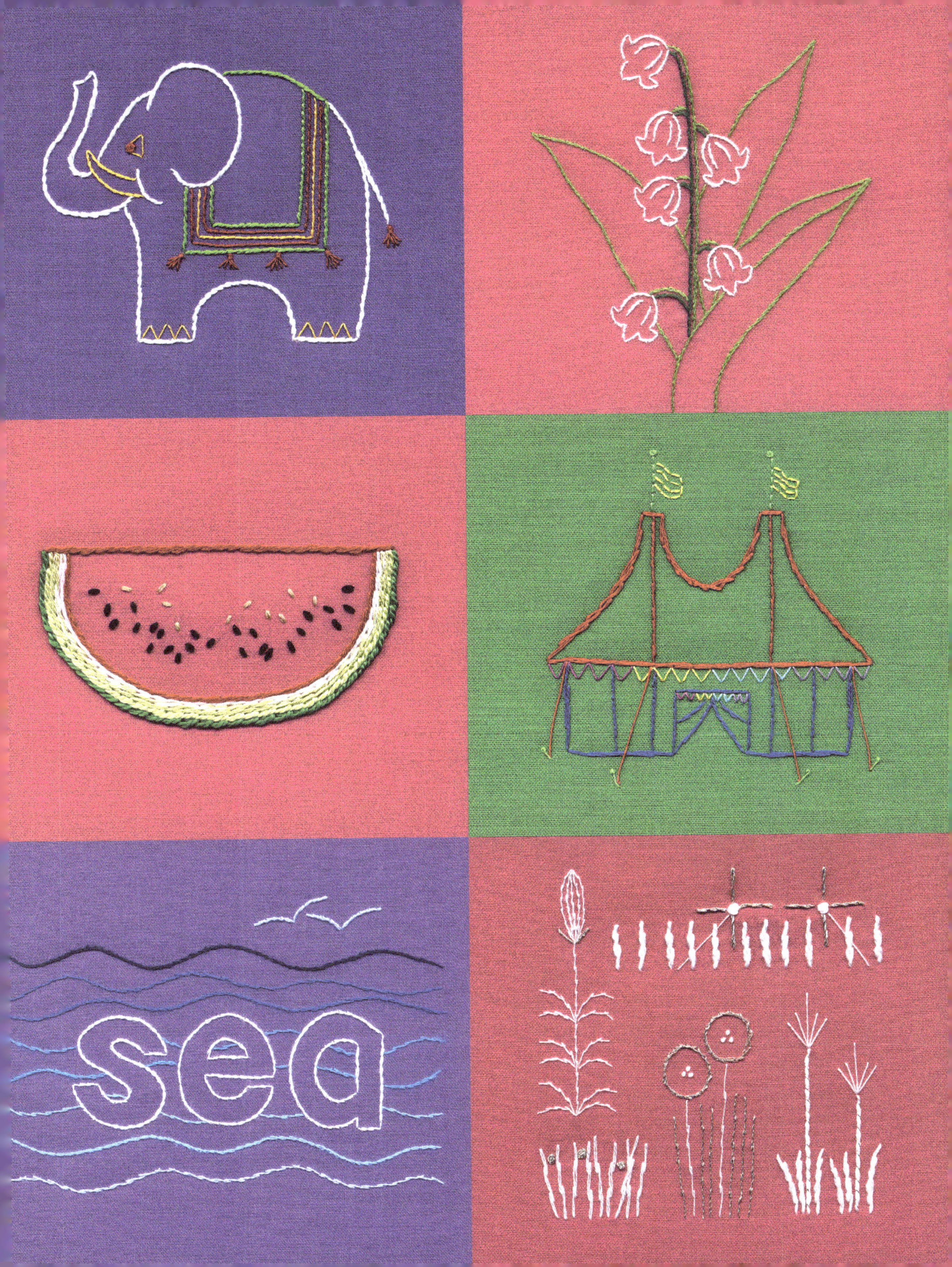
sea

# Ellie Elephant

Some say that an elephant never forgets. I wonder if it's true.

## The design

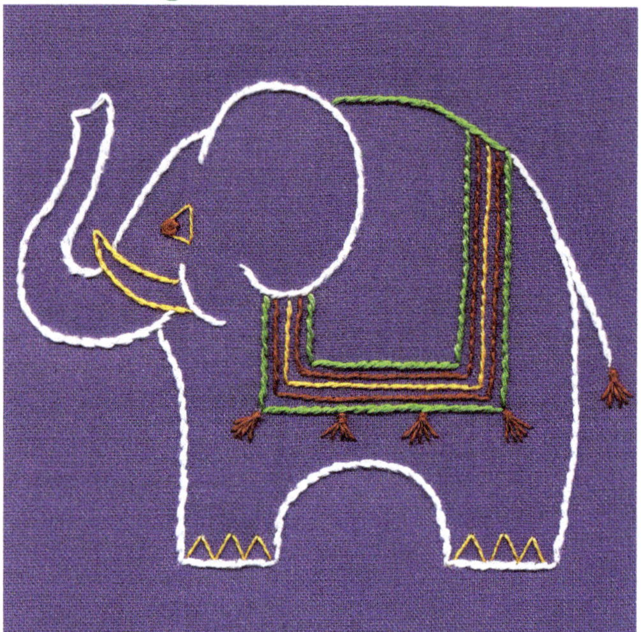

*Ellie Elephant*

This playful, easy design is worked mostly in stem stitch, while small details are added in straight stitch, back stitch, and French knot.

Follow the instructions on this page to work the design exactly as shown here on a violet background. To adapt the design for use on a cushion cover, see the project idea on the next page.

## The pattern

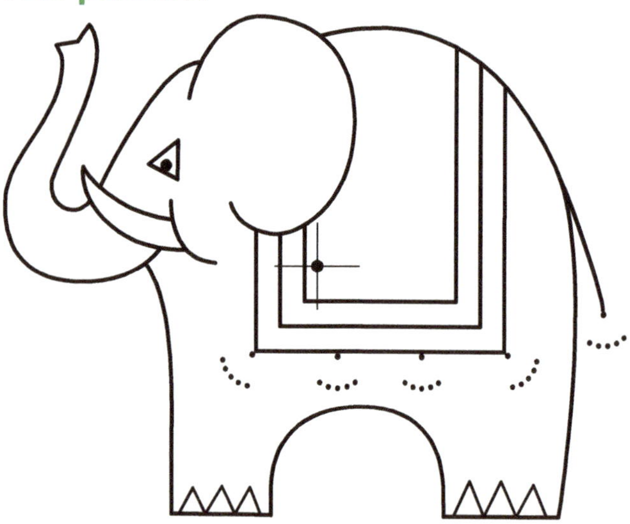

**Key:** Centre of design • **French knot** **Placement of straight stitches**

## Shopping list

- Violet cotton fabric for background: 25cm (10") square
- Fabric or interfacing for backing: 25cm (10") square
- Stranded cotton thread:
  (A) light green (B) medium yellow
  (C) dark red (D) white
- Tracing paper and other items for transferring the pattern onto the fabric

## Let's begin

Read page 15 for backing the fabric, and pages 22-25 for transferring the pattern onto the fabric, then select and use suitable methods for your fabric. For the violet fabric shown here, the pattern was transferred centrally onto the fabric by tracing with a water erasable fabric marker and then the backing fabric was tacked to the wrong side.

## Stitch!

For help, see pages 40-43 for straight stitch, 76-79 for back stitch, 94-97 for stem stitch, including turning a corner, and pages 184-187 for French knot. Work the stem stitch in this design with small stitches.

1. Beginning at the top of the head and leaving a space for the tusk, stitch the upper part of the trunk in stem stitch (2 strands D). Continuing with the same thread, work the end of the trunk with two back stitches, then complete the trunk in stem stitch.
2. Stitch the ear and cheek in stem stitch (2 strands D).
3. Work the body and legs in stem stitch (2 strands D).
4. Add the tail in stem stitch (2 strands D).
5. Stitch the tusk in stem stitch (1 strand B).
6. Work the toes in back stitch (1 strand B).
7. Outline the eye with three back stitches (1 strand B). Add the pupil with a two wrap French knot (3 strands C).
8. Using the photo as a guide, work the rug in stem stitch as follows. Begin with the green rows (2 strands A), then work the yellow row (1 strand B). Add the red rows in the spaces between the green and yellow rows (1 strand C).
9. Stitch four tassels on the rug and one on the tail (1 strand C). For each, stitch five straight stitches and bring the thread up between two stitches (Diagram 1). Take the needle and thread under the stitches out to one side (Diagram 2). With the thread wrapping the stitches, take the needle to the back where the thread emerged (Diagram 3). Pull to draw the stitches together. End off.

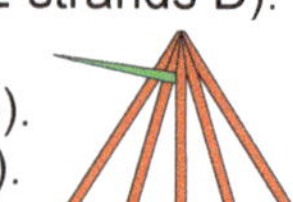

**Diagram 1**

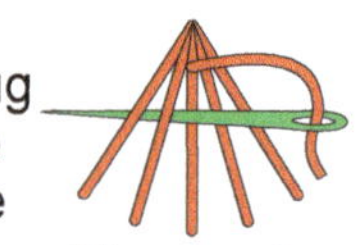

**Diagram 2**

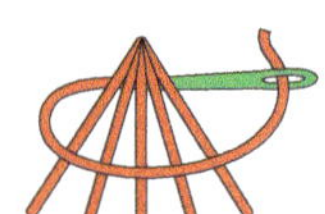

**Diagram 3**

## Let's finish

Take out the tacking. Rinse the work in cold water to remove the fabric marker. When partly dry, press or pin out work. See page 36 for pressing and for pinning out.

# Ellie Elephant Cushion Cover

Relax with this comfortable elephant cushion.

## The project

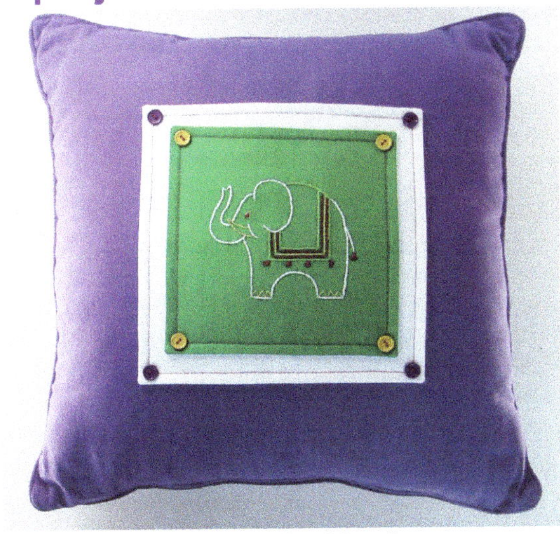

***Ellie Elephant Cushion Cover***

This purchased cushion cover features *Ellie Elephant* worked at a larger scale on a green patch. A larger patch, this time in white, is attached behind the green patch. Both are then stitched onto the violet cushion cover. Buttons are attached at the corners of each patch to add interest.
The size of this cushion is 42cm (16 1/2") square.
As this project uses buttons, it would not be safe for babies or very small children.

## Shopping list

- Violet cushion cover and insert
- Green cotton fabric for the green patch: two 18cm (7") squares
- White cotton fabric for the white patch: two 22cm (8 3/4") squares
- Lightweight iron-on interfacing for backing: one 18cm (7") square, and one 22cm (8 3/4") square
- Threads as listed for the original design on the page opposite
- Machine sewing thread: green, white, and red
- Four yellow buttons
- Four violet buttons
- Tracing paper and other items for transferring the pattern onto the fabric

## Let's begin

See the page opposite for the pattern. Prepare the pattern by enlarging it to 125% of its original size.
Following the instructions on page 15 for backing the fabric, attach one square of interfacing onto the wrong side of one green square and one white square.
Transfer the pattern centrally onto the right side of the backed green square using transfer paper. See page 24 for transferring the pattern using transfer paper.

## Stitch!

Work the elephant following steps 1-9 of the stitch instructions on the facing page.

## Let's finish

Rinse the work in cold water to remove the pattern markings. When almost dry, press. See page 36 for pressing.
With right sides together, pin the stitched square onto the second green square around the edge. Using matching machine sewing thread and a 1cm (3/8") seam allowance, machine stitch around the square, leaving an 8cm (3") opening in the lower side. Trim the seam allowances and cut away the excess fabric at the corners (Diagram 1).
Turn the patch to the right side through the opening and press.
Hand stitch the opening closed.
Make up the white patch in the same way.
With the design facing up, place the green patch centrally over the white patch and tack the patches together.
Using red machine sewing thread and stitching through both patches, machine stitch around the green patch 1cm (3/8") in from its edges, then take out the tacking (Diagram 2).
Remove the cushion insert.
Place the joined patches onto the centre of the front of the cushion cover and tack in place.
Again using the red machine sewing thread, attach the white patch to the front of the cushion cover by machine stitching 1cm (3/8") in from its edges (see Diagram 3). Take out the tacking. Using the red machine sewing thread, attach four yellow buttons at the corners of the green patch and four violet buttons at the corners of the white patch with hand stitches (Diagram 3).
Press, avoiding the buttons. Place cushion insert back inside the cover.

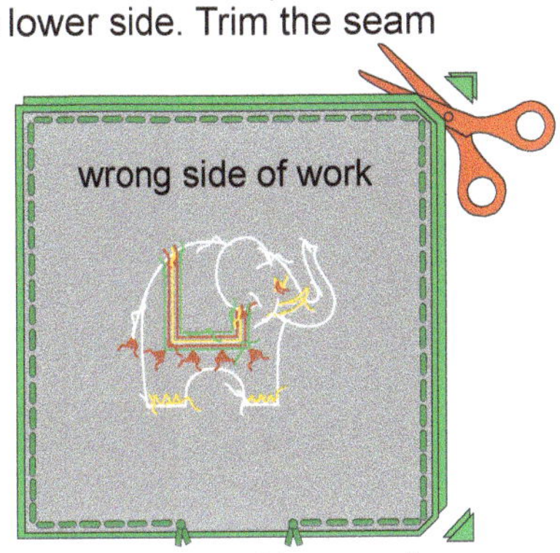


**Diagram 1**

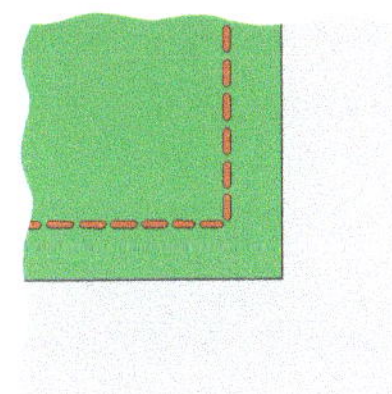

**Diagram 2**

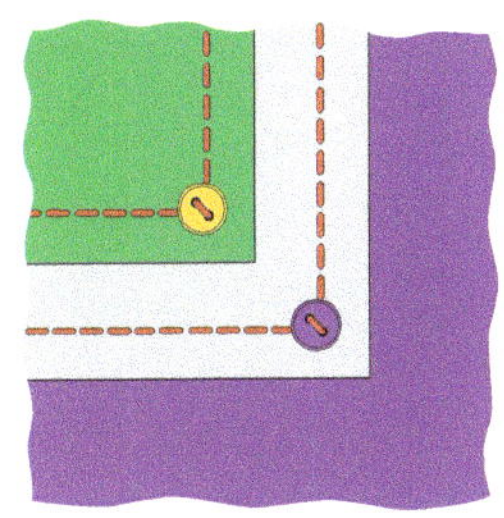

**Diagram 3**

# Lily of the Valley

Listen carefully and you may hear these tiny bells delicately chiming.

## The design

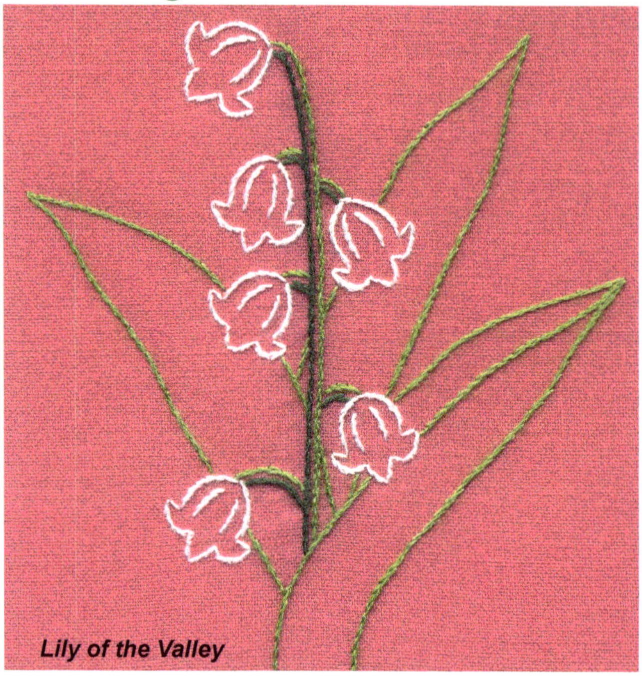


This design is worked mostly in small stem stitch, with the addition of single back stitches in the flowers. Silk threads, which have a beautiful sheen, are used throughout. Although the flowers are quite detailed, the design is easy to work. Follow the instructions on this page to work the design as shown here. To work the design on a greeting card, see the page opposite.

## The pattern

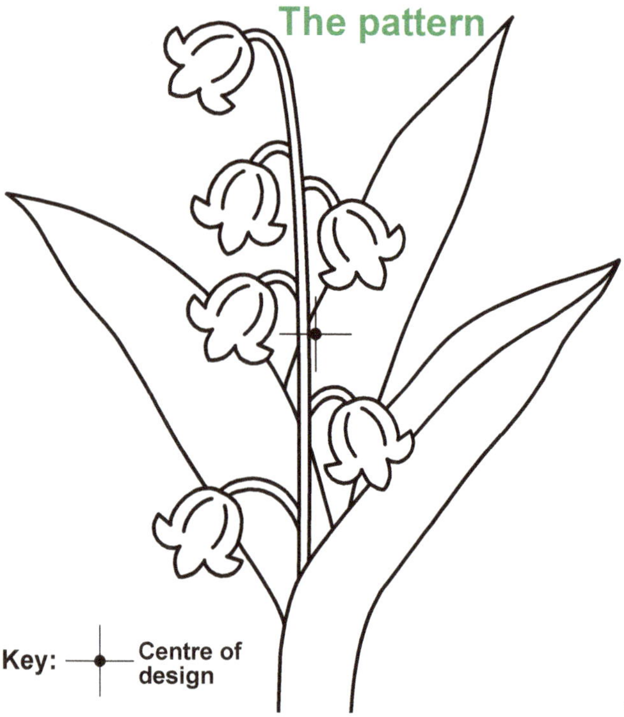

Key: Centre of design

## Shopping list

- Pink cotton fabric for background: 25cm (10") square
- Fabric or interfacing for backing: 25cm (10") square
- Stranded silk thread:
  (A) dark green (B) light green (C) white
- Tracing paper and other items for transferring the pattern onto the fabric

## Let's begin

Read page 15 for backing the fabric, and pages 22-25 for transferring the pattern onto the fabric, then select and use suitable methods for your fabric. For the pink fabric shown here, the pattern was transferred centrally onto the fabric by tracing with a water erasable fabric marker and then the backing fabric was tacked to the wrong side.

## Stitch!

For help, see pages 76-79 for back stitch and pages 94-97 for stem stitch, including turning a corner. Work the stem stitch in this design with small stitches.

1 Following the photo, stitch the light side of the main stem in stem stitch (1 strand B). Work the light side of the flower stems in the same way. Work the dark side of the stem and flower stems in stem stitch (1 strand A).

2 Following the diagram, work a flower in stem stitch down to the first petal (1 strand C). Take the needle to the back at the corner and emerge at the first petal tip (Diagram 1). Work a back stitch (Diagram 2).

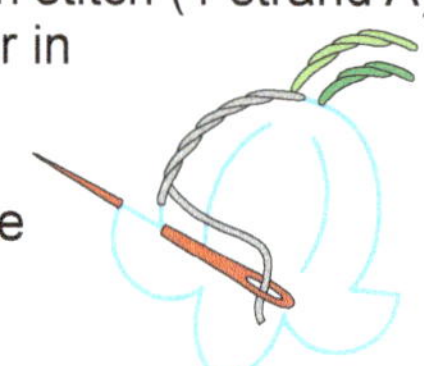

Diagram 1

3 Continue the curved side of the first petal in stem stitch. At the point between the first and second petals, work a corner and continue. At the central point work another corner. Work the remaining petals in a similar way, noting the change in slant of the stem stitches (See Diagram 3).

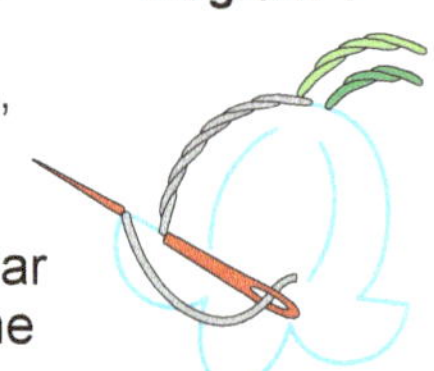

Diagram 2

4 Work a back stitch at the end of the third petal. Complete the second side, then work the internal lines, again noting the slant (Diagram 3).

5 Stitch the remaining flowers in the same way. Work the outlines of the leaves in stem stitch (1 strand B).

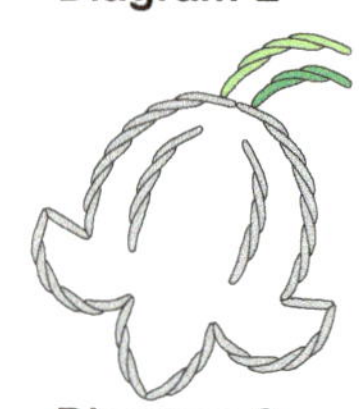

Diagram 3

## Let's finish

Take out the tacking. Rinse the work in cold water to remove the fabric marker. When partly dry, press or pin out work. See page 36 for pressing and for pinning out.

## Hint

**Realistic appearance**

Using light thread on one side of a stem and dark on the other creates an impression of sunlight on the plant.

# Lily of the Valley Greeting Card

Send a special message to a friend with this handmade greeting card.

## The project

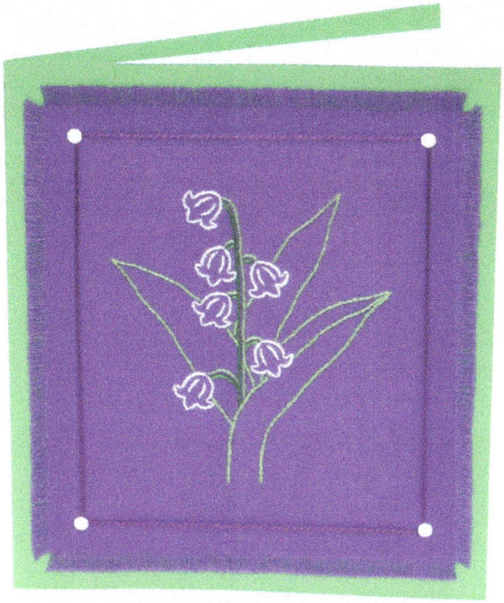

***Lily of the Valley Greeting Card***

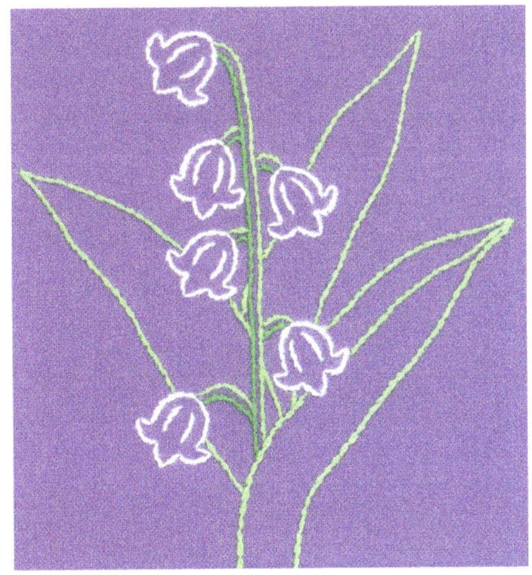

**Detail of *Lily of the Valley Greeting Card***

For this greeting card, *Lily of the Valley* is stitched on a piece of violet fabric that is then applied as a patch onto the front of the card.
The size of this greeting card is 18cm x 15cm wide (7" x 6").

## Shopping list

- Violet cotton fabric for background: 23cm x 20cm wide (9" x 8")
- Light weight iron-on interfacing for backing: 15cm x 12cm wide (5 3/4" x 4 3/4")
- Threads as listed for the original design on the page opposite
- No. 5 perlé cotton thread: dark violet
- Tracing paper and other items for transferring the pattern onto the fabric
- Green card: 18cm x 30cm wide (7" x 12")
- White paper: 17cm x 29cm wide (6 3/4" x 11 1/2")
- Archival single-sided and double-sided sticky tapes
- 4 small white paper fasteners

## Let's begin

See the page opposite for the *Lily of the Valley* pattern. Attach the iron-on interfacing centrally onto the wrong side of the violet fabric, noting that the fabric extends beyond the backing on all sides. See page 15 for backing the fabric. Transfer the pattern centrally onto the right side of the violet fabric by tracing with a water erasable fabric marker or by using transfer paper. See pages 22-25 for transferring the pattern onto the fabric.

## Stitch!

Work the design following steps 1-5 of the stitch instructions on the page opposite.

## Let's finish

Rinse the work in cold water to remove the pattern markings. When partly dry, press or pin out the work. See page 36 for pressing and for pinning out.
Place the stitched work with the wrong side facing up. Following the violet fabric threads, trim away the excess fabric around the work, leaving 1cm (3/8") outside the edge of the interfacing to make a rectangular patch that is centred around the design. Pull several fabric threads away from all sides to create a frayed edge but stop fraying just before reaching the edge of the interfacing.
To make the greeting card, fold the green card in half. Using the double-sided sticky tape, attach the stitched fabric centrally onto the front of the card.
Place the front of the card over a pad of folded fabric and, using a large needle, pierce a hole through the fabric and the card for the paper fastener near each corner. Attach a paper fastener through each of three of the holes. Thread a length of dark violet thread into a needle. Leaving a tail, take the thread up through the fourth hole, pass it around the three paper fasteners, and then take it down again through the fourth hole. Trim the thread ends and then secure them to the inside of the card with the single-sided sticky tape. Attach the last paper fastener through the fourth hole.
Fold the white paper in half, making the pages for the card. Secure the pages to the inside of the front of the card with the double-sided tape.

## Hint

**Variety of cards**

Using the designs in this book, or selected elements from many of them, an infinite variety of greeting cards could be made. Experimenting with different colour schemes, design sizes, and thread types and thicknesses would be extremely creative and great fun!

# Watery Watermelon

Enjoy the refreshing taste of summer.

## The design

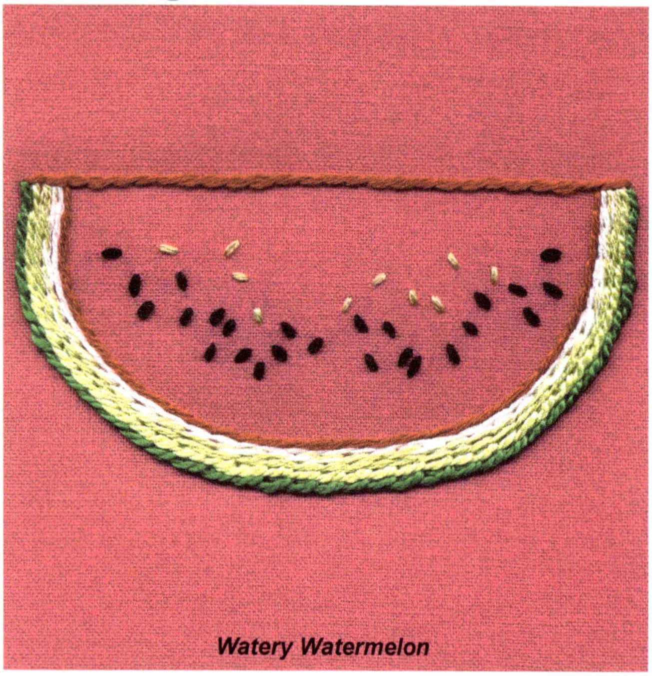

*Watery Watermelon*

This very easy design uses stem stitch and straight stitch. Bright pink fabric has been chosen for the background as it can represent the flesh of the watermelon. Texture is achieved by using both stranded cotton and perlé cotton threads.
Follow the instructions on this page to work the design exactly as shown here on a pink background. To apply the design to a garment, see the project idea on the next page where three slices of watermelon are featured on a stretch fabric summer top for a child.

## The pattern

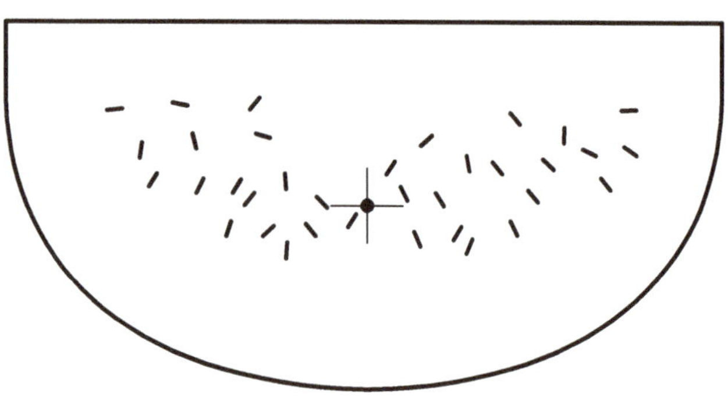

**Key:** **Centre of design**

## Shopping list

- Pink cotton fabric for background: 25cm (10") square
- Fabric or interfacing for backing: 25cm (10") square
- Stranded cotton thread: (A) black (B) very light green (C) dark red (D) white
- No. 5 perlé cotton thread: (E) medium green (F) very light green
- Tracing paper and other items for transferring the pattern onto the fabric

## Let's begin

Read page 15 for backing the fabric, and pages 22-25 for transferring the pattern onto the fabric, then select and use suitable methods for your fabric. For the pink fabric shown here, the pattern was transferred centrally onto the fabric by tracing with an HB pencil and then the backing fabric was tacked to the wrong side.

## Stitch!

For help, see pages 40-43 for straight stitch and pages 94-97 for stem stitch. Work the stem stitch with all the stitches slanting in the same direction.

1 Following the marked line, stitch the first row, which is the skin, in stem stitch (1 strand E).
2 Working inwards from the skin and referring to the diagram, stitch the flesh in stem stitch worked in parallel rows (Diagram 1) as follows:
   second row: very light green perlé cotton (1 strand F).
   third row: very light green stranded cotton (4 strands B).
   fourth row: very light green stranded cotton together with white stranded cotton (2 strands B mixed in the needle with 2 strands D).
   fifth row: white stranded cotton (3 strands D).
   sixth row: dark red stranded cotton (3 strands C).

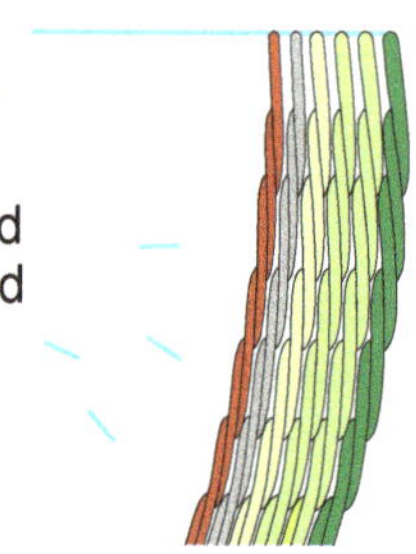

**Diagram 1**

3 Add the outline across the top of the watermelon in stem stitch (3 strands C).
4 Stitch each dark pip with three straight stitches worked through the same two holes in the fabric (2 strands A).
5 Work the pale pips in the same way (1 strand B).

## Let's finish

Take out the tacking. Press or pin out the work. See page 36 for pressing and for pinning out.

# Watery Watermelon Summer Top

Keep cool in this colourful summer top.

## The project

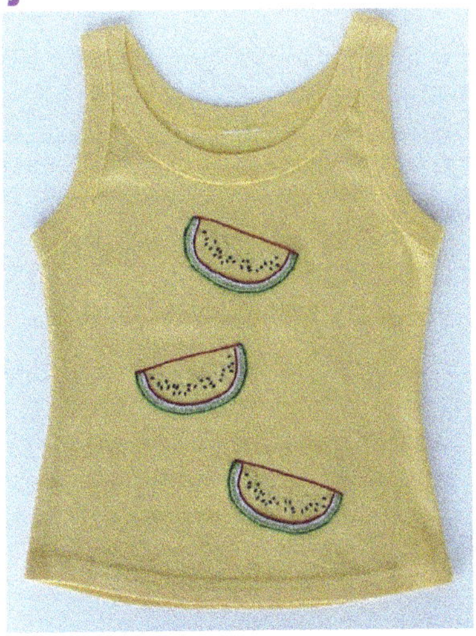

*Watery Watermelon Summer Top*

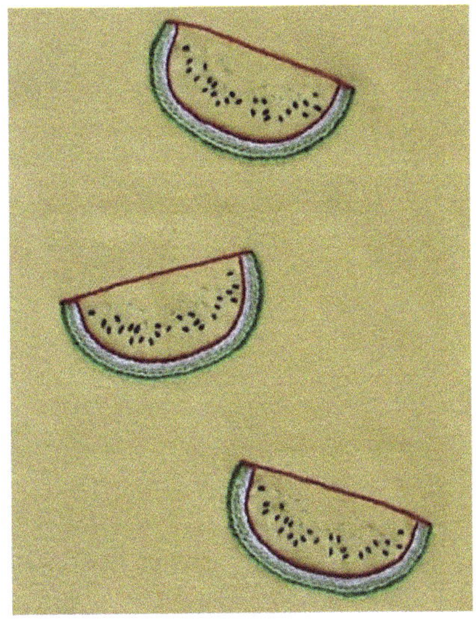

Detail of *Watery Watermelon Summer Top*

Three slices of watermelon are scattered on the front of this purchased summer top for a small child. The slices are all stitched in the same way as the original design on the page opposite.

## Shopping list

- Yellow stretch knit singlet top
- Lightweight iron-on interfacing for backing: three pieces 8cm x 12cm wide (3" x 5")
- Threads as listed for the original design on the page opposite
- Tracing paper and other items for transferring the pattern onto the garment

## Let's begin

See the page opposite for the *Watery Watermelon* pattern. Using three small pieces of tracing paper, make three separate tracings of the pattern. Referring to the photo, and the diagram, position the tracings on the front of the garment. Rotate the tracings and move them around until you are happy with their placement (Diagram 1). Using tacking stitches in a light colour, record the position at which each watermelon slice is to be stitched.

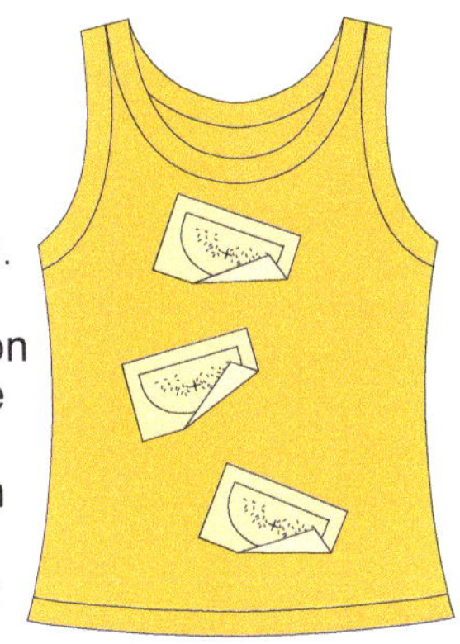

**Diagram 1**

From here on, each slice of watermelon is prepared and stitched before moving on to the next one. Begin with the watermelon that is closest to the neckline. Following the instructions on page 15 for backing the fabric, attach one piece of interfacing onto the wrong side of the front of the garment at the position for the watermelon. This will stabilize the area where the design is to be stitched.

Transfer the pattern onto the front of the garment by tracing with a water erasable fabric marker. See page 23 for transferring the pattern by tracing.

## Stitch!

Work this first watermelon following steps 1-5 of the stitch instructions for the original design on the previous page.

Continue in this way, preparing and completing the second watermelon before moving on to the third.

## Let's finish

Take out the tacking and turn the garment inside out. On the wrong side, peel back any excess interfacing from its outer edges and trim it back close to the stitches.

Rinse the garment in cold water to remove the water erasable fabric marker. When dry, turn it inside out and press it. See page 36 for pressing.

## Hint

**Change the colours**

For a honeydew melon use light green fabric for the background and instead of the red thread use a light green. For a rock melon, change to orange fabric and orange thread.

# The Big Top

We couldn't wait to see the circus performers.

## The design

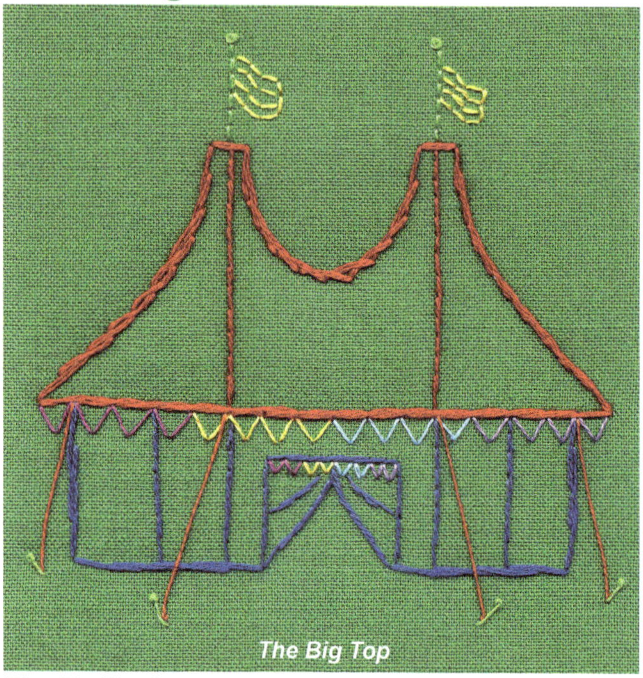


*The Big Top* features stem stitch as well as straight stitch, back stitch, French knot, and pistil stitch. It is worked in stranded cotton threads. The design is quite detailed, but the stitches are easy to work.
To work the design as shown here use the instructions on this page. To adapt the design for use on a journal cover, see the project idea on the next page.

## The pattern

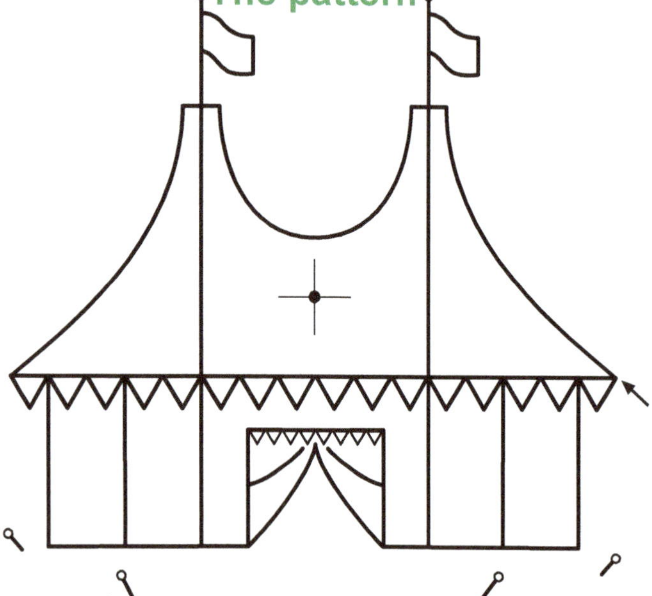

Key: Centre of design; • French knot; Pistil stitch; Begin roof outline here

## Shopping list

- Green cotton fabric for background: 25cm (10") square
- Fabric or interfacing for backing: 25cm (10") square
- Stranded cotton thread:
  (A) medium violet (B) medium blue (C) medium aqua
  (D) light green (E) medium yellow (F) medium orange
  (G) medium red (H) medium magenta
- Tracing paper and other items for transferring the pattern onto the fabric

## Let's begin

Read page 15 for backing the fabric, and pages 22-25 for transferring the pattern onto the fabric, then select and use suitable methods for your fabric. For the green fabric shown here, the pattern was transferred centrally onto the fabric by tracing with an HB pencil and then the backing fabric was tacked to the wrong side.

## Stitch!

For help, see pages 40-43 for straight stitch, 76-79 for back stitch, 94-97 for stem stitch, including turning a corner, and pages 184-187 for French knot and pistil stitch.

1 Beginning at the arrow, work the first side of the roof in stem stitch (2 strands G). Work a back stitch across the first peak (Diagrams 1 and 2), then continue in stem stitch. Work a back stitch at the second peak in the same way, and continue down the second side. Work a corner and continue across the lower edge.

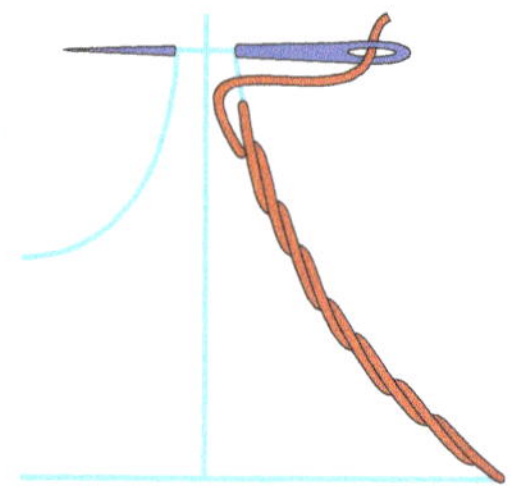

Diagram 1

2 Using smaller stitches, add the internal roof panels in stem stitch (1 strand G). On each half of the tent, stitch the wall and floor in stem stitch (2 strands B). Add the wall panels, doorway, and curtains with small stem stitch (1 strand B).

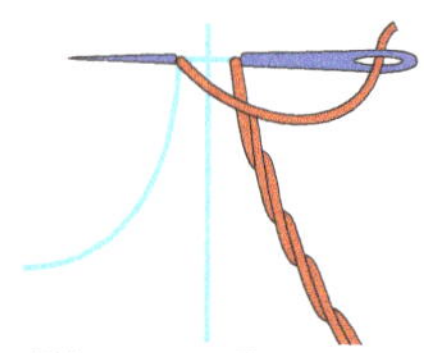

Diagram 2

3 Work the flagpoles in back stitch, then add a two wrap French knot to each (1 strand D). Using back stitch, work the flag outlines and add stripes (1 strand E).

4 Working eight stitches in each colour, add the zigzag to the roof in back stitch (1 strand A, C, E, and H).

5 Using smaller back stitches and working four stitches in each colour, add the zigzag to the top of the doorway (1 strand A, C, E, and H). Stitch each tent peg with a one wrap pistil stitch (1 strand D).

6 Add each guy rope with a long straight stitch worked from the tent peg to the roof (1 strand F).

## Let's finish

Take out the tacking. Press or pin out the work. See page 36 for pressing and for pinning out.

# The Big Top Journal Cover

Record your fun times in this journal.

## The project

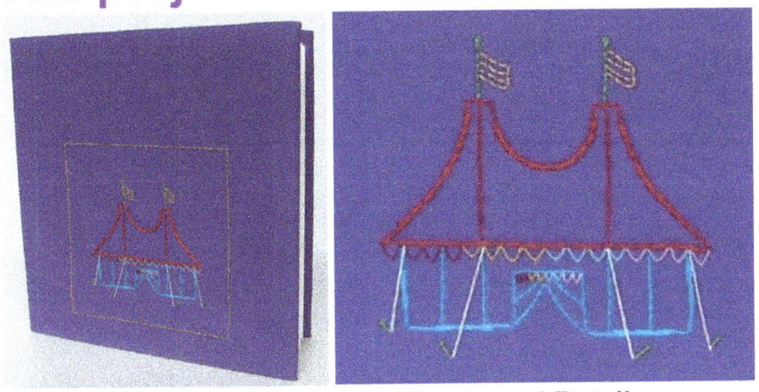

***The Big Top Journal Cover* and Detail**

*The Big Top* is worked on a piece of violet fabric that is then made up into a journal cover. The colour scheme has been changed, and a back stitch square border has been added to frame the circus tent. The size of this journal is 20.5cm (8") square.

## Shopping list

- Journal
- Violet cotton fabric and lightweight iron-on interfacing for the backing: See the Let's begin instructions on this page for calculating the dimensions
- Machine sewing thread: violet
- Tissue paper
- Stranded cotton thread:
  (A) light violet
  (B) dark aqua
  (C) medium aqua
  (D) light green
  (E) medium yellow
  (F) white
  (G) medium red
  (H) dark magenta
- Items for transferring the pattern onto the fabric

## Let's begin

See the page opposite for the circus tent pattern.

***Making the pattern for the cover***

Note that from this pattern we will estimate the amount of fabric and interfacing required. Measure the height of the front of the journal and add 3cm (1 1/4"). Measure the entire width of the front, spine and back of the journal and add 6mm (1/4"). Draw a rectangle using these measurements onto tissue paper and cut it out. Label this the lining pattern. On another piece of tissue paper, make a tracing of the lining pattern, then add 8cm (3") onto each end for the flaps. Cut this out and label it the outer layer pattern. Place this pattern onto the journal, aligning the flap fold line with the right hand side of the front of the journal.

Mark the position of the left hand side of the front onto the pattern with a dashed line (Diagram 1).

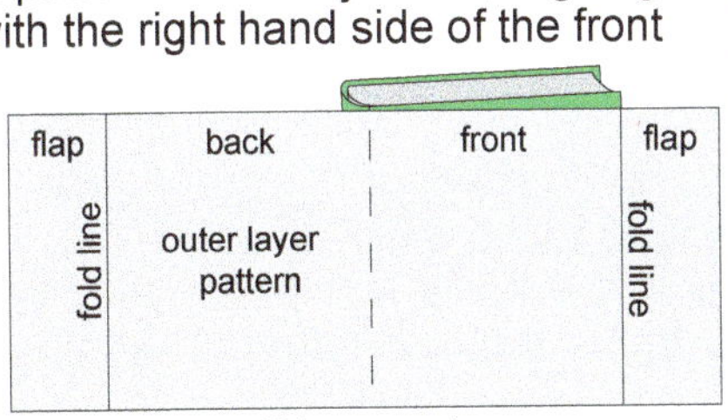


**Diagram 1**

Trace the pattern for the circus tent onto the front of the outer layer pattern, centred between the flap fold line and the dashed line. Draw a ruled square border around the circus tent (Diagram 2).

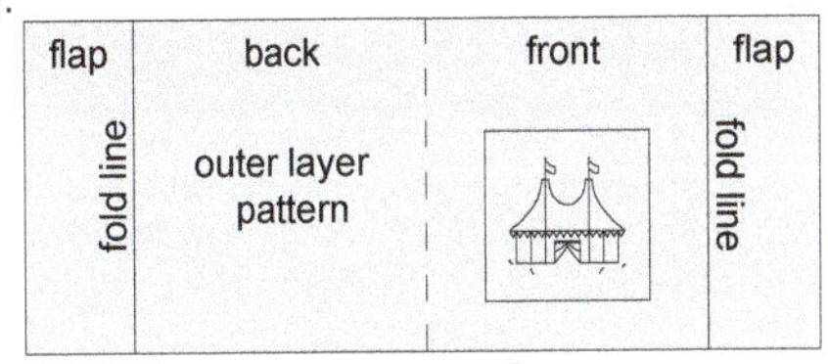


**Diagram 2**

***Preparing the fabric***

Cut out one piece of violet fabric using the lining pattern. Cut out one piece of violet fabric and one piece of interfacing using the outer layer pattern. Following the instructions on page 15 for backing the fabric, attach the iron-on interfacing onto the wrong side of the outer layer fabric. Referring to the outer layer pattern, work a row of tacking 8cm (3") in from each end to mark the flap fold lines. Transfer the circus tent and the border onto the front of the outer layer fabric using transfer paper. See page 24 for transferring the pattern using transfer paper.

## Stitch!

Work the circus tent following steps 1-6 of the stitch instructions for the original design on the previous page, substituting the alternative threads. Work the border around the design in back stitch (1 strand E).

## Let's finish

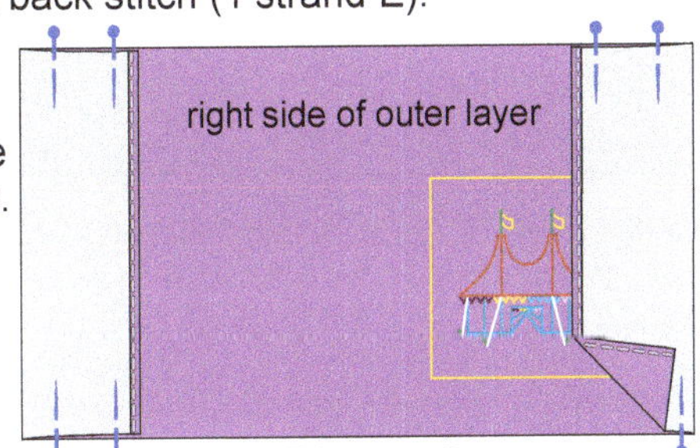


**Diagram 3**

Rinse the work in cold water to remove the pattern markings. When almost dry, press. See page 36 for pressing.

On the outer layer, fold under 6mm (1/4") to the wrong side on each end of the flaps and machine stitch with violet machine sewing thread. With right sides together, fold the flaps over at the tacked lines and pin (Diagram 3).

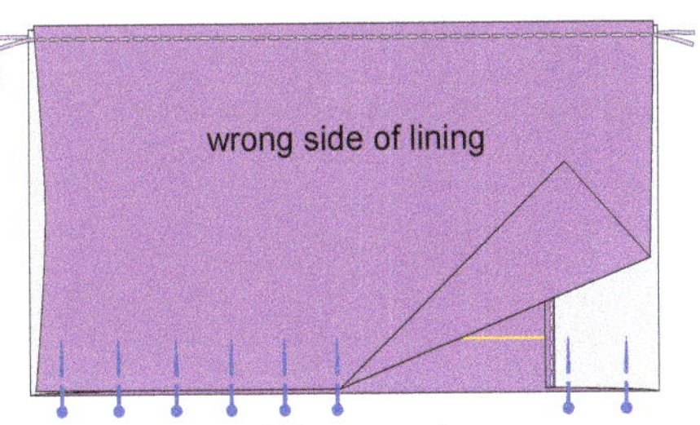


**Diagram 4**

With right sides together, pin the lining to the outer layer along the upper and lower edges. The flaps are between the layers. Using a 1cm (3/8") seam allowance, machine stitch along the upper edge (Diagram 4). Stitch along the lower edge in the same way. Turn the cover right side out through the tunnel formed. Re-fold the flaps over to the lining side of the cover. Take out the tacking and press. Place the journal into the completed fabric cover by slipping the front and back covers of the journal between the flaps and the lining.

# Sea Breeze

The breeze is cool, the seagulls are calling, and the rippling water is very, very blue.

## The design

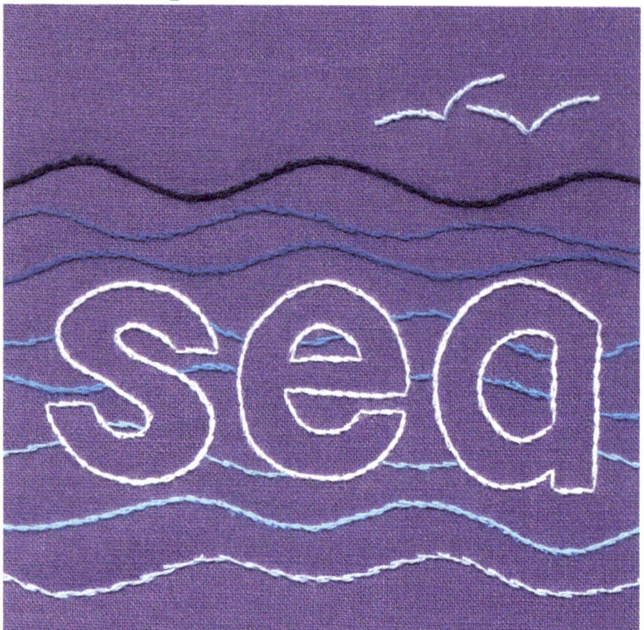

Sea Breeze

*Sea Breeze* is an easy design worked in stem stitch, spaced stem stitch, whipped stem stitch, and back stitch.

To work the design exactly as shown here on a violet background, follow the instructions on this page. To adapt the design for use as a trio of scrapbooking decorations, see the project idea on the next page.

## The pattern

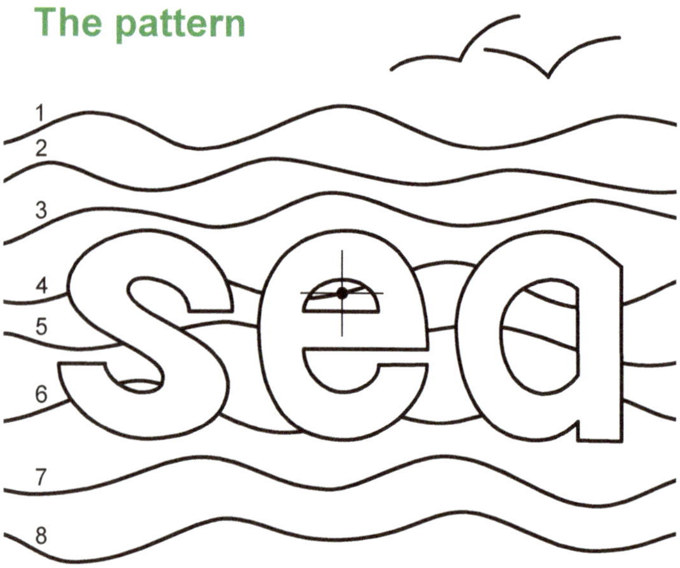


**Key:** Centre of design

## Shopping list

- Violet cotton fabric for background: 25cm (10") square
- Fabric or interfacing for backing: 25cm (10") square
- Stranded cotton thread:
  (A) dark blue (B) medium blue (C) light blue
  (D) dark aqua (E) medium aqua (F) white
- Tracing paper and other items for transferring the pattern onto the fabric

## Let's begin

Read page 15 for backing the fabric, and pages 22-25 for transferring the pattern onto the fabric, then select and use suitable methods for your fabric. For the violet fabric shown here, the pattern was transferred centrally onto the fabric by tracing with a water erasable fabric marker and then the backing fabric was tacked to the wrong side.

## Stitch!

For help, see pages 76-79 for back stitch, and pages 94-97 for stem stitch, including turning a corner, spaced stem stitch, and whipped stem stitch.

1. Stitch the letter outlines in small stem stitch, working smaller stitches around the tight curves (1 strand F). When stitching the letter 'a' work the tiny vertical line at the base of the letter with one back stitch.
2. Stitch **Wave 1** in stem stitch (1 strand A).
3. Work **Waves 2** and **3** (1 strand B), with **Wave 2** in spaced stem stitch, and **Wave 3** in stem stitch.
4. Stitch **Waves 4** and **5** (1 strand D), with **Wave 4** in spaced stem stitch and **Wave 5** in stem stitch.
5. Stitch **Waves 6** and **7** (1 strand E), with **Wave 6** in spaced stem stitch and **Wave 7** in stem stitch.
6. Work **Wave 8** in spaced stem stitch (1 strand C).
7. Using the diagram as a guide to the change in slant of the stitches (Diagram 1), stitch the seagulls in stem stitch (1 strand C). Using the same thread and changing to a tapestry needle, whip these stem stitches in the following way. Begin at a wing tip (Diagram 2), and whip to the middle of the seagull. Take the thread to the back just before the corner and emerge just after the corner. Continue whipping to the other wing tip, this time in the opposite direction (Diagram 3).

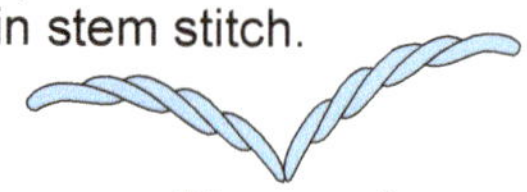

**Diagram 1**

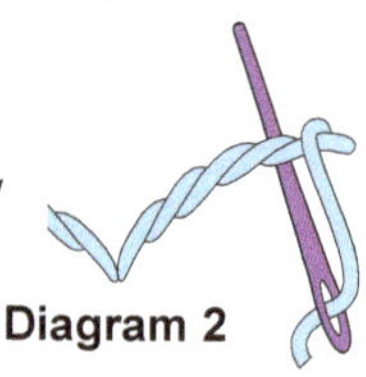

**Diagram 2**

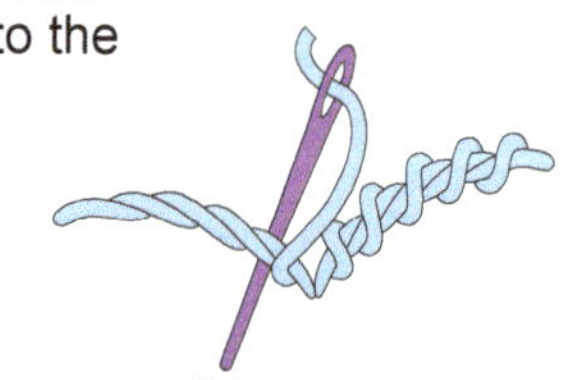

**Diagram 3**

## Let's finish

Take out the tacking. Rinse the work in cold water to remove the fabric marker. When partly dry, press or pin out work. See page 36 for pressing and for pinning out.

# Sea Breeze Scrapbooking Decorations

Add seaside charm to a page of beach memories.

## The project

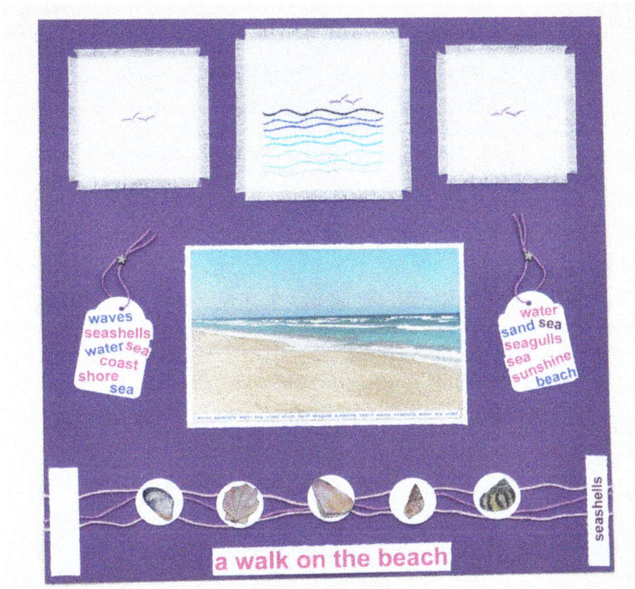


***Sea Breeze Scrapbooking Decorations***
**Featured on a page**

A trio of stitched decorations featuring the waves and seagulls from *Sea Breeze*, worked at a small scale, are used on a scrapbooking page that is dedicated to seashells and the beach.

## Shopping list

- White cotton fabric for background:
  one 15cm (6") square
  two 14cm (5 1/2") squares
- Medium weight iron-on interfacing for backing:
  one 8cm (3 1/8") square
  two 6cm (2 3/8") squares
- Threads (A), (B), (C), (D), and (E) as listed for the original design on the page opposite
- Stranded cotton thread in (F) medium violet
- Tracing paper and other items for transferring the pattern onto the fabric
- Archival double-sided sticky tape

## Let's begin

See the page opposite for the *Sea Breeze* pattern. Trace the pattern onto tracing paper, leaving out the lettering and continuing the waves across the spaces left by the omission of the letters. Reduce this pattern to 60% of its original size. Attach the squares of iron-on interfacing centrally onto the wrong side of the squares of white fabric, noting that the fabric extends beyond the backing on all sides in each case. See page 15 for backing the fabric.

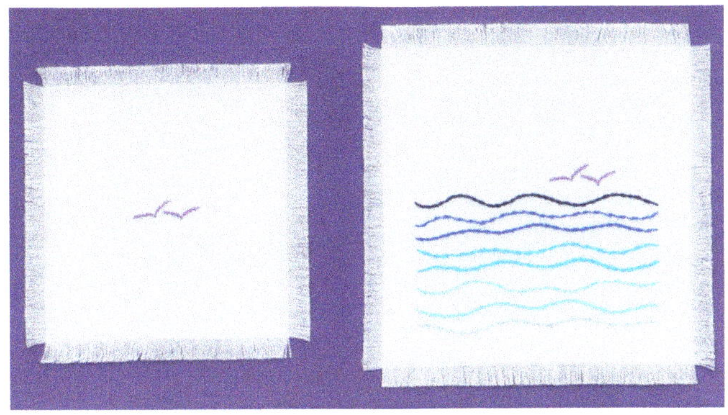

**Detail of two of the**
***Sea Breeze Scrapbooking Decorations***

Transfer the pattern centrally onto the right side of the larger square of white fabric by tracing with a water erasable fabric marker or by using transfer paper. In the same way, transfer the pattern for the seagulls centrally onto each of the smaller squares. See pages 22-25 for transferring the pattern onto the fabric.

## Stitch!

Work the designs following steps 2-7 of the stitch instructions on the facing page, substituting medium violet (F) for the seagulls in place of the original colour.

## Let's finish

Rinse the works in cold water to remove the pattern markings. When partly dry, press or pin out the works. See page 36 for pressing and for pinning out.
For each decoration, place the work with the wrong side facing up. Following the white fabric threads, trim away the excess fabric from around the work, leaving 1cm (3/8") extending outside the edge of the interfacing.
Pull several fabric threads away from all four sides of each decoration to create frayed edges, but stop fraying just before reaching the edge of the interfacing. Using archival sticky tape, attach the stitched works to the scrapbooking page in the chosen positions.

## Hint

**Other projects**
Stitched decorations like these could also be incorporated into journalling, or featured on tags or greeting cards.

# Starlit Garden

From evening twilight until dawn, the flowers shimmer in the exquisite starlight.

## The design

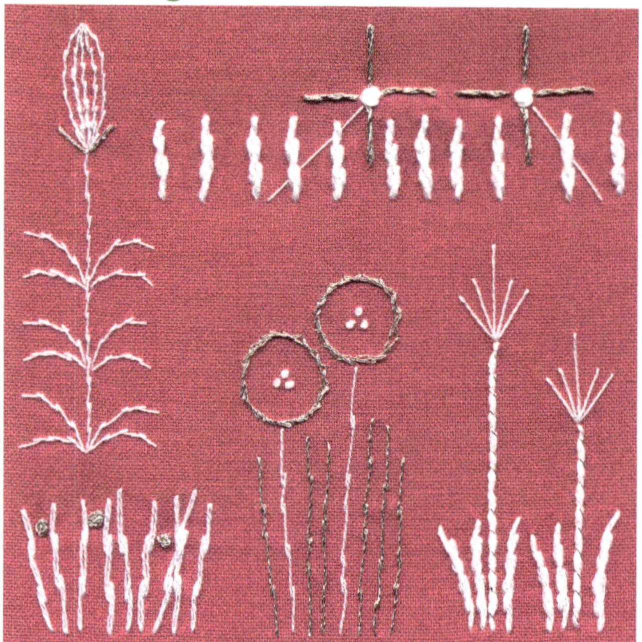

***Starlit Garden***

*Starlit Garden* is worked mostly in stem stitch, including spaced and whipped stem stitch. Straight stitch and French knot are also used. The stitches are worked in a limited colour scheme of silver metallic and white threads. Follow the instructions here to work the design as shown. To adapt for gift bags, see the next page.

## The pattern

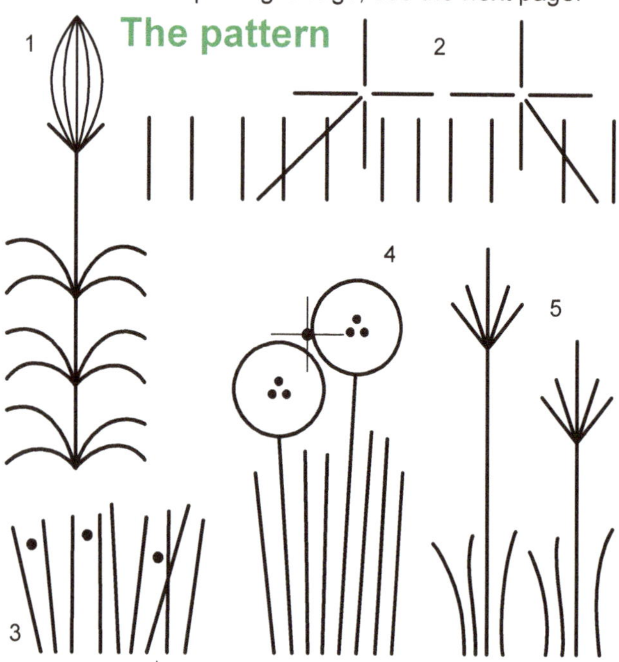


**Key:** ⊕ **Centre of design** • **French knot**

## Shopping list

- Pink cotton fabric for background: 25cm (10") square
- Fabric or interfacing for backing: 25cm (10") square
- Stranded cotton thread: (A) white
- No. 5 perlé cotton thread: (B) white
- No. 5 perlé metallic thread: (C) silver
- Tracing paper and other items for transferring the pattern onto the fabric

## Let's begin

Read page 15 for backing the fabric, and pages 22-25 for transferring the pattern onto the fabric, then select and use suitable methods for your fabric. For the pink fabric shown here, the pattern was transferred centrally onto the fabric by tracing with a water erasable fabric marker and then the backing fabric was tacked to the wrong side.

## Stitch!

For help, see pages 40-43 for straight stitch, 94-97 for stem stitch, including completing a shape, spaced stem stitch, and whipped stem stitch. See pages 184-187 for French knot, and also page 17 for preparing perlé metallic thread.

**Flower 1** Work the stem, leaves, and the five lines forming the bud in spaced stem stitch (1 strand A). Below the bud, add a straight stitch to each side (4 ply C).

**Flower 2** Work the petals in straight stitch (8 ply C). Add a two wrap French knot at each flower centre (1 strand B). Work the flower stems in straight stitch (1 strand A). Over the stems, work the leaves in stem stitch (1 strand B).

**Flower 3** Work the leaves in spaced stem stitch (2 strands A). Add French knots, each with two wraps, for the flowers (4 ply C).

**Flower 4** Work the two stems in uneven spaced stem stitch (1 strand A). Stitch the leaves in uneven spaced stem stitch (2 ply C). Work a circle of stem stitch for each flower (2 ply C). For the flower centres, add three French knots, each with two wraps (1 strand A).

**Flower 5** Work the flowers in straight stitch with the lower end of each stitch worked down through the same hole in the fabric (1 strand A). Work the stems and leaves in stem stitch (3 strands A), and then whip the stems (Diagram 1) with silver thread (1 ply C).

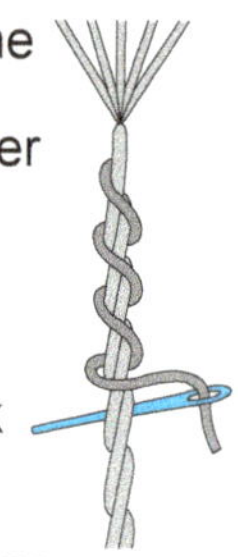

**Diagram 1**

## Let's finish

Take out the tacking. Rinse the work in cold water to remove the water erasable fabric marker. When partly dry, press or pin out the work. See page 36 for pressing and for pinning out.

## Hint

**Using perlé metallic thread**

Whipping a row of stitches with a tiny amount of silver thread creates a delicate shimmering effect.

# Starlit Garden Gift Bags

Create glittering charms to organza gift bags.

## The project

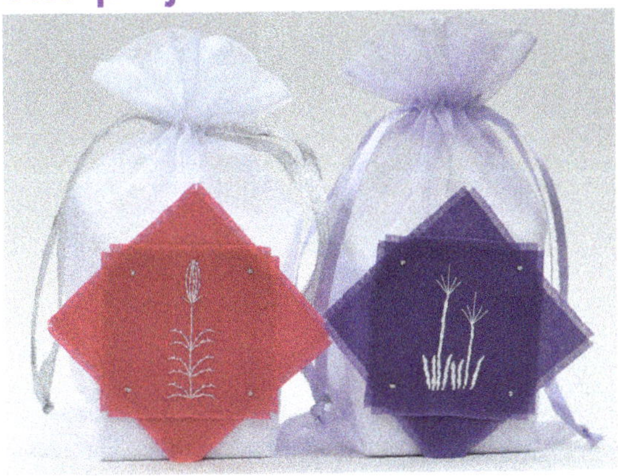

***Starlit Garden Gift Bags***

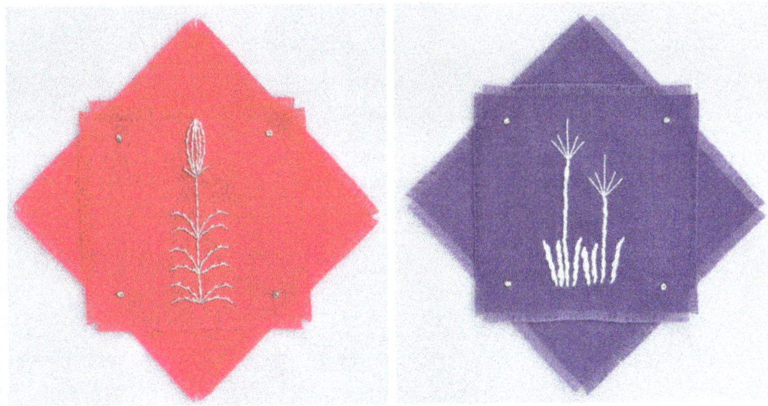

**Details of *Starlit Garden Gift Bags***

A patch, created from two layers of pink fabric, is worked with **Flower 1** and then attached to the purchased white organza bag. In a similar way, a violet patch is worked with **Flower 5** and attached to the violet bag. These bags are filled with soaps.

## Shopping list

***White bag***

- White organza bag: approximately 24cm x 15cm wide (9 1/2" x 6")
- Pink cotton fabric, cut along the fabric threads: one 7.5cm (3") square, and one 9cm (3 1/2") square
- Threads (A) and (C) as listed for the design on the page opposite
- Machine sewing thread: pink
- Tracing paper and other items for transferring the pattern onto the fabric

***Violet bag***

- Violet organza bag: approximately 24cm x 15cm wide (9 1/2" x 6")
- Violet cotton fabric, cut along the fabric threads: one 7.5cm (3") square, and one 9cm (3 1/2") square
- Threads (A) and (C) as listed for the design on the page opposite
- Machine sewing thread: violet
- Tracing paper and other items for transferring the pattern onto the fabric

## Let's begin

See the page opposite for the pattern.

***White bag***

Transfer the pattern for **Flower 1** centrally onto the small pink fabric square by tracing with a chalk-based pencil. See page 23 for transferring the pattern by tracing. Place this square centrally onto the large pink fabric square that has been rotated by 45 degrees. Tack these two layers together.

***Violet bag***

Transfer the pattern onto the fabric and tack the two layers together in the same way as for the white bag, this time using the pattern for **Flower 5** and the two squares of violet fabric.

## Stitch!

***White bag***

Stitch the flower following the stitch instructions for **Flower 1** on the page opposite.

Using 4 ply of (C), work a two wrap French knot through both layers in each corner of the small fabric square, securing the thread ends behind each. Take out the tacking and press this two-layered patch. See page 36 for pressing. Pull a few fabric threads away from all four sides of the two fabric squares to create frayed edges. Pin the patch centrally onto the front of the white organza bag. Carefully turn the bag inside out. Using the matching machine sewing thread, attach the patch to the bag by working small hand stitches through both the organza and the back of the French knots and the back of the stitches of the flower. Turn the bag through to the right side and remove the pins.

***Violet bag***

Work the violet bag in the same way as the white bag, instead working **Flower 5** from the original design on the page opposite and using violet fabric squares instead of the pink ones.

## Hints

**Not recommended to press organza bags**

As some organza fabrics will melt if pressed, even with the iron set to a low temperature, it is not recommended to press these gift bags.

**Use other designs**

Small elements from many of the designs in this book would be suitable to feature on a gift bag following these instructions, for example a chocolate from *Fine Chocolates* on page 68, or a heart from *Hearts and Flowers* on page 198.

# Herringbone stitch

## and variations

Herringbone stitch is quick and easy. It is worked as a row of crossing stitches, giving a plaited appearance. Herringbone stitch is particularly useful for borders or for filling spaces.

Herringbone stitch can take many forms. It can be worked with all stitches the same size and distance apart, giving an even look, or the stitches can vary freely along the row. When the stitches are worked so that they touch along the upper and lower edges of the row, it is called closed herringbone stitch.

This stitch is useful for representing textures ranging from thin and delicate to thick and chunky. For a dense version of herringbone stitch, a second row can be worked in the spaces between the stitches of the first row, using the same or different thread.

To create an interesting lattice pattern, herringbone stitch can be worked as stacked rows. Herringbone stitch can be used alone or with an outline of another stitch such as back stitch or stem stitch.

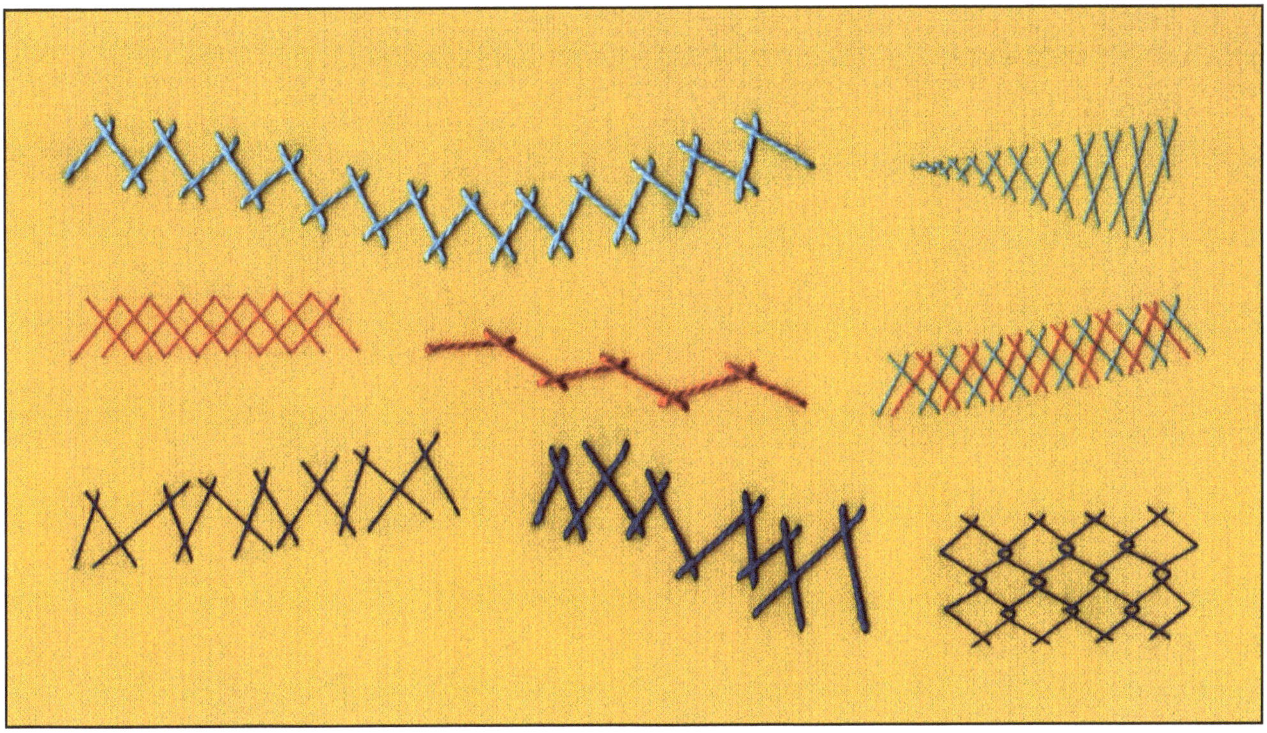

# Herringbone stitch and variations sampler

Herringbone stitch worked between two parallel lines

Herringbone stitch worked to fill a triangle

Closed herringbone stitch

Spaced herringbone stitch

Two rows of herringbone stitch, the second worked in the spaces of the first

Herringbone stitch with irregular spacing

Herringbone stitch with irregular spacing and irregular height

Stacked rows of herringbone stitch

# Herringbone stitch and variations

## Hints

Herringbone stitch is most commonly worked by skimming the needle in and out of the fabric before pulling the thread through.

Herringbone stitch is easily worked between two marked pattern lines. As this stitch will not cover these lines, use a removable transfer method for marking the pattern onto the fabric.

Do not work herringbone stitch with the tension of the thread too tight or the fabric will not lie flat.

## Herringbone stitch and variations: right-handed

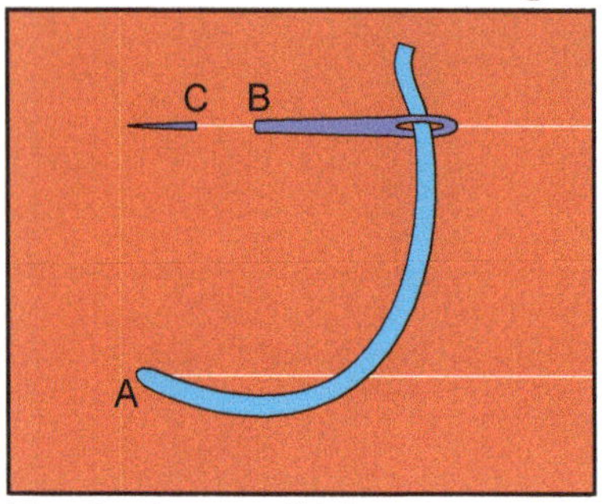


**Herringbone stitch**
**1** Come up at A. With thread below needle, take needle down at B and emerge at C. Note that B and C are both to the right of A.

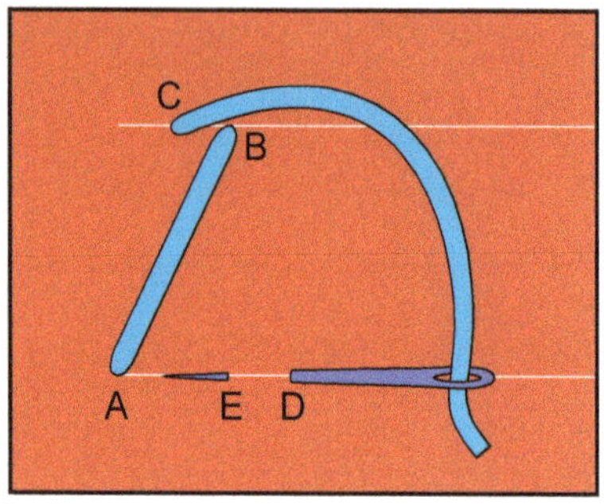


**2** Pull the thread through. With the thread above the needle, take the needle down at D and emerge at E, which is directly below B.

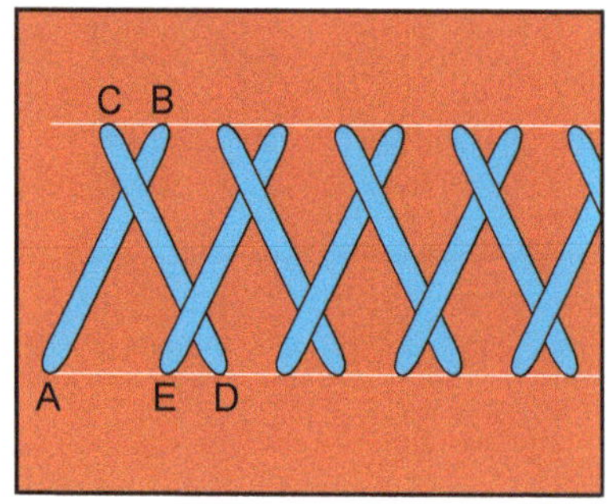


**3** Pull the thread through. Continue along the row, alternating between the upper and the lower marked pattern lines.

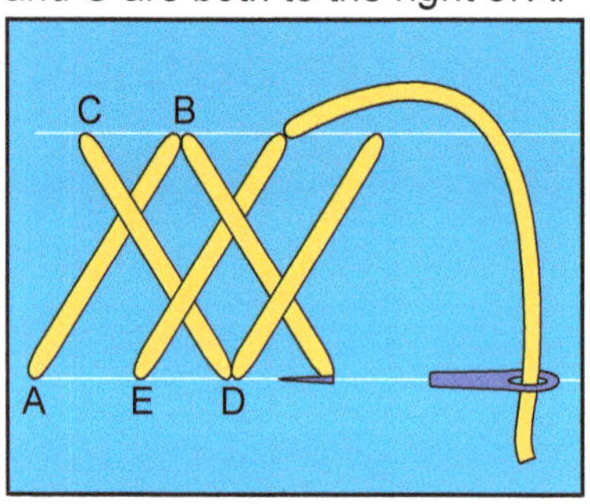


**Closed herringbone stitch**
Note that at B and D, and subsequent stitches, the needle emerges through the same fabric hole as a previously worked stitch.

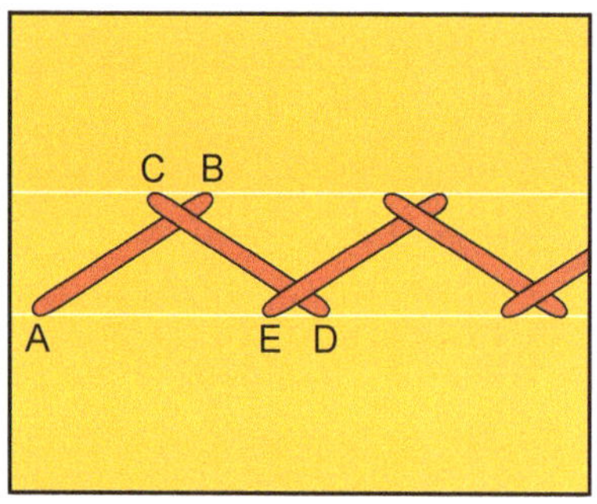


**Spaced herringbone stitch**
Work in a similar way to herringbone stitch, noting that this variation is elongated sideways.

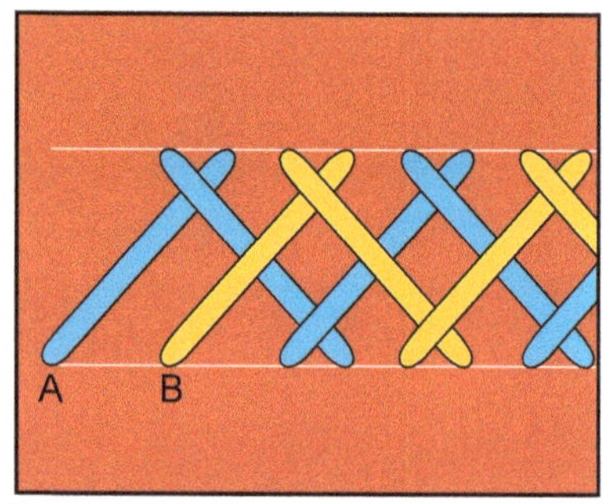


**Two rows of herringbone stitch**
Beginning at A, work a row of spaced herringbone stitch. Beginning at B with a new thread, work a second row in the spaces.

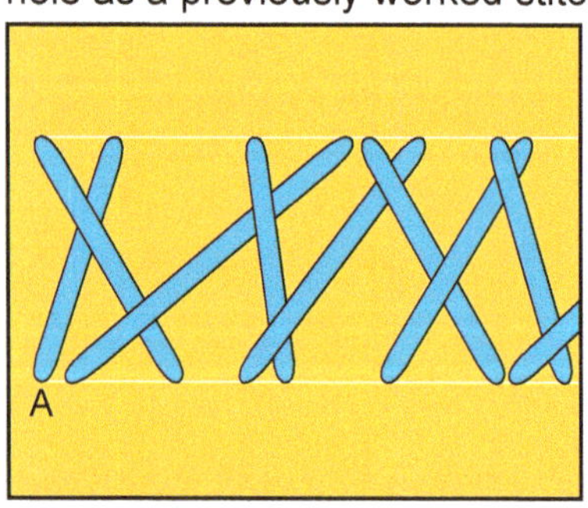


**Irregular spacing**
Vary the widths of the stitches and the distances between them. Note that the slant of the stitches varies along the row.

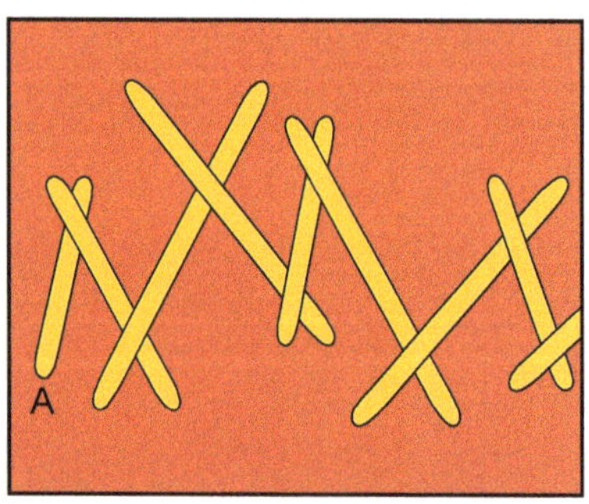


**Irregular spacing and height**
Vary widths and heights of stitches, and distances between them. Note that the slant of the stitches varies along the row.

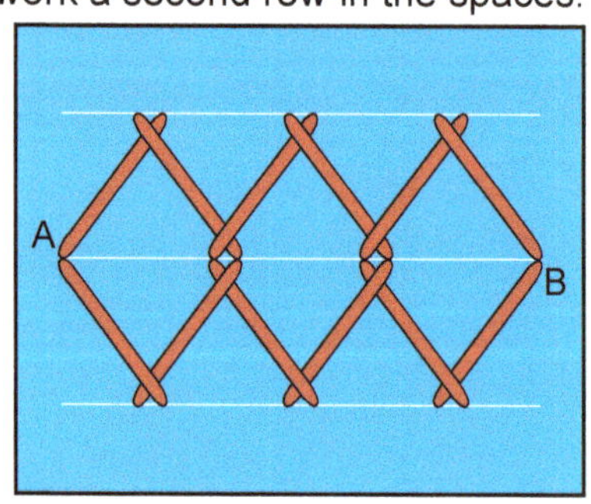


**Stacked rows**
Work two or more aligned rows of herringbone stitch by securing first row at B, then rotating work and stitching next row.

# Herringbone stitch and variations: left-handed

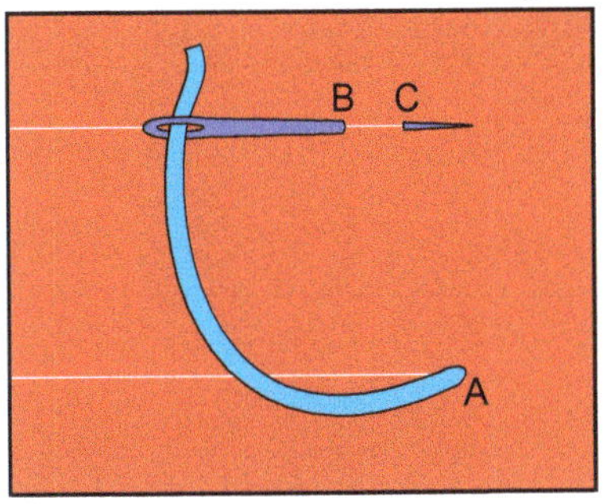


**Herringbone stitch**
**1** Come up at A. With thread below needle, take needle down at B and emerge at C. Note that B and C are both to the right of A.

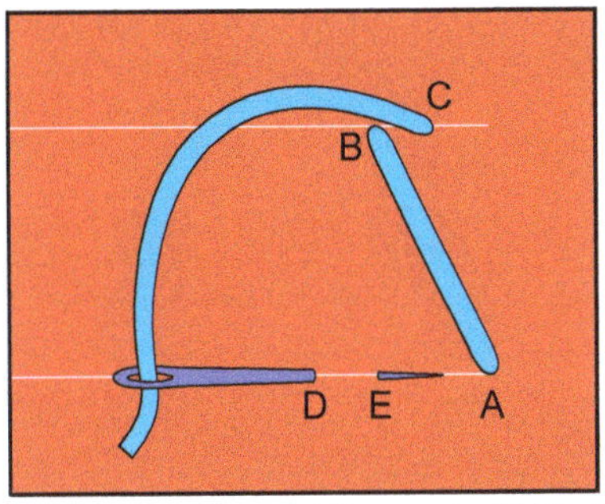


**2** Pull the thread through. With the thread above the needle, take the needle down at D and emerge at E, which is directly below B.

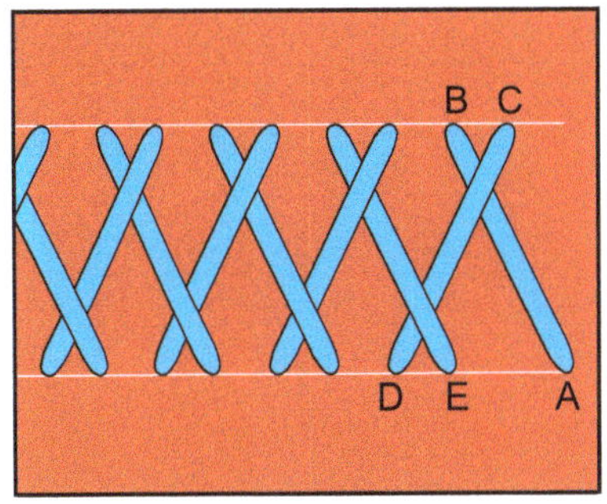


**3** Pull the thread through. Continue along the row, alternating between the upper and the lower marked pattern lines.

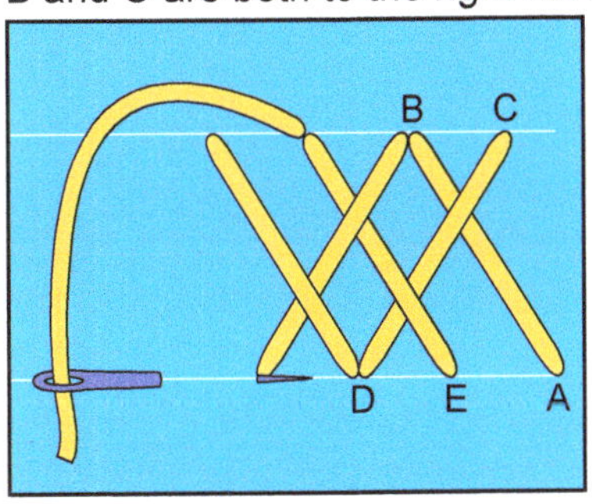


**Closed herringbone stitch**
Note that at B and D, and subsequent stitches, the needle emerges through the same fabric hole as a previously worked stitch.

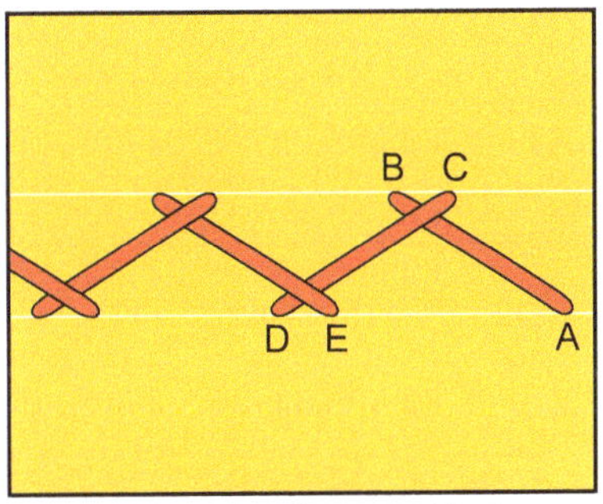


**Spaced herringbone stitch**
Work in a similar way to herringbone stitch, noting that this variation is elongated sideways.

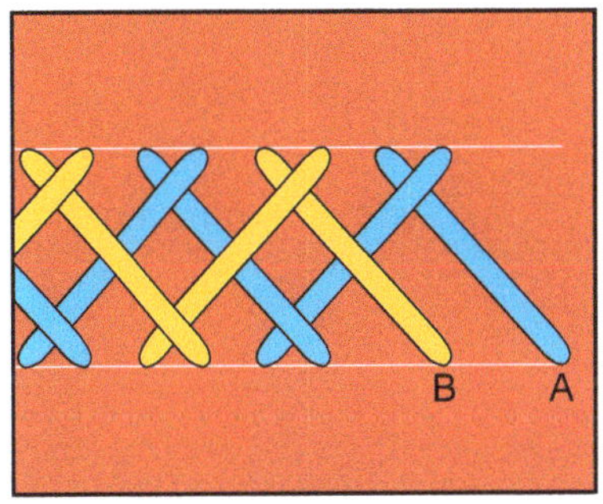


**Two rows of herringbone stitch**
Beginning at A, work a row of spaced herringbone stitch. Beginning at B with a new thread, work a second row in the spaces.

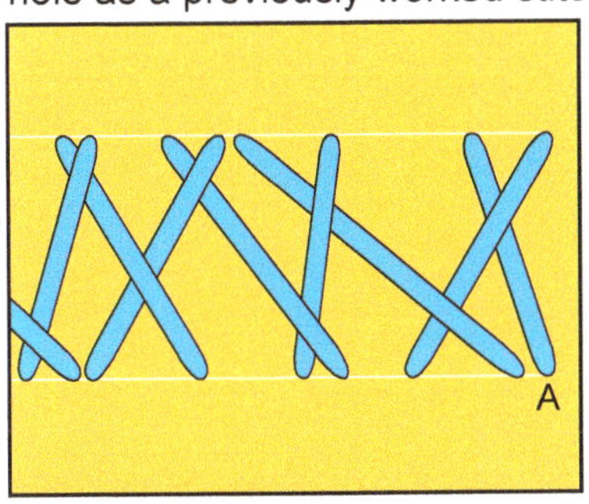


**Irregular spacing**
Vary the widths of the stitches and the distances between them. Note that the slant of the stitches varies along the row.

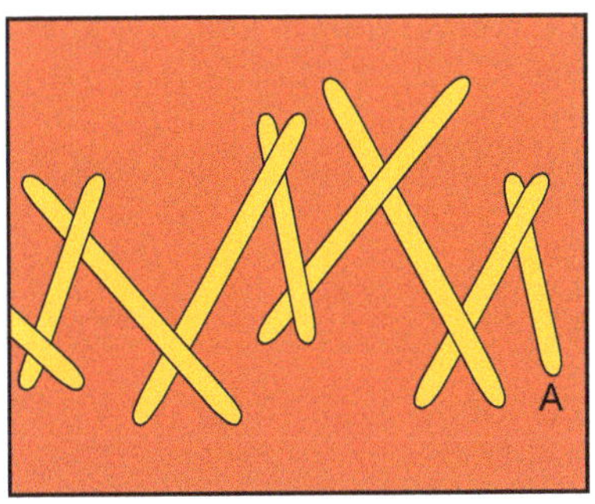


**Irregular spacing and height**
Vary widths and heights of stitches, and distances between them. Note that the slant of the stitches varies along the row.

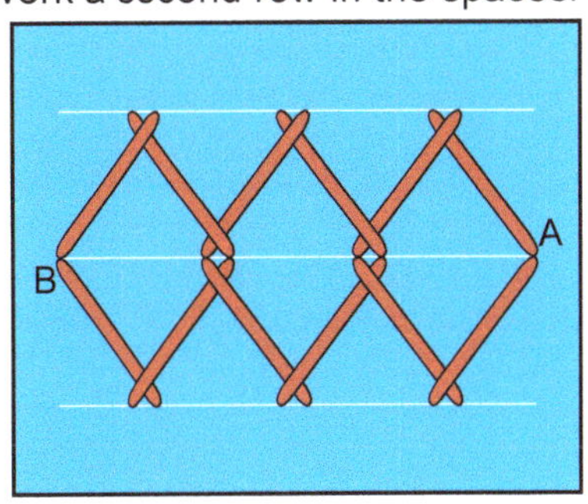


**Stacked rows**
Work two or more aligned rows of herringbone stitch by securing first row at B, then rotating work and stitching next row.

# Herringbone stitch
## and variations

# Designs and project ideas

## The designs

Trusty Tortoise

Ice Cream Treat

Cosmic Starburst

Sunshine Daffodils

Rainy Day

Tropical Palms

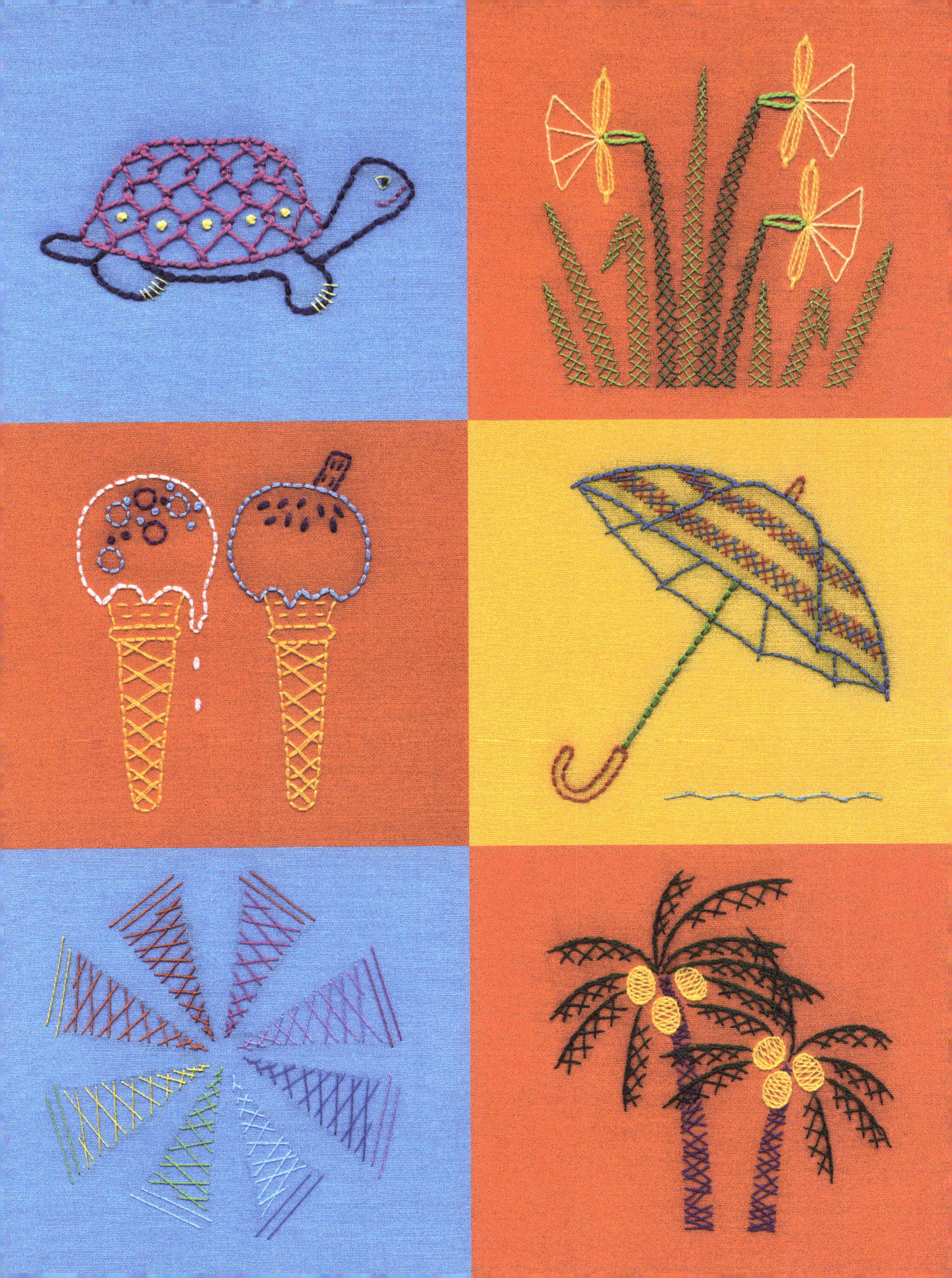

# Trusty Tortoise

Slow and steady wins the race!

## The design

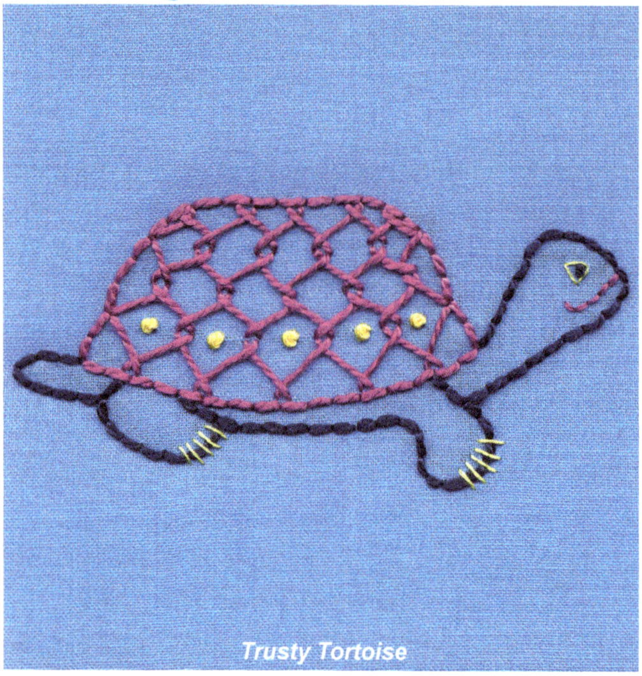

*Trusty Tortoise*

Stacked rows of spaced herringbone stitch using perlé cotton thread create the textured diamond pattern on the shell of the tortoise. Other details are worked in straight stitch, back stitch, and French knot.

This design may at first appear complicated, but actually it is easy to work. Use the instructions on this page to work *Trusty Tortoise* as shown here on an aqua background. To apply the design to a project, see the idea on the next page where it is worked as a patch on a cushion cover.

## The pattern

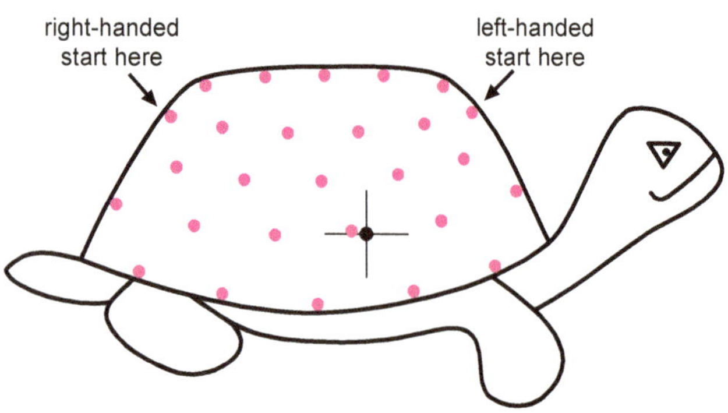


Key:
- ┼ Centre of design
- ➘ Begin herringbone stitch here
- • Place herringbone stitches here
- • French knot

## Shopping list

- Aqua cotton fabric for background: 25cm (10") square
- Fabric or interfacing for backing: 25cm (10") square
- Stranded cotton thread:
  (A) dark blue (B) light yellow (C) medium magenta
- No. 5 perlé cotton thread:
  (D) dark blue (E) medium magenta
- Tracing paper and other items for transferring the pattern onto the fabric

## Let's begin

Read page 15 for backing the fabric, and pages 22-25 for transferring the pattern onto the fabric, then select and use suitable methods for your fabric. For the aqua fabric shown here, the pattern was transferred centrally onto the fabric by tracing with a water erasable fabric marker and then the backing fabric was tacked to the wrong side.

## Stitch!

For help, see pages 40-43 for straight stitch, 76-79 for back stitch, 112-115 for spaced herringbone stitch, and pages 184-187 for French knot.

1. Work the outline for the shell of the tortoise in back stitch (1 strand E).
2. Starting at the marked dot, work a row of spaced herringbone stitch across the shell (1 strand E), placing the stitches either side of the dots. At the last dot take the thread to the back of the work (Diagram 1). Pass the thread under the back of a previously worked stitch, then take the thread to the front at the same dot (Diagram 2).
3. Turn the work upside down. Using the same lower holes as the first row, work a second row creating a diamond pattern (Diagram 3). Continue in the same way until four rows have been worked.
4. Add a row of two wrap French knots to the shell (4 strands B). Work the tail, legs, body and head in back stitch (1 strand D). Add five claws on each foot in straight stitch (1 strand B).
5. Stitch the eye with three back stitches (1 strand B), then add the pupil with a two wrap French knot (2 strands A).
6. Work the mouth in back stitch (2 strands C).

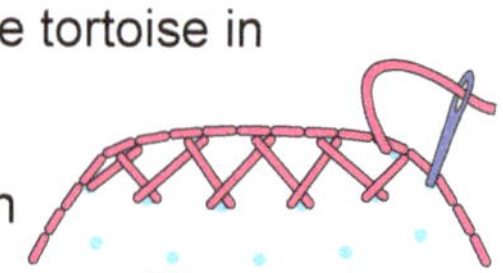

**Diagram 1**

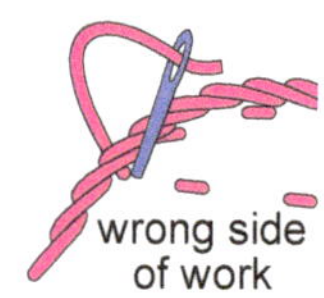


**Diagram 2**

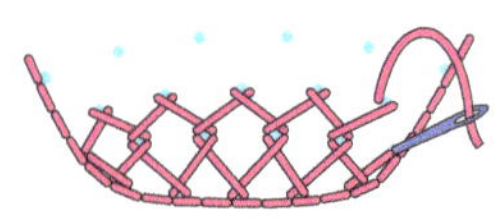

**Diagram 3**

## Let's finish

Take out the tacking. Rinse the work in cold water to remove the water erasable fabric marker. When partly dry, press or pin out the work. See page 36 for pressing and for pinning out.

# Trusty Tortoise Cushion Cover

Slow down and relax with this inviting cushion.

## The project

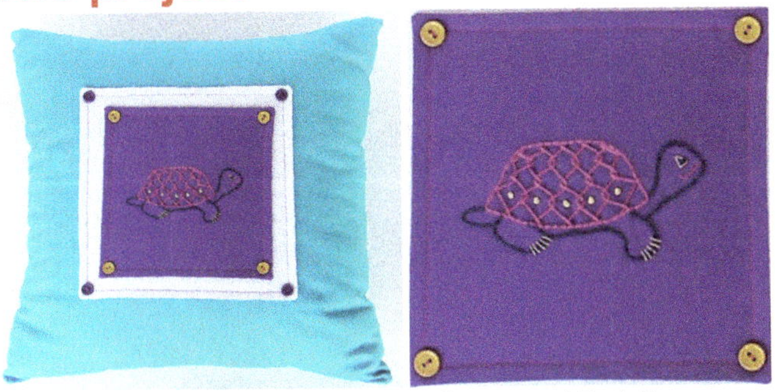

***Trusty Tortoise Cushion Cover*** **and Detail**

This purchased cushion cover features *Trusty Tortoise* worked at a larger scale on a violet patch. A larger patch, this time in white, is attached behind the violet patch. Both are then stitched onto the aqua cushion cover. Buttons are attached at the corners of each patch to add interest.
The size of this cushion is 40cm (16") square.

## Shopping list

- Aqua cushion cover and insert
- Violet cotton fabric for the violet patch: two 18cm (7") squares
- White cotton fabric for the white patch: two 22cm (8 3/4") squares
- Lightweight iron-on interfacing for backing: one 18cm (7") square one 22cm (8 3/4") square
- Threads as listed for the original design on the page opposite
- Machine sewing thread: violet, white, and magenta
- Four yellow buttons
- Four violet buttons
- Tracing paper and other items for transferring the pattern onto the fabric

## Let's begin

See the page opposite for the pattern.
Prepare the pattern by enlarging it to 125% of its original size.
Following the instructions on page 15 for backing the fabric, attach one square of interfacing onto the wrong side of one violet square and one white square.
Transfer the pattern centrally onto the right side of the backed violet square using transfer paper. See page 24 for transferring the pattern using transfer paper.

## Stitch!

Work the tortoise following steps 1-6 of the stitch instructions on the facing page.

## Let's finish

Rinse the work in cold water to remove the pattern markings. When almost dry, press. See page 36 for pressing.
With right sides together, pin the stitched square onto the second violet square around the edge. Using matching machine sewing thread and a 1cm (3/8") seam allowance, machine stitch around the square, leaving an 8cm (3") opening in the lower side. Trim the seam allowances and cut away the excess fabric at the corners (Diagram 1).

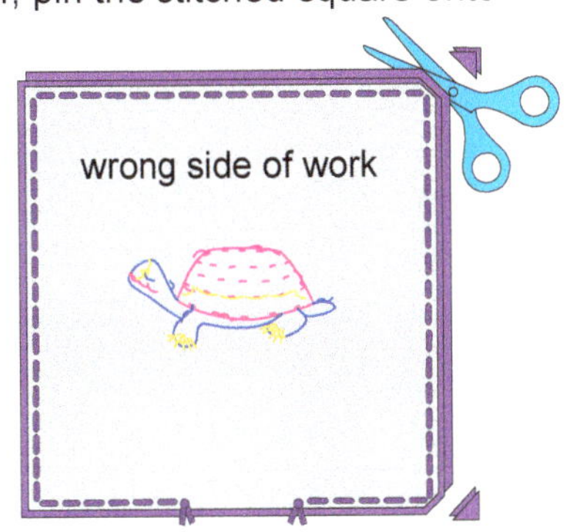


**Diagram 1**

Turn the patch to the right side through the opening and press.
Hand stitch the opening closed.
Make up the white patch in the same way.
With the design facing up, place the violet patch centrally over the white patch and tack the patches together.

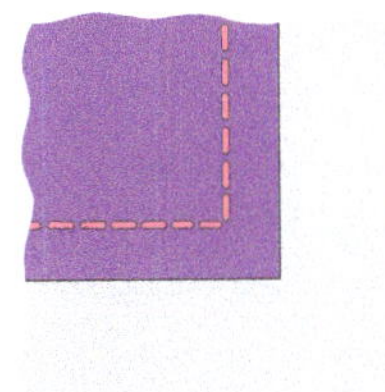

**Diagram 2**

Using magenta machine sewing thread and stitching through both patches, machine stitch around the violet patch 1cm (3/8") in from its edges, then take out the tacking (Diagram 2).
Remove the cushion insert.
Place the joined patches onto the centre of the front of the cushion cover and tack in place.

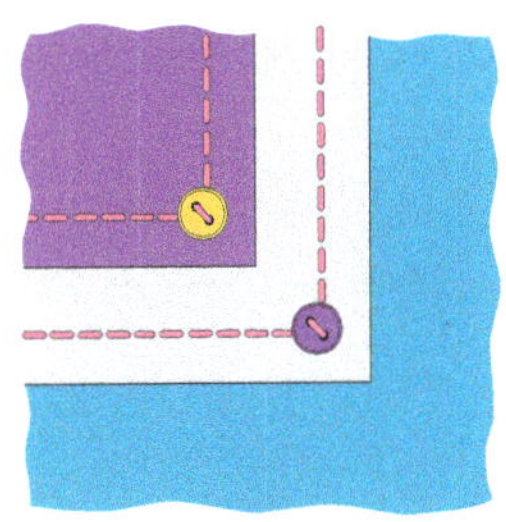

**Diagram 3**

Again using the magenta machine sewing thread, attach the white patch to the front of the cushion cover by machine stitching 1cm (3/8") in from its edges (see Diagram 3).
Take out the tacking. Using the magenta machine sewing thread, attach four yellow buttons at the corners of the violet patch and four violet buttons at the corners of the white patch with hand stitches (Diagram 3).
Press, avoiding the buttons. Place the cushion insert back inside the cover.

# Sunshine Daffodils

Beautiful daffodils dancing in the warm sunshine.

## The design

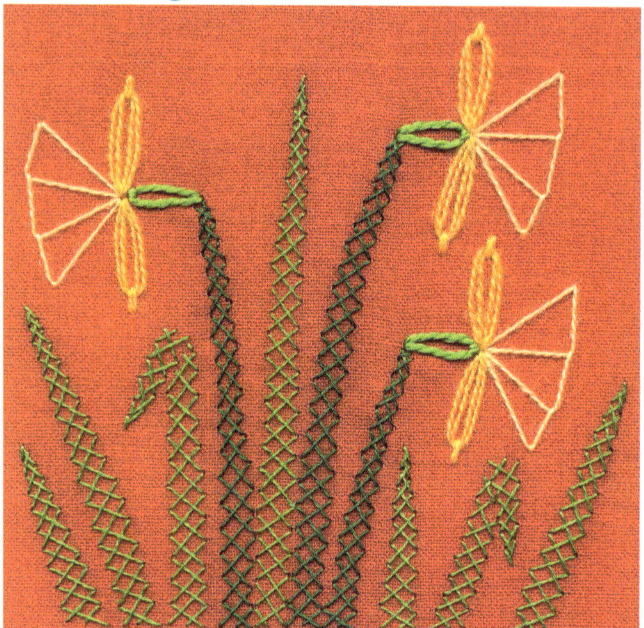

*Sunshine Daffodils*

Closed herringbone stitch is used in this design to quickly fill the shapes of the leaves and stems without any need for a stitched outline. The flowers are worked in straight stitch, blanket stitch, and detached chain stitch. Follow the instructions here to work the design as above. To adapt *Sunshine Daffodils* for use on a scrapbooking page, see opposite.

## The pattern

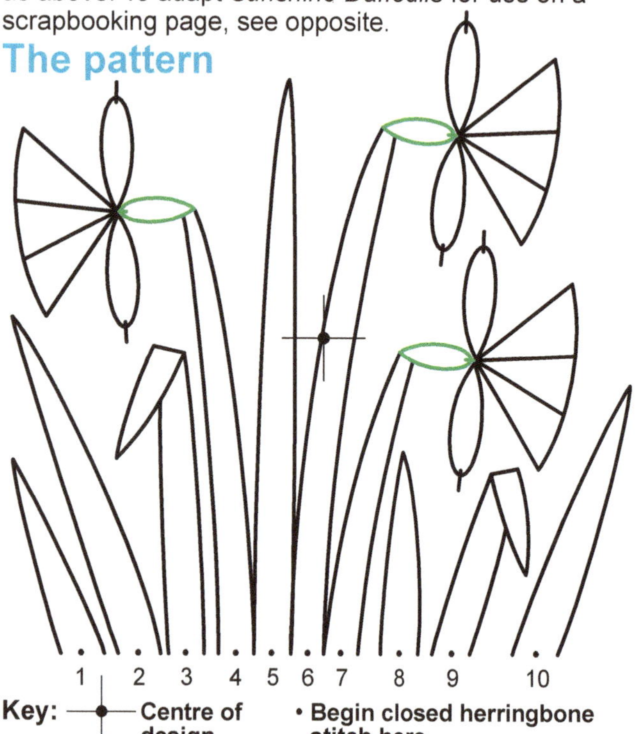


## Shopping list

- Red cotton fabric for background: 25cm (10") square
- Fabric or interfacing for backing: 25cm (10") square
- Stranded cotton thread:
  (A) medium green (B) light green
- No. 5 perlé cotton thread: (C) light green
- Fine 2 ply wool yarn:
  (D) light yellow (E) very light yellow
- Tracing paper and other items for transferring the pattern onto the fabric

## Let's begin

Read page 15 for backing the fabric, and pages 22-25 for transferring the pattern onto the fabric, then select and use suitable methods for your fabric. For the red fabric shown here, the pattern was transferred centrally onto the fabric by tracing with a water erasable fabric marker and then the backing fabric was tacked to the wrong side.

## Stitch!

For help, see pages 40-43 for straight stitch, 112-115 for closed herringbone stitch, 130-133 for blanket stitch, and pages 166-169 for detached chain stitch. Turn the work on its side when stitching the closed herringbone stitch.

1 Beginning at the base of **Leaf 1** at the marked dot (Diagram 1), stitch the leaf in closed herringbone stitch (1 strand B). Towards the leaf tip, work the stitches closer together and more angled, to fit the shape. End the last stitch at the tip (Diagram 2). Work **Leaves 2**, **5**, **8**, and **10** in the same way.

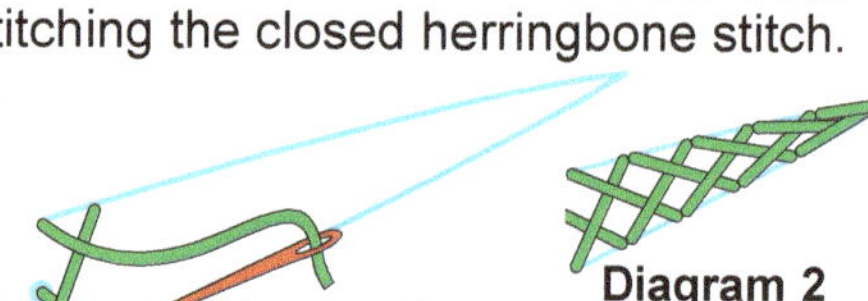

Diagram 1

Diagram 2

2 In closed herringbone stitch, work **Leaves 3** and **9**, which have folded tips, in two stages (1 strand B). First stitch the upper section, beginning at the fold and stitching towards the tip. Then work the lower section, beginning at the base and tapering to fit the shape.

3 Stitch **Flower stems 4**, **6**, and **7** in closed herringbone stitch, tapering to fit the shape (1 strand A).

4 At the top of each stem, work a green detached chain stitch (1 strand C).

5 At the anchor of the green stitch, add two detached chain stitch petals (2 strands D). Begin each daffodil trumpet with one straight stitch (1 strand E), worked from A to the base of the petals.

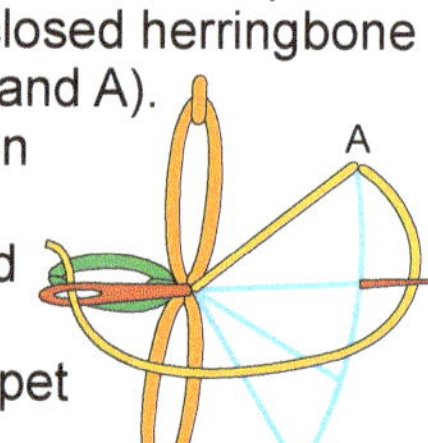


Diagram 3

6 Emerge again at A (Diagram 3) and stitch three blanket stitches worked through the same hole in the fabric at the bases of the petals. Anchor the third blanket stitch.

## Let's finish

Take out tacking. Rinse the work gently in cold water to remove fabric marker. When partly dry, press or pin out the work. See page 36 for pressing and for pinning out.

# Sunshine Daffodils Scrapbooking Decorations

Decorate a scrapbooking page with these sunny spring daffodils.

## The project

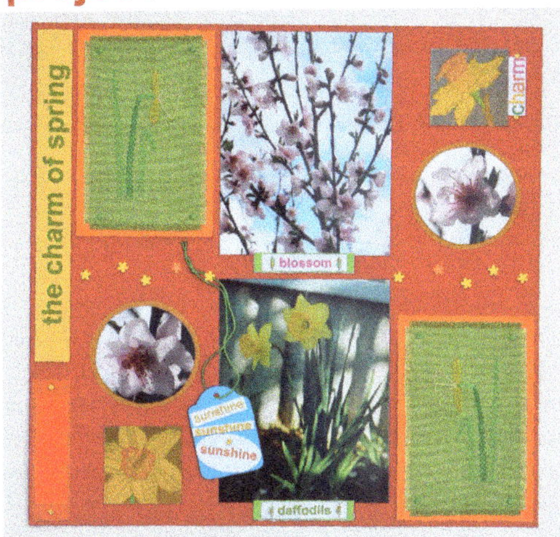


***Sunshine Daffodils Scrapbooking Decorations*** **Featured on a page**

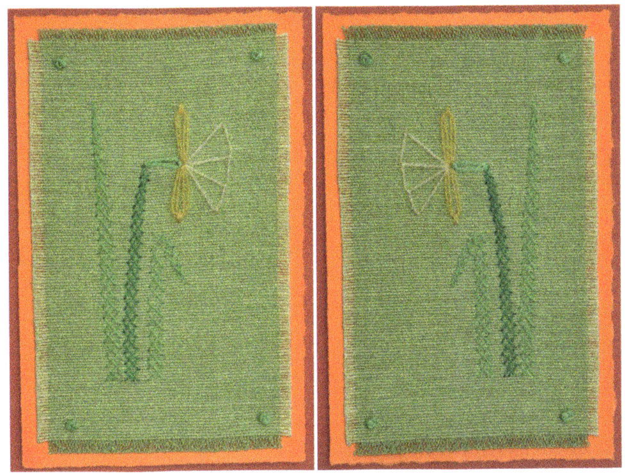

**Details of** ***Sunshine Daffodils Scrapbooking Decorations***

A pair of stitched decorations, each featuring a single daffodil from the design, are used on a scrapbooking page that is dedicated to spring flowers. French knots are added to the corners of the decorations for interest.

## Shopping list

- Light green cotton fabric for background: two pieces 17cm x 13cm wide (6 1/2" x 5")
- Medium weight iron-on interfacing for backing: two pieces 11cm x 6.5cm wide (4 1/4" x 2 1/2")
- Threads as listed for the original design on the page opposite
- Tracing paper and other items for transferring the pattern onto the fabric
- Orange card, torn to size: two pieces 13cm x 8.5cm wide (5" x 3 1/4")
- Archival double-sided and single-sided sticky tapes

## Let's begin

See the page opposite for the pattern.
Attach the pieces of iron-on interfacing centrally onto the wrong side of the pieces of green fabric, noting that the green fabric extends beyond the backing on all sides. See page 15 for backing the fabric. Transfer the left hand daffodil and **Leaves 3** and **5** centrally onto the right side of one piece of green fabric by tracing with a water erasable fabric marker or by using transfer paper. Transfer a mirrored copy of the same daffodil and leaves centrally onto the other. See pages 22-25 for transferring the pattern onto the fabric and page 20 for information on mirroring the pattern.

## Stitch!

Work the leaves and flowers following the relevant steps of the stitch instructions on the previous page.

## Let's finish

Rinse the works very gently in cold water to remove the pattern markings. When partly dry, press or pin them out. See page 36 for pressing and for pinning out. Place each work with the wrong side facing up. Following the fabric threads, trim away excess fabric from around each work, leaving 5mm (1/4") extending outside the edge of the interfacing. Pull several fabric threads away from all four sides of each to create patches with frayed edges, but stop fraying just before reaching the edge of the interfacing. Using archival sticky tape, attach each stitched work centrally onto one of the pieces of torn orange card. Add a green one wrap French knot (1 strand C) at each corner of the two decorations by working the French knots through all layers and securing the threads on the back of the orange card with single sided sticky tape. See pages 184-187 for French knot. Attach these decorations to the background of the scrapbooking page in their chosen positions.

## Hints

**Using wool yarn**

Items stitched with wool yarn should only be washed very gently by hand in cold water to avoid shrinkage or matting of the wool.

**Use other designs**

Many of the designs in this book, or selected elements from them, can be worked as decorations for scrapbooking pages.

# Ice Cream Treat

Nothing is better than an icy cold ice cream on a hot summer's day.

## The design

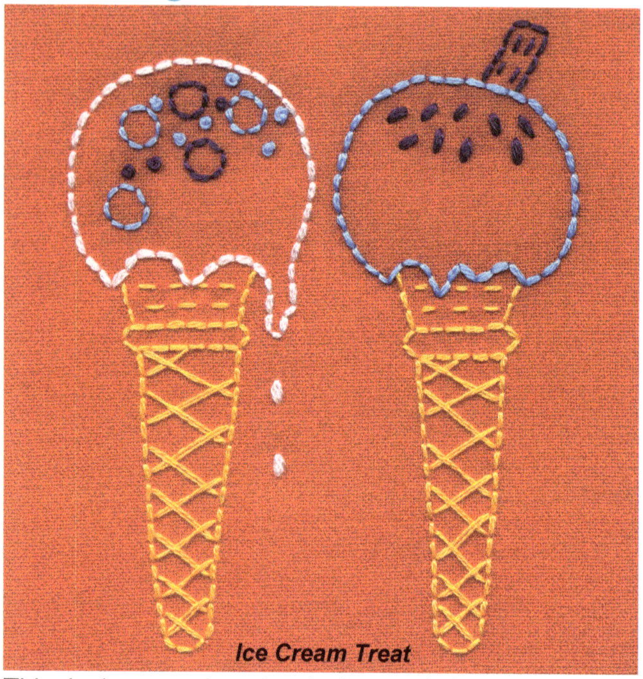


This design uses long herringbone stitches to represent the surface pattern on the ice cream cones. Other details are worked in straight stitch, running stitch, back stitch, and French knot.

To work the design as shown here, use the instructions on this page. To adapt the design for a project, see the idea on the following page where ice creams are featured as decorations for a child's room.

## The pattern

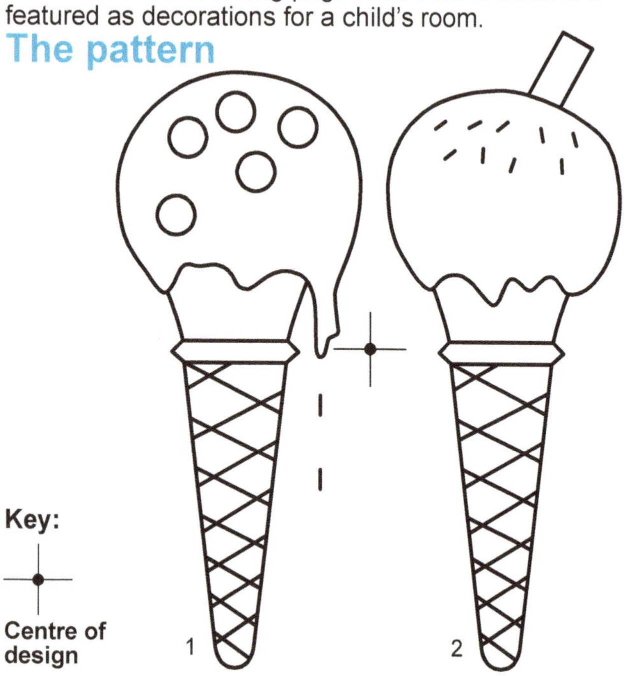


## Shopping list

- Red cotton fabric for background: 25cm (10") square
- Fabric or interfacing for backing: 25cm (10") square
- Stranded cotton thread:
  (A) dark violet (B) medium aqua
  (C) medium yellow (D) white
- Tracing paper and other items for transferring the pattern onto the fabric

## Let's begin

Read page 15 for backing the fabric, and pages 22-25 for transferring the pattern onto the fabric, then select and use suitable methods for your fabric. For the red fabric shown here, the pattern was transferred centrally onto the fabric by tracing with a water erasable fabric marker and then the backing fabric was tacked to the wrong side.

## Stitch!

For help, see pages 40-43 for straight stitch, 58-61 for running stitch, 76-79 for back stitch, 112-115 for herringbone stitch, and pages 184-187 for French knot. Turn the design on its side for working the herringbone stitch on the ice cream cones.

**Ice cream 1**

1 Work the cone outline, including the ridge, in back stitch (2 strands C).
2 Referring to the photo, stitch the broken lines across the top section of the cone with two rows of running stitch (2 strands C).
3 Following the marked lines, fill the lower section of the cone with long herringbone stitches (2 strands C).
4 Work the outline for the ice cream in back stitch (3 strands D).
5 Add two drips, each with two straight stitches worked through the same two holes in the fabric (3 strands D).
6 Using the photo as a guide, add the large lollies in back stitch, then scatter French knots, each worked with two wraps, for the sprinkles (2 strands A or B).

**Ice cream 2**

1 Work the cone following steps 1-3 for **Ice cream 1**.
2 Work the outline for the ice cream in back stitch (3 strands B).
3 Stitch the outline for the chocolate stick in back stitch, then add four running stitches inside the outline (2 strands A).
4 Stitch the choc chips, each with three straight stitches worked through the same two holes in the fabric (2 strands A).

## Let's finish

Take out the tacking. Rinse the work in water to remove the fabric marker. When partly dry, press or pin out the work. See page 36 for pressing and for pinning out.

# Ice Cream Treat Decorations

Decorate a child's room with these colourful ice creams.

## The project

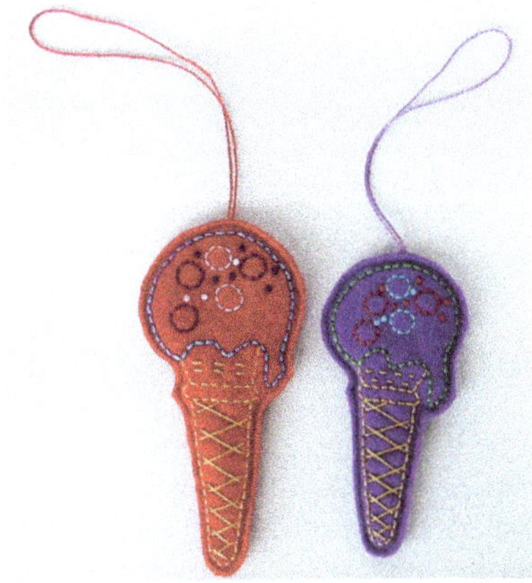

*Ice Cream Treat Decorations*

These felt decorations are playful ways to adapt **Ice cream 1** from the design. They are worked on felt pieces that are later made up into double-sided shapes. For both decorations, the ice cream drips have been omitted, the pattern has been enlarged, and new colour schemes are used. The violet ice cream is 11cm (4 1/4") in height, and the red ice cream is 13cm (5").

## Shopping list

***Violet ice cream***

- Violet felt fabric for the ice cream shape: two pieces 15cm x 10cm wide (6" x 4")
- Grey lightweight iron-on interfacing for backing: two pieces 15cm x 10cm wide (6" x 4")
- Thin wadding: one piece 13cm x 7cm wide (5" x 3")
- Stranded cotton thread: (A) medium aqua (B) medium red (C) medium yellow (D) light green
- No. 5 perlé cotton thread: medium violet
- Machine sewing thread: violet
- Tracing paper and other items for transferring the pattern onto the felt

***Red ice cream***

- Red felt fabric for the ice cream shape: two pieces 17cm x 10cm wide (7" x 4")
- Grey lightweight iron-on interfacing for backing: two pieces 17cm x 10cm wide (7" x 4")
- Thin wadding: one piece 15cm x 8cm wide (6" x 3")
- Stranded cotton thread: (A) white (B) dark violet (C) medium yellow (D) medium aqua
- No. 5 perlé cotton thread: medium red
- Machine sewing thread: red
- Tracing paper and other items for transferring the pattern onto the felt

## Let's begin

Use the following instructions for either ice cream unless otherwise indicated.

See the page opposite for the pattern.

Prepare the pattern by enlarging **Ice cream 1**, omitting the drips, to 125% of its original size for the violet ice cream, and to 150% for the red ice cream.

Following the instructions on page 15 for backing the fabric, attach one piece of interfacing onto the wrong side of each piece of felt.

Transfer the pattern centrally onto the right side of one of the two felt pieces by the pierce and dot method using a chalk-based pencil. See page 25 for transferring the pattern using the pierce and dot method. The remaining felt piece can be left plain or can be stitched using a mirror image of the enlarged pattern. See page 20 for information on mirroring the pattern.

## Stitch!

Using the alternative thread colours, work the ice creams following steps 1-6, omitting step 5, of the stitch instructions for **Ice cream 1** on the previous page. Note that when working the sprinkles on the red ice cream, three strands of stranded cotton should be used for the French knots as they need to be bigger due to the fact that the pattern has been enlarged.

## Let's finish

Cut a 28cm (11") length of the perlé cotton thread for the hanging loop. Fold the thread in half and knot the ends together. Firmly attach the knotted end onto the wrong side centrally at the top of the ice cream using small hand stitches.

Cut the piece of wadding exactly to the enlarged pattern shape. Aligning the wadding with the back of the stitched design, place it onto the wrong side of the ice cream. With wrong sides together, place the remaining piece of felt behind the wadding.

Tack the felt pieces together 1.5cm (5/8") outside the design.

Using a zipper foot on the machine and with matching machine sewing thread, stitch around the ice cream close to the design. Being careful not to cut the thread hanging loop, trim away the excess felt from around the edge of the ice cream (Diagram 1).

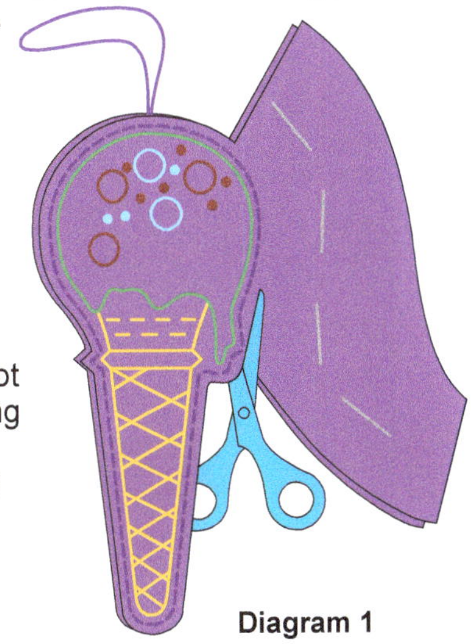

**Diagram 1**

# Rainy Day

We ran through the rain with our gumboots on, splashing in the puddles as we went.

## The design

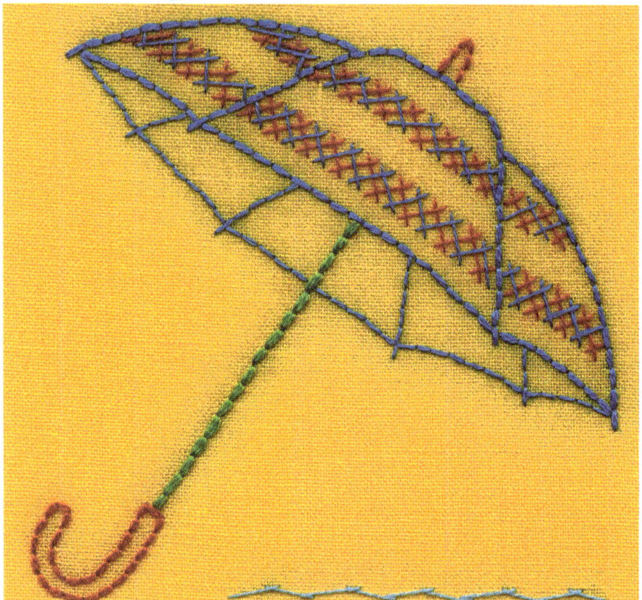

*Rainy Day*

Each stripe on the umbrella is created by first working a row of spaced herringbone stitch in red. A second row in aqua is then worked over the red row. As the stitches are worked densely, an outline for the stripes is not needed. Back stitch and widely spaced herringbone stitch are also included. To work this as shown, use the instructions here. To adapt the design for a child's library bag, see the page opposite.

## The pattern

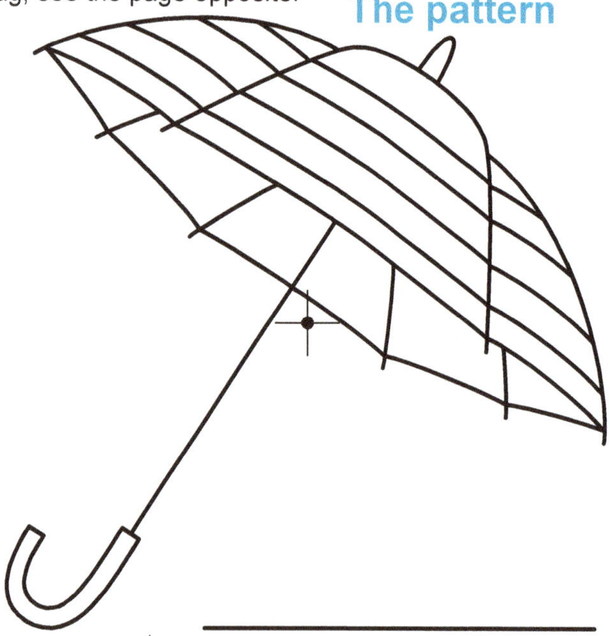

**Key:** ✛ **Centre of design**

## Shopping list

- Yellow cotton fabric for background: 25cm (10") square
- Fabric or interfacing for backing: 25cm (10") square
- Stranded cotton thread:
  (A) dark aqua (B) medium aqua
  (C) light green (D) medium red
- Tracing paper and other items for transferring the pattern onto the fabric

## Let's begin

Read page 15 for backing the fabric, and pages 22-25 for transferring the pattern onto the fabric, then select and use suitable methods for your fabric. For the yellow fabric shown here, the pattern was transferred centrally onto the fabric by tracing with a water erasable fabric marker and then the backing fabric was tacked to the wrong side.

## Stitch!

For help, see pages 76-79 for back stitch and pages 112-115 for spaced herringbone stitch, and also for how to stitch two rows of herringbone stitch with the second row worked in the spaces of the first.

1 Work the outline for the three panels at the front of the umbrella in back stitch (2 strands A).

2 Stitch the outline for the five panels at the back of the umbrella in back stitch (1 strand A).

3 Following the marked lines for each stripe, work a row of spaced herringbone stitch on each of the three front panels (1 strand D), working partial stitches at the beginning and end of the rows as needed (Diagram 1).

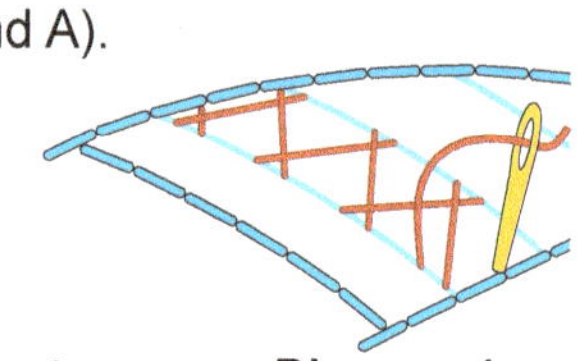

**Diagram 1**

4 Work a row of spaced herringbone stitch over each of the first rows (1 strand A), placing the stitches in the spaces between the previous stitches and working partial stitches at the beginning and end of the rows as needed (Diagram 2).

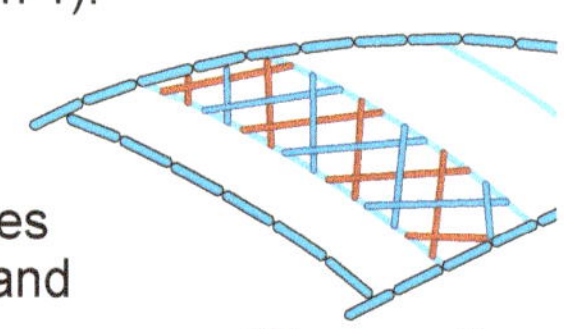

**Diagram 2**

5 Stitch the umbrella pole in back stitch (4 strands C).

6 Add the tip of the umbrella, and also the curved handle, in back stitch (2 strands D).

7 Working each stitch from just below the marked line to just above the line, stitch the puddle with shallow, widely spaced herringbone stitch (1 strand B).

## Let's finish

Take out the tacking. Rinse the work in cold water to remove the water erasable fabric marker. When partly dry, press or pin out the work. See page 36 for pressing and for pinning out.

# Rainy Day Library Bag

Make a colourful splash at your next library visit.

## The project

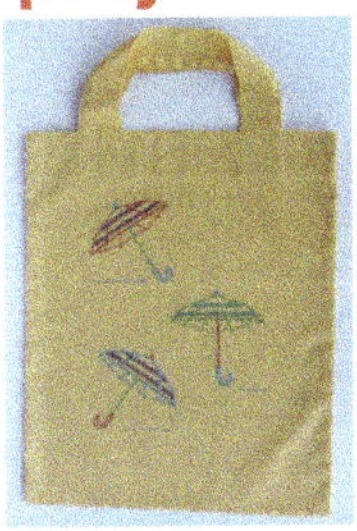

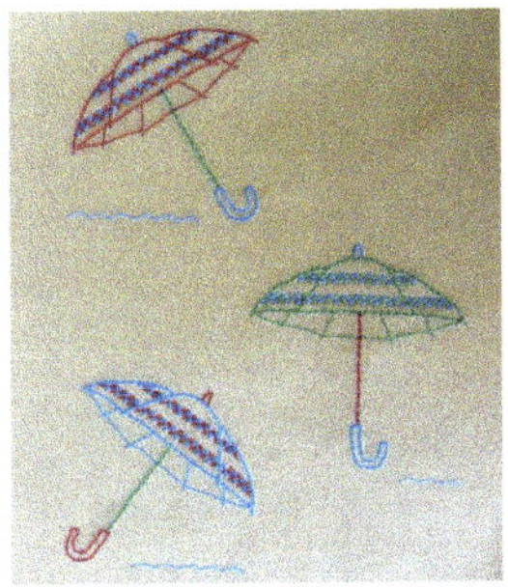

***Rainy Day Library Bag*** **and Detail**

For this project, three umbrellas are worked on a piece of yellow fabric that is then made up into a library bag. The umbrellas are all worked in the same way as the original design, but two of them have the colours and orientation changed around.

The finished size of the library bag is 39cm x 31cm wide (15 1/2" x 12 1/4"), not including the handles.

## Shopping list

- Yellow cotton drill fabric for the bag: one piece 86cm x 33cm wide (34" x 13")
- Yellow cotton drill fabric for the handles: two pieces 40cm x 10cm wide (16" x 4")
- Threads as listed for the original design opposite
- Machine sewing thread: yellow
- Tracing paper and other items for transferring the pattern onto the fabric

## Let's begin

See opposite for the umbrella pattern. Using tracing paper, make three tracings of the pattern for the umbrella, two of which are mirror images. See page 20 for mirroring patterns.

Place the bag fabric out flat with one short end at the top and right side facing up. Beginning at the top, measure half way down and tack across the width of the fabric. This will be the fold line at the base of the bag. Measure down from the top edge again, and tack across 4cm (1 1/2") for the top hem fold line. Work a row of tacking from the upper fold line to the lower fold line, 1cm (3/8") in from each long side to indicate the seam allowances (see Diagram 1).

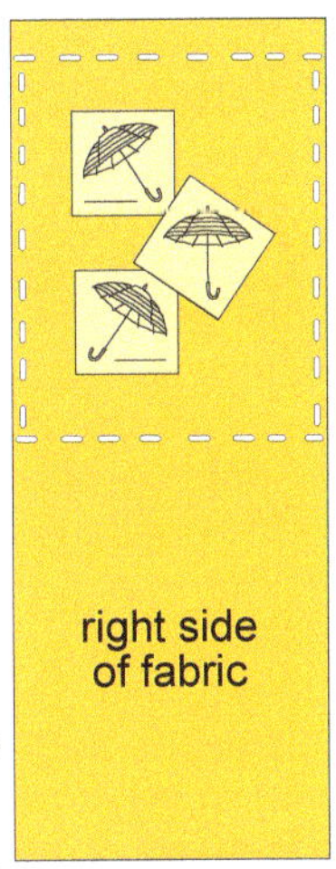


**Diagram 1**

Place the umbrella tracings onto the top half of the bag, positioned within the four lines of tacking. Move the tracings around to achieve a balanced placement (Diagram 1). Mark the position of each tracing with pins. Transfer the umbrella patterns onto the right side of the fabric by tracing with a water erasable fabric marker or by using transfer paper, changing the position of the puddle as necessary. See pages 22-25 for transferring the pattern onto the fabric.

## Stitch!

Work the three umbrellas following steps 1-7 of the stitch instructions opposite, keeping the colours in the same position for the aqua umbrella, and swapping them around for the two mirrored designs as follows:

***Red umbrella*** (A) medium red (B) medium aqua (C) light green (D) dark aqua

***Green umbrella*** (A) light green (B) medium aqua (C) medium red (D) dark aqua

## Let's finish

Take out the tacking indicating the seam allowances along the two long sides. Rinse the work in cold water to remove the pattern markings. When partly dry, press or pin out the work. See page 36 for pressing and for pinning out.

With right sides together, fold the work in half along the tacked fold line at the base of the bag. Pin the two layers together along the long sides. With machine sewing thread and a straight stitch on the machine, stitch the side seams with a 1cm (3/8") seam allowance. Prevent fraying of the seams by sewing along the edges of the fabric with a machine zigzag or overlock stitch (Diagram 2).

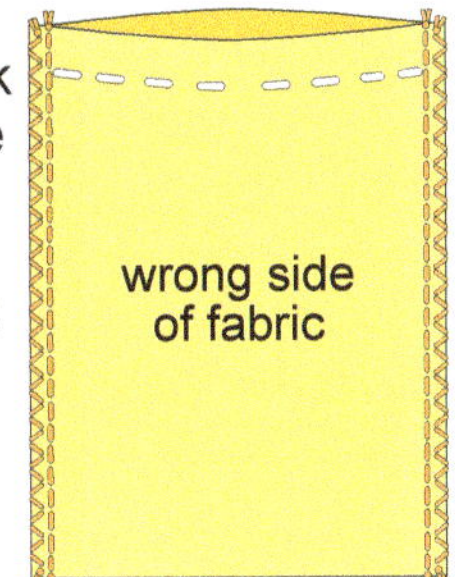


**Diagram 2**

Take out the tacking from the base of the bag. Turn the bag through to the right side and press. Fold under and press 1cm (3/8") on the long sides of the strips for the handles. With wrong sides together, fold each handle in half lengthwise. Stitch along both long edges of each handle (Diagram 3 shows these two steps). Press.

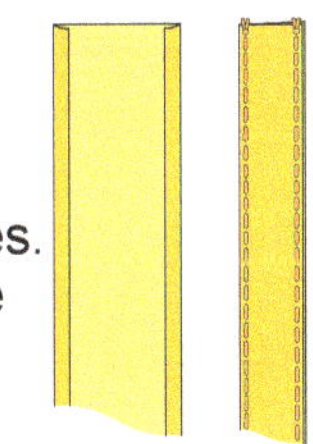

**Diagram 3**

With raw edges even, pin one handle onto the right side of the bag front at the top, with its outer edges 6cm (2 1/2") in from the side seams (see Diagram 4). Stitch the handle to the bag 4cm (1 1/2") down from the upper raw edges (Diagram 4).

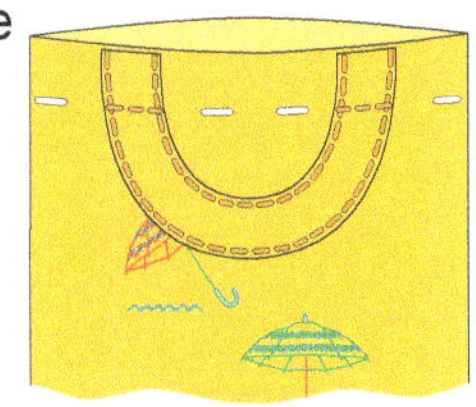

**Diagram 4**

Attach the second handle onto the back of the bag in the same way.

Prevent fraying of the upper raw edge of the bag, including handles, with a machine zigzag or overlock stitch.

Fold the upper edge to the inside along the tacked fold line for the top hem and press. Take out the tacking from the upper edge of the bag.

Stitching through both layers, work one row of machine straight stitch around the top edge of the bag close to the fold and a second row 2cm (3/4") below the first (Diagram 5).

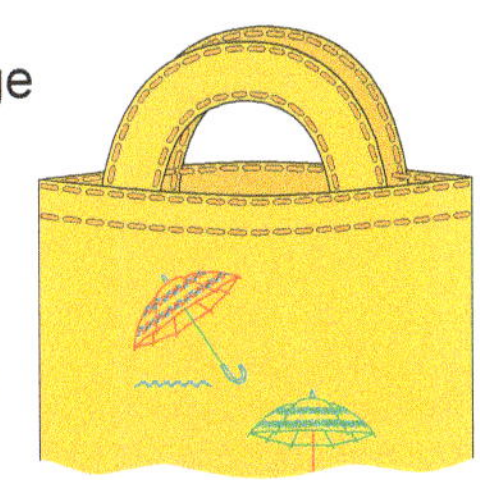

**Diagram 5**

# Cosmic Starburst

What a massive explosion of colour!

## The design

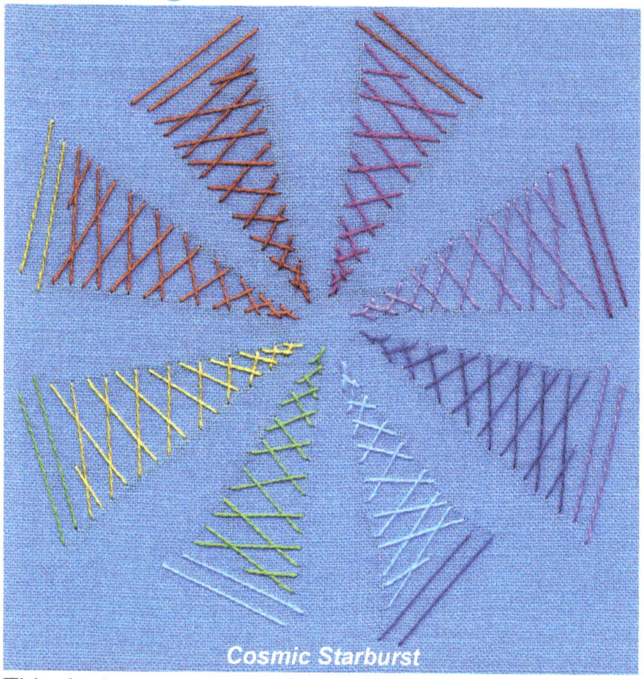

*Cosmic Starburst*

This design uses herringbone stitch to quickly fill the triangles without any need for a stitched outline. The long straight stitches at the outer edges of the triangles create a feeling of movement. *Cosmic Starburst* features eight colours arranged in rainbow order. To work the design as shown here, follow the instructions on this page. To adapt the design for a cushion cover, see the next page.

## The pattern

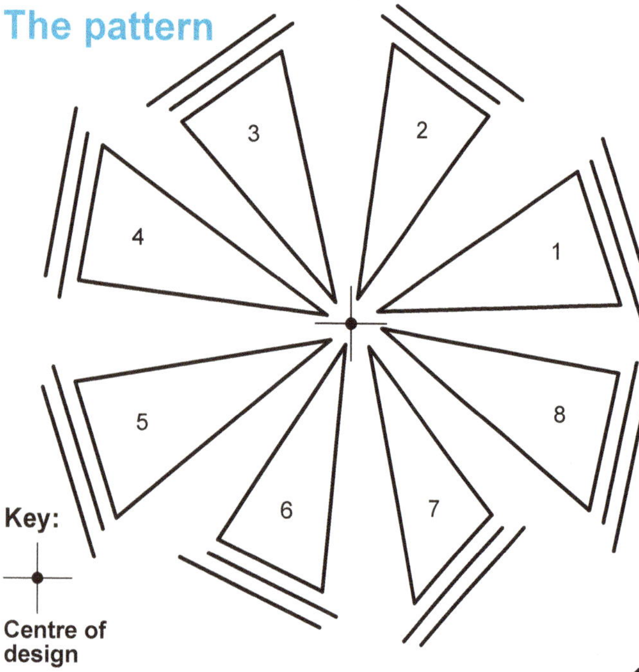


## Shopping list

- Aqua cotton fabric for background: 25cm (10") square
- Fabric or interfacing for backing: 25cm (10") square
- Stranded cotton thread:
  (A) medium violet (B) medium magenta
  (C) medium red (D) medium orange
  (E) medium yellow (F) light green
  (G) medium aqua (H) medium blue
- Tracing paper and other items for transferring the pattern onto the fabric

## Let's begin

Read page 15 for backing the fabric, and pages 22-25 for transferring the pattern onto the fabric, then select and use suitable methods for your fabric. For the aqua fabric shown here, the pattern was transferred centrally onto the fabric by tracing with a water erasable fabric marker and then the backing fabric was tacked to the wrong side.

## Stitch!

For help, see pages 40-43 for straight stitch and pages 112-115 for herringbone stitch. When working the herringbone stitch, turn the design so that each triangle lies horizontally as you work. This design may be easier to work if the fabric is placed in a hoop.

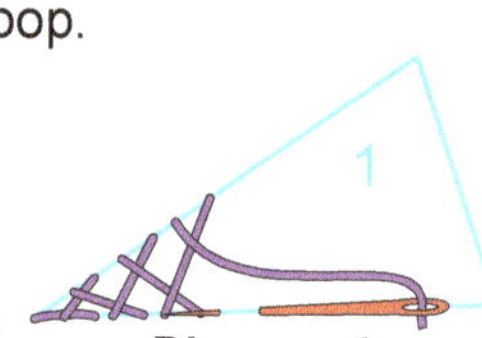


Diagram 1

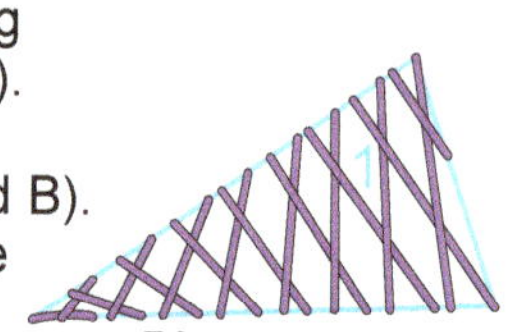


Diagram 2

1. Following the ruled outline and beginning at the inner point (Diagram 1), stitch **Triangle 1** in herringbone stitch (1 strand A). Work the stitches a little larger as you move towards the outer edge and follow the diagram for working the last three stitches (Diagram 2).
2. Work two straight stitches at the outer edge of **Triangle 1** (1 strand B).
3. Continue working the herringbone stitch triangles and the straight stitches at their outer edges, using one strand in the following colours:

**Triangle 2**: herringbone stitch (B), straight stitch (C)
**Triangle 3**: herringbone stitch (C), straight stitch (D)
**Triangle 4**: herringbone stitch (D), straight stitch (E)
**Triangle 5**: herringbone stitch (E), straight stitch (F)
**Triangle 6**: herringbone stitch (F), straight stitch (G)
**Triangle 7**: herringbone stitch (G), straight stitch (H)
**Triangle 8**: herringbone stitch (H), straight stitch (A)

## Let's finish

Take out the tacking. Rinse the work in cold water to remove the water erasable fabric marker. When partly dry, press or pin out the work. See page 36 for pressing and for pinning out.

# Cosmic Starburst Cushion Cover

Decorate a cushion with colourful starbursts.

## The project

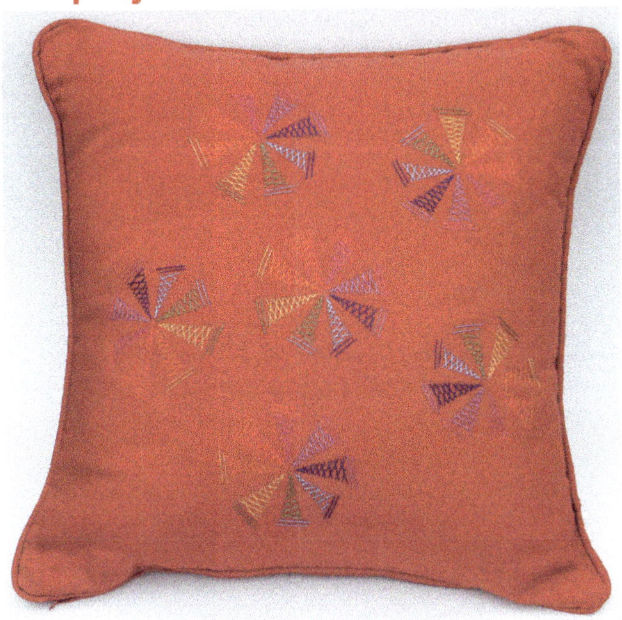

***Cosmic Starburst Cushion Cover***

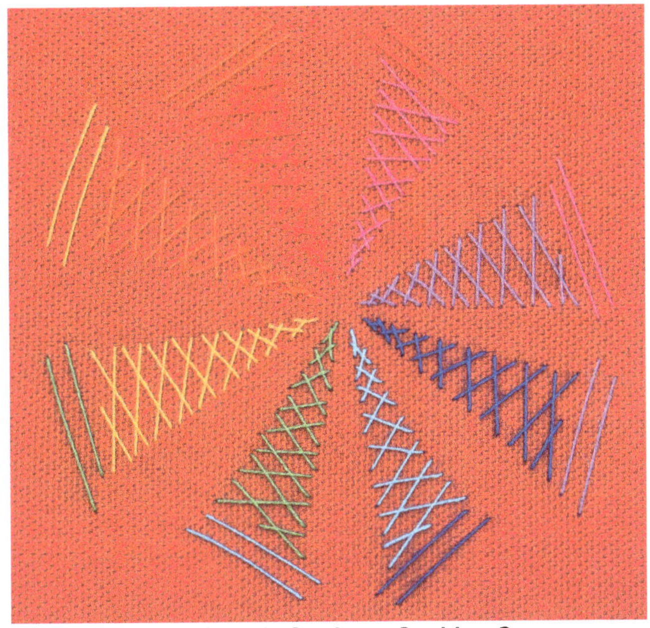

**Detail of *Cosmic Starburst Cushion Cover***

*Cosmic Starburst* is worked six times in its original coloured threads on a purchased red cushion cover. This project demonstrates that a multi-coloured design can look different on an alternative coloured background, as some colours may show up more and other colours may show up less.

The size of this cushion is 43cm (17") square.

## Shopping list

- Red cushion cover and insert
- Iron-on interfacing for backing: same size as the front of the cushion cover
- Threads as listed for the original design on the page opposite
- Tracing paper and other items for transferring the pattern onto the cushion cover

## Let's begin

See the page opposite for the pattern.

Remove the cushion insert and turn the cover inside out. Attach the iron-on interfacing onto the wrong side of the front of the cushion cover. See page 15 for backing the fabric.

Turn the cover through to the right side and place it with the front facing up. Transfer the pattern, including the numbers, centrally onto the right side of the front of the cushion cover using water erasable transfer paper. See page 24 for transferring the pattern using transfer paper. Transfer the pattern, including the numbers, five more times, placing them evenly around the first starburst and changing their orientation each time.

## Stitch!

Work the six designs following steps 1-3 of the stitch instructions on the page opposite.

## Let's finish

Rinse the work in cold water to remove the pattern markings. When almost dry, press with the cushion cover turned inside out. See page 36 for pressing. Turn through to the right side. Place the insert back into the cover.

## Hints

**Change the colours**

As an alternative design, choose any six colours and stitch the central starburst completely in one of these colours. Work each of the remaining starbursts in the same way, changing the colour each time.

**White on black**

Working the starbursts in white on a black background would be an impressive colour scheme.

# Tropical Palms

Gently swaying coconut palms, and peaceful idyllic beaches.

## The design

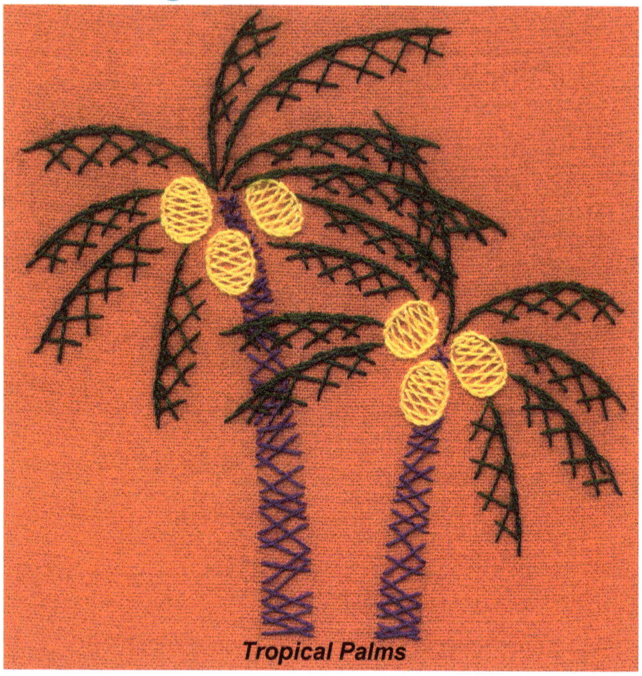


The textures on the coconuts, palm trunks, and leaves in this design are created by using three different forms of herringbone stitch. Stem stitch is also used.
Follow the instructions on this page to work the design as shown here. To work this easy design on a pair of shorts for a child, see the project idea on the next page.

## The pattern

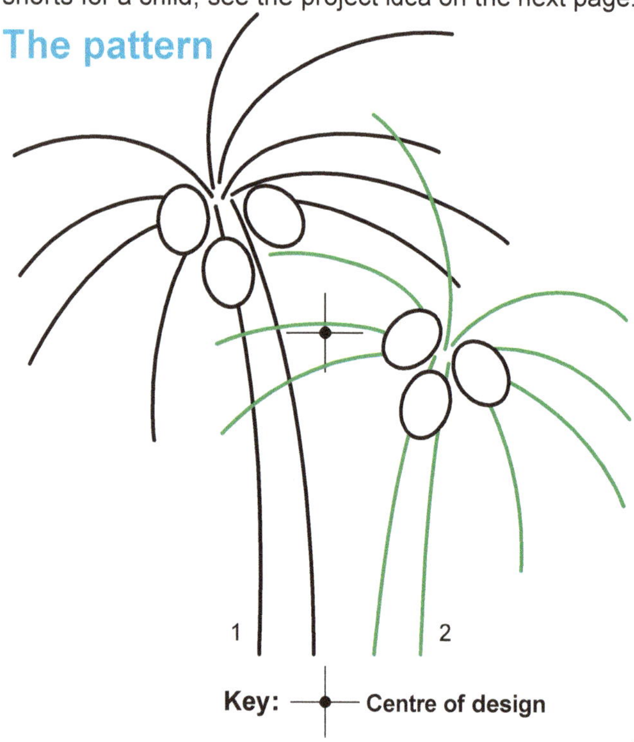


## Shopping list

- Red cotton fabric for background: 25cm (10") square
- Fabric or interfacing for backing: 25cm (10") square
- Stranded cotton thread:
  (A) dark violet (B) dark green (C) medium yellow
- Tracing paper and other items for transferring the pattern onto the fabric

## Let's begin

Read page 15 for backing the fabric, and pages 22-25 for transferring the pattern onto the fabric, then select and use suitable methods for your fabric. For the red fabric shown here, the pattern was transferred centrally onto the fabric by tracing with a water erasable fabric marker and then the backing fabric was tacked to the wrong side.

## Stitch!

For help, see pages 94-97 for stem stitch, including completing a shape, and pages 112-115 for herringbone stitch, including closed and irregular. Turn the design on its side for working the herringbone stitch on the coconuts and the palm trunks.

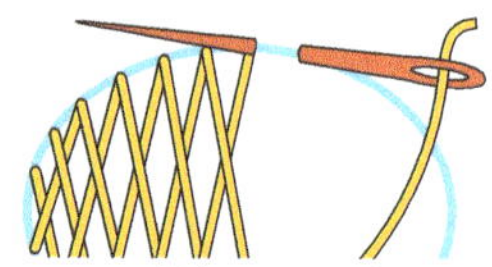

Diagram 1

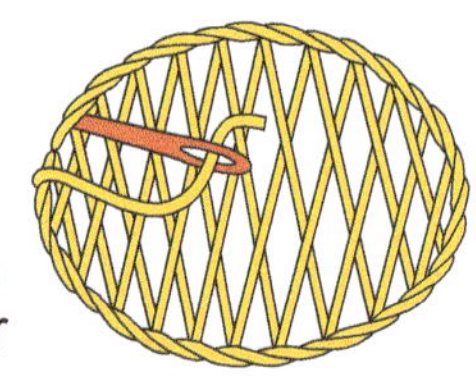

Diagram 2

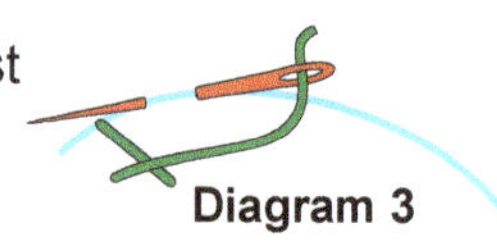

Diagram 3

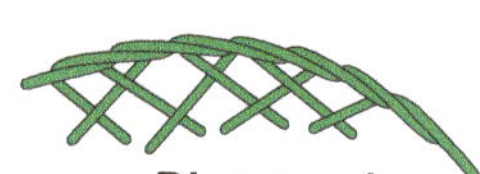

Diagram 4

1 Work each coconut in closed herringbone stitch (1 strand C), following the marked outline and working the stitches densely (Diagram 1). Stitch the outline of each coconut in small stem stitch (1 strand C), overlapping the last stitch with the first to complete the outline (Diagram 2).
2 Beginning at the base of the palm trunk, stitch each trunk in irregular herringbone stitch following the marked outline (1 strand A).
3 Stitch the leaves of **Tree 1** by first working a row of irregular herringbone stitch for each leaf (1 strand B) with the top of the stitches worked along the marked line (Diagram 3). Using the same thread, complete each leaf on **Tree 1** by working a row of stem stitch along the marked line (Diagram 4).
4 In the same way, work the leaves of **Tree 2** (1 strand B), with the overlapping leaves worked over the top of the trunk and leaves of **Tree 1**. When working the overlapping leaves, avoid splitting the threads of the previously worked stitches.

## Let's finish

Take out the tacking. Rinse the work in cold water to remove the fabric marker. When partly dry, press or pin out the work. See page 36 for pressing and for pinning out.

# Tropical Palms Shorts

Add some tropical fun to a pair of holiday shorts.

## The project

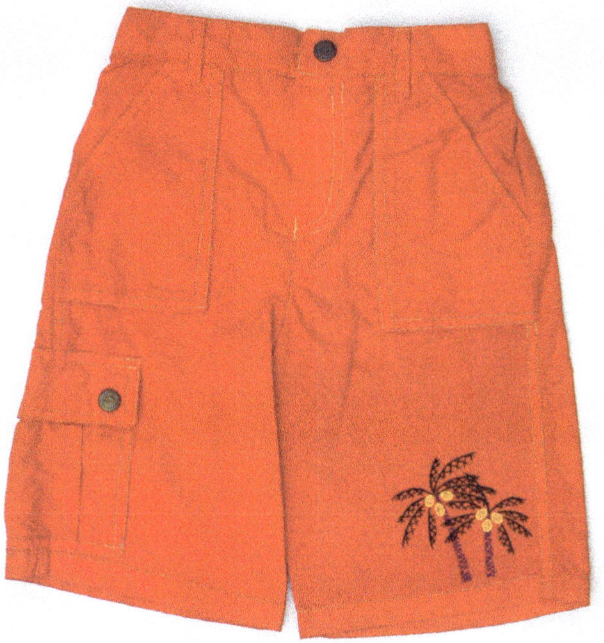

*Tropical Palms Shorts*

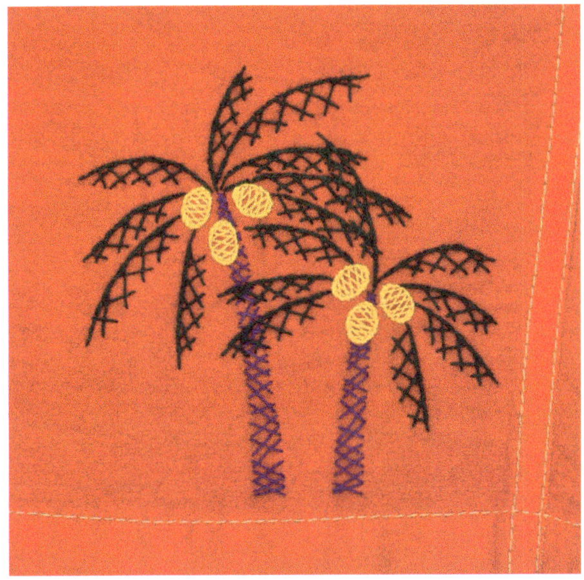

**Detail of**
***Tropical Palms Shorts***

*Tropical Palms* is worked on a purchased pair of child's shorts in exactly the same colours, threads and stitching as the original design.

## Shopping list

- Red shorts
- Lightweight iron-on interfacing for backing: 11cm (4 1/2") square
- Threads as listed for the original design on the page opposite
- Tracing paper and other items for transferring the pattern onto the shorts

## Let's begin

See the page opposite for the *Tropical Palms* pattern. To make it easier to decide on the placement of the palms design on the shorts, give consideration to the practicality of the position and how the stitched design will look when the shorts are worn.
Attach the square of iron-on interfacing onto the wrong side of the front of the shorts at the selected position. This will stabilize the area where the design is to be stitched. See page 15 for backing the fabric.
Transfer the pattern onto the front of the shorts using water erasable transfer paper. See page 24 for transferring the pattern using transfer paper.

## Stitch!

Work the design following steps 1-4 of the stitch instructions on the page opposite.

## Let's finish

Turn the shorts inside out. On the wrong side, peel back any excess interfacing from its outer edge and trim it back close to the stitches. Rinse the shorts in cold water to remove the pattern markings. When almost dry, turn the shorts inside out and press them. See page 36 for pressing.

## Hints

### Using irregular stitches

Irregular herringbone stitch is worked for these palm trunks and leaves with its stitches purposely lying at many different angles, creating a free, sketchy look.

### Another project idea

For an alternative project, you could stitch a row of palm trees as a border on a child's skirt.

# Blanket stitch

## and variations

Blanket stitch, one of the best-known loop stitches, is fast and easy to work. It is formed with a continuous row of linked open loops that can be worked either left to right or right to left.

Having a corded or scroll-like base, blanket stitch is commonly used for finishing the edges of blankets and appliqué pieces. It is also useful for working borders and outlining and filling shapes.

Blanket stitch can be worked as a row along a line or as several rows worked in various combinations of stitch direction. It can also be formed into shapes such as circles and squares. The stitches can be of even size or they can be worked with variable distances apart and heights of their uprights.

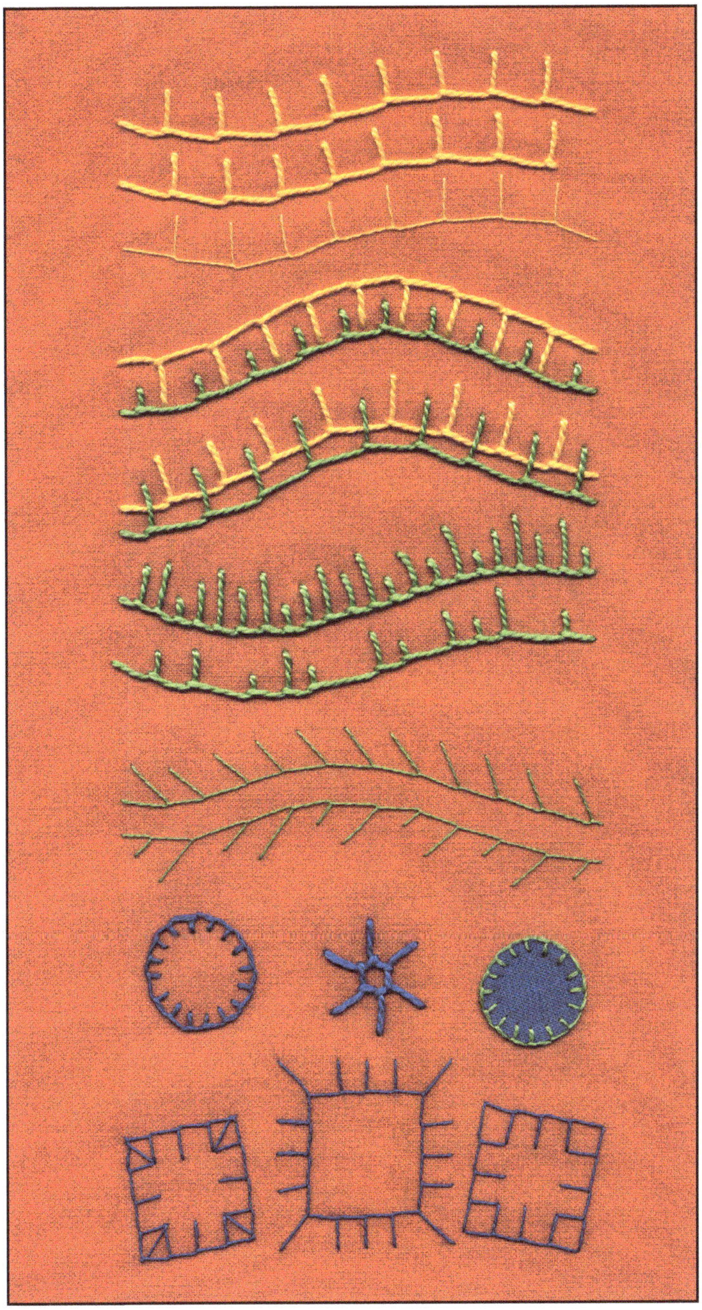

Blanket stitch ended with a long anchor stitch

Blanket stitch ended with a short anchor stitch

Blanket stitch worked in opposite direction

Two rows of blanket stitch that interlock

Two rows of blanket stitch that overlap

Blanket stitch worked with irregular height

Blanket stitch worked with irregular spacing and irregular height

Rows of blanket stitch worked with slanted stitches

Blanket stitch worked as inward circle, outward circle, and to appliqué a shape

Three alternatives for using blanket stitch to work a square

## Blanket stitch and variations sampler

# Blanket stitch and variations

## Hints

Blanket stitch is most commonly worked by skimming the needle in and out of the fabric before pulling the thread through. The stitch can be worked either left to right or right to left, with the needle pointing down, or similarly, left to right or right to left, with the needle pointing up.

When working blanket stitch, each new loop is secured by the next stitch, and the last loop in the row is secured with a straight stitch as an anchor. The length of the anchor can vary depending on the desired effect. As you work, keep the tension of the thread even so that each stitch is formed correctly and lies flat against the fabric.

## Blanket stitch and variations: right-handed or left-handed

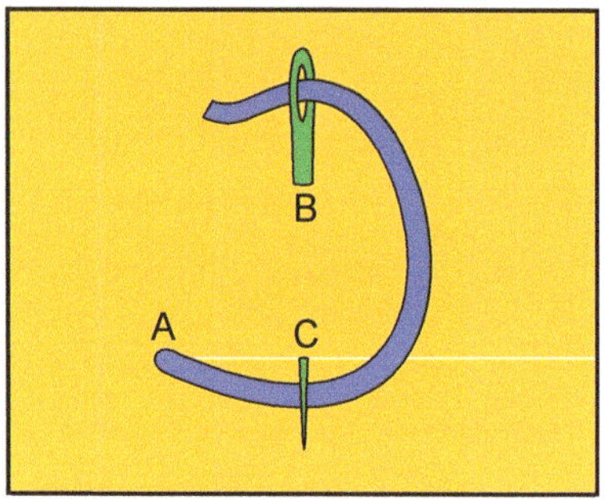


**Blanket stitch**
**1** Come up at A at start of line. Take needle down at B and emerge at C. Keep thread under tip of needle, forming a loop.

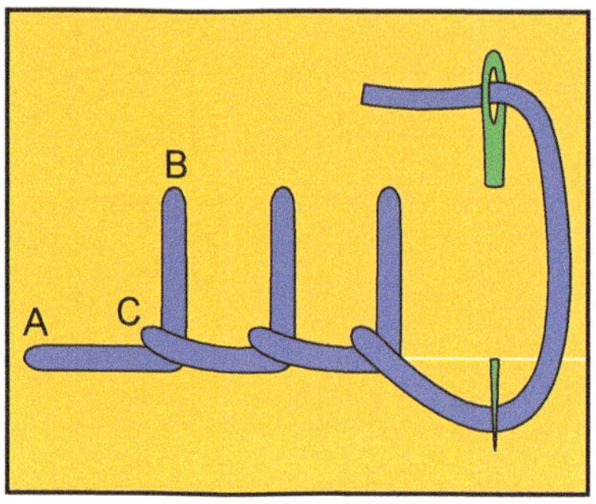


**2** Pull the thread through, allowing the loop to settle in place. Continue along the row with evenly spaced stitches.

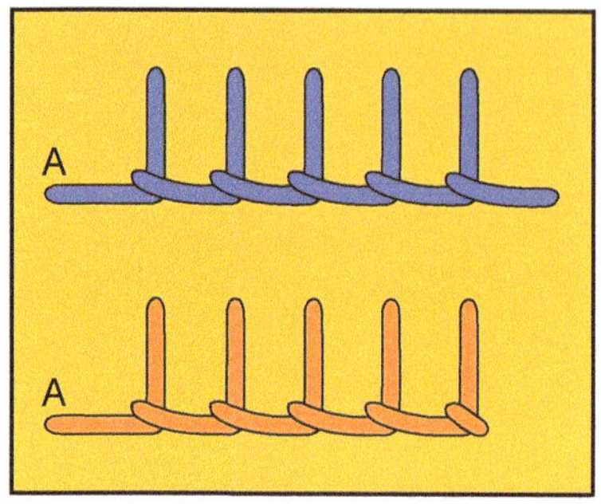


**3** To end off, work a straight stitch as an anchor and secure on the back. Upper example shows a long anchor, lower example shows a short anchor.

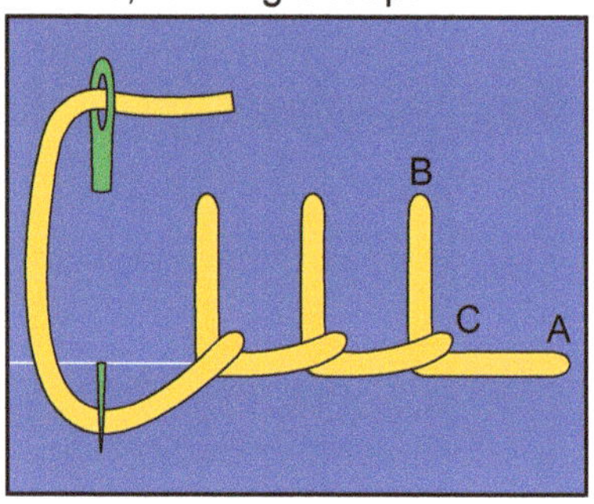


**Alternative direction 1**
Come up at A at the start of the line. Take the needle down at B and emerge at C. Continue along row.

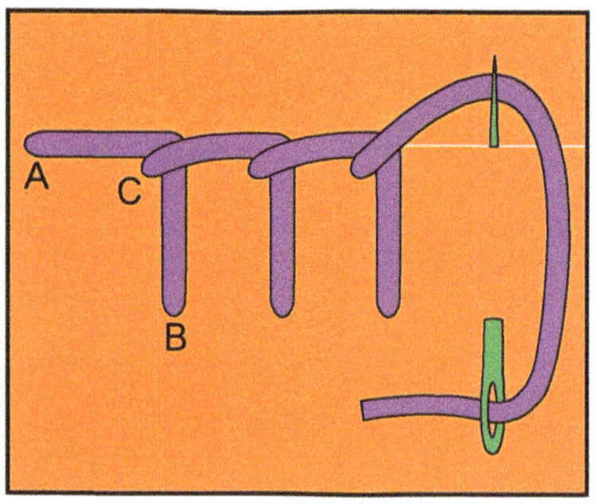


**Alternative direction 2**
Come up at A at the start of the line. Take the needle down at B and emerge at C. Continue along row.

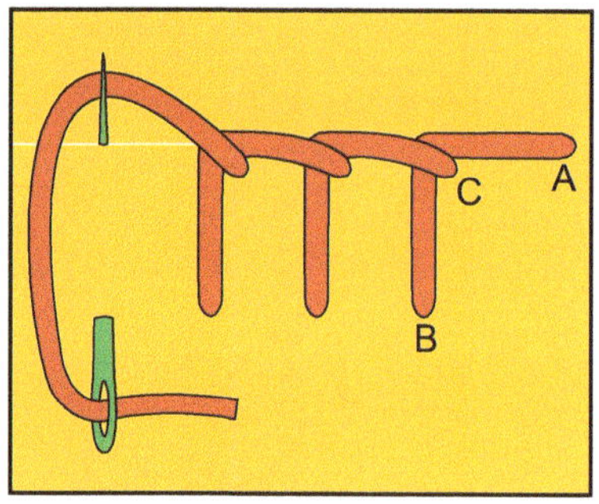


**Alternative direction 3**
Come up at A at the start of the line. Take the needle down at B and emerge at C. Continue along row.

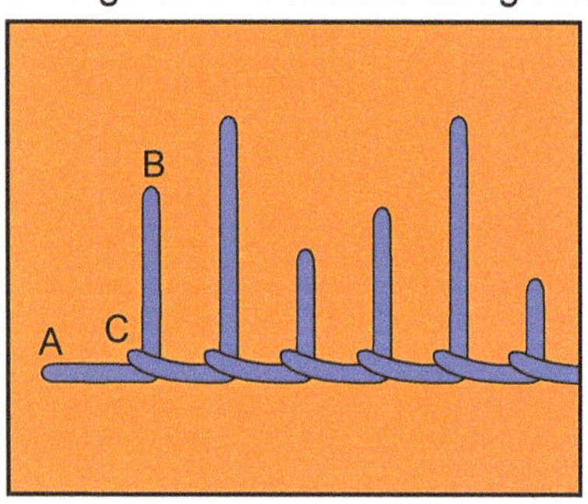


**Irregular height**
Work this variation in a similar way, but vary the height of B to C along the row.

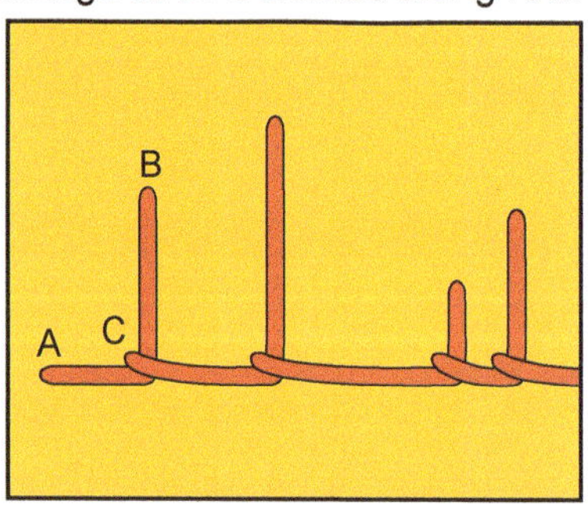


**Irregular spacing and height**
Work this variation in a similar way, but vary the space between A to C, and the height of B to C.

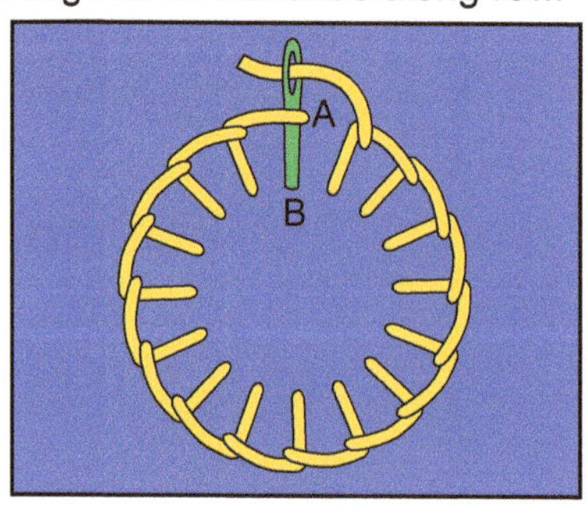


**Completing a shape**
Begin at A. Stitch shape anti-clockwise. For last stitch, pass thread under first stitch, then take it to back at B and secure.

## Blanket stitch and variations: right-handed or left-handed

**Joining in a new thread**
If it is necessary to join in a new thread, rather than anchoring the old one and beginning again with a new one, a method for an invisible join is shown here.

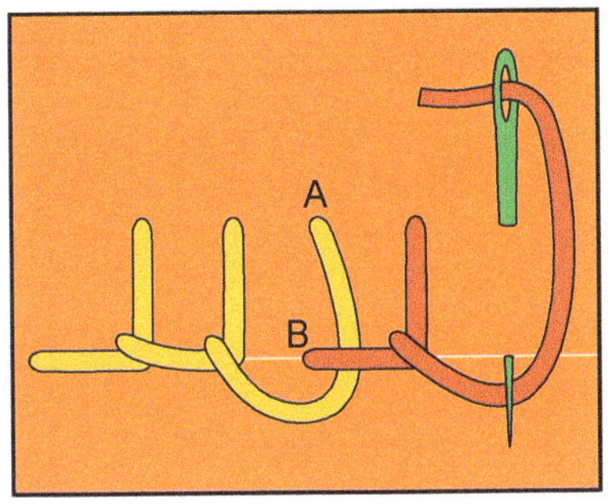


**Joining in a new thread**
**1** Take old thread down at A, leaving loop loose and thread hanging. Bring new thread up at B and continue.

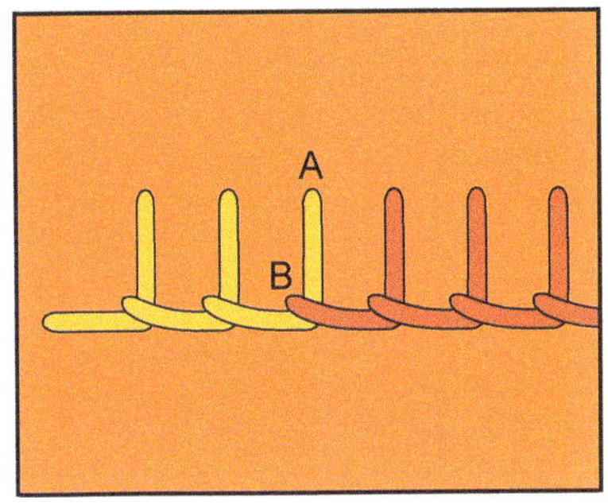


**2** After working several stitches, tighten the last loop of the old thread and end it off.

**Turning a corner**
When working blanket stitch around an angular shape, avoid the problem of the stitches collapsing at the corners by choosing one of the methods shown here for turning a corner. The resulting corners are neat and well defined.

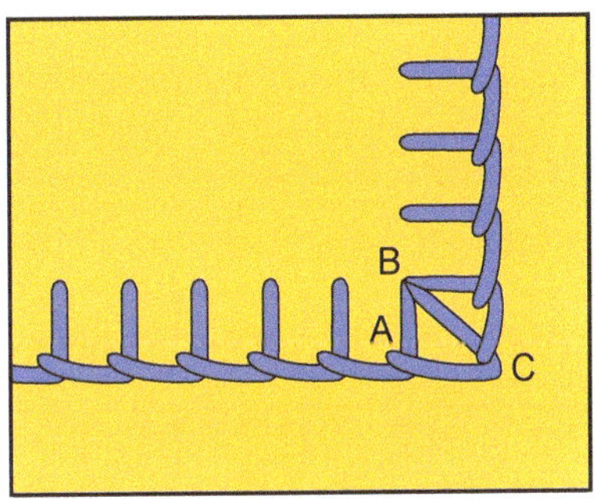


**Method 1: Turning a corner**
For an inward corner, work B to C diagonally, then work second side. Three stitches at the corner share same hole at B.

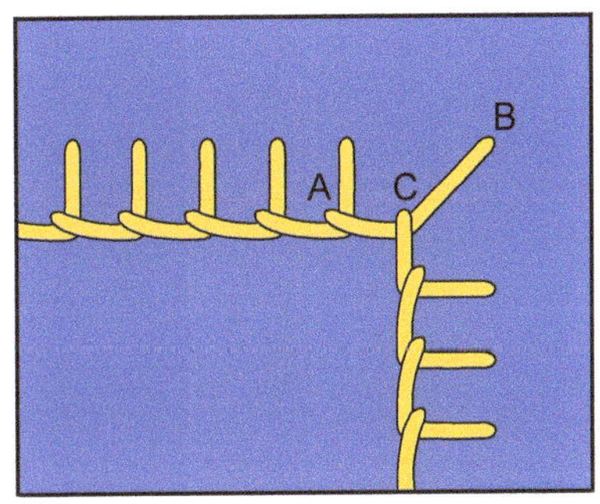


**Method 2: Turning a corner**
For an outward corner, work B to C diagonally, and then work along the second side.

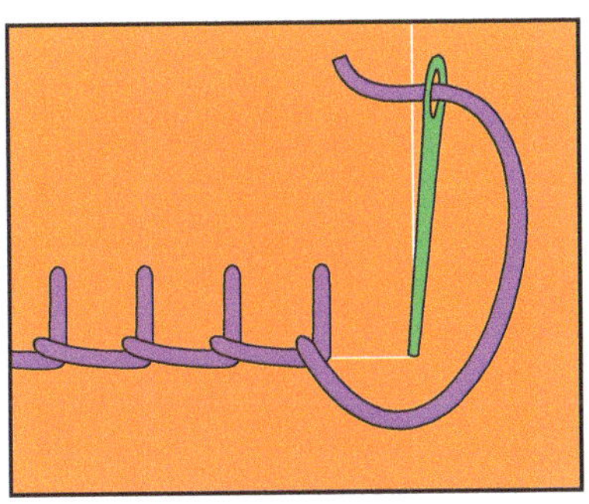

**Method 3: Turning a corner**
**1** Work blanket stitch along the first side. At the corner, take the thread to the back of the work.

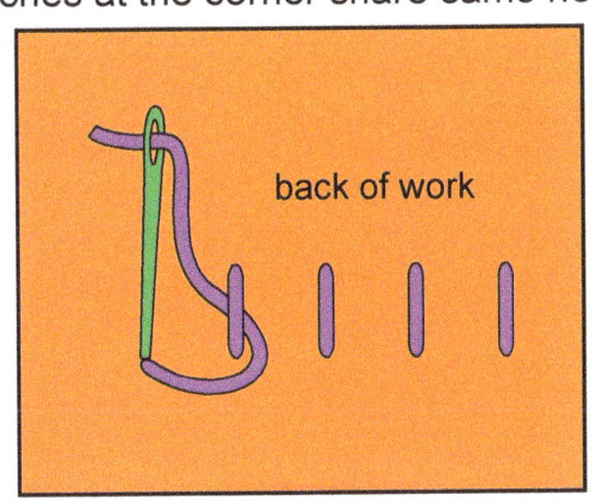


**2** Pass the thread under the last stitch on the back of the work. Return the thread to the front at the corner through the same hole in the fabric.

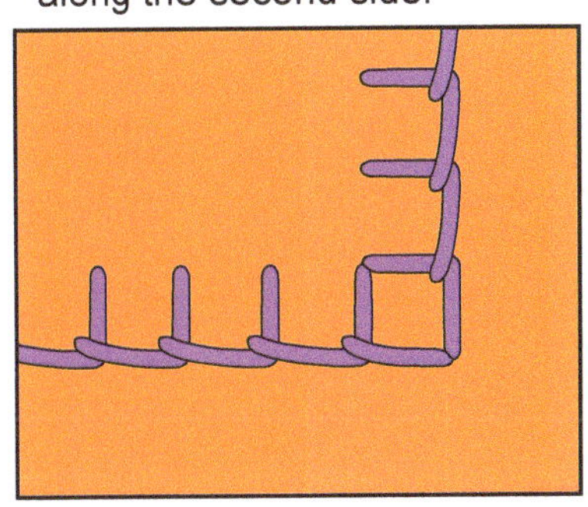

**3** On the front, work along the second side.

# Blanket stitch
## and variations

# Designs and project ideas

## The designs

Creepy Caterpillars

Red Hot Chilli

Amazing Planets

Frangipani Fantasy

The Penny-farthing Bicycle

Sunlit Garden

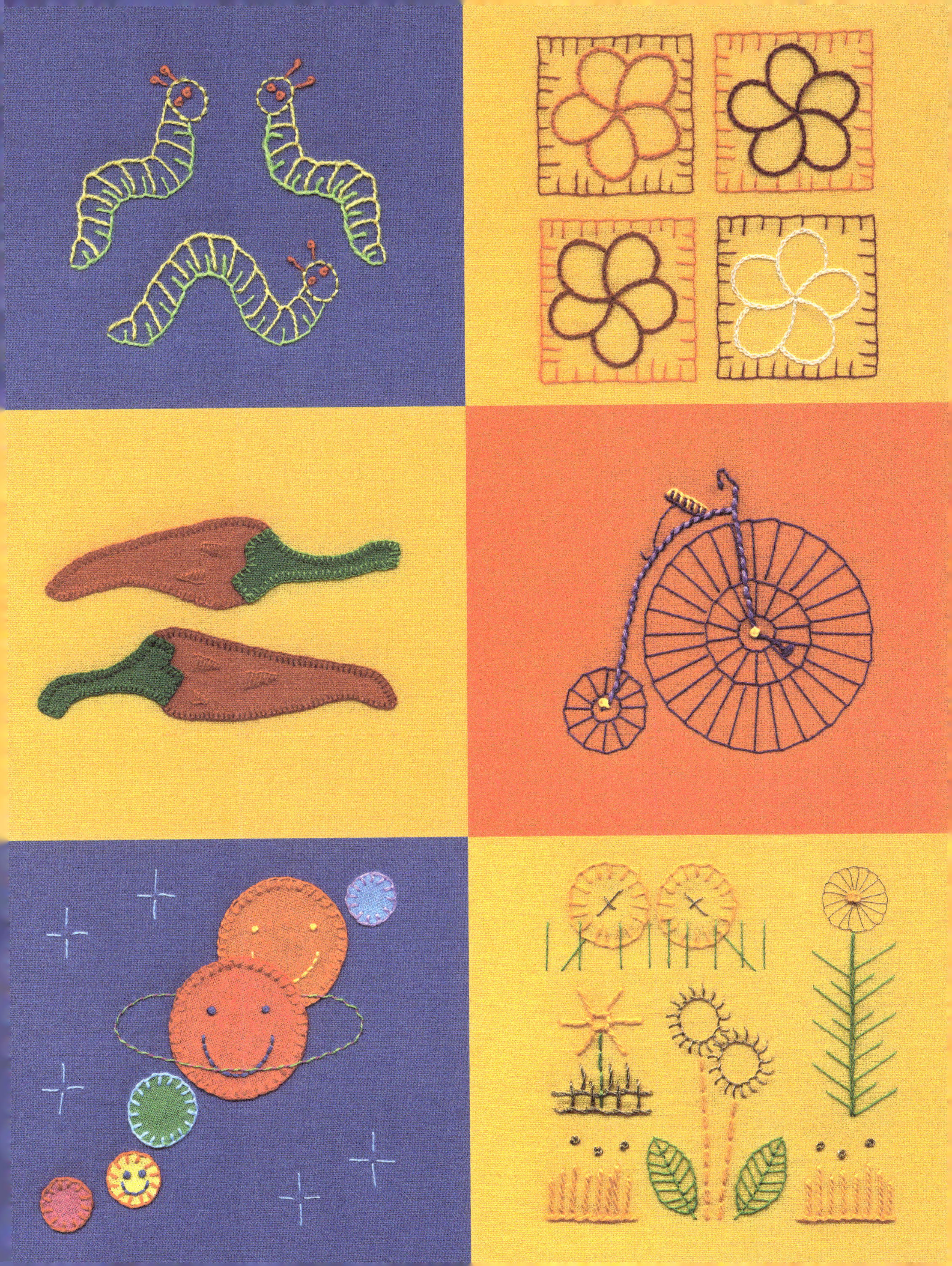

# Creepy Caterpillars

We might look frightening, but we're actually quite friendly!

## The design

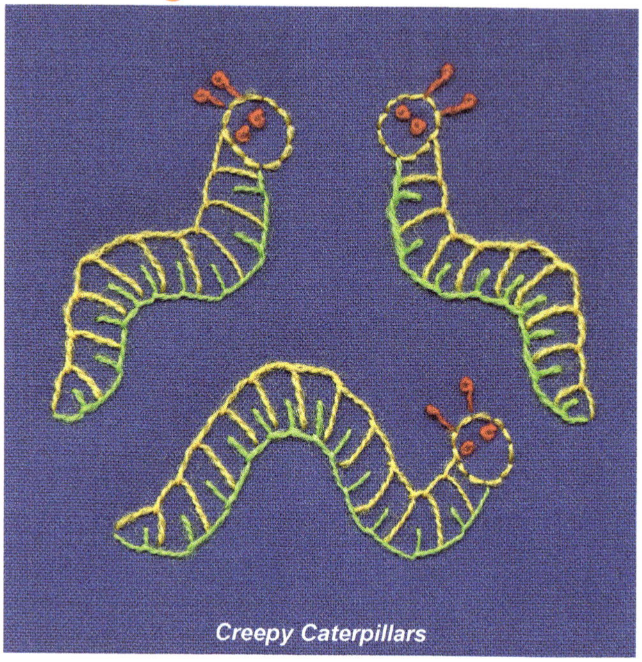


The caterpillars are formed with large blanket stitches, and the details are worked in back stitch, French knot, and pistil stitch. This design is worked completely in wool yarn, giving a furry appearance.
Use the instructions on this page to work the design as shown here. To adapt the design for a project, see the idea on the following page where many caterpillars are creeping around the band of a child's hat.

## The pattern

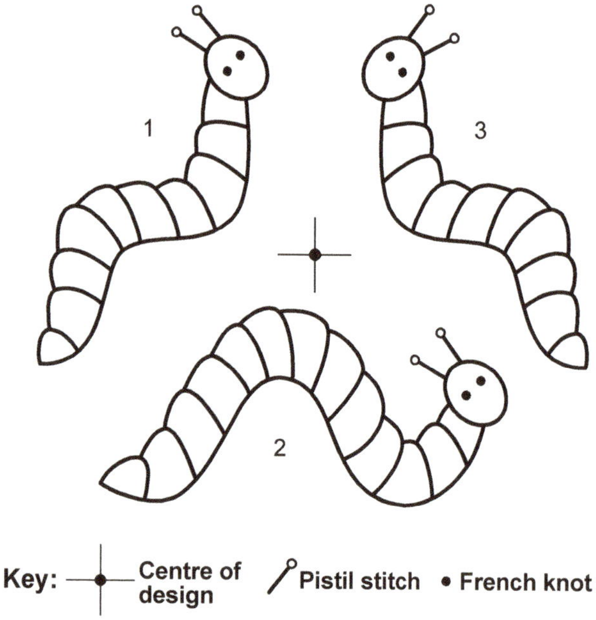


## Shopping list

- Blue cotton fabric for background: 25cm (10") square
- Fabric or interfacing for backing: 25cm (10") square
- Fine 2 ply wool yarn:
  (A) light green (B) light yellow (C) medium red
- Tracing paper and other items for transferring the pattern onto the fabric

## Let's begin

Read page 15 for backing the fabric, and pages 22-25 for transferring the pattern onto the fabric, then select and use suitable methods for your fabric. For the blue fabric shown here, the pattern was transferred centrally onto the fabric by tracing with a chalk-based pencil and then the backing fabric was tacked to the wrong side.

## Stitch!

For help, see pages 76-79 for back stitch, 130-133 for blanket stitch, and pages 184-187 for French knot and pistil stitch. All three caterpillars are worked with the same stitch combinations and thread colours. Work the blanket stitches in the same direction for **Caterpillars 1** and **2** and in the opposite direction for **Caterpillar 3**.

1 Work the outline for the head in back stitch (1 strand B).

2 Following the marked divisions and beginning at the tail end (Diagram 1), stitch the top part of the body in blanket stitch (1 strand B). Finish the row of blanket stitch with a long anchor (Diagram 2).

3 Beginning at the tail end, work the lower edge of the body in blanket stitch (1 strand A). Place the stitches halfway between the long arms of the yellow stitches and only half as high (Diagram 3).

4 Stitch each of the antennae with a two wrap pistil stitch (1 strand C).

5 Work each eye with a two wrap French knot (1 strand C).

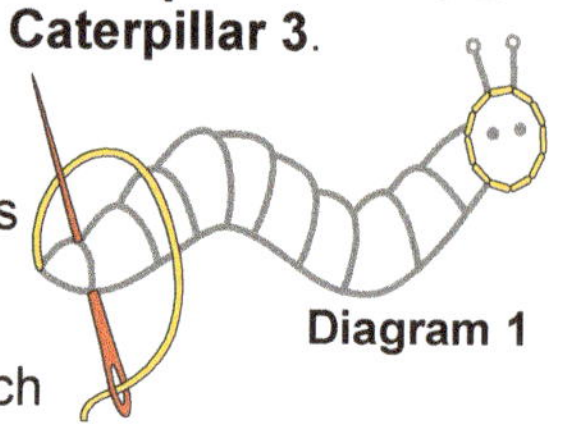
**Diagram 1**

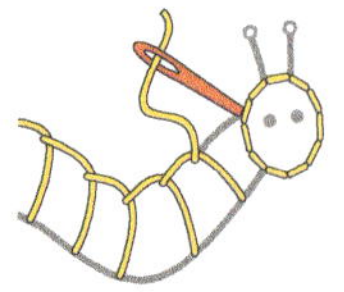
**Diagram 2**

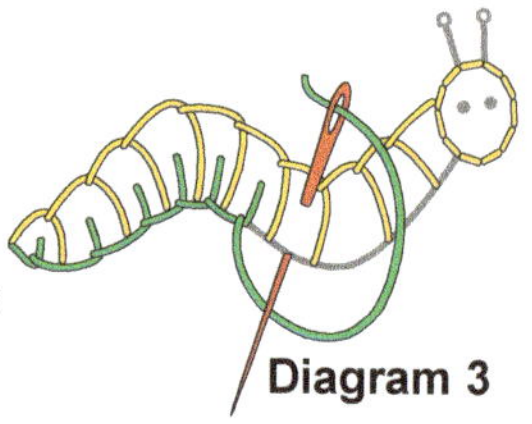
**Diagram 3**

## Let's finish

Take out the tacking. Press or pin out the work. See page 36 for pressing and for pinning out.

## Hint

**Using wool yarn**

As wool yarn is springy, it is best to work with a looser tension than you would use with cotton or silk threads. This looser tension allows for the stitches to settle correctly and the fabric to remain flat.

# Creepy Caterpillars Hat

Be safe in the sun – wear a caterpillar hat.

## The project

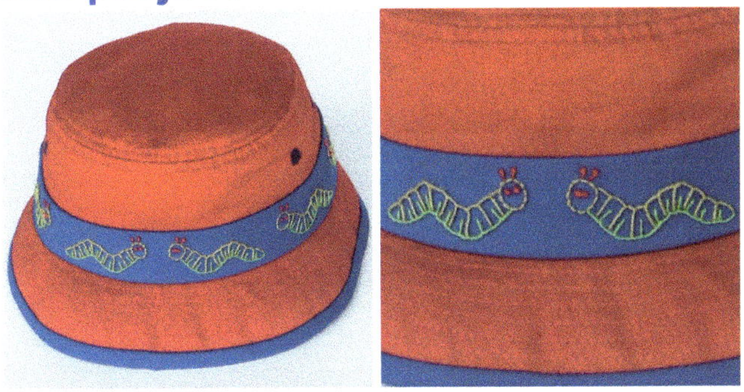

***Creepy Caterpillars Hat* and Detail**

This hat features caterpillars worked on a strip of blue fabric that is then made into a hatband. The same blue fabric, attached as a bias strip binding, trims the brim of the hat. The finished hatband is 3.5cm (1 3/8") wide.

## Shopping list

- Child's red hat
- Blue cotton fabric for the band and lightweight iron-on interfacing for backing: one piece of each, 6.5cm (2 5/8") wide and 3cm (1 1/4") longer than the circumference of the crown
- Blue cotton fabric strip cut on the bias (Diagram 3): 4.5cm (1 3/4") wide and 5cm (2") longer than the circumference of the outer edge of the hat's brim
- Threads as listed for the original design opposite
- Machine sewing thread: blue
- Tissue paper
- Items for transferring the pattern onto the fabric

## Let's begin

See the page opposite for the pattern.

***Making the pattern for the band***

Make a tissue paper pattern for the band by ruling lines to form a rectangle that is the circumference of the crown of the hat in length, and 3.5cm (1 3/8") in width. Add 1.5cm (5/8") on all sides for the seam allowances. Cut out this tissue paper pattern. Arranging caterpillars evenly along the band pattern, trace **Caterpillar 1** four times onto half the length of the band, and **Caterpillar 3** four times onto the other half (Diagram 1).

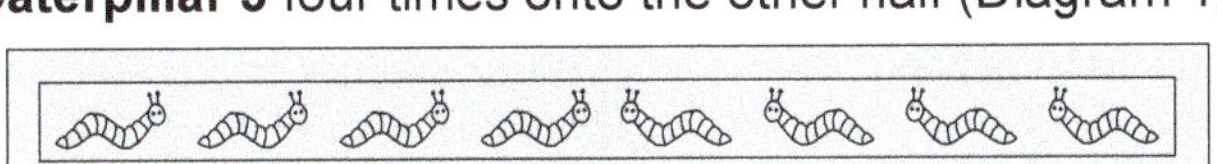

**Diagram 1**

***Preparing the fabric***

Following the instructions on page 15 for backing the fabric, attach the iron-on interfacing onto the wrong side of the blue fabric for the band.

Using the prepared tissue paper pattern, transfer the caterpillars onto the right side of the interfaced fabric using water erasable transfer paper. See page 24 for transferring the pattern using transfer paper.

## Stitch!

Work the caterpillars following steps 1-5 of the stitch instructions for the original design on the facing page.

## Let's finish

***Making the band***

Rinse the band very gently in cold water to remove the pattern markings. When dry, press. See page 36 for pressing. With right sides together, fold the band in half and pin and tack the short ends together. Test the size of the band on the hat and adjust if necessary. Using the machine sewing thread, machine stitch the ends together, then take out the tacking (Diagram 2). Trim the seam allowances and press the seam open. Fold under 1.5cm (5/8") on the upper and lower raw edges and press. Turn the band to the right side and place it onto the crown of the hat. Attach the band to the hat along the upper and lower edges with hand stitches worked invisibly.

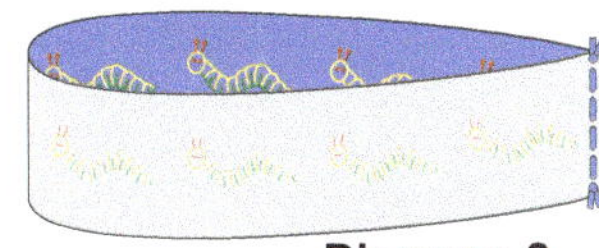

**Diagram 2**

***The bias strip binding***

A fabric strip cut on the bias, called a bias strip, will stretch and fit well when attached as a binding around a curve. To make the bias strip binding for this hat, rule a rectangle of the required size on the fabric at a 45 degree angle to the grain (warp and weft) of the fabric (Diagram 3). Cut out bias strip.

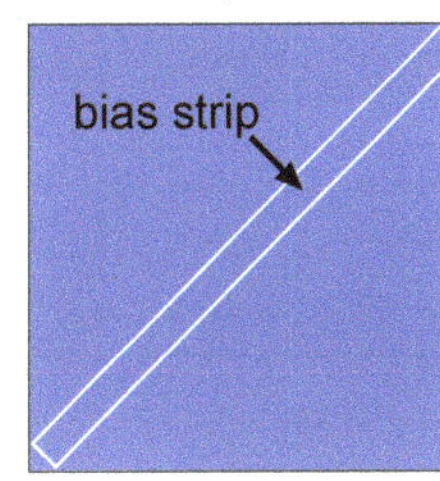


**Diagram 3**

***Attaching the binding***

On one short end of the bias strip, fold under a 1cm (3/8") seam allowance to the wrong side. With right sides together, align the folded end with the seam on the brim, then pin the bias strip binding around the edge of the brim (Diagram 4). On reaching the beginning again, overlap the ends of the binding. Trim away any excess binding extending beyond the 1cm (3/8") seam allowance (Diagram 5). Attach the binding to the brim by machine stitching through all layers 1cm (3/8") away from the edge of the brim. Fold the binding over to the underside of the brim. Turning under 1cm (3/8") on the long edge and aligning the folded edge of the binding with the previous row of machine stitching, hand stitch the binding in place (Diagram 6).

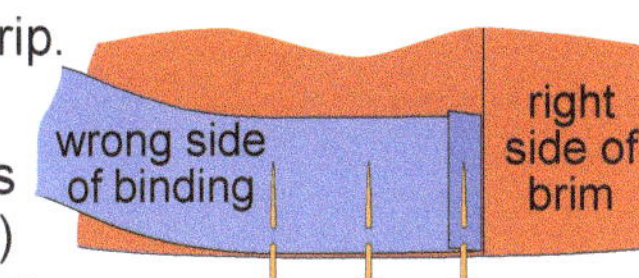


**Diagram 4**

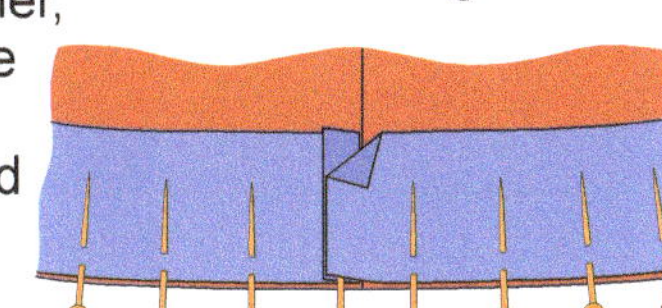

**Diagram 5**

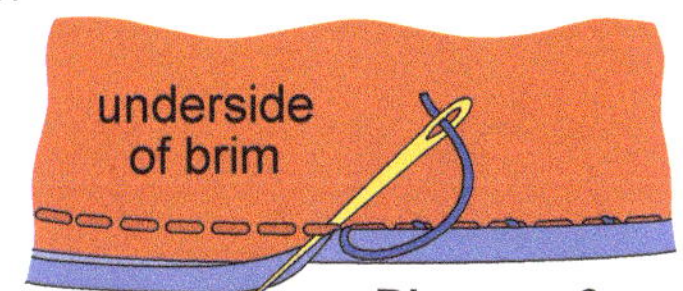


**Diagram 6**

# Frangipani Fantasy

The wonderful perfume of frangipani flowers fills the air.

## The design

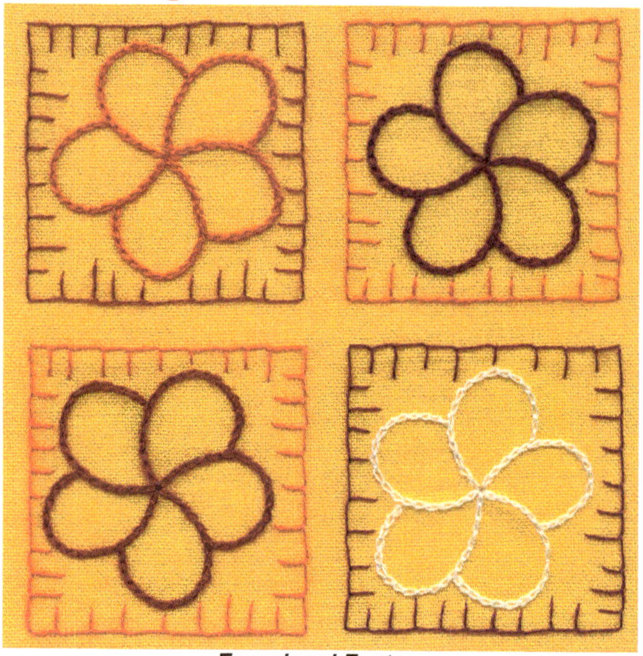

***Frangipani Fantasy***

Irregular blanket stitch is used here to frame the chain stitch flowers. Follow the instructions on this page to work the design as shown above. To stitch part of the design as a repeating pattern on a T-shirt, see opposite.

## The pattern

1 2

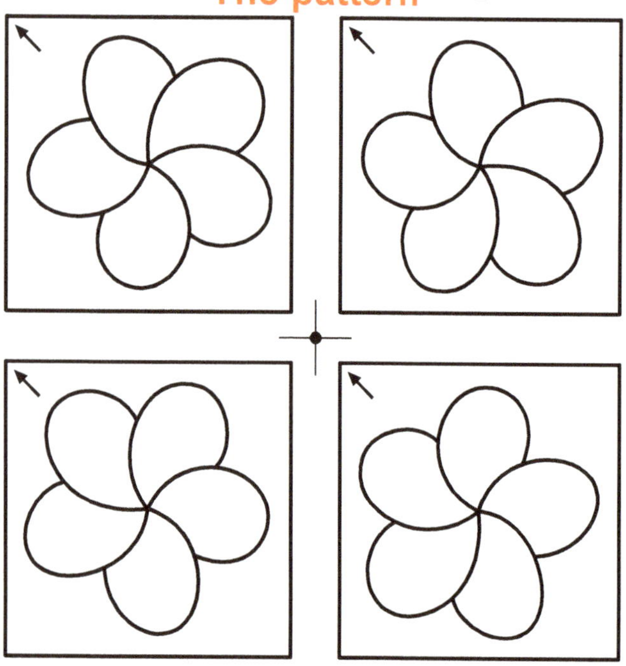

3 4

**Key:** **Centre of design** **→ Begin frame here**

## Shopping list

- Yellow cotton fabric for background: 25cm (10") square
- Fabric or interfacing for backing: 25cm (10") square
- Stranded cotton thread:
  (A) medium orange (B) dark red (C) light red
  (D) dark magenta (E) white
- Tracing paper and other items for transferring the pattern onto the fabric

## Let's begin

Read page 15 for backing the fabric, and pages 22-25 for transferring the pattern onto the fabric, then select and use suitable methods for your fabric. For the yellow fabric shown here, the pattern was transferred onto the fabric by tracing with a water erasable fabric marker and then the backing fabric was tacked to the wrong side.

## Stitch!

For help, see pages 130-133 for blanket stitch, including turning a corner, and pages 166-169 for chain stitch. Work all the blanket stitches that create these frames with irregular height and spacing.

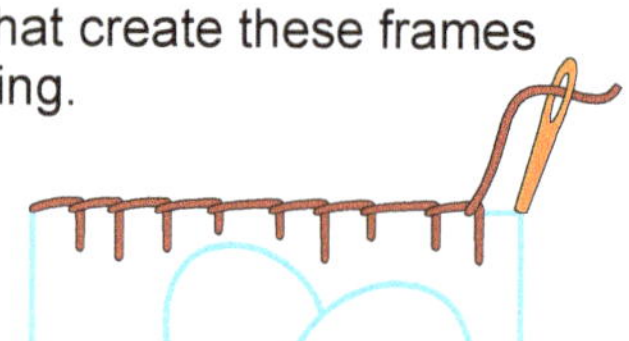

**Diagram 1**

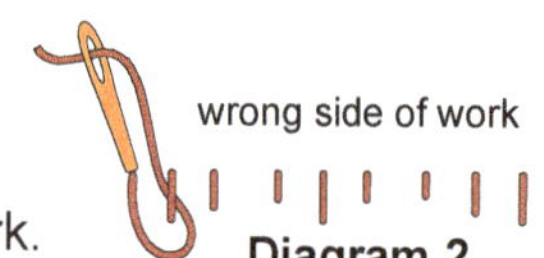


**Diagram 2**

**Framed flower 1**

Beginning at the marked corner, stitch along the top side of the frame in irregular blanket stitch (1 strand B). Work the anchor of the last stitch into the second corner (Diagram 1). Take the thread through to the back of the work. Pass the thread under the back of a previously worked stitch, then take the thread to the front at the corner (Diagram 2). Continue stitching the frame, working the next two corners in the same way. To complete the frame, work an anchor into the marked corner and end off. For the flower, stitch the petals in small chain stitch (1 strand A), beginning each petal at the same hole in the fabric at the flower centre and ending with a tiny anchor.

**Framed flower 2**

Work the frame in irregular blanket stitch (1 strand A) and the petals in small chain stitch (1 strand D).

**Framed flower 3**

Work the frame in irregular blanket stitch (1 strand C) and the petals in small chain stitch (1 strand B).

**Framed flower 4**

Work the frame in irregular blanket stitch (1 strand D) and the petals in small chain stitch (1 strand E).

## Let's finish

Take out the tacking. Rinse the work in cold water to remove the fabric marker. When partly dry, press or pin out work. See page 36 for pressing and for pinning out.

# Frangipani Fantasy T-shirt

Add tropical flowers to a joyful summer T-shirt.

## The project

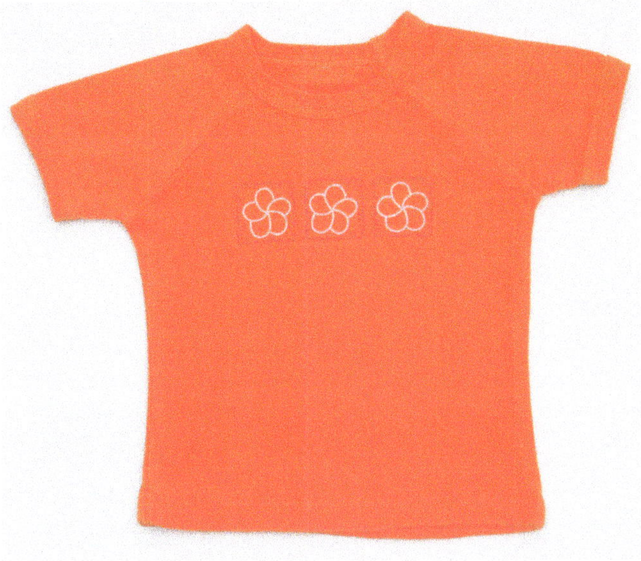

*Frangipani Fantasy T-shirt*

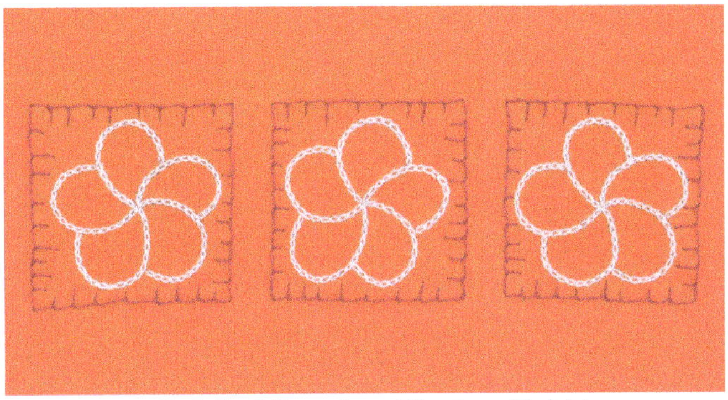

Detail of *Frangipani Fantasy T-shirt*

This project illustrates how a stitched design can be adapted for use as a repeating pattern. **Framed flower 4** from *Frangipani Fantasy* is repeated three times in a row across a purchased T-shirt.

## Shopping list

- Orange T-shirt for a child
- Lightweight iron-on interfacing for backing: 6cm x 15cm wide (2 1/2" x 6")
- Threads (D) and (E) as listed for the original design on the page opposite
- Tracing paper and other items for transferring the pattern onto the T-shirt

## Let's begin

See the page opposite for the frangipani pattern. Make a pattern for the row of framed flowers by drawing a line 13cm (5") long, close to the lower edge of the piece of tracing paper. Trace **Framed flower 4**, evenly spaced, three times along the line.

Attach the piece of iron-on interfacing onto the wrong side of the front of the T-shirt at the selected position. This will stabilize the area where the design is to be stitched. See page 21 for placing the pattern and page 15 for backing the fabric. Transfer the pattern onto the front of the T-shirt by tracing with a water erasable fabric marker or by using transfer paper. See pages 22-25 for transferring the pattern onto the fabric.

## Stitch!

Work the row of framed flowers following the stitch instructions for **Framed flower 4** on the page opposite.

## Let's finish

Turn the T-shirt inside out. On the wrong side, peel back any excess interfacing from its outer edge and trim it back close to the stitches. Rinse the T-shirt in cold water to remove the pattern markings. When almost dry, turn the T-shirt inside out and press it. See page 36 for pressing.

## Hint

**Change the colours**

These framed flowers could be worked entirely with a dark coloured thread on a light background fabric, or entirely in a light coloured thread on a dark background fabric, each giving dramatically different effects.

# Red Hot Chilli

The smaller they are, the hotter they seem to be!

## The design

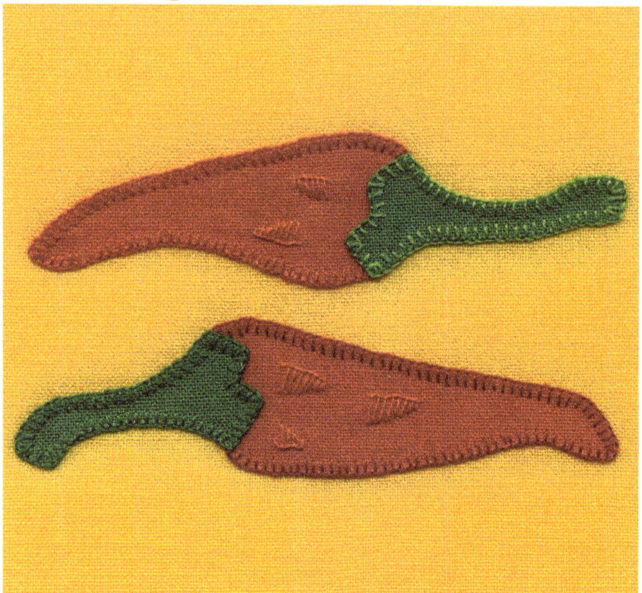

*Red Hot Chilli*

The technique of appliqué is used for this design. Fabrics, cut to the shapes of the chillies, are fused to the background fabric. The edges of the shapes are then worked with blanket stitch. Surface detail is also done in blanket stitch.

To work the design exactly as shown here, use the instructions on this page. To adapt the design for use on a project, see the next page where a chilli is featured on each of three table napkins.

## The pattern

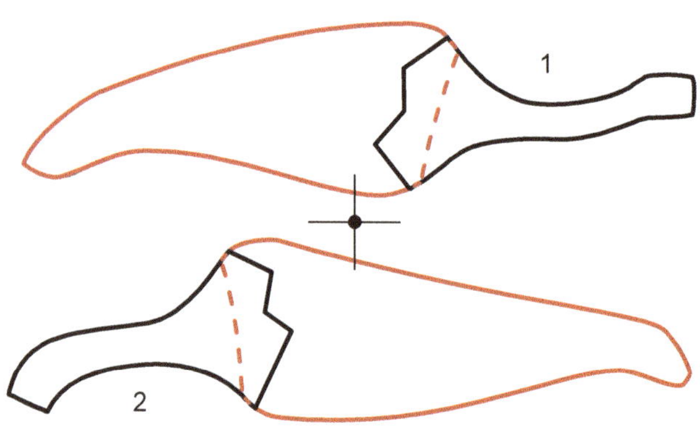


**Note: Trace each fabric shape separately**

**Key:** **Centre of design** **Edge of red shapes**

## Shopping list

- Yellow cotton fabric for background: 25cm (10") square
- Fabric or interfacing for backing: 25cm (10") square
- Red and green cotton fabrics for the appliqué shapes: 8cm (3") square of each colour
- Paper-backed fusible webbing: 9cm x 12cm wide (3 1/2" x 4 3/4")
- Stranded cotton thread: (A) medium green (B) light green (C) medium orange (D) dark red (E) medium red
- Tracing paper and other items for transferring the pattern onto the fabric

## Let's begin

Read page 15 for backing the fabric, and pages 22-25 for transferring the pattern onto the fabric, then select and use suitable methods for your fabric. For the yellow fabric shown here, the outlines for the chillies were transferred onto the background fabric by tracing with an HB pencil and then the backing fabric was tacked to the wrong side. Referring to pages 220-223 for appliqué and following steps 3-6 of Method 2, prepare and cut out the shapes for the chillies from the red fabric, and the stalks from the green fabric.

## Stitch!

For help, see pages 130-133 for blanket stitch, including turning a corner and completing a shape.

Complete the first chilli before working the second.

**Chilli 1** Peel off the paper backing from the red shape. Place the shape, glue side down, onto the background fabric over the marked outline. Cover with a pressing cloth. Fuse the red shape to the background with a hot iron. Stitch around the edge in blanket stitch (1 strand E), working the point with three stitches sharing the same inner hole (Diagram 1). Do not stitch where the red shape will be covered by the stalk.

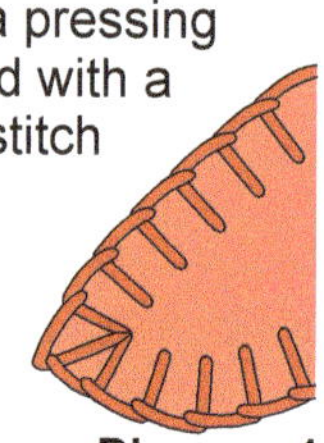

**Diagram 1**

Peel off the paper backing from the green stalk. Place the stalk overlapping the red shape. Fuse in place. Stitch around the edge in blanket stitch (1 strand B), working each corner with three stitches sharing the same inner hole (Diagram 2). To complete the outline, pass the last stitch under the first.

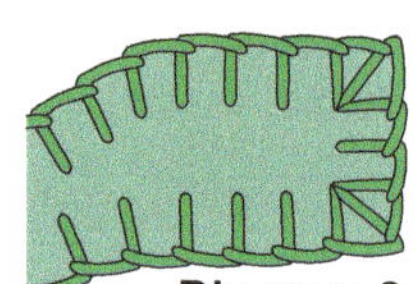

**Diagram 2**

Using the photo as a guide, work two highlights on the red shape in blanket stitch (1 strand C).

**Chilli 2** Fuse and stitch the red shape (1 strand D) and the green shape (1 strand A) in the same way as **Chilli 1**. Add three highlights in blanket stitch (1 strand C).

## Let's finish

Take out the tacking. Press or pin out the work. See page 36 for pressing and for pinning out.

# Red Hot Chilli Table Napkins

Create a hot topic of conversation with this trio of table napkins.

## The project

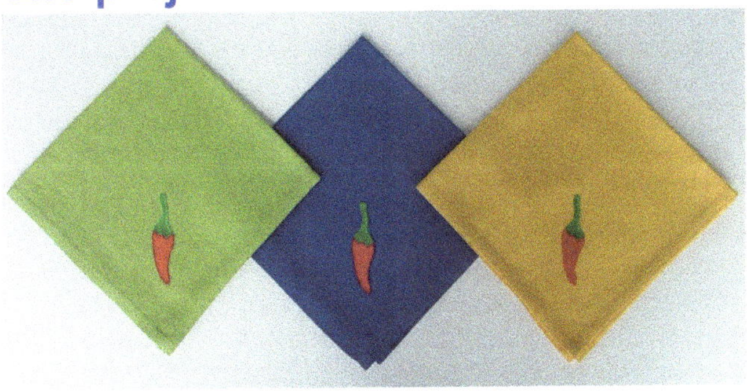

*Red Hot Chilli Table Napkins*

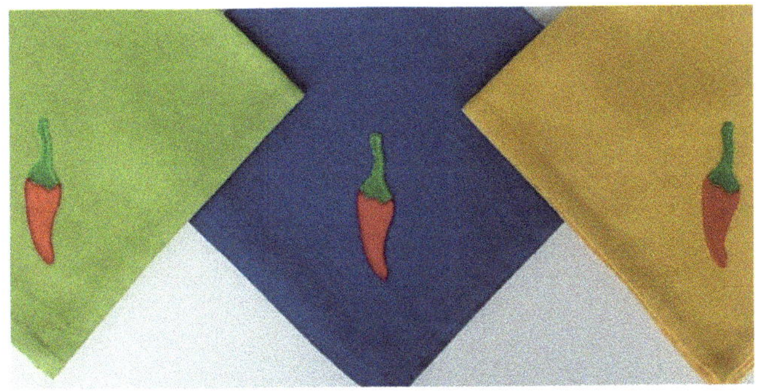

Detail of *Red Hot Chilli Table Napkins*

For this project, **Chilli 1** from the original design is featured separately on three table napkins. The chillies on the green and blue napkins are the same as the original design, while the yellow napkin features a chilli worked in an alternative colour scheme.

## Shopping list

- Green, blue, and yellow table napkins
- Red, green, and orange cotton fabrics for the appliqué shapes:
  8cm (3") square each of red and green
  5cm x 8cm wide (2" x 3") rectangle of orange
- Paper-backed fusible webbing:
  12cm (5") square
- Threads (B), (C), and (E) as listed for the original design on the page opposite
- Tracing paper and other items for transferring the pattern onto the napkins

## Let's begin

See the page opposite for the pattern.
Positioning the design diagonally on one corner, transfer the outline for **Chilli 1** onto the right side of each napkin using transfer paper. See page 24 for transferring the pattern using transfer paper.
Referring to pages 220-223 for appliqué and following steps 3-6 of Method 2, prepare and cut out the shapes from the fabrics as follows:

***Green and blue napkins***
red and green fabrics

***Yellow napkin***
orange and green fabrics

## Stitch!

Attach the shapes and stitch the chillies on the green and blue napkins following the stitch instructions for **Chilli 1** on the page opposite. Work the chilli on the yellow napkin in a similar way, but use (C) medium orange for the blanket stitch around the orange fabric shape, and (E) medium red for the blanket stitch highlights.

## Let's finish

Press the napkins on the wrong side of the fabric using a well-padded surface. See page 36 for pressing.

## Hint

**Change the colours**
Try new colour combinations on three extra napkins for a setting for six people.

# The Penny-farthing Bicycle

Imagine the days of long ago when Great Grandpa was a boy.

## The design

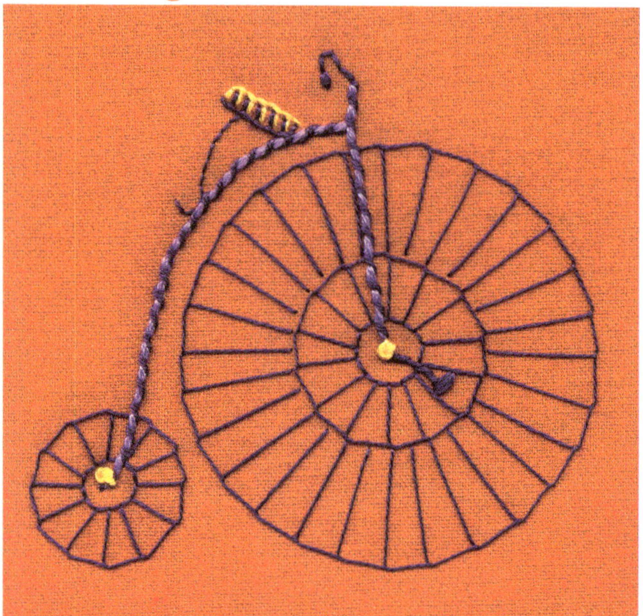

*The Penny-farthing Bicycle*

Blanket stitch is worked in circles to represent the wheels and spokes on this olden day bicycle. Smaller blanket stitches create the seat. Other details are added with straight stitch, back stitch, whipped back stitch, and French knot. Follow the instructions on this page to work the design exactly as shown here on an orange background. To apply the design to a project, see the facing page where the bicycle is featured on a cover for a notebook.

## The pattern

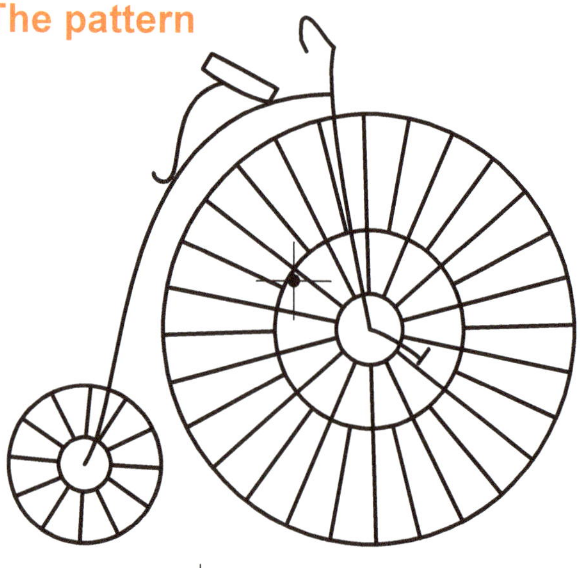

**Key:** Centre of design

## Shopping list

- Orange cotton fabric for background: 25cm (10") square
- Fabric or interfacing for backing: 25cm (10") square
- Stranded cotton thread:
  (A) dark violet (B) medium violet (C) medium yellow
- Tracing paper and other items for transferring the pattern onto the fabric

## Let's begin

Read page 15 for backing the fabric, and pages 22-25 for transferring the pattern onto the fabric, then select and use suitable methods for your fabric. For the orange fabric shown here, the pattern was transferred onto the fabric by tracing with a water erasable fabric marker and then the backing fabric was tacked to the wrong side.

## Stitch!

For help, see pages 40-43 for straight stitch, 76-79 for back stitch and whipped back stitch, 130-133 for blanket stitch, including completing a shape, and pages 184-187 for French knot.

1 Starting at the rim, work the outer section of spokes for the front wheel in blanket stitch (1 strand A). To complete the circle, loop the last stitch behind the first stitch (Diagram 1). Using the same holes at the ends of every second stitch of the previous row (Diagram 2), work the inner section of spokes (1 strand A).

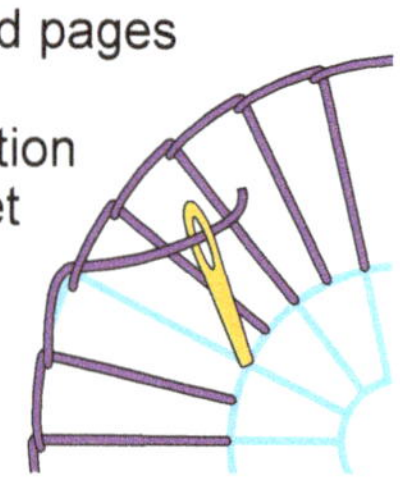

**Diagram 1**

2 Using the same holes at the ends of the smaller blanket stitches, stitch the small circle in back stitch (1 strand A). Stitch the back wheel in a similar way to the front wheel, noting that there is only one row of spokes.

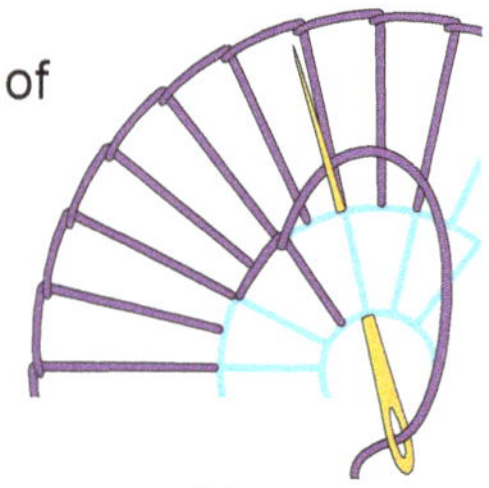

**Diagram 2**

3 Work the frame in back stitch (4 strands B), then whip these back stitches (2 strands A). Stitch the pedal crank in back stitch, then whip these back stitches (2 strands A). Add the pedal with three straight stitches worked through the same two holes in the fabric. Work the handlebar in back stitch, adding the handle with three straight stitches worked through the same two holes (2 strands A). Stitch the curved seat support in back stitch (1 strand A). Work the lower edge of the seat (2 strands A), then the upper edge (2 strands C), both in blanket stitch (Diagram 3). Add the wheel bolts, each with a two wrap French knot (4 strands C).

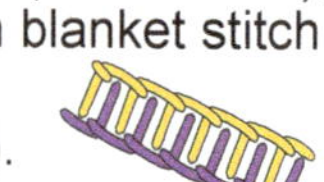

**Diagram 3**

## Let's finish

Take out the tacking. Rinse the work in cold water to remove the fabric marker. When partly dry, press or pin out the work. See page 36 for pressing and for pinning out.

# The Penny-farthing Bicycle Notebook Cover

Travel to the past with this old-fashioned notebook cover.

## The project

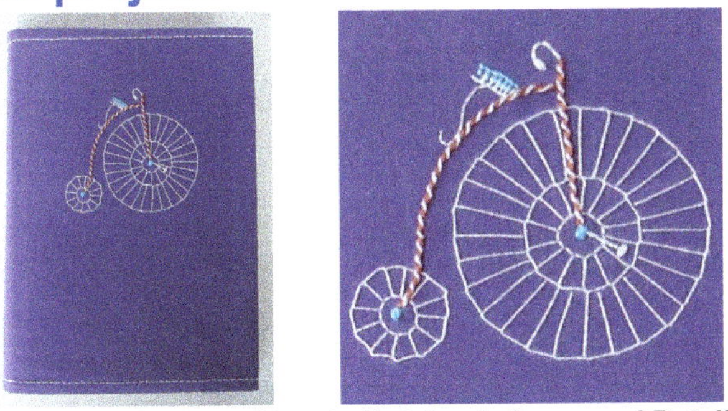

***The Penny-farthing Bicycle Notebook Cover* and Detail**

This project features *The Penny-farthing Bicycle* worked in a different colour scheme. The design is worked on a piece of cotton fabric that is then made up into a notebook cover once the design is stitched.
This notebook is 20cm x 14cm wide (8" x 5 1/2") in size.

## Shopping list

- Notebook
- Violet cotton fabric for the cover and lightweight iron-on interfacing for backing:
  see the Let's begin instructions below for calculating the dimensions
- Stranded cotton thread:
  (A) white (B) medium orange (C) medium aqua
- Machine sewing thread: violet
- Tissue paper
- Items for transferring the pattern onto the fabric

## Let's begin

See opposite for *The Penny-farthing Bicycle* pattern.
As follows, make a tissue paper pattern for the cover and its lining. This pattern can then be used to estimate the fabric and interfacing required.

***Making the pattern for the cover***

Measure the height of the front of the notebook and add 3cm (1 1/4"). Measure the entire width of the front, spine, and back of the notebook and add 6mm (1/4") for ease. Draw a rectangle using these measurements onto a piece of tissue paper and cut it out. Label this the lining pattern.
On another piece of tissue paper, make a tracing of the lining pattern, then add 8cm (3") onto each end for the flaps. Cut this out and label it the outer layer pattern.
Place this pattern onto the notebook, aligning the flap fold line with the right hand side of the front of the notebook. Mark the position of the left hand side of the front onto the pattern with a dashed line (Diagram 1).

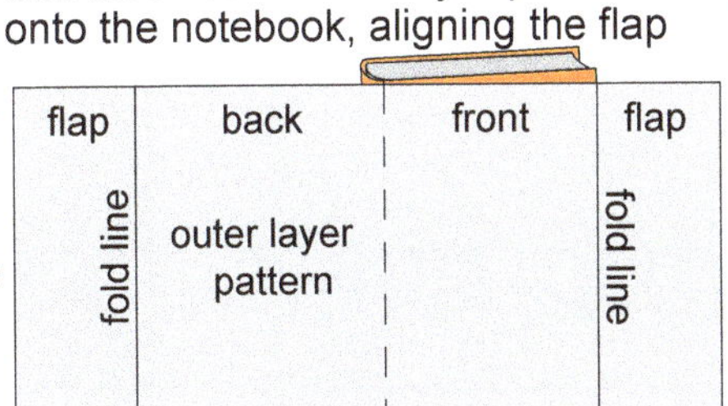


**Diagram 1**

Trace the pattern for the bicycle onto the front of the outer layer pattern, centred between the flap fold line and the dashed line, and with the marked centre of the design 8cm (3") down from the upper edge (Diagram 2).

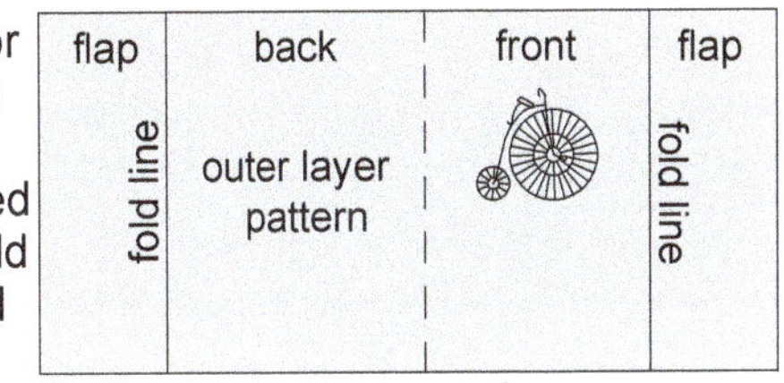


**Diagram 2**

***Preparing the fabric***

Cut out one piece of violet fabric using the lining pattern. Cut out one piece of violet fabric and one piece of interfacing using the outer layer pattern. Following the instructions on page 15 for backing the fabric, attach the iron-on interfacing onto the wrong side of the outer layer fabric. Referring to the outer layer pattern, work a row of tacking 8cm (3") in from each end to mark the flap fold lines. Transfer the bicycle onto the front of the outer layer fabric using transfer paper. See page 24 for transferring the pattern using transfer paper.

## Stitch!

Work the bicycle following steps 1-3 of the stitch instructions for the original design on the previous page, substituting the alternative threads.
Work a row of back stitch 2cm (3/4") away from the entire upper and lower raw edges (1 strand A).

## Let's finish

Rinse the work in cold water to remove the pattern markings. When almost dry, press. See page 36 for pressing.
On the outer layer, fold under 6mm (1/4") to the wrong side on each end of the flaps and machine stitch with violet machine sewing thread. With right sides together, fold the flaps over at the tacked lines and pin (Diagram 3).

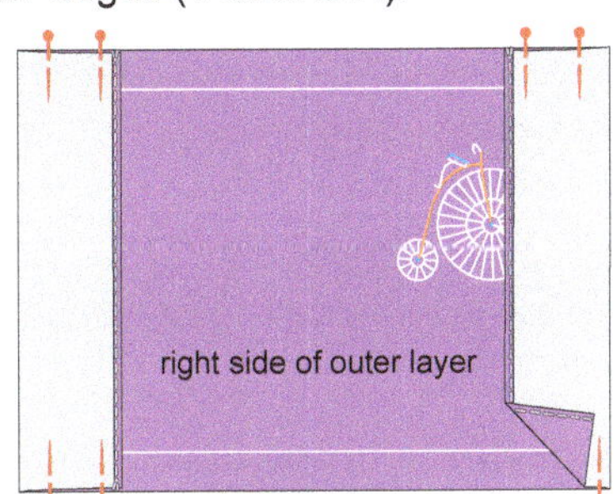


**Diagram 3**

With right sides together, pin the lining to the outer layer along the upper and lower edges. The flaps are between the layers.
Using a 1cm (3/8") seam allowance, machine stitch along the upper edge (Diagram 4). Stitch along the lower edge in the same way.

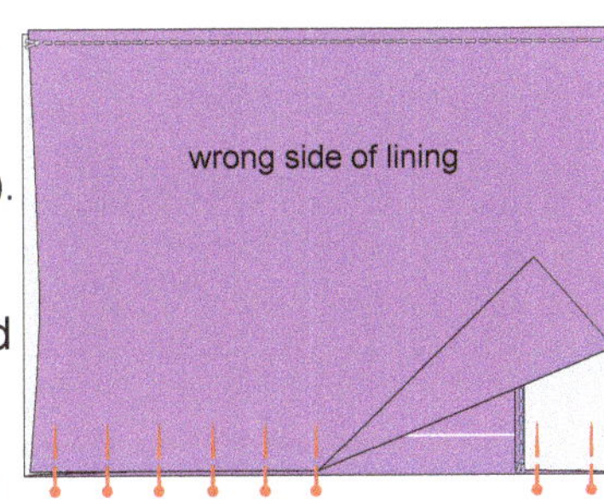


**Diagram 4**

Turn the cover right side out. Re-fold the flaps over to the lining side of the cover. Take out the tacking and press.
Insert the notebook into the fabric cover.

# Amazing Planets

Let's take a space flight and visit some planets.

## The design

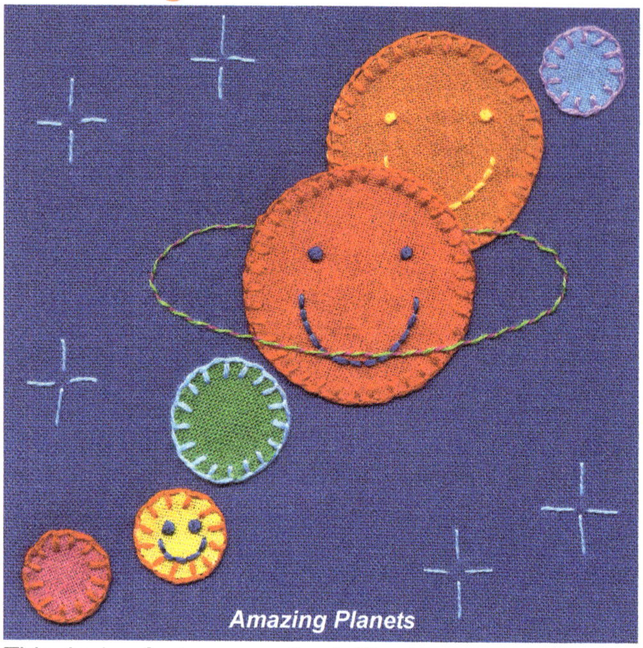

*Amazing Planets*

This design features appliqué. The planets are edged with blanket stitch. Also used are straight stitch, whipped running stitch, back stitch, and French knot. Follow the instructions on this page to work the design as above. For a child's winter top, see the next page.

## The pattern

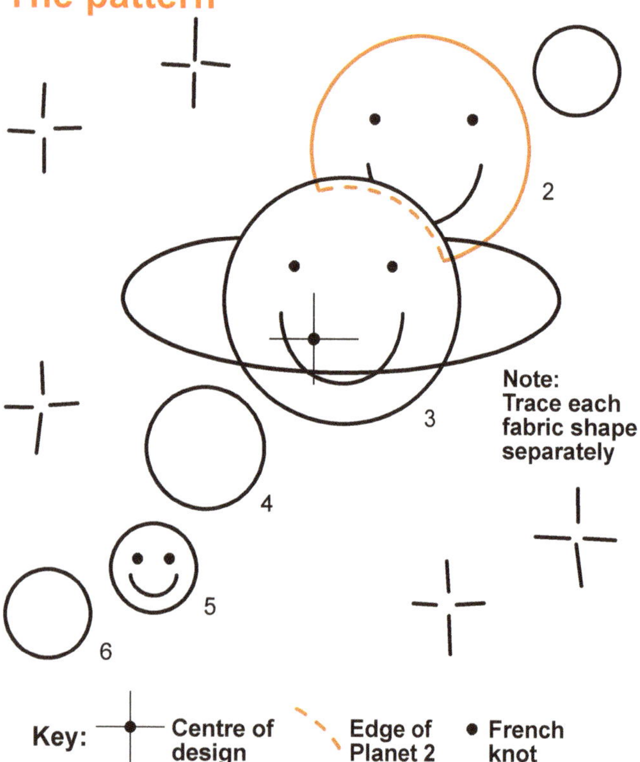


## Shopping list

- Blue cotton fabric for background: 25cm (10") square
- Fabric or interfacing for backing: 25cm (10") square
- Aqua, orange, red, green, yellow, and pink cotton fabrics for the appliqué: 5cm (2") square of each colour
- Paper-backed fusible webbing: 10cm (4") square
- Stranded cotton thread:
  (A) medium violet (B) medium blue (C) medium aqua
  (D) light green (E) medium yellow (F) medium orange
  (G) medium red (H) medium magenta
- Tracing paper and other items for transferring the pattern onto the fabric

## Let's begin

Read page 15 for backing the fabric, and pages 22-25 for transferring the pattern onto the fabric, then select and use suitable methods for your fabric. For the blue fabric shown here, the pattern, not including the faces, was transferred centrally onto the background fabric by tracing with a chalk-based pencil and then the backing fabric was tacked to the wrong side.

Referring to pages 220-223 for appliqué and following steps 3-7 of Method 2, prepare and cut out the fabric shapes for the planets. Transfer the faces, and the ring where it crosses **Planet 3**, onto the fabric shapes.

## Stitch!

For help, see pages 40-43 for straight stitch, 58-61 for whipped running stitch, 76-79 for back stitch, 130-133 for blanket stitch, including completing a shape, and pages 184-187 for French knot. When working this design, complete the blanket stitch edging of each planet before fusing and edging the next. The faces, the ring around **Planet 3**, and the stars are worked later in steps 3 and 4.

1 Place **Planet 1**, glue side down, onto the background fabric over the marked outline. Cover with a pressing cloth and fuse the fabric shape on with a hot iron. Work around the edge in blanket stitch (2 strands A), passing the last stitch under the first so that the join is not visible.

2 Similarly, work **Planet 2** (2 strands F). Do not stitch where **Planet 2** will be covered by **Planet 3**. Then work **Planet 3** (2 strands G), **Planet 4** (2 strands C), **Planet 5** (2 strands F) and **Planet 6** (2 strands G).

3 On **Planet 2**, work the mouth in back stitch and each eye with a two wrap French knot (2 strands E). For **Planets 3** and **5**, work the faces in a similar way (2 strands B). Stitch the ring around **Planet 3** in running stitch (1 strand H), then whip these running stitches (1 strand D).

4 Work each star with four slightly uneven straight stitches (1 strand C).

## Let's finish

Take out the tacking. Press or pin out the work. See page 36 for pressing and for pinning out.

# Amazing Planets Winter Top

Bring a love of astronomy to a child with these colourful planets and twinkling stars.

## The project

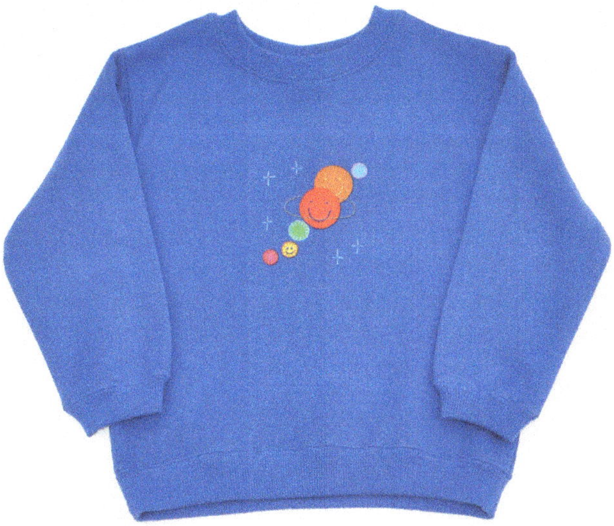

***Amazing Planets Winter Top***

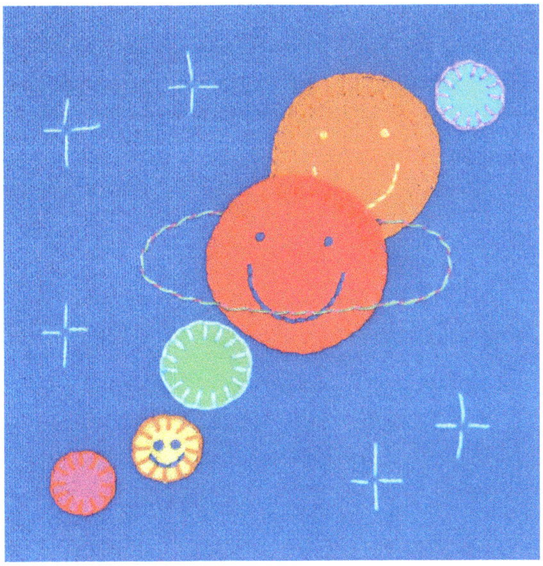

**Detail of *Amazing Planets Winter Top***

Working this design on a purchased winter top is a simple, yet effective, way to add visual impact and excitement to an item of clothing.
This blue winter top features *Amazing Planets* worked with exactly the same colours, threads, and stitching as the original design on the page opposite.

## Shopping list

- Blue stretch knit winter top
- Lightweight iron-on interfacing for backing: 10cm (4") square
- Fabric for the appliqué shapes, paper-backed fusible webbing, and threads as listed for the original design on the page opposite
- Tracing paper and other items for transferring the pattern onto the garment

## Let's begin

See the page opposite for the *Amazing Planets* pattern. Attach the piece of iron-on interfacing onto the wrong side of the front of the garment at the selected position. This will stabilize the area where the design is to be stitched. See page 21 for placing the pattern and page 15 for backing the fabric. Transfer the pattern, not including the faces, onto the front of the garment using transfer paper. See page 24 for transferring the pattern using transfer paper.
Referring to pages 220-223 for appliqué and following steps 3-7 of Method 2, prepare and cut out the fabric shapes for the planets. Transfer the faces, and the ring where it crosses **Planet 3**, onto the fabric shapes.

## Stitch!

Attach the shapes and stitch the design following the stitch instructions for the original design on the page opposite.

## Let's finish

Rinse the winter top in cold water to remove the pattern markings. When almost dry, turn the top inside out and press it. See page 36 for pressing.

## Hint

**Stitch at a larger scale**

*Amazing Planets* would be a fun design to work at a larger scale, in fact you could add some extra planets to this design as well if you'd like to!

# Sunlit Garden

This garden is radiant in the golden sunlight.

## The design

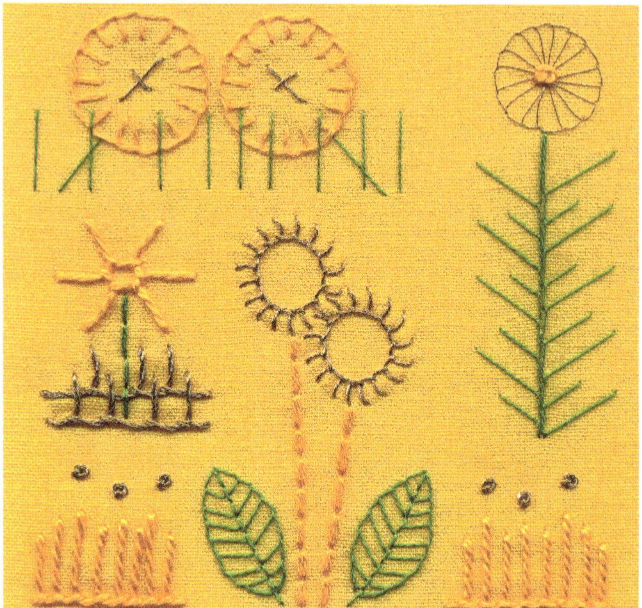

*Sunlit Garden*

*Sunlit Garden* features various forms of blanket stitch with the addition of straight stitch, back stitch, and French knot. The design includes gold metallic thread, adding shimmer. Follow the instructions on this page to work the design as shown here. To adapt elements of the design for a framed picture, see the next page.

## The pattern

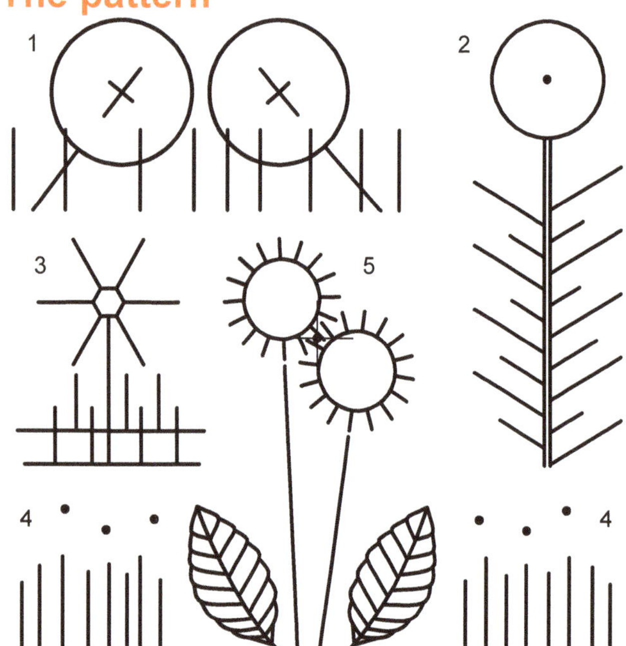


**Key:** Centre of design • French knot

## Shopping list

- Yellow cotton fabric for background: 25cm (10") square
- Fabric or interfacing for backing: 25cm (10") square
- Stranded cotton thread:
  (A) light green (B) medium yellow
- No. 5 perlé cotton thread: (C) medium yellow
- No. 5 perlé metallic thread: (D) gold
- Tracing paper and other items for transferring the pattern onto the fabric

## Let's begin

Read page 15 for backing the fabric, and pages 22-25 for transferring the pattern onto the fabric, then select and use suitable methods for your fabric. For the yellow fabric shown here, the pattern was transferred onto the fabric by tracing with a water erasable fabric marker and then the backing fabric was tacked to the wrong side.

## Stitch!

For help, see pages 40-43 for straight stitch, 76-79 for back stitch, 130-133 for blanket stitch, including completing a shape, and pages 184-187 for French knot. See also page 17 for preparing perlé metallic thread.

**Flower 1** Work each flower with an inward circle of blanket stitch (2 strands B). Add centres with crossed straight stitches (4 ply D). Add the stems and leaves in straight stitch (1 strand A).

**Flower 2** Work the flower with an inward circle of blanket stitch (1 ply D). Add a two wrap French knot for the centre (1 strand C). Beginning below the flower (Diagram 1), work row of slanted blanket stitch on right (1 strand A). Repeat on left.

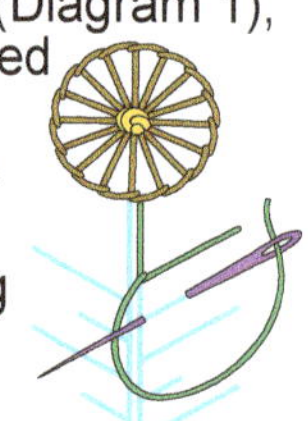

Diagram 1

**Flower 3** Starting at the left, work the upper row of gold leaves and then the lower row in blanket stitch (8 ply D). Add the stem in back stitch (2 strands A). Work the flower (1 strand C) with an outward circle of blanket stitch (Diagram 2). Pass the last stitch under the first to complete flower (Diagram 3).

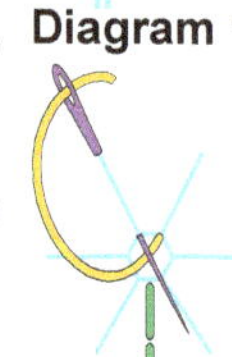

Diagram 2

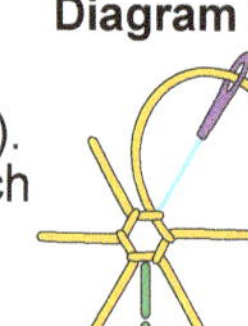

Diagram 3

**Flower 4** Work the leaves in blanket stitch (1 strand C). Add French knots, each with two wraps, for the flowers (4 ply D).

**Flower 5** Stitch each flower with an outward circle of blanket stitch (4 ply D). Work the stems in back stitch (4 strands B). Stitch the leaf stem and central vein in back stitch (1 strand A). Working from the leaf tip, stitch down each side of the leaf in blanket stitch, forming the outline and side veins (1 strand A). Work the last stitch with its anchor ending at the central vein (Diagram 4).

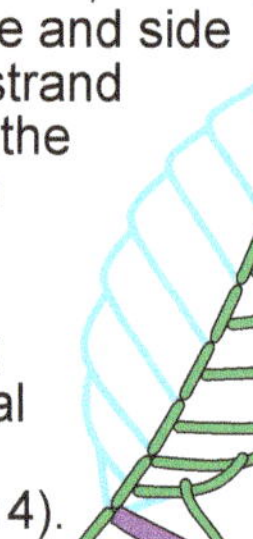

Diagram 4

## Let's finish

Take out tacking. Rinse the work in cold water to remove the fabric marker. When partly dry, press or pin out the work. See page 36 for pressing and for pinning out.

# Sunlit Flowers Framed Picture

Introduce blue and white décor with this floral picture.

## The project

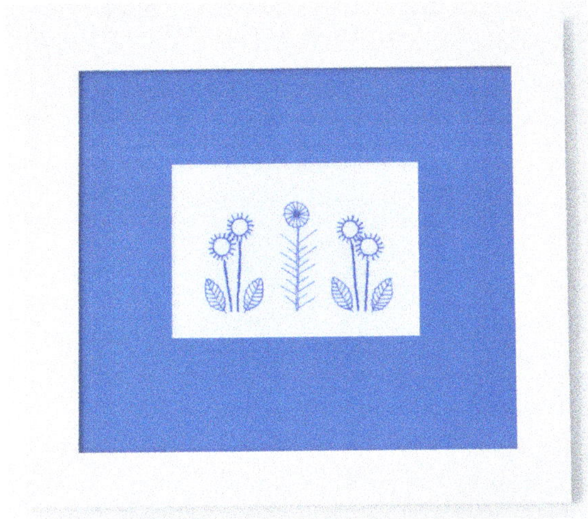

*Sunlit Flowers Framed Picture*

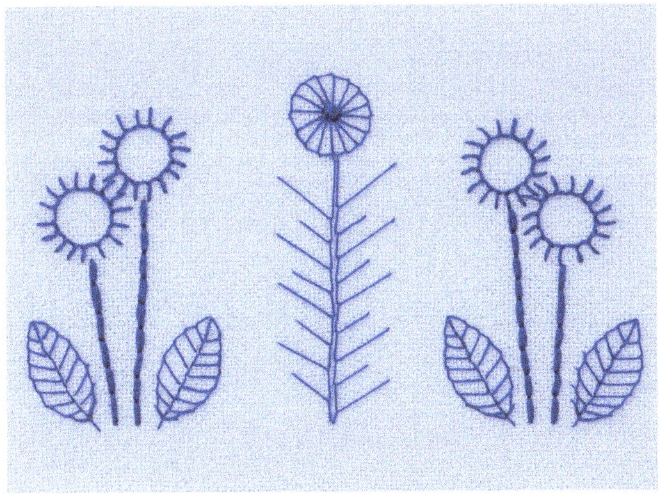

Detail of *Sunlit Flowers Framed Picture*

Here's a refreshing blue and white artwork! In many art media, blue and white has been a popular colour combination for many hundreds of years.

For this project, **Flowers 2** and **5** from *Sunlit Garden* are worked entirely in blue thread on a white background. This project illustrates that a completely different look can be achieved by stitching with a single colour of thread on a white background.

The measurements given in the shopping list on this page are suitable for a picture frame with window dimensions of 22cm x 25cm wide (8 1/2" x 10"). If your picture frame has different dimensions, you will need to adjust the shopping list measurements accordingly. The dimensions of the wadding, the foam core board, or similar, and the mat board, are determined by the size of the backing board of the frame you select.

## Shopping list

- White picture frame:
  22cm x 25cm wide (8 1/2" x 10") window
- White linen-look fabric for background:
  40cm x 45cm wide (16" x 18")
- Fabric or interfacing for backing:
  40cm x 45cm wide (16" x 18")
- Stranded cotton thread:
  medium blue
- Strong thread for lacing
- Tracing paper and other items for transferring the pattern onto the fabric
- Thin wadding
- Foam core board, or similar
- Blue mat board

## Let's begin

See the page opposite for the pattern.

Transfer the pattern for **Flower 2** centrally onto the fabric by tracing with a water erasable fabric marker or by using transfer paper. Transfer the pattern for **Flower 5** onto the fabric to the right of **Flower 2**, and then a mirror image of **Flower 5** to the left of **Flower 2**. See pages 22-25 for transferring the pattern onto the fabric, and see page 20 for information on mirroring the pattern.

Tack the piece of backing fabric to the wrong side of the white fabric. See page 15 for backing the fabric.

## Stitch!

Work the flowers following the stitch instructions for **Flowers 2** and **5** on the page opposite, replacing all threads with medium blue stranded cotton thread as follows:

**Flower 2**

Flower, stem, and leaves: 1 strand

Centre: 4 strands

**Flower 5**

Flowers: 2 strands

Stems: 4 strands

Leaves: 1 strand

## Let's finish

Take out the tacking. Rinse the work in cold water to remove the pattern markings. When partly dry, press or pin out the work. See page 36 for pressing and for pinning out.

Pad, lace, and frame the work. See page 37 for lacing.

Alternatively, take the work to a professional framer who specializes in framing textiles.

# Fly stitch

## and variations

Fly stitch is an isolated loop stitch that is very easy to work. It is formed with an open loop held down with a straight stitch anchor. Depending on the length of the anchor, the result is a Y or V shaped stitch. The two sides of the loop can be different lengths, making an asymmetrical stitch.

Fly stitches can be used singly, or scattered over an area. Also, they can be worked side-by-side or stacked, forming rows or patterns. The stitches can be worked spaced apart, or they can meet or overlap each other.

Fly stitches are particularly suited to portraying sharp points, such as on stars or flower petals.

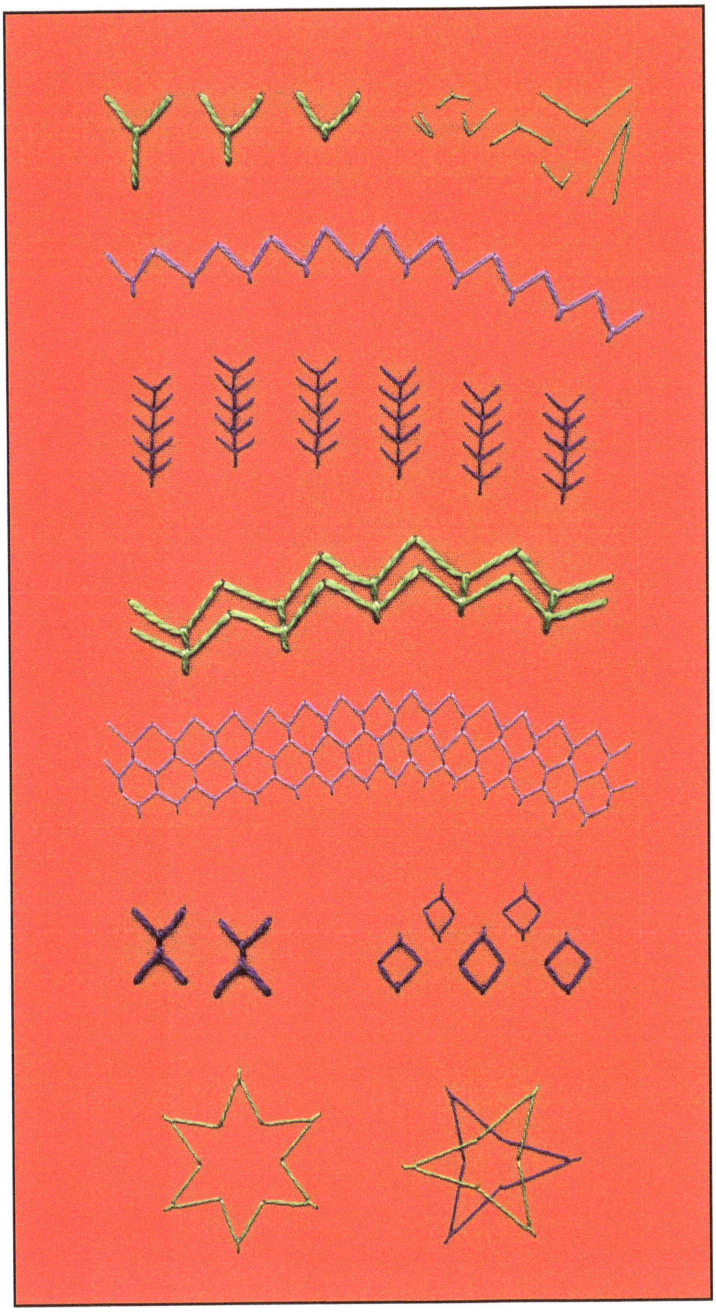

Fly stitches worked with varying anchor stitch lengths, and fly stitches worked with varying angles and lengths of sides

Fly stitch worked as a horizontal row

Fly stitch worked as vertical rows

Fly stitch worked as stacked rows

Fly stitch worked as stacked rows, offset to form hexagons

Fly stitches worked with anchors meeting, and fly stitches worked with sides meeting

Fly stitches worked to form a star shape, and fly stitches worked to form overlapping shapes

**Fly stitch and variations sampler**

# Fly stitch and variations

## Hints

Fly stitch is most commonly worked by skimming the needle in and out of the fabric before pulling the thread through.

Aim to keep the thread tension of the two sides of the loop and the anchor equal so that the stitch lies flat against the fabric.

When working fly stitch, the length of the anchor can vary from short to long depending on the desired effect.

Many different effects can be achieved when working horizontal, vertical, and stacked rows of fly stitch.

When working fly stitches that meet, at each junction take the needle through the same hole in the fabric as the previously worked stitch, but do not split the thread.

## Fly stitch and variations: right-handed

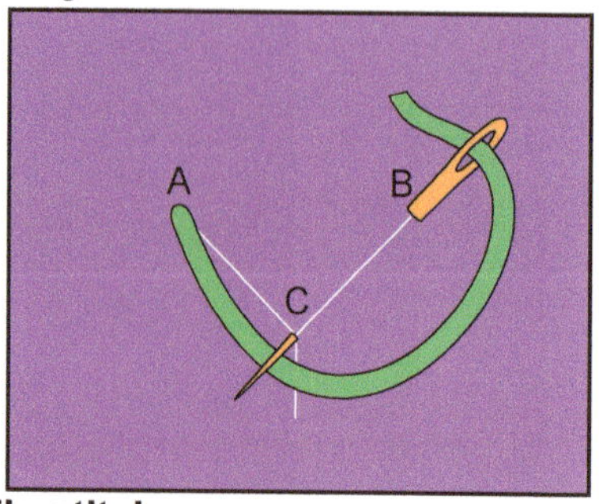


**Fly stitch**
**1** Come up at A. Take needle down at B and emerge at C. Keep thread under tip of needle, forming a loop.

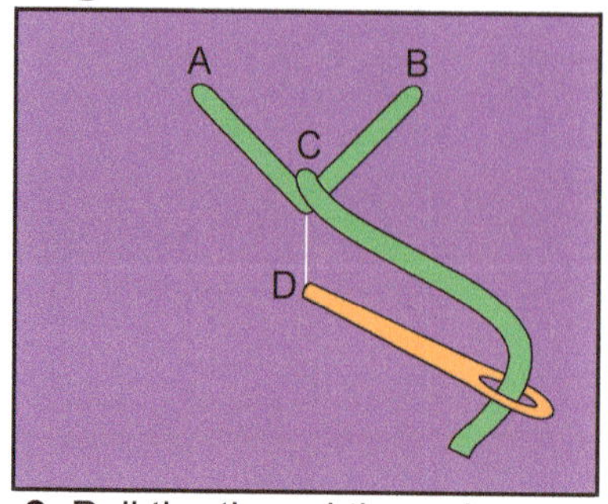


**2** Pull the thread through, allowing loop to settle in place. Take the thread to the back at D, forming a straight stitch anchor.

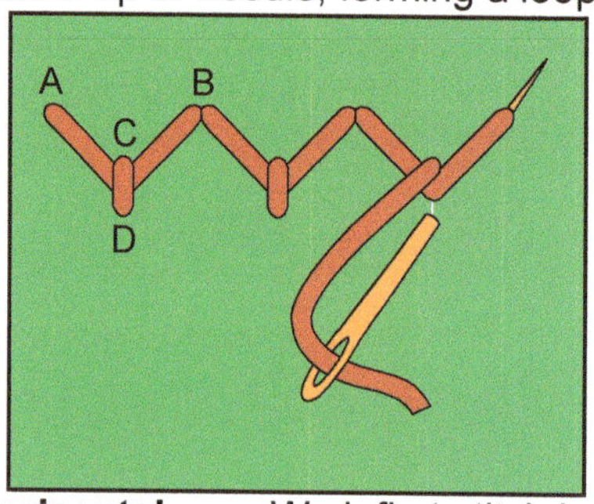


**Horizontal row** Work first stitch in order shown. Begin second stitch at B, through same hole in fabric as previous stitch. Continue along row.

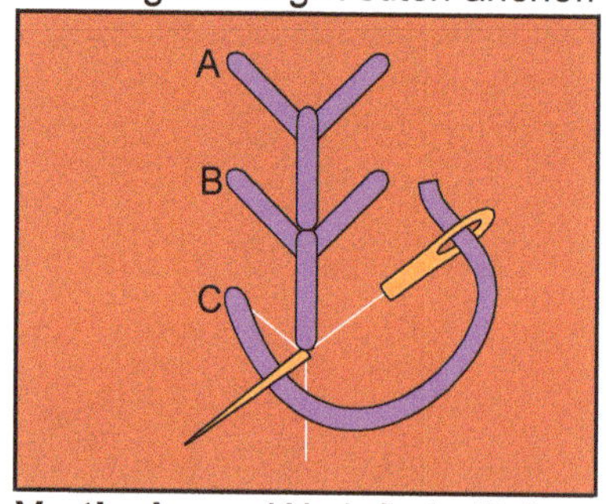


**Vertical row** Work first stitch starting at A. Work second stitch starting at B, third stitch starting at C. Continue down the row.

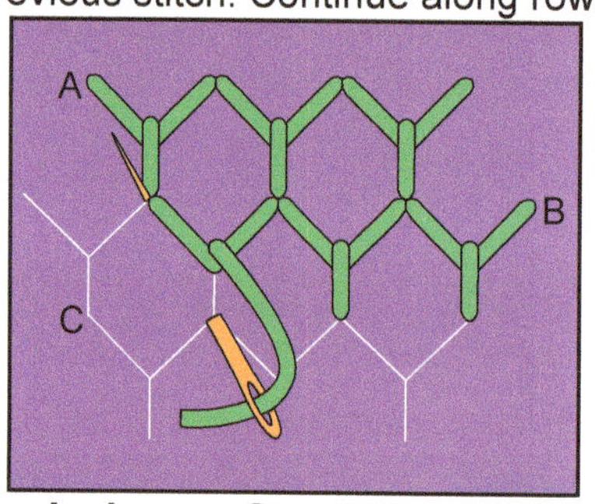


**Stacked rows** Start at A, work a horizontal row. Start at B, work second row in opposite direction. Secure thread on back. For third row, start at C.

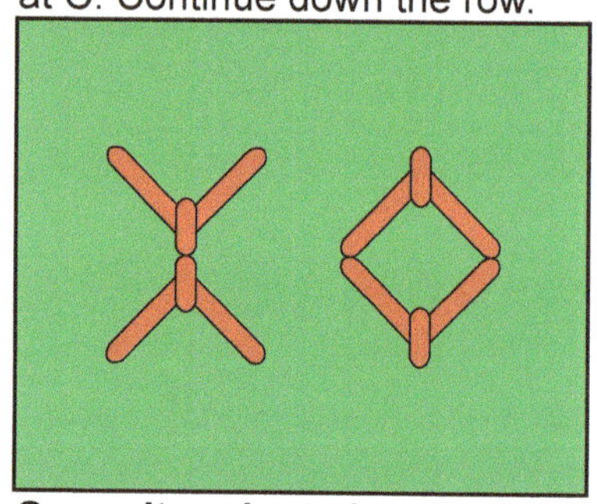

**Opposite orientation** Work a fly stitch. Work a second fly stitch in opposite orientation. Examples show anchors or sides meeting.

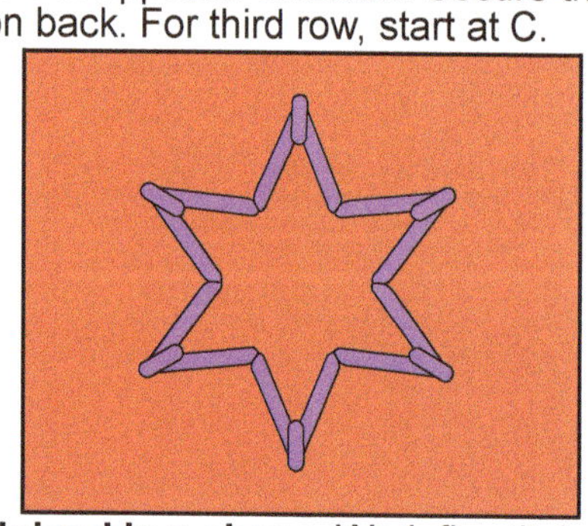

**Joined in a shape** Work fly stitches anti-clockwise, using the same hole in the fabric where each stitch meets the previous stitch.

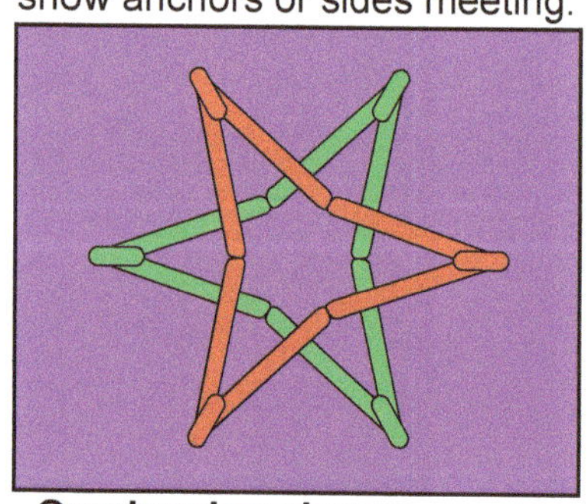

**Overlapping shapes**
Working anti-clockwise, stitch the green fly stitches first, then stitch the red fly stitches.

# Fly stitch and variations: left-handed

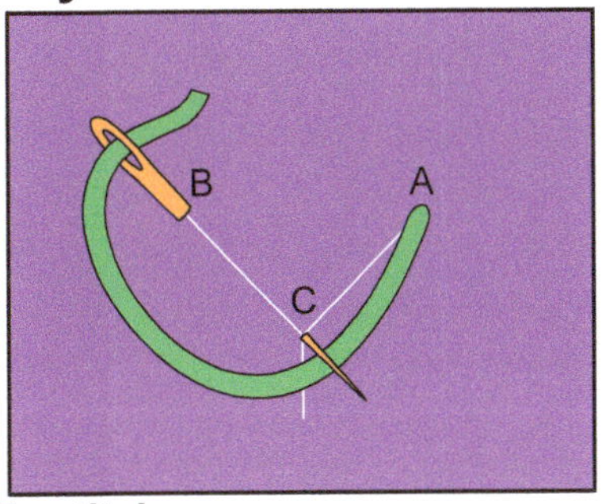


**Fly stitch**
**1** Come up at A. Take needle down at B and emerge at C. Keep thread under tip of needle, forming a loop.

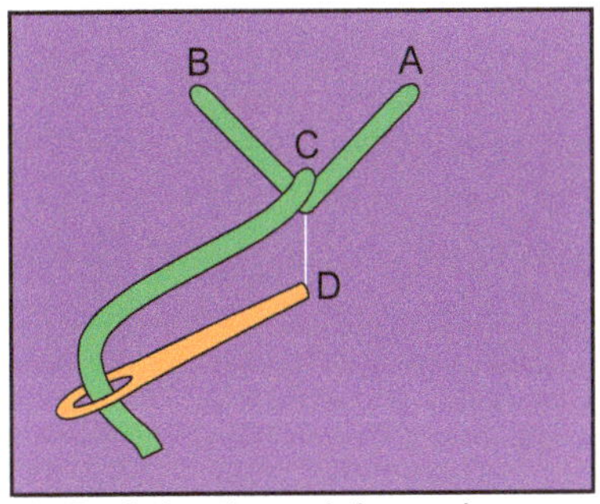


**2** Pull the thread through, allowing loop to settle in place. Take the thread to the back at D, forming a straight stitch anchor.

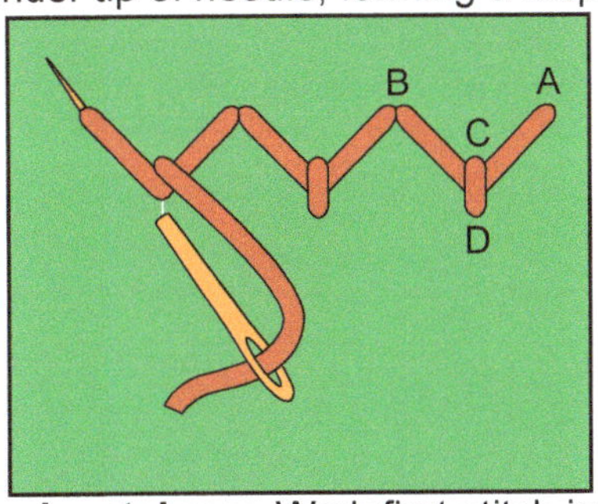


**Horizontal row** Work first stitch in order shown. Begin second stitch at B, through same hole in fabric as previous stitch. Continue along row.

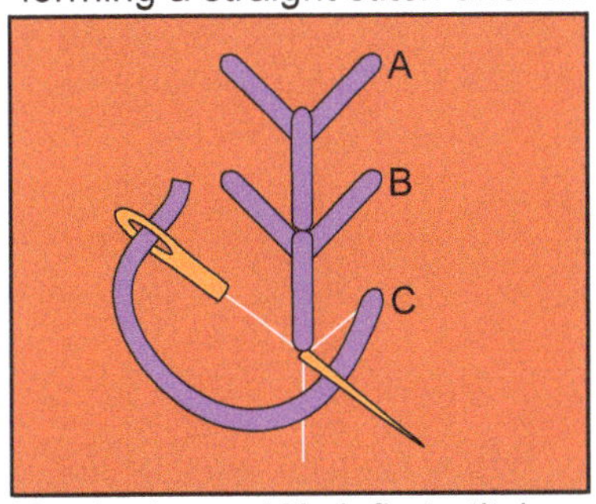


**Vertical row** Work first stitch starting at A. Work second stitch starting at B, third stitch starting at C. Continue down the row.

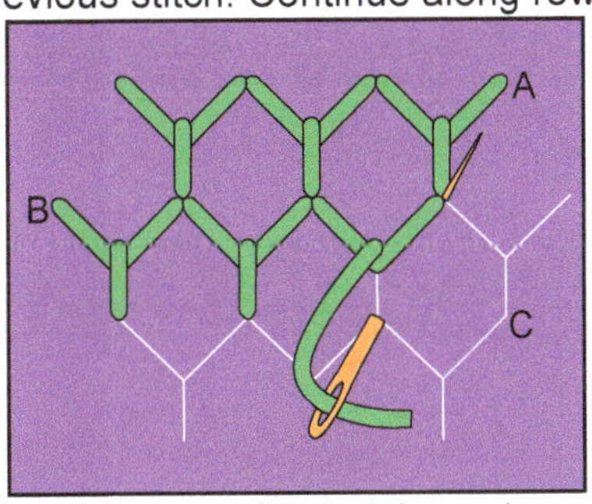


**Stacked rows** Start at A, work a horizontal row. Start at B, work second row in opposite direction. Secure thread on back. For third row, start at C.

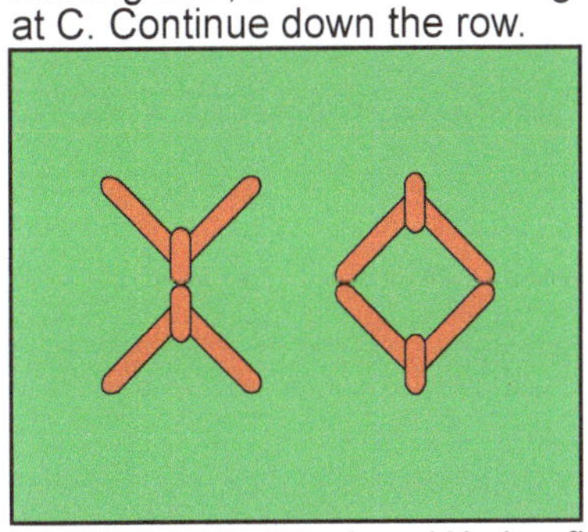

**Opposite orientation** Work a fly stitch. Work a second fly stitch in opposite orientation. Examples show anchors or sides meeting.

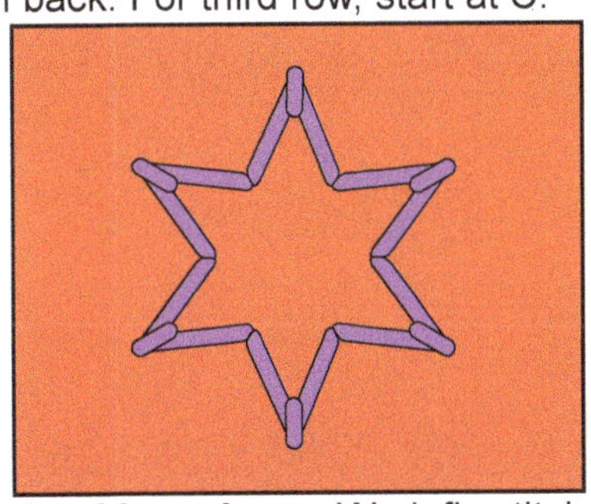

**Joined in a shape** Work fly stitches clockwise, using the same hole in the fabric where each stitch meets the previous stitch.

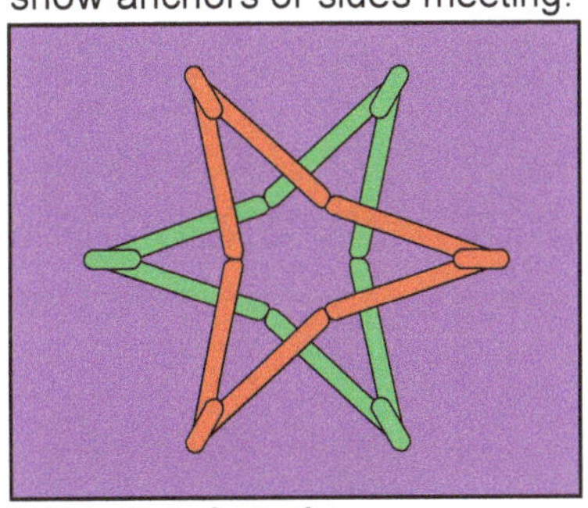

**Overlapping shapes**
Working clockwise, stitch the green fly stitches first, then stitch the red fly stitches.

# Fly stitch
## and variations

# Designs and project ideas

## The designs

Eric Echidna

Prickly Pineapple

Glittering Snowflakes

Violet Essence

Hot-air Balloon

Lily Garden

# Eric Echidna

I'm rather shy and very prickly, and I really, really love ants!

## The design

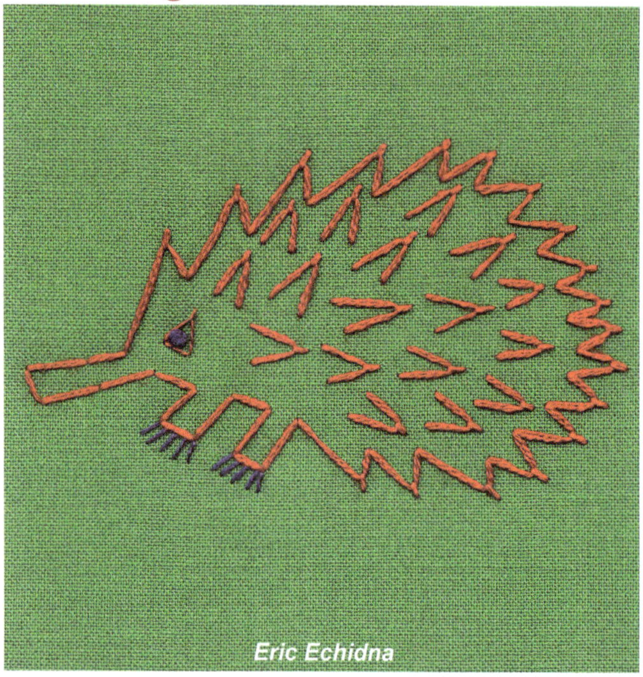

*Eric Echidna*

The echidna, or spiny anteater, is a much-loved Australian mammal. In this easy design, the prickly spines covering Eric's body are depicted with fly stitch. Details are added with straight stitch, back stitch, and French knot.

To work the design exactly as shown here on a green background, use the instructions on this page. To apply the echidna to a T-shirt for a child, see the project idea on the following page.

## The pattern

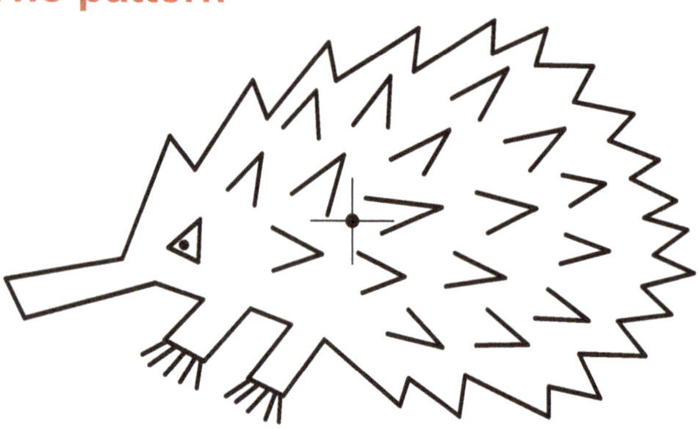

**Key:** **Centre of design** **Fly stitch** **• French knot**

## Shopping list

- Green cotton fabric for background: 25cm (10") square
- Fabric or interfacing for backing: 25cm (10") square
- Stranded silk thread: (A) dark violet (B) medium red
- Tracing paper and other items for transferring the pattern onto the fabric

## Let's begin

Read page 15 for backing the fabric, and pages 22-25 for transferring the pattern onto the fabric, then select and use suitable methods for your fabric. For the green fabric shown here, the pattern was transferred centrally onto the fabric by tracing with a water erasable fabric marker and then the backing fabric was tacked to the wrong side.

## Stitch!

For help, see pages 40-43 for straight stitch, 76-79 for back stitch, 148-151 for fly stitch, including working a row, and pages 184-187 for French knot.

When working this design, work the fly stitches following the marked V shapes with the anchors extending beyond the marked points. Vary the size of the anchors to make some spines appear more prickly than others.

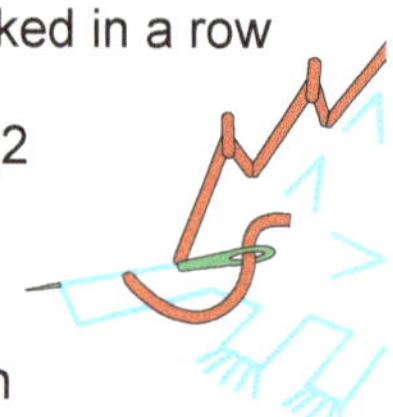

**Diagram 1**

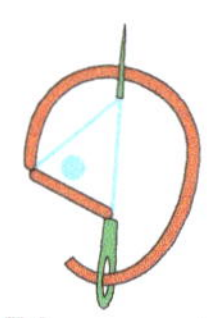

**Diagram 2**

1. Stitch the spiny outline in fly stitch worked in a row (2 strands B).
2. Add the snout with long back stitches (2 strands B), working two stitches along each long side (Diagram 1) and one across the end of the snout.
3. Continuing with the same thread, stitch the legs in long back stitch.
4. Stitch the spines on the body in fly stitch, carrying the thread on the back of the work between stitches (2 strands B).
5. Outline the eye (1 strand B) with a straight stitch at the base and a fly stitch above it (Diagram 2).
6. Complete the eye with a two wrap French knot for the pupil (4 strands A).
7. Stitch the claws with five straight stitches on each foot (1 strand A).

## Let's finish

Take out tacking. Rinse the work in cold water to remove the fabric marker. When partly dry, press or pin out the work. See page 36 for pressing and for pinning out.

## Hint

**Carrying the thread**

When working the isolated fly stitches depicting the spines, work them so that the distance that the thread is carried between stitches is as short as possible.

# Eric Echidna T-shirt

Add some prickly characters to a child's T-shirt.

## The project

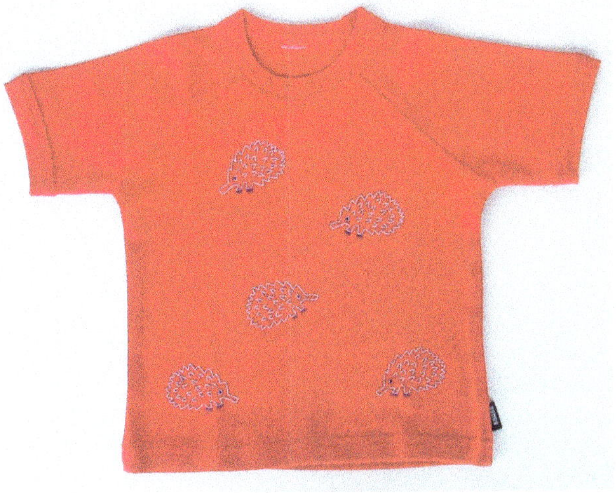

*Eric Echidna T-shirt*

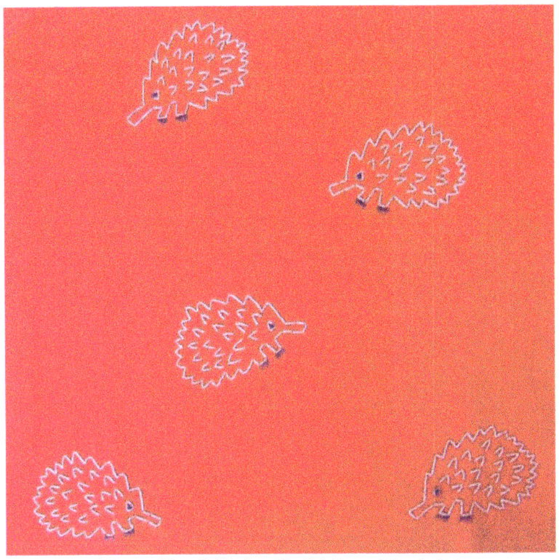

Detail of *Eric Echidna T-shirt*

Five echidnas scattered over the front of this garment have transformed an otherwise plain T-shirt into a piece of wearable art. All the echidnas are reduced in size and two are a mirror image.

## Shopping list

- Red stretch knit T-shirt
- Lightweight iron-on interfacing for backing: five pieces 5cm x 7cm wide (2" x 2 3/4")
- Stranded cotton thread: (A) dark violet (B) white
- Tracing paper and other items for transferring the pattern onto the T-shirt

## Let's begin

Prepare the pattern by reducing it to 65% of its original size. Using separate pieces of tracing paper for each, make three tracings of the reduced pattern. Make two extra tracings that are a mirror image of the reduced pattern. See page 20 for information on mirroring the pattern. Referring to the photo and the diagram, position the tracings on the front of the garment. Rotate the tracings and move them around until you are happy with their placement (Diagram 1). Using tacking stitches in a light colour, record the position at which each echidna is to be stitched.

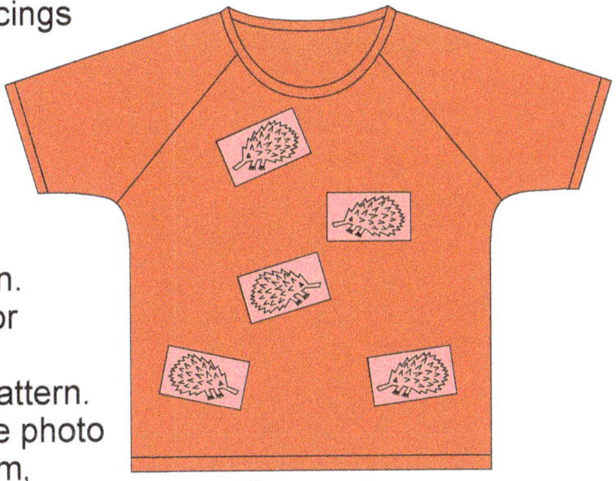

Diagram 1

From here on, each echidna is prepared and stitched before moving on to the next echidna. Begin with the echidna that is closest to the neckline.

Following the instructions on page 15 for backing the fabric, attach one piece of iron-on interfacing onto the wrong side of the front of the garment at the position for the first echidna. This will stabilize the area where the design is to be stitched.

Transfer the pattern onto the front of the T-shirt by tracing with a water erasable fabric marker or by using transfer paper. See pages 22-25 for transferring the pattern onto the fabric.

## Stitch!

Work this first echidna following the stitch instructions for the original design on the previous page, using the alternative coloured threads with the following number of strands:

Body, eye outline, and claws: 1 strand

Pupil: 2 strands

Continue in this way, preparing and completing each echidna before moving to the next.

## Let's finish

Take out the tacking and turn the T-shirt inside out. On the wrong side, peel back any excess interfacing from its outer edges and trim it back close to the stitches. Rinse the T-shirt in cold water to remove the water erasable fabric marker. When dry, turn it inside out and press. See page 36 for pressing.

## Hint

**Adapt the design**

As an alternative to scattering the echidnas on the T-shirt, consider placing just three echidnas in a row across the front.

# Violet Essence

Violet, a colour so regal.

## The design

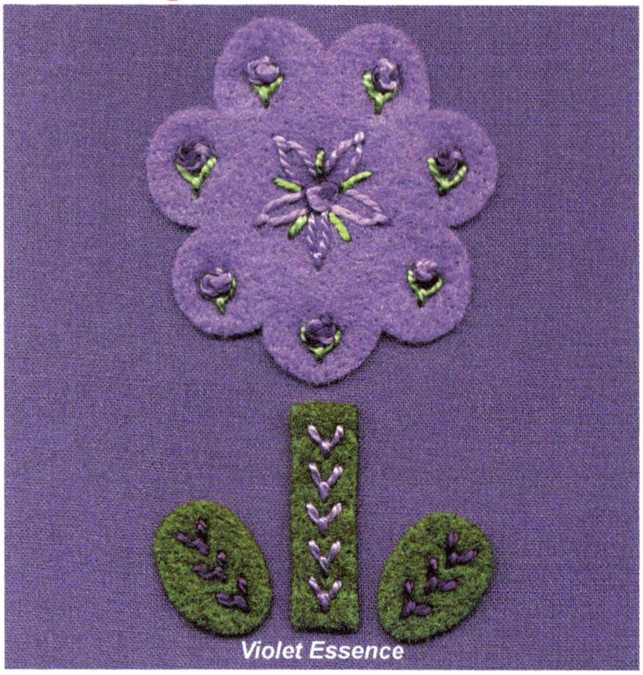


The technique of appliqué is used for this design. The stem, leaf and flower shapes are cut from felt and attached to the background using fly stitch, straight stitch, and French knot. The edges of the felt shapes remain free. Follow the instructions here to work the design as above. To feature elements of the design on pincushions, see the project ideas opposite.

## The pattern

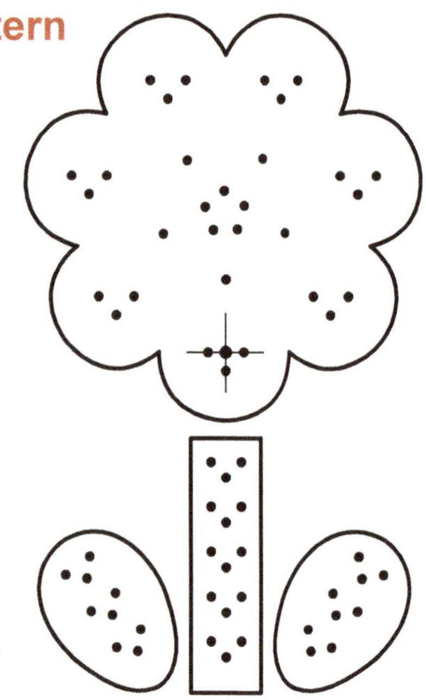

**Key:**

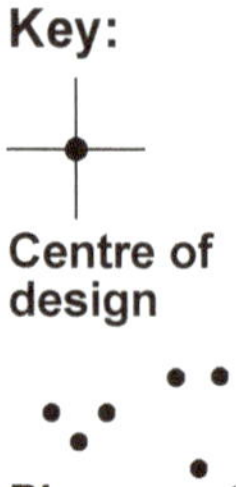

**Centre of design**

**Placement of fly stitches**

## Shopping list

- Violet cotton fabric for background: 25cm (10") square
- Fabric or interfacing for backing: 25cm (10") square
- Violet and green felt fabrics for the appliqué shapes: 7cm (2 3/4") square of each colour
- No. 5 perlé cotton thread:
  (A) dark violet (B) medium violet (C) light green
- Tracing paper and other items for preparing the felt shapes

## Let's begin

In this design the pattern is not transferred onto the background fabric. Attach the backing fabric to the wrong side of the violet background fabric. See page 15 for backing the fabric. Referring to pages 220-223 for appliqué and following steps 1 and 3-5 of Method 1, prepare and cut out the shapes for the stem, leaves, and flower from green and violet felt fabrics. Remove tracings. Alternatively, the shapes can all be cut out and marked freehand, simply using the pattern as a visual guide.

## Stitch!

For help, see pages 40-43 for straight stitch, 148-151 for fly stitch, and pages 184-187 for French knot.

Use the photo as a guide when placing the felt shapes. Due to the thickness of the fabrics, work stitches with a stabbing motion. Work each fly stitch with a medium anchor extending beyond the marked dot. Complete the stitching on each shape, and then pin and work the next.

1 Pin the stem onto the violet background fabric.

2 Using the marked dots (Diagram 1), work a row of fly stitches (1 strand B). These stitches secure the stem to the background. Remove the pins.

3 Pin one leaf onto the background fabric next to the stem. Work a row of fly stitches (1 strand A). Remove the pins. Repeat for the other leaf.

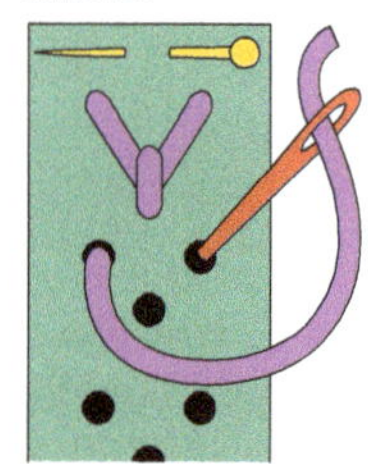

**Diagram 1**

4 Pin and tack the felt flower shape onto the background fabric. Remove the pins.

5 Using the marked dots for the flower (Diagram 2), work each petal in fly stitch (1 strand B). Add a two wrap French knot at the centre (1 strand A mixed in the needle with 1 strand B).

6 Add straight stitches (1 strand C) between the fly stitch petals.

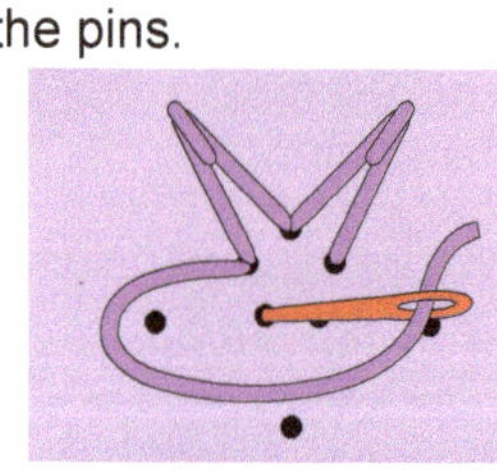

**Diagram 2**

7 Using the marked dots, work the tiny buds on each felt petal with a fly stitch (1 strand C), then complete the buds by adding a two wrap French knot above each fly stitch (1 strand A mixed in the needle with 1 strand B).

## Let's finish

Take out tacking. Press the background fabric only. See page 36 for pressing.

# Violet Essence Pincushions

Mix and match elements of the design to create these embellished pincushions.

## The projects

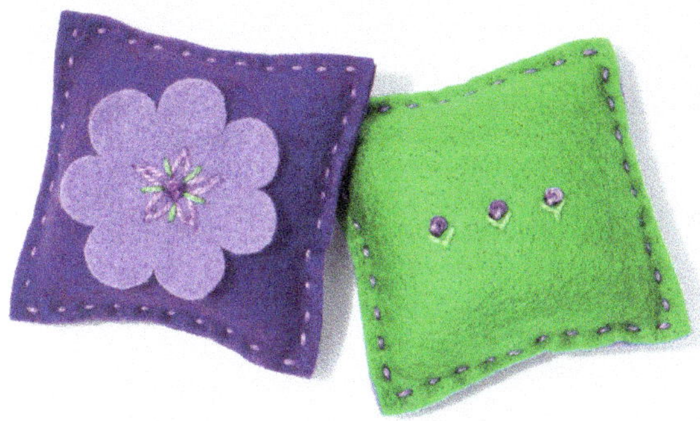

*Violet Essence Pincushions*

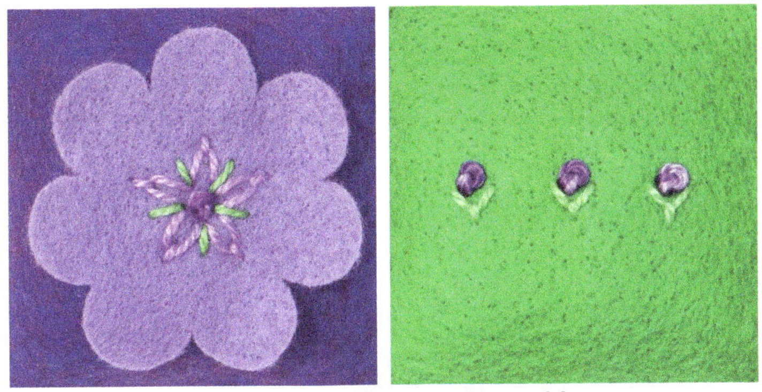

Details of *Violet Essence Pincushions*

***Violet Pincushion***

The felt flower shape and the central stitched flower from *Violet Essence* are featured on this constructed pincushion.
The finished size of this pincushion is 8cm (3") square.

## Shopping list

- Dark violet felt fabric for the pincushion: two 8cm (3") squares
- Medium violet felt fabric for the flower shape: one 7cm (2 3/4") square
- Threads as listed for the original design on the page opposite
- Tracing paper and other items for preparing the felt shape
- Fibre filling

## Let's begin

See the page opposite for the pattern.
Referring to pages 220-223 for appliqué and following steps 1 and 3-5 of Method 1, prepare and cut out the felt flower shape from the medium violet felt fabric. When transferring the internal pattern markings onto the felt, omit the dots for the buds. Remove the tracing. Alternatively, the shapes can be cut out and marked freehand, simply using the pattern as a visual guide.

## Stitch!

Place the felt flower shape and work the stitching following steps 4-6 of the stitch instructions on the page opposite.

## Let's finish

With wrong sides together, pin the worked felt square onto the remaining dark violet square around the edge. Work running stitch (1 strand B) through both layers close to the edge, leaving a 4cm (1 5/8") opening in the middle of one side. See pages 58-61 for running stitch. Fill the pincushion with fibre filling. Stitch the opening closed by continuing with running stitch.

***Green Pincushion***

Three tiny buds from *Violet Essence* are featured in a row on this constructed pincushion.
The finished size of this pincushion is 8cm (3") square.

## Shopping list

- Green and medium violet felt fabrics for the pincushion: one 8cm (3") square of each colour
- Threads as listed for the original design on the page opposite
- Tracing paper and other items for transferring the pattern onto the felt
- Fibre filling

## Let's begin

See the page opposite for the pattern.
Transfer three sets of dots depicting buds in a row centrally onto the green square of felt using the pierce and dot method with an HB pencil. See page 25 for transferring the pattern using the pierce and dot method.
Alternatively, the dots can be marked freehand, simply using the pattern as a visual guide.

## Stitch!

Work the buds following step 7 of the stitch instructions on the page opposite.

## Let's finish

With wrong sides together, pin the worked green felt square onto the violet square around the edge. Work running stitch (1 strand B) through both layers close to the edge, leaving a 4cm (1 5/8") opening in the middle of one side. See page 58-61 for running stitch. Fill the pincushion with fibre filling. Stitch the opening closed by continuing with running stitch.

# Prickly Pineapple

Let's go on an island holiday and feast on this deliciously sweet tropical fruit.

## The design

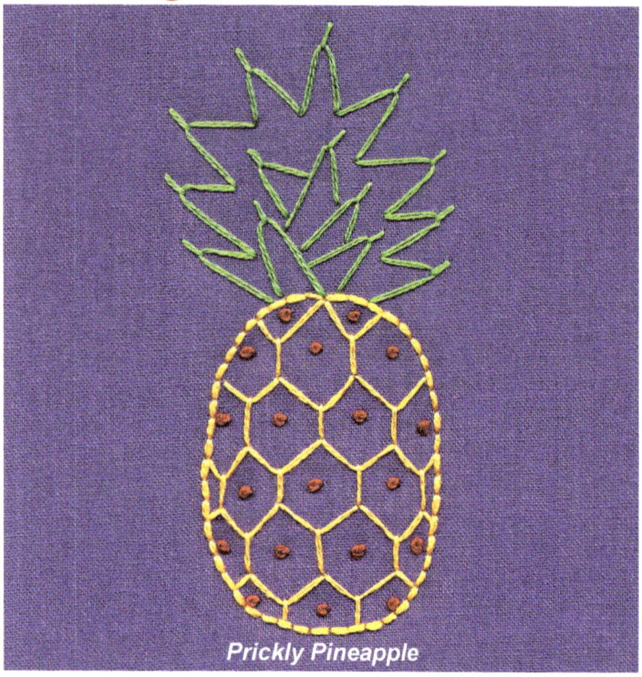

*Prickly Pineapple*

The versatility of fly stitch can be seen in this easy design. The diamond pattern on the skin is formed with fly stitches worked in stacked rows, while the leaves are formed with fly stitches worked either as a row or grouped together. Back stitch and French knot are also used.
Use the instructions on this page to work the design exactly as shown here on a violet background. To use the design on babywear, see the next page.

## The pattern

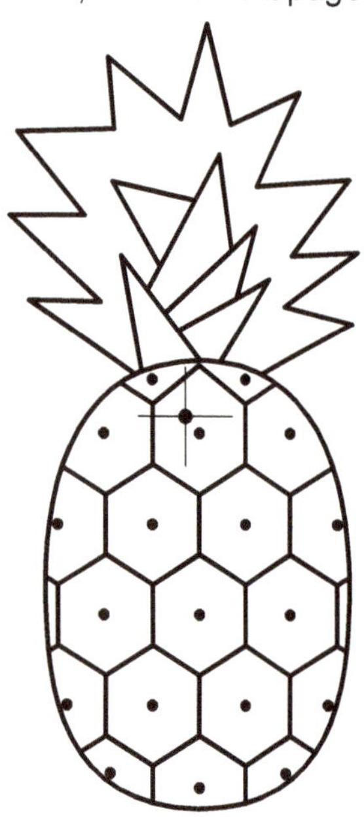

**Key:**

**Centre of design**

**Fly stitch leaf**

**Fly stitch on skin**

• **French knot**

## Shopping list

- Violet cotton fabric for background: 25cm (10") square
- Fabric or interfacing for backing: 25cm (10") square
- Stranded cotton thread:
  (A) light green (B) medium yellow (C) dark red
- Tracing paper and other items for transferring the pattern onto the fabric

## Let's begin

Read page 15 for backing the fabric, and pages 22-25 for transferring the pattern onto the fabric, then select and use suitable methods for your fabric. For the violet fabric shown here, the pattern was transferred centrally onto the fabric by tracing with a water erasable fabric marker and then the backing fabric was tacked to the wrong side.

## Stitch!

For help, see pages 76-79 for back stitch, 148-151 for fly stitch, including working rows, and pages 184-187 for French knot.

1 Stitch the marked oval outline for the pineapple in back stitch (3 strands B).

2 Referring to the diagram and following the marked lines for the skin (Diagram 1), work the first row of fly stitch (2 strands B). Working back in the opposite direction, stitch a second row of fly stitch below the first (Diagram 2), forming diamonds (2 strands B).

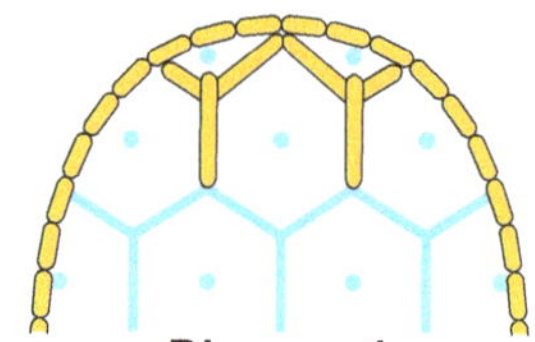

**Diagram 1**

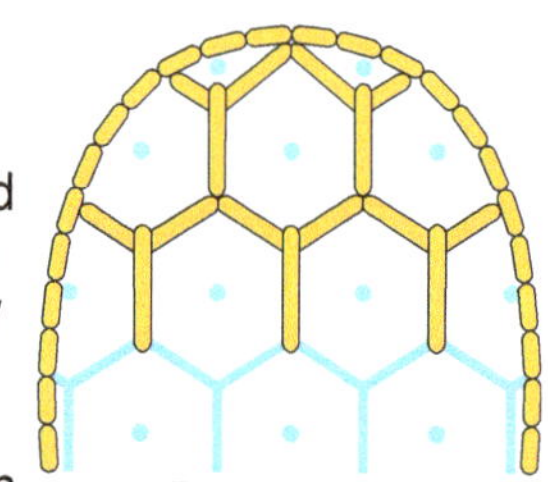

**Diagram 2**

3 Continuing with the same thread and changing direction for each row, work three more rows of fly stitch to fill the shape.

4 Add the spot inside each diamond with a two wrap French knot (2 strands C).

5 Anchoring the stitches with long anchors that extend beyond the marked lines, work the outer row of leaves in fly stitch (2 strands A).

6 Continuing with the same thread, stitch the five inner leaves in fly stitch, also worked with long anchors.

## Let's finish

Take out tacking. Rinse the work in cold water to remove the fabric marker. When partly dry, press or pin out the work. See page 36 for pressing and for pinning out.

## Hint

**Realistic appearance of leaves**

The long anchors on the fly stitches give a prickly appearance to the leaves.

# Prickly Pineapple Babywear

Brighten clothing for a baby by adding a colourful pineapple.

## The project

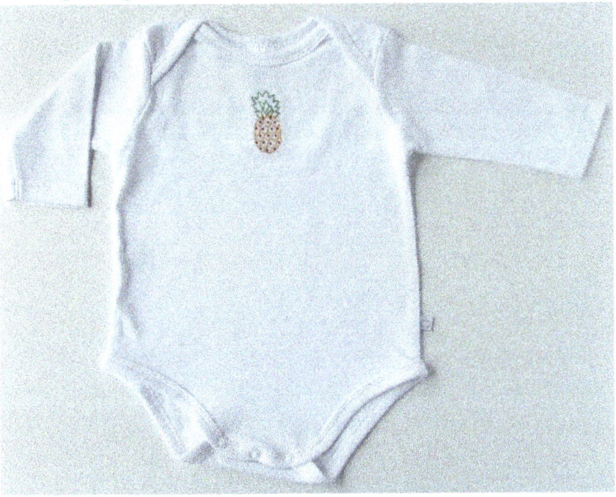

***Prickly Pineapple Babywear***

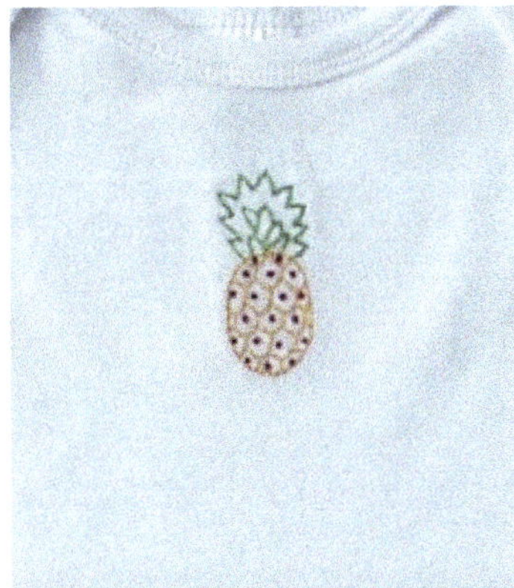

**Detail of *Prickly Pineapple Babywear***

This quick and easy project uses the *Prickly Pineapple* design to decorate a purchased white stretch knit suit for a baby. The design has been reduced in size so that the fly stitches can be worked smaller than the original, and are therefore less likely to be caught and pulled.

## Shopping list

- White stretch knit baby's suit
- Lightweight iron-on interfacing for backing: 8cm x 5cm wide (3" x 2")
- Threads as listed for the original design on the page opposite
- Tracing paper and other items for transferring the pattern onto the baby's suit

## Let's begin

See the page opposite for the pattern. Prepare the pattern by reducing it to 65% of its original size. Trace the reduced pattern onto tracing paper.

To help in deciding the placement of the design on the baby's suit, fold the garment in half and mark the centre front with pins (Diagram 1).

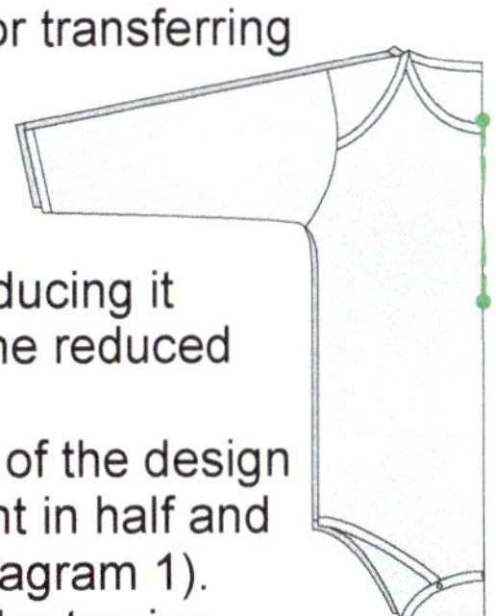

**Diagram 1**

Open out the garment and place the tracing, centred over the pins, an appropriate distance below the front neckline (Diagram 2).

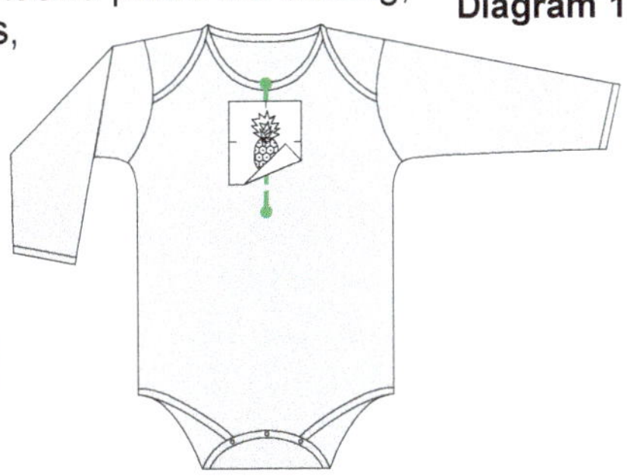

**Diagram 2**

Move the tracing up or down until it is visually appealing and note its position with pins.

Following the instructions on page 15 for backing the fabric, attach the piece of iron-on interfacing onto the wrong side of the front of the garment at the selected position. This will stabilize the area where the design is to be stitched.

Transfer the pattern onto the front of the garment by tracing with a water erasable fabric marker. See page 23 for transferring the pattern by tracing.

## Stitch!

Work the pineapple following steps 1-6 of the stitch instructions for the original design on the facing page.

## Let's finish

Turn the garment inside out. On the wrong side, peel back any excess interfacing from its outer edge and trim it back close to the stitches. Rinse the garment in cold water to remove the water erasable fabric marker. When dry, turn the garment inside out and press it. See page 36 for pressing.

## Hints

**Using stretch knit fabrics**

Knit fabrics are designed to stretch, allowing ease of movement when worn. However, this stretching is usually not desirable on the area where the design is stitched. By attaching interfacing onto the wrong side of the fabric, the amount of stretch on the area to be worked is minimised and controlled. This makes the stitching much easier to manage.

**Change the colours**

For a different colour scheme, choose yellow fabric for the background and work the stitches for the pineapple in dark orange instead of yellow.

# Hot-air Balloon

Shall we go floating high above the hills?

## The design

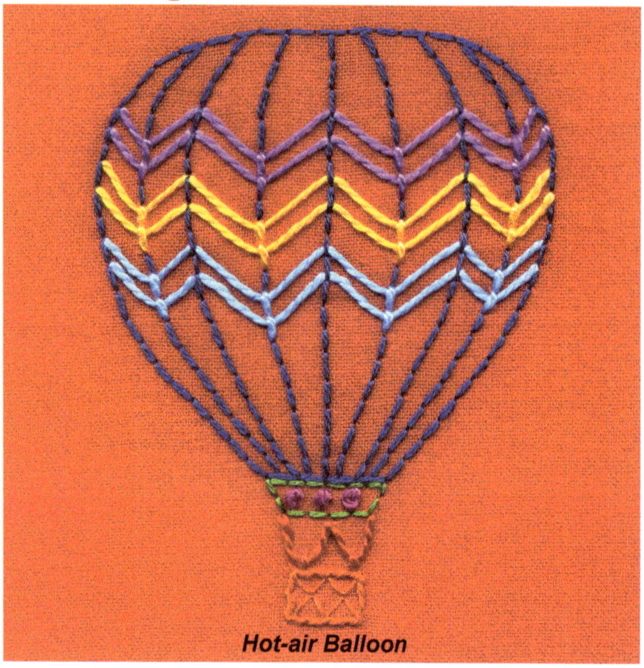

*Hot-air Balloon*

Three sizes of fly stitch are used in this design. Rows of large fly stitches form the zigzag pattern on the balloon, medium fly stitches depict the basket support ropes and small fly stitches create the weave on the basket. Back stitch, whipped back stitch, and French knot are also used.

To work the design as above, use the instructions on this page. See the following page where hot-air balloons are featured on a mobile for a child's room.

## The pattern

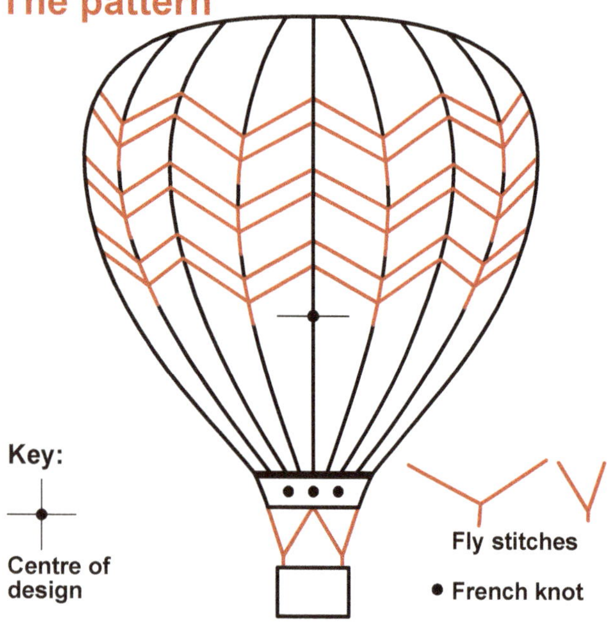


## Shopping list

- Red cotton fabric for background: 25cm (10") square
  Fabric or interfacing for backing: 25cm (10") square
- Stranded cotton thread:
  (A) medium blue (B) light green (C) medium orange
- No. 5 perlé cotton thread:
  (D) medium violet (E) medium aqua
  (F) medium yellow (G) medium red
  (H) medium magenta
- Tracing paper and other items for transferring the pattern onto the fabric

## Let's begin

Read page 15 for backing the fabric, and pages 22-25 for transferring the pattern onto the fabric, then select and use suitable methods for your fabric. For the red fabric shown here, the pattern was transferred centrally onto the fabric by tracing with a water erasable fabric marker and then the backing fabric was tacked to the wrong side.

## Stitch!

For help, see pages 76-79 for back stitch and whipped back stitch, 148-151 for fly stitch, including a horizontal row, and pages 184-187 for French knot.

1 On the balloon, work the upper row of the violet stripe with large fly stitches (1 strand D).

2 Working in the opposite direction, stitch the lower violet row, noting that a space is left between the anchors and the yellow fly stitch row to be worked next (Diagram 1).

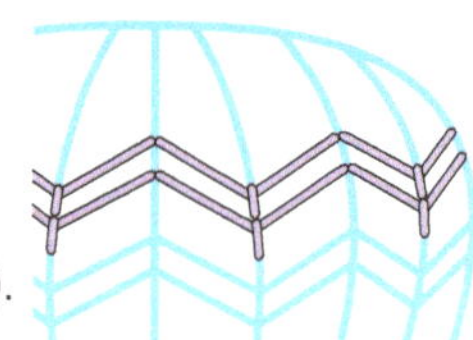

**Diagram 1**

3 Stitch two rows of yellow fly stitch (1 strand F), then two rows of aqua (1 strand E) in the same way.

4 Work the outline for the balloon in back stitch (2 strands A), then add the panels using isolated back stitches where the panels are broken by the fly stitch anchors on each alternate line (Diagram 2).

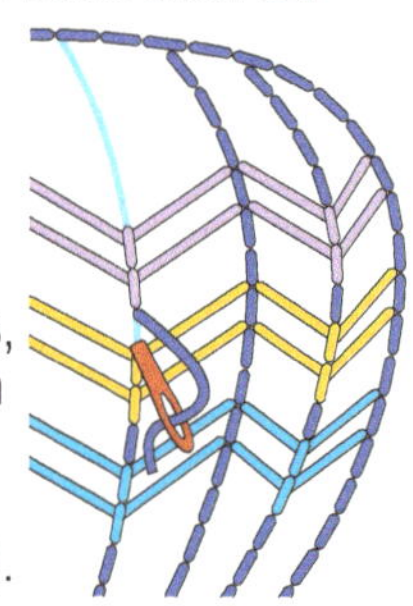

**Diagram 2**

5 At the base of the balloon panels, work the green band in back stitch (2 strands B). Add three French knots, each with two wraps, inside the green band (1 strand H).

6 Stitch two fly stitches side by side for the basket support ropes (1 strand G). Outline the basket with back stitch, then whip the stitches (2 strands C).

7 Add the basket weave (Diagram 3) with fly stitch (1 strand C).

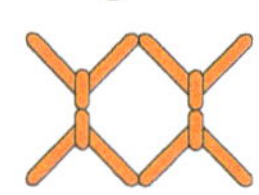

**Diagram 3**

## Let's finish

Take out tacking. Rinse the work in cold water to remove the fabric marker. When partly dry, press or pin out the work. See page 36 for pressing and for pinning out.

# Hot-air Balloon Mobile

Catch the breeze with this cheerful mobile.

## The project

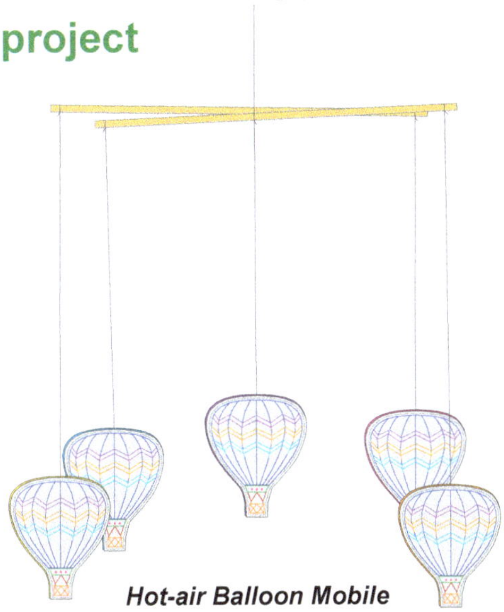

***Hot-air Balloon Mobile***

This mobile for a child's room features hot-air balloons worked on white felt. The design has been enlarged and then worked five times in the original colours. Pieces of felt, in colours matching five of the threads used in the design, are attached on the reverse sides of the balloons.

Each balloon is 11cm (4 1/4") in height.

## Shopping list

- White felt fabric for the balloon shapes:
  five pieces 15cm x 13cm wide (6" x 5")
- Violet, aqua, yellow, magenta, and orange felt fabric for the reverse sides:
  one piece of each colour 15cm x 13cm wide (6" x 5")
- Lightweight iron-on interfacing for backing:
  ten pieces 15cm x 13cm wide (6" x 5")
- Thin wadding: one piece 13cm x 50cm wide (5" x 20")
- Threads as listed for the original design on the page opposite
- Machine sewing thread:
  white, violet, aqua, yellow, magenta, and orange
- Tracing paper and other items for transferring the pattern onto the felt
- Clear fishing line: one piece 33cm (13") and four pieces 38cm (15") for the balloons, and one piece 40cm (16") for the central hanger
- Square wooden rods: two pieces 45cm (18") long
- Glue

## Let's begin

See the page opposite for the pattern.

Enlarge the pattern to 125% of its original size.

Transfer the pattern centrally onto each of the white felt pieces by tracing with a chalk-based pencil. See page 23 for transferring the pattern by tracing. The coloured felt pieces are left plain.

Following the instructions on page 15 for backing fabric, attach the iron-on interfacing onto the wrong side of the five white felt pieces and the five coloured felt pieces.

## Stitch!

Work the five balloons following steps 1-7 of the stitch instructions on the page opposite, however use 4 strands of thread when stitching with stranded cotton threads (A) and (B).

## Let's finish

***Making up the balloons***

The following instructions are for making up the central balloon. Make up the remaining balloons in the same way, using the four longer lengths of fishing line.

Tie a small loop at one end of the short piece of fishing line. Using small hand stitches, firmly attach the loop onto the back of the work just below the centre of the upper edge of the balloon.

Cut a piece of wadding exactly to the enlarged pattern shape. Place the wadding onto the wrong side of the white felt, aligning it with the back of the stitched balloon. With wrong sides together, place one piece of coloured felt behind the wadding. Pin in place. Tack the layers together about 1cm (3/8") outside the design. Using a zipper foot on the machine, and with white machine sewing thread on the top, and thread to match the coloured felt in the bobbin, straight stitch around the balloon close to the design. Being careful not to cut the fishing line, trim away excess felt from around the edge of the balloon (Diagram 1).

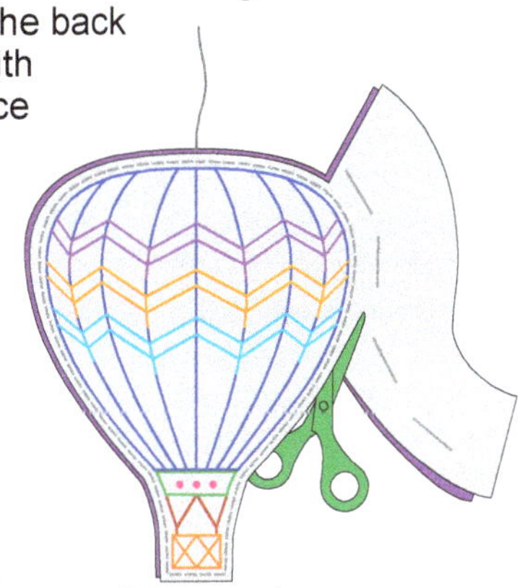

**Diagram 1**

***Assembling the mobile***

Mark the centre point of each wooden rod. With the rods placed at right angles to each other, glue the rods together at the marked centres.

Tie the balloon that has the short piece of fishing line to the centre of the rods. Tie the remaining four balloons to the ends of the rods.

For the hanger, tie a small loop at one end of the remaining piece of fishing line, and attach the other end to the centre of the rods.

Check to see that the mobile hangs correctly.

If necessary, adjust the position of the pieces of fishing line by sliding them along the rods. Once balanced, apply tiny amounts of glue to secure each knot in place.

# Glittering Snowflakes

Delicate icy snowflakes are fluttering from the sky, turning the landscape sparkling white.

## The design

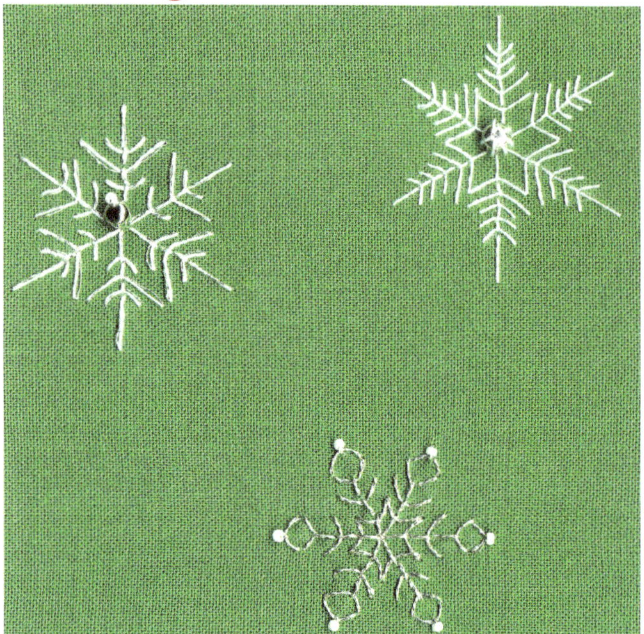

*Glittering Snowflakes*

For this design, three different snowflakes are worked in fly stitch, with the addition of straight stitch and beading. *Glittering Snowflakes* is quite detailed, but it is easy to stitch. To work the design as above, follow the instructions on this page. To feature individual snowflakes on greeting cards, see the project ideas on the next page. As this design uses beads, it is not considered safe for use on projects for babies or very small children.

## The pattern

1

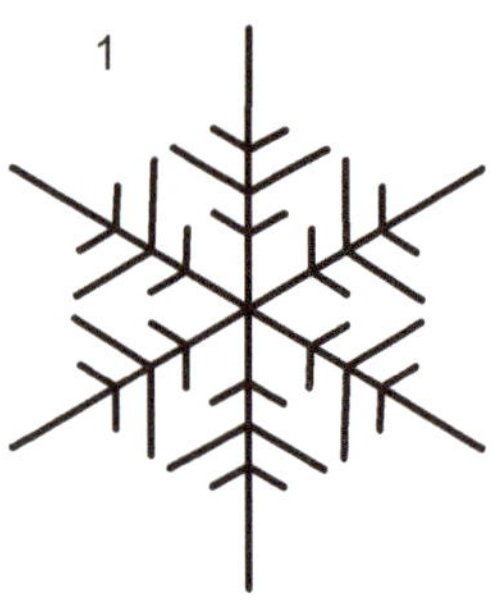

2

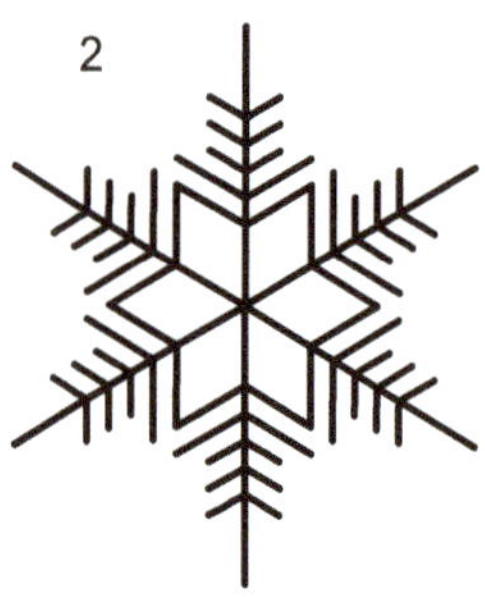

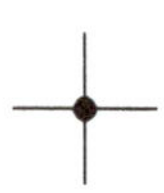

3

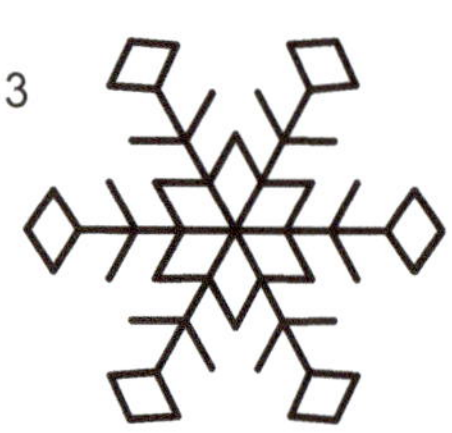

**Key:**

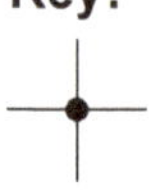

**Centre of design**

## Shopping list

- Green cotton fabric for background: 25cm (10") square
- Fabric or interfacing for backing: 25cm (10") square
- Stranded cotton thread: (A) white
- No. 5 perlé metallic thread: (B) silver
- 2 medium size beads: (C) silver
- 7 very small beads: (D) white
- Tracing paper and other items for transferring the pattern onto the fabric

## Let's begin

Read page 15 for backing the fabric, and pages 22-25 for transferring the pattern onto the fabric, then select and use suitable methods for your fabric. For the green fabric shown here, the pattern was transferred centrally onto the fabric by tracing with a water erasable fabric marker and then the backing fabric was tacked to the wrong side.

## Stitch!

For help, see pages 40-43 for straight stitch, 148-151 for fly stitch, including a vertical row, and pages 238-241 for beading. See also page 17 for preparing perlé metallic thread. If your threaded needle will not pass through the very small bead, just pass the thread on its own through the bead, then re-thread your needle and continue.

**Snowflake 1**

1 At one spoke tip, work a straight stitch from the tip to the first junction (1 strand A mixed in the needle with 1 ply B). Complete this spoke with a vertical row of fly stitches, anchoring the last stitch at the centre (Diagram 1). Repeat for remaining spokes.

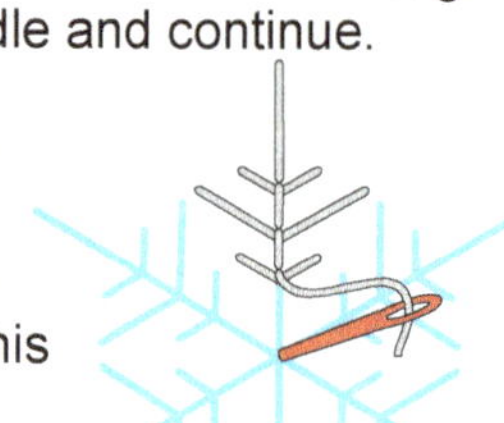

**Diagram 1**

2 At the centre (Diagram 2) attach a silver bead with a white bead above it (C and D, attached with 1 strand A).

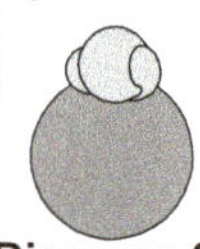

**Diagram 2**

**Snowflake 2**

1 Follow step 1 of snowflake 1 (1 strand A).

2 At the centre, attach a silver bead (Diagram 3) with six straight stitches worked down through the centre (C, attached with 1 strand A).

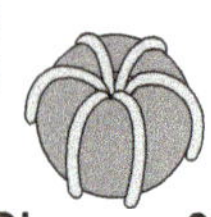

**Diagram 3**

**Snowflake 3**

1 At one spoke tip, work a fly stitch (3 ply B) with a bead (D) added to a short anchor (Diagram 4). Secure by working a small stitch on the reverse side behind the bead. Complete this spoke with a vertical row of fly stitches, anchoring last stitch at centre.

2 Repeat step 1 for the other five spokes.

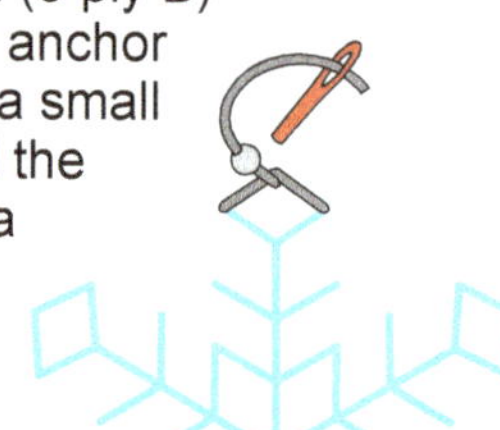

**Diagram 4**

## Let's finish

Take out tacking. Rinse the work in cold water to remove the fabric marker. When partly dry, press or pin out the work. See page 36 for pressing and for pinning out.

# Glittering Snowflakes Greeting Cards

Try this different technique – these greeting cards are stitched without using any fabric!

## The projects

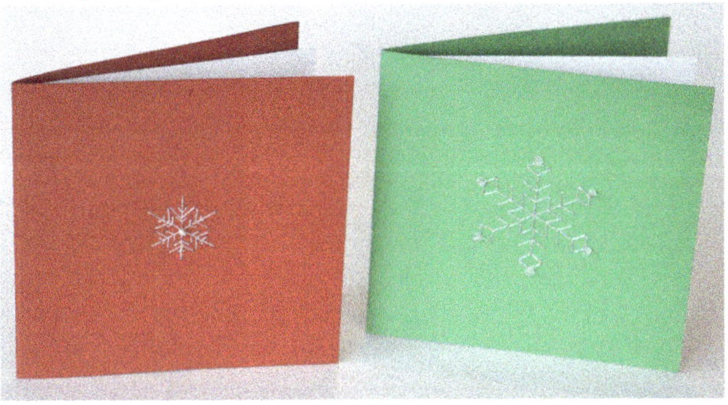

***Glittering Snowflakes Greeting Cards***

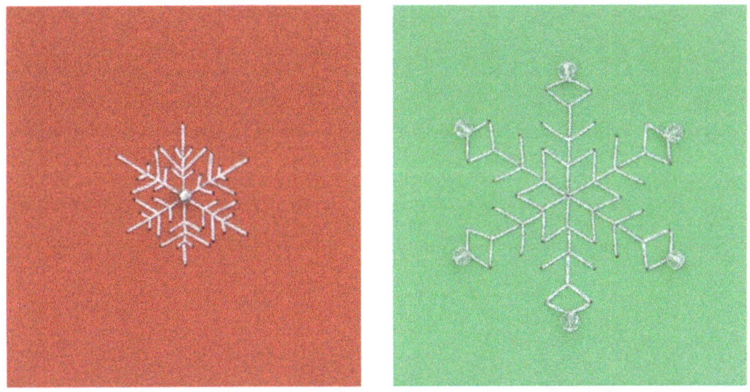

**Details of *Glittering Snowflakes Greeting Cards***

***Red card***

At the same scale as the original design, **Snowflake 1** is stitched through holes pierced in the front of this card. No fabric is used.

The size of this greeting card is 15cm (6") square.

## Shopping list

- Stranded cotton thread: (A) white
- No. 5 perlé metallic thread: (B) silver
- 1 medium size bead: (C) silver
- 1 very small bead: (D) white
- Tracing paper and other items for transferring the pattern onto the card
- Red card: 15cm x 30cm wide (6" x 12")
- White paper: 14cm x 29cm wide (5 1/2" x 11 1/2")
- Archival single-sided and double-sided sticky tapes

## Let's begin

See the page opposite for the pattern.

Trace the pattern for **Snowflake 1** onto tracing paper.

To make the greeting card, fold the red card in half. Open out the card and place a pad of folded fabric under the front of the card. Position the tracing centrally onto the front of the card. Using a fine needle, pierce holes through the tracing and the card at the ends and junctions of all the lines. Make sure that the holes pierced for the stitches of adjacent spokes are not too close together or the card may tear between them.

## Stitch!

Work **Snowflake 1** on the card following the stitch instructions on the page opposite, securing the thread ends on the wrong side with the single-sided sticky tape. No beginning or ending off required!

## Let's finish

Fold the white paper in half, making the pages for the card. Secure the pages to the inside of the front of the card with the double-sided sticky tape.

***Green card***

Worked at a larger scale, **Snowflake 3** is stitched through holes pierced in the front of this card.

No fabric is used.

The size of this greeting card is 15cm (6") square.

## Shopping list

- No. 5 perlé metallic thread: (B) silver
- 6 medium size faceted beads: (D) clear
- Tracing paper and other items for transferring the pattern onto the card
- Green card: 15cm x 30cm wide (6" x 12")
- White paper: 14cm x 29cm wide (5 1/2" x 11 1/2")
- Archival single-sided and double-sided sticky tapes

## Let's begin

See the page opposite for the pattern.

Prepare the pattern by enlarging **Snowflake 3** to 200% of its original size. Trace the enlarged pattern onto tracing paper.

To make the greeting card, fold the green card in half. Open out the card and place a pad of folded fabric under the front of the card. Rotating the snowflake until two of the spokes are vertical, position the tracing centrally onto the front of the card. Using a fine needle, pierce holes through the tracing and the card at the ends and junctions of all the lines. Pierce one extra hole 3mm (1/8") beyond the end of each spoke for the fly stitch anchors.

## Stitch!

Using the alternative beads, work **Snowflake 3** on the card following the stitch instructions on the facing page, securing the thread ends on the wrong side with the single-sided sticky tape. No beginning or ending off required!

## Let's finish

Fold the white paper in half, making the pages for the card. Secure the pages to the inside of the front of the card with the double-sided sticky tape.

# Lily Garden

This garden is filled with graceful lilies in warm glowing colours.

## The design

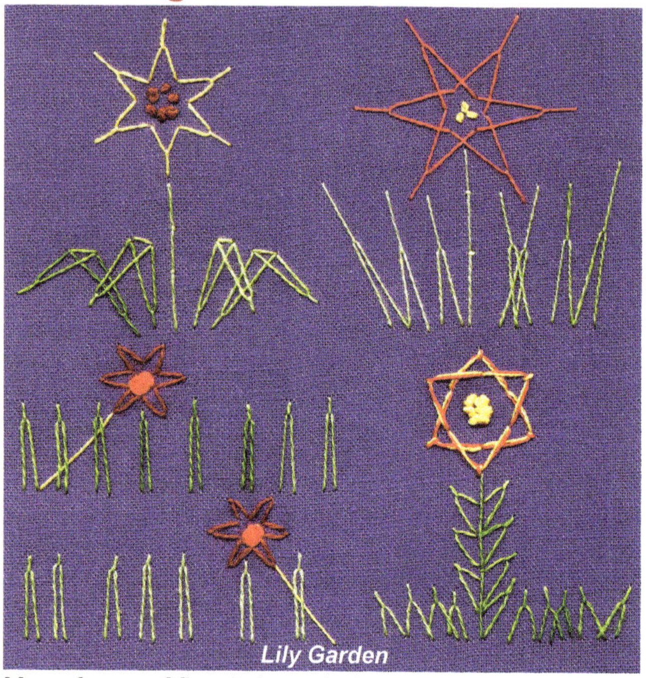


Many forms of fly stitch are included in *Lily Garden*. Straight stitch and French knot are also used. This design features variegated thread for all the foliage. Although the design has many elements, it is easy to work. Follow these instructions to work the design as above. To work lilies on babywear, see opposite.

## The pattern

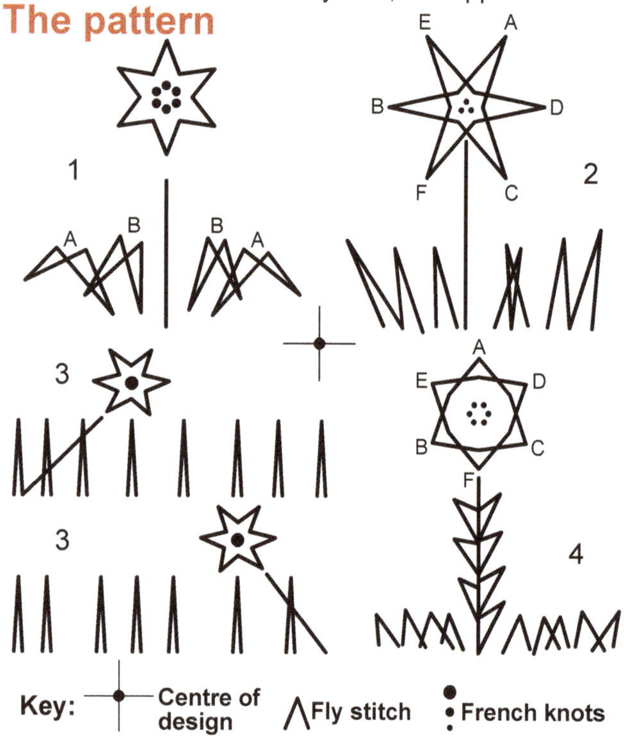


## Shopping list

- Violet cotton fabric for background: 25cm (10") square
- Fabric or interfacing for backing: 25cm (10") square
- Stranded cotton thread: (A) variegated green (B) light yellow (C) dark red (D) light red
- No. 5 perlé cotton thread: (E) light red
- Tracing paper and other items for transferring the pattern onto the fabric

## Let's begin

Read page 15 for backing the fabric, and pages 22-25 for transferring the pattern onto the fabric, then select and use suitable methods for your fabric. For the violet fabric shown here, the pattern was transferred centrally onto the fabric by tracing with a water erasable fabric marker and then the backing fabric was tacked to the wrong side.

## Stitch!

For help, see pages 40-43 for straight stitch, 148-151 for fly stitch, and pages 184-187 for French knot.
When working the fly stitches, use the photo as a guide to the lengths of the anchors.

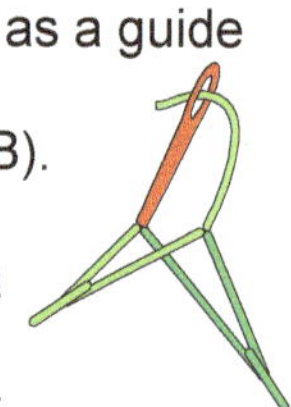

Diagram 1

**Lily 1** Work the petals in fly stitch (1 strand B). At the centre add French knots, each with one wrap (2 strands C). For the stem, work a long straight stitch held in place with two tiny straight stitches (1 strand A). Stitch the lower half of leaf A, and then the upper half, with fly stitches (1 strand A), adding a straight stitch for the fold (Diagram 1). Work leaf B in front of leaf A. Repeat in mirror image for the remaining leaves.

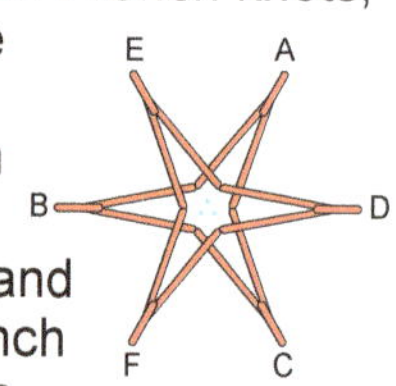


Diagram 2

**Lily 2** Work fly stitch petals (1 strand D) in the order indicated (Diagram 2). At the centre, stitch French knots, each with one wrap (1 strand B). For the stem, work a long straight stitch held in place with two tiny straight stitches, then add the leaves in fly stitch (1 strand A).

**Lily 3** Work the petals in fly stitch (1 strand C) and each centre with a two wrap French knot (1 strand E). Work each stem with a long straight stitch (1 strand B) and then the leaves in fly stitch (1 strand A).

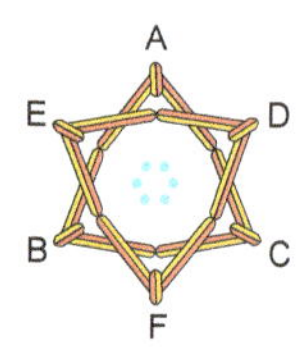


Diagram 3

**Lily 4** Work the petals (1 strand B mixed in the needle with 1 strand D) in the order indicated (Diagram 3). At the centre, stitch French knots, each with one wrap (3 strands B). For the stem, work a long straight stitch held in place with two tiny straight stitches, then add the leaves in fly stitch (1 strand A).

## Let's finish

Take out tacking. Rinse the work in cold water to remove the fabric marker. When partly dry, press or pin out the work. See page 36 for pressing and for pinning out.

# Lily Babywear

Add special lilies to singlets for a baby.

## The projects

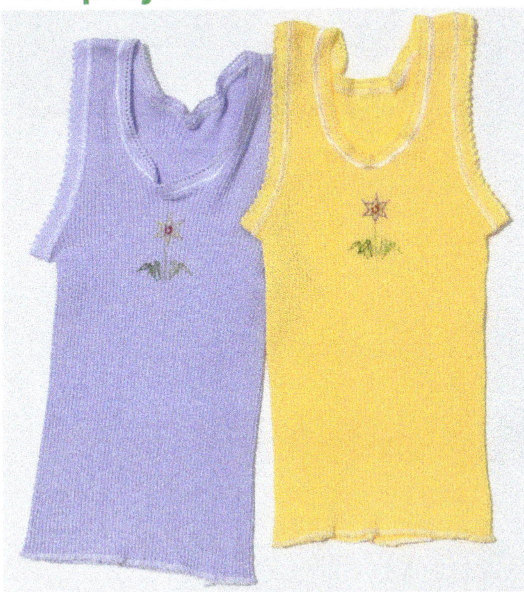

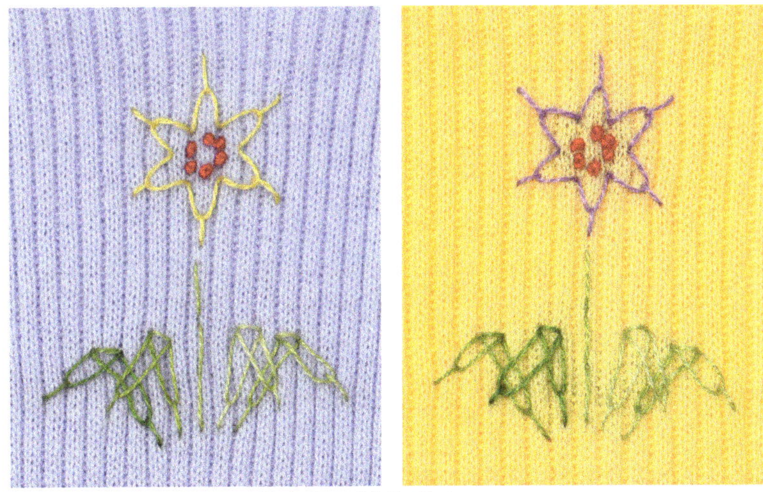

**Details of *Lily Babywear***

***Lily Babywear***

Delicate lilies are worked on these purchased singlets for a baby. **Lily 1** is stitched in its original colour scheme on the violet singlet. As an alternative colour scheme, the same lily is stitched with violet petals on the yellow singlet.

## Shopping list

***Violet singlet***

- Violet singlet
- Stranded cotton thread:
  (A) variegated green (B) light yellow (C) dark red
- Tracing paper and other items for transferring the pattern onto the singlet

***Yellow singlet***

- Yellow singlet
- Stranded cotton thread:
  (A) variegated green (B) medium violet (C) dark red
- Tracing paper and other items for transferring the pattern onto the singlet

## Let's begin

See the page opposite for the pattern.
Trace the pattern for **Lily 1** onto tracing paper, leaving out the dots for the centre of the flower. Tape each singlet, very slightly stretched sideways, to a table surface. Transfer the traced pattern onto the front of each singlet using the pierce and dot method with a water erasable fabric marker. See page 25 for transferring the pattern using the pierce and dot method.

## Stitch!

Following the stitch instructions for **Lily 1** on the page opposite, work the flower on each singlet, keeping the thread tension fairly loose and using the alternative coloured thread for the petals on the yellow singlet. Use the pattern as a guide to the position of the six French knots for the flower centre.

## Let's finish

Rinse the singlets in cold water to remove the water erasable fabric marker. When dry, turn the singlets inside out and lightly press them. See page 36 for pressing.

# Chain stitch

## and variations

Chain stitch is a widely used stitch that is fast and easy to work. It is formed with a continuous row of linked closed loops creating a broad textured line.

As chain stitch is worked, each new loop secures the previous loop. The last loop in the row is secured with a straight stitch as an anchor.

Chain stitch is useful for working lines and for outlining shapes effectively. When worked in close rows, it can be used to quickly fill a shape.

An isolated chain stitch is called a detached chain stitch. It is formed as a single, closed loop secured with a straight stitch anchor. This stitch can be used on its own, scattered as a filling, or worked in groups to create patterns such as flowers.

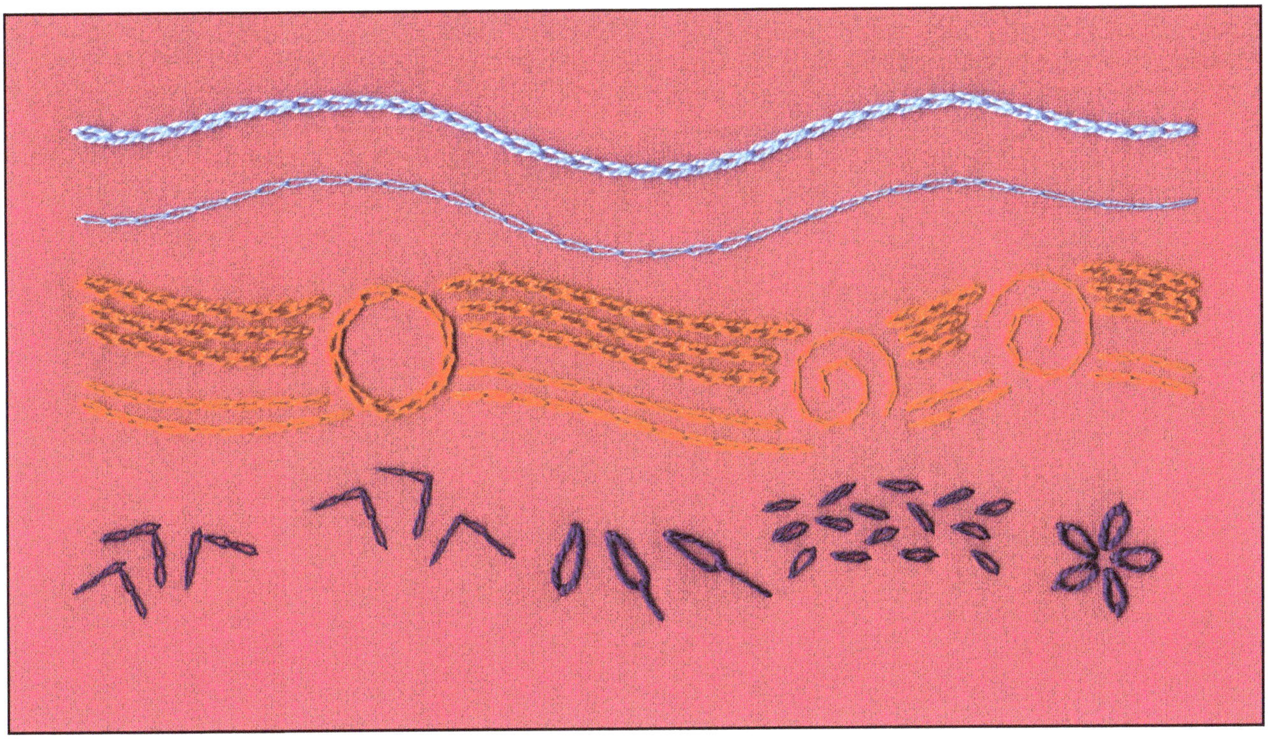

# Chain stitch and variations sampler

Chain stitch

Chain stitch

Chain stitch rows worked to fill areas, chain stitch worked in a circle and worked in spirals

Chain stitch rows worked in different directions

| Chain stitch with an anchored corner | Chain stitch with a continuous corner | Detached chain stitches with short, medium, and long anchor stitch | Scattered detached chain stitches | Detached chain stitches worked as a flower |
|---|---|---|---|---|

# Chain stitch and variations

## Hints

Chain stitch is most commonly worked by skimming the needle in and out of the fabric before pulling the thread through. When working chain stitch or detached chain stitch, the length of the anchor can vary from short to long depending on the desired effect.

Do not work chain stitch or detached chain stitch with the tension of the thread too tight or the stitch will not form correctly and the fabric will not lie flat.

When working stacked rows of chain stitch, different effects can be achieved by lining up the stitches, staggering them, or by working the rows in opposite directions.

## Chain stitch and variations: right-handed

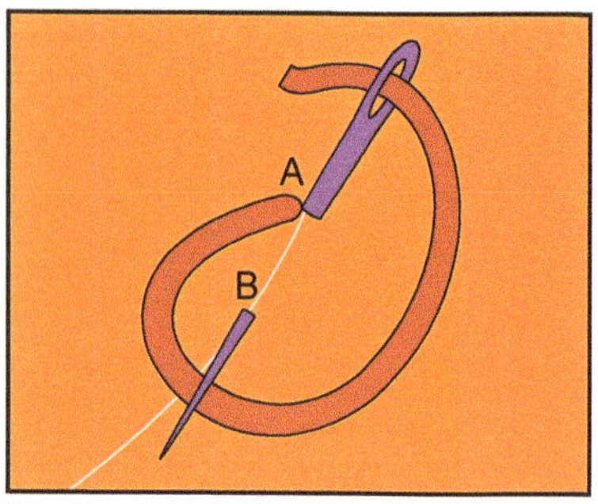


**Chain stitch**
**1** Come up at A. Forming thread into a loop, take needle down at A and up at B. Keep thread under tip of needle.

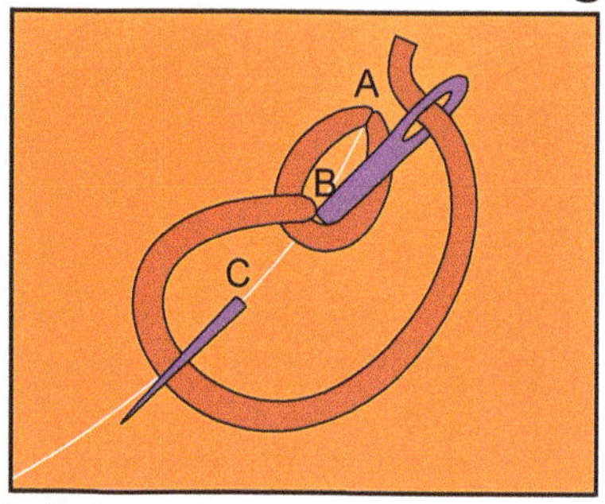


**2** Pull the thread through, allowing the loop to settle in place. Forming a loop for the next stitch, take the needle down at B and emerge at C.

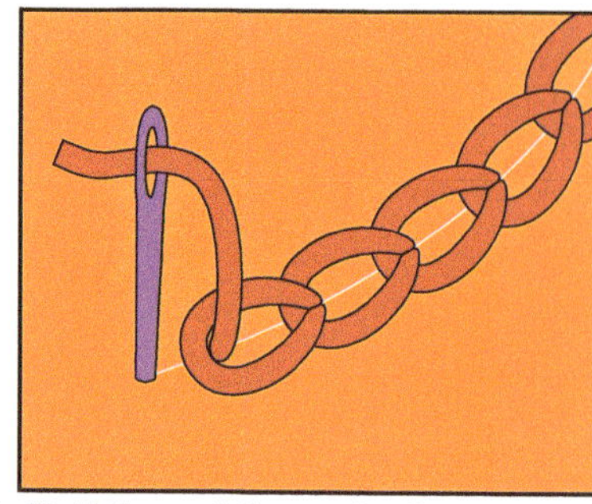

**3** Pull thread through. Continue along row. Complete last stitch by working a straight stitch as an anchor. Secure thread on the back.

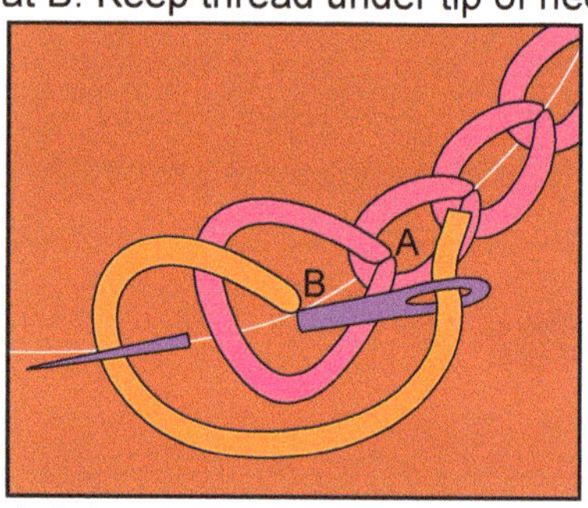


**Joining in a new thread**
Take old thread down at A, leave loop loose. Bring new thread up at B and continue. Tighten last loop of old thread later and end it off.

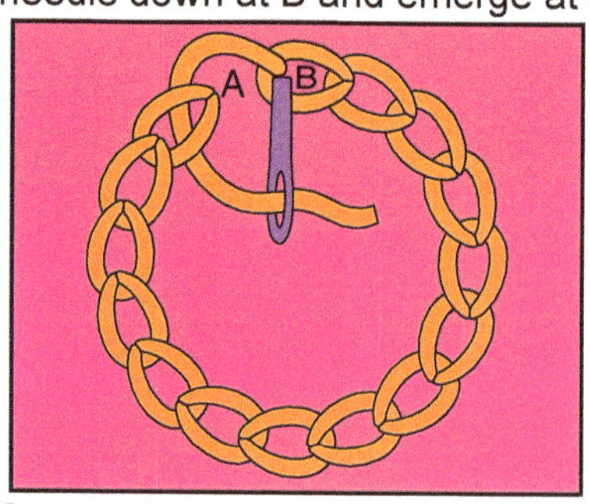


**Completing a shape**
Begin at A. Stitch shape anti-clockwise. For last stitch, pass thread under first stitch, then take it to the back at B and secure.

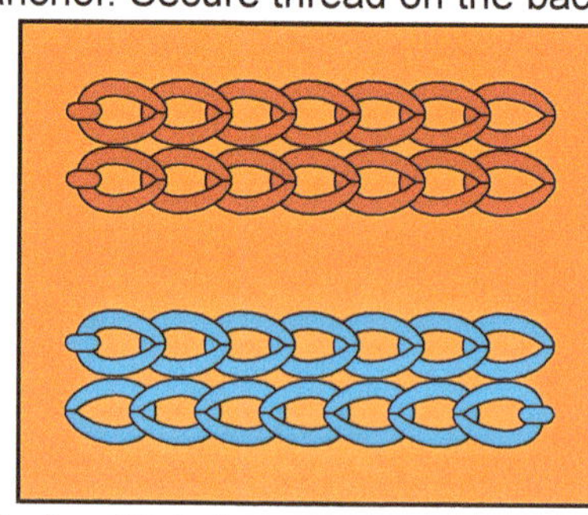

**Chain stitch in rows**
Upper example shows rows worked in the same direction. Lower example shows rows worked in opposite directions.

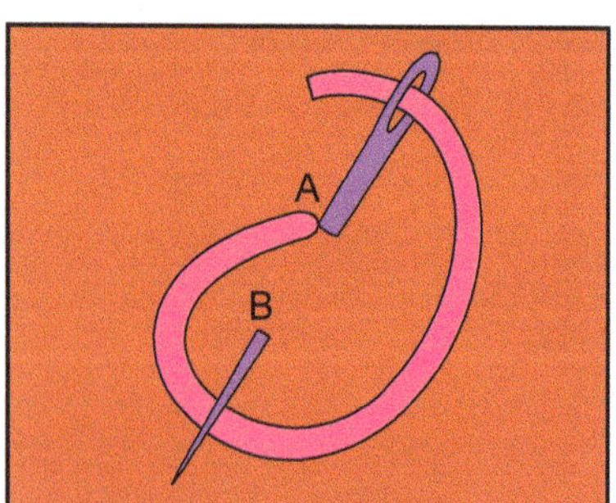


**Detached chain stitch**
**1** Come up at A. Forming thread into a loop, take needle down at A and emerge at B. Keep thread under tip of needle.

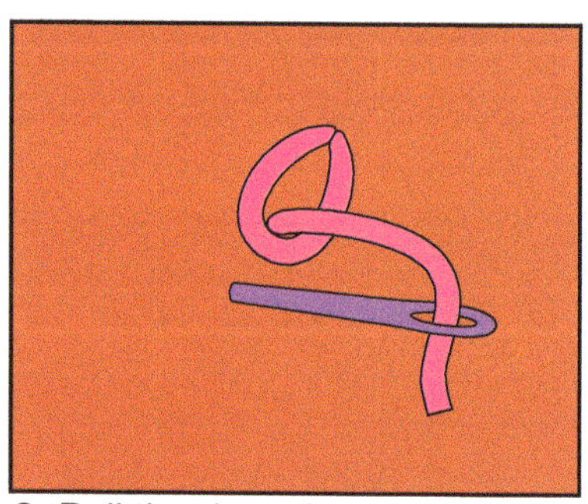

**2** Pull the thread through, allowing loop to settle in place. Complete the stitch by working a straight stitch anchor. Secure the thread on the back.

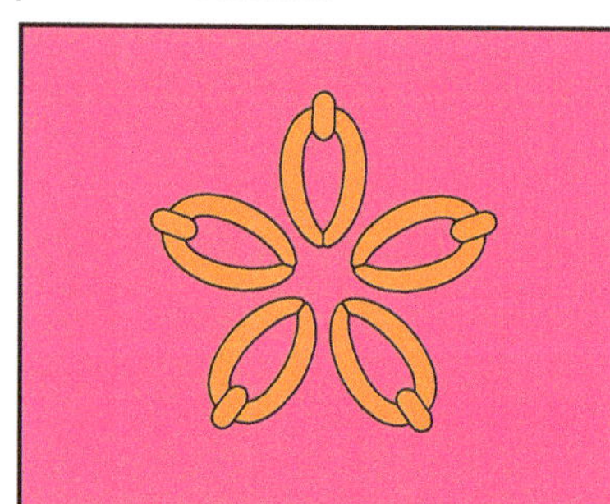

**Detached chain stitch flower**
Work a detached chain stitch for each petal.

## Chain stitch and variations: left-handed

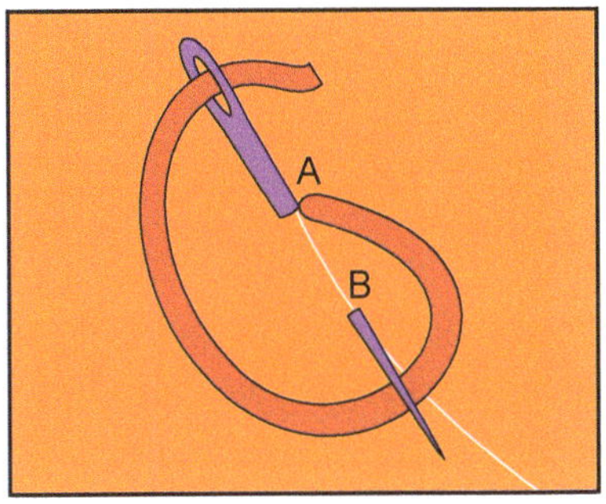


**Chain stitch**
**1** Come up at A. Forming thread into a loop, take needle down at A and up at B. Keep thread under tip of needle.

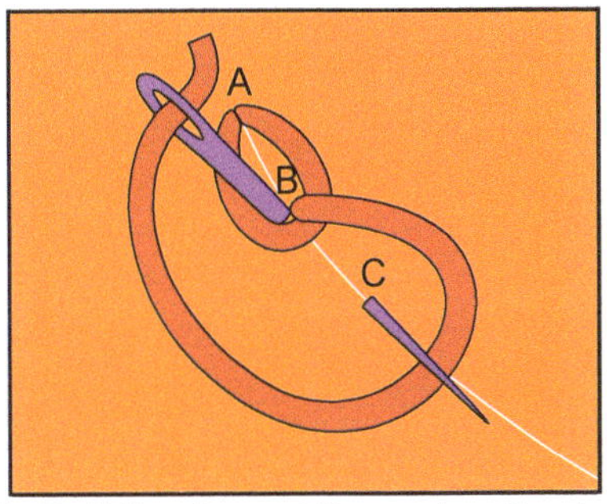


**2** Pull the thread through, allowing the loop to settle in place. Forming a loop for the next stitch, take the needle down at B and emerge at C.

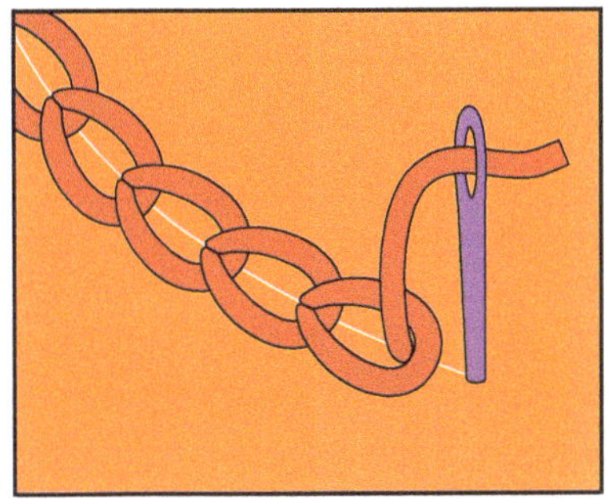

**3** Pull thread through. Continue along row. Complete last stitch by working a straight stitch as an anchor. Secure thread on the back.

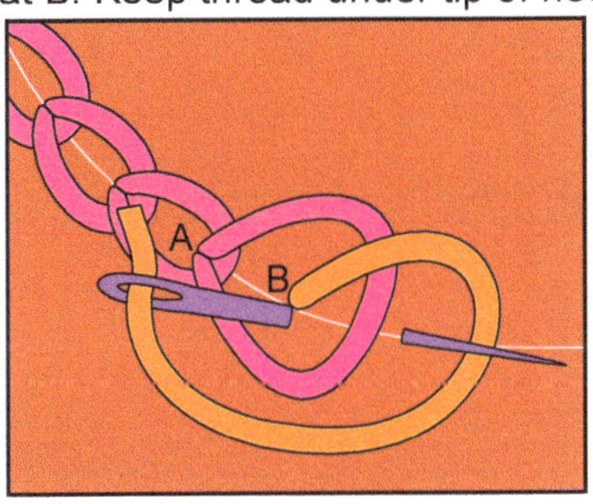


**Joining in a new thread**
Take old thread down at A, leave loop loose. Bring new thread up at B and continue. Tighten last loop of old thread later and end it off.

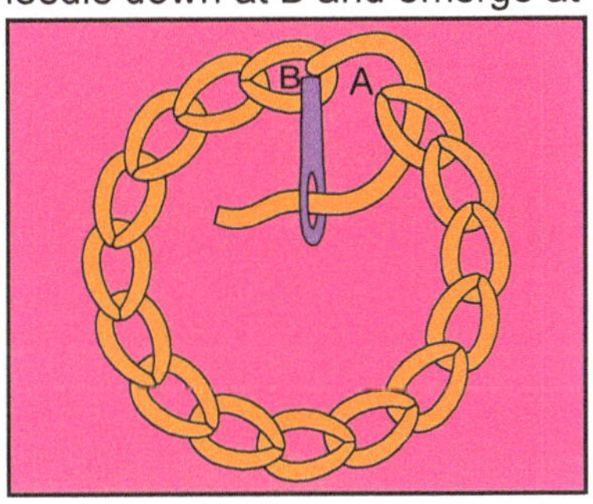


**Completing a shape**
Begin at A. Stitch shape clockwise. For last stitch, pass thread under first stitch, then take it to the back at B and secure.

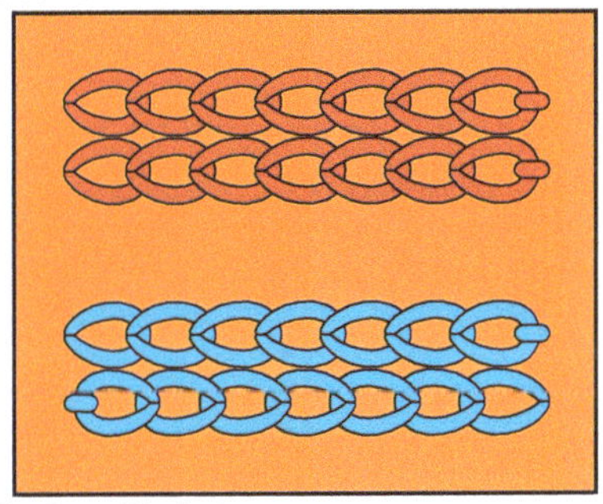

**Chain stitch in rows**
Upper example shows rows worked in the same direction. Lower example shows rows worked in opposite directions.

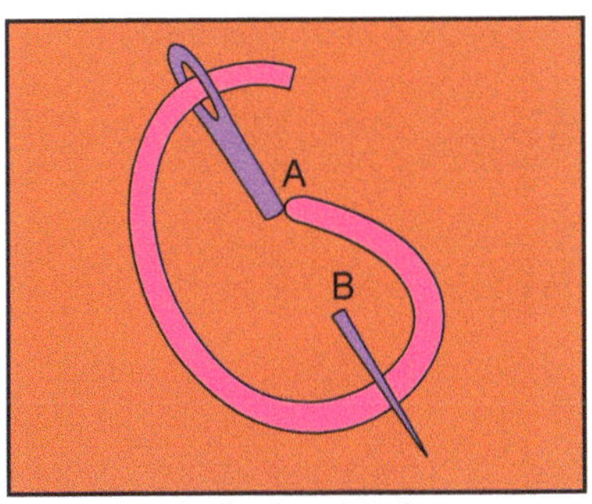


**Detached chain stitch**
**1** Come up at A. Forming thread into a loop, take needle down at A and emerge at B. Keep thread under tip of needle.

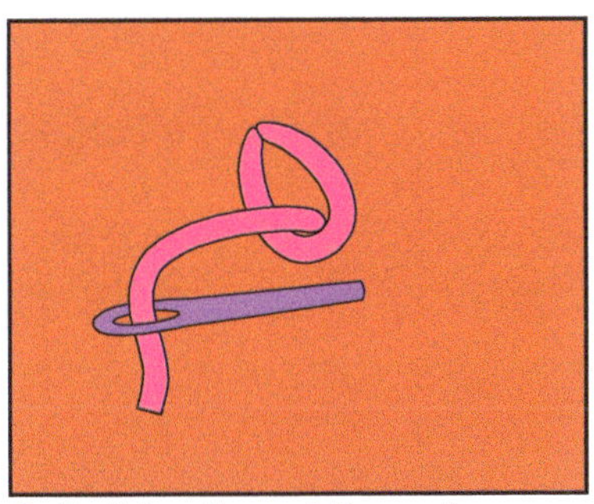

**2** Pull the thread through, allowing loop to settle in place. Complete the stitch by working a straight stitch anchor. Secure the thread on the back.

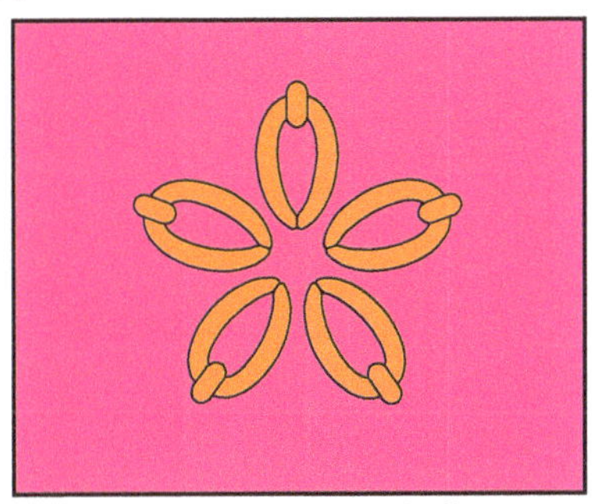

**Detached chain stitch flower**
Work a detached chain stitch for each petal.

# Chain stitch
## and variations

# Designs and project ideas

## The designs

| | |
|---|---|
| Quack Quack | Flower Diamond |
| Lollipops | Vroom Vroom |
| Rainbow Magic | Moonlit Forest |

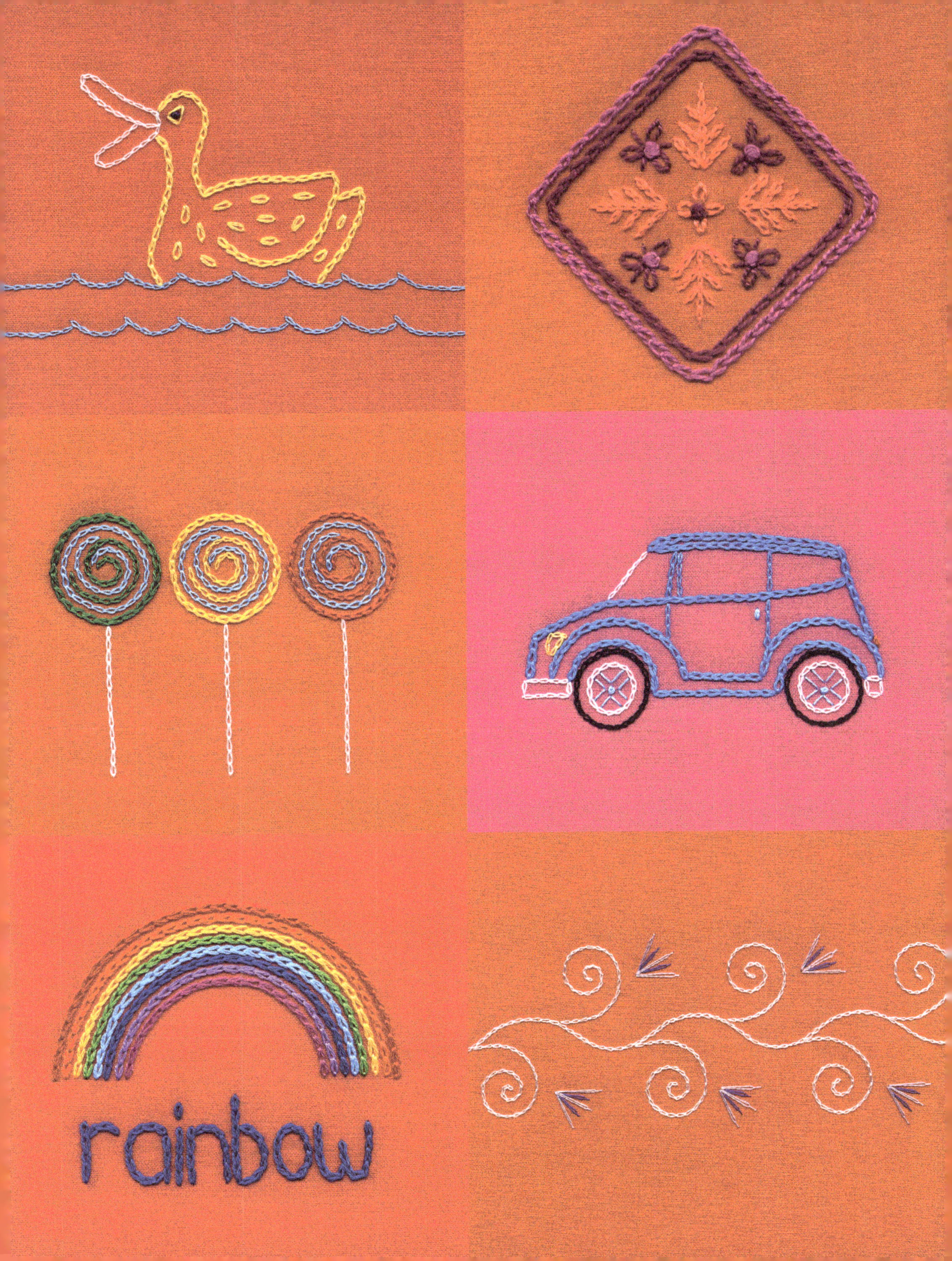
rainbow

# Quack Quack

Paddling in a pond is always so much fun.

## The design

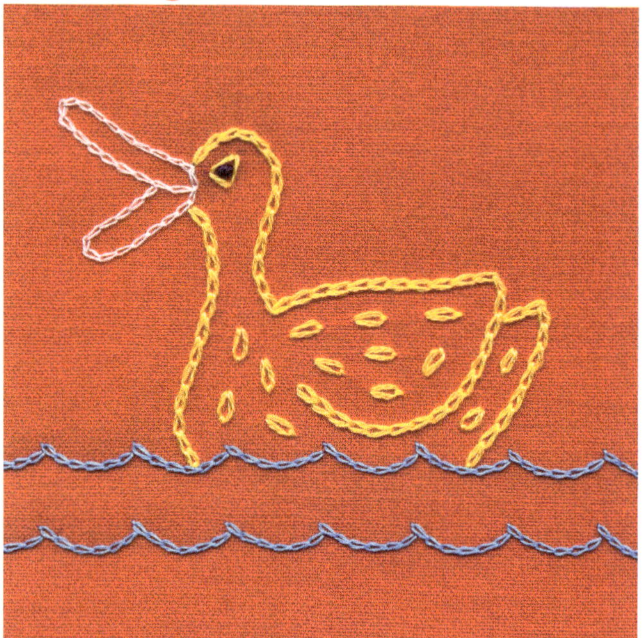

*Quack Quack*

This easy design is stitched mostly in chain stitch, which is used to outline the duck and to form each wave. Detached chain stitches are used to depict the feathers on the duck's body and wing. The eye is added with back stitch and French knot.

Follow the instructions on this page to work the design exactly as shown here on a red background. To use the design on a project, see the idea on the next page where the duck is featured on a play rug for a baby.

## The pattern

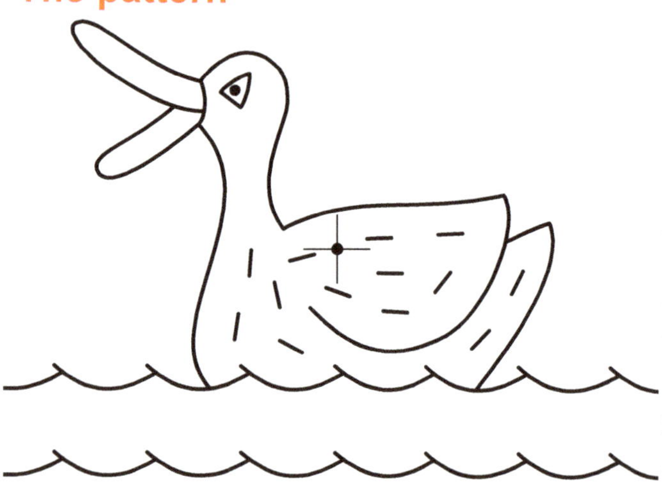

**Key:** Centre of design — Detached chain stitch for feather — • French knot

## Shopping list

- Red cotton fabric for background: 25cm (10") square
- Fabric or interfacing for backing: 25cm (10") square
- Stranded cotton thread:
  (A) dark violet (B) medium aqua (C) light yellow
  (D) white
- Tracing paper and other items for transferring the pattern onto the fabric

## Let's begin

Read page 15 for backing the fabric, and pages 22-25 for transferring the pattern onto the fabric, then select and use suitable methods for your fabric. For the red fabric shown here, the pattern was transferred centrally onto the fabric by tracing with a water erasable fabric marker and then the backing fabric was tacked to the wrong side.

## Stitch!

For help, see pages 76-79 for back stitch, 166-169 for chain stitch, including completing a shape and detached chain stitch, and pages 184-187 for French knot.

1 Stitch the beak in chain stitch, working down the front of the face first, then the lower beak followed by the upper beak (1 strand D). Complete the beak by passing the last stitch under the first stitch (Diagram 1).

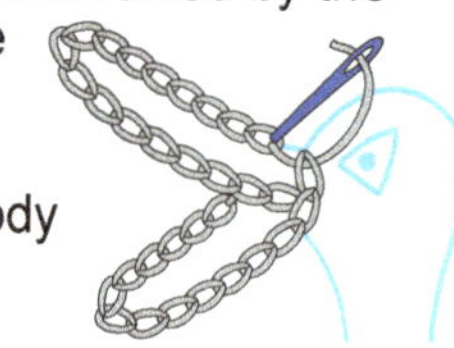

**Diagram 1**

2 Outline the head, wing, tail, and body in chain stitch (2 strands C).

3 Referring to the photo for the direction of the stitches, work the feathers on the body, wing and tail with detached chain stitch, working each stitch with a small anchor extending beyond the marked line (2 strands C).

4 Work the eye outline with three back stitches (2 strands C). Add the pupil with a two wrap French knot (4 strands A).

5 Beginning each wave on the right hand side and anchoring the last stitch at the peak of the wave (Diagram 2), work the waves with six chain stitches for each (1 strand B).

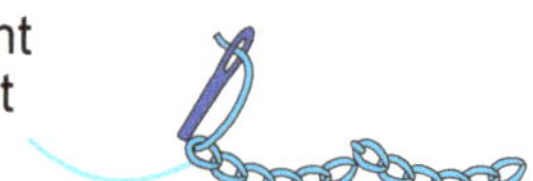

**Diagram 2**

## Let's finish

Take out the tacking. Rinse the work in cold water to remove the water erasable fabric marker. When partly dry, press or pin out the work. See page 36 for pressing and for pinning out.

## Hint

**Achieving evenness**

The waves are designed in a uniform repeating pattern, so keep the number and length of the chain stitches in each wave the same.

# Quack Quack Play Rug for a Baby

Have fun at playtime.

## The project

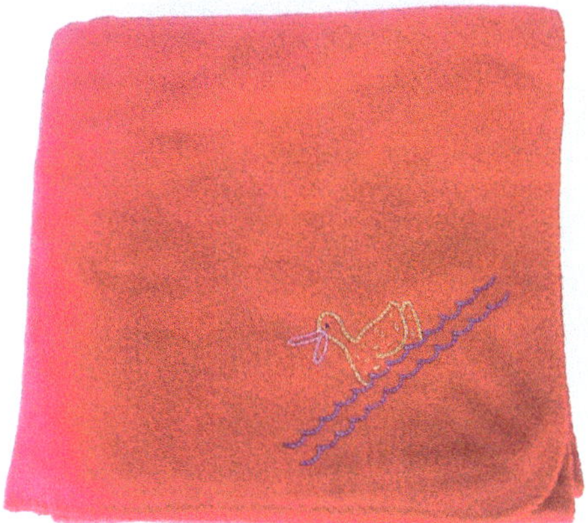

***Quack Quack Play Rug for a Baby***

This colourful project is designed as a floor rug to be used when the baby is supervised in play. Its use is not recommended when the baby is sleeping.

For this project, the design is worked on one corner of a piece of polar fleece fabric that is then made into a rug. Alternatively, a purchased plain rug could be decorated with the design.

The finished size of this play rug is 148cm (58") square.

## Shopping list

- Red polar fleece fabric:
  approximately 148cm (58") square, with any selvedges removed
- Threads as listed for the original design on the page opposite
- No. 5 perlé cotton thread:
  (E) red
- Medium weight tracing paper and other items for transferring the pattern onto the fabric

## Let's begin

See the page opposite for the pattern.

Prepare the pattern by enlarging it to 125% of its original size. Trace the enlarged pattern onto tracing paper. Add extra waves at either side of the design.

Place the tracing over a pad of folded fabric and pierce holes through the tracing at regular intervals along the pattern lines using a large needle.

Prepare the fabric by trimming all four corners of the polar fleece so that they are slightly rounded.

Pin the tracing diagonally onto the right side of the fabric on one corner. See page 21 for placing the pattern diagonally on a corner. Using a water erasable fabric marker, draw dots onto the fabric through the holes in the tracing paper to transfer the pattern, and then remove the tracing. See page 25 for transferring the pattern using the pierce and dot method.

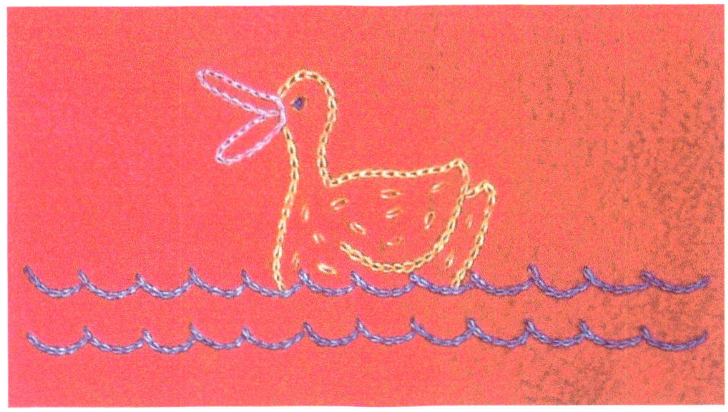

**Detail of *Quack Quack Play Rug for a Baby***

## Stitch!

Work the duck and waves following steps 1-5 of the stitch instructions for the original design on the page opposite. For this project, since the pattern has been enlarged, use stitches that are slightly larger than those shown in the original design.

Using the red perlé cotton thread (E), work around the raw edges of the rug in blanket stitch (Diagrams 1 and 2). Space the stitches evenly, and secure the beginnings and endings of the thread as invisibly as possible behind the back of the stitches on the wrong side.

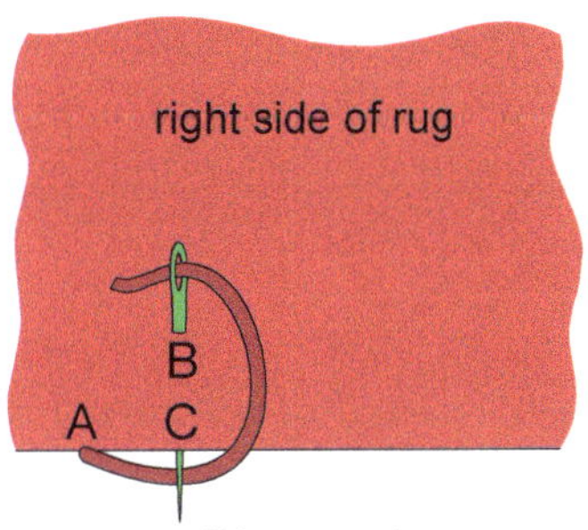


**Diagram 1**

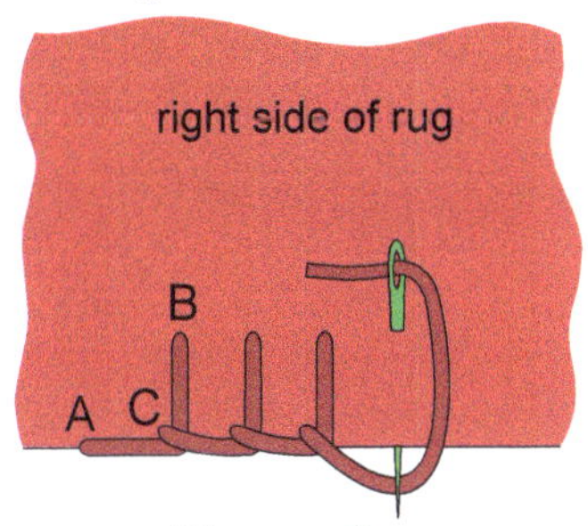


**Diagram 2**

## Let's finish

Rinse the work in cold water to remove the water erasable fabric marker. Allow to dry.

## Hint

**Adapt the design**

The design could be worked on all four corners of the rug. Alternatively, continuous rows of waves and several ducks could be worked across the lower edge or as a border on all four sides.

# Flower Diamond

Decorations featuring flowers are everywhere!

## The design

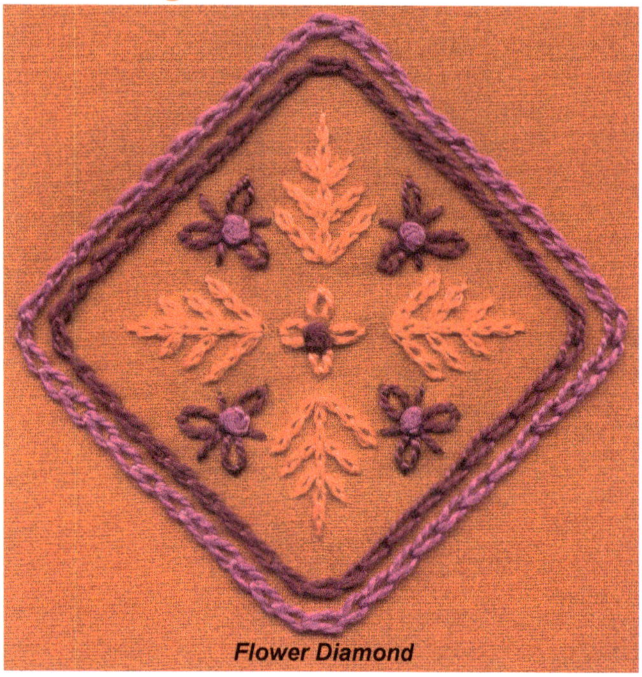

*Flower Diamond*

Chain stitch and detached chain stitch are both used in this quick and easy design. Straight stitch and French knot are also included.

Use the instructions on this page to work the design as shown here on an orange background. See the project idea on the facing page where an element from the design is used on socks for a baby or young child.

## The pattern

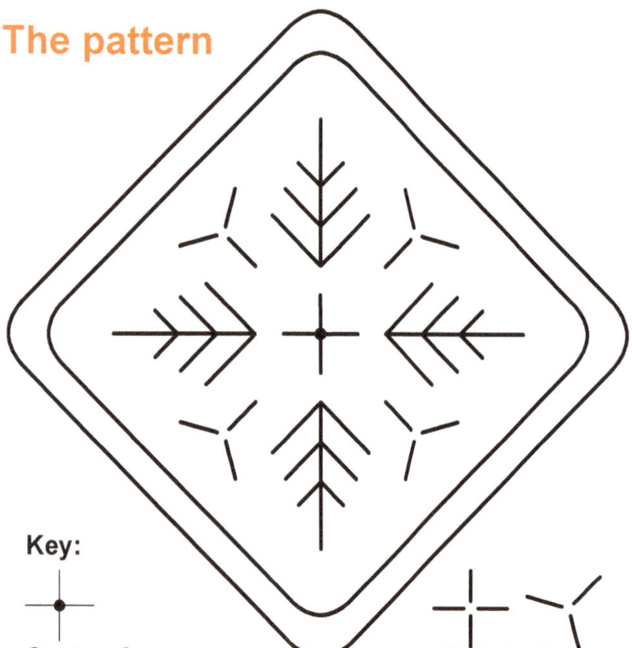

**Key:**

**Centre of design**

**Detached chain stitches**

## Shopping list

- Orange cotton fabric for background: 25cm (10") square
- Fabric or interfacing for backing: 25cm (10") square
- Stranded cotton thread: (A) light red
- No. 5 perlé cotton thread:
  (B) light red (C) dark magenta (D) medium magenta
- Tracing paper and other items for transferring the pattern onto the fabric

## Let's begin

Read page 15 for backing the fabric, and pages 22-25 for transferring the pattern onto the fabric, then select and use suitable methods for your fabric. For the orange fabric shown here, the pattern was transferred centrally onto the fabric by tracing with a water erasable fabric marker and then the backing fabric was tacked to the wrong side.

## Stitch!

For help, see pages 40-43 for straight stitch, 166-169 for chain stitch, including completing a shape and detached chain stitch, and pages 184-187 for French knot. When stitching the flowers and leaves, work each anchor extending a little beyond the marked pattern line.

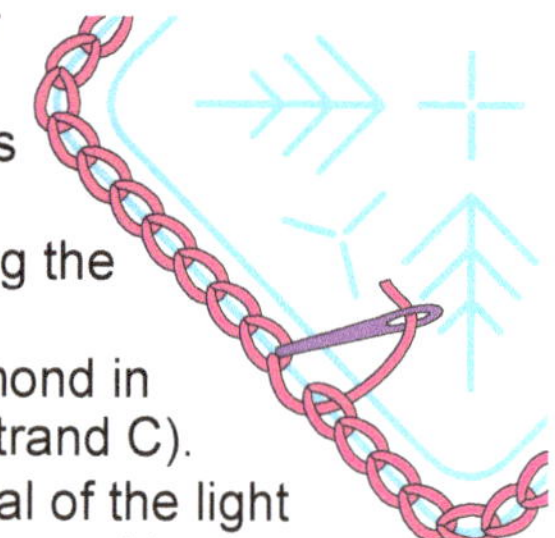

**Diagram 1**

**Diamond frame** Stitch the outer diamond in chain stitch (1 strand D), working a stitch evenly across each of the rounded corners.
Complete the diamond by passing the last stitch under the first stitch (Diagram 1). Work the inner diamond in chain stitch in the same way (1 strand C).

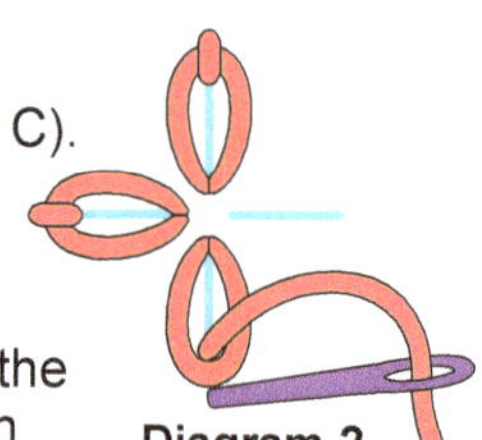

**Diagram 2**

**Light red flower** Work each petal of the light red flower at the centre of the diamond in detached chain stitch (1 strand B), leaving a space at the centre (Diagram 2).
Complete the flower with a two wrap French knot for the centre (2 strands C).

**Magenta flowers** Following the marked lines, work the petals in detached chain stitch (1 strand C), leaving a space at the centre. Using the photo as a guide, add a straight stitch between each petal with the same thread. Complete each flower with a two wrap French knot for the centre (2 strands D).

**Leaves** For each leaf, start at the base and stitch the central stem in small chain stitch. Using the photo as a guide to the number of stitches, work the leaflets with one, two, or three chain stitches (3 strands A).

## Let's finish

Take out the tacking. Rinse work in cold water to remove the fabric marker. When partly dry, press or pin out the work. See page 36 for pressing and for pinning out.

# Flower Socks

Imagine these adorable socks as a gift for a baby or young child.

## The projects

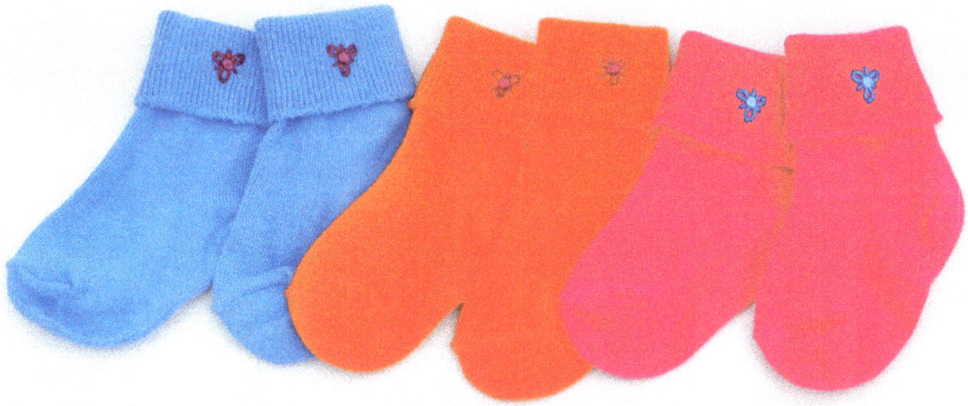

*Flower Socks*

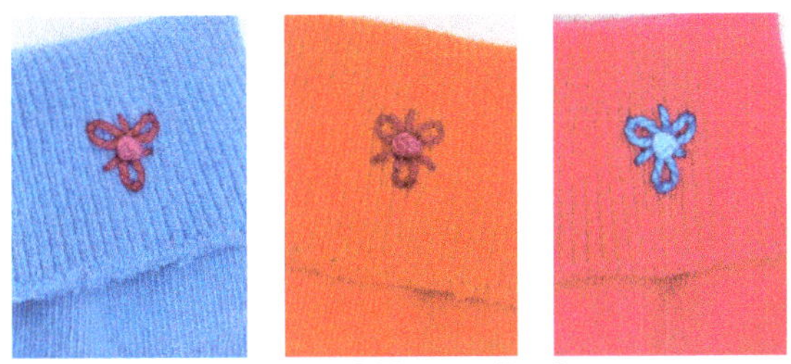

**Details of** ***Flower Socks***

These socks for a baby or young child are very quick to work. You can add small details like this to a pair of socks within minutes. Two flowers are stitched on each sock. They are worked on the wrong side of the sock fabric so that they are visible on the socks when the cuffs are turned down.

## Shopping list

***For all three pairs of socks***

- Medium weight tracing paper and other items for transferring the pattern onto the socks

***Blue socks***

- Pair of blue socks
- Threads (C) and (D) as listed for the original design on the page opposite

***Orange socks***

- Pair of orange socks
- Threads (C) and (D) as listed for the original design on the page opposite

***Pink socks***

- Pair of pink socks
- No. 5 perlé cotton thread in the following colours: (C) dark aqua (D) medium aqua

## Let's begin

See the page opposite for the pattern.

Use the following instructions for any of the three pairs of socks.

Trace the pattern for one of the three-petalled **Magenta flowers** onto the medium weight tracing paper. Place the tracing over a pad of folded fabric and pierce holes through the tracing at each end of the pattern lines using a large needle. Turn the socks inside out and place them on their sides. Slightly stretch the socks sideways as they will be when they are being worn.

Place the tracing with the flower centre 2cm (3/4") down from the upper edge, centrally on the side of one of the socks. Holding the tracing in place, use a chalk-based pencil to draw dots through the holes in the tracing onto the sock fabric (Diagram 1). See page 25 for transferring the pattern using the pierce and dot method. Still with the sock inside out, turn it over so that the other side faces up. Transfer a flower to this side in the same way as the first. Repeat for the second sock.

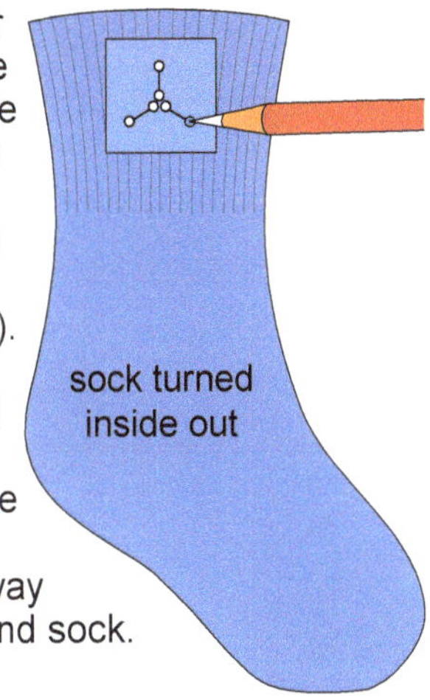


**Diagram 1**

## Stitch!

Work the stitches with a slightly loose thread tension to allow for stretching of the socks when they are worn. Stitch the flowers on the socks following the stitch instructions for the **Magenta flowers** on the page opposite. Use the original coloured threads for the blue and the orange socks, and work with the alternative coloured threads for the pink socks.

## Let's finish

Turn the socks right side out. Fold down the cuffs so that the flowers are visible.

# Lollipops

Here's some colourful confectionery!

## The design

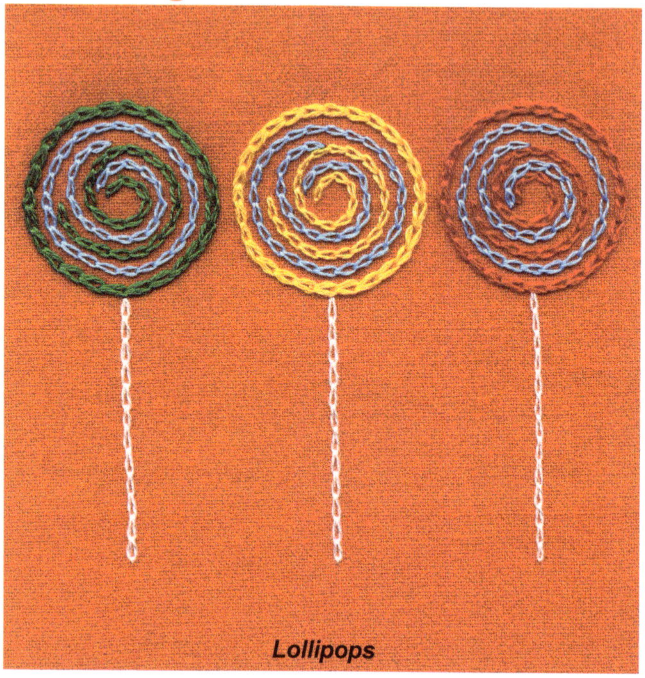

*Lollipops*

This simple design features a repeated pattern of lollipops worked entirely in chain stitch.
To work the design exactly as shown here on an orange background, use the instructions on this page. See the project idea on the next page to adapt the design for use as a border on a pillowcase.

## The pattern

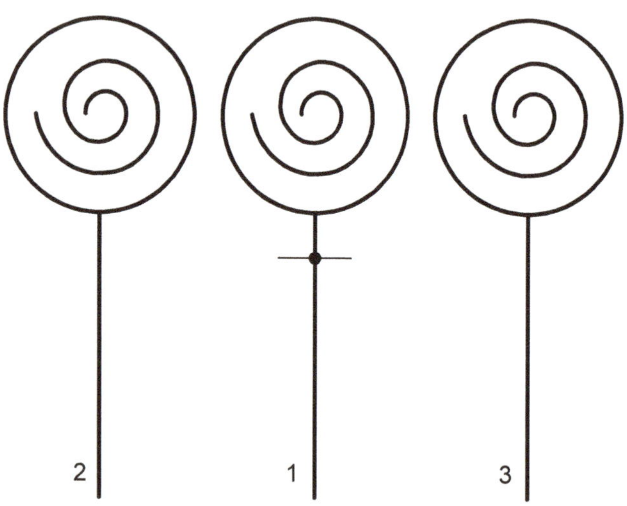


**Key:** Centre of design

## Shopping list

- Orange cotton fabric for background: 25cm (10") square
- Fabric or interfacing for backing: 25cm (10") square
- Stranded cotton thread:
  (A) medium aqua (B) medium green
  (C) medium yellow (D) medium red (E) white
- Tracing paper and other items for transferring the pattern onto the fabric

## Let's begin

Read page 15 for backing the fabric, and pages 22-25 for transferring the pattern onto the fabric, then select and use suitable methods for your fabric. For the orange fabric shown here, the pattern was transferred centrally onto the fabric by tracing with a water erasable fabric marker and then the backing fabric was tacked to the wrong side.

## Stitch!

For help, see pages 166-169 for chain stitch, including completing a shape.

**Lollipop 1**

1. Work a circle of chain stitch for the lollipop outline (2 strands C), completing the circle by passing the last stitch under the first stitch (Diagram 1).
2. To work the yellow centre detail, stitch along the marked spiral in chain stitch, beginning at the outer edge and working in towards the centre (1 strand C).
3. Using the photo as a guide, work a circle of chain stitch between the outline and the spiral (1 strand A).

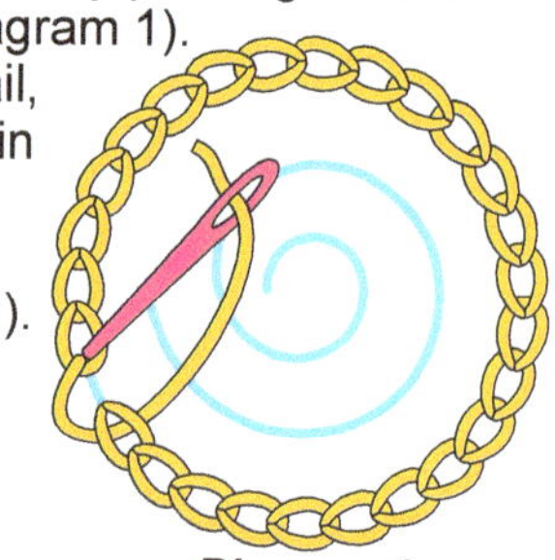

**Diagram 1**

4. Using the photo as a guide, work an aqua spiral in chain stitch, beginning at the top of the yellow spiral and finishing level with the yellow spiral at the centre (1 strand A).
5. Beginning at the lower edge of the lollipop, add a row of chain stitch for the stick (1 strand E).

**Lollipops 2 and 3**

Referring to the photo for placing the colours, work these lollipops in the same way as **Lollipop 1**, substituting the yellow thread with green thread (B) or red thread (D).

## Let's finish

Take out the tacking. Rinse work in cold water to remove the fabric marker. When partly dry, press or pin out the work. See page 36 for pressing and for pinning out.

## Hint

**Change the colours**

This design lends itself to experimenting with colours. Try different colours for the outlines and spirals or alternatively work the whole lollipop with variegated thread to give a gradually changing colour scheme.

# Lollipops Pillowcase

Enjoy sweet dreams with this pillowcase.

## The project

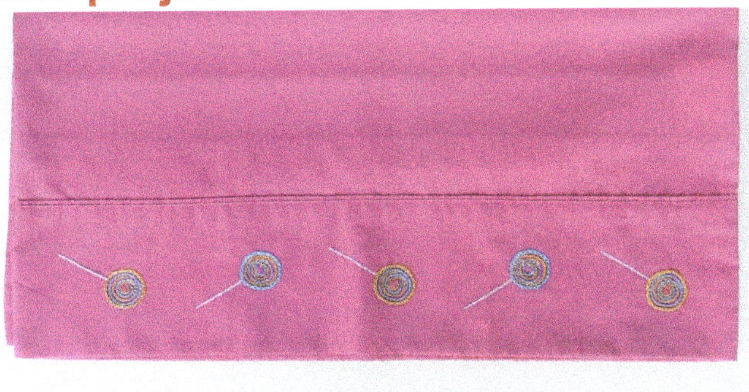

*Lollipops Pillowcase*

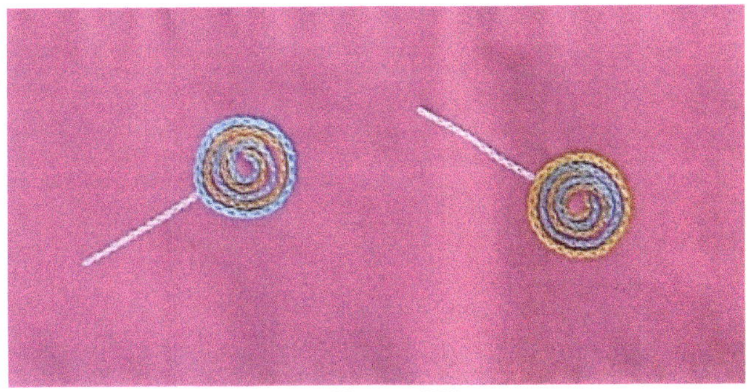

Detail of *Lollipops Pillowcase*

This brightly coloured pillowcase features five lollipops spaced evenly along the border. All the lollipops use the same colours as **Lollipop 1** in the original design, but on two of the lollipops the colours are reversed.

## Shopping list

- Pink pillowcase with a border along one side
- Stranded cotton thread:
  (A) medium aqua (C) medium yellow (E) white
- Tracing paper and other items for transferring the pattern onto the pillowcase

## Let's begin

See the page opposite for the pattern.
Using the pattern, and with a separate piece of tracing paper for each, make five tracings of **Lollipop 1**. Position the tracings on the right side of the pillowcase, evenly along the border, with the first, third and fifth lollipops angled in one direction and the second and fourth lollipops angled in the opposite direction. Pin the tracings in place (Diagram 1).

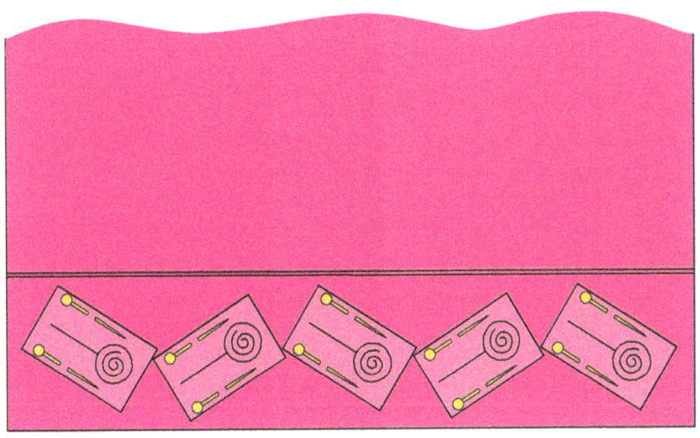

Diagram 1

Placing transfer paper between the pinned tracings and the fabric, transfer the pattern for the five lollipops onto the border using transfer paper. See page 24 for transferring the pattern using transfer paper.

## Stitch!

Work the first, third, and fifth lollipop following steps 1-5 of the stitch instructions for **Lollipop 1** from the original design on the page opposite. Work the second and fourth lollipop in a similar way, reversing the aqua and yellow threads.

## Let's finish

Rinse the pillowcase in cold water to remove the pattern markings. When almost dry, turn the pillowcase inside out and lightly press it. See page 36 for pressing.

## Hint

**More project ideas**

To create a matching set of bed linen, work the same lollipops on the border of a sheet, and larger lollipops scattered on a quilt cover.

# Vroom Vroom

This sporty little two-seater will have you holding on to your hat!

## The design

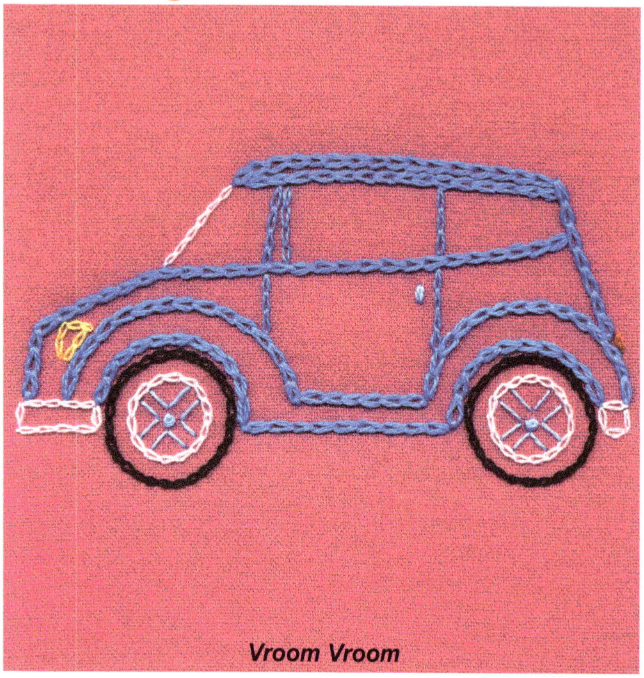

*Vroom Vroom*

Chain stitch is used for most of this design. Details are added with straight stitch, detached chain stitch, and French knot. This design is quite detailed, but it is easy to work.

Follow the instructions on this page to work the design exactly as shown here on a pink background.

To apply the design, see the project idea on the facing page where the car is worked as a patch that is then attached to a baseball cap.

## The pattern

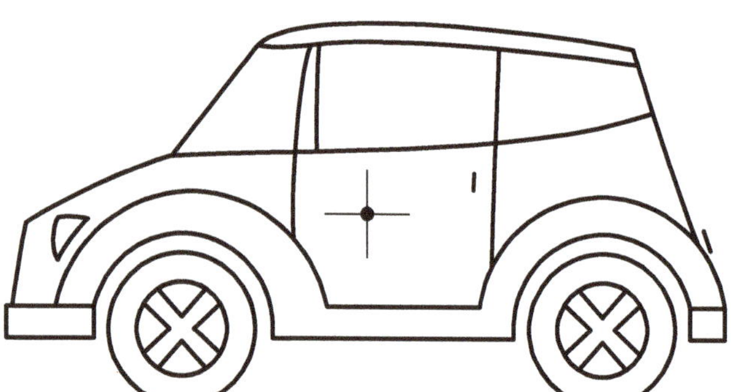

**Key:** ┼ **Centre of design**

## Shopping list

- Pink cotton fabric for background: 25cm (10") square
- Fabric or interfacing for backing: 25cm (10") square
- Stranded cotton thread:
  (A) black (B) dark aqua (C) medium aqua
  (D) light yellow (E) medium red (F) white
- Tracing paper and other items for transferring the pattern onto the fabric

## Let's begin

Read page 15 for backing the fabric, and pages 22-25 for transferring the pattern onto the fabric, then select and use suitable methods for your fabric. For the pink fabric shown here, the pattern was transferred centrally onto the fabric by tracing with a water erasable fabric marker and then the backing fabric was tacked to the wrong side.

## Stitch!

For help, see pages 40-43 for straight stitch, 166-169 for chain stitch and detached chain stitch, and pages 184-187 for French knot.

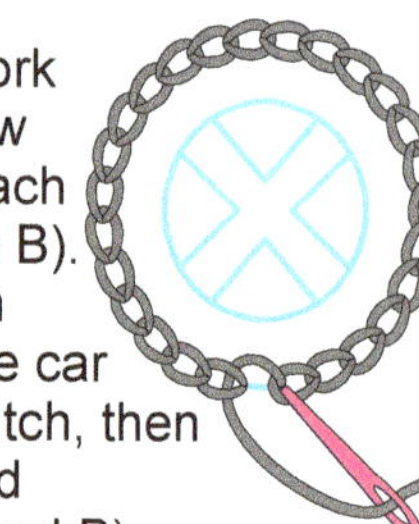

**Diagram 1**

1 Beginning at the back of the roof, work the upper row and then the lower row of the roof in chain stitch, working each row in opposite directions (2 strands B).

2 Starting at the back of the roof again and using the same thread, stitch the car body and the mudguards in chain stitch, then add the vertical lines for the door and window frames in chain stitch (1 strand B).

3 Work a circle of chain stitch for each tyre (1 strand A), completing the circle by passing the last stitch under the first stitch (Diagram 1).

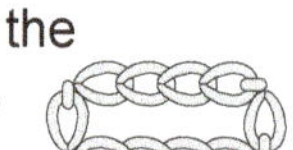

**Diagram 2**

4 Add the rims for the wheels in chain stitch (1 strand F). Stitch the front bumper bar in chain stitch (1 strand F), working each short end with a detached chain stitch (Diagram 2).

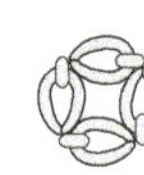

**Diagram 3**

5 Using same thread, work the back bumper bar with four detached chain stitches (Diagram 3).

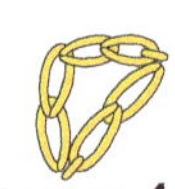

**Diagram 4**

6 Work the windscreen in chain stitch (1 strand F). Stitch the headlight (1 strand D) in chain stitch (Diagram 4). Add the tail light with two straight stitches worked through the same two holes (3 strands E).

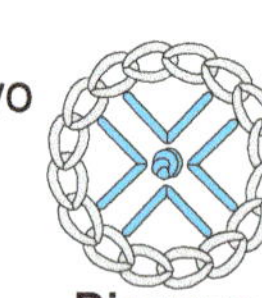

**Diagram 5**

7 Work the spokes on each wheel with straight stitch (1 strand C). Add a two wrap French knot (2 strands C) at the centre of each wheel (Diagram 5). Stitch the door handle with two straight stitches worked through the same two holes in the fabric (2 strands C).

## Let's finish

Take out tacking. Rinse the work in cold water to remove the fabric marker. When partly dry, press or pin out. See page 36 for pressing and for pinning out.

# Vroom Vroom Baseball Cap

Be on trend with this sporty cap.

## The project

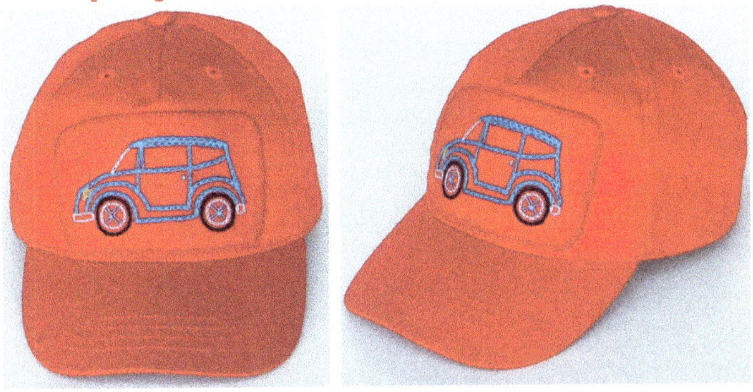

***Vroom Vroom Baseball Cap***

This project features *Vroom Vroom* worked on a fabric patch that is then attached to a purchased baseball cap. When choosing the colour of the fabric for the patch, match the colour to the cap so the emphasis is on the design and not on the patch itself. To avoid any excess dye running from the cap onto the patch when it is laundered, it is recommended to wash the cap before attaching the patch.

## Shopping list

- Red baseball cap
- Red cotton fabric for the patch:
  13cm x 18cm wide (5" x 7")
- Medium weight iron-on interfacing:
  13cm x 18cm wide (5" x 7")
- Threads as listed for the original design on the page opposite
- Machine sewing thread: red
- Tracing paper and other items for transferring the pattern onto the fabric
- Cardboard:
  13cm x 18cm wide (5" x 7")

## Let's begin

See the page opposite for the pattern.
Following the instructions on page 15 for backing the fabric, attach the interfacing onto the wrong side of the red fabric. This will stabilize the area where the design is to be stitched and will also make the patch easier to handle when attaching it to the cap.
Transfer the pattern centrally onto the right side of the red fabric using transfer paper. See page 24 for transferring the pattern using transfer paper.

## Stitch!

Work the car following steps 1-7 of the stitch instructions on the page opposite.

## Let's finish

Rinse the work in cold water to remove the pattern markings. When partly dry, press or pin out the work. See page 36 for pressing and for pinning out.
From the cardboard, make a template that has a centrally placed cut-out window measuring 7cm x 11cm wide (2 3/4" x 4 3/8") with rounded corners (Diagram 1).

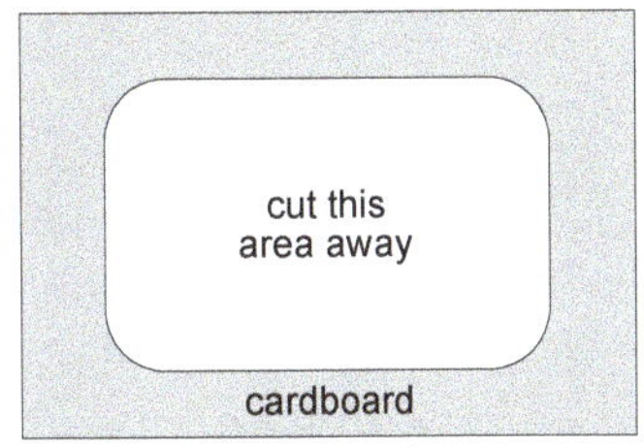


**Diagram 1**

Place this template so that the window is positioned centrally over the stitched car.
Trace around the window with a chalk-based pencil.
Using a close zigzag stitch on the machine, and with red machine sewing thread, stitch around the patch over the marked line.
Carefully cut away the excess fabric close to the zigzag stitching (Diagram 2).

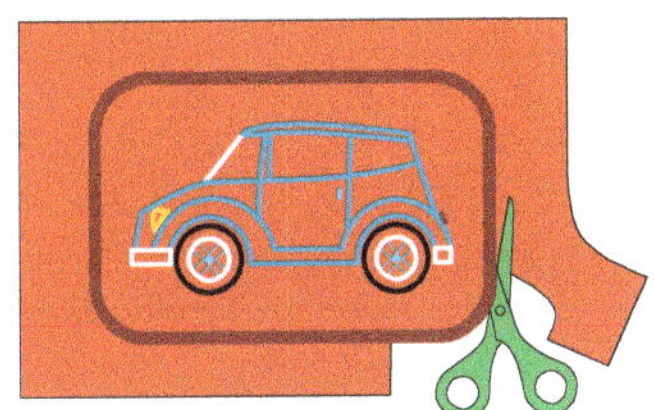

**Diagram 2**

Position the patch onto the centre front of the cap and tack it firmly in place. Using the machine sewing thread, sew the patch to the cap with small hand stitches placed over the zigzag stitches.

## Hint

**More project ideas**

As an alternative project, decorate the border on a sheet and pillowcase set with many cars worked in a variety of colours.

# Rainbow Magic

A rainbow is so captivating and magnificent, and yet so fleeting.

## The design

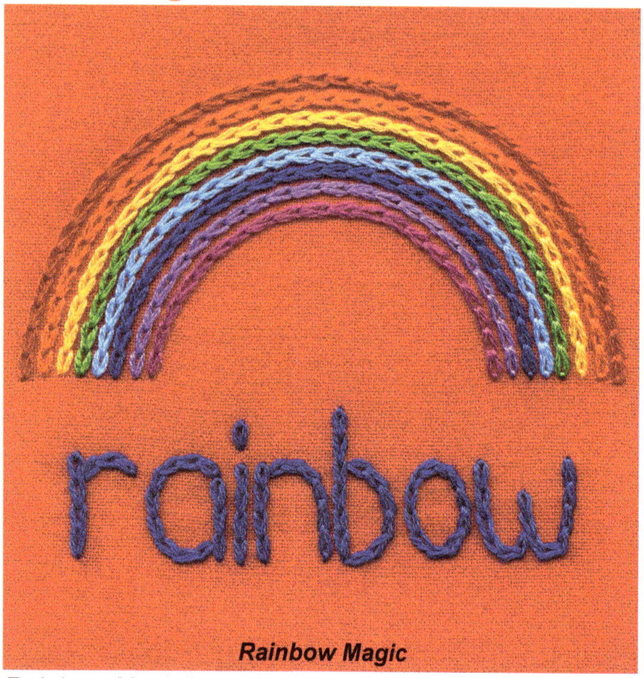

*Rainbow Magic*

*Rainbow Magic* is worked mainly in chain stitch, with one detached chain stitch. The rows of coloured stitching in this design achieve a rainbow effect. Follow the instructions on this page to work the design exactly as shown here on a red background. To feature the rainbow from the design as a mobile, see the project idea on the page opposite.

## The pattern

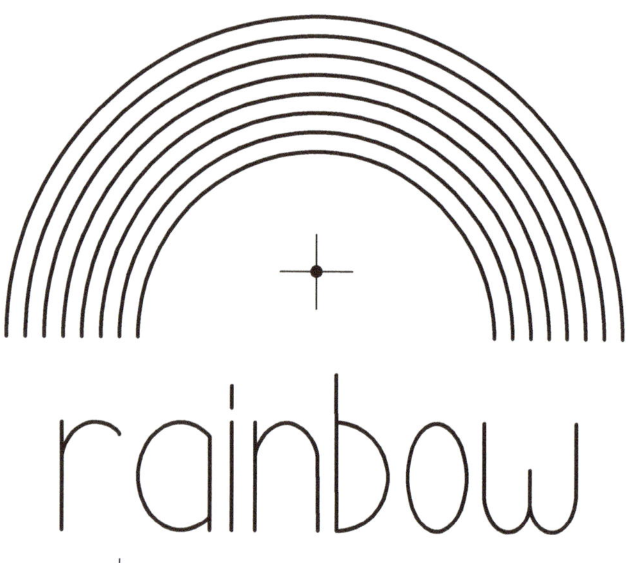

Key: Centre of design | Detached chain stitch for the dot on the 'i'

## Shopping list

- Red cotton fabric for background: 25cm (10") square
- Fabric or interfacing for backing: 25cm (10") square
- Stranded cotton thread:
  (A) medium violet (B) medium blue (C) medium aqua (D) light green (E) medium yellow (F) medium orange (G) medium red (H) medium magenta
- Tracing paper and other items for transferring the pattern onto the fabric

## Let's begin

Read page 15 for backing the fabric, and pages 22-25 for transferring the pattern onto the fabric, then select and use suitable methods for your fabric. For the red fabric shown here, the pattern was transferred centrally onto the fabric by tracing with an HB pencil and then the backing fabric was tacked to the wrong side.

## Stitch!

For help, see pages 166-169 for chain stitch, including completing a shape and detached chain stitch.

1 Work the inner row of the rainbow in chain stitch (3 strands H).

2 Working outwards, and beginning every row on the same side of the rainbow, stitch the remaining rows in chain stitch in the following order (3 strands A, B, C, D, E, F, and G).

3 Referring to the diagram for stitch direction (Diagram 1), work each letter in reasonably small chain stitch, adding the dot on the letter 'i' with a detached chain stitch (3 strands B). When stitching the letter 'o' complete the oval shape by passing the last stitch under the first stitch (Diagram 2).

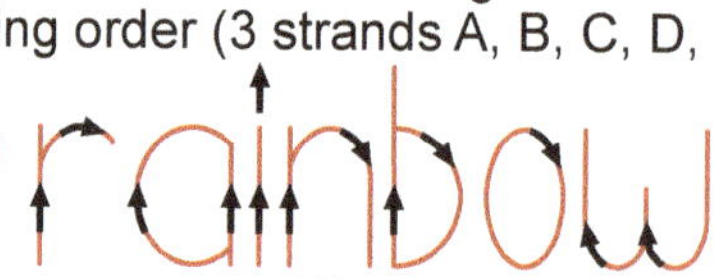

Diagram 1

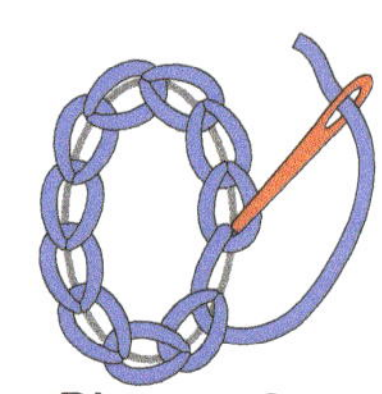

Diagram 2

## Let's finish

Take out the tacking. Press or pin out the work. See page 36 for pressing and for pinning out.

## Hint

**Lettering**

Feel free to experiment with using any stitch for working lettering on an embroidered work, particularly those stitches that form a distinct line. Whipping the stitches can add even more definition to the letters, for example see pages 76-79 for whipped back stitch. It may be easiest to create an even curve on any rounded letters by working with very small stitches.

Remember to try out a few different writing styles, including both handwriting and printing fonts!

# Rainbow Magic Mobile

Create a mobile with the magic of rainbows.

## The project

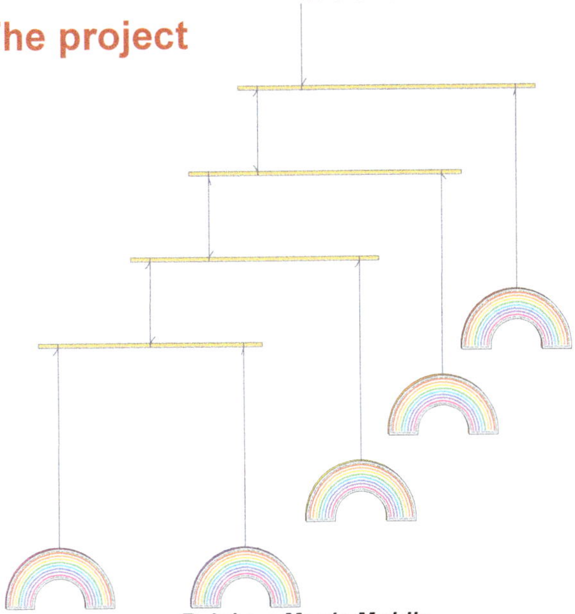

***Rainbow Magic Mobile***

For this mobile, the rainbow from *Rainbow Magic* has been enlarged and then worked five times in the original colours on white felt. Different coloured felt pieces are attached on the reverse sides of the rainbows. Each rainbow is 11.5cm (4 1/2") in width.

## Shopping list

- White felt fabric for the rainbow shapes:
  five pieces 10cm x 15cm wide (4" x 6")
- Violet, pink, red, orange, and yellow felt fabric for the reverse sides:
  one piece of each colour 10cm x 15cm wide (4" x 6")
- Lightweight iron-on interfacing for backing:
  ten pieces 10cm x 15cm wide (4" x 6")
- Thin wadding: one piece 8cm x 66cm wide (3" x 26")
- Threads as listed for the original design opposite
- Machine sewing thread:
  white, violet, pink, red, orange, and yellow
- Tracing paper and other items for transferring the pattern onto the felt
- Clear fishing line: 2.7m (106")
- Wooden rod in the following four lengths:
  23cm, 25.5cm, 28cm, 30.5cm (9", 10", 11", 12")
- Glue

## Let's begin

See the page opposite for the pattern. Enlarge the pattern, excluding the letters, to 125% of its original size. Following the instructions on page 15 for backing fabric, attach one piece of iron-on interfacing onto the wrong side of each piece of felt. Transfer the enlarged rainbow centrally onto the right side of each of the white felt pieces using the pierce and dot method with an HB pencil. See page 25 for transferring the pattern using the pierce and dot method.

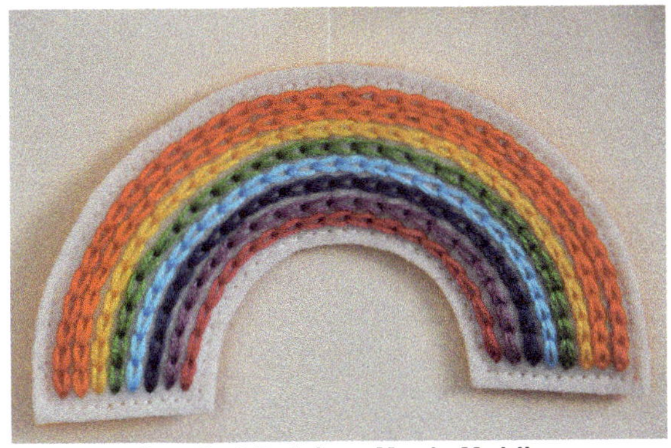

**Detail of *Rainbow Magic Mobile***

## Stitch!

Work each rainbow following steps 1 and 2 of the stitch instructions on the page opposite, however use 4 strands of thread for each colour.

## Let's finish

***Making up the rainbows***

The following instructions are for making up one rainbow. Make up the remaining rainbows in the same way.

Cut a 32cm (12 1/2") length of fishing line and tie a small loop at one end. Using small hand stitches, firmly attach the loop onto the back of the stitches centrally at the top of the rainbow.

Cut a piece of wadding exactly to the enlarged pattern shape. Place the wadding onto the wrong side of the white felt, aligning it with the back of the stitched rainbow. With wrong sides together, place one piece of coloured felt behind the wadding.

Tack the layers together 1cm (3/8") outside the design. Using a zipper foot on the machine, and with white machine sewing thread on the top, and thread to match the coloured felt in the bobbin, straight stitch around the rainbow close to the design. Being careful not to cut the fishing line, trim away the excess felt from around the edge of the rainbow (Diagram 1).

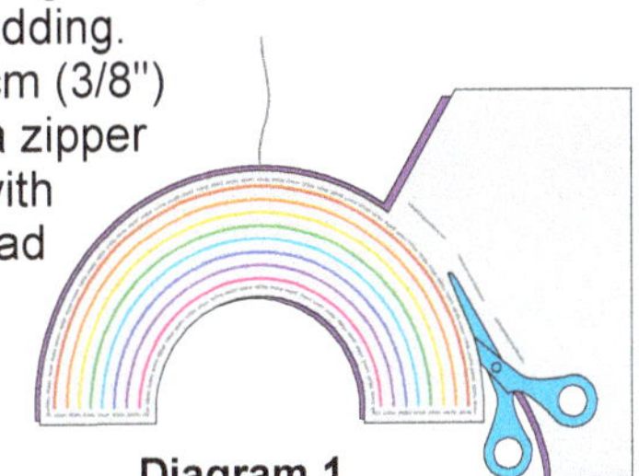

**Diagram 1**

***Assembling the mobile***

Knotting the remaining fishing line around the wooden rods, assemble the mobile. Begin with the lowest rod, which is the shortest, and work upwards, ending with the longest rod. Check to see that the mobile hangs correctly. If necessary, adjust the position of the pieces of fishing line by sliding them along the rods. Once balanced, apply small amounts of glue to secure each knot in place.

# Moonlit Forest

The leaves and flowers are dancing in the soft light of the full moon.

## The design

*Moonlit Forest*

*Moonlit Forest* features chain stitch and detached chain stitch. It is worked entirely in rayon thread, which has a lustrous shine. The curving stem and spiral leaves, accented by delicate flowers, are highly stylized and form a repeating pattern. Follow the instructions on this page to work the design as shown here. To use this design as a repeating pattern on a cushion cover, see the project idea on the next page.

## The pattern

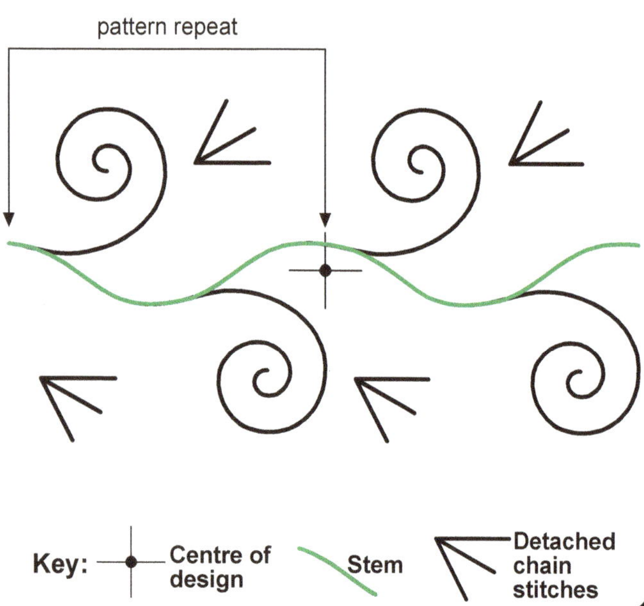


## Shopping list

- Orange cotton fabric for background: 25cm (10") square
- Fabric or interfacing for backing: 25cm (10") square
- Stranded rayon thread: (A) dark violet (B) light violet (C) white
- Tracing paper and other items for transferring the pattern onto the fabric

## Let's begin

Read page 15 for backing the fabric, and pages 22-25 for transferring the pattern onto the fabric, then select and use suitable methods for your fabric. For the orange fabric shown here, the pattern was transferred centrally onto the fabric by tracing with a water erasable fabric marker and then the backing fabric was tacked to the wrong side.

## Stitch!

For help, see pages 166-169 for chain stitch and detached chain stitch.

1 Beginning at the left-hand end, work the stem in chain stitch, finishing with a small anchor (1 strand C).

2 Stitch the spirals in chain stitch, working outward from the stem to the centre of each spiral, and ending each with a small anchor (1 strand C).

3 For each flower, stitch three detached chain stitch petals worked through the same hole in the fabric at the base (1 strand B), ending each stitch with a medium anchor beyond the marked line (Diagram 1).

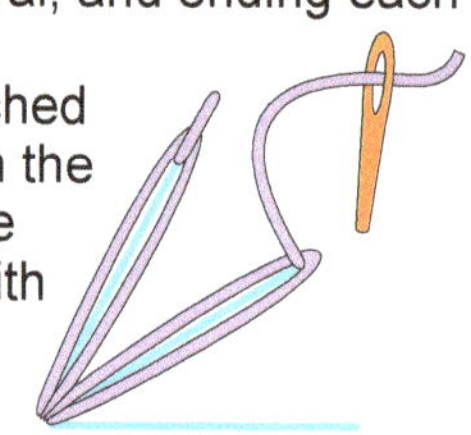

Diagram 1

4 Work a detached chain stitch (1 strand A) in each of the spaces formed between the previously worked petals, ending each stitch with a medium anchor (Diagram 2).

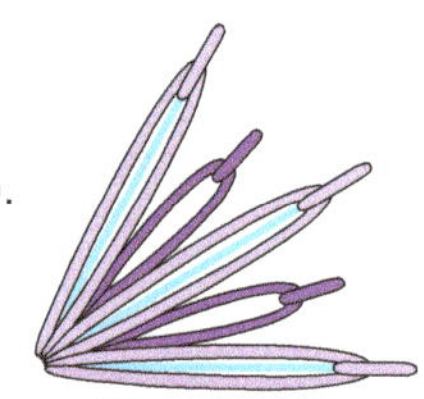

Diagram 2

## Let's finish

Take out the tacking. Rinse the work in cold water to remove the water erasable fabric marker. When partly dry, press or pin out the work. See page 36 for pressing and for pinning out.

## Hint

**Using rayon thread**

When stitching with rayon thread, begin and end off the thread extra securely on the back of the work as it is springy and can easily work loose.

Use shorter lengths of rayon thread than you would normally use for cotton thread because rayon is easily damaged every time it is pulled through the fabric.

# Moonlit Forest Cushion Cover

Add elegance to a cushion with this trailing vine.

## The project

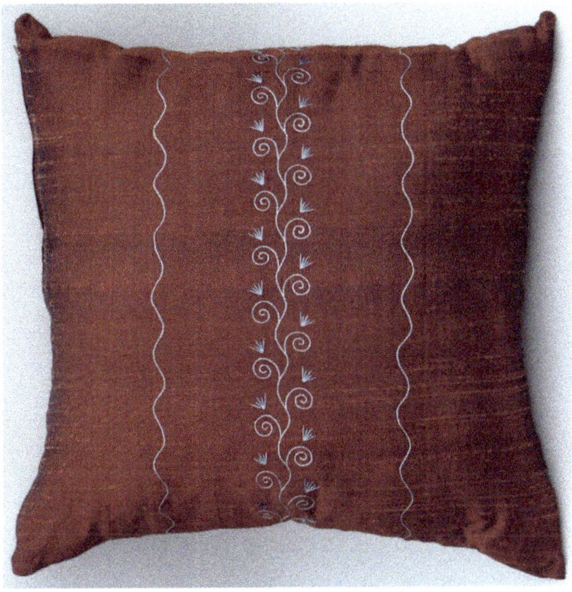

***Moonlit Forest Cushion Cover***

**Detail of *Moonlit Forest Cushion Cover***

*Moonlit Forest* is worked as a repeating pattern in an alternative colour scheme on a purchased dark orange cushion cover. Two extra stems are added to form the edges of the decoration.
The size of this cushion is 46cm (18") square.

## Shopping list

- Dark orange cushion cover and insert.
- Iron-on interfacing for backing:
  25cm (10") wide by the height of the cushion cover
- Stranded rayon thread:
  (A) medium aqua (B) light violet (C) white
- Tracing paper and other items for transferring the pattern onto the cushion cover

## Let's begin

See the page opposite for the pattern.
Remove the cushion insert and turn the cover inside out. Attach the iron-on interfacing centrally, from seam to seam, onto the wrong side of the front of the cushion cover. See page 15 for backing the fabric. Turn the cover through to the right side and place it with the front facing up. Rule a line from the upper to the lower edge through the centre of the interfaced area of the front using a water erasable fabric marker. Rule a line 9cm (3 1/2") at left of the central line, and then another the same distance at right of the central line. Using transfer paper, transfer the pattern along the central line, repeating it along the whole height of the cushion cover from seam to seam. Along the left and right lines, transfer the pattern for the stem only. See page 24 for transferring the pattern using transfer paper.

## Stitch!

Work the design along the central line following steps 1-4 of the stitch instructions on the page opposite, using the alternative colour scheme. Work the two extra stems, to form the edges of the panel, following step 1.

## Let's finish

Turn the cover inside out. On thc wrong side, peel back any excess interfacing from the outer edges of the stitched area and trim it back close to the stitches. Rinse the cover in cold water to remove the pattern markings. When almost dry, press with the cushion cover turned inside out. See page 36 for pressing. Turn through to the right side. Place the insert back into the cover.

## Hint

**Different colour schemes**

The design could be worked on a whole set of cushions, featuring a different colour scheme for each one.

# French knot

## and variations

French knot is one of the best known of the knotted stitches. Each stitch is an isolated round knot that gives a raised textured appearance.

The knots can be worked singly, scattered over a surface, packed closely together to fill a shape, or stitched in a row to make a line. When massed together, they can create an interesting knobbly texture. French knots, which can range from very tiny to quite large depending on the thread used, are particularly useful for portraying features such as eyes and flower centres.

French knots can be worked in combination with other stitches such as running stitch, or used as anchors on fly stitches or detached chain stitches.

A useful variation of French knot is pistil stitch, which is worked as a French knot with a stalk.

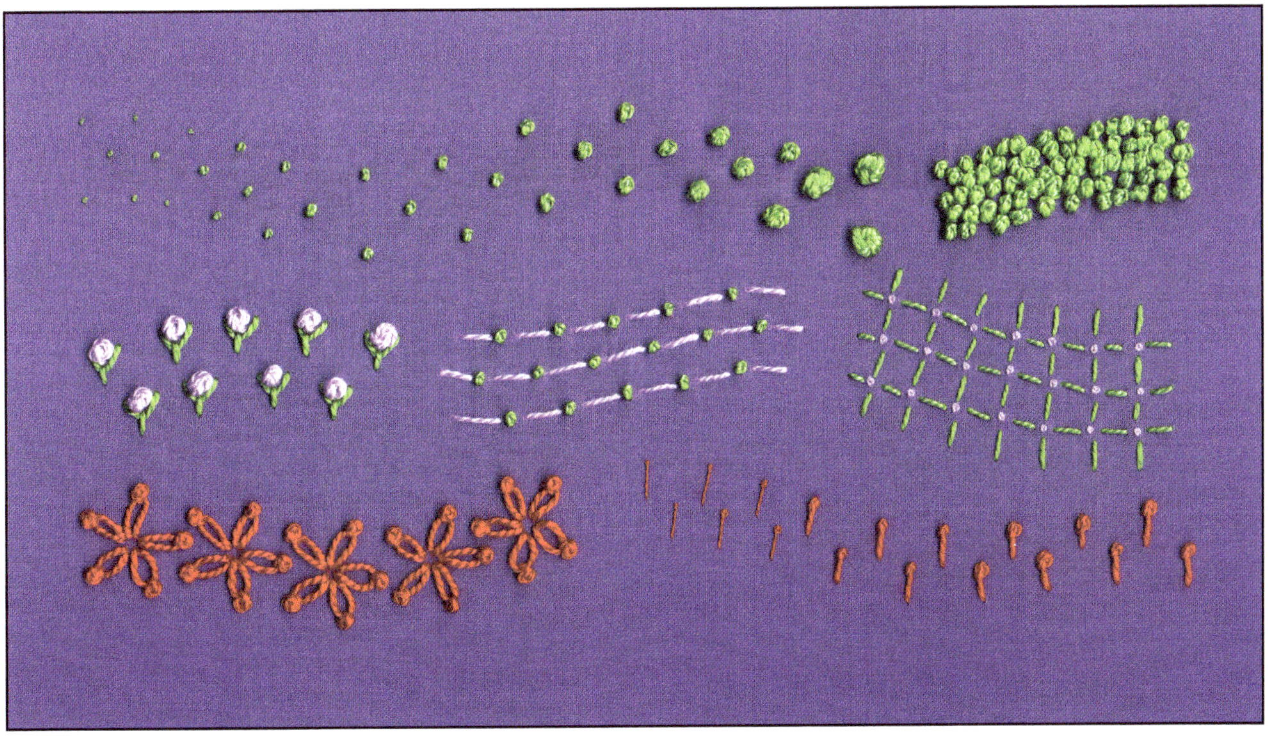

## French knot and variations sampler

French knots, small to large in size

French knots worked in a dense group to fill a shape

French knots combined with fly stitches to form a bud design

French knots combined with running stitch

French knots combined with running stitch worked at right angles

French knots worked as anchors on detached chain stitches

Pistil stitch, small to large in size

# French knot and variations

## Hints

A French knot is created by wrapping a secured thread around the needle one or more times, and then, with the thread tension taut and the wraps held in place, pulling the thread through the wraps and the background fabric. The more wraps there are, the larger the knot. Also the thicker the thread is, the larger the knot.

A pistil stitch is created in a similar way to a French knot, but the needle is taken through to the back of the fabric a greater distance away from the starting point, forming a stalk. The more wraps there are, the larger the knot of the pistil stitch. Also, as with French knots, the thicker the thread is, the larger the knot.

Before working large French knots or large pistil stitches that are worked with two or more strands of thread, consider experimenting on a scrap of fabric. Keep the same tension on all the strands so that the finished knot is even in appearance.

## French knot and variations: right-handed

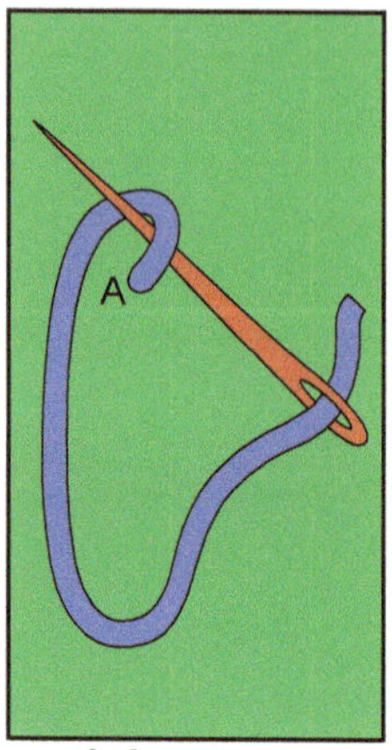


**French knot – one wrap**
**1** Come up at A. Holding thread in your left hand, wrap the thread once around the needle.

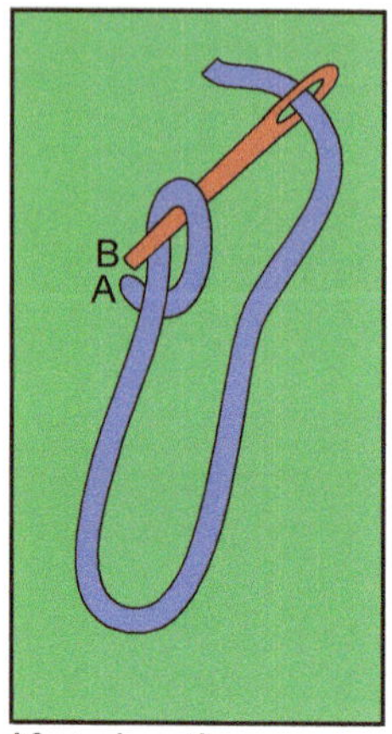


**2** Keeping the wrap on the needle, take the needle partly down into the fabric at B, a short distance above A.

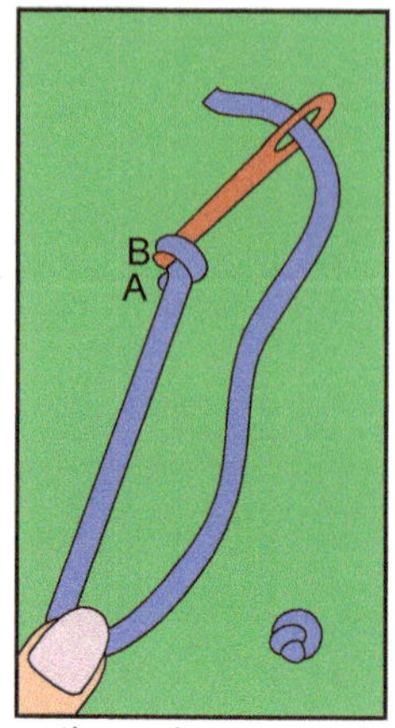


**3** Tighten thread so wrap hugs needle. Hold thread taut and wraps in place as you pull needle through to the back, forming the knot. Secure.

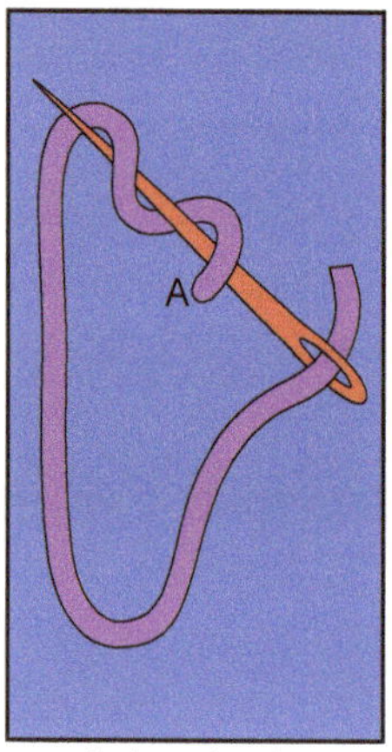


**French knot – two wraps**
**1** Come up at A. Holding the thread in your left hand, wrap the thread twice around the needle.

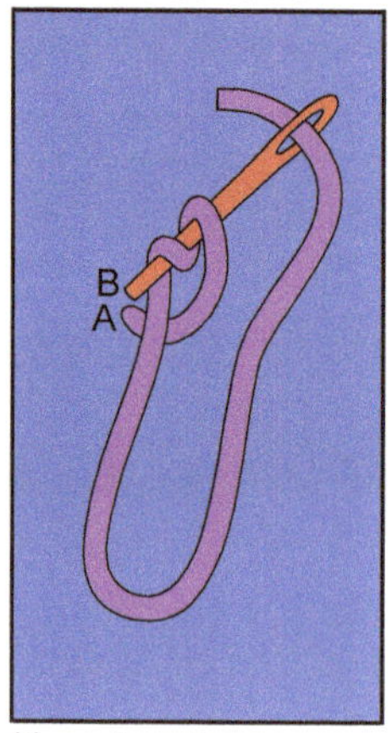


**2** Keeping the wraps on the needle, take the needle partly down into the fabric at B, a short distance above A.

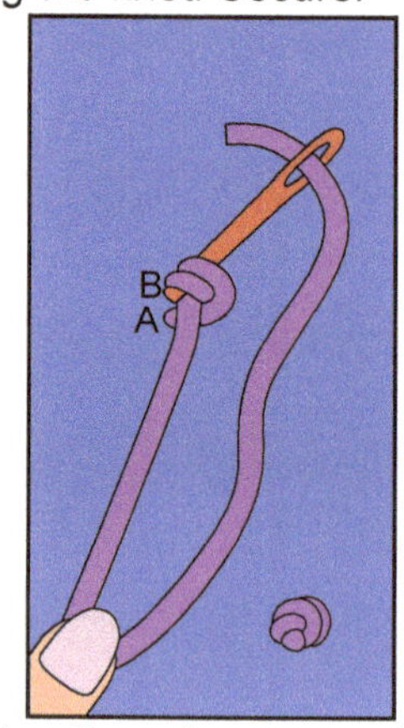


**3** Tighten thread so wraps hug needle. Hold thread taut and wraps in place as you pull needle through to the back, forming the knot. Secure.

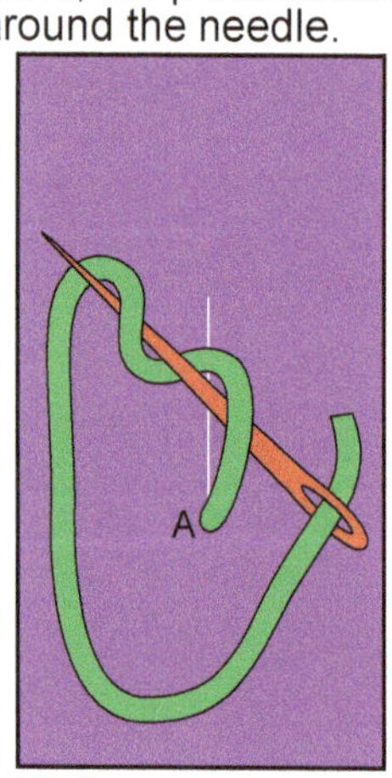


**Pistil stitch – one or two wraps**
**1** Come up at A. Holding the thread in your left hand, wrap the thread once or twice around the needle.

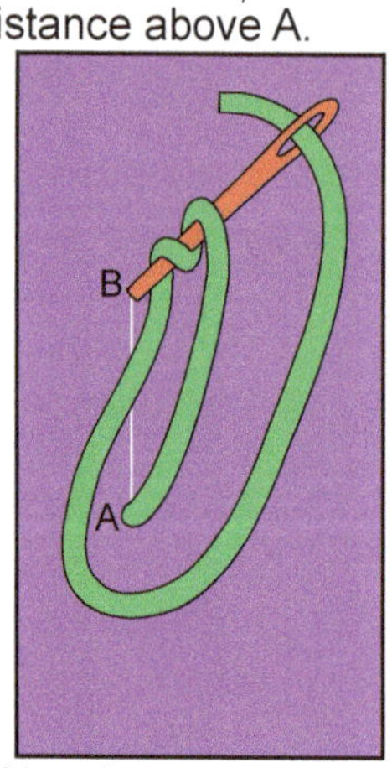


**2** Keeping wraps on needle, take needle partly down at B, the required distance from A.

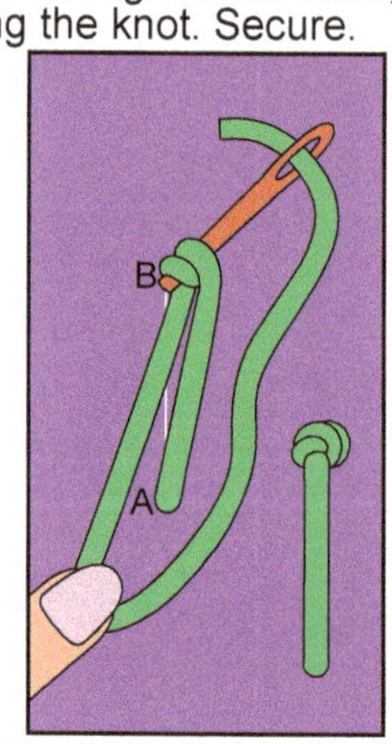


**3** Tighten thread so wraps hug needle. Hold thread taut and wraps in place as you pull needle through to the back, forming the stitch. Secure.

# French knot and variations: left-handed

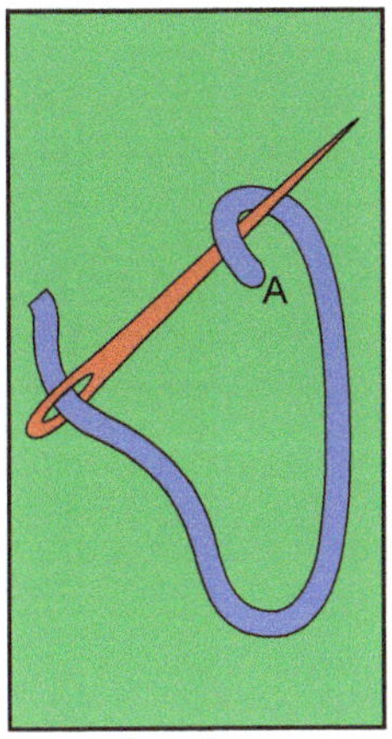


**French knot – one wrap**
**1** Come up at A. Holding thread in your right hand, wrap the thread once around the needle.

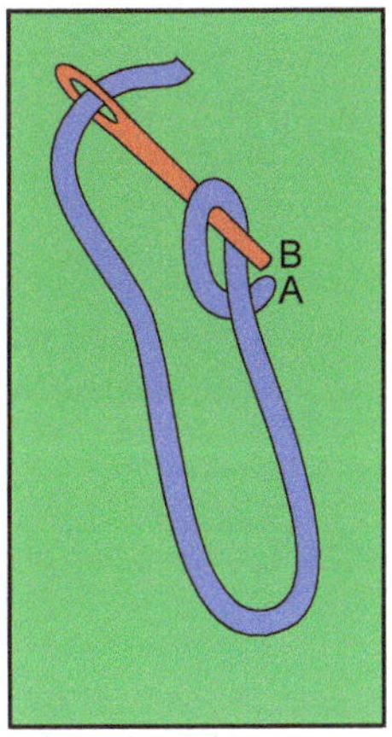


**2** Keeping the wrap on the needle, take the needle partly down into the fabric at B, a short distance above A.

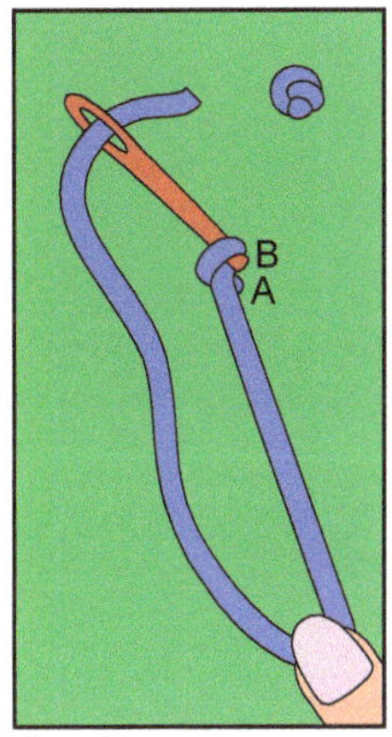


**3** Tighten thread so wrap hugs needle. Hold thread taut and wraps in place as you pull needle through to the back, forming the knot. Secure.

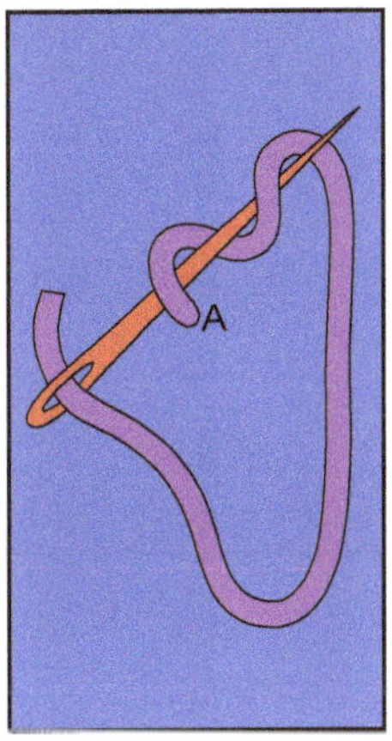


**French knot – two wraps**
**1** Come up at A. Holding the thread in your right hand, wrap the thread twice around the needle.

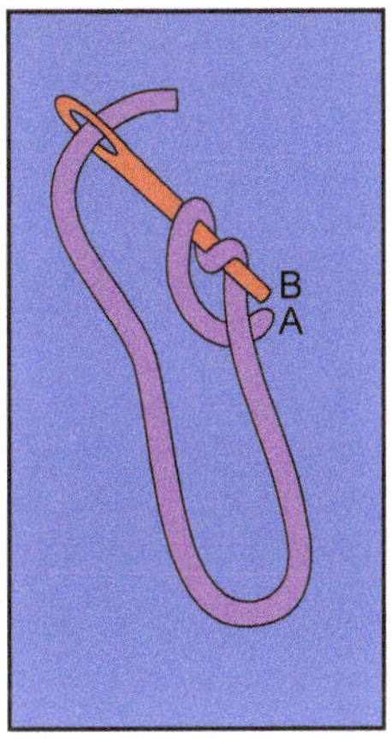


**2** Keeping the wraps on the needle, take the needle partly down into the fabric at B, a short distance above A.

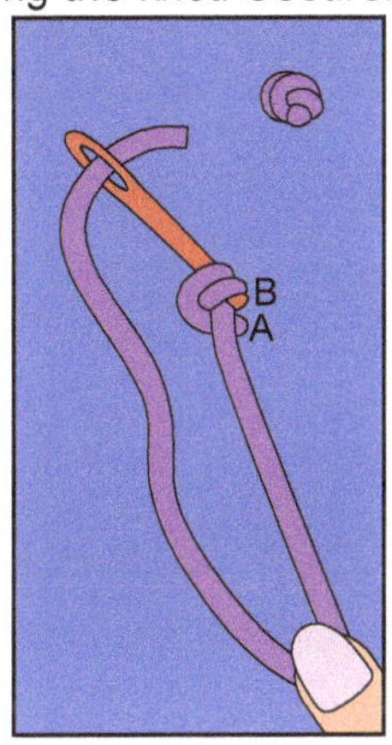


**3** Tighten thread so wraps hug needle. Hold thread taut and wraps in place as you pull needle through to the back, forming the knot. Secure.

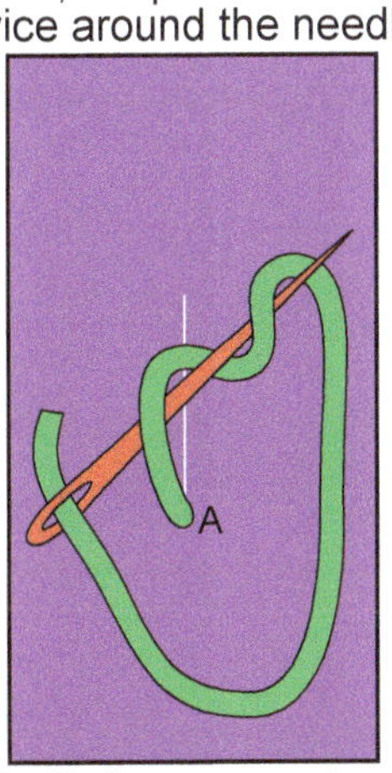


**Pistil stitch – one or two wraps**
**1** Come up at A. Holding the thread in your right hand, wrap the thread once or twice around the needle.

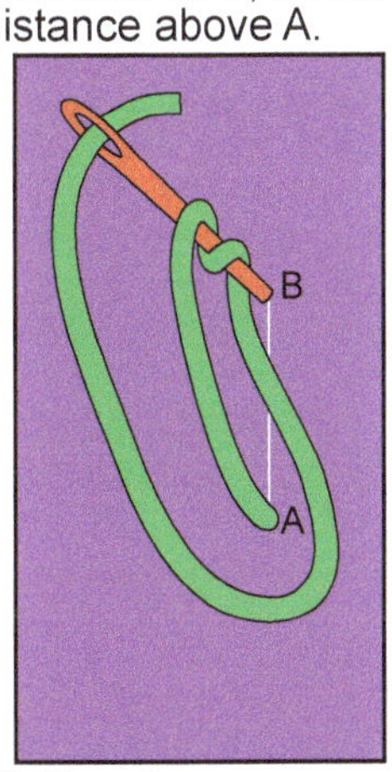


**2** Keeping wraps on needle, take needle partly down at B, the required distance from A.

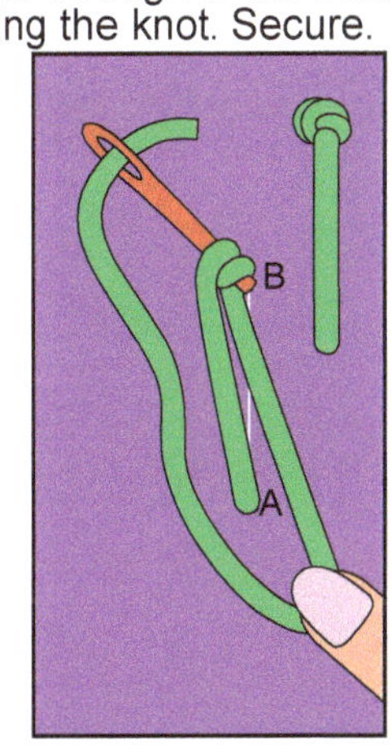


**3** Tighten thread so wraps hug needle. Hold thread taut and wraps in place as you pull needle through to the back, forming the stitch. Secure.

# French knot
## and variations

# Designs and project ideas

### The designs

Pompom Poodle

Cherry Tart

Hearts and Flowers

Golden Wattle

Red Telephone

Summer Garden

# Pompom Poodle

The ultimate companion, with stylish perfection.

## The design

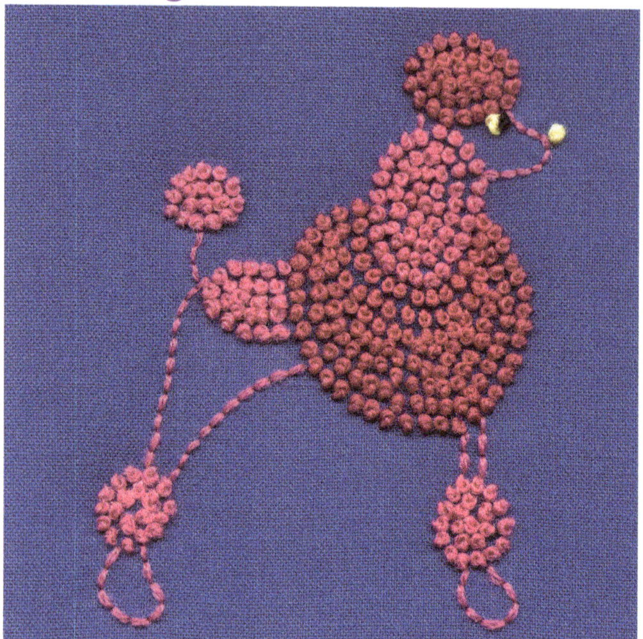

*Pompom Poodle*

This poodle design, using only French knots and back stitch, is worked mostly in wool to achieve a fluffy texture. French knots are stitched in groups to depict the pompom shapes seen typically on poodles. As the French knots are placed densely, this design may take some time to complete, but it is easy to work.
Follow the instructions on this page to work the design as above. To apply the design, see the handbag on the page opposite.

## The pattern

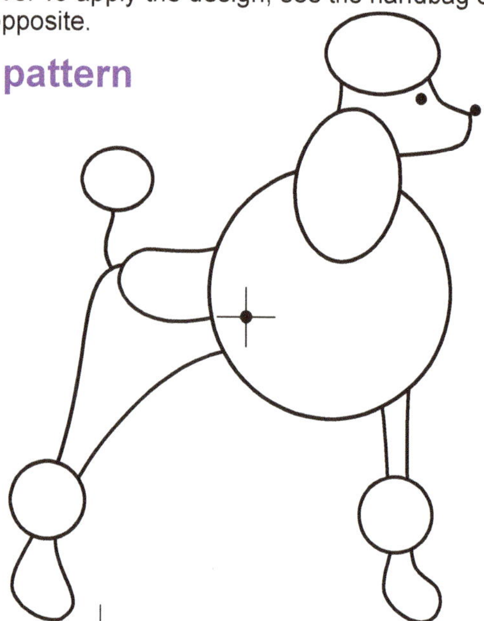

**Key:** ┼ **Centre of design** • **French knot**

## Shopping list

- Blue cotton fabric for background: 25cm (10") square
- Fabric or interfacing for backing: 25cm (10") square
- Stranded cotton thread: (A) black
- Fine 2 ply wool yarn:
  (B) very light yellow (C) dark magenta
  (D) medium magenta
- Tracing paper and other items for transferring the pattern onto the fabric

## Let's begin

Read page 15 for backing the fabric, and pages 22-25 for transferring the pattern onto the fabric, then select and use suitable methods for your fabric. For the blue fabric shown here, the pattern was transferred centrally onto the fabric by tracing with a chalk-based pencil and then the backing fabric was tacked to the wrong side.

## Stitch!

For help, see pages 76-79 for back stitch, and pages 184-187 for French knot. This design may be easier to work if the fabric is placed in a hoop. When working the French knots in this design, use two wraps.

1. Work the outline for the head, legs, feet, and tail in back stitch (2 strands D). Do not outline the pompoms.
2. Stitch the pompom on the head with French knots (2 strands C) as follows. Begin with an outer row of knots, placing them close together along the marked outline (Diagram 1). Work a second row inside the first (Diagram 2). Continue with further rows of closely worked French knots until the shape is filled.

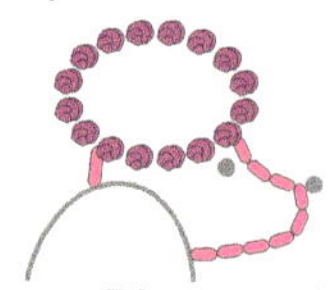

**Diagram 1**

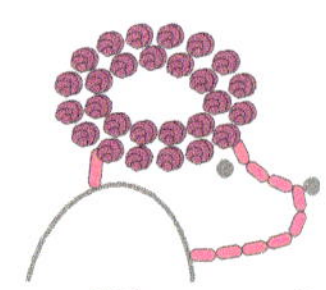

**Diagram 2**

3. Leaving the space for the lower part of the ear, stitch the pompom on the chest with French knots in the same way (2 strands C).
4. Stitch the ear, then work the pompoms on the back of the body, tail, and legs with French knots (2 strands D).

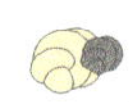

**Diagram 3**

5. Add the nose with a French knot (2 strands B). Work the eye, first with a French knot placed at the marked dot (2 strands B), then with a second French knot (3 strands A) piercing the front edge of the yellow knot (Diagram 3).

## Let's finish

Take out the tacking. Press or pin out the work. See page 36 for pressing and for pinning out.

## Hint

**Shades of one colour**

By using medium magenta for the ear and dark magenta for the pompom on the body, the shapes can be distinguished one from another without the need for an outline.

# Pompom Poodle Handbag

Add a playful poodle to this little handbag.

## The project

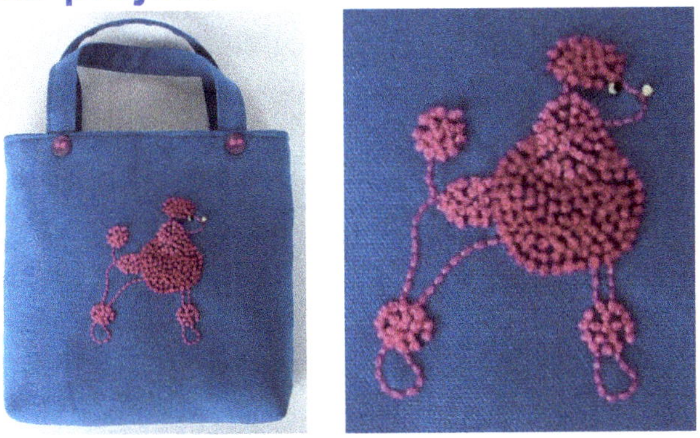

***Pompom Poodle Handbag* and Detail**

For this project the poodle is worked on a piece of fabric that is then made up into a handbag. Buttons decorated with French knots add a special finish. The finished size of the handbag is 16cm x 15cm wide (6 1/4" x 6"), not including the handles.

As this project uses buttons, it is not considered safe for babies or very small children.

## Shopping list

- Blue cotton fabric for outer layer and lining: two pieces 40cm x 23cm wide (16" x 9")
- Blue cotton fabric for the handles: two pieces 24cm x 5cm wide (9 1/2" x 2")
- Medium weight iron-on interfacing for backing: one piece 40cm x 23cm wide (16" x 9")
- Thin wadding: one piece 40cm x 23cm wide (16" x 9")
- Threads as listed for the original design opposite
- Machine sewing thread: blue and magenta
- 4 small magenta two-hole buttons
- Tracing paper and other items for transferring the pattern onto the fabric

## Let's begin

See the page opposite for the pattern. Following the instructions on page 15 for backing the fabric, attach the iron-on interfacing onto the wrong side of the outer layer fabric. Measuring down from one short end on the right side of the fabric, work two rows of tacking, the first 9.5cm (3 3/4") down, and the second 20cm (8") down. Aligning the centre of the design with the upper row of tacking (Diagram 1), transfer the pattern onto the fabric by tracing or by using the pierce and dot method with a chalk-based pencil, then remove this tacking. See pages 22-25 for transferring the pattern onto fabric.

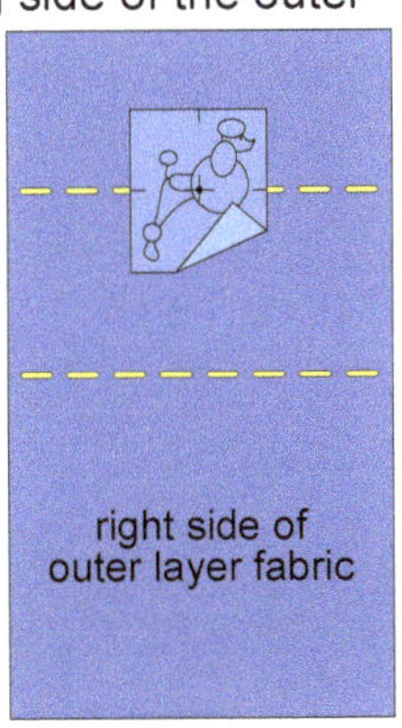


**Diagram 1**

## Stitch!

Work poodle following steps 1-5 on page opposite.

## Let's finish

Place the work face down on a well-padded surface and gently press. See page 36 for pressing.

Tack the wadding onto the wrong side of the outer layer and treat both layers as one layer from now on.

### *Assembling the handbag*

Use a 1cm (3/8") seam allowance unless otherwise specified.

With right sides together, fold the outer layer in half along the row of tacking at the base and pin the sides together. Using a machine straight stitch and matching thread, stitch the side seams (Diagram 2). Press the seam allowances open.

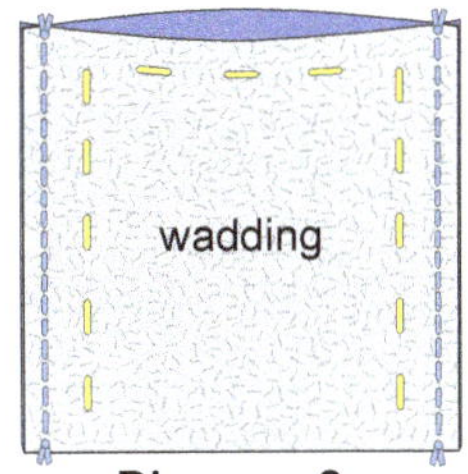


**Diagram 2**

To form the base, align one side seam with the tacking along the base of the handbag. Stitch across the side seam 2cm (3/4") in from the point (Diagram 3). Trim away the excess fabric at the corner (Diagram 4).

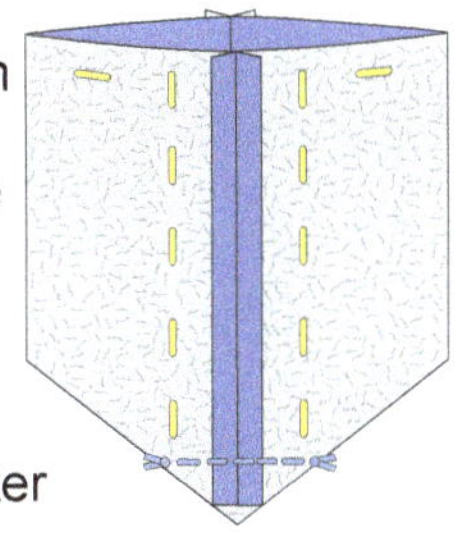

**Diagram 3**

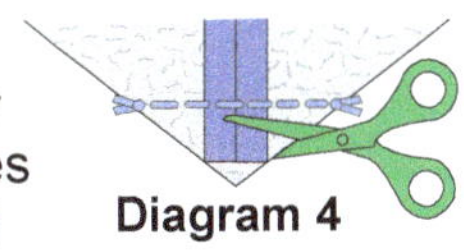

**Diagram 4**

Repeat for the second side seam at the base of the handbag. Turn the outer layer through to the right side and press. Make the lining in a similar way, but leave it inside out.

With wrong sides together, fold under and press 1cm (3/8") on the long sides of the strips for the handles, then fold each handle in half lengthwise. Stitch along both long edges of each handle (Diagram 5). Press. With raw edges even, stitch one handle onto the right side of the outer layer at the top, positioning its outer edges 4cm (1 1/2") in from the side seams (Diagram 6). Attach the second handle in the same way.

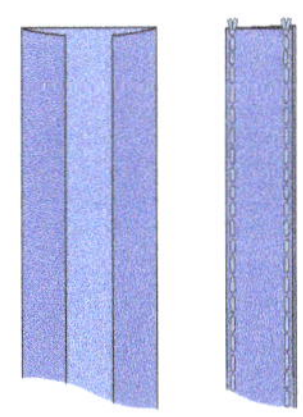

**Diagram 5**

Fold under 1cm (3/8") to the wrong side along the upper raw edge of the bag and press. Repeat for the lining.

Place the lining inside the outer layer and tack together around the top edges. Machine stitch the layers together close to the folded edges (see Diagram 7). Take out the tacking.

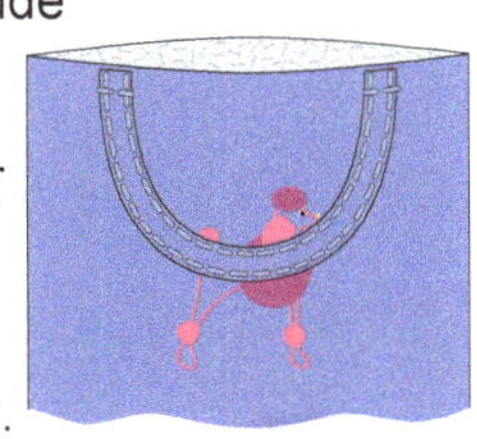

**Diagram 6**

Attach a button at the base of each handle with magenta machine sewing thread. Using two strands of medium magenta (D), work a three wrap French knot through each hole in the buttons (Diagrams 7 and 8).

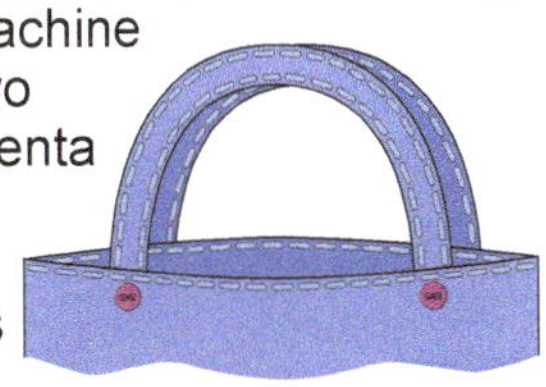

**Diagram 7**

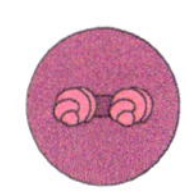

**Diagram 8**

# Golden Wattle

The golden wattle, with its fluffy yellow flowers, is Australia's floral emblem.

## The design

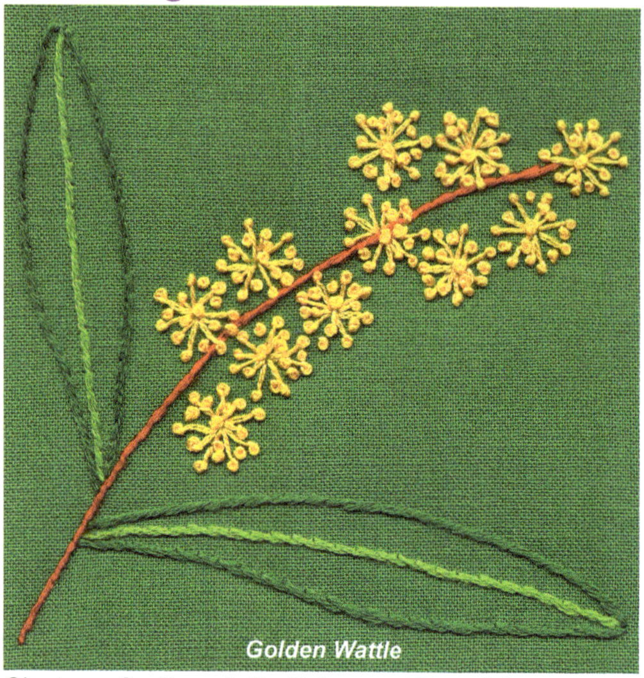

*Golden Wattle*

Clusters of yellow pistil stitches and French knots are worked to create the round fluffy flowers in this easy design. Stem stitch is also included.

Follow the instructions on this page to work the design exactly as shown here on a green background. See the project idea on the facing page to feature this wattle on a sachet for dried flowers.

## The pattern

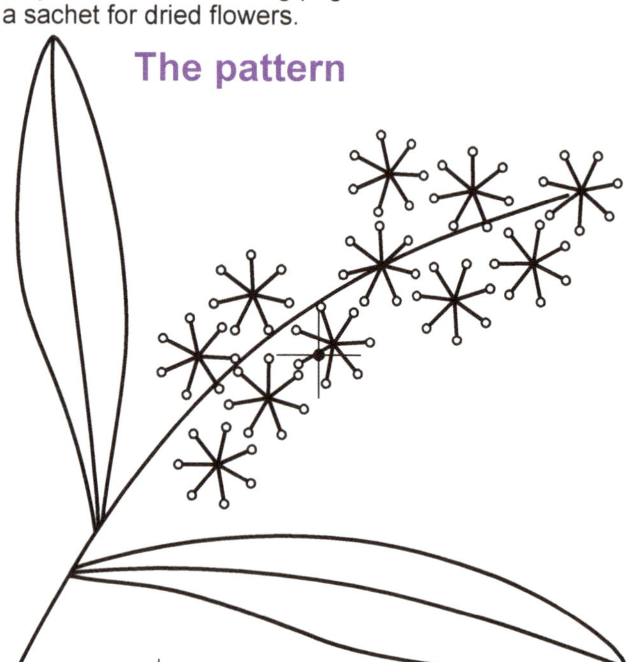

Key: Centre of design | Pistil stitch

## Shopping list

- Green cotton fabric for background: 25cm (10") square
- Fabric or interfacing for backing: 25cm (10") square
- Stranded cotton thread: (A) medium green (B) light green (C) medium yellow (D) medium orange
- Tracing paper and other items for transferring the pattern onto the fabric

## Let's begin

Read page 15 for backing the fabric, and pages 22-25 for transferring the pattern onto the fabric, then select and use suitable methods for your fabric. For the green fabric shown here, the pattern was transferred onto the fabric by tracing with a water erasable fabric marker and then the backing fabric was tacked to the wrong side.

## Stitch!

For help, see pages 94-97 for stem stitch, including turning a corner, and pages 184-187 for French knot and pistil stitch. To minimize carrying the thread on the back of the work when stitching the flowers, complete one cluster of pistil stitches and French knots before moving on to the next. This design has a more realistic, natural appearance if the clusters are all slightly different.

1 Work the stem in stem stitch (2 strands D). Do not leave spaces for the flowers.

2 Work the central vein of each leaf in stem stitch (2 strands B). Beginning at the base, stitch the outline for each leaf in stem stitch (2 strands A), working a corner at the leaf tip as follows. Take the thread through to the wrong side at the tip. Pass the needle under the back of a previously worked stitch. Take the needle to the front at the leaf tip (Diagram 1). Continue stitching the leaf outline.

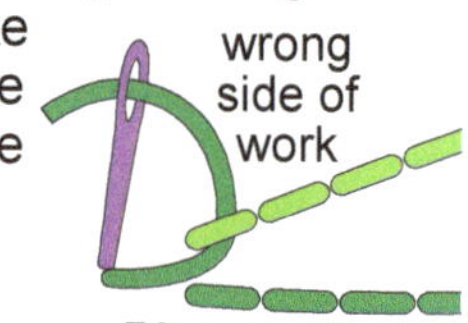


Diagram 1

3 Beginning with the lowest flower, stitch seven pistil stitches, each with two wraps (2 strands C), following the marked lines and working the stitches through the same hole at the centre (Diagram 2). Add three shorter pistil stitches, each with two wraps, placing them randomly between the previous pistil stitches (Diagram 3). Add six French knots, each with two wraps, in some of the spaces. Add one extra French knot at, or near, the flower centre (Diagram 4).

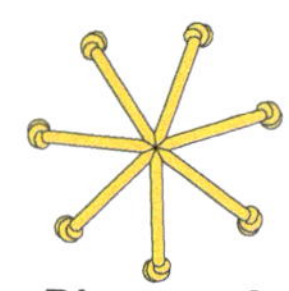

Diagram 2

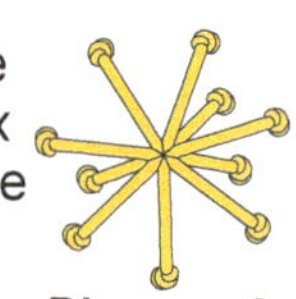

Diagram 3

4 Work all of the remaining flowers in the same way.

## Let's finish

Take out the tacking. Rinse the work in cold water to remove the fabric marker. When partly dry, press or pin out the work. See page 36 for pressing and for pinning out.

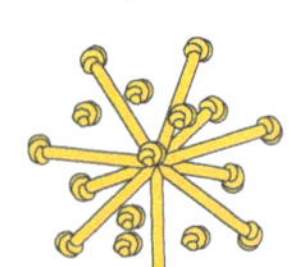

Diagram 4

# Golden Wattle Sachet

Perfume a room with this golden floral sachet!

## The project

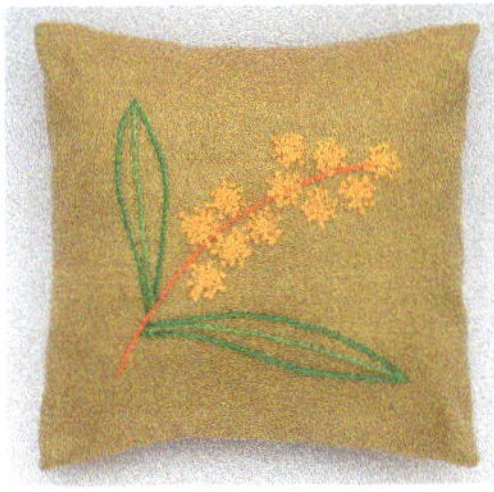

*Golden Wattle Sachet*

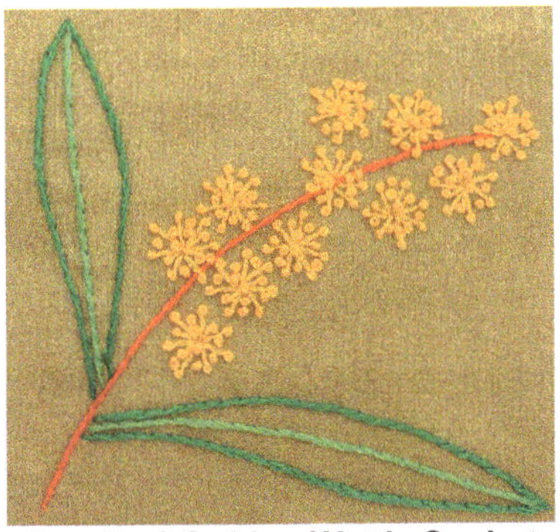

Detail of *Golden Wattle Sachet*

*Golden Wattle* is worked on a piece of gold fabric that is then made up into a perfumed sachet.
The finished size of the sachet is 14cm (5 1/2") square.

## Shopping list

- Gold polycotton fabric for the sachet: 16cm x 37cm wide (6 1/4" x 14 1/2")
- Fabric or interfacing for backing: 16cm x 34cm wide (6 1/4" x 13 1/4")
- White closely-woven cotton fabric for the insert: two 16cm (6 1/4") squares
- Threads as listed for the original design on the page opposite
- Machine sewing thread: gold and white
- Tracing paper and other items for transferring the pattern onto the fabric
- Dried rose petals, rosebuds, or lavender flowers

## Hints

**An alternative filling for the sachets**
You could fill the insert with cloves and small pieces of cinnamon stick.

**Themed series**
On any projects of your choice, *Golden Wattle* could be worked as a pair to *Red Flowering Gum* on page 48, which is also an Australian plant.

## Let's begin

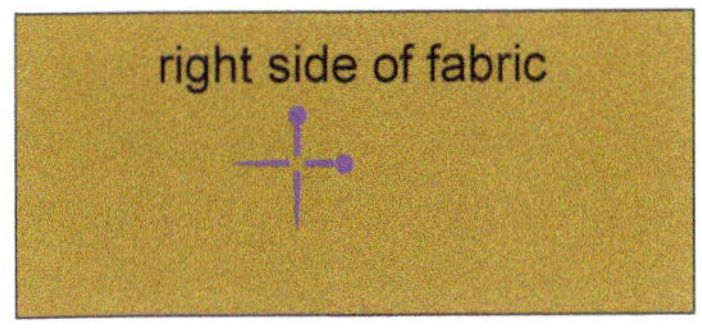


**Diagram 1**

See the page opposite for the pattern. Place the gold fabric with the right side facing up. Place pins at a point that is 15.5cm (6 1/8") in from the left hand short side and half way between the two long sides (Diagram 1).
Centering the pattern at the point marked by the pins, transfer the pattern by tracing with a water erasable fabric marker or by using transfer paper. See pages 22-25 for transferring the pattern. Tack the backing fabric centrally to the wrong side, noting that the gold fabric extends beyond the backing at each short end. See page 15 for backing the fabric.

## Stitch!

Work the design following steps 1-4 of the stitch instructions on the page opposite.

## Let's finish

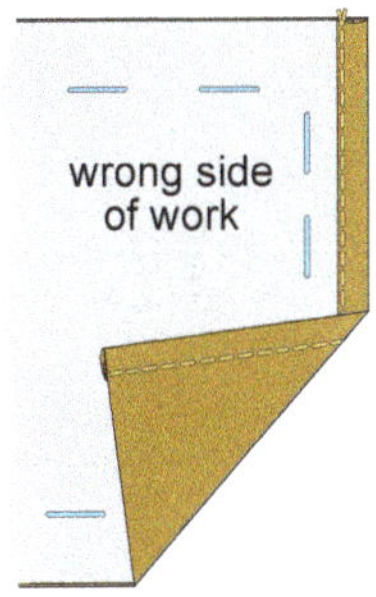


**Diagram 2**

***Making the sachet*** Rinse the work in cold water to remove the pattern markings. When almost dry, press. See page 36 for pressing. On each short end, fold the raw edge 5mm (1/4") to the wrong side and press. Fold again 1cm (3/8") and press. Using gold machine sewing thread, machine stitch near the first fold through all layers (Diagram 2).
Place the work with the stitched design facing up. With right sides together, fold the hemmed end that is closest to the stitched design over for 7cm (2 3/4") and pin (Diagram 3). Fold the remaining hemmed end over for 13cm (5"), overlapping the first end, and pin. Machine stitch through all layers 1cm (3/8") from the upper and lower edges. Take out the tacking and trim the corners (Diagram 4). Turn the sachet through to the right side and press.

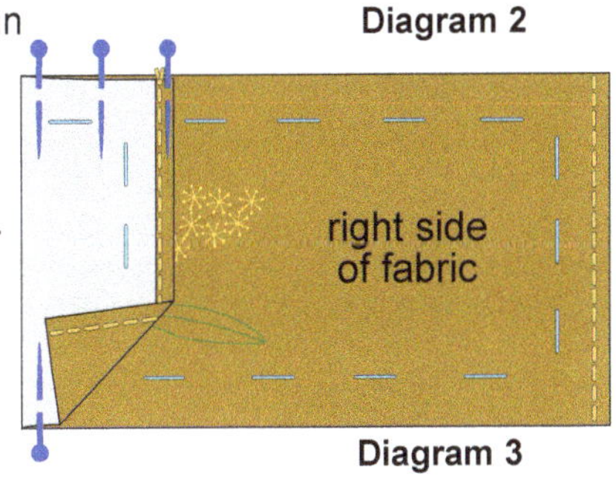


**Diagram 3**

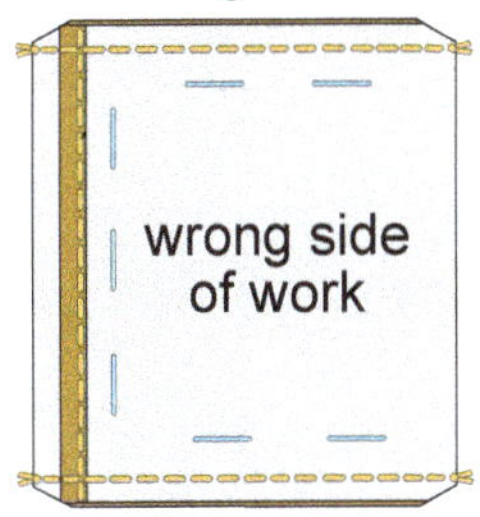


**Diagram 4**

***Making the insert*** Place the two squares of fabric right sides together and pin around the edge. Using white machine sewing thread and a 1cm (3/8") seam allowance, machine stitch around the square, leaving a 5cm (2") opening in the middle of one side. Ensure that 20cm (8") of machine thread length remains before cutting it. Knot the machine sewing threads and trim three of them, leaving one of the long ends. Trim the corners (Diagram 5).
Turn the insert to the right side through the opening and press. Fill with the dried filling. Using the long end of machine sewing thread, hand stitch the opening closed.
Place the filled insert into the sachet.

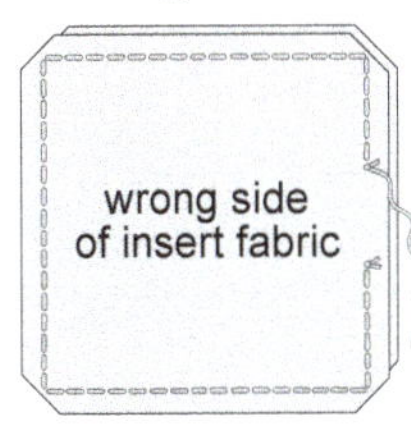


**Diagram 5**

# Cherry Tart

Would you like a slice of cherry tart?

## The design

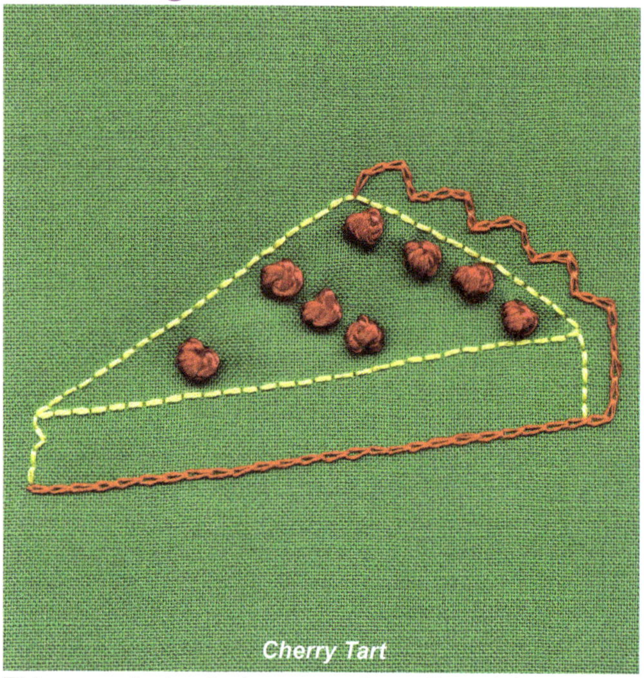

*Cherry Tart*

This easy design features very large French knots depicting the cherries on the tart. Their chunky appearance is achieved with four strands of perlé thread. Back stitch and chain stitch are used for the remainder of the design.

Use the instructions on this page to work the design exactly as shown here on a green background. To apply the design, see the project idea on the next page where the tart is featured on a child's apron.

## The pattern

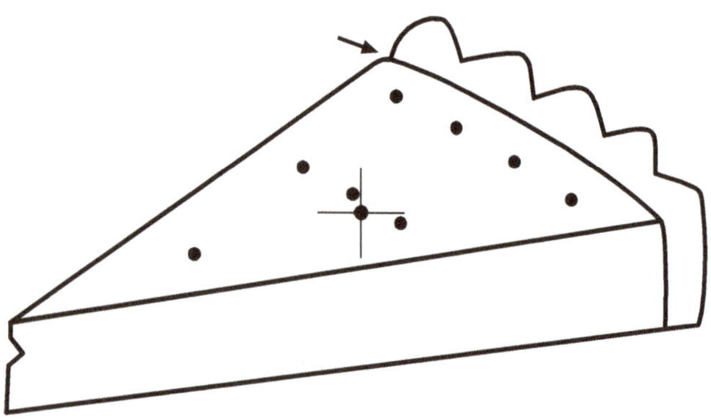

**Key:** Centre of design

**Begin pastry here**

• **French knot**

## Shopping list

- Green cotton fabric for background: 25cm (10") square
- Fabric or interfacing for backing: 25cm (10") square
- Stranded cotton thread:
  (A) light yellow (B) medium orange
- No. 5 perlé cotton thread:
  (C) dark red
- Tracing paper and other items for transferring the pattern onto the fabric

## Let's begin

Read page 15 for backing the fabric, and pages 22-25 for transferring the pattern onto the fabric, then select and use suitable methods for your fabric. For the green fabric shown here, the pattern was transferred centrally onto the fabric by tracing with a water erasable fabric marker and then the backing fabric was tacked to the wrong side.

## Stitch!

For help, see pages 76-79 for back stitch, 166-169 for chain stitch, and pages 184-187 for French knot.

1 Beginning at the marked point, work the scalloped edge of the pastry in chain stitch (1 strand B), changing the direction of the chain stitches at the valley of each scallop (Diagram 1).

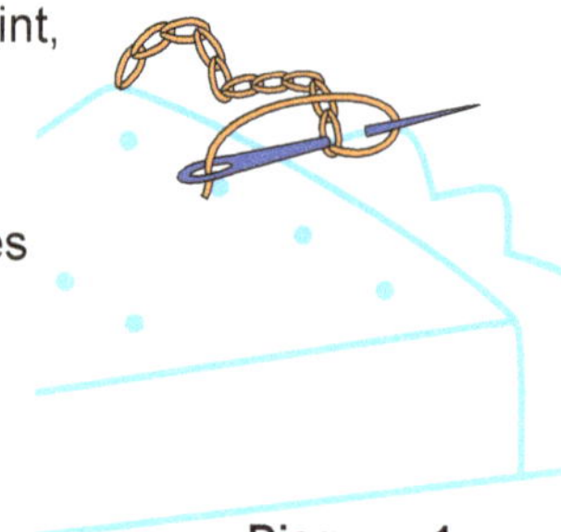

**Diagram 1**

2 Continuing with the same thread, complete the pastry. Secure the last stitch with a small anchor.

3 Stitch the tart filling in back stitch (2 strands A).

4 Placing a cherry at each marked dot, add eight cherries, working each with a two wrap French knot (4 strands C). To lessen the bulk resulting from threading four strands of perlé thread into the needle, thread just two longer strands and double them over, giving four strands in total (Diagram 2).

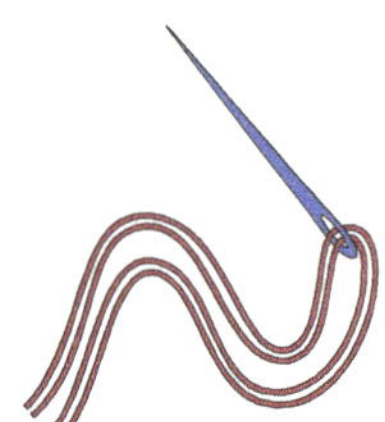

**Diagram 2**

## Let's finish

Take out the tacking. Rinse the work in cold water to remove the water erasable fabric marker. When partly dry, press or pin out the work. See page 36 for pressing and for pinning out.

## Hint

**Stitch tension**

Before working the large French knots in this design, experiment with four strands of the perlé thread on a scrap piece of fabric. Keep the same tension on all the strands so that the finished knot is even in appearance.

# Blackberry Tart Apron

Cook up a tasty treat – make an apron.

## The project

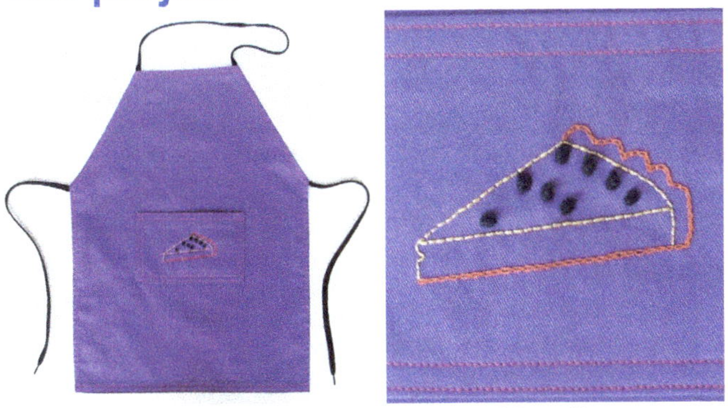

***Blackberry Tart Apron* and Detail**

For this project, a slice of tart is worked on a piece of fabric that is then attached as a pocket on a constructed apron. The original design has been changed to represent a blackberry tart by altering the thread colour used for the fruit.
The finished size of the apron is 52cm x 36cm wide (20 1/2" x 14").

## Shopping list

- Violet cotton fabric for the apron: 57cm x 39cm wide (22 1/2" x 15 1/2")
- Violet cotton fabric for the pocket: 14cm x 19cm wide (5 1/2" x 7 1/2")
- Lightweight iron-on interfacing for backing: 11cm x 16cm wide (4 1/4" x 6 1/4")
- Stranded cotton thread: (A) light yellow (B) medium orange
- No. 5 perlé cotton thread: (C) black
- Machine sewing thread: violet and orange
- Flat black shoelaces: two 100cm (39 1/2") in length
- Tracing paper and other items for transferring the pattern onto the fabric

## Let's begin

See the page opposite for the pattern. Following the instructions on page 15 for backing the fabric, attach the iron-on interfacing centrally onto the wrong side of the pocket fabric, noting that the violet fabric extends beyond the interfacing on all sides. Using the violet machine sewing thread, prevent fraying of the raw edges of the pocket by sewing along the edges with a machine zigzag or overlock stitch.
Transfer the tart pattern centrally onto the right side of the pocket using transfer paper. See page 24 for transferring the pattern using transfer paper.

## Stitch!

Work the blackberry tart following steps 1-4 of the stitch instructions for the original design on the facing page, replacing the red thread with black thread.

## Let's finish

Rinse the pocket in cold water to remove the pattern markings. When almost dry, press, avoiding the French knots.

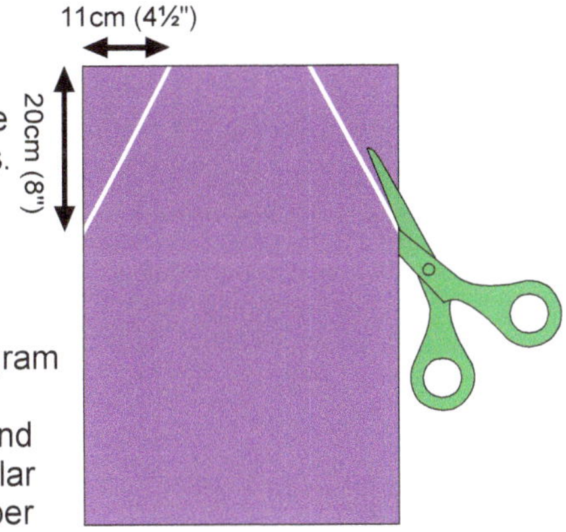


**Diagram 1**

***Making the apron***

Referring to the diagram for measurements (Diagram 1), mark and cut away the triangular shapes from the upper two corners of the violet fabric for the apron. Fold under 6mm (1/4") to the wrong side on both the diagonal sides of the apron and press. Fold under a further 1cm (3/8") and press. Using the orange machine sewing thread and a machine straight stitch, sew the hems in place. Repeat for the two vertical sides (Diagram 2). Fold under 1cm (3/8") on both the upper and lower edges of the apron and press. Fold under a further 1.5cm (5/8") and press. Stitch each hem with two rows of machine stitching placed 1cm (3/8") apart (Diagram 3). For the waist ties, cut one shoelace in half, leaving the plastic end on each half. Folding under the raw edge and using small hand stitches with the violet sewing thread, attach one piece onto the wrong side of the apron at the side. Attach the second piece to the other side. From the other shoelace, cut one 51cm (20") length for the neck band. Attach each raw end to the wrong side of the apron at the upper corners in the same way as the ties.

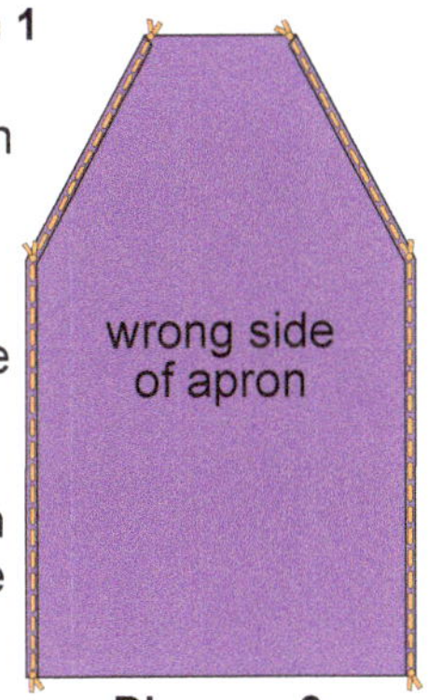


**Diagram 2**

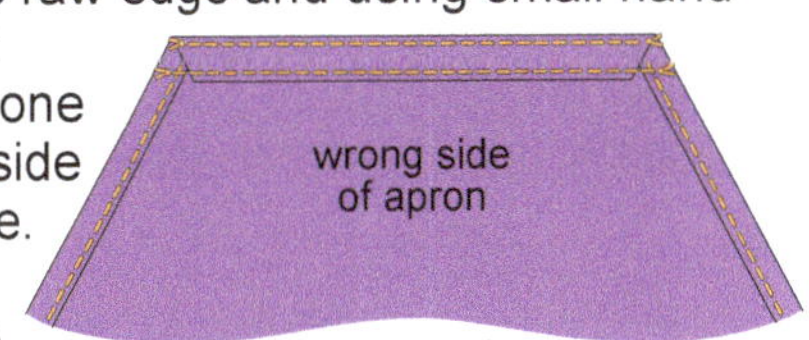


**Diagram 3**

***Making the pocket***

Fold under 1.5cm (5/8") on all sides of the pocket and press. Using the orange sewing thread, stitch two rows placed 1cm (3/8") apart across the upper edge only. Position the pocket onto the apron and tack in place. Attach the pocket to the apron by stitching two rows placed 1cm (3/8") apart along the remaining three sides through all layers (Diagram 4). Remove tacking.

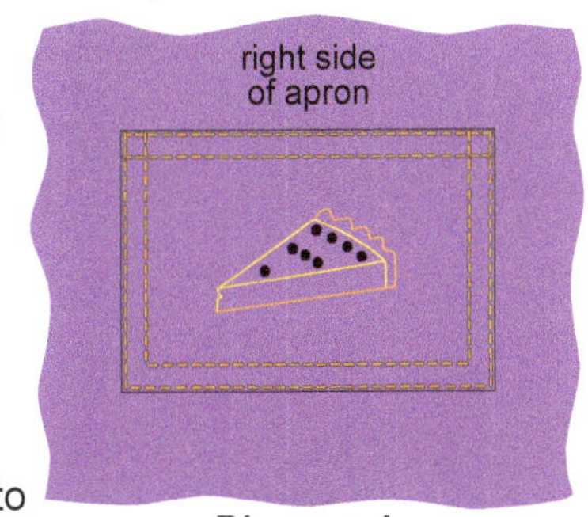


**Diagram 4**

# Red Telephone

Ring ring, ring ring, ...

## The design

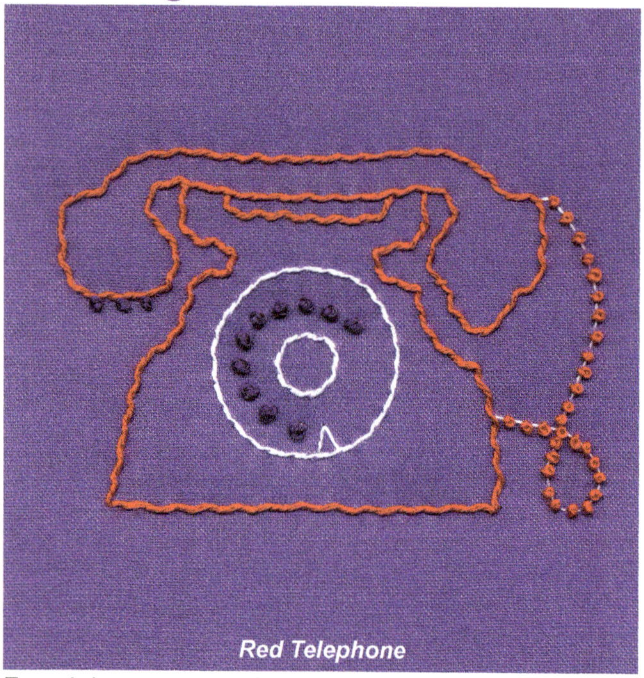

*Red Telephone*

French knots are used in this design to depict the numbers on the dial, the holes on the earpiece, and to add detail to the cord. Running stitch, whipped running stitch, and straight stitch are also included. The design is quite detailed, but the stitches are easy to work. Use the instructions on this page to work the design exactly as shown here on a violet background. To apply the design to a project, see the idea on the next page where the telephone is featured on clothing for a baby.

## The pattern

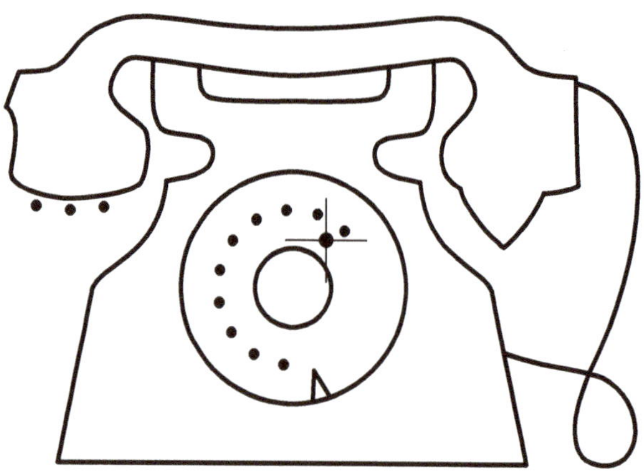

**Key:** Centre of design • **French knot**

## Shopping list

- Violet cotton fabric for background: 25cm (10") square
- Fabric or interfacing for backing: 25cm (10") square
- Stranded cotton thread:
  (A) dark violet (B) medium red (C) white
- Tracing paper and other items for transferring the pattern onto the fabric

## Let's begin

Read page 15 for backing the fabric, and pages 22-25 for transferring the pattern onto the fabric, then select and use suitable methods for your fabric. For the violet fabric shown here, the pattern was transferred centrally onto the fabric by tracing with a water erasable fabric marker and then the backing fabric was tacked to the wrong side.

## Stitch!

For help, see pages 40-43 for straight stitch, 58-61 for running stitch and whipped running stitch, and pages 184-187 for French knot. Use a tapestry needle for all the whipping.

1. Work the whipped running stitch outlines for the telephone base and receiver by firstly working running stitch, leaving small spaces between the stitches (2 strands B). Then, using the same thread, whip the running stitches. This makes the outline more defined.
2. Stitch the outer circle for the dial, then the inner circle, both in running stitch, leaving small spaces between the stitches (2 strands C). Changing to 1 strand, whip the running stitch on both circles (1 strand C).
3. Work two straight stitches on the outer circle for the stopper (1 strand C).
4. Stitch a row of running stitches for the cord (1 strand C), keeping the stitches even, as the spaces between the stitches determine the placement of the French knots to be worked in step 5 (Diagram 1).
5. Work a two wrap French knot (2 strands B) in each space between the running stitches on the cord (Diagram 2).
6. Stitch three French knots, each with two wraps, on the lower edge of the earpiece (2 strands A). Work ten French knots, each with two wraps, on the dial for the numbers (4 strands A).

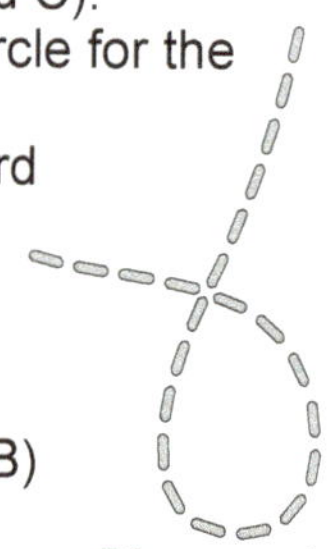

**Diagram 1**

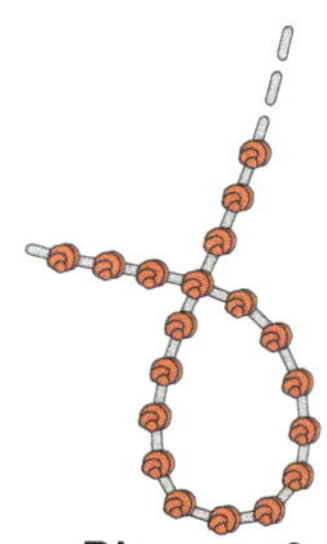

**Diagram 2**

## Let's finish

Take out the tacking. Rinse the work in cold water to remove the fabric marker. When partly dry, press or pin out the work. See page 36 for pressing and for pinning out.

# Red Telephone Babywear

Decorate a baby's suit with a red telephone.

## The project

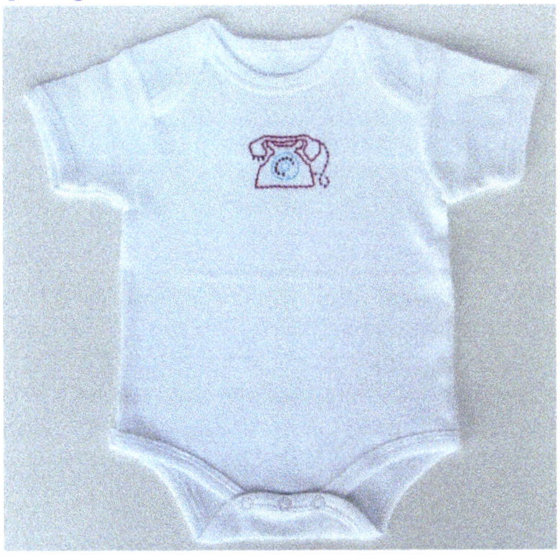

***Red Telephone Babywear***

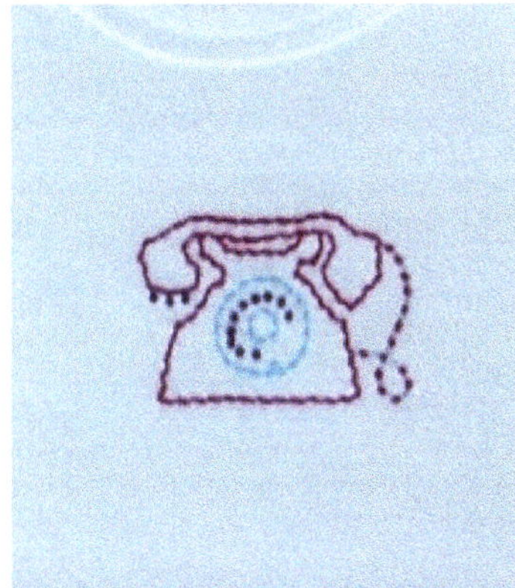

**Detail of *Red Telephone Babywear***

This quick and easy project uses the *Red Telephone* design to decorate a purchased white stretch knit suit for a baby. The design has been reduced in size and a slightly different colour scheme has been used.

## Shopping list

- White stretch knit baby's suit
- Lightweight iron-on interfacing for backing: 7cm x 9cm wide (2 3/4" x 3 1/2")
- Stranded cotton thread: (A) dark violet (B) medium red (C) medium aqua
- Tracing paper and other items for transferring the pattern onto the baby's suit

## Let's begin

See the page opposite for the pattern. Prepare the pattern by reducing it to 80% of its original size. Trace the reduced pattern onto tracing paper.

To help in deciding the placement of the design on the baby's suit, fold the garment in half and mark the centre front with pins (Diagram 1).

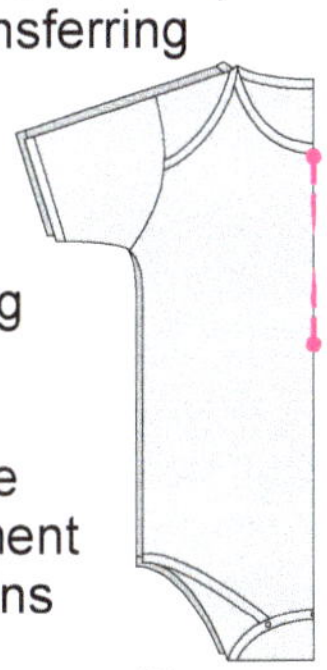

**Diagram 1**

Open out the garment and place the tracing, centred over the pins, an appropriate distance below the front neckline (Diagram 2). Move the tracing up or down until it is visually appealing and note its position with pins.

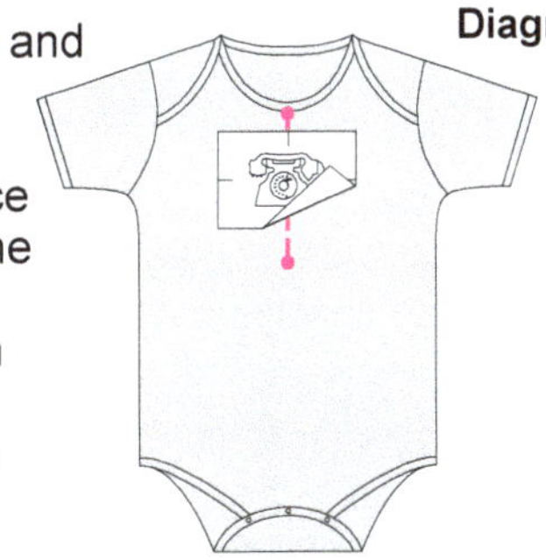

**Diagram 2**

Following the instructions on page 15 for backing the fabric, attach the piece of iron-on interfacing onto the wrong side of the front of the garment at the selected position. This will stabilize the area where the design is to be stitched.

Transfer the pattern onto the front of the garment by tracing with a water erasable fabric marker. See page 23 for transferring the pattern by tracing.

## Stitch!

Work the telephone following steps 1-6 of the stitch instructions on the facing page, replacing the white thread with medium aqua thread. As the design is reduced in size, use fewer stitches when working the running stitch and French knots on the cord, and only two strands of thread for the French knots representing the numbers on the dial.

## Let's finish

Turn the garment inside out. On the wrong side, peel back any excess interfacing from its outer edge and trim it back close to the stitches. Rinse the garment in cold water to remove the water erasable fabric marker. When dry, turn the garment inside out and press it. See page 36 for pressing.

## Hints

**Using stretch knit fabrics**

Knit fabrics are designed to stretch, allowing ease of movement when worn. However, this stretching is usually not desirable on the area where the design is stitched. By attaching interfacing onto the wrong side of the fabric, the amount of stretch on the area to be worked is minimised and controlled. This makes the stitching much easier to manage.

# Hearts and Flowers

Romantic hearts decorated with petite flowers.

## The design

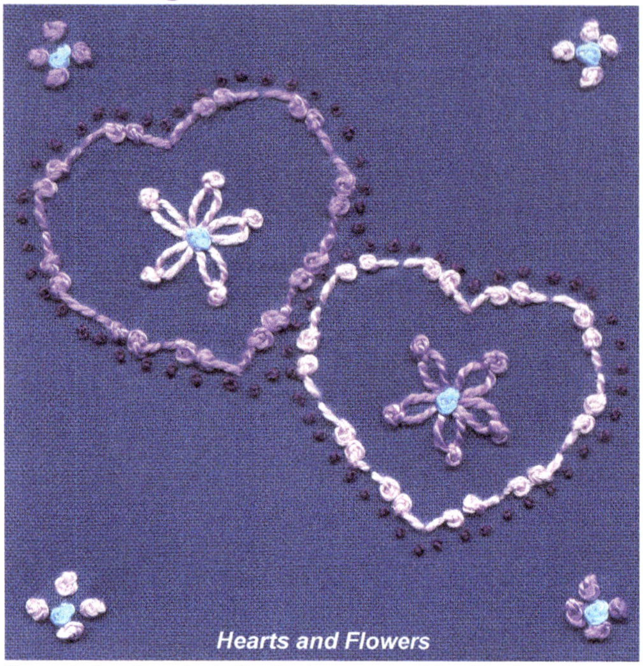

*Hearts and Flowers*

French knot and pistil stitch are used for the heart outlines. Detached chain stitches in combination with French knots create the central flowers, and French knots used alone form the corner flowers. To work the design as shown, follow the instructions on this page. To feature flowers from this design on a felt jewellery purse, see the page opposite.

## The pattern

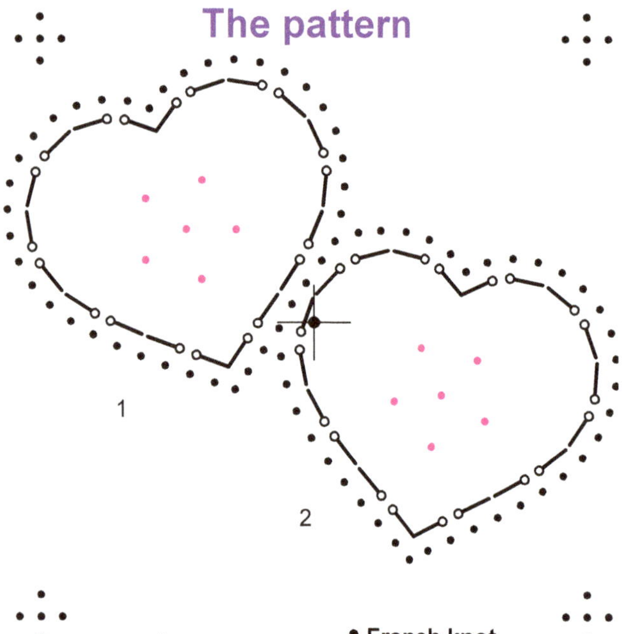


**Key:** **Centre of design** · **French knot** · **Pistil stitch** · **Detached chain stitch**

## Shopping list

- Blue cotton fabric for background: 25cm (10") square
- Fabric or interfacing for backing: 25cm (10") square
- Stranded cotton thread: (A) dark violet
- No. 5 perlé cotton thread:
  (B) medium violet (C) light violet (D) medium aqua
- Tracing paper and other items for transferring the pattern onto the fabric

## Let's begin

Read page 15 for backing the fabric, and pages 22-25 for transferring the pattern onto the fabric, then select and use suitable methods for your fabric. For the blue fabric shown here, the pattern was transferred centrally onto the fabric by tracing with a chalk-based pencil and then the backing fabric was tacked to the wrong side.

## Stitch!

For help, see pages 166-169 for detached chain stitch, and pages 184-187 for French knot and pistil stitch.

**Heart 1**

1. Placing a knot at each dot, work the outer heart shape with a row of one wrap French knots (2 strands A).
2. Beginning at the lower point of the heart and following the marked symbols for placing the stitches, stitch the inner heart shape with a row of two wrap pistil stitches (1 strand B).
3. Leaving a space at the flower centre, work the petals of the flower (1 strand C) with detached chain stitches, each anchored at the outer dot with a two wrap French knot (Diagrams 1 and 2).
4. Add a two wrap French knot at the flower centre (1 strand D).

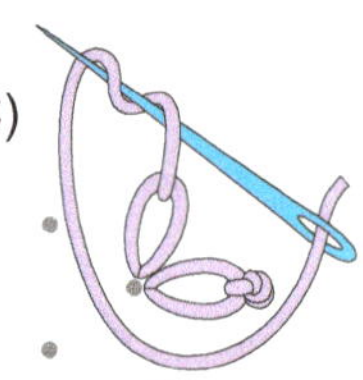

**Diagram 1**

**Heart 2**

Work **Heart 2** in the same way as **Heart 1** but instead work the pistil stitch heart shape in light violet (1 strand C) and the flower petals in medium violet (1 strand B).

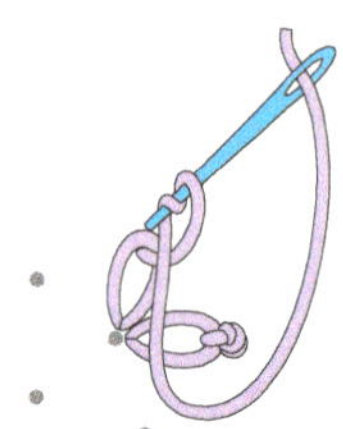

**Diagram 2**

**Corner flowers**

1. Work the petals of the darker flowers (1 strand B) and the petals of the lighter flowers (1 strand C), each with a two wrap French knot.
2. Add a two wrap French knot at the centre of each of the flowers (1 strand D).

## Let's finish

Take out the tacking. Press or pin out the work. See page 36 for pressing and for pinning out.

## Hint

**Stitch tension**

Work the pistil stitch heart shapes with a loose tension or the fabric may not lie flat.

# Flowers Jewel Purse

Keep your most precious jewellery in a decorated purse.

## The project

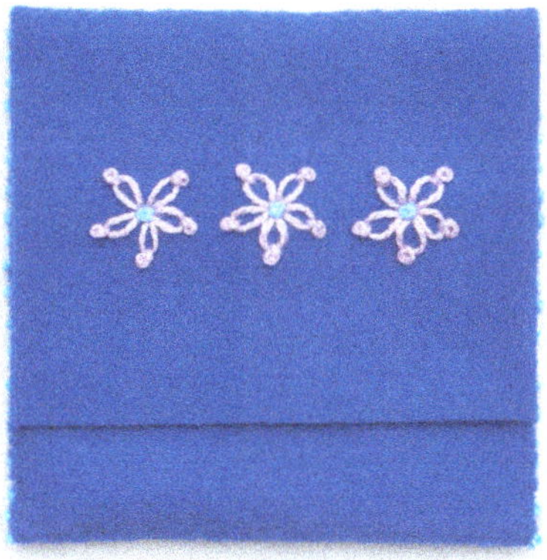

***Flowers Jewel Purse***

The central flower from **Heart 1** is worked three times on a piece of blue felt fabric that is then made up into a miniature purse suitable for keeping jewellery in. The finished size of this purse is 10cm (4") square.

## Shopping list

- Blue felt fabric for the purse: 28cm x 10cm wide (11" x 4")
- Threads (C) and (D) as listed for the original design opposite
- Machine sewing thread: blue
- Tracing paper and other items for transferring the pattern onto the felt
- Self-adhesive hook and loop dot

## Let's begin

See the page opposite for the pattern. On the felt fabric, draw a dot with a chalk-based pencil at a point that is 4cm (1 1/2") up from the lower short end and 5cm (2") in from one long side.
Transfer the pattern for the flower from **Heart 1** centrally over the marked dot using the pierce and dot method with a chalk-based pencil (Diagram 1). See page 25 for transferring the pattern using the pierce and dot method. In the same way, transfer the pattern for additional flowers onto the felt fabric on either side of the first.

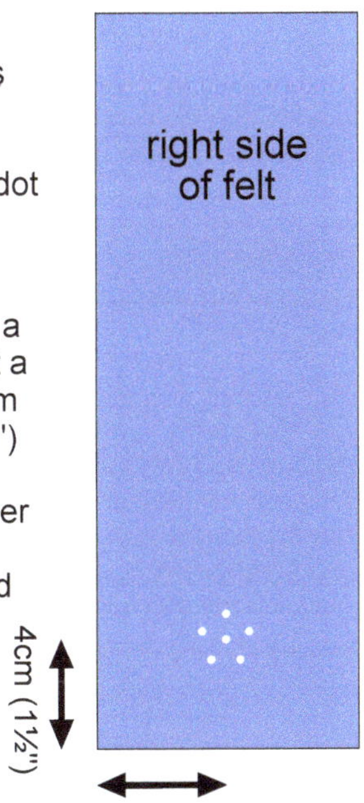


**Diagram 1**

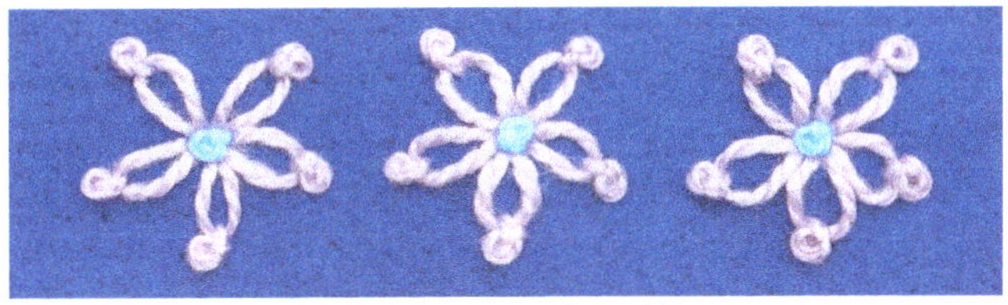

**Detail of *Flowers Jewel Purse***

## Stitch!

Stitch each flower following steps 3 and 4 of the stitch instructions for **Heart 1** on the previous page.

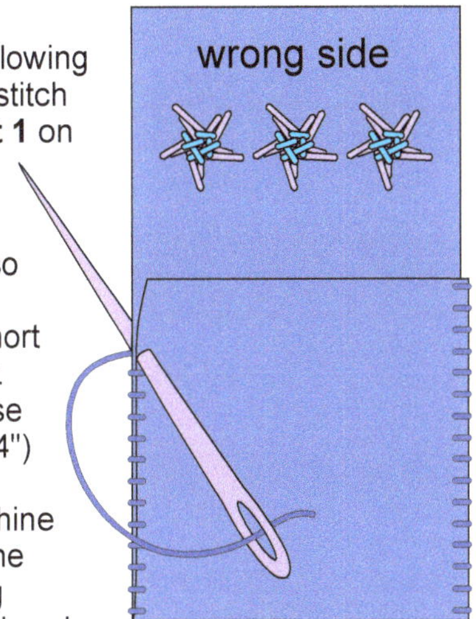


**Diagram 2**

## Let's finish

Place the felt fabric so that the flowers are towards the upper short end, then turn it over. Create a square purse by folding up 10cm (4") from the lower end.
Using matching machine sewing thread, join the layers together along each side with small hand stitches (Diagram 2).
Using the medium aqua thread (D) and beginning and ending off invisibly inside the seam, work a row of two wrap French knots along each seam (Diagram 3). Fold down the purse flap. Attach the self-adhesive hook and loop dot under the flap as a closure for the purse.

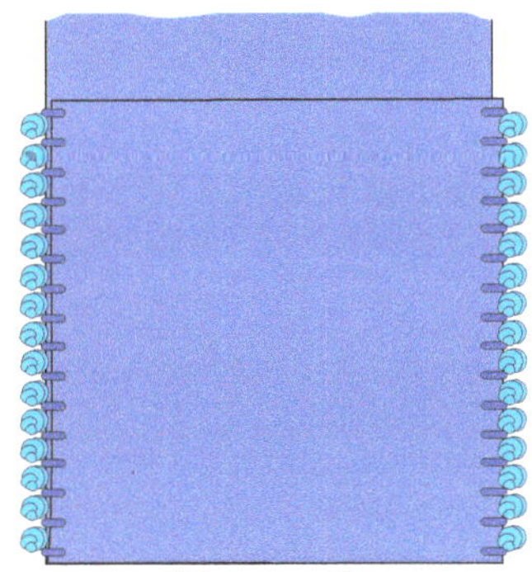

**Diagram 3**

## Hint

**Another project idea**

Here a corner flower from *Hearts and Flowers* was worked three times on a very small green rectangle of felt. This was then made up into a tiny purse, which is the perfect size for a ring or a tiny pendant.

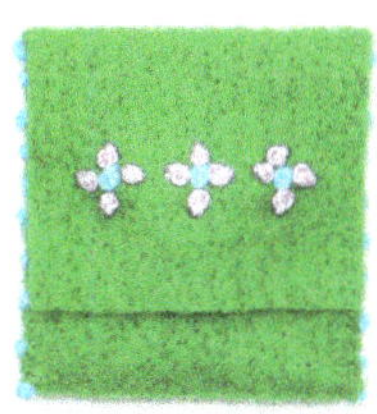

***Flowers Tiny Jewel Purse***

# Summer Garden

The flowers in this garden are glowing in the brilliant summer sunshine.

## The design

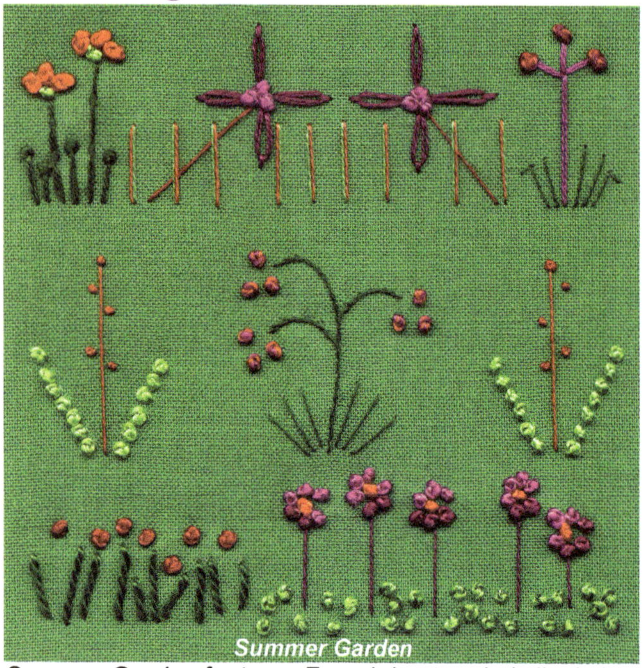


*Summer Garden* features French knot and pistil stitch. Also included are straight stitch, stem stitch, and detached chain stitch. Follow the instructions here to work the design as shown above. See opposite to adapt an element from the design for a child's T-shirt.

## The pattern

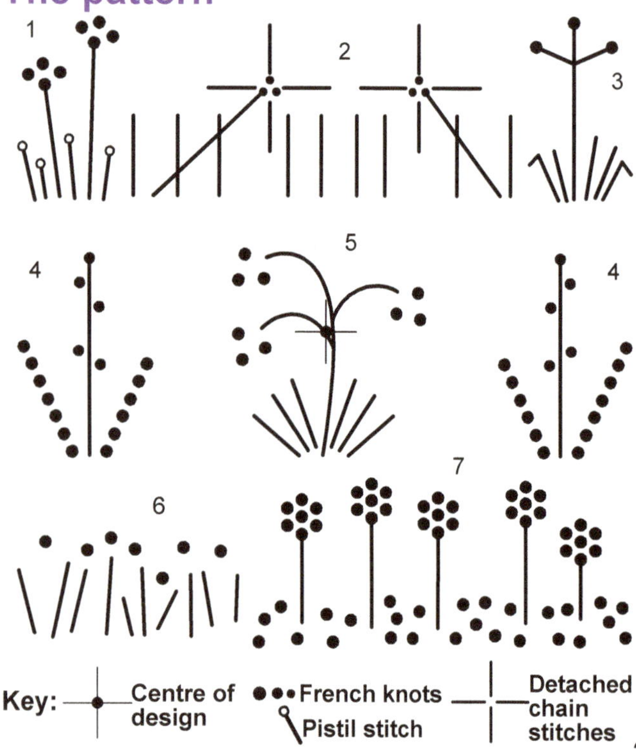


## Shopping list

- Green cotton fabric for background: 25cm (10") square
- Fabric or interfacing for backing: 25cm (10") square
- Stranded cotton thread:
  (A) dark green (B) light green (C) medium orange
  (D) dark red (E) dark magenta (F) medium magenta
- No. 5 perlé cotton thread:
  (G) dark green (H) light green (I) medium orange
  (J) dark red (K) dark magenta (L) medium magenta
- Tracing paper and other items for transferring the pattern onto the fabric

## Let's begin

Read page 15 for backing the fabric, and pages 22-25 for transferring the pattern onto the fabric, then select and use suitable methods for your fabric. For the green fabric shown here, the pattern was transferred centrally onto the fabric by tracing with a water erasable fabric marker and then the backing fabric was tacked to the wrong side.

## Stitch!

For help, see pages 40-43 for straight stitch, 94-97 for stem stitch, 166-169 for detached chain stitch, and pages 184-187 for French knot and pistil stitch.

**Flower 1** Stitch petals with two wrap French knots (1 strand I) and base with a one wrap French knot (1 strand H). Work stem with a long straight stitch held in place with two straight stitches, and work each leaf with a two wrap pistil stitch (3 strands A).

**Flower 2** Work petals in detached chain stitch (2 strands E). Using one wrap French knots, add centres (1 strand L). Work stems (1 strand D) and leaves (1 strand B mixed in the needle with 1 strand C) in straight stitch.

**Flower 3** Work the stem and branches (2 strands F) and the leaves (1 strand A) in straight stitch. Work each flower with a one wrap French knot (2 strands E mixed in the needle with 1 strand J).

**Flower 4** Stitch leaves with French knots, each with one wrap (1 strand H). Stitch each stem with a straight stitch (1 strand C). Work flowers with French knots, each with one wrap (1 strand C mixed in the needle with 1 strand D).

**Flower 5** Work the stems in small stem stitch (1 strand A). Add the leaves in straight stitch (1 strand A). Work flowers with one wrap French knots (2 strands each of C and E, mixed in the needle with 1 strand F).

**Flower 6** Stitch the leaves in straight stitch (1 strand G). Add a one wrap French knot for each flower (1 strand J).

**Flower 7** Using one wrap French knots, work petals (1 strand K or L) and flower centres (1 strand I). Add stems in straight stitch (1 strand E). Stitch each leaf with a one wrap French knot (1 strand A mixed in the needle with 4 strands B).

## Let's finish

Take out tacking. Rinse the work in cold water to remove the fabric marker. When partly dry, press or pin out the work. See page 36 for pressing and for pinning out.

# Summer Flowers T-shirt

Sprinkle colourful flowers on a summer T-shirt.

## The project

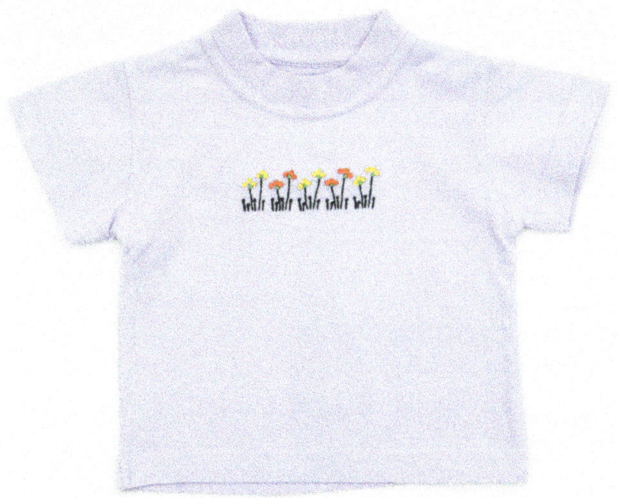

*Summer Flowers T-shirt*

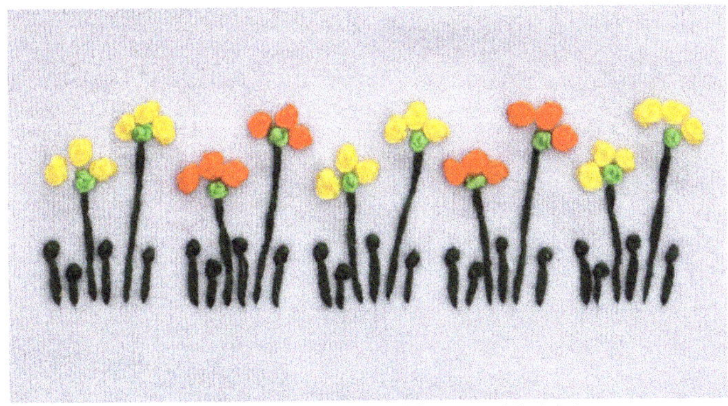

**Detail of *Summer Flowers T-shirt***

**Flower 1** from the design is repeated five times in a row across the front of a purchased stretch knit T-shirt. The petals are worked alternately along the row in yellow and orange.

## Shopping list

- Light violet stretch knit T-shirt for a baby or child
- Lightweight iron-on interfacing for backing: 5cm x 10cm wide (2" x 4")
- Threads (A), (H) and (I) as listed for the original design on the page opposite
- No. 5 perlé cotton thread:
  (M) light yellow
  Tracing paper and other items for transferring the pattern onto the T-shirt

## Let's begin

See the page opposite for the pattern.
Make a pattern for the row of flowers required by drawing a line 8cm (3") long, close to the lower edge of the piece of tracing paper. Trace **Flower 1**, evenly spaced, five times along the line.
Attach the piece of iron-on interfacing onto the wrong side of the front of the T-shirt at the selected position. This will stabilize the area where the design is to be stitched. See page 21 for placing the pattern and page 15 for backing the fabric. Transfer the pattern onto the front of the T-shirt by tracing with a water erasable fabric marker or by using transfer paper. See pages 22-25 for transferring the pattern onto the fabric.

## Stitch!

Work the row of flowers following the instructions for **Flower 1** on the page opposite, using (M) light yellow instead of (I) medium orange when stitching the petals of the first, third, and fifth flowers.

## Let's finish

Turn the T-shirt inside out. On the wrong side, peel back any excess interfacing from its outer edge and trim it back close to the stitches. Rinse the T-shirt in cold water to remove the pattern markings. When dry, turn it inside out and press it. See page 36 for pressing.

## Hints

### Using stretch knit fabrics

Knit fabrics are designed to stretch, allowing ease of movement when worn. However, this stretching is usually not desirable on the area where the design is stitched. By attaching interfacing onto the wrong side of the fabric, the amount of stretch on the area to be worked is minimised and controlled. This makes the stitching much easier to manage.

### Another project idea

Below, a single element from *Summer Garden* has been worked as a framed picture. This was created in a similar way to the *Blue Flowers Framed Picture*, the instructions for which are on page 57.

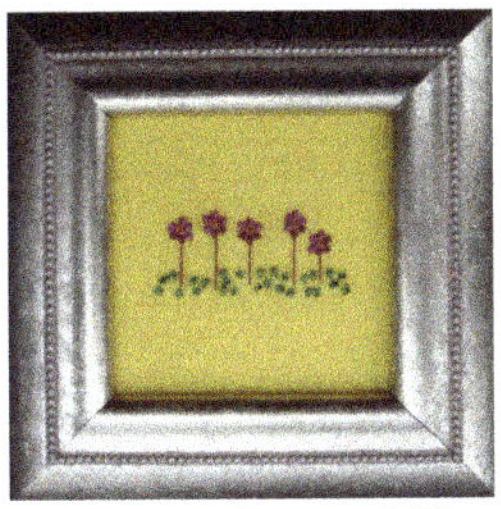

***Pink Flowers Framed Picture*, featuring Flower 7 from *Summer Garden***

# Couching

Couching is formed by placing a foundation thread, or laid thread, on the surface of the fabric and then attaching it with stitches. The couching stitches can be either straight or slanted and can be worked at regular intervals. Alternatively, they can be worked irregularly, or in pairs or groups, often forming patterns. Stitches such as blanket stitch can be used to attach the laid thread to the fabric, giving a decorative effect.

As couching forms a continuous line, it is well suited to working lines, especially intricate patterns such as zigzags or spirals. It is often used as an outline, and it can also be worked so that it covers the raw edges of appliqué shapes. When worked in rows it can be used to fill an area.

The laid thread and the thread used for the couching stitches can be of the same or different colours and textures. Threads that are too thick, too highly textured, or too fragile to be stitched directly into the fabric can be used as the laid thread, with a different thread used to attach them.

For added texture, a string of beads can be laid onto the fabric and couched between the beads to hold them in place.

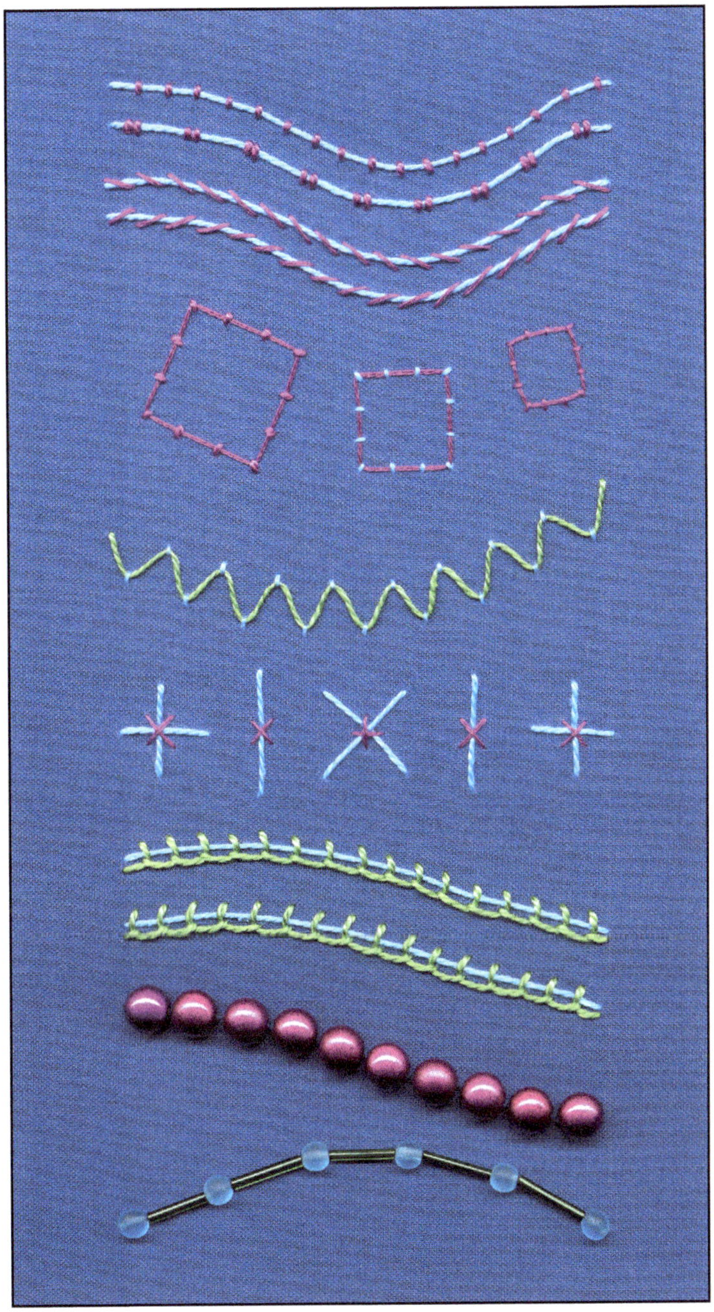

Couching

Couching with pairs of stitches

Couching with slanted stitches, in two directions

Couching to form shapes

Couching to create a zigzag

Couching with crossed stitches to attach long threads

Couching with blanket stitch, in two directions

Couching a string of large beads

Couching a string of two types of bead

**Couching sampler**

# Couching

## Hints

When attaching the laid thread onto the fabric, the couching stitches can be worked by skimming the needle in and out of the fabric before pulling the thread through. Alternatively, the stitches can be worked in two stabbing movements by taking the needle and thread up through the fabric, and then taking the needle and thread down through the fabric. Couching can be quite heavy, so choose a background fabric that is strong enough to support the weight of the threads.

To avoid joining in a new laid thread, measure the length required before you begin, or use the thread straight from the skein. If, however, you ever do need to join in a new laid thread, cover the join with a couching stitch. When working couching around tight curves, place the couching stitches closer together so that the curve of the laid thread is as smooth as possible.

## Couching: right-handed

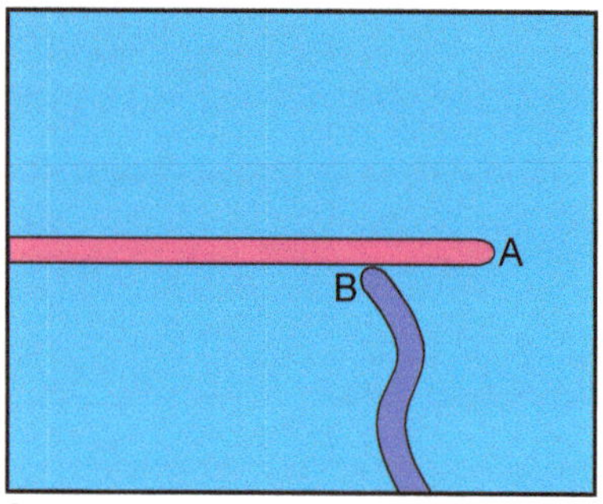


**Couching with straight stitches**
**1** Bring thread to be laid to the front at A. Lay thread along marked line. Come up at B with couching thread.

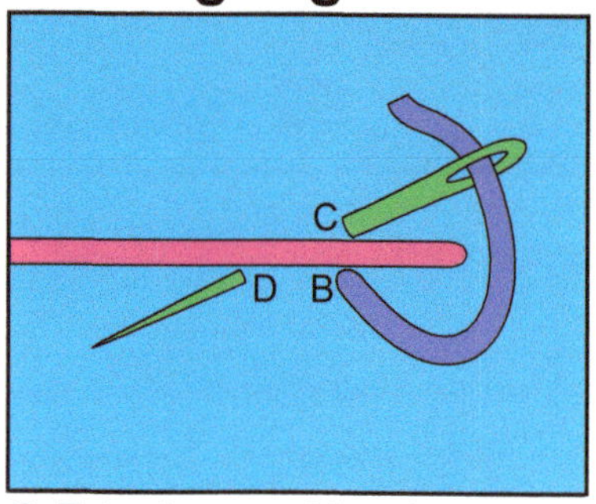


**2** Take the couching thread down at C, which is aligned above B. Emerge at D.

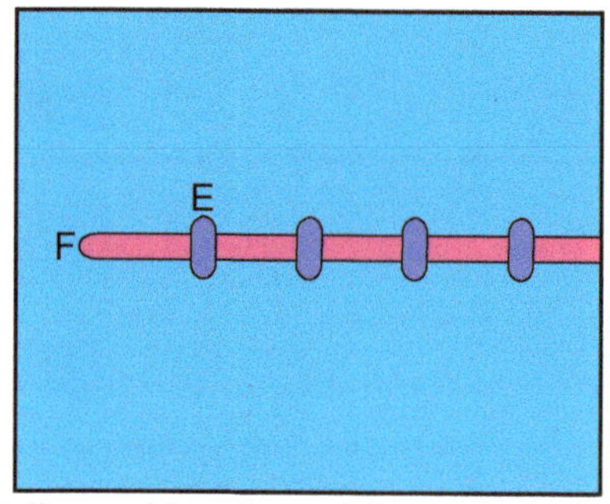


**3** Pull couching thread through and continue. To end off, take couching thread to back at E and secure. Take laid thread to back at F and secure.

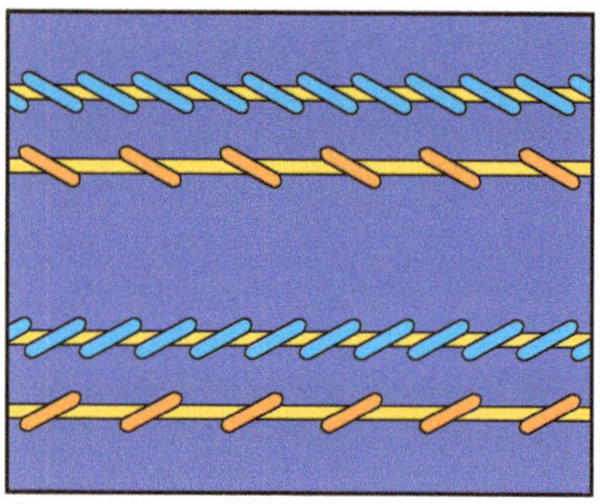

**Couching with slanted stitches**
Examples show slanted couching stitches worked in two directions with stitches placed close together or further apart.

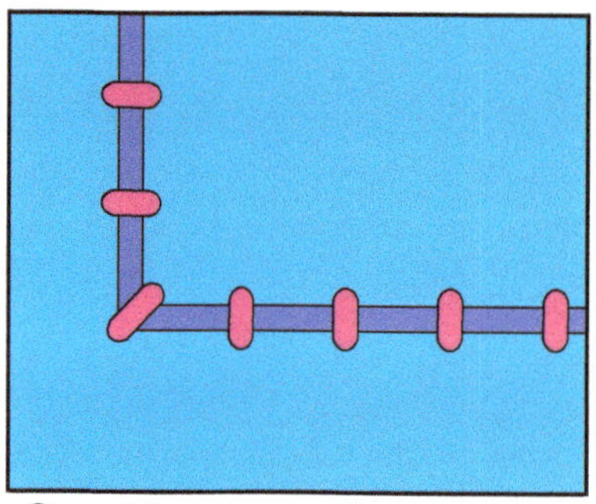

**Couching around a corner**
Work a stitch diagonally at the corner before changing the direction of the laid thread.

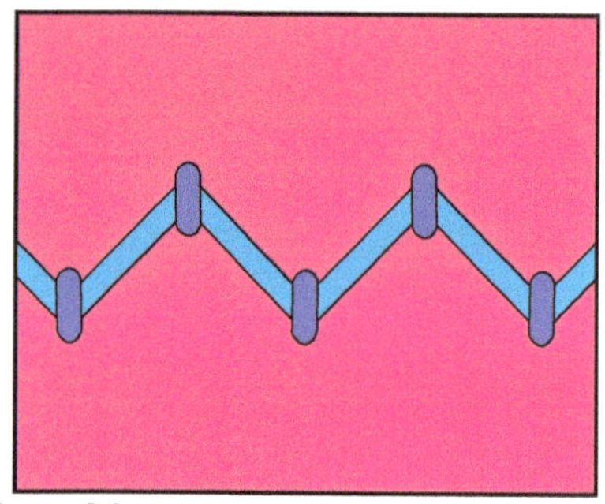

**Couching a zigzag line**
Work a couching stitch at each change in the direction of the laid thread.

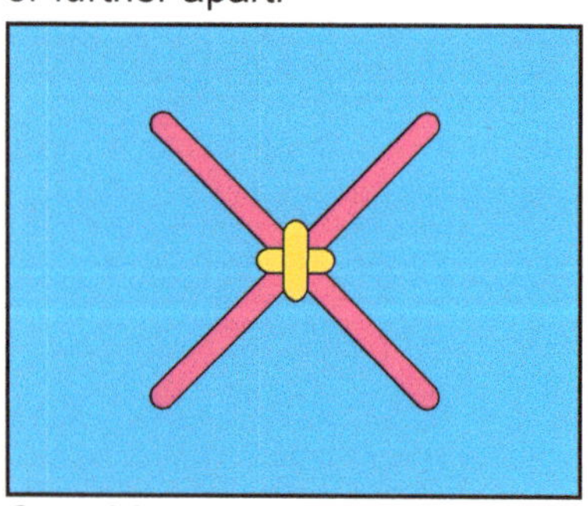

**Couching an intersection**
Stitch two crossed diagonal straight stitches as laid thread. Add couching stitches in a cross over the diagonal stitches.

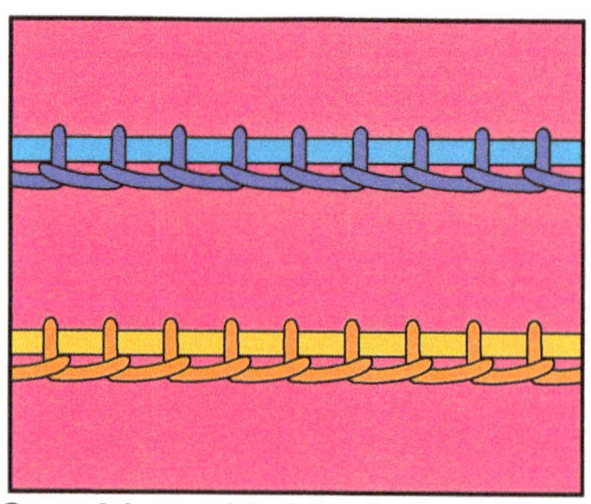

**Couching with blanket stitch**
Examples show blanket stitch used to couch the laid thread. Blanket stitch can be worked in either direction.

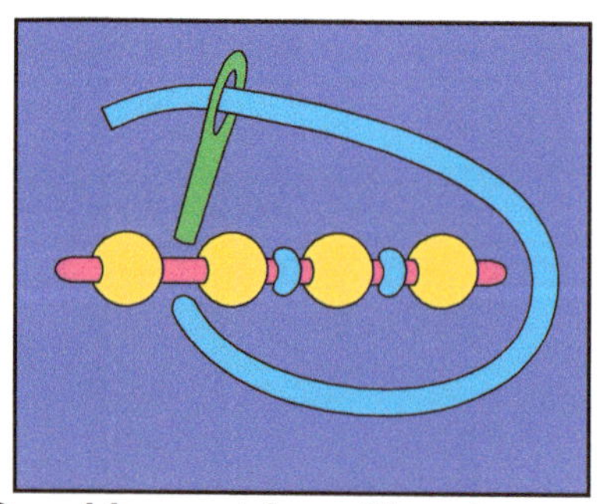

**Couching a string of beads**
Bring thread to front of fabric. Pass needle and thread through all the beads. Take thread to back and secure. Bring new thread to front and couch between beads.

# Couching: left-handed

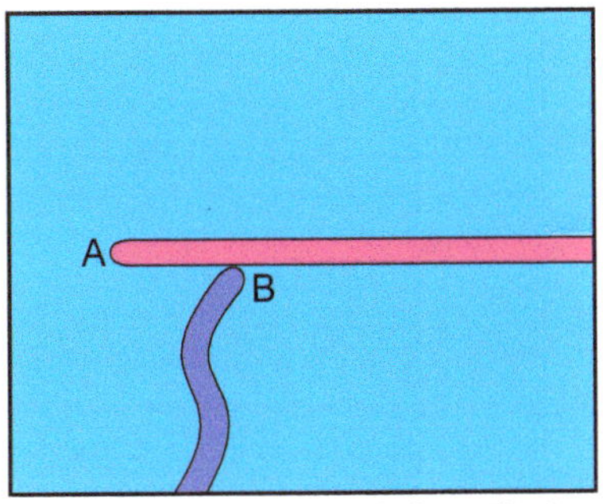


**Couching with straight stitches**
**1** Bring thread to be laid to the front at A. Lay thread along marked line. Come up at B with couching thread.

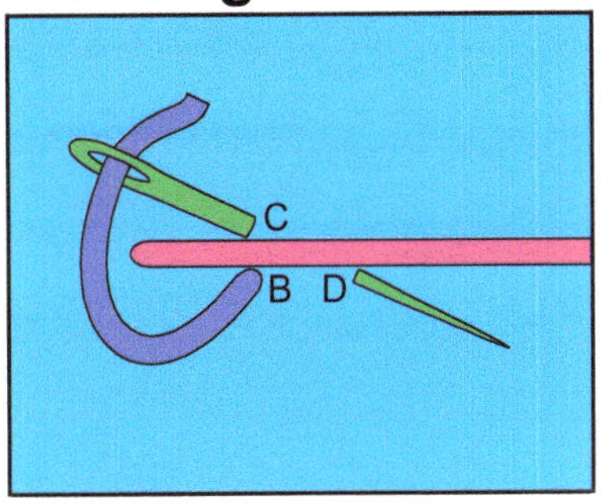


**2** Take the couching thread down at C, which is aligned above B. Emerge at D.

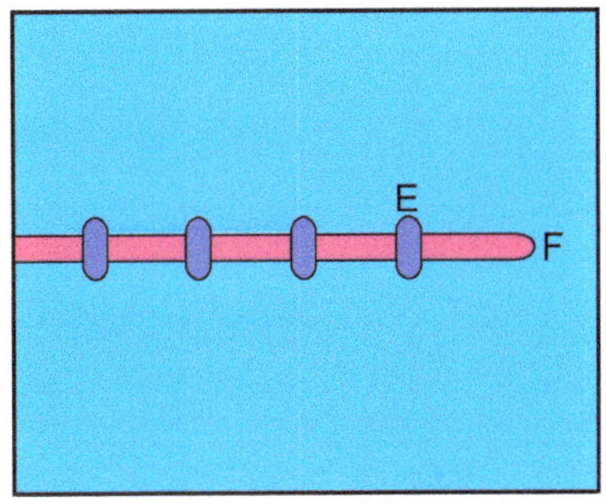


**3** Pull couching thread through and continue. To end off, take couching thread to back at E and secure. Take laid thread to back at F and secure.

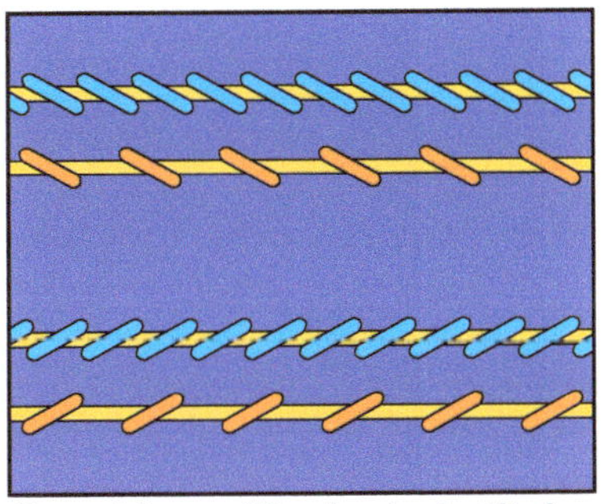

**Couching with slanted stitches**
Examples show slanted couching stitches worked in two directions with stitches placed close together or further apart.

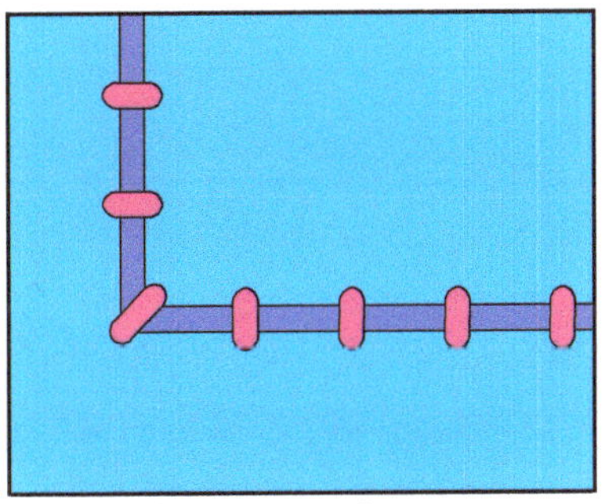

**Couching around a corner**
Work a stitch diagonally at the corner before changing the direction of the laid thread.

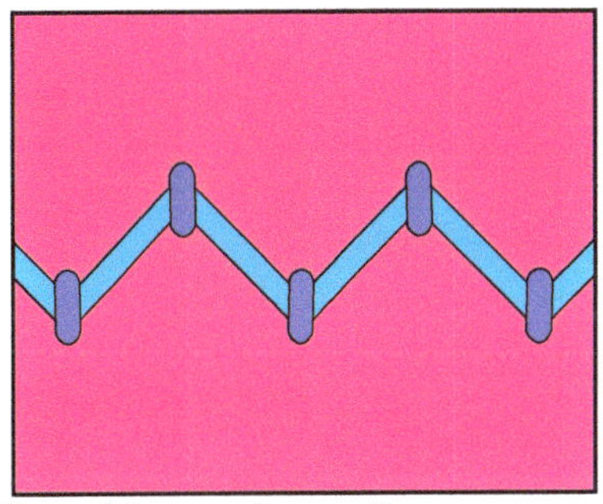

**Couching a zigzag line**
Work a couching stitch at each change in the direction of the laid thread.

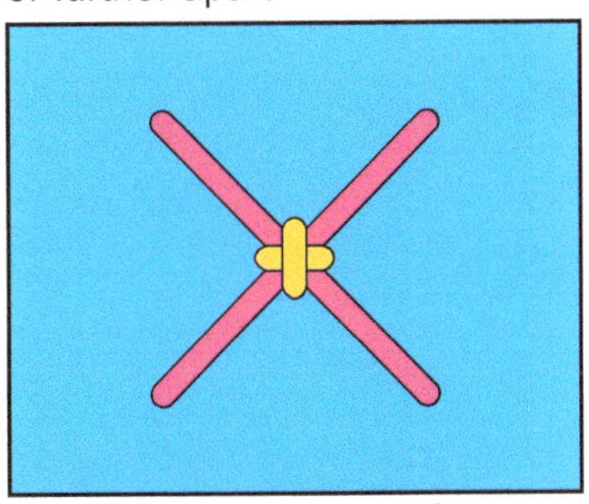

**Couching an intersection**
Stitch two crossed diagonal straight stitches as laid thread. Add couching stitches in a cross over the diagonal stitches.

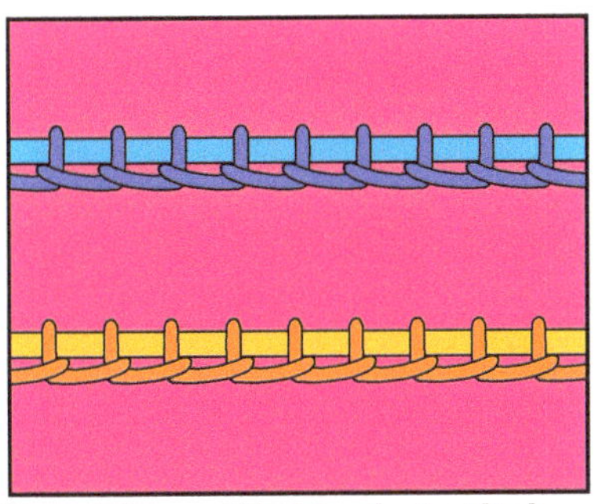

**Couching with blanket stitch**
Examples show blanket stitch used to couch the laid thread. Blanket stitch can be worked in either direction.

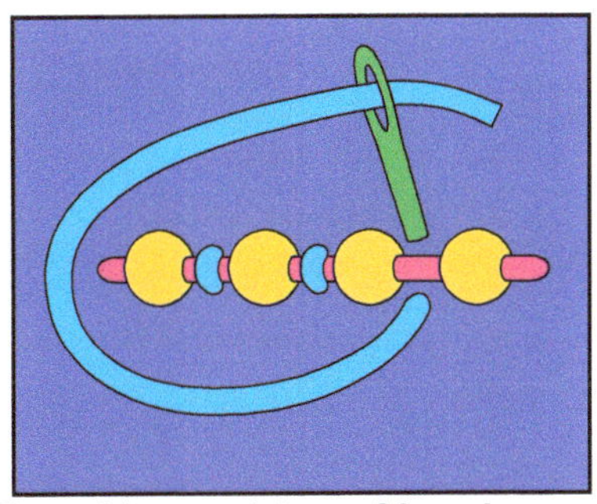

**Couching a string of beads**
Bring thread to front of fabric. Pass needle and thread through all the beads. Take thread to back and secure. Bring new thread to front and couch between beads.

# Couching

# Designs and project ideas

## The designs

| | |
|---|---|
| Fishy Fish | Fuchsia Magic |
| Juicy Red Apple | Beach Boxes |
| Seaspray | Golden Garden |

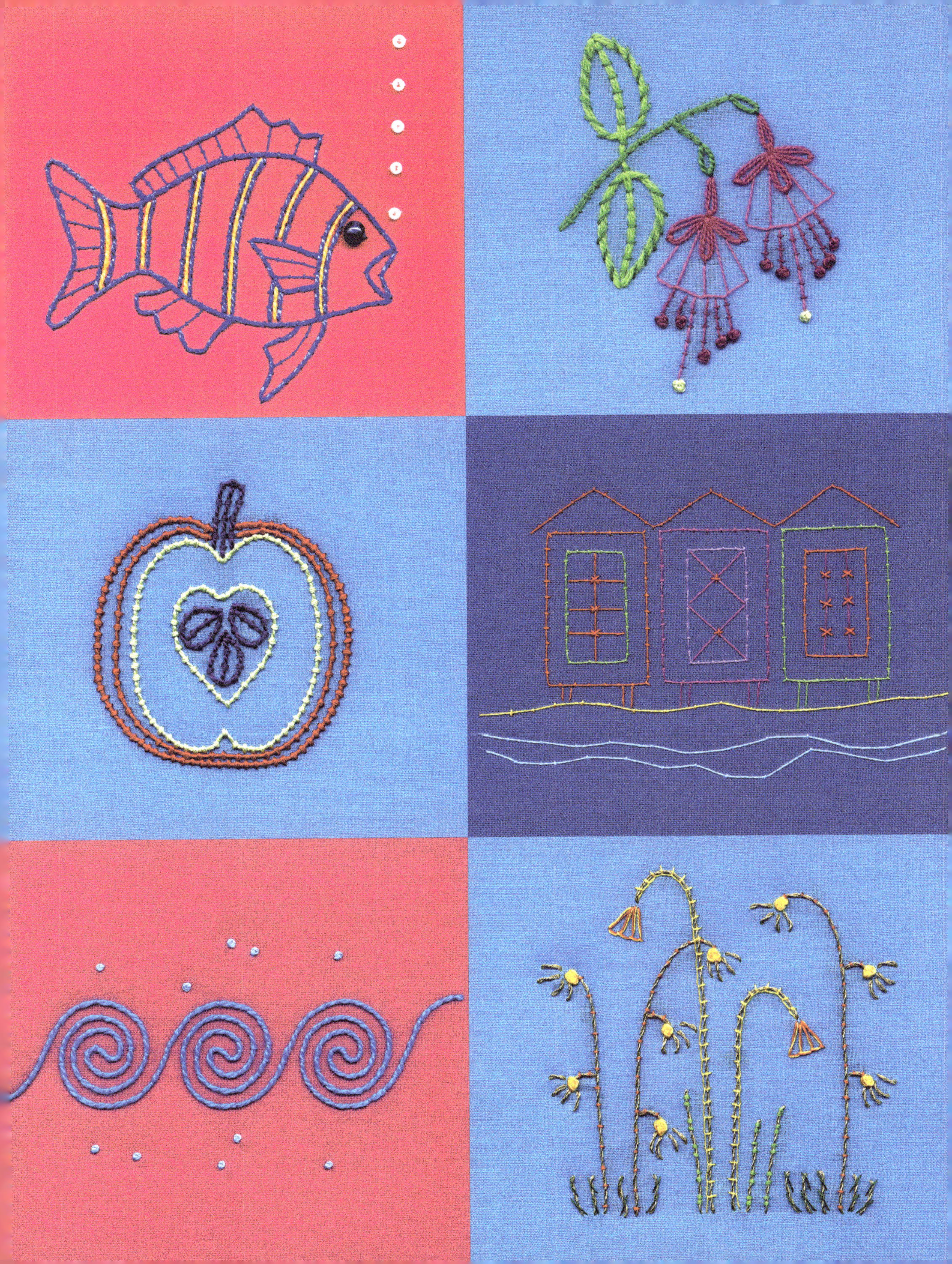

# Fishy Fish

Something is fishy here!

## The design

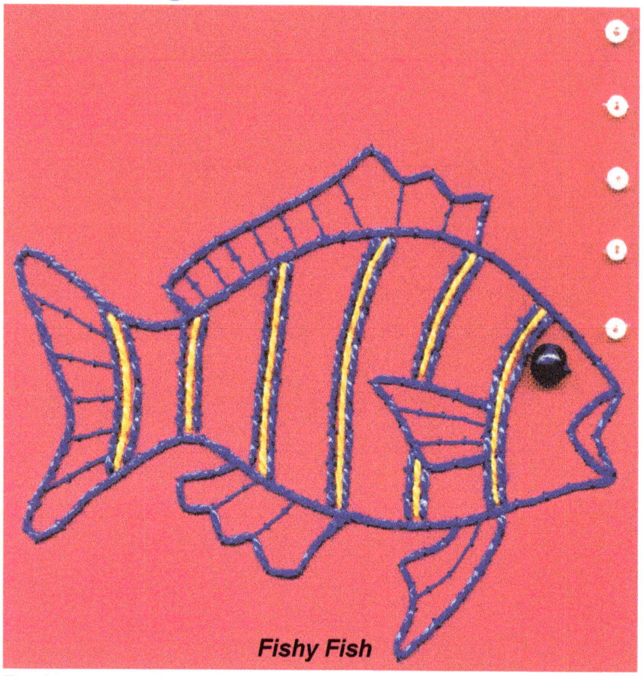

*Fishy Fish*

Perlé cotton thread, couched with straight stitches in stranded cotton thread, is used for the outline of the fish and its stripes. The details on the tail and fins are worked with couching in stranded cotton thread. Beads are added for the eye and bubbles. To work the design exactly as shown here, use the instructions on this page. On the facing page, the fish is featured on a child's library bag.

As this design uses beads, it is not considered safe for use on projects for babies or very small children.

## The pattern

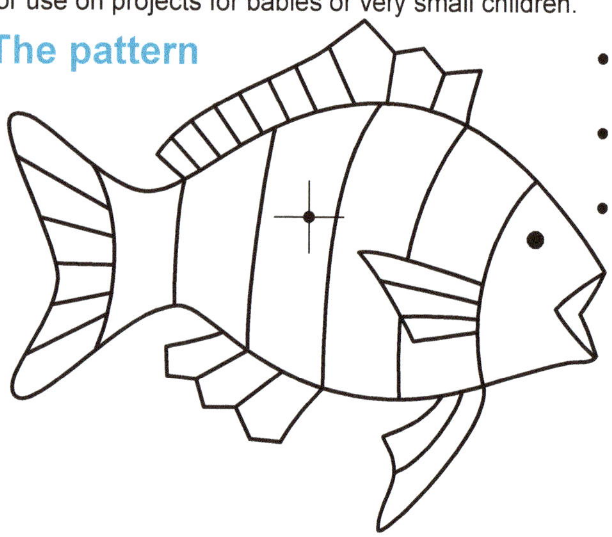

Key: Centre of design · Bead for eye · Bead for bubble

## Shopping list

- Pink cotton fabric for background: 25cm (10") square
- Fabric or interfacing for backing: 25cm (10") square
- Stranded cotton thread:
  (A) medium blue (B) medium yellow (C) white
- No. 5 perlé cotton thread:
  (D) medium blue (E) medium yellow
- 1 medium size round bead: (F) medium blue
- 5 small flattened round beads: (G) white
- Tracing paper and other items for transferring the pattern onto the fabric

## Let's begin

Read page 15 for backing the fabric, and pages 22-25 for transferring the pattern onto the fabric, then select and use suitable methods for your fabric. For the pink fabric shown here, the pattern was transferred centrally onto the fabric by tracing with a water erasable fabric marker and then the backing fabric was tacked to the wrong side.

## Stitch!

For help, see pages 40-43 for straight stitch, 202-205 for couching, including a zigzag line, and pages 238-241 for beading, including a bead attached on its end. When working the couching, attach the laid thread with small evenly spaced straight stitches.

1. Beginning at the mouth, work the outline for the head, body, and tail of the fish in couching (1 strand D, attached with 1 strand A). On returning to the beginning, take the laid thread to the back of the work and secure. Bring the laid thread to the front again and complete the mouth.
2. Outline the fins in couching (1 strand D, attached with 1 strand A), working the zigzag lines with a couching stitch placed at each change in direction.
3. Following the marked lines, work the yellow stripes on the body with couching (1 strand E, attached with 1 strand B).
4. Work a row of couching on each side of the yellow stripes (1 strand D, attached with 1 strand A).
5. Add the internal lines on the tail and fins in couching (1 strand A, attached with 1 strand A).
6. For the eye, attach the blue bead with several straight stitches (F, attached with two strands A). Secure firmly on the back of the work.
7. For each bubble, attach a white bead on its end (G, attached with 1 strand C). Secure the thread firmly on the back of the work after attaching each bead.

## Let's finish

Take out the tacking. Rinse the work in cold water to remove the water erasable fabric marker. When partly dry, press or pin out the work. See page 36 for pressing and for pinning out.

# Fishy Fish Library Bag

Have fun at the library with this fishy library bag.

## The project

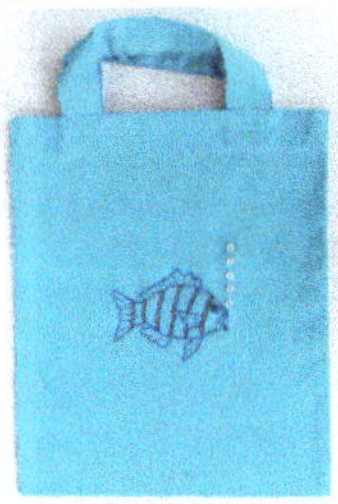

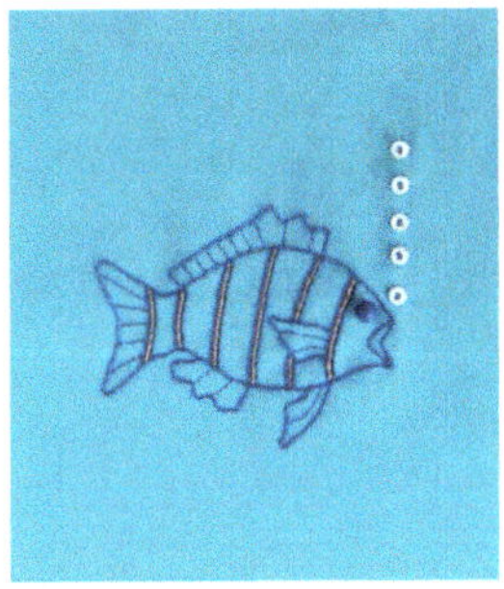

***Fishy Fish Library Bag*** **and Detail**

For this project, the fish is worked on a piece of aqua fabric that is then made up into a library bag. The fish is worked in the same way as the original design, but the pattern has been enlarged. The finished size of the library bag is 39cm x 31cm wide (15 1/2" x 12 1/4"), not including the handles. As this project uses beads, it is not considered safe for babies or very small children.

## Shopping list

- Aqua cotton drill fabric for the bag: one piece 86cm x 33cm wide (34" x 13")
- Aqua cotton drill fabric for the handles: two pieces 40cm x 10cm wide (16" x 4")
- Threads as listed for the original design opposite
- 1 large round bead: (F) medium blue
- 5 medium flattened round beads: (G) white
- Machine sewing thread: aqua
- Tracing paper and other items for transferring the pattern onto the fabric

## Let's begin

See opposite for the fish pattern. Prepare the pattern by enlarging it to 130% of its original size.
Place the bag fabric out flat with one short end at the top and right side facing up. Beginning at the top, measure half way down the rectangle and tack a line across the width of the fabric. This indicates the fold line at the base of the bag. Measure down from the top edge again, and tack a line 4cm (1 1/2") for the top hem fold line. On the right side of the fabric, transfer the pattern onto the upper section centrally between the tacked lines (Diagram 1) by tracing with a water erasable fabric marker or by using transfer paper. See pages 22-25 for transferring the pattern onto the fabric.

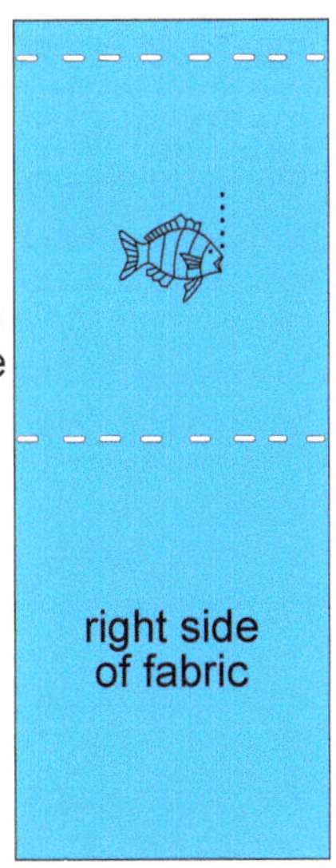


**Diagram 1**

## Stitch!

Work the fish following steps 1-7 of the stitch instructions for the original design on the previous page. When attaching the white beads (G), use two strands of thread (C).

## Let's finish

Rinse the work in cold water to remove the pattern markings. When partly dry, press or pin out the work. See page 36 for pressing and for pinning out.
With right sides together, fold the work in half along the tacked fold line indicating the base of the bag. Pin the layers together along the two long sides. With the machine sewing thread and a straight stitch on the machine, stitch the side seams using a 1cm (3/8") seam allowance. Sew along the edge of the seams with a machine zigzag or overlock stitch (Diagram 2). Take out the tacking from the base of the bag. Turn the bag through to the right side and press.

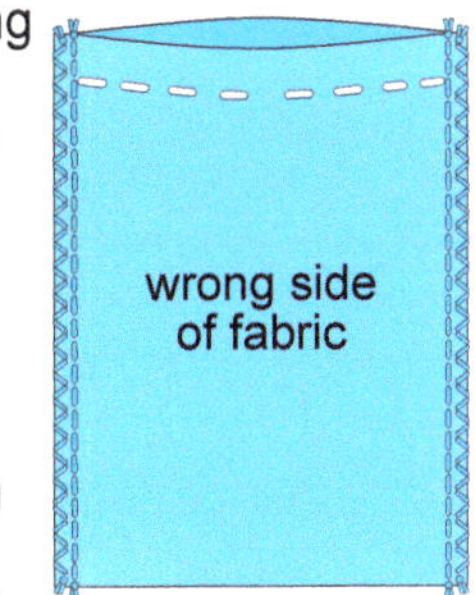


**Diagram 2**

Fold under and press 1cm (3/8") on the long sides of the strips for the handles. With wrong sides together, fold each handle in half lengthwise. Stitch along both long edges of each handle (Diagram 3). Press.
With raw edges even, pin one handle onto the right side of the front of the bag at the top, with its outer edges 6cm (2 1/2") in from the side seams (see diagram 4). Stitch the handle to the bag 4cm (1 1/2") down from the upper raw edges (Diagram 4). Attach the second handle onto the back of the bag in the same way.

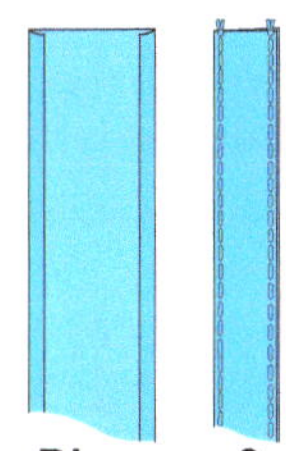

**Diagram 3**

Sew along the upper raw edge of the bag, including the handles, with a machine zigzag or overlock stitch. Fold the upper edge to the inside along the tacked fold line for the top hem and press. Take out the tacking from the upper edge of the bag. Stitching through both layers, work one row of machine straight stitch around the top edge of the bag close to the fold and a second row 2cm (3/4") below the first (Diagram 5).

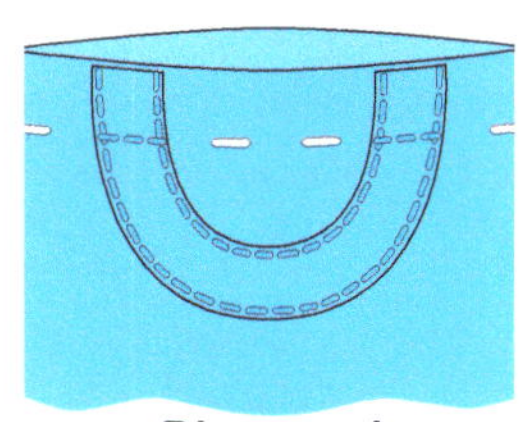

**Diagram 4**

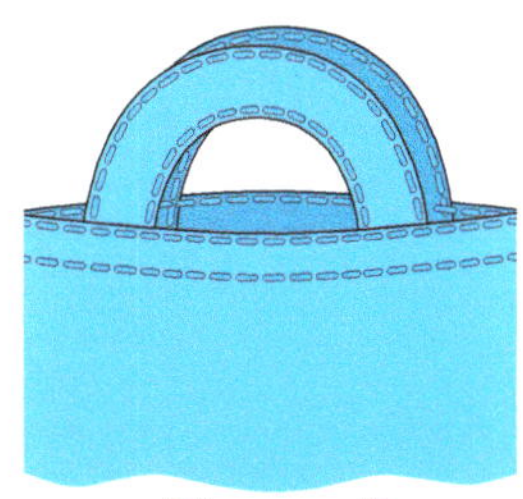

**Diagram 5**

# Fuchsia Magic

Glorious fuchsia blossoms dancing in the gentle breeze.

## The design

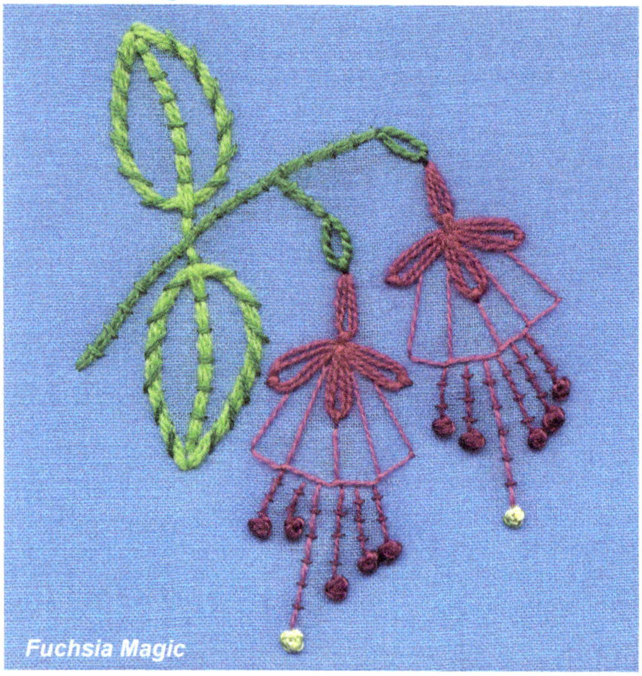


Couching is featured in this design, creating textural detail on the stems, leaves and flower centres. Straight stitch, blanket stitch, detached chain stitch, and French knot are also used. This design is worked in thin and thick cotton threads and wool yarns.

Follow the instructions on this page to work the design as shown above. See the project idea on the facing page where the design is featured on the lid of a tin.

## The pattern

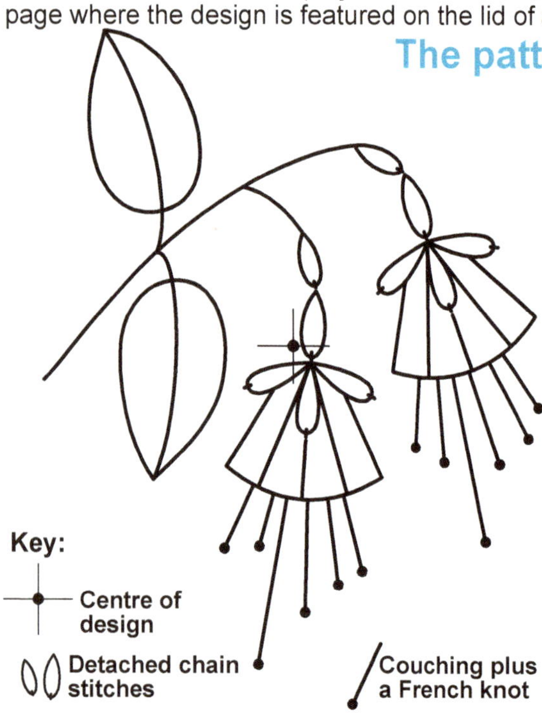


## Shopping list

- Aqua cotton fabric for background: 25cm (10") square
- Fabric or interfacing for backing: 25cm (10") square
- Stranded cotton thread:
  (A) medium green (B) dark magenta
- No. 5 perlé cotton thread: (C) medium green
  (D) very light green (E) dark magenta
- Fine 2 ply wool yarn: (F) medium green (G) light green
  (H) dark magenta (I) medium magenta
- Tracing paper and other items for transferring the pattern onto the fabric

## Let's begin

Read page 15 for backing the fabric, and pages 22-25 for transferring the pattern onto the fabric, then select and use suitable methods for your fabric. For the aqua fabric shown here, the pattern was transferred centrally onto the fabric by tracing with a water erasable fabric marker and then the backing fabric was tacked to the wrong side.

## Stitch!

For help, see pages 40-43 for straight stitch, 130-133 for blanket stitch, 166-169 for detached chain stitch, 184-187 for French knot, and pages 202-205 for couching.

When working the couching, attach the laid wool yarn with small straight stitches unless otherwise stated.

1 Work the main stem and the lower flower stem in couching (2 strands F, attached with 2 strands A).
2 Beginning and ending at the tip, work the outline of one leaf in couching using slanted straight stitches (3 strands G, attached with 2 strands A).
3 Continuing with the same threads, work the leaf stem and vein in couching. Work the other leaf.
4 Stitch a detached chain stitch for each green flower base (1 strand C). Work four dark magenta detached chain stitches (2 strands H) (Diagram 1).
5 Begin the magenta petals with a single straight stitch on the left (1 strand I), worked from A to the chain stitch above. Emerge at A (Diagram 2) and work four blanket stitches. End with a tiny anchor.
6 Work a line of couching for the longest part of the flower centre (1 strand I, attached with 1 strand B). Add the remaining lines of couching for the flower centre (1 strand H, attached with 1 strand B).
7 Add a two wrap French knot (1 strand D) at the end of the longest part of the flower centre and a two wrap French knot (1 strand E) to the others.

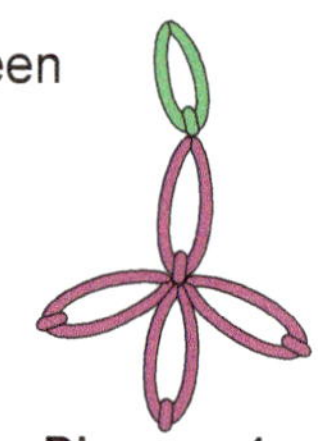

Diagram 1

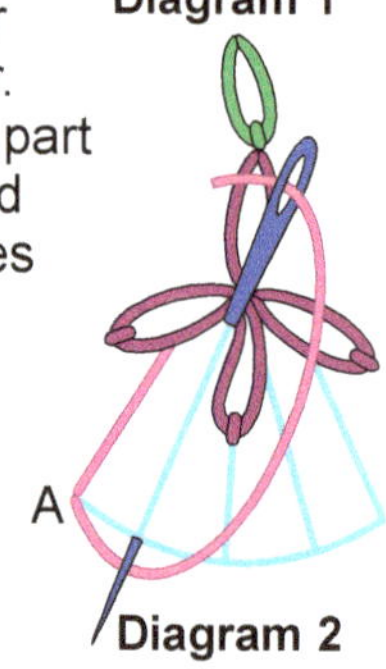


Diagram 2

## Let's finish

Take out tacking. Rinse work very gently in cold water to remove the marker. When partly dry, press or pin out the work. See page 36 for pressing and for pinning out.

# Fuchsia Magic Treasures Container

Keep some special treasures in a tin decorated with fuchsias.

## The project

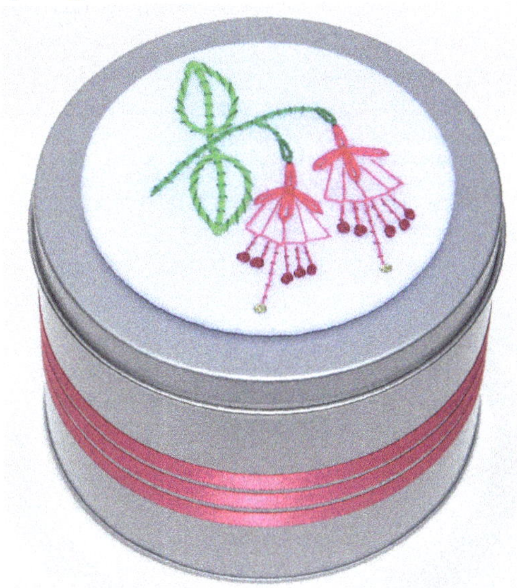

***Fuchsia Magic Treasures Container***

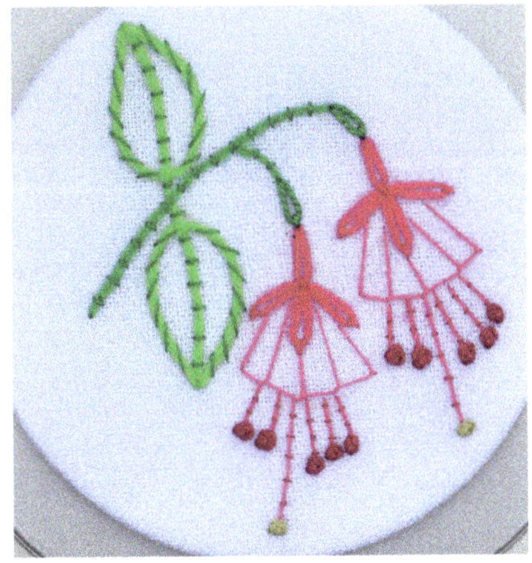

**Detail of *Fuchsia Magic Treasures Container***

*Fuchsia Magic* is stitched in the original thread colours on a white background for this project. The work is then laced over cardboard and attached to the lid of a tin. This tin is 13cm (5") in diameter.

## Shopping list

- Silver tin
- White linen-look fabric for background: 25cm (10") square
- Fabric or interfacing for backing: 25cm (10") square
- Threads as listed for the original design on the page opposite
- Machine sewing thread for gathering
- Strong thread for lacing
- Tracing paper and other items for transferring the pattern onto the fabric
- Thin wadding: one circle 10cm (4") in diameter
- White cardboard: one circle 10cm (4") in diameter
- Medium magenta ribbon: three pieces, each measuring the length around the tin plus 6cm (2 1/2")
- Archival double-sided sticky tape or glue

## Let's begin

See the page opposite for the pattern.
Transfer the pattern centrally onto the white fabric by tracing with a water erasable fabric marker or by using transfer paper. See pages 22-25 for transferring the pattern onto the fabric. Tack the backing to the wrong side of the fabric. See page 15 for backing the fabric.

## Stitch!

Work the design following the stitch instructions on the page opposite.

## Let's finish

Rinse the work very gently in cold water to remove the pattern markings. When partly dry, press or pin out the work. See page 36 for pressing and for pinning out.
Trim the white fabric and the backing to a circle 14cm (5 1/2") in diameter, centred over the stitched design.
Using machine sewing thread, and leaving both ends of the thread dangling, work a row of running stitch around the edge of the backing and the fabric together. See pages 58-61 for running stitch. Take out any remaining tacking. Place the wadding and then the cardboard centrally onto the wrong side of the stitched work (Diagram 1).

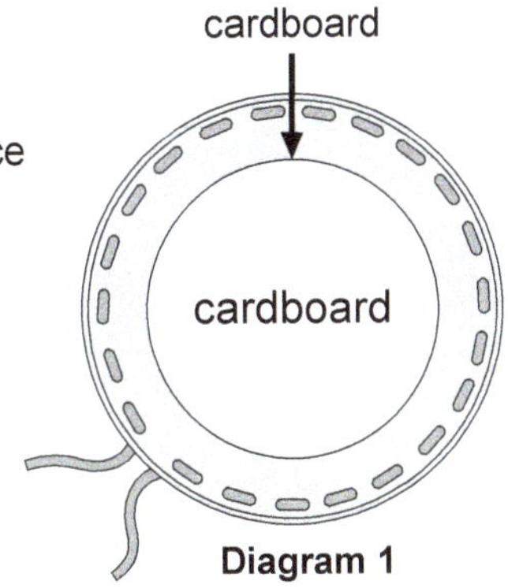


**Diagram 1**

Pull the two thread ends to gather the fabric over the padded cardboard, then tie them in a knot. Trim the excess length of threads. Lace the work tightly. As a guide, see page 37 for lacing.
Using archival double-sided sticky tape or glue, adhere the laced side of the work centrally onto the lid of the tin.
Decorate the sides of the tin with the three lengths of medium magenta ribbon.

## Hint

**Use other designs**

Many of the designs in this book, or selected elements from them, can be used to decorate the lid of a tin or other container. The creative possibilities are infinite!

# Juicy Red Apple

An apple a day...

## The design

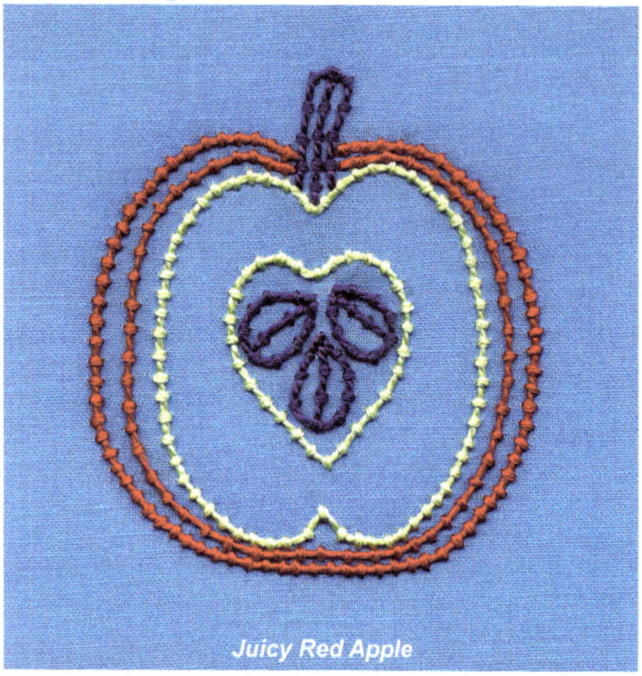


The apple is couched entirely using perlé cotton thread attached with straight stitches in stranded silk thread. This combination of threads gives an interesting textured appearance.
Use the instructions on this page to work the design exactly as shown here on an aqua background.
To feature the design on two bibs for a baby, see the following page.

## The pattern

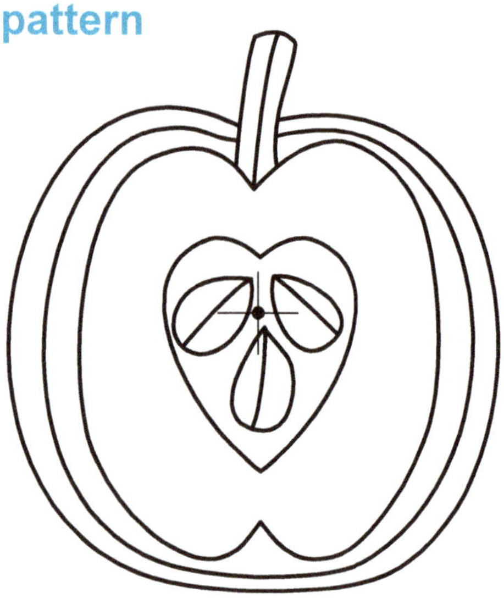

**Key:** ┼ **Centre of design**

## Shopping list

- Aqua cotton fabric for background: 25cm (10") square
- Fabric or interfacing for backing: 25cm (10") square
- No. 5 perlé cotton thread:
  (A) dark violet (B) very light green (C) medium red
- Stranded silk thread:
  (D) dark violet (E) very light green (F) medium red
- Tracing paper and other items for transferring the pattern onto the fabric

## Let's begin

Read page 15 for backing the fabric, and pages 22-25 for transferring the pattern onto the fabric, then select and use suitable methods for your fabric. For the aqua fabric shown here, the pattern was transferred centrally onto the fabric by tracing with a water erasable fabric marker and then the backing fabric was tacked to the wrong side.

## Stitch!

For help, see pages 40-43 for straight stitch, and pages 202-205 for couching. When couching the laid threads, work evenly spaced straight stitches using the silk thread.

1 Leaving the space for the stalk, work the two rows for the apple skin in couching (1 strand C, attached with 4 strands F).

2 Stitch the next row, which represents the apple flesh, in couching (1 strand B, attached with 4 strands E), beginning at the top of the shape and couching down one side. At the peak, work a couching stitch at the change of direction (Diagram 1). Continue up the other side.

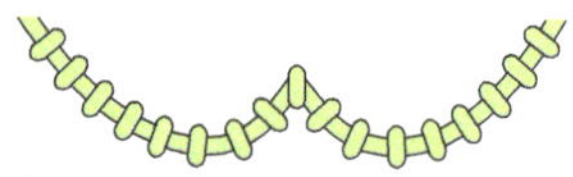

**Diagram 1**

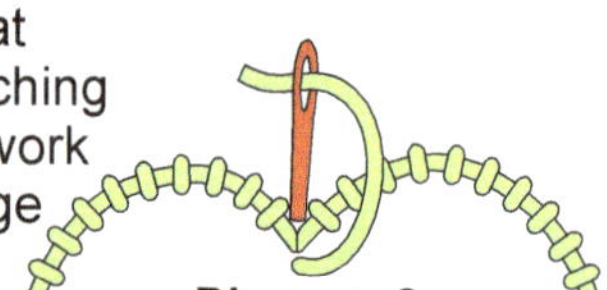

**Diagram 2**

At the top, take the perlé thread down through the same hole in the fabric as the beginning. Cover the join with a couching stitch (Diagram 2). Continuing with the same threads, couch the heart shape for the apple core.

3 Couch the outline for each pip (1 strand A, attached with 4 strands D). Cover the join with a couching stitch. Couch the centre line on each pip.

4 Add the outline, and then the centre line, for the stalk in couching (1 strand A, attached with 4 strands D).

## Let's finish

Take out the tacking. Rinse the work in cold water to remove the water erasable fabric marker. When partly dry, press or pin out the work. See page 36 for pressing and for pinning out.

## Hint

**Length of couching stitches**

Working the straight stitches slightly longer than the thickness of the laid thread will make the couching stitches a visible feature.

# Juicy Red Apple Bibs

Enjoy mealtimes with these decorated bibs.

## The projects

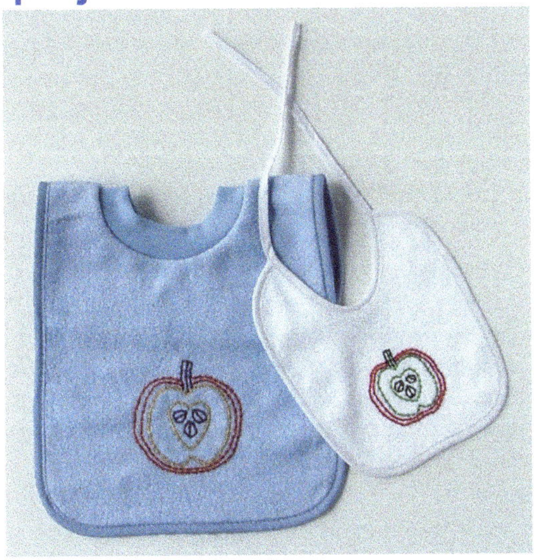

***Juicy Red Apple Bibs***

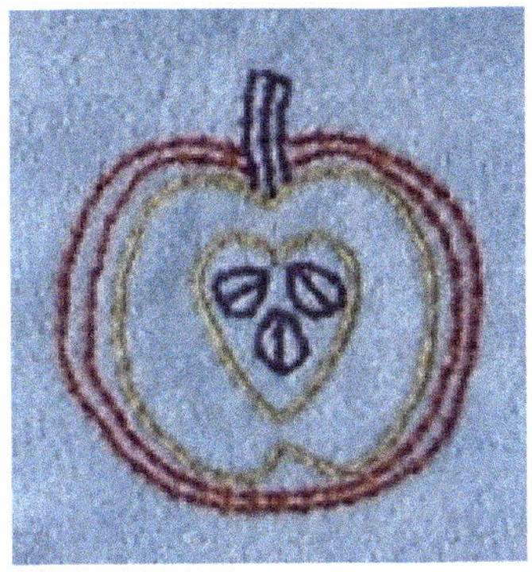

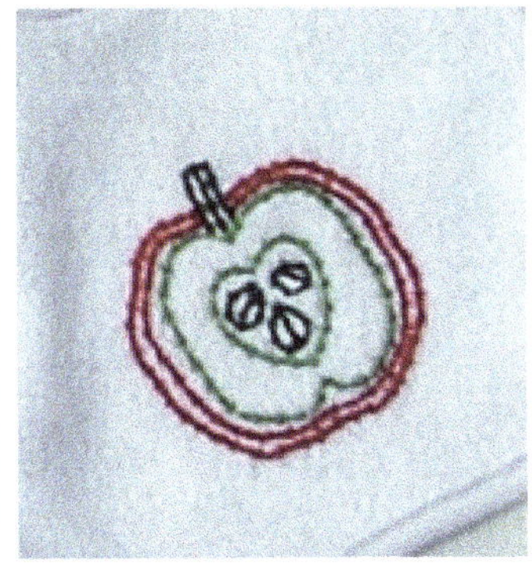

**Details of *Juicy Red Apple Bibs***

This design is perfect to quickly and easily decorate purchased plain towelling bibs.
For the blue bib, the design has been enlarged, and for the white bib, the design has been reduced in size.
Both bibs feature colour schemes that are different from the original, and stranded cotton thread is used in place of silk thread for the couching stitches.

## Shopping list

***Blue bib***

- Large blue towelling bib
- No. 5 perlé cotton thread:
  (A) dark violet (B) medium yellow (C) medium orange
- Stranded cotton thread:
  (D) dark violet (E) medium yellow (F) medium orange
- Tracing paper and other items for transferring the pattern onto the bib

***White bib***

- Small white towelling bib
- No. 5 perlé cotton thread:
  (A) dark green (B) light green (C) medium red
- Stranded cotton thread:
  (D) dark green (E) light green (F) medium red
- Tracing paper and other items for transferring the pattern onto the bib

## Let's begin

See the page opposite for the apple pattern.
Prepare the pattern by enlarging it to 120% for the blue bib, and by reducing it to 85% of its original size for the white bib. Trace the reduced or enlarged pattern onto tracing paper.
Transfer the pattern onto the front of the bibs at a chosen position using the pierce and dot method with a water erasable fabric marker. See page 25 for transferring the pattern using the pierce and dot method.

## Stitch!

Stitch both the bibs following steps 1-4 of the stitch instructions on the facing page, using the alternative threads.

## Let's finish

Rinse the bibs in cold water to remove the water erasable fabric marker. When almost dry, press the bibs lightly on the wrong side. See page 36 for pressing.

## Hint

**Other food designs**

Many of the different food designs in this book would be fun to work on bibs!

# Beach Boxes

Brightly painted beach boxes stand in a row beside the ocean.

## The design

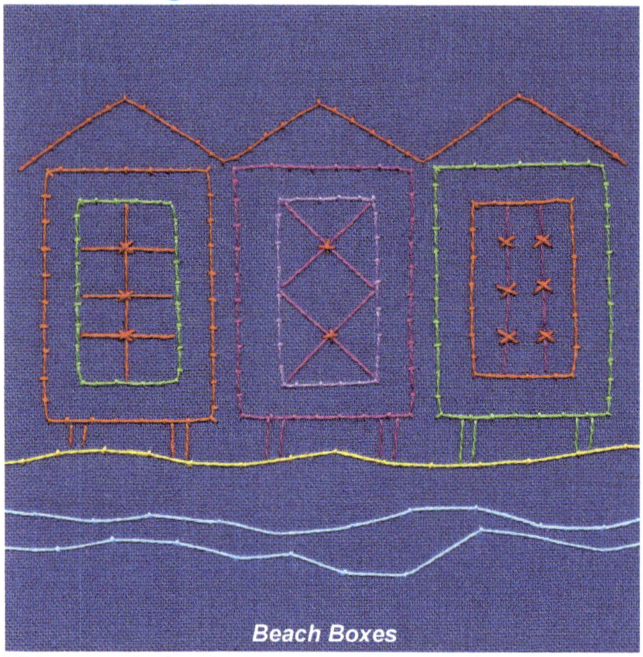

*Beach Boxes*

This easy design features couching. Straight stitch is also included. For most of the design, the laid thread is attached with small straight stitches using the same thread, while on the door panels straight stitches of contrasting colour are worked in crosses.

To work the design as shown here, use the instructions on this page. To apply the design to a project, see the idea on the following page where one beach box is worked on a scrapbooking tag.

## The pattern

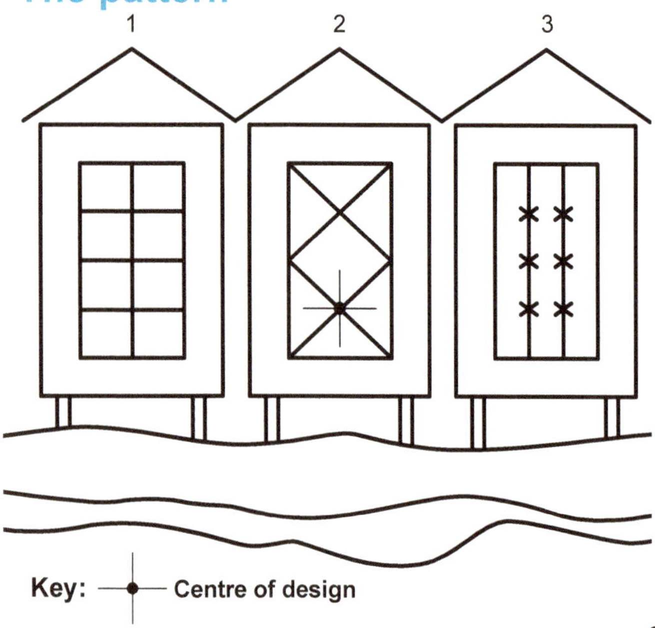


## Shopping list

- Blue cotton fabric for background: 25cm (10") square
- Fabric or interfacing for backing: 25cm (10") square
- Stranded cotton thread:
  (A) medium violet (B) medium aqua (C) light green
  (D) medium yellow (E) medium orange
  (F) medium red (G) medium magenta
- Tracing paper and other items for transferring the pattern onto the fabric

## Let's begin

Read page 15 for backing the fabric, and pages 22-25 for transferring the pattern onto the fabric, then select and use suitable methods for your fabric. For the blue fabric shown here, the pattern was transferred centrally onto the fabric by tracing with a chalk-based pencil and then the backing fabric was tacked to the wrong side.

## Stitch!

For help, see pages 40-43 for straight stitch, and pages 202-205 for couching, including corners and intersections. Attach the laid thread with the same thread using small straight stitches unless otherwise stated.

**Beach box 1** Beginning and ending at one corner, stitch the outline for the box in couching (1 strand E), placing a couching stitch at the corners (Diagram 1). Add the legs in straight stitch (1 strand E). Outline the door in couching (1 strand C). Stitch three horizontal straight stitches and then one vertical straight stitch for the door panels (1 strand E). Add small straight stitches in a cross (1 strand F) over the long stitches where they intersect (Diagram 2).

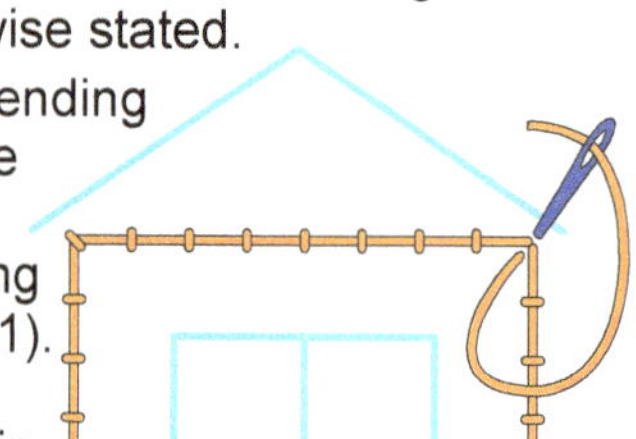

Diagram 1

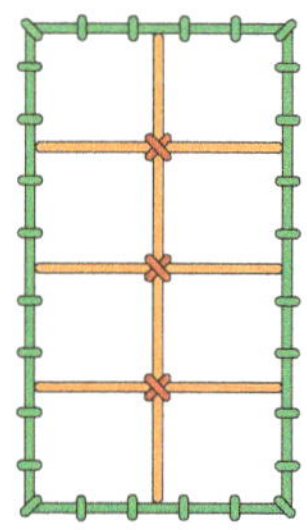

Diagram 2

**Beach box 2** Work the box outline and legs (1 strand G), and the door outline (1 strand A), in the same way as the first box. Stitch diagonal straight stitches for the door panels (1 strand G). Add small straight stitches in a cross (1 strand F) over the long stitches where they intersect.

**Beach box 3** Work the box outline and legs (1 strand C), and the door outline (1 strand E), in the same way as the first box. Stitch vertical straight stitches for the door panels (1 strand G). Add small crossed straight stitches (1 strand F) over the long stitches.

**Roofs, sand, and ocean** Work the roofs (1 strand F), sand (1 strand D), and ocean (1 strand B) in couching.

## Let's finish

Take out the tacking. Press or pin out the work. See page 36 for pressing and for pinning out.

# Beach Boxes Scrapbooking Tag

Bring a beach scene to life with this scrapbooking tag.

## The project

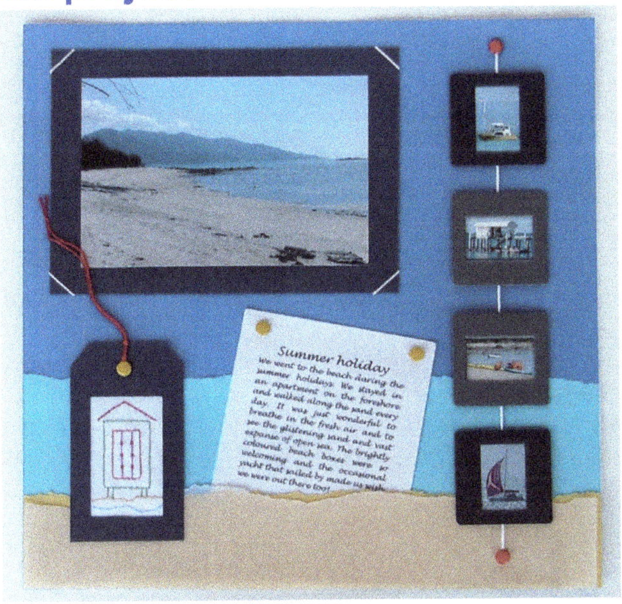

***Beach Boxes Scrapbooking Tag***
**Featured on a page**

This scrapbooking page, dedicated to a beach holiday, features **Beach box 3** worked on a piece of white fabric that is then framed by a tag shaped piece of card. The size of the tag is 10cm x 6cm wide (4" x 2 1/2"), not including the hanging loop.

## Shopping list

- White cotton fabric for background: 16.5cm x 14cm wide (6 1/2" x 5 1/2")
- Medium weight iron-on interfacing for backing: 16.5cm x 14cm wide (6 1/2" x 5 1/2")
- Threads (B), (C), (D), (E), (F), and (G) as listed for the original design on the page opposite
- No. 5 perlé cotton thread: medium red
- Tracing paper and other items for transferring the pattern onto the fabric
- Dark grey card: 10cm x 6cm wide (4" x 2 1/2")
- Archival double-sided sticky tape
- Yellow paper fastener

## Let's begin

See the page opposite for the pattern.
Following the instructions on page 15 for backing the fabric, attach the iron-on interfacing onto the wrong side of the white fabric.
Transfer the pattern for **Beach box 3**, plus the sand and first wave, centrally onto the right side of the fabric by tracing with a water erasable fabric marker. See page 23 for transferring the pattern by tracing.

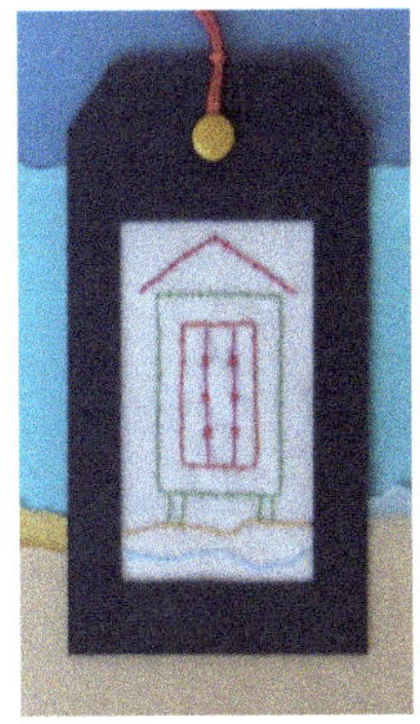

**Detail of**
***Beach Boxes Scrapbooking Tag***

## Stitch!

Work the beach box following the stitch instructions for **Beach box 3** and the **Roof, sand, and ocean** from the original design on the previous page.

## Let's finish

Rinse the work in cold water to remove the water erasable fabric marker. When almost dry, press. See page 36 for pressing.
Using the photo as a guide, create a tag shape by diagonally cutting away the two upper corners from the dark grey card, then cut out a window that is 6.5cm x 4cm wide (2 1/2" x 1 1/2"). Place the tag shape centrally over the stitched work and trace around the outer edge of the tag. Remove the tag. Cutting 5mm (1/4") inside the marked shape, cut away the excess fabric from around the design. Using archival double-sided sticky tape, attach the stitched work centrally to the back of the tag.
Make a small hole centrally near the top of the tag using a hole punch. Cut a 25cm (10") length of the perlé thread. Double it over forming a loop and knot the ends together. With the right side of the tag facing, pass the looped end through the hole (Diagram 1).
Pass the knotted ends through the loop (Diagram 2). Pull the knotted ends to tighten the thread around the tag. Attach the tag to the scrapbooking page with the yellow paper fastener.

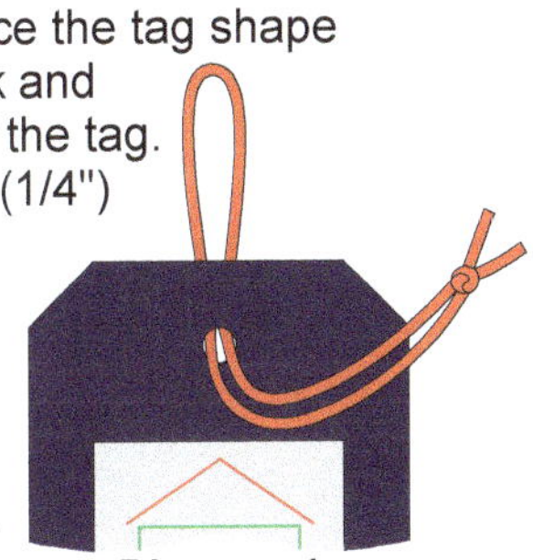

**Diagram 1**

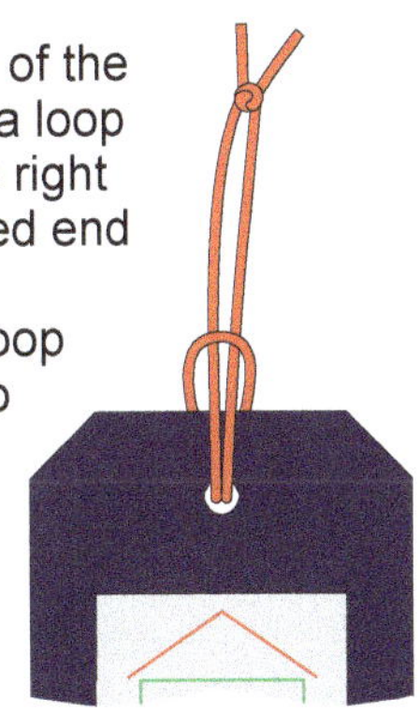

**Diagram 2**

## Hint

**Alternative projects**
Feature this tag as part of a greeting card, or back it to use it as a gift tag.

# Seaspray

Listen to the tumbling of the waves and breathe the cool, fresh sea air.

## The design

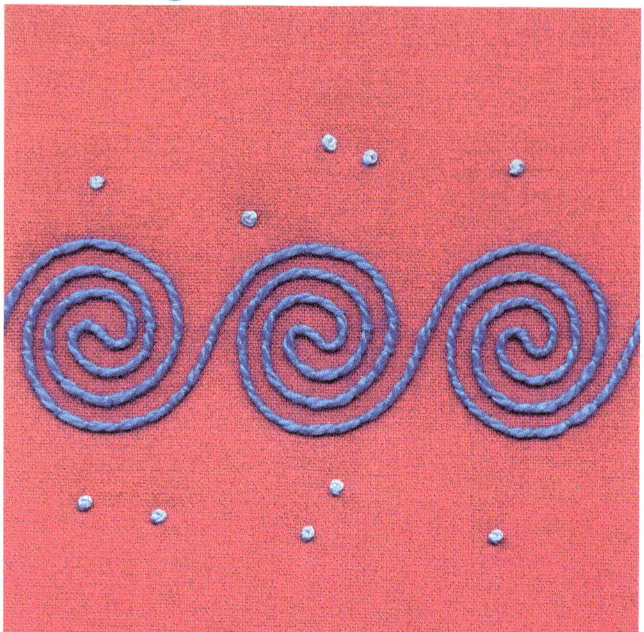

*Seaspray*

The spiral waves in this stylized design are worked with couched perlé cotton thread, creating a corded scroll. French knots are also included, representing seawater droplets splashing.

To work the design on a pink background as above, follow the instructions on this page. See the project idea on the next page to adapt the design for use as a repeating pattern along the band of a bath towel.

## The pattern

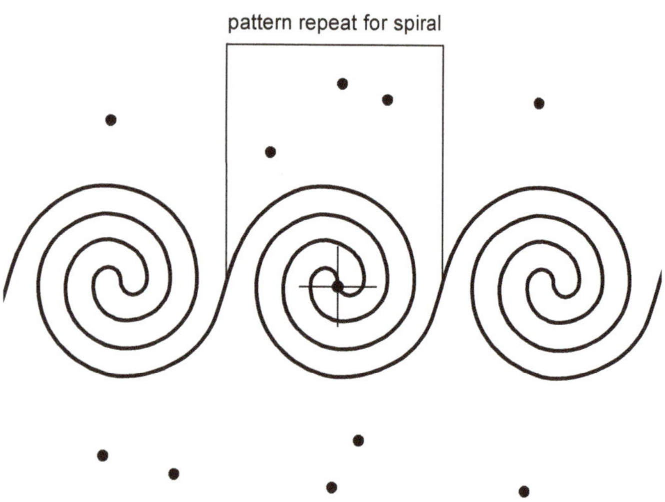


**Key:** Centre of design • French knot

## Shopping list

- Pink cotton fabric for background: 25cm (10") square
- Fabric or interfacing for backing: 25cm (10") square
- Stranded cotton thread:
  (A) dark aqua (B) medium aqua
- No. 5 perlé cotton thread:
  (C) dark aqua
- Tracing paper and other items for transferring the pattern onto the fabric

## Let's begin

Read page 15 for backing the fabric, and pages 22-25 for transferring the pattern onto the fabric, then select and use suitable methods for your fabric. For the pink fabric shown here, the pattern was transferred centrally onto the fabric by tracing with a water erasable fabric marker and then the backing fabric was tacked to the wrong side.

## Stitch!

For help, see pages 40-43 for straight stitch, 184-187 for French knot, and pages 202-205 for couching. To work three waves, 80cm (32") of perlé thread is sufficient length. When working the couching, attach the perlé cotton thread with small, closely worked straight stitches using the stranded cotton thread.

1 Starting at one end, work the waves in couching (1 strand C, attached with 1 strand A). It may be easier to stitch with a stabbing motion in order to work along this spiralling line rather than rotating the work. When couching closer to the centre of each spiral, work the couching stitches with smaller spaces between them (Diagram 1).

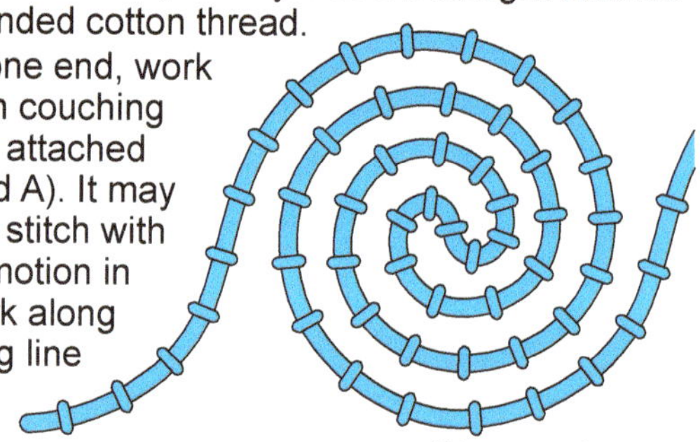

**Diagram 1**

2 Stitch each of the seawater droplets with a two wrap French knot (2 strands B).

## Let's finish

Take out the tacking. Rinse the work in cold water to remove the water erasable fabric marker. When partly dry, press or pin out the work. See page 36 for pressing and for pinning out.

## Hint

**Managing the laid thread**

If working more waves, wind the skein of thread that is to be laid into a ball first and then, without cutting any lengths, couch this thread straight from the ball.

# Seaspray Bath Towel

Add an artistic seaside element to a bath towel.

## The project

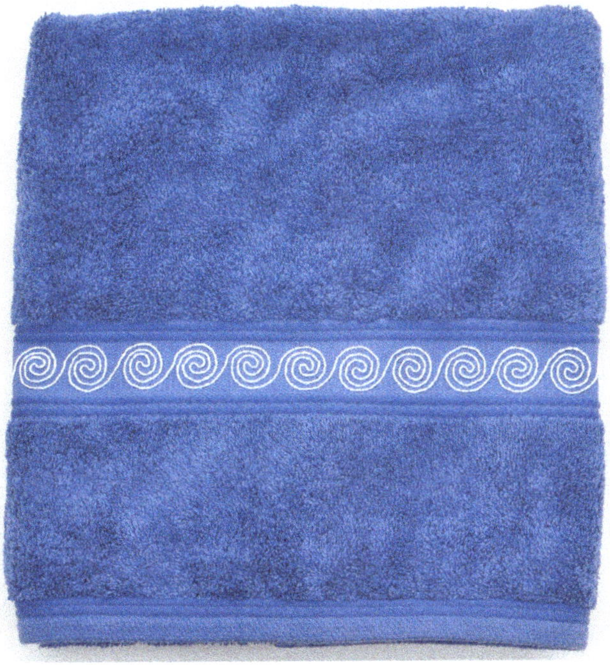

*Seaspray Bath Towel*

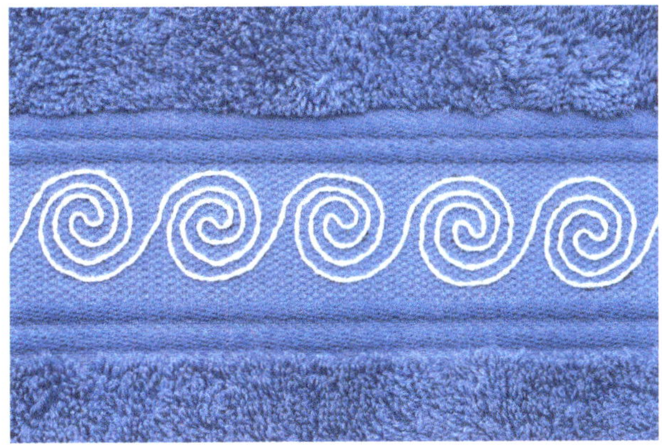

Detail of *Seaspray Bath Towel*

The spiral waves from the original design are worked entirely in white threads as a repeating scroll pattern along the band of a bath towel. The seawater droplets have been left out.

## Shopping list

- Blue bath towel with a plain band at least 3.5cm (1 3/8") in width
- Stranded cotton thread:
  (A) white
- No. 5 perlé cotton thread:
  (C) white
- Tracing paper, a fine permanent black pen, and other items for transferring the pattern onto the towel

## Let's begin

See the page opposite for the pattern.
Place the towel with the right side facing up. Transfer the pattern, without the seawater droplets, continuously along the band using the pierce and dot method with a fine permanent black pen. Repeat as many times as is necessary to cover the whole length of the band. See page 25 for transferring the pattern using the pierce and dot method.

## Stitch!

Wind the skein of perlé thread into a ball and then, without cutting any lengths, work the couched scroll design following **Step 1** of the stitch instructions on the page opposite.
It is important to weave in any thread ends securely and as neatly as possible along the back of the stitches on the wrong side. This will ensure that the stitching will not undo when the towel is frequently machine washed and that the border looks neat when it is occasionally viewed from the wrong side.

## Let's finish

Press the bath towel lightly from the wrong side. See page 36 for pressing.

# Golden Garden

The plants are shimmering in the late afternoon sunlight.

## The design

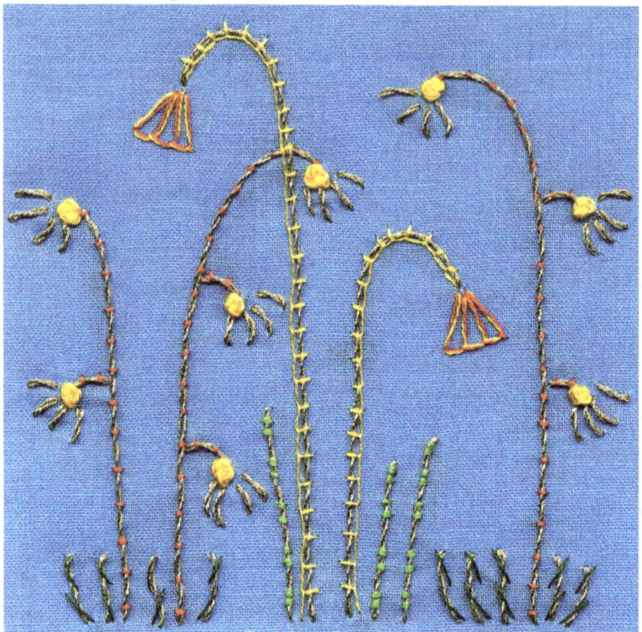

*Golden Garden*

The stems and leaves in *Golden Garden* are worked in metallic thread couched with stranded cotton thread using a variety of stitches. The flowers are added in straight stitch, blanket stitch and French knots. Follow the instructions on this page to work the design as shown here. See the project idea on the following page to feature the design on the front of an album.

## The pattern

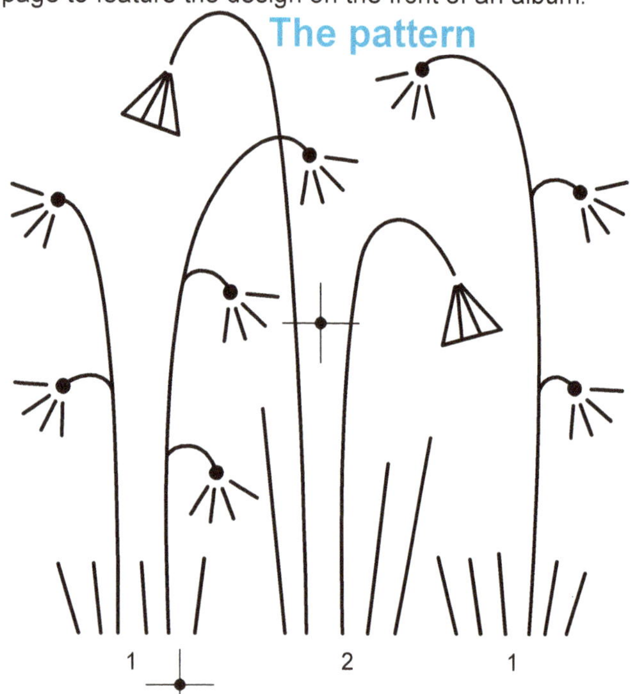


## Shopping list

- Aqua cotton fabric for background: 25cm (10") square
- Fabric or interfacing for backing: 25cm (10") square
- Stranded cotton thread: (A) dark green (B) light green (C) medium yellow (D) medium orange
- No. 5 perlé cotton thread: (E) medium yellow
- No. 5 perlé metallic thread: (F) gold
- Tracing paper and other items for transferring the pattern onto the fabric

## Let's begin

Read page 15 for backing the fabric, and pages 22-25 for transferring the pattern onto the fabric, then select and use suitable methods for your fabric. For the aqua fabric shown here, the pattern was transferred centrally onto the fabric by tracing with a water erasable fabric marker and then the backing fabric was tacked to the wrong side.

## Stitch!

For help, see pages 40-43 for straight stitch, 130-133 for blanket stitch, 184-187 for French knot, and pages 202-205 for couching, including couching with slanted stitches and couching with blanket stitch.

**Flower 1** Work the stem and flower stems in couching using small straight stitches (8 ply F, attached with 1 strand D), weaving the gold thread on the back of each plant without ending off. Add four straight stitches for the petals of each flower (8 ply F). Work the leaves in couching using slanted straight stitches (8 ply F, attached with 1 strand A). Add a two wrap French knot at each marked dot, forming the base of each flower (1 strand E).

**Flower 2** Beginning at the top, work each stem in couching using blanket stitch (8 ply F, attached with 1 strand C), working the blanket stitch with the loops of the stitches below the curve of the stem (Diagram 1). Work each leaf in couching using straight stitches worked in pairs (8 ply F, attached with 2 strands B). Begin each flower with a single straight stitch on the left (1 strand C mixed in the needle with 1 strand D), worked from A towards the stem. Emerge at A (Diagram 2) and work three blanket stitches. Complete the last stitch with a tiny anchor.

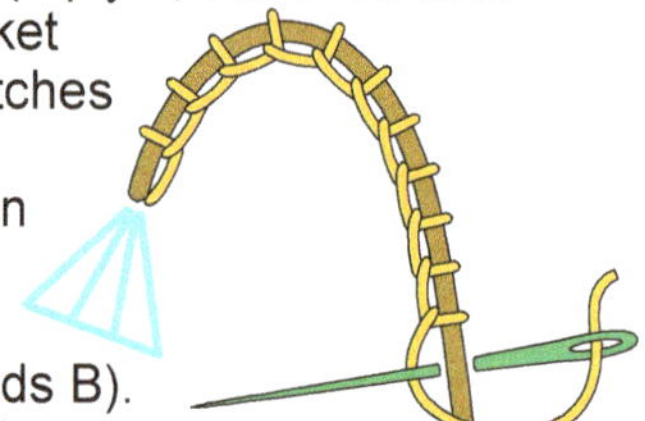

Diagram 1

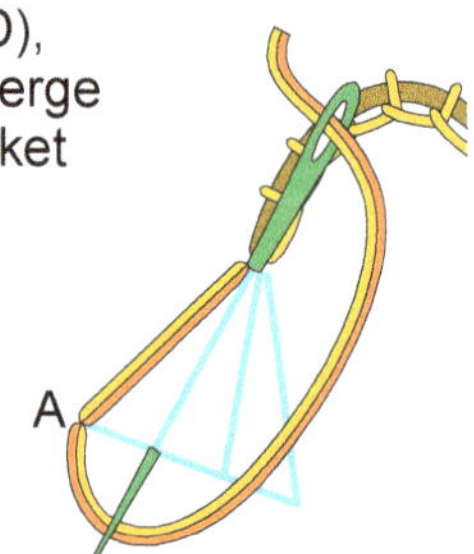


Diagram 2

## Let's finish

Take out the tacking. Rinse the work in cold water to remove the fabric marker. When partly dry, press or pin out the work. See page 36 for pressing and for pinning out.

# Golden Garden Album Cover

Preserve memories forever in this album.

## The project

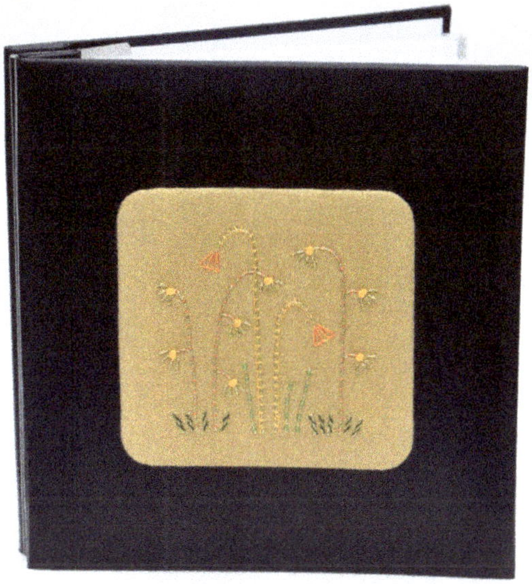

***Golden Garden Album Cover***

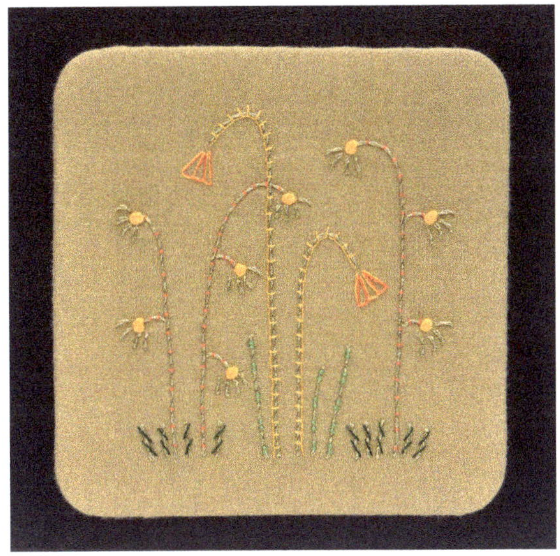

**Detail of**
***Golden Garden Album Cover***

For this project, *Golden Garden* is worked in the original thread colours on an alternative coloured background. The work is then laced over cardboard and attached to the front cover of an album.
This album is 21cm x 20cm wide (8 1/2" x 8") in size.

## Shopping list

- Black album
- Gold fabric for background: 25cm (10") square
- Fabric or interfacing for backing: 25cm (10") square
- Threads as listed for the original design on the page opposite
- Machine sewing thread for gathering
- Strong thread for lacing
- Tracing paper and other items for transferring the pattern onto the fabric
- Thin wadding: 11.5cm (4 1/2") square
- White cardboard: 11.5cm (4 1/2") square
- Archival double-sided sticky tape or glue

## Let's begin

See the page opposite for the pattern.
Transfer the pattern centrally onto the gold fabric by tracing with a water erasable fabric marker or by using transfer paper. See pages 22-25 for transferring the pattern onto the fabric. Tack the backing to the wrong side of the fabric. See page 15 for backing the fabric.

## Stitch!

Work the design following the stitch instructions on the page opposite.

## Let's finish

Rinse the work in cold water to remove the pattern markings. When partly dry, press or pin out the work. See page 36 for pressing and for pinning out.
Trim the corners of the gold fabric and the backing, and also the corners of the cardboard and the wadding, so that they are rounded.
Using machine sewing thread, and leaving both ends of the thread dangling, work a row of running stitch around the edge of the backing and the fabric together. See pages 58-61 for running stitch. Take out remaining tacking. Place the wadding and then the cardboard centrally onto the wrong side of the stitched work (Diagram 1). Pull the two thread ends to gather the fabric over the padded cardboard, then tie them in a knot. Trim the threads. Lace the work tightly. As a guide, see page 37 for lacing. Using archival double-sided sticky tape or glue, adhere the laced side of the work centrally onto the album front.

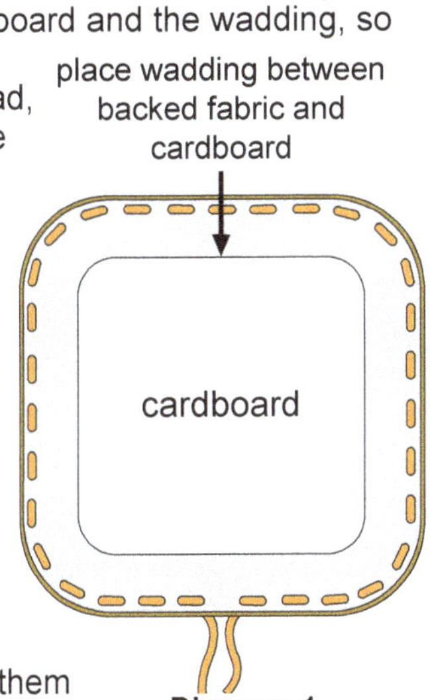


**Diagram 1**

## Hint

**Use other designs on an album cover**
Many of the designs in this book would be excellent featured on the front of an album.

# Appliqué

Appliqué is a process by which separate pieces of fabric, cut to the shapes in the design, are attached onto a background fabric. This process is easy to work and areas are filled quickly with the fabric shapes. Appliqué is an effective way of adding colour, surface texture, and patterning. Very different results can be created with the use of either matching or contrasting fabrics and threads.

There are many methods for working appliqué. Two easy methods are featured in this book.

In the first, felt fabric shapes are attached to the background fabric with stitches.

In the second, fabric shapes are fused to the background fabric with fusible webbing, also called adhesive webbing, and then the edges are covered with stitches. Other stitched details may also be added within the fabric shape.

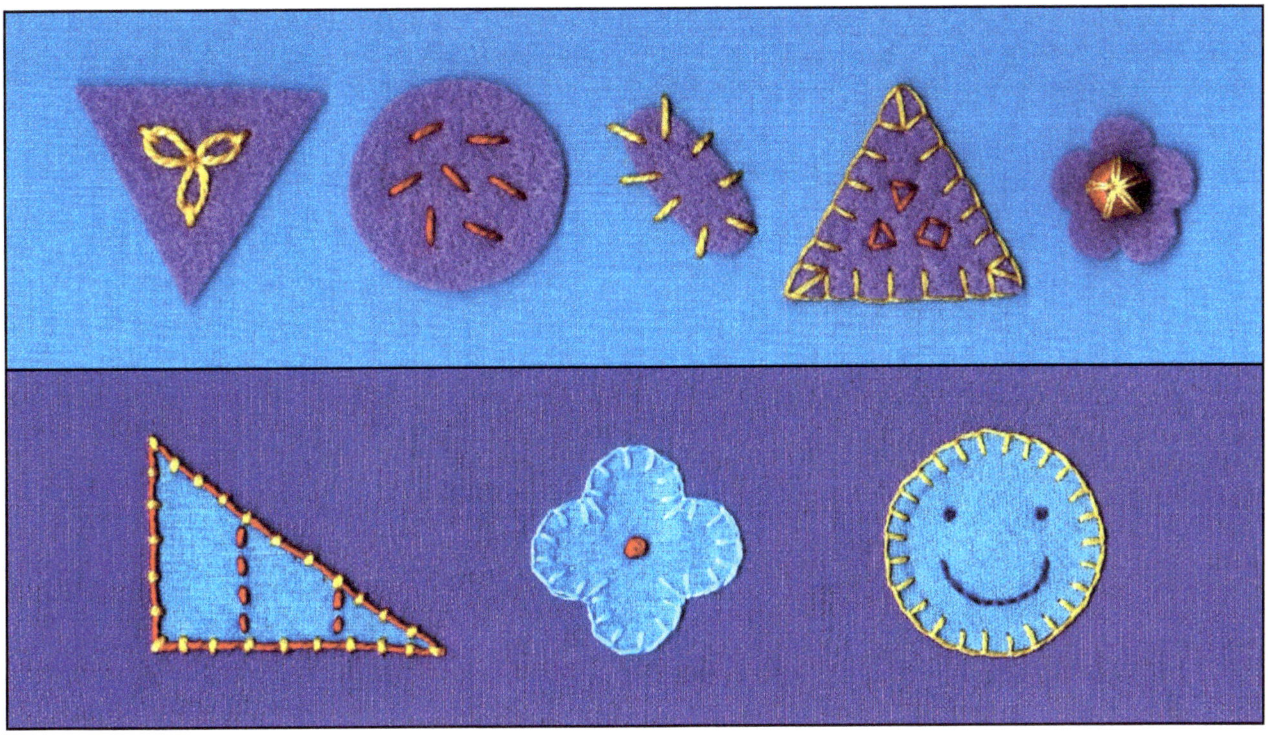

## Appliqué sampler

**Felt shapes attached with stitches:**

Felt attached with detached chain stitches

Felt attached with isolated back stitches

Felt attached with straight stitches

Felt attached with blanket stitch and back stitch shapes

Felt attached with beading

**Fabric shapes attached by fusing and then with stitches:**

Fabric attached by fusing, and then with couching and running stitch

Fabric attached by fusing, and then with blanket stitch and French knot

Fabric attached by fusing, and then with blanket stitch, French knot, and back stitch

# Appliqué

## Hints

### Appliqué Method 1: Felt shape attached with stitches

With this method, a felt shape can be attached to the background fabric simply with the stitches worked within the shape, leaving the cut edges of the felt loose. Alternatively, stitches can be worked over the cut edges to hold the felt in place.

To prepare, some designs may require pattern marks to be transferred onto the background fabric to indicate the placement of the appliqué shapes. See pages 22-25 for transferring the pattern onto the fabric.

## Appliqué: right-handed or left-handed

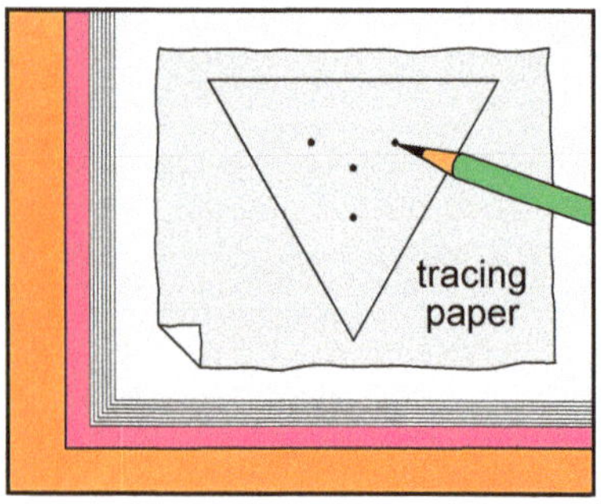


**Appliqué Method 1**
**1** Trace the pattern outline and any internal markings onto tracing paper using an HB pencil.

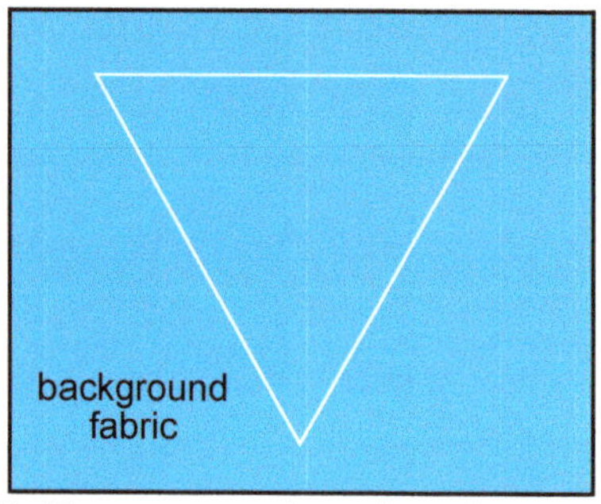


**2** If necessary, transfer relevant pattern marks onto the background fabric to indicate the placement of the appliqué shape.

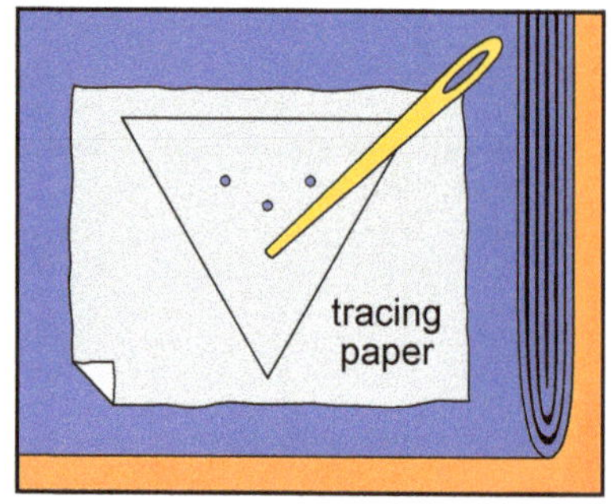


**3** Place the traced pattern over a pad of folded fabric. Using a large needle, pierce holes through the tracing at any internal markings.

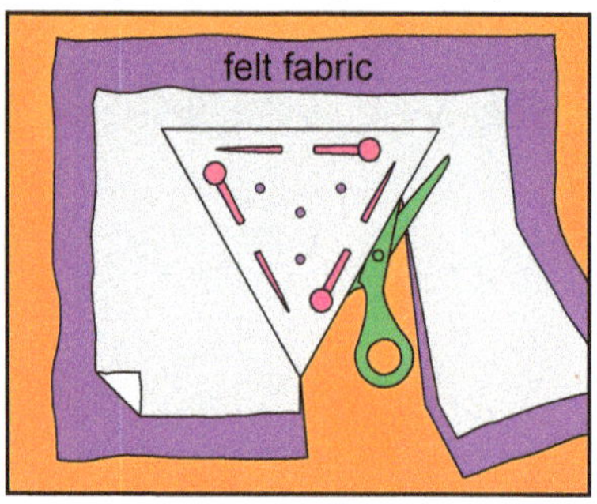


**4** Pin the tracing to the felt. Cut out the shape along the pattern outline.

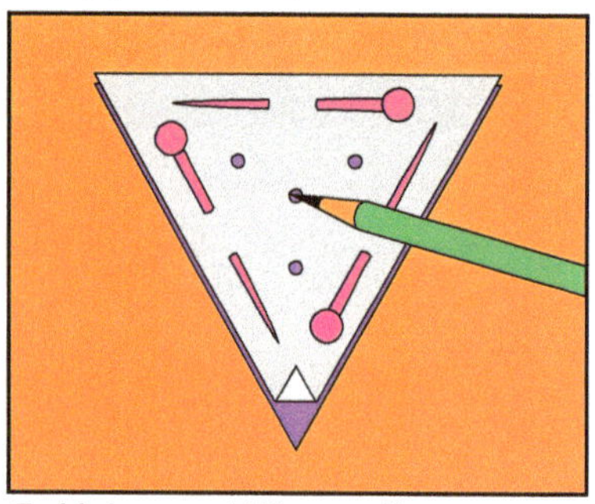

**5** Using an HB pencil or a chalk-based pencil, transfer internal pattern markings onto felt by marking a dot through each pierced hole.

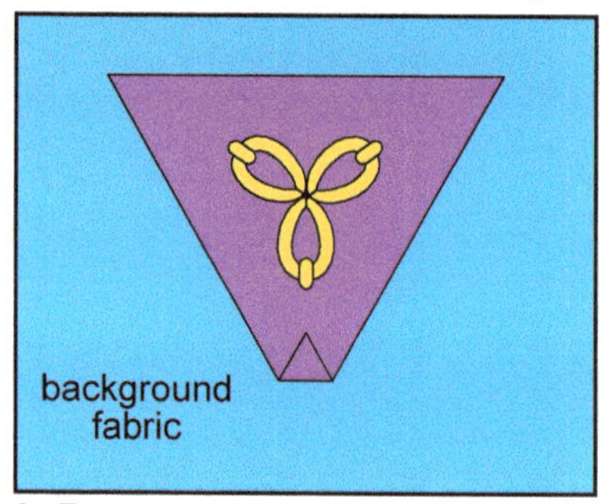


**6** Remove tracing. Pin and tack felt onto background fabric, matching any placement marks. Work decorative stitches through both layers. Remove tacking.

## Hints

**Appliqué Method 2: Fabric shape attached by fusing and then with stitches**

With this method, the fabric shape is fused, or glued, onto the background fabric using paper-backed fusible webbing, also called adhesive webbing. The cut edge of the shape is covered with stitching. Additional stitching can be worked within the shape. The fusible webbing holds the shape securely in place, and it helps to reduce fraying of the cut fabric edge. If the project is to be laundered, wash both the background fabric and the fabrics to be used for the shapes before beginning, as some fabrics shrink more than others.

To prepare, some designs may require pattern marks to be transferred onto the background fabric to indicate the placement of the appliqué shapes. See pages 22-25 for transferring the pattern onto the fabric.

# Appliqué: right-handed or left-handed

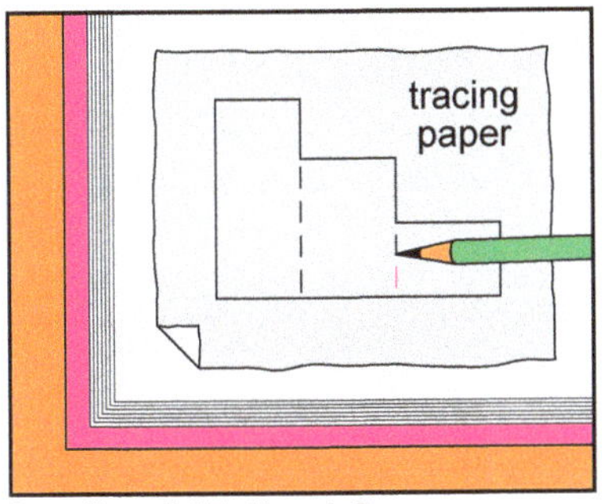


**Appliqué Method 2**

**1** Trace the pattern outline and any internal markings onto tracing paper using an HB pencil.

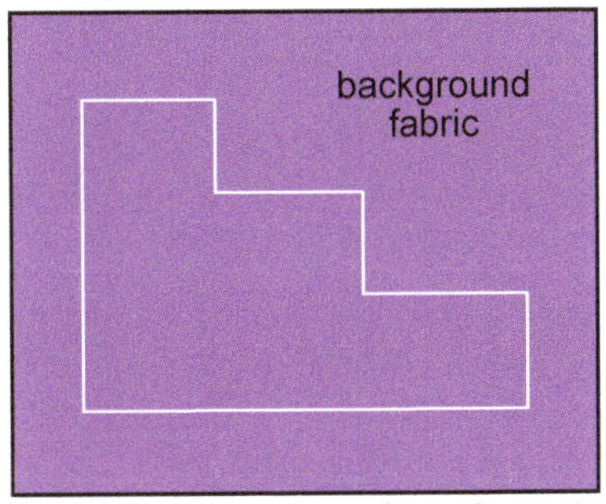


**2** If necessary, transfer relevant pattern marks onto the background fabric to indicate the placement of the appliqué shape.

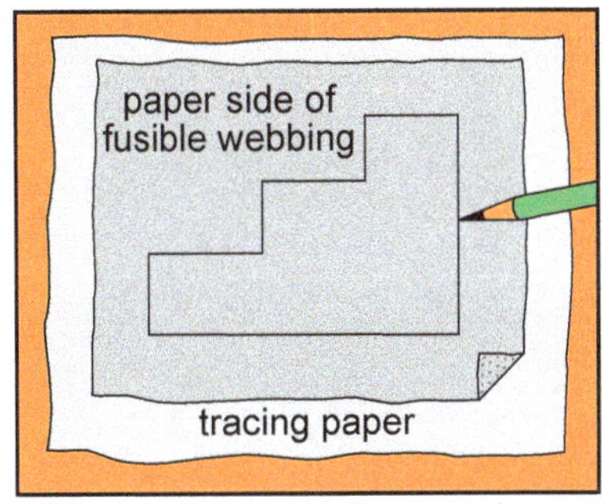


**3** Flip tracing over. Trace mirrored shape onto paper side of fusible webbing. Omit internal pattern markings.

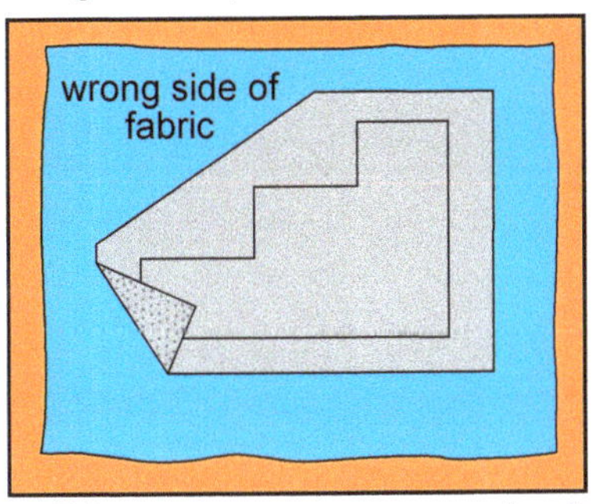


**4** Trim away excess paper-backed webbing. Place the glue side of the paper onto the wrong side of the appliqué fabric.

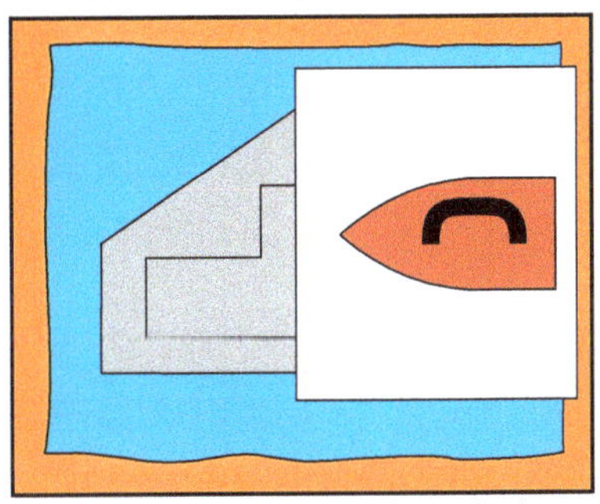

**5** Cover with a pressing cloth and fuse the webbing onto the wrong side of the fabric with a hot iron.

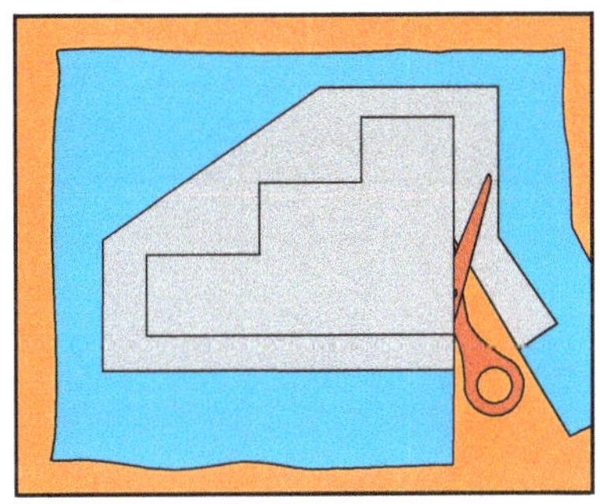

**6** Cut out the shape along the marked pattern line.

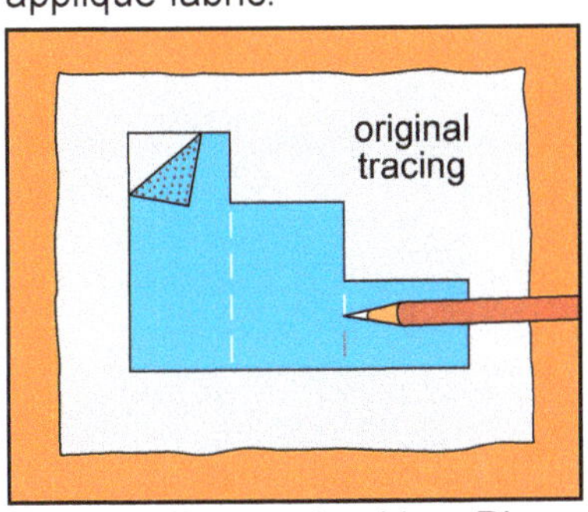


**7** Peel off paper backing. Place fabric shape, glue side down, over original tracing and transfer any internal markings onto fabric using a chalk-based pencil.

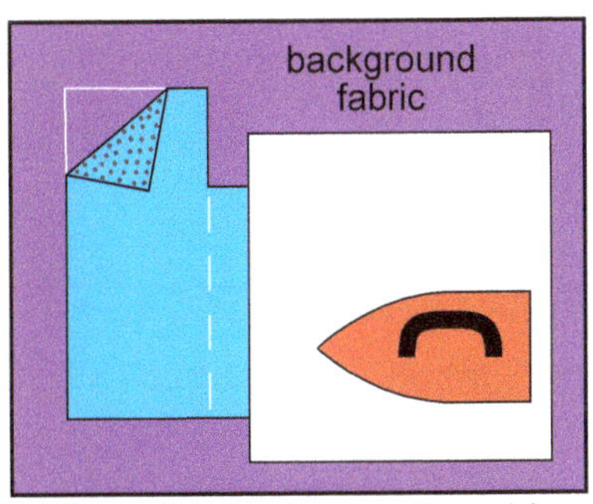


**8** Place fabric shape, glue side down, onto background fabric, matching any placement marks. Cover with pressing cloth and fuse fabric shape on with a hot iron.

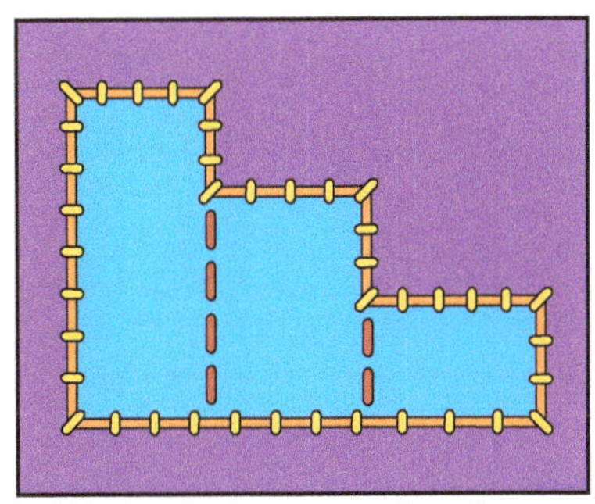

**9** Work stitches covering the raw edges, then work any internal stitches. This example shows couching covering the edges and running stitch worked internally.

# Appliqué

# Designs and project ideas

## The designs

Georgina Giraffe

Liquorice Allsorts

Lightning and Thunder

Orange Essence

Sail Away

Terracotta Garden

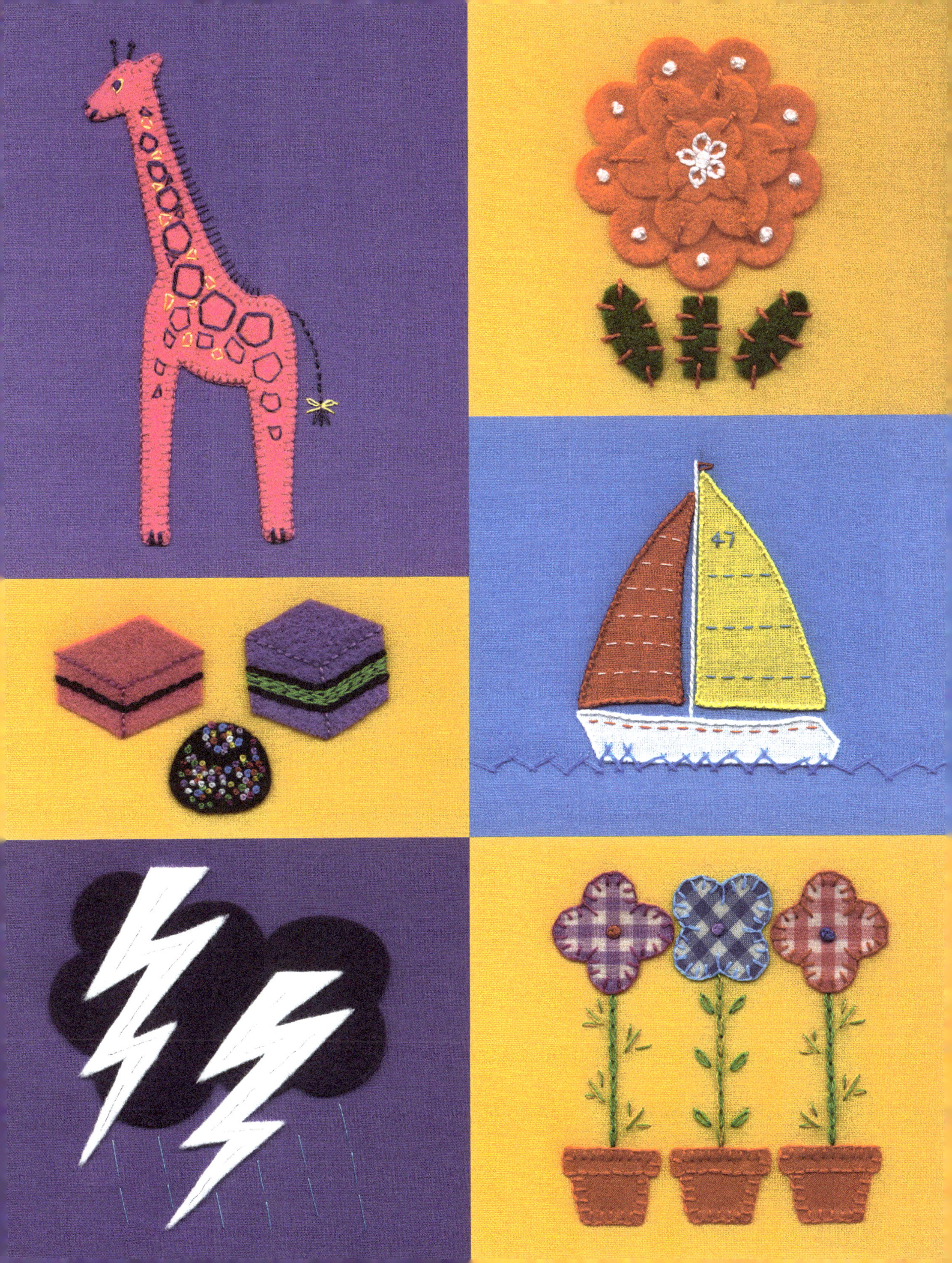
47

# Georgina Giraffe

Look at my patchwork coat and my pretty yellow bow!

## The design

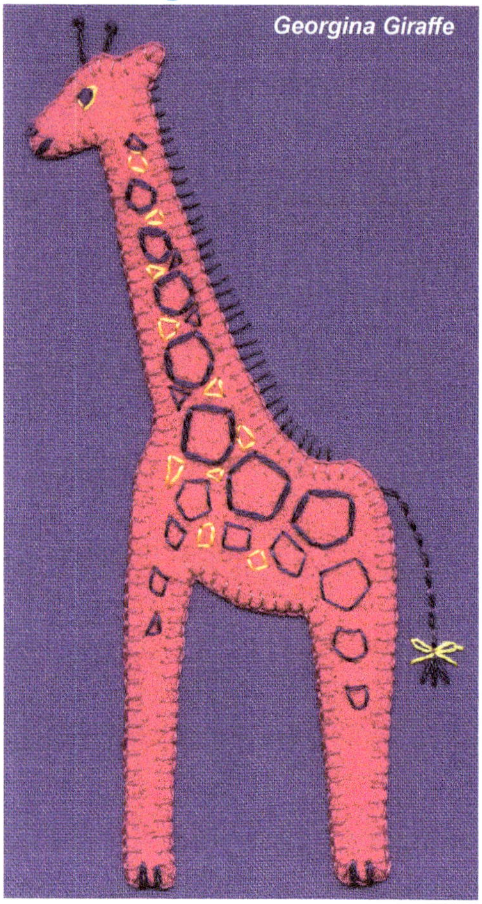


This appliqué design features felt attached to the fabric with blanket stitch and other stitches. To work *Georgina Giraffe* as above, use the instructions on this page. To adapt the design for a cushion, see the next page.

## Shopping list

- Violet cotton fabric for background: 25cm (10") square
- Iron-on interfacing for backing: 25cm (10") square
- Pink felt fabric: 14cm x 7cm wide (5 1/2" x 2 3/4")
- Stranded cotton thread:
  (A) dark violet (B) light yellow (C) medium magenta
- Tracing paper for transferring the pattern to the fabric

## Let's begin

See the pattern above right. Read page 15 for backing the fabric, and pages 22-25 for transferring the pattern, then select and use suitable methods for your fabric. For the violet fabric shown here, the pattern for the giraffe was transferred onto the fabric by tracing with an HB pencil and then the backing was attached to the wrong side. Referring to pages 220-223 for appliqué and following steps 3-5 of Method 1, cut out the giraffe shape from the felt and mark the eye and nostril. Remove the tracing.

## The pattern

**Key:** **Centre of design** — **Pistil stitch** — **Placement of straight stitches** — **French knot**

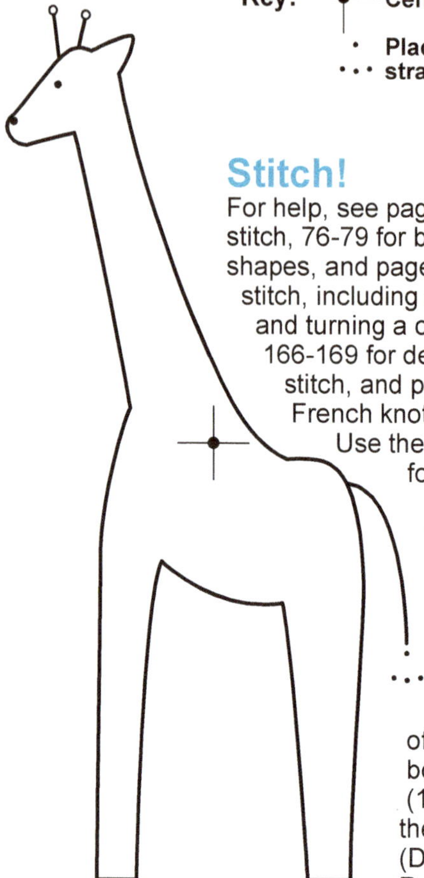

## Stitch!

For help, see pages 40-43 for straight stitch, 76-79 for back stitch, including shapes, and pages 130-133 for blanket stitch, including completing a shape and turning a corner. See pages 166-169 for detached chain stitch, and pages 184-187 for French knot and pistil stitch. Use the photo as a guide for working the giraffe's details.

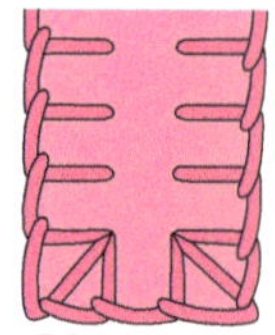

**Diagram 1**

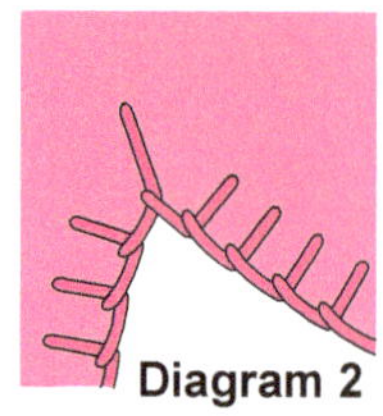

**Diagram 2**

1 Pin and tack the felt shape onto the background fabric. Work blanket stitches around the edge of the giraffe through both felt and fabric (1 strand C). Work the corners as shown (Diagrams 1 and 2). Remove the tacking.

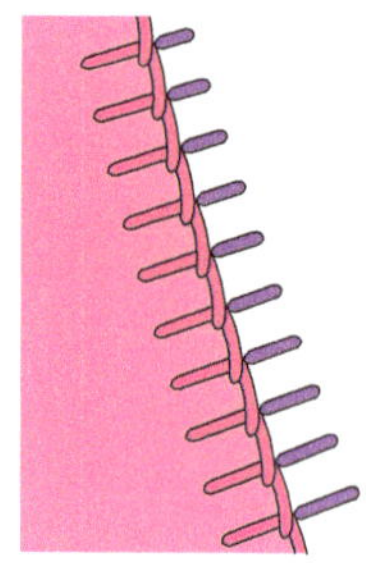

**Diagram 3**

2 Working on the fabric only, stitch the mane with straight stitch (1 strand A), aligning the straight stitches with the previously worked blanket stitches (Diagram 3).

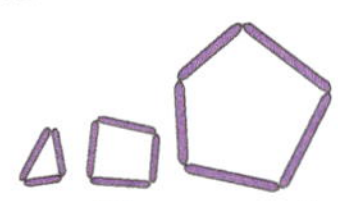

**Diagram 4**

3 Stitch the tail in back stitch, adding three straight stitches on the end, then add the horns, each with a two wrap pistil stitch (2 strands A). Add the nostril with a one wrap French knot, then work the mouth and toes in straight stitch. Add the pupil with a two wrap French knot (3 strands A).

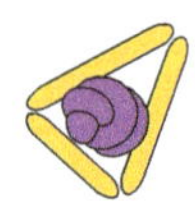

**Diagram 5**

4 Using three, four or five stitches (Diagram 4), work dark violet spots on the body in back stitch (2 strands A for large spots, 1 strand A for small).

5 Using three or four back stitches, stitch yellow spots (1 strand B), then complete the eye with three back stitches worked around the French knot (Diagram 5). Add the bow on the tail (1 strand B) with detached chain stitch and straight stitch (Diagram 6).

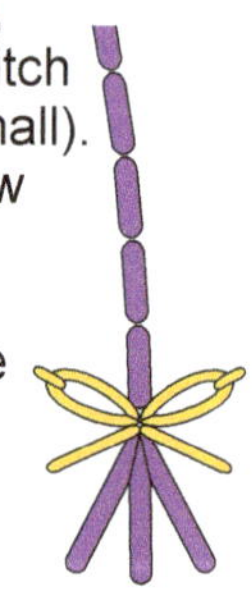

**Diagram 6**

## Let's finish

Press the background fabric only. See page 36 for pressing.

# Georgina Giraffe Cushion Cover

Relax with these three friendly giraffes.

## The project

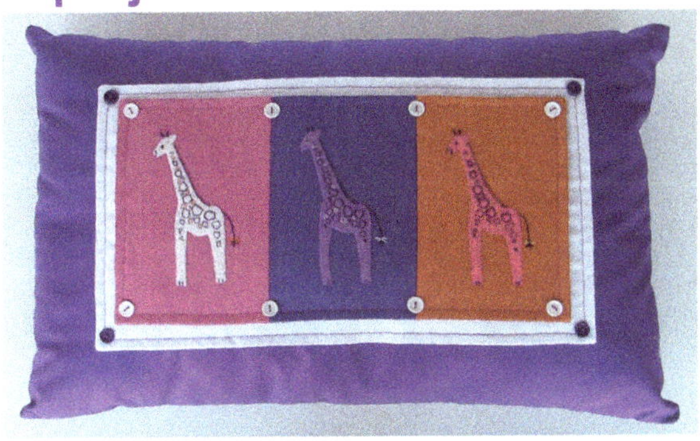

***Georgina Giraffe Cushion Cover***

This project features three giraffes worked on separate fabric pieces that are joined into a multi-coloured patch. A white patch is attached behind it and both are then stitched onto a purchased cushion cover. Buttons are attached to the patches. The size of this cushion is 34cm x 52cm wide (13 1/2" x 20 1/2"). As buttons are included, it is unsafe for babies or very small children.

## Shopping list

- Violet rectangular cushion cover and insert
- Pink, violet, and orange fabrics for the sections of the multi-coloured patch: one piece of each colour 19cm x 13cm wide (7 1/2" x 5")
- Violet fabric for lining the multi-coloured patch: one piece 19cm x 35cm wide (7 1/2" x 13 1/2")
- White cotton fabric for the white patch: two pieces 22cm x 38cm wide (9" x 15")
- Lightweight iron-on interfacing for backing the patches: three pieces 19cm x 13cm wide (7 1/2" x 5"), and one piece 22cm x 38cm wide (9" x 15")
- Machine sewing thread: violet, white, and magenta
- 8 white buttons and 4 violet buttons
- Tracing paper and other items for transferring the pattern onto the fabric
- Felt fabric and threads for the multi-coloured patch as follows:

***Pink section***

- White felt fabric for the appliqué shape: 14cm x 7cm wide (5 1/2" x 2 3/4")
- Stranded cotton thread: (A) dark violet (B) medium orange (C) white

***Violet section***

- Medium violet felt fabric for the appliqué shape: 14cm x 7cm wide (5 1/2" x 2 3/4")
- Stranded cotton thread: (A) dark violet (B) white (C) medium violet

***Orange section***

- Pink felt fabric for the appliqué shape: 14cm x 7cm wide (5 1/2" x 2 3/4")
- Stranded cotton thread: (A) dark violet (B) light yellow (C) medium magenta

## Let's begin

Follow the Let's begin instructions on the previous page to prepare the three background fabrics and the three felt shapes.

## Stitch!

Work the three giraffes following steps 1-5 of the stitch instructions for the original design on the page opposite, working the orange section with the original felt and thread colours, and the pink and violet sections with the alternative colours.

## Let's finish

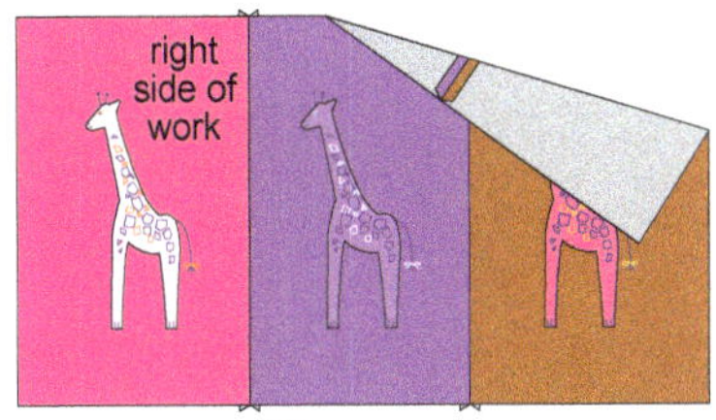


**Diagram 1**

Press the three stitched sections. Using violet machine sewing thread and 1cm (3/8") seam allowances, stitch the three sections together to make a multi-coloured patch. Press the seam allowances open (Diagram 1).

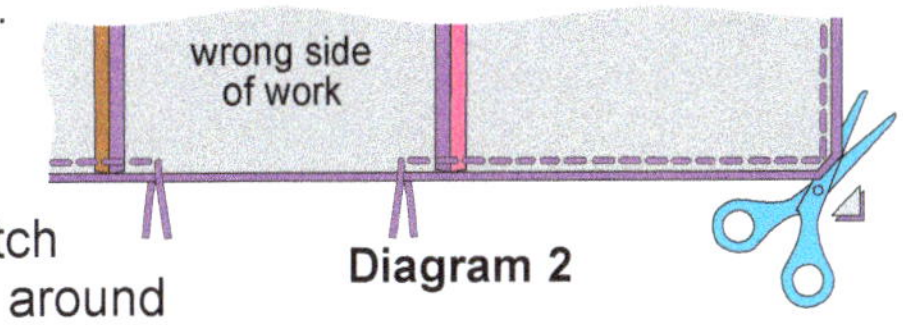


**Diagram 2**

With right sides together, pin and stitch the multi-coloured patch to the violet lining around the edge, leaving an 8cm (3") opening in the lower side. Trim the seam allowances and cut away the excess fabric at the corners (Diagram 2). Turn the patch to the right side and press. Hand stitch the opening closed.

Attach the remaining piece of interfacing onto one piece of the white fabric, then make up the white patch.

With the giraffes facing up, place the multi-coloured patch centrally over the white patch and tack the patches together. Using magenta sewing thread, and stitching through both patches, machine stitch around the multi-coloured patch 1cm (3/8") in from its edges.

Take out the tacking.

Remove the cushion insert. Place the joined patches centrally onto the front of the cushion cover and tack in place. With magenta sewing thread, attach the white patch to the cushion cover by machine stitching 1cm (3/8") in from its edges (see Diagram 3).

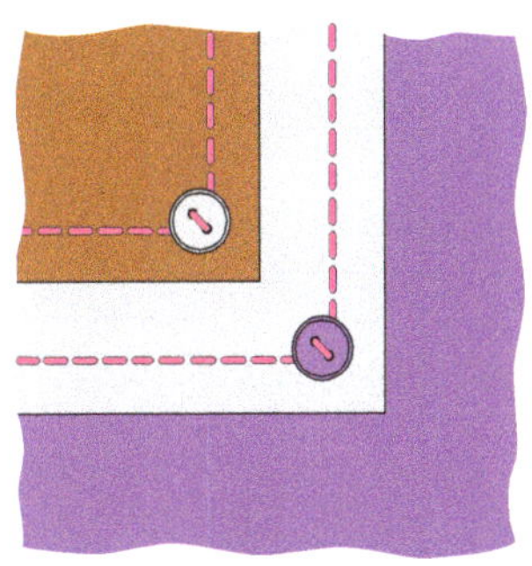

**Diagram 3**

Take out the tacking. Using magenta sewing thread, attach the buttons to the patches (Diagram 3).

Press, avoiding the buttons.

Place the cushion insert back inside the cover.

# Orange Essence

Orange. What a lovely citrus tang!

## The design

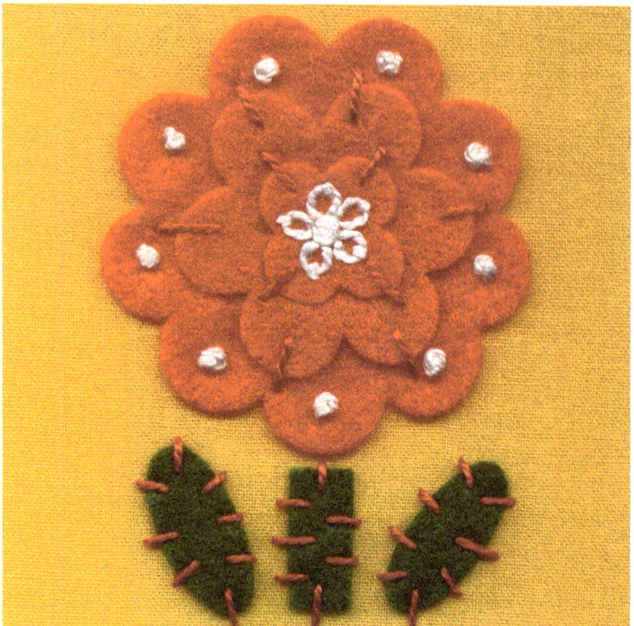

*Orange Essence*

*Orange Essence* is created using appliqué. The stem and leaves, and the three-layered flower, are cut from felt and attached onto the background fabric using straight stitch, detached chain stitch, and French knot. Follow the instructions here to work the design as above. To adapt elements of *Orange Essence* for decorations on organza bags, see the page opposite.

## The pattern

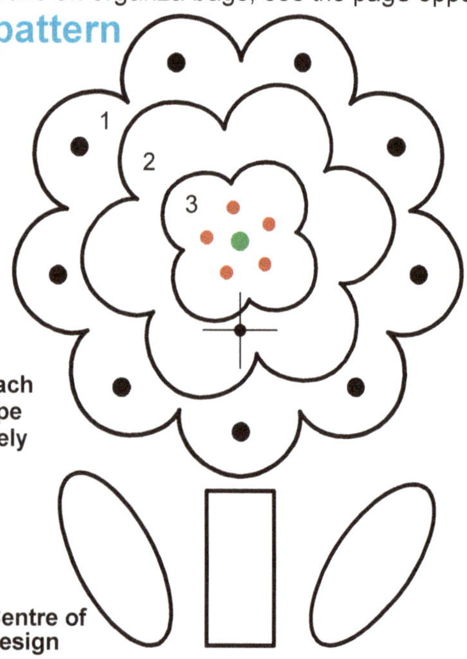


**Note: Trace each felt shape separately**

**Key:**

- **Centre of design**
- **French knot**
- **Centre of felt flower shapes**
- **Detached chain stitch petal**

## Shopping list

- Yellow cotton fabric for background: 25cm (10") square
- Fabric or interfacing for backing: 25cm (10") square
- Green felt fabric for the stem and leaf shapes: 5cm x 8cm wide (2" x 3")
- Orange felt fabric for the flower shapes: 8cm x 20cm wide (3" x 8")
- No. 5 perlé cotton thread: (A) medium orange (B) white
- Tracing paper and other items for transferring the pattern onto the fabric

## Let's begin

For this design, the pattern is not transferred onto the background fabric.

Attach the backing fabric to the wrong side of the yellow background fabric. See page 15 for backing the fabric. Referring to pages 220-223 for appliqué and following steps 1 and 3-5 of Method 1, prepare and cut out the shapes for the stem, leaves, and the three layers of the flower from the green and orange felt fabrics. When following step 5, mark each layer of the flower with the central dot. On layer 1 mark the placement of the French knot on each scallop, and on layer 3 the five dots surrounding the centre. Remove the tracings. Alternatively, the shapes can all be cut out and marked freehand, simply using the pattern as a visual guide.

## Stitch!

For help, see pages 40-43 for straight stitch, 166-169 for detached chain stitch, and pages 184-187 for French knot. Use the photo as a guide when placing the felt shapes. Complete the stitching on each shape before pinning and working the next shape. When stitching through layers of felt, do not pull the thread too tightly or the stitches may sink into the felt.

1. Pin the stem onto the yellow background fabric.
2. Attach the stem with straight stitches (1 strand A). Remove the pins. Attach the leaves in the same way.
3. Pin layer 1 of the flower in position above the stem.
4. At each dot that is marked on layer 1, work a two wrap French knot (2 strands B). Remove pins.
5. Bring needle and thread up through centre of layer 1 (2 strands B). Take the needle and thread through the centre of layers 2 and 3 (Diagram 1). Position shapes.
6. Work a two wrap French knot through all layers. Around the central French knot, work the white petals in detached chain stitch (1 strand B).
7. Work a straight stitch over the end of each scallop of layer 3, then of layer 2 (1 strand A).

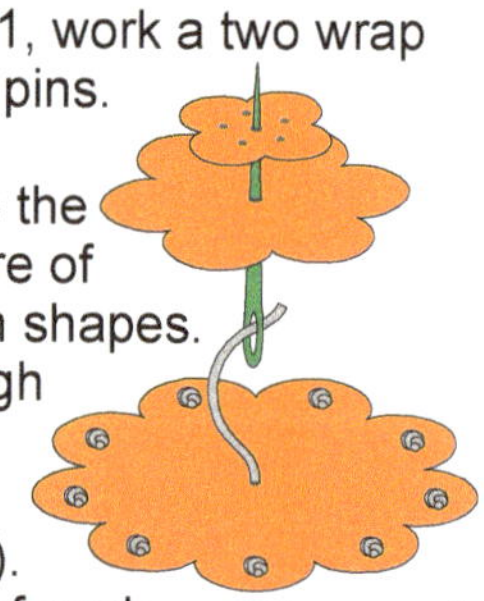

**Diagram 1**

## Let's finish

Take out tacking. Press the background fabric only. See page 36 for pressing.

# Orange Essence Gift Bags

Appliqué brightly coloured flowers onto these organza bags.

## The project

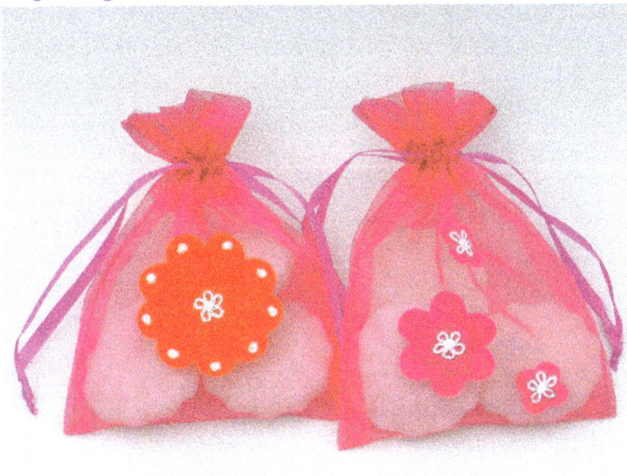

*Orange Essence Gift Bags*

The three-layered felt flower from *Orange Essence* is created and then attached to the first purchased organza bag. Three felt flowers based on the design are created and then attached to the other purchased organza bag. These bags are filled with soaps.

## Shopping list

***Bag with orange flower***

- Pink organza bag: approximately 17cm x 12cm wide (6 3/4" x 4 3/4")
- Orange felt fabric for the flower shapes: 8cm x 20cm (3" x 8")
- Threads as listed for the original design opposite
- Machine sewing thread: orange
- Tracing paper

***Bag with pink flowers***

- Pink organza bag: approximately 17cm x 12cm wide (6 3/4" x 4 3/4")
- Pink felt fabric for the flower shapes: 6cm x 15cm (2 1/2" x 6")
- No. 5 perlé cotton thread: (B) white
- Machine sewing thread: pink
- Tracing paper

## Let's begin

See the page opposite for the pattern. Referring to pages 220-223 for appliqué and following steps 1 and 3-5 of Method 1, prepare and cut out the felt shapes as follows below. Alternatively, the shapes can all be cut out and marked freehand.

***Bag with orange flower***

Cut out the three layers of the flower from the orange felt. When following step 5, mark each layer with the central dot. On layer 1 mark the placement of the French knot on each scallop, and on layer 3 the five dots surrounding the centre. Remove the tracings.

***Bag with pink flowers***

Cut out one shape using the pattern for layer 2 and three shapes using the pattern for layer 3 from the pink felt. When following step 5, mark all the shapes with the central dot and the three small shapes with the five dots surrounding the centre. Remove the tracings.

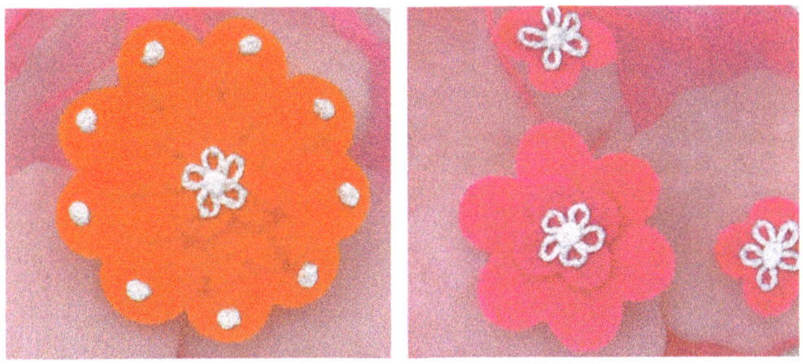

**Details of *Orange Essence Gift Bags***

## Stitch!

***Bag with orange flower*** Noting that for this project the orange flower is first worked without any background fabric, stitch the flower following steps 4-7 of the stitch instructions on the previous page.

***Bag with pink flowers*** Noting that these flowers are first created without any background fabric, stitch the flowers as follows below:

***Large two-layered flower*** Secure the thread (2 strands B) on the wrong side of layer 2 and then bring the needle and thread through the centre of layers 2 and 3 (Diagram 1). Position the shapes. Work a two wrap French knot through both layers and work petals of the flower following step 6 of the stitch instructions opposite.

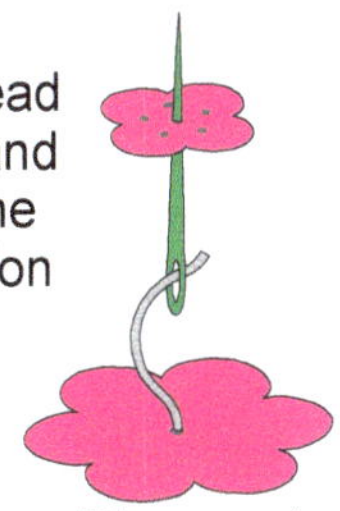

**Diagram 1**

***Small single-layered flowers*** For each, through layer 3 only, work a two wrap French knot at the centre (2 strands B) and work petals of the flower following step 6 of the stitch instructions opposite.

## Let's finish

***Bag with orange flower*** Using the photo as a guide for positioning the flower onto the bag, pin the flower onto the front. Turn the bag inside out. Using the orange machine sewing thread, attach the flower to the bag by working small stitches through the organza and the back of the stitched flower. Turn the bag through to the right side and remove the pins.

***Bag with pink flowers*** Using the photo as a guide for positioning the flowers onto the bag, pin the flowers onto the front. Turn the bag inside out. Using the pink machine sewing thread, attach the flowers to the bag by working small stitches through the organza and the back of the stitched flowers. Turn the bag through to the right side and remove the pins.

## Hint

**Not recommended to press organza bags**

As some organza fabrics will melt if pressed, even with the iron set to a low temperature, it is not recommended to press these gift bags.

# Liquorice Allsorts

Yummy! Let's have some!

## The design

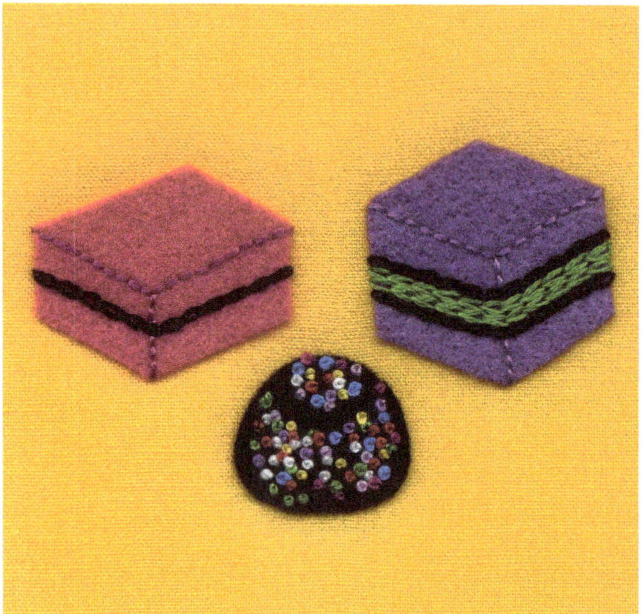

*Liquorice Allsorts*

This design uses the technique of appliqué. Felt fabric shapes are attached onto the background fabric using back stitch, chain stitch, and French knot. The outer edges of the felt shapes remain free.
Use the instructions on this page to work the design exactly as shown here on a yellow background. To use the design on a project, see the idea on the next page where many liquorice allsorts are featured on a border decorating a scrapbooking page.

## The pattern

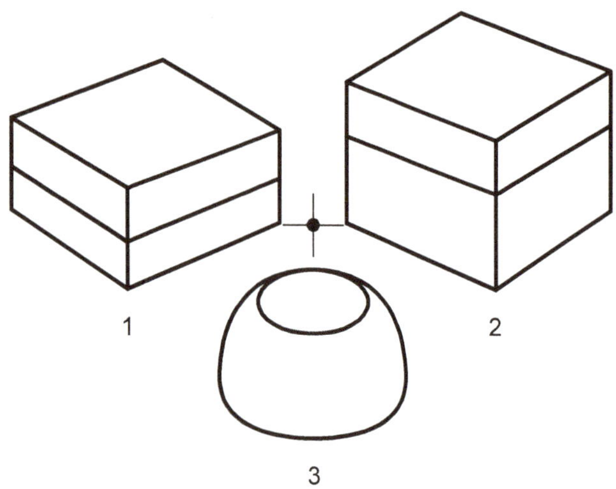


**Key:** — **Centre of design**

## Shopping list

- Yellow cotton fabric for background: 25cm (10") square
- Fabric or interfacing for backing: 25cm (10") square
- Pink, violet, and black felt fabric for appliqué shapes: 5cm (2") square of each colour
- Stranded cotton thread:
  (A) black (B) medium violet (C) light violet
  (D) dark aqua (E) light green (F) light yellow
  (G) medium red (H) medium magenta (I) white
- Tracing paper and other items for preparing the felt shapes

## Let's begin

In this design the pattern is not transferred onto the background fabric.
Attach the backing fabric to the wrong side of the yellow background fabric. See page 15 for backing the fabric.
Referring to pages 220-223 for appliqué and following steps 1 and 3-5 of Method 1, prepare and cut out the shapes for the allsorts from the pink, violet, and black felt fabric and transfer the internal pattern lines with dots. Remove the tracing paper and join the dots to complete the pattern lines on the felt.

## Stitch!

For help, see pages 76-79 for back stitch, 166-169 for chain stitch, and pages 184-187 for French knot.
Refer to the photo as a guide when placing the felt shapes. Work the stitches by stabbing through all the layers.

**Allsort 1** Pin and tack the pink shape onto the yellow fabric. Stitch the lines of the allsort shape in back stitch (2 strands H). Remove the tacking. Add the liquorice layer (Diagram 1) in chain stitch (2 strands A).

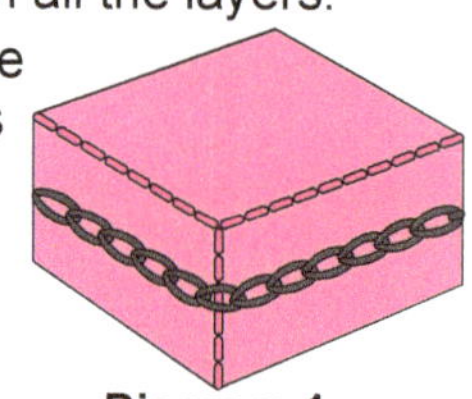

**Diagram 1**

**Allsort 2** Work the violet allsort as for the first stages of the pink allsort (2 strands B). Following the marked line, add the upper liquorice layer in chain stitch (2 strands A). Below this layer, add the green layer with two rows of chain stitch (2 strands E), then add the lower liquorice layer (Diagram 2) in chain stitch (2 strands A).

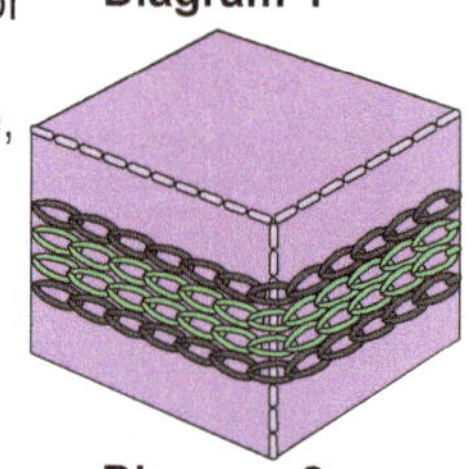

**Diagram 2**

**Allsort 3** Pin and tack the black shape in place. Work the internal line in back stitch (2 strands A). Remove tacking. Add the hundreds and thousands (Diagram 3), with two wrap French knots (2 strands B, C, D, E, F, G, H, and I).

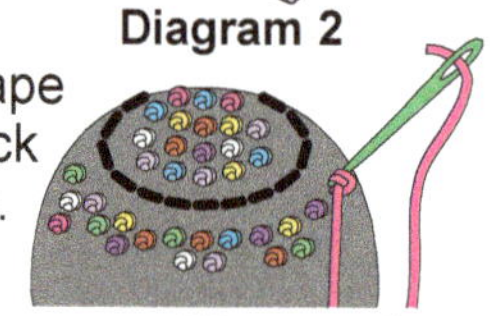

**Diagram 3**

## Let's finish

Take out the tacking. Press the background fabric only. See page 36 for pressing.

# Liquorice Allsorts Scrapbooking Decoration

Have fun decorating a scrapbooking page with liquorice allsorts.

## The project

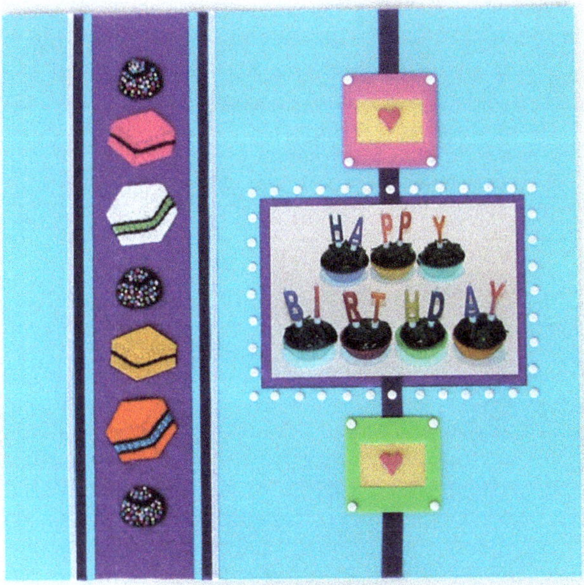


***Liquorice Allsorts Scrapbooking Border***
**Featured on a page**

This decorative border is featured on a scrapbooking page that is dedicated to a birthday celebration. To create the border, seven colourful liquorice allsorts are worked on a felt background. The black allsorts and the pink allsort are the same as those on the original design. The remaining allsorts are worked using different coloured felt and threads. The finished size of this border is 30.5cm x 5cm wide (12" x 2").

## Shopping list

- Violet felt fabric for background:
  one piece 32cm x 7cm wide (12 1/2" x 2 3/4")
- Lightweight iron-on interfacing for backing:
  one piece 32cm x 7cm wide (12 1/2" x 2 3/4")
- Black felt fabric for the appliqué shapes:
  three 5cm (2") squares
- Pink, white, yellow, and orange felt fabric for the appliqué shapes:
  one 5cm (2") square of each colour
- Threads as listed for the original design on the page opposite
- Stranded cotton thread:
  (J) medium yellow (K) medium orange
- Tracing paper and other items for preparing the felt shapes
- Archival double-sided sticky tape

## Let's begin

See the page opposite for the pattern.
In this project, the pattern is not transferred onto the background felt fabric. The felt shapes are spaced evenly down the border.

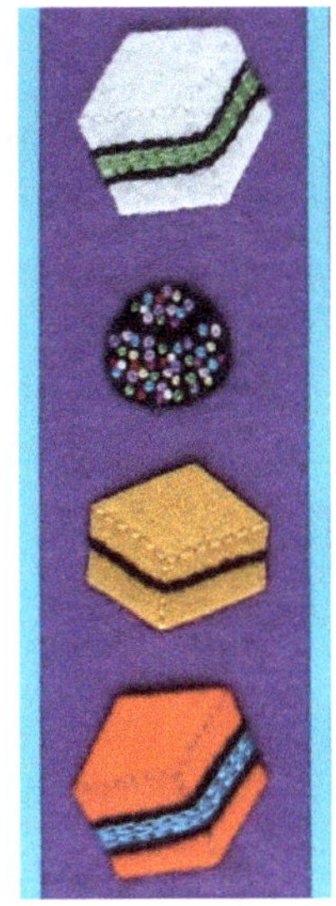

**Detail of**
***Liquorice Allsorts Scrapbooking Border***

Attach the iron-on interfacing to the wrong side of the violet felt fabric. See page 15 for backing the fabric. Trim the upper and lower edges of the backed felt so that it is the same height as your scrapbooking page.
Referring to pages 220-223 for appliqué and following steps 1 and 3-5 of Method 1, cut out the allsort shapes from the felt pieces and mark the internal lines using the pattern as follows:
**Allsort 1** – one pink shape, one yellow shape
**Allsort 2** – one white shape, one orange shape
**Allsort 3** – three black shapes

## Stitch!

Use the photo as a guide for placement when tacking the felt shapes onto the violet felt background.

1. Work the black allsorts following the instructions for **Allsort 3** on the previous page.
2. Work the pink allsort following the instructions for **Allsort 1**.
3. Work the white allsort following the instructions for **Allsort 2**, using (I) white for the lines representing the allsort shape.
4. Work the yellow allsort following the instructions for **Allsort 1**, using (J) medium yellow for the lines representing the allsort shape.
5. Work the orange allsort following the instructions for **Allsort 2**, using (K) orange for the lines representing the allsort shape, and (D) dark aqua for the layer between the liquorice.

## Let's finish

Attach the border to the scrapbooking page with the double-sided sticky tape.

# Sail Away

Imagine the glistening white sand and crystal clear waters!

## The design

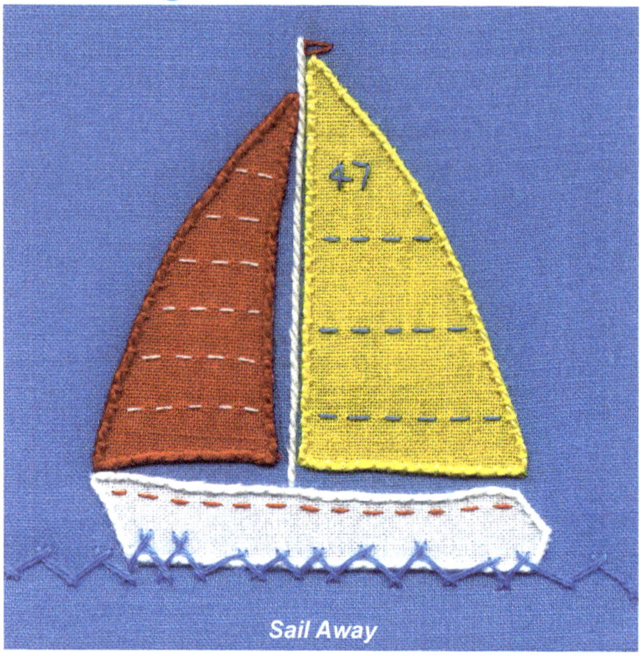


*Sail Away*

In this appliqué design the fabric shapes are fused to the background fabric. Laid perlé thread is then couched around the shapes, covering the raw edges of the fabric. Details are added in running stitch, back stitch, irregular herringbone stitch, and couching. Use the instructions on this page to work the design exactly as shown here on an aqua background. To use the design as a framed picture, see the project idea on the following page.

## The pattern

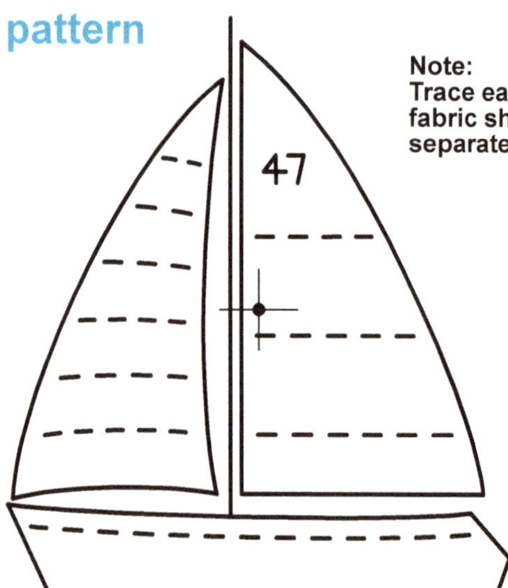


**Note: Trace each fabric shape separately**

**Key:** ─┼─ **Centre of design**

## Shopping list

- Aqua cotton fabric for background: 25cm (10") square
- Fabric or interfacing for backing: 25cm (10") square
- Red and yellow cotton fabric for the sail shapes: one piece of each colour 8cm x 5cm wide (3" x 2")
- White cotton fabric for the hull shape: one piece 3cm x 8cm wide (1" x 3")
- Paper-backed fusible webbing: 12cm (5") square
- Stranded cotton thread: (A) dark aqua (B) light yellow (C) medium red (D) white
- No. 5 perlé cotton thread: (E) light yellow (F) medium red (G) white
- Tracing paper and other items for transferring the pattern onto the fabric

## Let's begin

Read page 15 for backing the fabric, and pages 22-25 for transferring the pattern onto the fabric, then select and use suitable methods for your fabric. For the aqua fabric shown here, the mast and the outlines for the sails and hull were transferred centrally onto the fabric by tracing with an HB pencil and then the backing fabric was tacked to the wrong side. Referring to pages 220-223 for appliqué, and following steps 3-7 of Method 2, prepare and cut out the fabric shapes for the sails and hull.

## Stitch!

For help, see pages 40-43 for straight stitch, 58-61 for running stitch, 76-79 for back stitch, 112-115 for irregular herringbone stitch, and pages 202-205 for couching. When working the couching, attach the perlé thread with small, evenly spaced straight stitches.

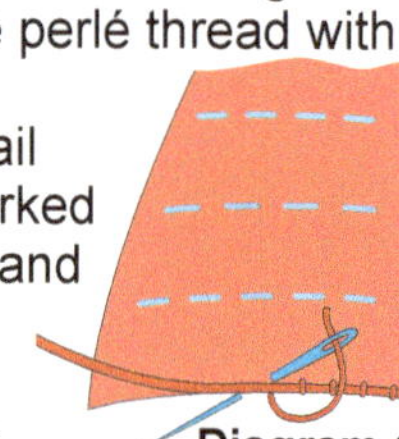

**Diagram 1**

1 With glue side down, place the red sail onto the background fabric at the marked position. Cover with a pressing cloth and fuse the shape on with a hot iron. Couch around the edge of the sail (1 strand F, attached with 1 strand C), placing the perlé thread just inside the raw edge (Diagram 1). Work stripes in running stitch (1 strand D).

2 Attach the yellow sail, then outline it with couching (1 strand E, attached with 1 strand B). Add stripes in running stitch and the number 47 with back stitch (1 strand A). Attach the hull, then outline it with couching (1 strand G, attached with 1 strand D). Add the red stripe in running stitch (1 strand C).

3 Couch the mast (1 strand G, attached with 1 strand D) with slanted straight stitches (Diagram 2).

4 Judging by eye, add the flag at the top of the mast in back stitch (1 strand C). Work the waves in irregular herringbone stitch (2 strands A).

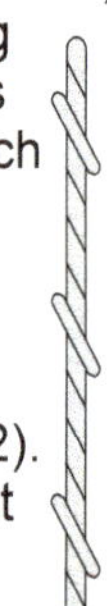

**Diagram 2**

## Let's finish

Take out the tacking. Press or pin out the work. See page 36 for pressing and for pinning out.

# Sail Away Framed Picture

Decorate a wall with this nautical themed picture.

## The project

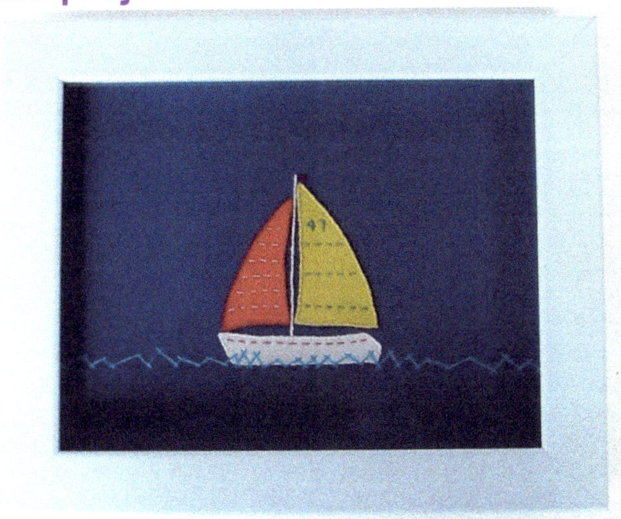


***Sail Away Framed Picture***

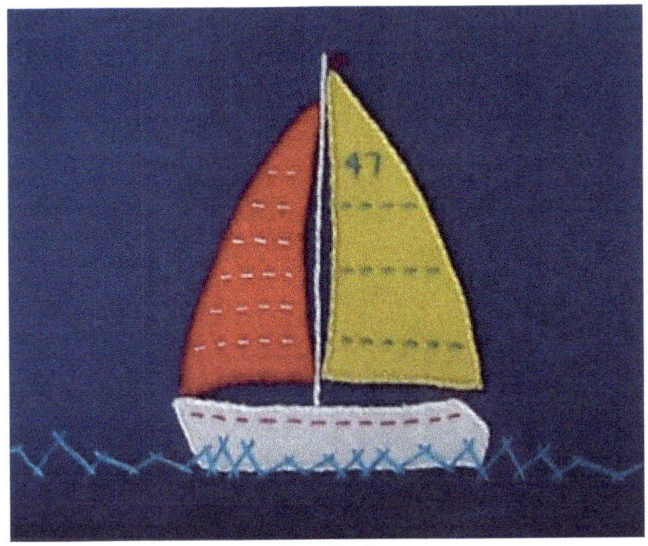


**Detail of**
***Sail Away Framed Picture***

This sailing boat design is an ideal subject for decorating a beach house. It is worked in the same way as the original design, but the background fabric colour has been changed.

The measurements given in the shopping list on this page are suitable for a picture frame with window dimensions of 15cm x 19cm wide (6" x 7 1/2"). If your picture frame has different dimensions, you will need to adjust the shopping list measurements accordingly.

The dimensions of the wadding and foam core board, or similar, are determined by the size of the backing board of the frame you select.

## Shopping list

- Light blue box picture frame:
  15cm x 19cm wide (6" x 7 1/2") window
- Blue cotton fabric for background:
  25cm x 33cm wide (10" x 13")
- Lightweight iron-on interfacing for backing:
  25cm x 33cm wide (10" x 13")
- Fabric for the appliqué shapes, paper-backed fusible webbing, and threads as listed for the original design on the page opposite
- Strong thread for lacing
- Tracing paper and other items for transferring the pattern onto the fabric
- Thin wadding
- Foam core board, or similar

## Let's begin

See the page opposite for the pattern.

Attach the iron-on interfacing onto the wrong side of the blue fabric. See page 15 for backing the fabric.

Using the pattern, transfer the mast and the outlines for the sails and hull centrally onto the right side of the blue fabric using transfer paper. See page 24 for transferring the pattern using transfer paper.

Referring to pages 220-223 for appliqué, and following steps 3-7 of Method 2, prepare and cut out the fabric shapes for the sails and hull.

## Stitch!

Work the boat and waves following steps 1-4 of the stitch instructions for the original design on the previous page. When working the waves, extend the row of herringbone stitches across the entire width of the picture.

## Let's finish

Press or pin out the work. See page 36 for pressing and for pinning out.

Pad, lace, and frame the work. See page 37 for lacing. Alternatively, take the work to a professional framer who specializes in framing textiles.

# Lightning and Thunder

Storm clouds gather, lightning illuminates the sky, then listen for the rumble of thunder.

## The design

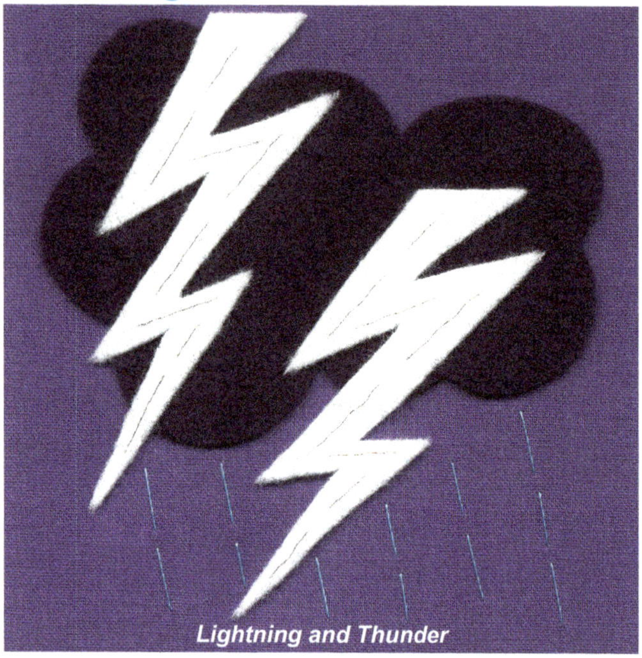

*Lightning and Thunder*

*Lightning and Thunder* is worked using an appliqué technique. The lightning bolts and storm cloud are cut from felt fabric and attached onto the background fabric with large running stitches. The rain is added in running stitch. To work the design as shown above, follow the instructions on this page. See opposite for the design in an alternative colour scheme worked as a wall hanging.

## The pattern

**Note: Trace each felt shape separately**

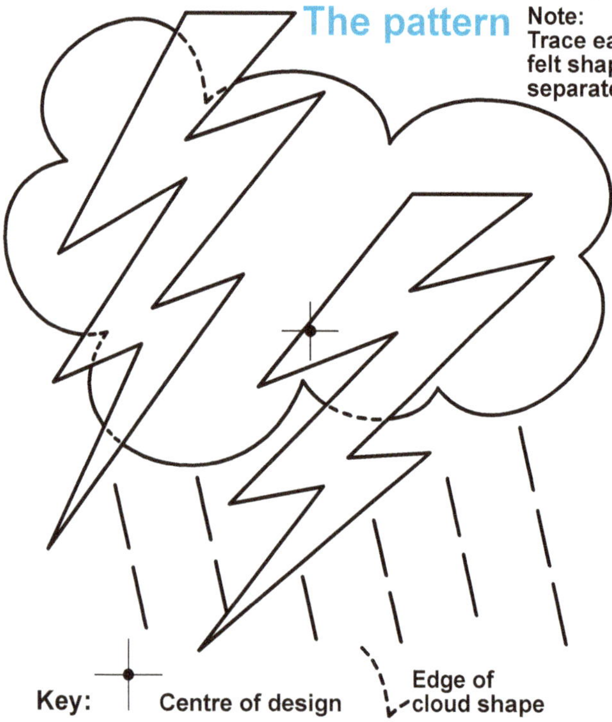


## Shopping list

- Violet cotton fabric for background: 25cm (10") square
- Fabric or interfacing for backing: 25cm (10") square
- Dark violet and white felt fabrics for the shapes: 10cm (4") square of each colour
- White iron-on interfacing for backing the white felt: 10cm (4") square
- Stranded rayon thread: (A) medium aqua
- No. 5 perlé metallic thread: (B) silver
- Tracing paper and other items for transferring the pattern onto the fabric

## Let's begin

For this design, transfer only the pattern for the cloud and the rain onto the background fabric.

Read page 15 for backing the fabric, and pages 22-25 for transferring the pattern onto the fabric, then select and use suitable methods for your fabric. For the violet fabric shown here, the pattern for the cloud and the rain was transferred centrally onto the fabric by tracing with a chalk-based pencil and then the backing fabric was tacked to the wrong side.

Referring to pages 220-223 for appliqué and following step 4 of Method 1, prepare and cut out the cloud from the dark violet felt fabric. Attach the iron-on interfacing to the white felt and then cut out the lightning bolts from this in a similar way.

Alternatively, the shapes can be cut out freehand, simply using the pattern as a visual guide.

## Stitch!

For help, see pages 58-61 for running stitch. See also page 17 for preparing perlé metallic thread.

1. Work the rain in large running stitch (1 strand A).
2. Place the cloud over the marked outline on the background fabric. Pin and tack in place.
3. Using the photo as a guide, pin one lightning bolt over the cloud.
4. Working through all layers and stitching with a stabbing motion, attach the felt pieces to the background fabric with large running stitches worked along the lightning bolt (1 ply B). Remove the pins.
5. Attach the remaining lightning bolt over the cloud in the same way.

## Let's finish

Take out the tacking. Press the background fabric only. See page 36 for pressing.

## Hint

**Using rayon and perlé metallic threads**

Make sure that the ends of the rayon and perlé metallic threads are ended off very securely on the back of the work as they may easily work loose.

# Lightning and Thunder Wall Hanging

Create a dramatic, stormy wall hanging.

## The project

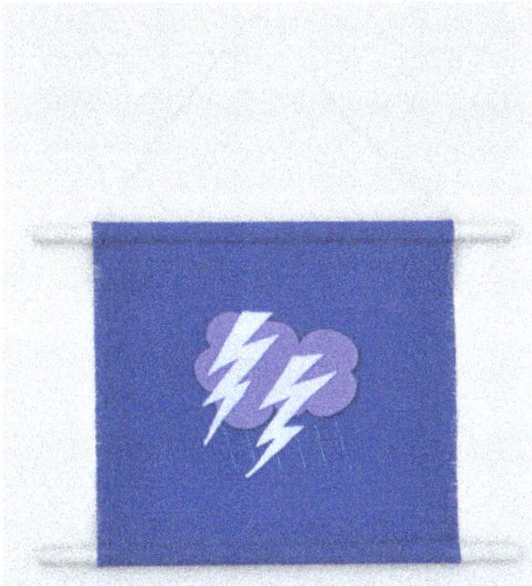

***Lightning and Thunder Wall Hanging***

The design is worked in an alternative colour scheme on a piece of fabric that is then constructed into a wall hanging.

The finished size of this wall hanging, excluding the rods and thread for hanging, is 19cm (7 1/2") square.

## Shopping list

- Blue linen-look fabric for background: 27cm x 23cm wide (10 5/8" x 9")
- Lightweight iron-on interfacing for backing: 27cm x 23cm wide (10 5/8" x 9")
- Violet and white felt fabrics for the appliqué shapes: 10cm (4") square of each colour
- White iron-on interfacing for backing the white felt: 10cm (4") square
- Threads as listed for the original design on the page opposite
- No. 5 perlé cotton thread: (C) white
- Machine sewing thread: blue
- Tracing paper and other items for transferring the pattern onto the fabric
- Wooden rods: two pieces 25cm (10") in length and 1cm (3/8") in diameter

## Let's begin

See the page opposite for the pattern.

Attach the iron-on interfacing onto the wrong side of the background fabric. See page 15 for backing the fabric. Transfer the pattern for the cloud and the rain, omitting the lightning bolts, centrally onto the right side of the fabric by tracing with a chalk-based pencil or by using the pierce and dot method. See pages 22-25 for transferring the pattern onto the fabric. Referring to pages 220-223 for appliqué and following step 4 of Method 1, prepare and cut out the cloud from the violet felt fabric. Attach the iron-on interfacing to the white felt and then cut out the lightning bolts from this in a similar way. Alternatively, the shapes can be cut out freehand, simply using the pattern as a visual guide.

**Detail of**
***Lightning and Thunder Wall Hanging***

## Stitch!

Work the design following steps 1-5 of the stitch instructions on the previous page.

## Let's finish

Take out the tacking. Place the work face down on a padded surface and gently press the fabric surrounding the design. See page 36 for pressing. Using the straight stitch on the machine, and the blue machine sewing thread, stitch along each of the two long sides of the work, 4cm (1 1/2") away from the raw edges.

On the wrong side, peel back and trim the interfacing to just outside the machine stitching on each side.

Following the fabric threads, cut 2cm (3/4") off both sides of the work. Pull five or six fabric threads away from each of the two sides to create frayed edges (Diagram 1).

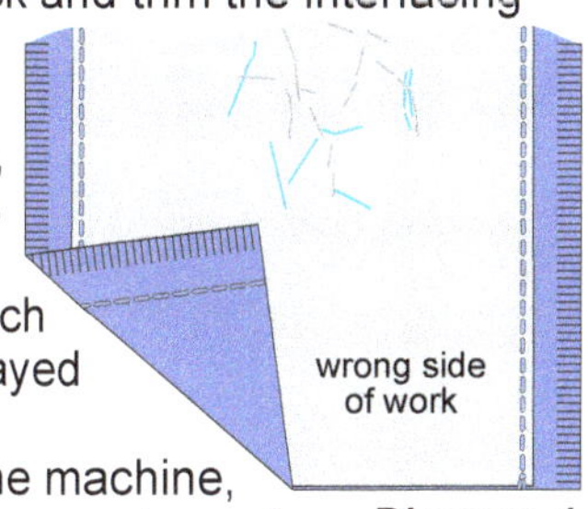


**Diagram 1**

Using the zigzag stitch on the machine, stitch along the upper and lower edges of the work 1cm (3/8") away from each raw edge. Cut away the excess fabric close to the zigzag stitches. Fold 3cm (1 1/4") to the back on the upper and lower edges.

Pin and machine straight stitch 2cm (3/4") away from the fold, forming casings (Diagram 2).

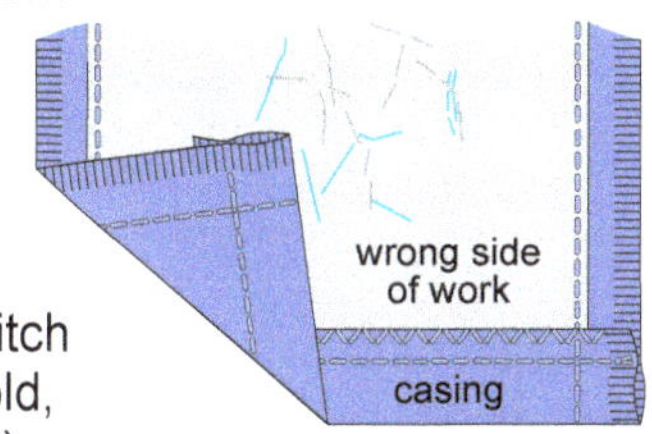


**Diagram 2**

Insert the wooden rods into the casings and use the white perlé thread (C), knotted around the ends of the rods, to hang the work.

# Terracotta Garden

In the courtyard the day is warm and the plants in their terracotta pots are blooming.

## The design

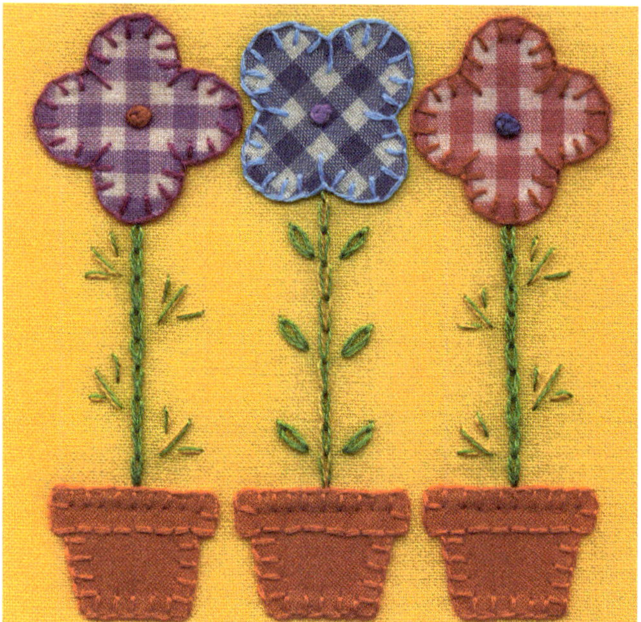

*Terracotta Garden*

These appliqué shapes are fused onto the background fabric and edged with blanket stitch. Follow the instructions here to work the design as above. To adapt the design for a set of placemats, see the next page.

## The pattern

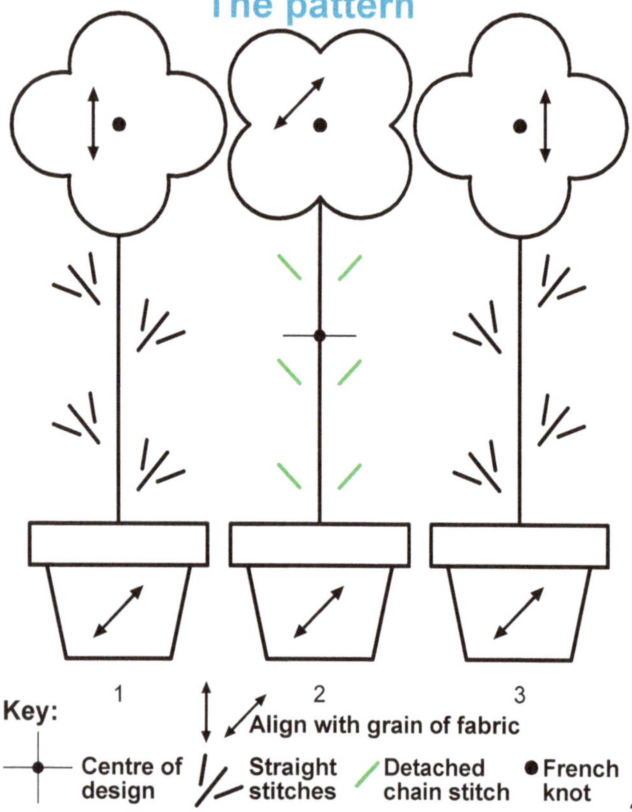


## Shopping list

- Yellow cotton fabric for background: 25cm (10") square
- Fabric or interfacing for backing: 25cm (10") square
- Orange cotton fabric for the flowerpots: 5cm x 15cm wide (2" x 6")
- Violet, blue, and pink gingham fabric for the flowers: 5cm (2") square of each
- Paper-backed fusible webbing: 13cm (5") square
- Stranded cotton thread: (A) medium aqua (B) light green (C) medium yellow (D) medium orange (E) medium red (F) medium magenta
- No. 5 perlé cotton thread: (G) medium violet (H) medium blue (I) medium red
- Tracing paper and other items for transferring the pattern onto the fabric

## Let's begin

Read page 15 for backing the fabric, and pages 22-25 for transferring the pattern onto the fabric, then select and use suitable methods for your fabric. For the yellow fabric shown here, the pattern was transferred centrally onto the fabric by tracing with a chalk-based pencil and then the backing fabric was tacked to the wrong side.

Referring to pages 220-223 for appliqué and following steps 3-7 of Method 2, prepare and cut out the shapes for the orange flowerpots and the gingham flowers

## Stitch!

For help, see pages 40-43 for straight stitch, 76-79 for back stitch, 130-133 for blanket stitch, including completing a shape and turning a corner, Methods 2 and 3, 166-169 for chain stitch and detached chain stitch, and pages 184-187 for French knot.

**Flower 1** Place a flowerpot, glue side down, onto the background fabric at the marked outline. Cover with a pressing cloth and fuse the shape in place with a hot iron. Work the lower edge of the rim in back stitch (2 strands D). With the same thread, and beginning below the back stitch row, work around the pot in blanket stitch. Fuse the violet flower in place and work around its edge in blanket stitch (2 strands F). Add a two wrap French knot at centre (1 strand I). Work the stem in chain stitch (2 strands B) and the leaves in straight stitch (1 strand B mixed in the needle with 1 strand C).

**Flower 2** Work pot and flower as for **Flower 1**, but with a blue flower (2 strands A) and a violet centre (1 strand G). Work the stem in chain stitch (1 strand B mixed in the needle with 1 strand C) and each leaf in detached chain stitch, worked with a small anchor (2 strands B).

**Flower 3** Work all parts as for **Flower 1**, but with a pink flower (2 strands E) and a blue centre (1 strand H).

## Let's finish

Take out the tacking. Press or pin out the work. See page 36 for pressing and for pinning out.

# Terracotta Garden Placemats

What's for dinner? Let's have fun making and using these flowery placemats!

## The project

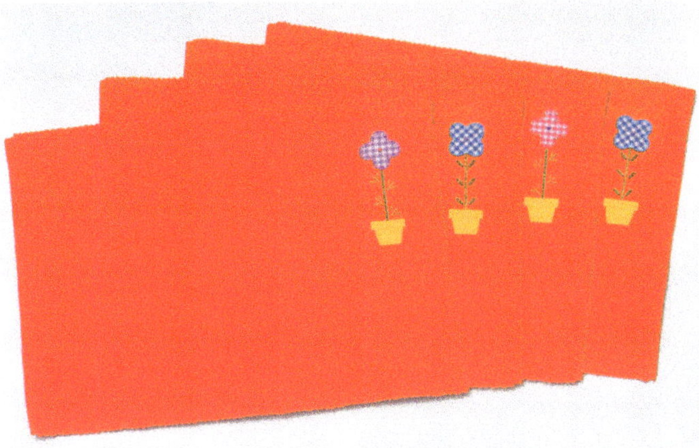

***Terracotta Garden Placemats***

Flowers from *Terracotta Garden* are enlarged in size and worked in an alternative colour scheme on a set of four placemats. Two blue flowers, and one each of the violet and pink flowers, make up the set.

## Shopping list

- Four orange fabric placemats
- Yellow cotton fabric for the flowerpots: 7cm x 24cm wide (2 3/4" x 9 1/2")
- Gingham fabric for the flowers: one 7cm (3") square each of violet and pink two 7cm (3") squares of blue
- Paper-backed fusible webbing: 14cm x 24cm wide (5 1/2" x 9 1/2")
- Threads as listed for the original design on the page opposite, omitting (D) medium orange
- Medium weight tracing paper and other items for transferring the pattern onto the fabric

## Let's begin

See the page opposite for the pattern.
Prepare the pattern by enlarging it to 150% of its original size. Trace the three enlarged flowers onto separate pieces of the tracing paper.
Transfer **Flowers 1** and **3** onto the upper right corner of two of the placemats, and **Flower 2** onto the remaining two placemats, using the pierce and dot method with a chalk based pencil. See page 25 for transferring the pattern using the pierce and dot method.
Referring to pages 220-223 for appliqué and following steps 3-7 of Method 2, prepare and cut out the shapes for the yellow flowerpots and the four gingham flowers.

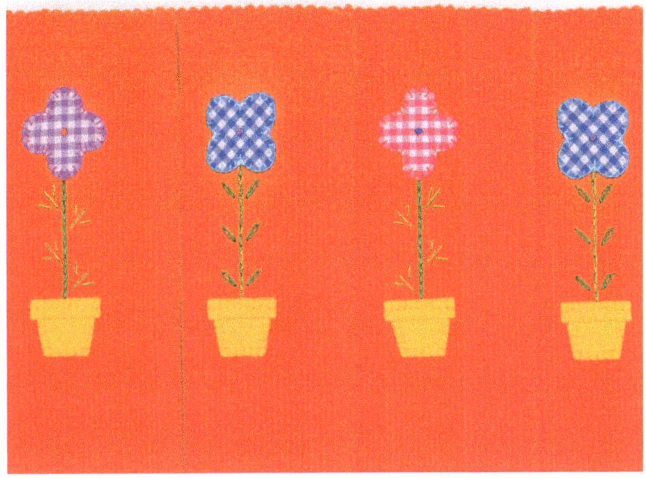

**Detail of**
***Terracotta Garden Placemats***

## Stitch!

Work the pots and flowers following the stitch instructions on the page opposite, using the yellow fabric and (C) medium yellow thread for the pots.
Due to the thickness of the placemats, it may be easier to work the stitches with a stabbing motion.

## Let's finish

Press the placemats on the wrong side. See page 36 for pressing. Enjoy your dining experience!

# Beading

Beading in textile art is a technique by which stitches can be used to attach beads to a background. Beads can add an extra dimension to a design by creating textural interest and adding subtle or intense colour as well as sparkle and shimmer. An entire design can be worked in beading, or beads can be used on parts of a design where they are grouped, scattered, or worked in rows. A single bead can very effectively highlight a small detail.

Beads are available in many sizes and can be made from a large variety of materials including glass, plastic, metal, wood, clay, pearl, and shell. Ranging in appearance from transparent to opaque, and from matt to shiny, they are made in many shapes, such as round, flattened round, square, and tubular. Tubular shaped beads are called bugle beads, while beads of any shape with many flat sides are called faceted beads.

When selecting thread for attaching a bead, the thread can be the same colour as the bead so that the stitching is almost invisible. Alternatively, the thread can be of a contrasting colour as a feature. Always make sure that the chosen thread is strong enough to hold the bead in place.

Note that it is not considered safe to use beads or buttons on clothing or other projects for babies and very small children.

There are many ways to attach beads to fabric, and some easy methods are shown on the following pages.

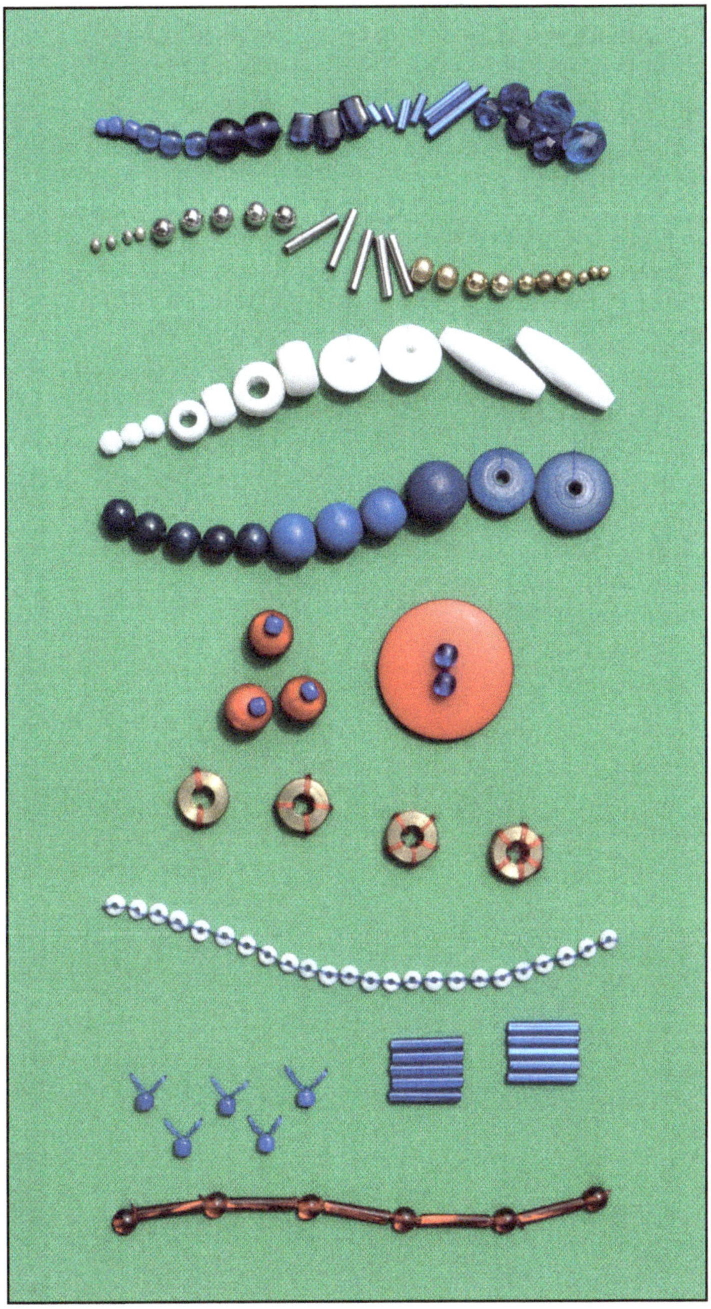

Glass beads

Metal beads

Plastic beads

Wooden beads

Beads attached with a second bead, and button attached with beads

Large beads attached on their ends

Row of beads attached on their ends

Beads attached using anchors of fly stitches, and rows of bugle beads

Couched string of beads

**Beading sampler**

# Beading

## Hints

As beads are often heavy, consider how the background fabric will be affected by the added weight of the beading. If a backing layer of fabric or interfacing is added, this will give extra support to the background fabric.

A beading needle, which is long and thin and has a narrow eye, is specifically designed for working with beads. Although not essential for the designs in this book, a beading needle is useful when working with very small beads, or when forming long strings of beads.

To prevent an isolated bead from becoming loose, begin and end off the thread extra securely on the back of the work. When attaching a group of beads, secure each bead by working one or two small stitches on the reverse side of the fabric behind the bead before attaching the next bead.

## Beading: right-handed

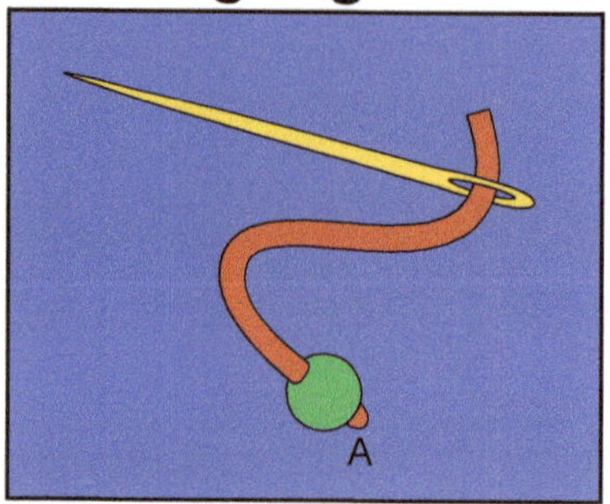


**Bead attached with one stitch**
**1** Come up at A. Thread a bead onto needle and pull thread through. Allow the bead to settle on the fabric.

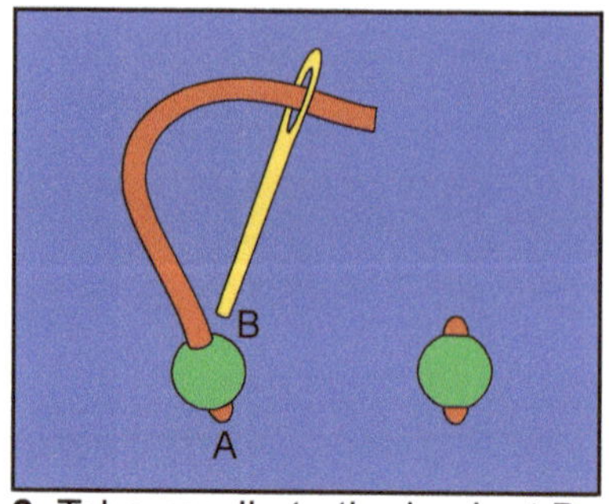


**2** Take needle to the back at B, a bead length away from A. Pull thread through. Settle the bead. Secure the thread on the back.

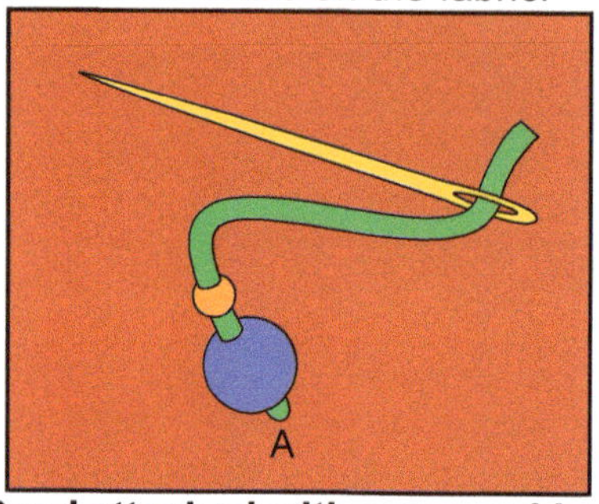


**Bead attached with a second bead**
**1** Come up at A. Thread a large bead and a smaller bead onto needle. Pull thread through and allow bead to settle.

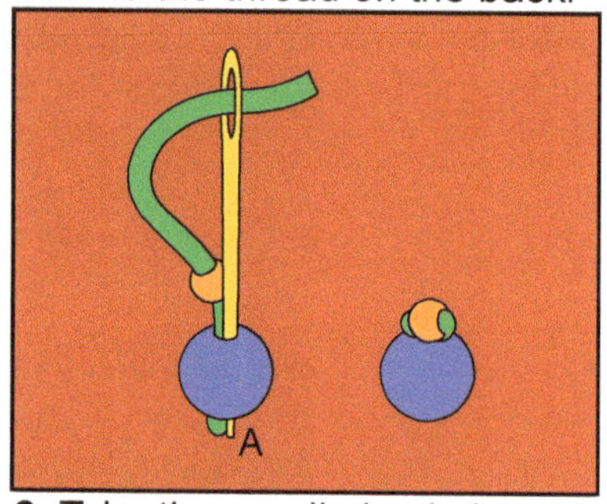


**2** Take the needle back through the large bead and down through the fabric close to A. Pull the thread through and secure.

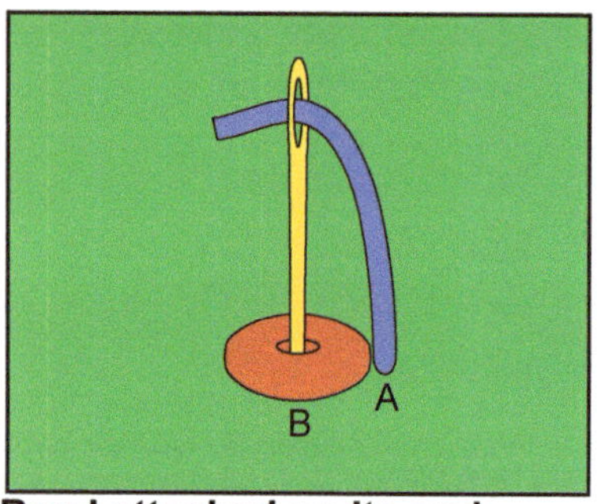


**Bead attached on its end**
**1** Place the bead on its end. Come up at A. Take the needle down at B, through the centre of the bead.

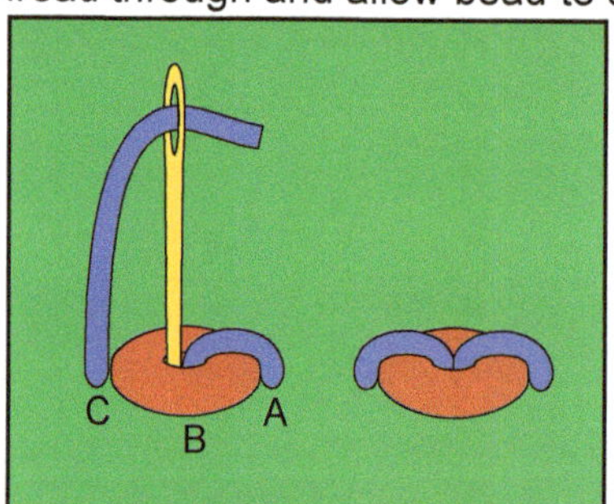


**2** Pull thread through. Come up at C. Take the needle down at B, through the centre of the bead again and to the back. Secure.

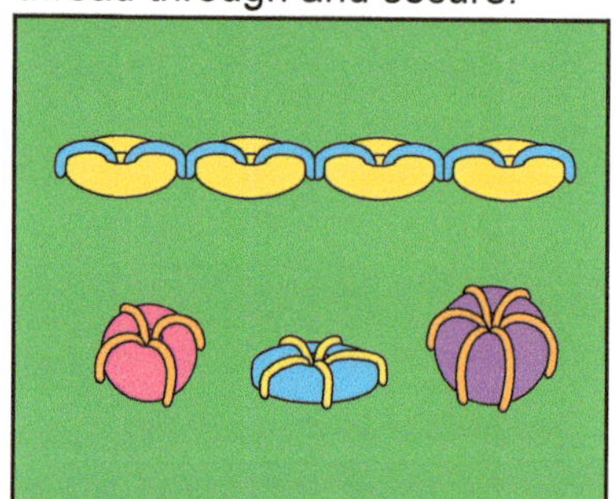

**3** Upper example shows a row of beads attached with two stitches for each bead. Lower examples show beads attached with several stitches.

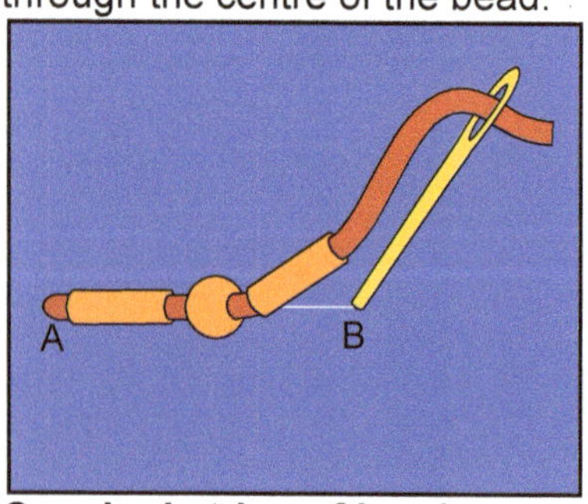


**Couched string of beads**
**1** Come up at A. Thread beads onto needle and allow them to settle on fabric. Take thread to back at B and end off securely.

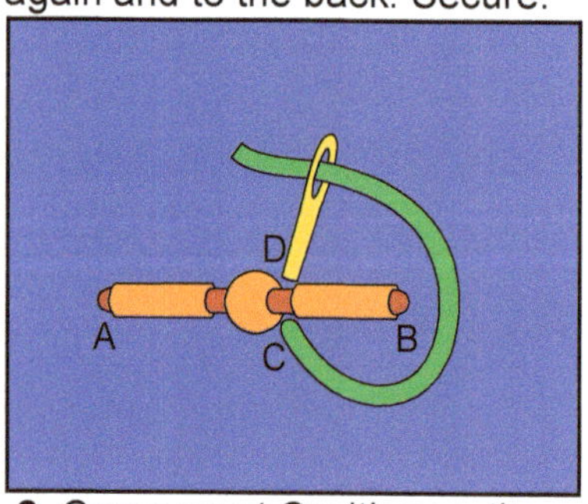


**2** Come up at C with new thread. Take needle to back at D, which is aligned above C.

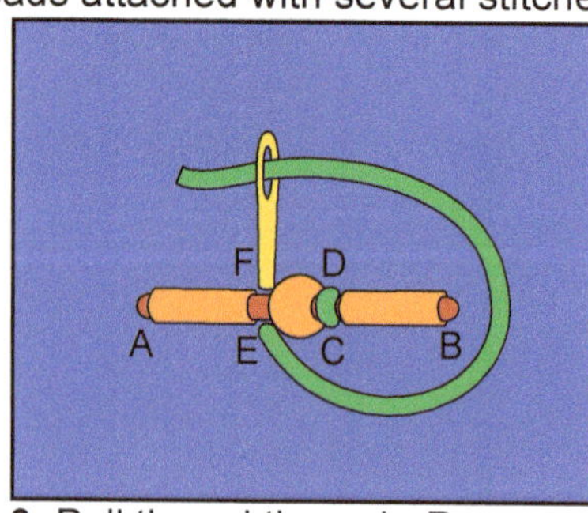


**3** Pull thread through. Repeat at E and F and end off securely.

# Beading: left-handed

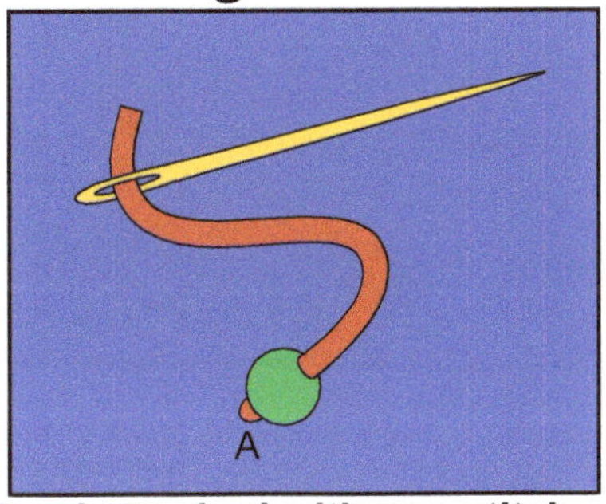


**Bead attached with one stitch**
**1** Come up at A. Thread a bead onto needle and pull thread through. Allow the bead to settle on the fabric.

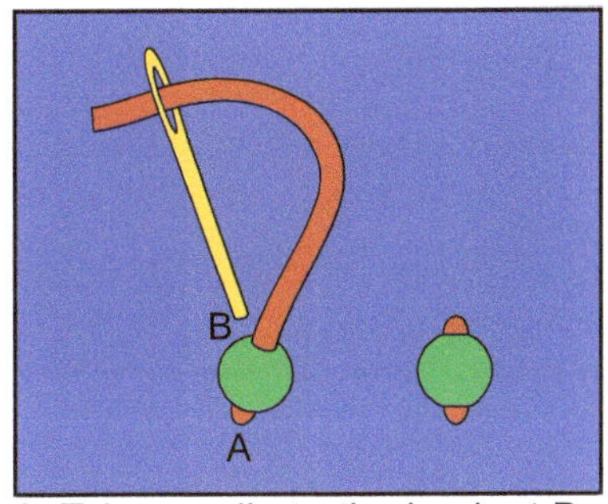


**2** Take needle to the back at B, a bead length away from A. Pull thread through. Settle the bead. Secure the thread on the back.

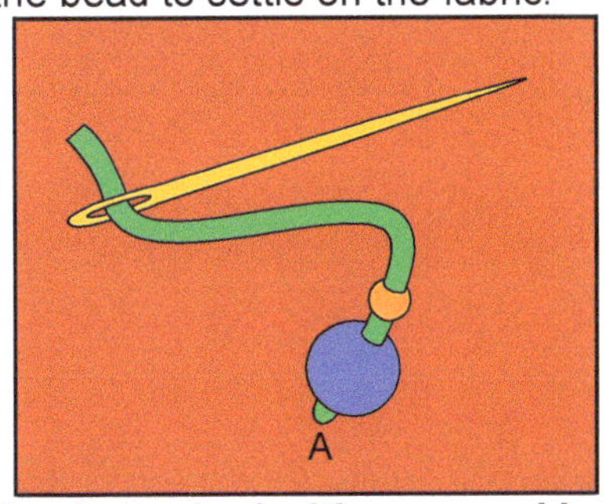


**Bead attached with a second bead**
**1** Come up at A. Thread a large bead and a smaller bead onto needle. Pull thread through and allow bead to settle.

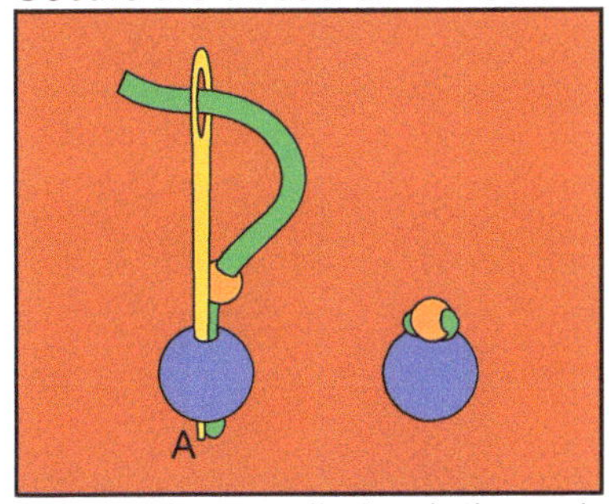


**2** Take the needle back through the large bead and down through the fabric close to A. Pull the thread through and secure.

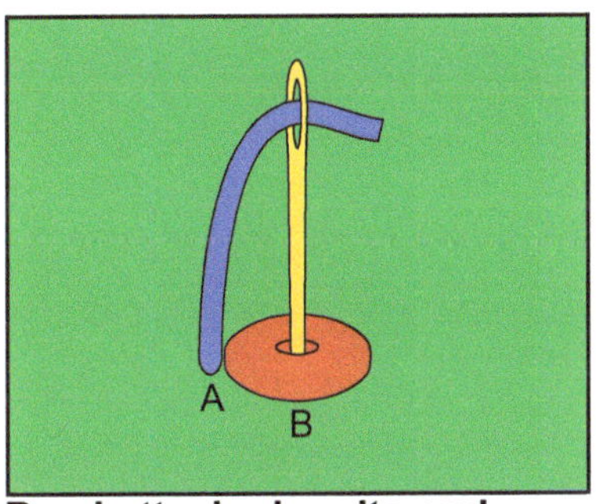


**Bead attached on its end**
**1** Place the bead on its end. Come up at A. Take the needle down at B, through the centre of the bead.

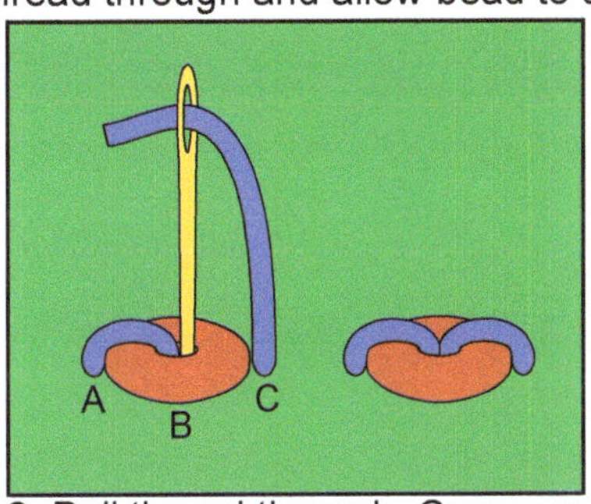


**2** Pull thread through. Come up at C. Take the needle down at B, through the centre of the bead again and to the back. Secure.

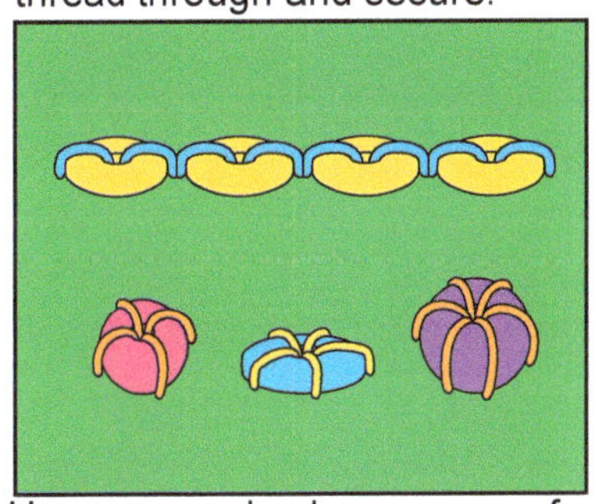

**3** Upper example shows a row of beads attached with two stitches for each bead. Lower examples show beads attached with several stitches.

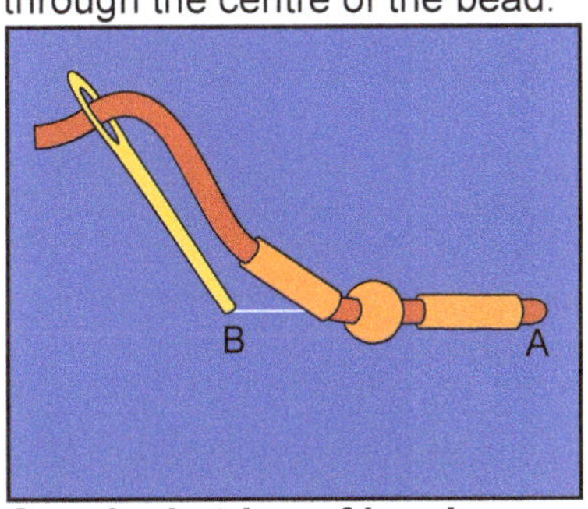


**Couched string of beads**
**1** Come up at A. Thread beads onto needle and allow them to settle on fabric. Take thread to back at B and end off securely.

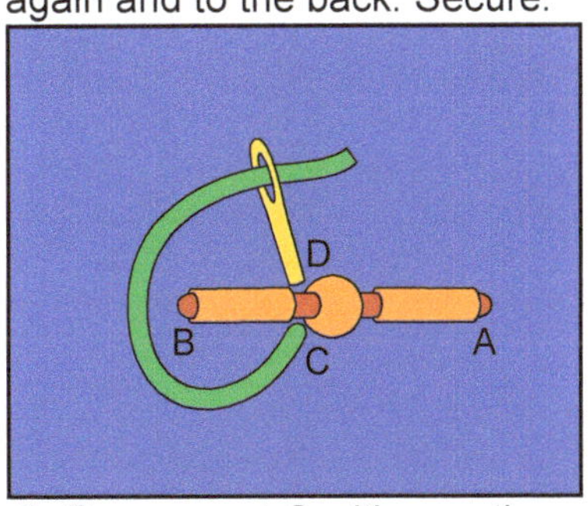


**2** Come up at C with new thread. Take needle to back at D, which is aligned above C.

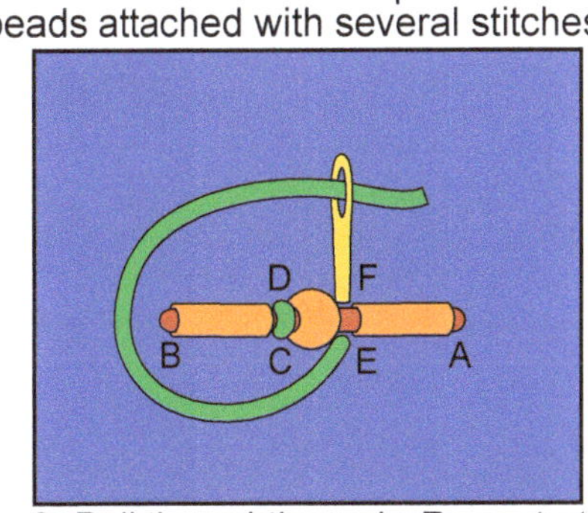


**3** Pull thread through. Repeat at E and F and end off securely.

# Beading

# Designs and project ideas

## The designs

Beautiful Butterfly

Ripe Cherries

Starlight Magic

Rose Essence

Tick Tock, Tick Tock

Crystal Forest

# Beautiful Butterfly

Beautiful butterfly – please visit my garden.

## The design

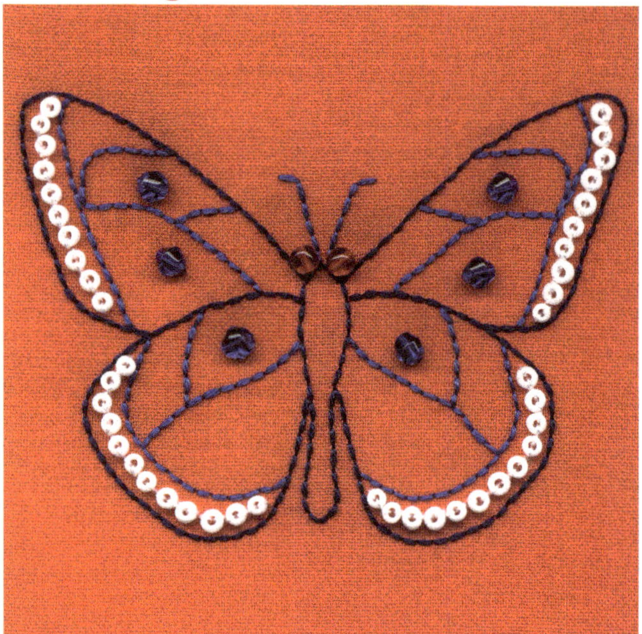

*Beautiful Butterfly*

Three types of beads are featured in this design. Beads depict the eyes and wing markings on the butterfly, while the remaining details are worked in back stitch.

Use the instructions on this page to work the design exactly as shown here on a red background. To apply the design to a project, see the idea on the facing page where the butterfly is featured on a T-shirt.

As this design uses beads, it is not considered safe for use on projects for babies or very small children.

## The pattern

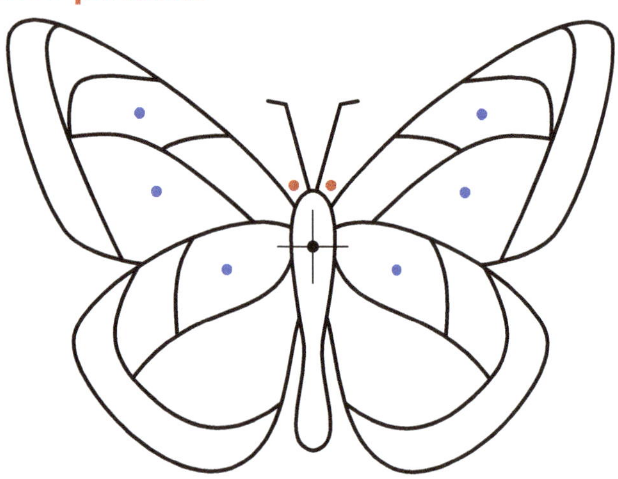

**Key:** ✛ **Centre of design** • • **Blue or red bead**

## Shopping list

- Red cotton fabric for background: 25cm (10") square
- Fabric or interfacing for backing: 25cm (10") square
- Stranded cotton thread: (A) dark blue (B) medium blue (C) medium red (D) white
- 6 medium size faceted beads: (E) medium blue
- 2 medium size round beads: (F) medium red
- Approx. 60 small flattened round beads: (G) white
- Tracing paper and other items for transferring the pattern onto the fabric

## Let's begin

Read page 15 for backing the fabric, and pages 22-25 for transferring the pattern onto the fabric, then select and use suitable methods for your fabric. For the red fabric shown here, the pattern was transferred centrally onto the fabric by tracing with a water erasable fabric marker and then the backing fabric was tacked to the wrong side.

## Stitch!

For help, see pages 40-43 for straight stitch, 76-79 for back stitch, and pages 238-241 for beading.

1. Using back stitch, work the outlines for the body and wings (2 strands A), then add the internal lines on the wings (2 strands B).
2. Stitch the antennae with back stitch (2 strands B).
3. Working in the space along the edge of each wing, attach the white beads (G, attached with 1 strand D) as follows. Place the first bead on its end. Work one straight stitch down through the hole (Diagram 1).
   Work a second stitch down through the hole (Diagram 2). Secure the thread on the back of the work with a small stitch. Continue adding beads along the row (Diagram 3).
4. Using straight stitch, attach a blue bead at each marked dot on the wings (E, attached with 1 strand B). Secure each bead by working a small stitch on the reverse side of the fabric behind the bead.
5. For the eyes, attach a red bead at each marked dot with straight stitch (F, attached with 1 strand C).

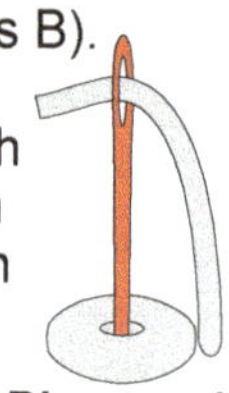

**Diagram 1**

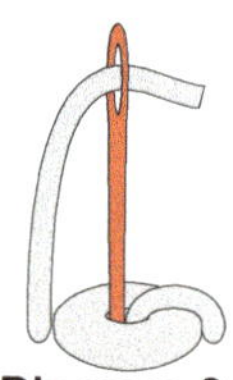

**Diagram 2**

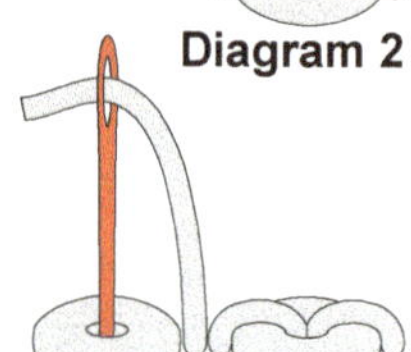

**Diagram 3**

## Let's finish

Take out the tacking. Rinse the work in cold water to remove the water erasable fabric marker. When partly dry, press or pin out the work. See page 36 for pressing and for pinning out.

# Beautiful Butterfly T-shirt

Decorate a T-shirt with a fluttering butterfly.

## The project

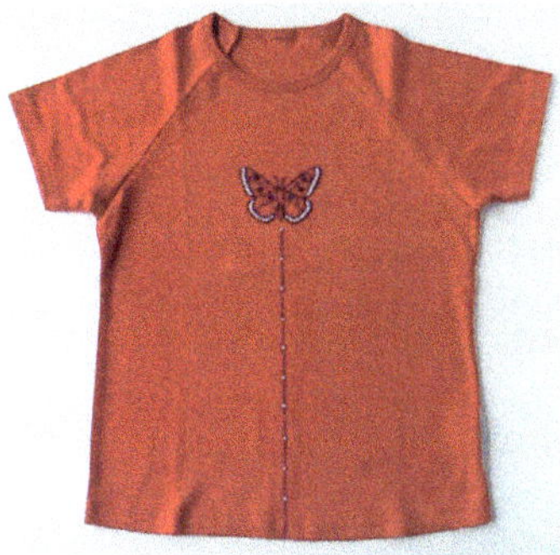

***Beautiful Butterfly T-Shirt***

The butterfly worked on the front of this T-shirt has transformed an otherwise plain stretch knit top into a delightful fashion item. The row of back stitch and beads adds an extra design element.

As the butterfly design uses beads, it is not considered safe for use on clothing for babies or very small children.

## Shopping list

- Red stretch knit T-shirt
- Lightweight iron-on interfacing for backing: 9cm x 11cm wide (3 1/2" x 4 1/2")
- Threads and beads as listed for the original design on the page opposite
- Additional white beads (G) for the trail below the butterfly
- Tracing paper and other items for transferring the pattern onto the T-shirt

## Let's begin

See the page opposite for the *Beautiful Butterfly* pattern. To help in deciding the placement of the design on the T-shirt, first trace the pattern onto tracing paper. Fold the T-shirt in half and mark the entire centre front with a row of tacking (Diagram 1).

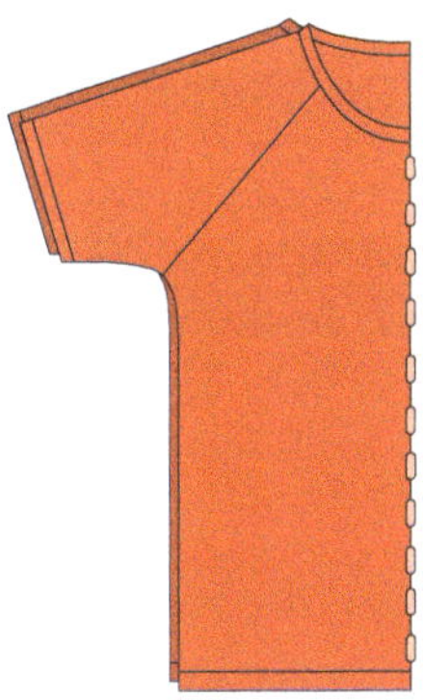

**Diagram 1**

Open out the T-shirt and place the butterfly tracing, centred over the tacking, an appropriate distance below the front neckline (Diagram 2). Move the tracing up or down until it is visually appealing and note its position with pins.

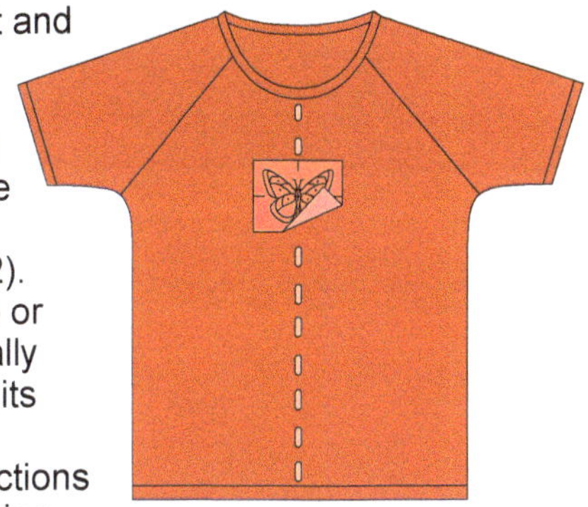

**Diagram 2**

Following the instructions on page 15 for backing the fabric, attach the piece of iron-on interfacing onto the wrong side of the front of the T-shirt at the selected position. This will stabilize the area where the butterfly is to be stitched. Transfer the pattern onto the front of the T-shirt by tracing with a water erasable fabric marker or by using transfer paper. See pages 22-25 for transferring the pattern onto the fabric.

Following the tacking that marks the centre front, rule a guideline beginning at the hemline and finishing 1cm (3/8") below the marked butterfly design. Remove the tacking.

## Stitch!

Work the butterfly following steps 1-5 of the stitch instructions on the facing page. Following the ruled guideline that marks the centre front of the T-shirt, work a row of back stitch (2 strands B). Beginning at the end below the butterfly, attach white beads on their ends 3cm (1 1/4") apart along the row of back stitches (G, attached with 1 strand D). End off the thread securely after attaching each bead.

## Let's finish

Turn the T-shirt inside out. On the wrong side, peel back any excess interfacing from its outer edge and trim it back close to the stitches. Rinse the T-shirt in cold water to remove the pattern markings. When dry, turn the T-shirt inside out and press it, avoiding the beads. See page 36 for pressing.

# Rose Essence

Roses. Wow! What fantastic colours and fragrances.

## The design

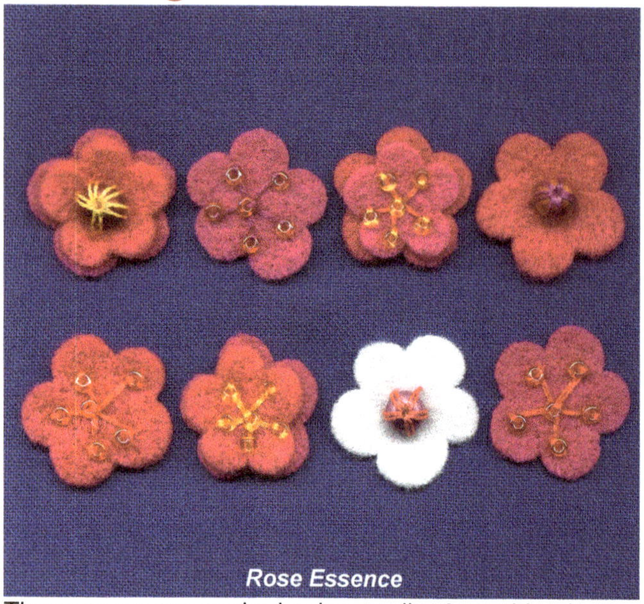

*Rose Essence*

These roses are worked using appliqué combined with beading. The flowers are created using either one or two felt shapes that are attached to the background fabric with stitches and beads. The edges of the felt shapes remain free. Follow the instructions on this page to work *Rose Essence* as shown here on a blue background. To adapt roses from the design for use on gift cards, see the next page.

As this design uses beads, it is not considered safe for use on projects for babies or very small children.

## The pattern

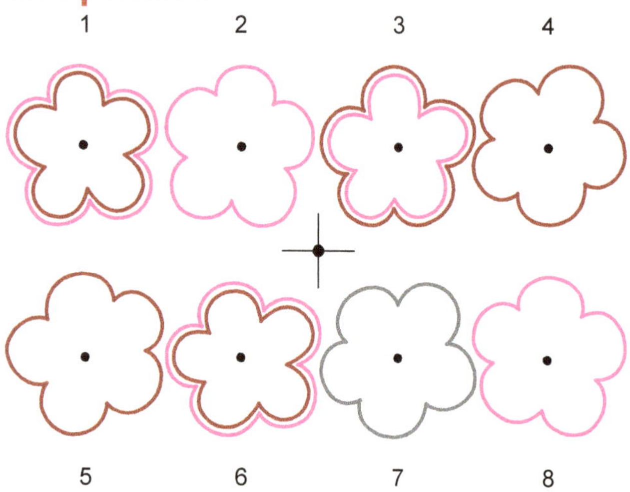


**Key:** **Centre of design** • **Flower centre** **Two layers of felt**

**Note: Trace each felt shape separately**

## Shopping list

- Blue cotton fabric for background: 25cm (10") square
- Fabric or interfacing for backing: 25cm (10") square
- Pink, light red, and white felt fabrics for the roses: 5cm x 18cm wide (2" x 7") each of pink and light red, and 5cm (2") square of white
- Stranded cotton thread:
  (A) medium yellow (B) light red (C) medium magenta
- 1 large round bead in each of the following colours:
  (D) dark yellow (E) medium red (F) light magenta
- 12 small beads: (G) light yellow
- 18 small beads: (H) light red
- Tracing paper and other items for preparing felt shapes

## Let's begin

Read page 15 for backing the fabric, and pages 22-25 for transferring the pattern onto the fabric, then select and use suitable methods for your fabric. For the blue fabric shown here, the eight dots for the flower centres were transferred onto the fabric by tracing with a chalk-based pencil. The backing fabric was tacked to the wrong side. Referring to pages 220-223 for appliqué and following steps 3-5 of Method 1, cut out five pink, five light red, and one white rose shape, then mark the centre dot on each. Alternatively, the shapes can all be cut out and marked freehand, simply using the pattern as a visual guide.

## Stitch!

For help, see pages 40-43 for straight stitch, and pages 238-241 for beading. Begin each rose by pinning one or two felt layers onto the background fabric, matching dots.

**Roses 1, 4, and 7** Using the threads and beads listed below, attach the large bead at the centre dot (Diagram 1) with five straight stitches, all worked down through the hole in the bead, and through all layers.

*Rose 1*: beading (E, attached with 2 strands A).
*Rose 4*: beading (D, attached with 2 strands C).
*Rose 7*: beading (F, attached with 2 strands B).

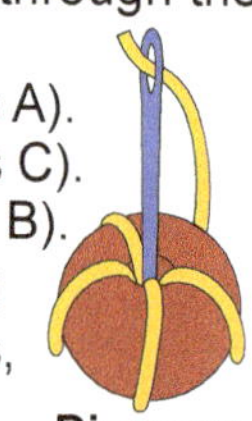

**Diagram 1**

**Roses 2, 3, 5, 6, and 8** With the threads and beads listed below, stitch five straight stitches, all worked down through the flower centre. Using a small straight stitch, attach a bead at the centre, then a bead at the end of each straight stitch.

*Rose 2*: straight stitches (2 strands C) and beading (H, attached with 2 strands C).
*Rose 3*: straight stitches (2 strands B) and beading (G, attached with 2 strands A).
*Rose 5*: straight stitches (2 strands B) and beading (H, attached with 2 strands B).
*Rose 6*: straight stitches (2 strands A) and beading (G, attached with 2 strands A).
*Rose 8*: straight stitches (2 strands B) and beading (H, attached with 2 strands B).

## Let's finish

Take out the tacking. Press the background fabric only.

# Rose Essence Gift Cards

Spread the joy of roses by sending these gift cards.

## The projects

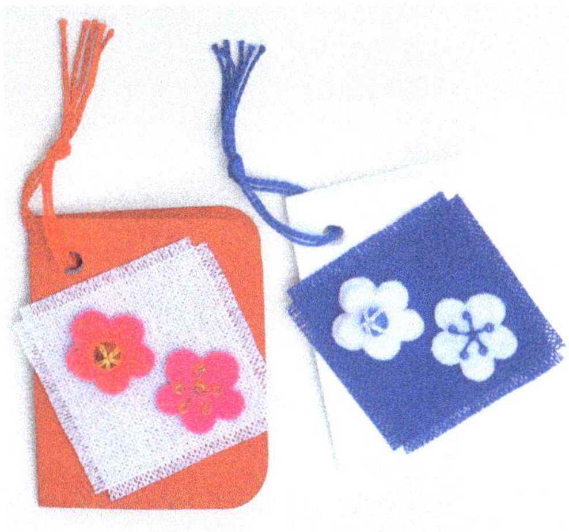

*Rose Essence Gift Cards*

**Roses 1** and **2** from *Rose Essence* are worked in two different colour schemes on frayed edge patches to create decorated gift cards.
Each of these small cards is 7cm x 5.5cm wide (2 3/4" x 2 1/4") in size.

## Shopping list

***Red gift card***

- White linen-look fabric for the patch: 5cm (2") square, cut following the fabric threads
- Pink and light red felt fabrics for the roses: 5cm (2") square of each colour
- Threads (A) and (C) as listed for the original design on the page opposite
- No. 5 perlé cotton thread: medium red
- 1 large round bead: (E) medium red
- 6 small beads: (H) light red
- Tracing paper and other items for preparing the felt shapes
- Red card: 7cm x 11cm wide (2 3/4" x 4 1/2")
- White paper: 6cm x 10cm wide (2 3/8" x 4")
- Archival double-sided sticky tape or glue

***White gift card***

- Blue linen-look fabric for the patch: 5cm (2") square, cut following the fabric threads
- White felt fabric for the roses: 8cm (3") square
- Stranded cotton thread: (A) white (C) medium blue
- No. 5 perlé cotton thread: medium blue
- 1 large round bead: (E) medium blue
- 6 small beads: (H) medium blue
- Tracing paper and other items for preparing the felt shapes
- White card: 7cm x 11cm wide (2 3/4" x 4 1/2")
- White paper: 6cm x 10cm wide (2 3/8" x 4")
- Archival double-sided sticky tape or glue

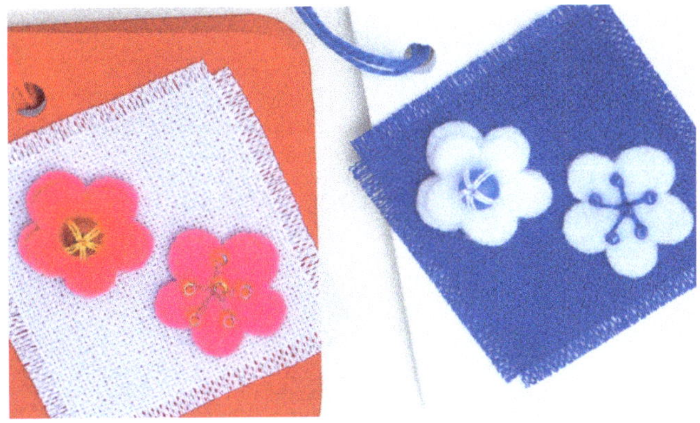

**Details of *Rose Essence Gift Cards***

## Let's begin

See the page opposite for the pattern.
Referring to pages 220-223 for appliqué and following steps 3-5 of Method 1, cut out the rose shapes from the felt fabrics as follows, and mark the centre dot on each. Alternatively, the shapes can all be cut out and marked freehand, simply using the pattern as a visual guide.

***Red gift card*** Cut the shapes for **Roses 1** and **2** following the felt colours indicated on the pattern.

***White gift card*** Cut all the shapes for **Roses 1** and **2** from the white felt.

## Stitch!

Using the photo as a guide for placement, work the two flowers on the square of fabric for each card following the instructions for **Rose 1** and **Rose 2** on the page opposite.

## Let's finish

For each gift card, pull a few fabric threads away from all sides of the square of fabric to create frayed edges. Trim the corners of the piece of card and of the piece of paper so that they are rounded.
Fold both pieces in half, making the gift card and the pages. Secure the pages to the inside of the front of the card with sticky tape or glue.
Punch a hole in the upper left corner of the closed card though all four layers. Thread three strands of the perlé cotton thread through the holes and knot the ends together, forming the tie. Using sticky tape or glue, attach the patch to the front of the card at an angle so that it hangs over some of the edges.

## Hint

**Other project ideas**

Make a matching set of greeting cards, or you could work these patches on gift bags, or as tags or decorations for scrapbooking pages.

# Ripe Cherries

Two ripe red cherries ready for harvesting.

## The design

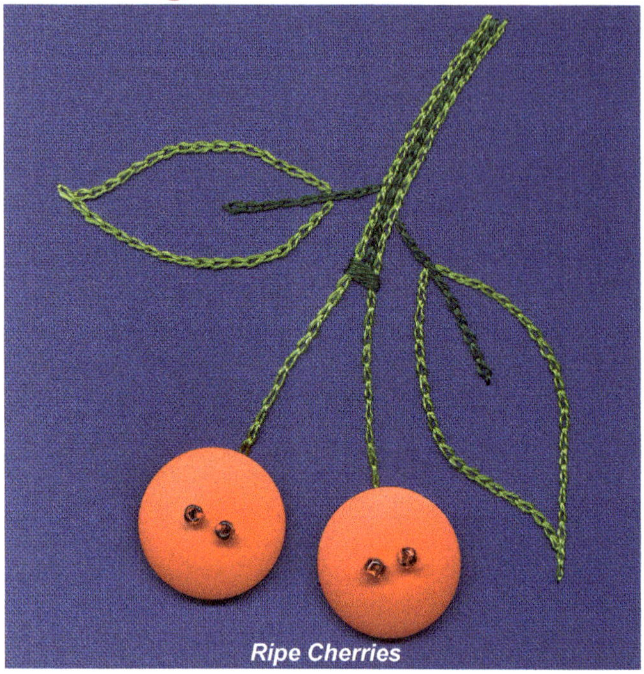

*Ripe Cherries*

The cherries are simply created with buttons attached to the fabric with thread and beads. Rows of chain stitch in silk thread depict the stem and leaves. Straight stitch is also used. Use the instructions on this page to work the design as above. See opposite to feature the cherries on a small handbag. As this design uses buttons and beads, it is not considered safe to use on projects for babies or very small children.

## The pattern

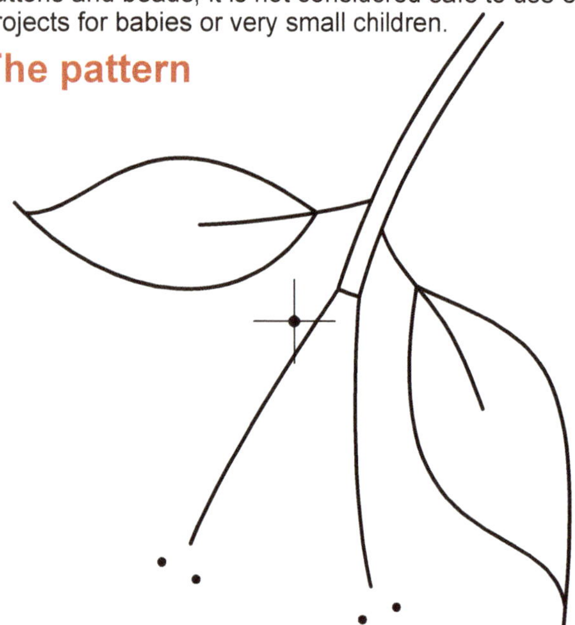

**Key:** ✚ **Centre of design** • **Placement of button**

## Shopping list

- Blue cotton fabric for background: 25cm (10") square
- Fabric or interfacing for backing: 25cm (10") square
- Stranded cotton thread: (A) medium red
- Stranded silk thread: (B) dark green (C) light green
- 2 large round two-hole buttons: (D) red
- 4 small round beads, larger than holes in buttons: (E) red
- Tracing paper and other items for transferring the pattern onto the fabric

## Let's begin

Read page 15 for backing the fabric, and pages 22-25 for transferring the pattern onto the fabric, then select and use suitable methods for your fabric. For the blue fabric shown here, the pattern was transferred centrally onto the fabric by tracing with a chalk-based pencil and then the backing fabric was tacked to the wrong side.

## Stitch!

For help, see pages 40-43 for straight stitch, 166-169 for chain stitch, and pages 238-241 for beading.

1 Following the marked lines, work the two rows forming the main stem in chain stitch, beginning at the top of the design and ending at the marked positions for the cherries (1 strand C).

2 Beginning at the top and stopping at the line where the stem divides, work a row of chain stitch between the previous rows (1 strand B).

3 Work five straight stitches (1 strand B) over the chain stitches at the divide (Diagram 1).

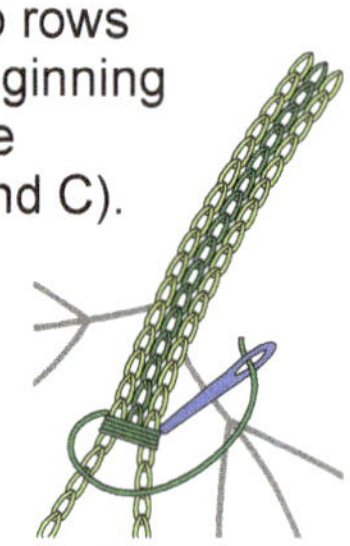

**Diagram 1**

4 Stitch the leaf stem, then continue for the vein of each leaf in chain stitch (1 strand B).

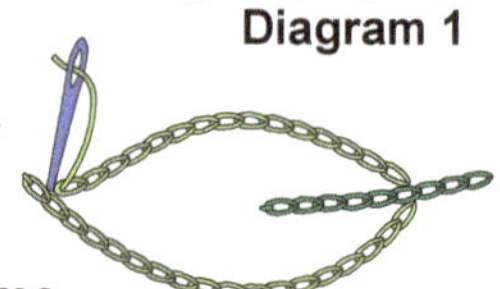

**Diagram 2**

5 Beginning at the leaf base each time, work the sides of the leaves in chain stitch (1 strand C), following the diagram for working the leaf tips (Diagram 2).

6 Add the cherries (Diagram 3) by securing each button (D) with a single bead at each hole (E, attached with 2 strands A). Secure each bead by working several small stitches on the reverse side of the fabric before moving to the next bead.

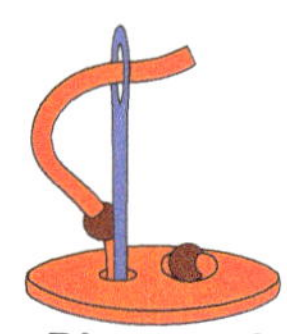

**Diagram 3**

## Let's finish

Take out the tacking. Press the work, avoiding the buttons. Alternatively, pin out the work. See page 36 for pressing and for pinning out.

# Ripe Cherries Handbag

Add luscious cherries to a little handbag.

## The project

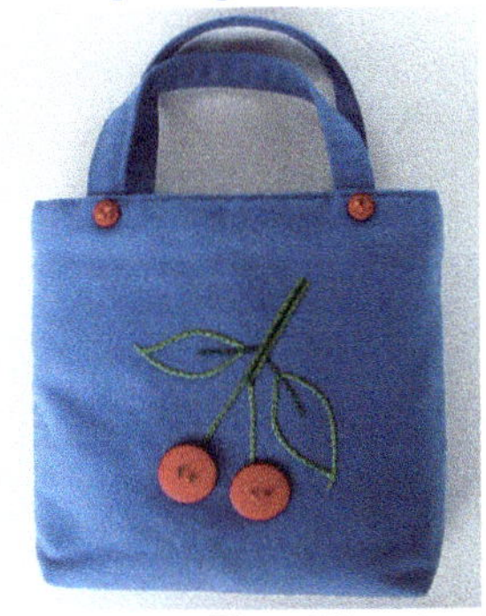

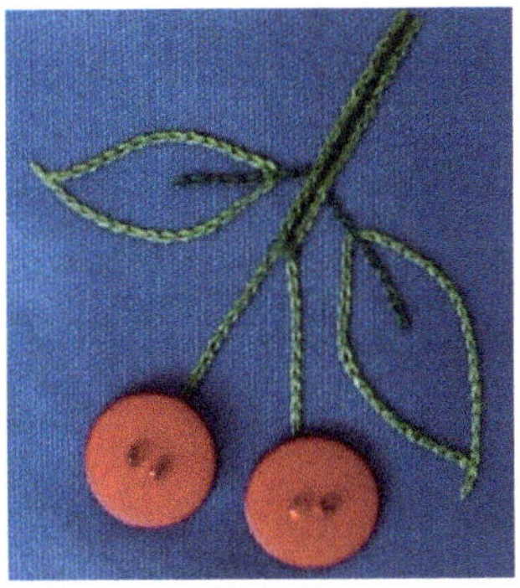

***Ripe Cherries Handbag* and Detail**

The cherries are worked on a piece of fabric that is then made up into a charming handbag. Additional small buttons attached with beads add extra interest. The finished size of the handbag is 16cm x 15cm wide (6 1/4" x 6"), not including the handles.

As this project uses buttons and beads, it would not be safe for babies or very small children.

## Shopping list

- Blue cotton fabric for outer layer and lining: two pieces 40cm x 23cm wide (16" x 9")
- Blue cotton fabric for the handles: two pieces 24cm x 5cm wide (9 1/2" x 2")
- Medium weight iron-on interfacing for backing: one piece 40cm x 23cm wide (16" x 9")
- Thin wadding: one piece 40cm x 23cm wide (16" x 9")
- Threads as listed for the original design opposite
- 2 large round two-hole buttons: (D) red
- 4 small round four-hole buttons: (F) red
- 20 small round beads, larger than holes in buttons: (E) red
- Machine sewing thread: blue
- Tracing paper and other items for transferring the pattern onto the fabric

## Let's begin

See opposite for the pattern. Following the instructions on page 15 for backing the fabric, attach the iron-on interfacing onto the wrong side of the outer layer fabric. Measuring down from one short end on the right side of the fabric, work two rows of tacking, the first 9.5cm (3 3/4") down, and the second 20cm (8") down. Aligning the centre of the design with the upper row of tacking (Diagram 1), transfer the pattern onto the fabric by tracing or by using the pierce and dot method with a chalk-based pencil, then remove this tacking. See pages 22-25 for transferring the pattern onto fabric.

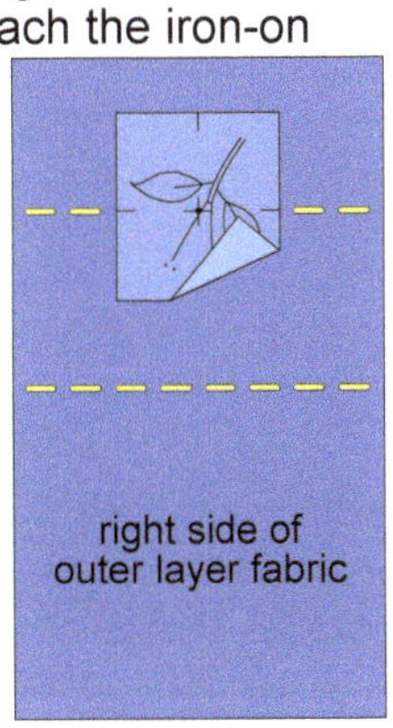


**Diagram 1**

## Stitch!

Work cherries following steps 1-6 on page opposite.

## Let's finish

Place the work face down on a well-padded surface and press. Tack the wadding onto the wrong side of the outer layer and treat both layers as one layer from now on.

***Assembling the handbag***

Use a 1cm (3/8") seam allowance unless otherwise specified.

With right sides together, fold the outer layer in half along the row of tacking at the base and pin the sides together. Using a machine straight stitch and matching thread, stitch the side seams (Diagram 2). Press the seam allowances open.

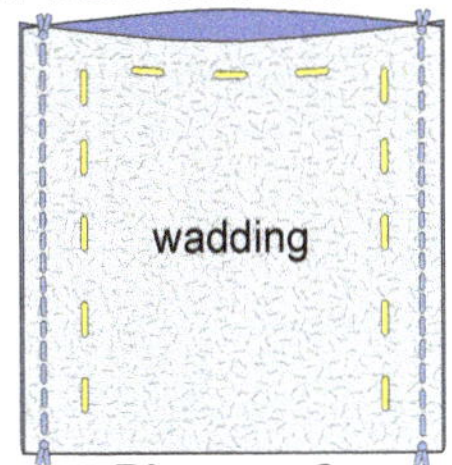


**Diagram 2**

To form the base, align one side seam with the tacking along the base of the handbag. Stitch across the side seam 2cm (3/4") in from the point (Diagram 3). Trim away the excess fabric at the corner (Diagram 4).

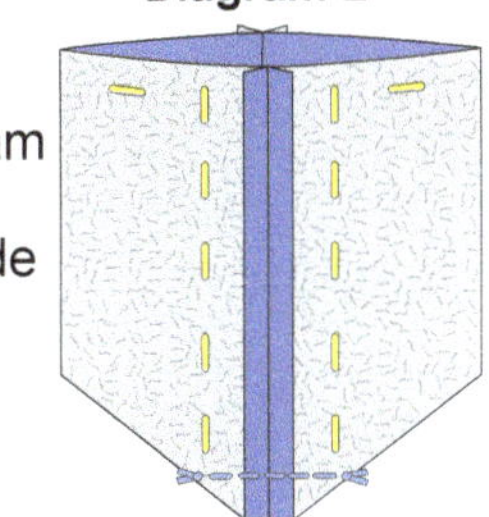

**Diagram 3**

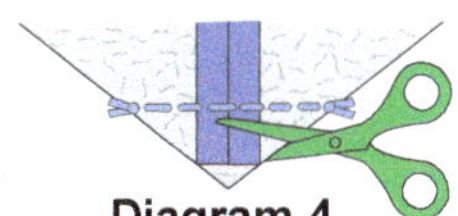

**Diagram 4**

Repeat for the second side seam at the base of the handbag. Turn the outer layer through to the right side and press. Make the lining in a similar way, but leave it inside out.

With wrong sides together, fold under and press 1cm (3/8") on the long sides of the strips for the handles, then fold each handle in half lengthwise. Stitch along both long edges of each handle (Diagram 5). Press. With raw edges even, stitch one handle onto the right side of the outer layer at the top, positioning its outer edges 4cm (1 1/2") in from the side seams (Diagram 6). Attach the second handle in the same way.

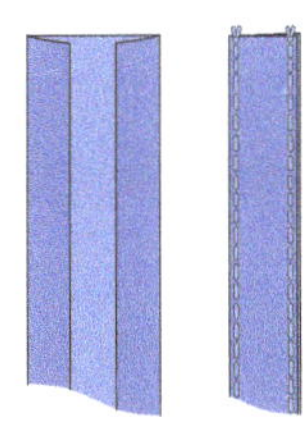

**Diagram 5**

Fold under 1cm (3/8") to the wrong side along the upper raw edge of the bag and press. Repeat for the lining.

Place the lining inside the outer layer and tack together around the top edges. Machine stitch the layers together close to the folded edges (see Diagram 7). Take out the tacking.

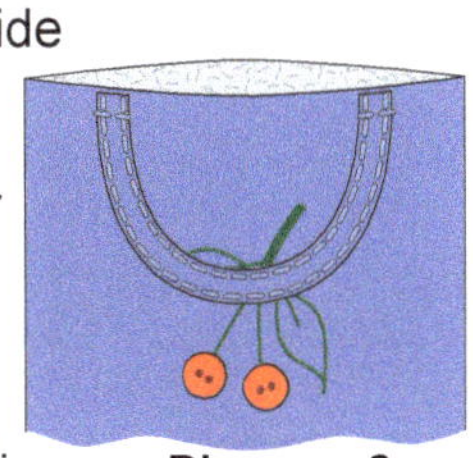

**Diagram 6**

Attach a button (F) at the base of each handle (Diagram 7) adding a single bead at each hole (E, attached with 2 strands A) (Diagram 8).

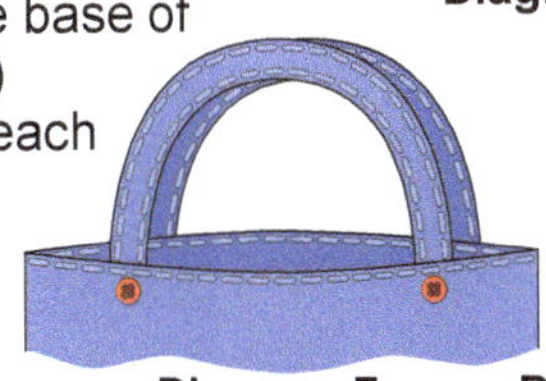

**Diagram 7**

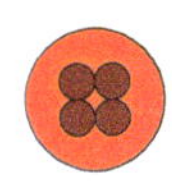

**Diagram 8**

# Tick Tock, Tick Tock

Time flies!

## The design

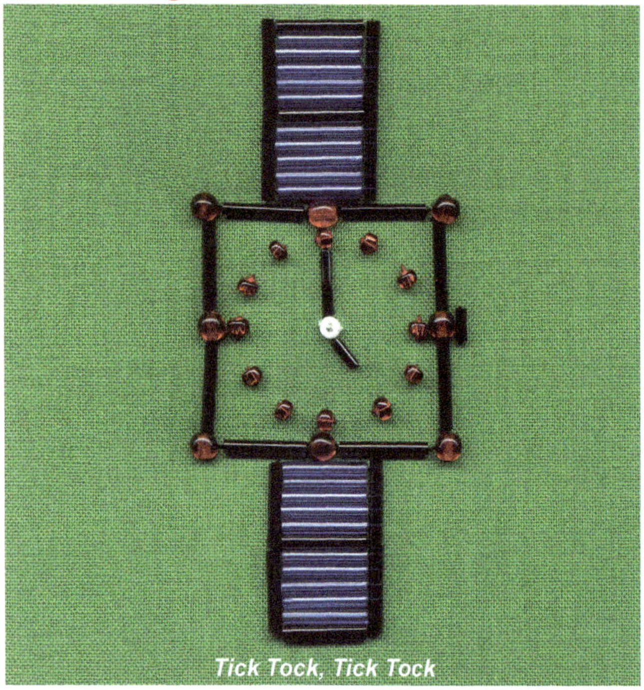

*Tick Tock, Tick Tock*

This entire design is worked in beading. Bugle beads, attached singly and in rows, are combined with round beads for dramatic effect. Use the instructions on this page to work the design as above. To feature the watch on the cover of a photo album, see the page opposite. As this design uses beads, it is not considered safe for use on projects for babies or very small children.

## The pattern

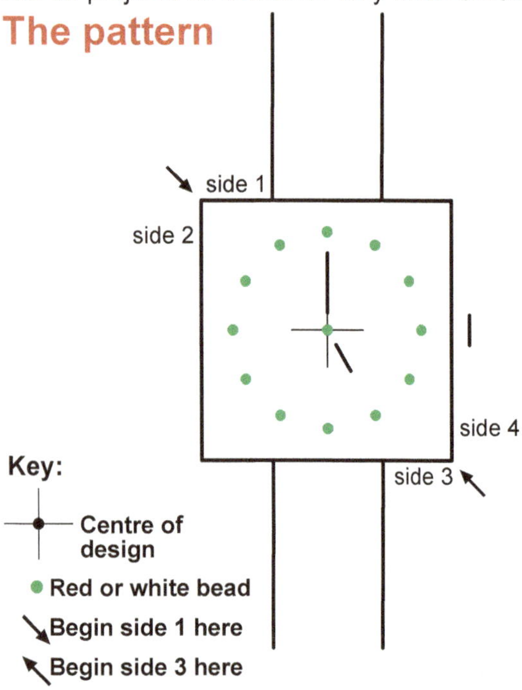


## Shopping list

- Green cotton fabric for background: 25cm (10") square
- Fabric or interfacing for backing: 25cm (10") square
- 20 x 12mm (1/2") bugle beads: (A) black
- 20 x 12mm (1/2") bugle beads: (B) blue
- 4 x 5mm (3/16") bugle beads: (C) black
- 8 medium size round beads: (D) red
- 12 small round beads: (E) red
- 1 small flattened round bead: (F) white
- Polyester sewing thread: (G) black (H) medium blue (I) medium red (J) white
- Tracing paper and other items for transferring the pattern onto the fabric

## Let's begin

Read page 15 for backing the fabric, and pages 22-25 for transferring the pattern onto the fabric, then select and use suitable methods for your fabric. For the green fabric shown here, the pattern was transferred centrally onto the fabric by tracing with a chalk-based pencil and then the backing fabric was tacked to the wrong side.

## Stitch!

For help, see pages 40-43 for straight stitch, 202-205 for couching, and pages 238-241 for beading. Attach all the beads with one strand of thread unless otherwise stated. Secure each bead, or string of beads, by working a small stitch on the reverse side of the fabric behind the bead before continuing.

1. Beginning at the arrow for side 1, thread beads onto needle (D, A, D, A, D, attached with G). Take thread to back at corner and secure. With same thread, couch along string of beads with small straight stitches (Diagram 1).

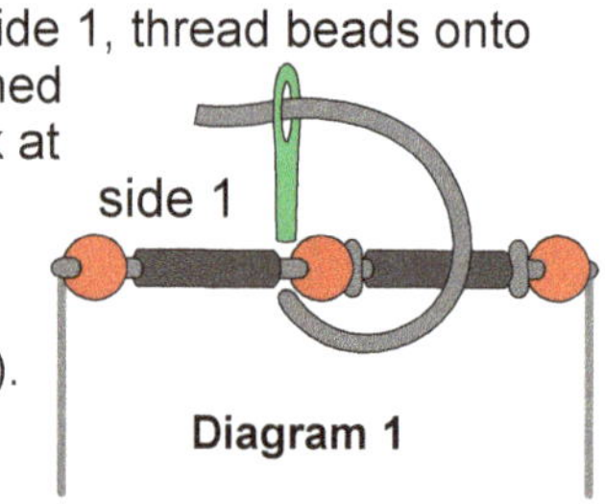


**Diagram 1**

2. For side 2, thread beads onto needle (A, D, A, D, attached with G). Take thread to back at corner and secure. Couch the string of beads and end off.
3. Beginning at the arrow, work side 3 (D, A, D, A, attached with G) then side 4 (A, D, A, attached with G).
4. Using straight stitch, attach a bead at each dot for the numbers (E, attached with 2 strands I). At the centre dot, add a white bead attached on its end (F, attached with J). Using one straight stitch for each hand, attach one bugle bead for the short hand and two for the long hand, then add the winder (C, attached with G).
5. Referring to the photo, work the band with bugle beads placed horizontally (B and A, attached with H).
6. Outline the band with strings of bugle beads (A, attached with G). Couch between the beads.

## Let's finish

Take out the tacking. Press or pin out the work. See page 36 for pressing and for pinning out.

# Tick Tock, Tick Tock Album Cover

Record all your good times in this album.

## The project

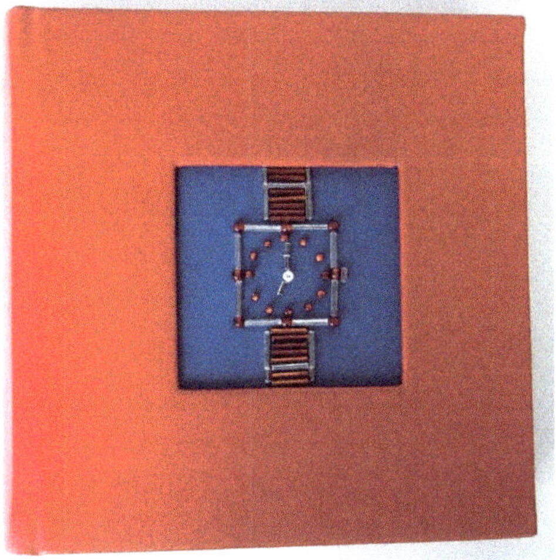

***Tick Tock, Tick Tock Album Cover***

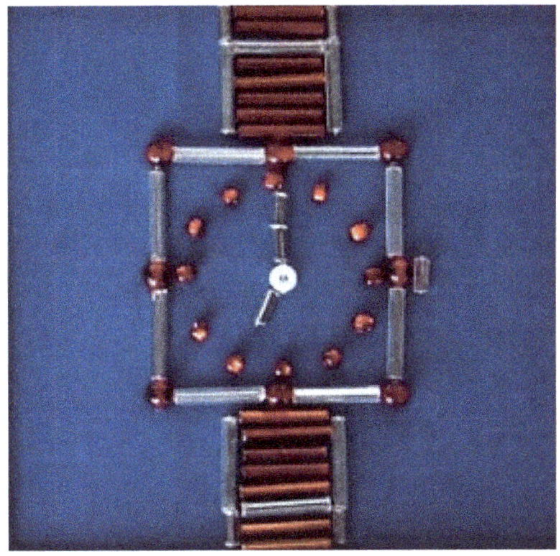

**Detail of**
***Tick Tock, Tick Tock Album Cover***

This album features the watch displayed on the front cover. The design is worked with the same type of beads as the original, but a new colour scheme is used. The clock can be set to any time of day!
Requirements given in the shopping list on this page are suitable for an album that has a cut out display window on the front cover measuring 7.5cm (3") square. If your album has different dimensions, you will need to adjust the shopping list accordingly.

## Shopping list

- Red album with window
- Blue cotton fabric for background: 13cm (5") square
- Lightweight iron-on interfacing for backing: 13cm (5") square
- 20 x 12mm (1/2") bugle beads: (A) silver
- 20 x 12mm (1/2") bugle beads: (B) red
- 4 x 5mm (3/16") bugle beads: (C) silver
- 8 medium size round beads: (D) red
- 12 small round beads: (E) red
- 1 small flattened round bead: (F) white
- Polyester sewing thread: white and red
- Tracing paper and other items for transferring the pattern onto the fabric
- White cardboard: 14cm (5 1/2") square
- Archival double-sided sticky tape
- Wide archival single-sided sticky tape

## Let's begin

See the page opposite for the pattern.
Adjust the length of the watchband according to the size of the window in your album.
Transfer the pattern centrally onto the right side of the blue fabric by tracing with a chalk-based pencil. See page 23 for transferring the pattern by tracing.
Attach the iron-on interfacing onto the wrong side of the blue fabric. See page 15 for backing the fabric.

## Stitch!

Work the watch following steps 1-6 of the stitch instructions on the previous page, substituting the alternative coloured beads and attaching them with threads as follows. Use the red thread for attaching the string of red and silver beads outlining the watch, the red beads on the band and those depicting the numbers. Use the white sewing thread for attaching the silver beads on the band, and the beads depicting the hands and the winder. Depending on the size of the window, work more or less of the band.

## Let's finish

Press the fabric, avoiding the beads. Alternatively, pin out the work. See page 36 for pressing and for pinning out.
Using archival double-sided sticky tape, attach the stitched design centrally onto the cardboard.
Position the watch centrally behind the window on the front of the album. Firmly attach the edges of the cardboard to the wrong side of the cover with the single-sided sticky tape.

# Starlight Magic

The stars of the Southern Cross are twinkling delicately in the night sky.

## The design

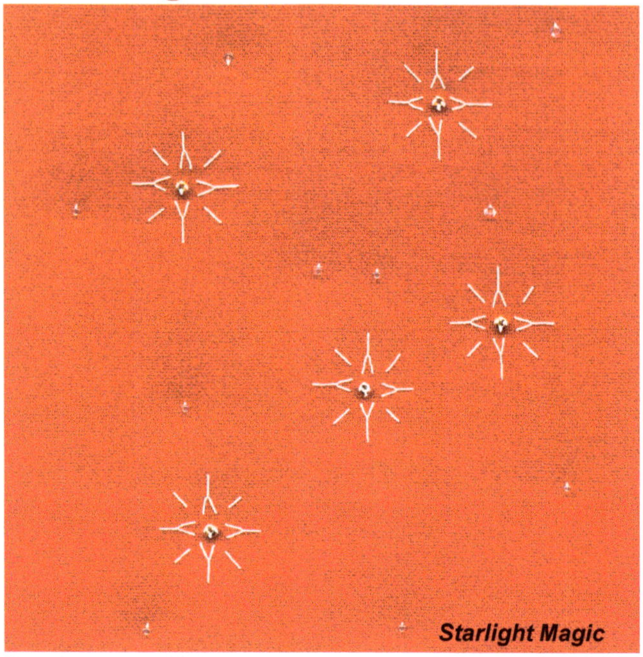

*Starlight Magic*

Beading, in addition to straight stitch and fly stitch, is used in this design. Metallic beads and clear glass beads are featured, creating glimmer and sparkle.
To work the design as above, follow the instructions on this page. To adapt elements of *Starlight Magic* for use on greeting cards, see the project ideas opposite.
As this design uses beads, it is not considered safe for use on projects for babies or very small children.

## The pattern

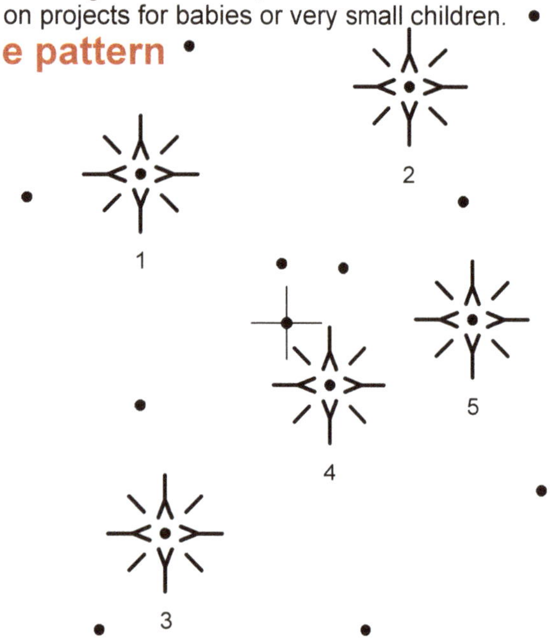


**Key:** Centre of design Fly stitch • Bead

## Shopping list

- Red cotton fabric for background: 25cm (10") square
- Fabric or interfacing for backing: 25cm (10") square
- Stranded cotton thread: (A) white
- 4 small beads: (B) gold metallic
- 1 small bead: (C) silver metallic
- 10 very small beads: (D) clear glass
- Tracing paper and other items for transferring the pattern onto the fabric

## Let's begin

Read page 15 for backing the fabric, and pages 22-25 for transferring the pattern onto the fabric, then select and use suitable methods for your fabric. For the red fabric shown here, the pattern was transferred centrally onto the fabric by tracing with a water erasable fabric marker and then the backing fabric was tacked to the wrong side.

## Stitch!

For help, see pages 40-43 for straight stitch, 148-151 for fly stitch, and pages 238-241 for beading. If the threaded needle will not pass through the bead, then unthread the needle and pass just the thread through the bead. Re-thread the needle and continue.

**Stars 1, 2, 3, and 5**

1. Following the marked lines, work the straight stitch rays (1 strand A). With the same thread, work the fly stitch rays, each with a long anchor.
2. At the centre, attach a bead on its end (Diagram 1) with four straight stitches, all worked down through the hole (B, attached with 1 strand A). End off securely.

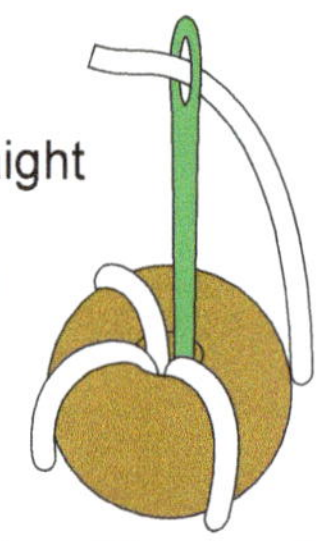

**Diagram 1**

**Star 4**

Work the straight stitch and fly stitch rays (1 strand A) and attach the bead (C, attached with 1 strand A) in the same way as for the previously worked stars.

**Background stars**

Attach each very small bead (D, attached with 1 strand A) with a small vertical straight stitch. Secure each bead by working a small stitch or two on the reverse side of the work before moving on to the next star.

## Let's finish

Take out the tacking. Rinse the work in cold water to remove the water erasable fabric marker. When partly dry, press or pin out the work. See page 36 for pressing and for pinning out.

# Starlight Magic Greeting Cards

Enjoy creating these greeting cards – They're stitched without using any fabric.

## The projects

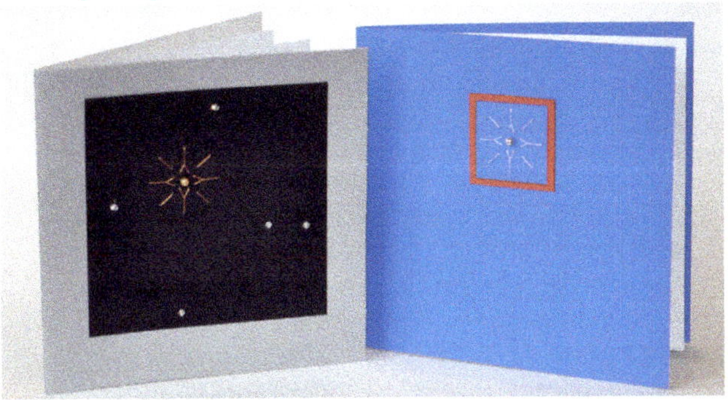

***Starlight Magic Greeting Cards***

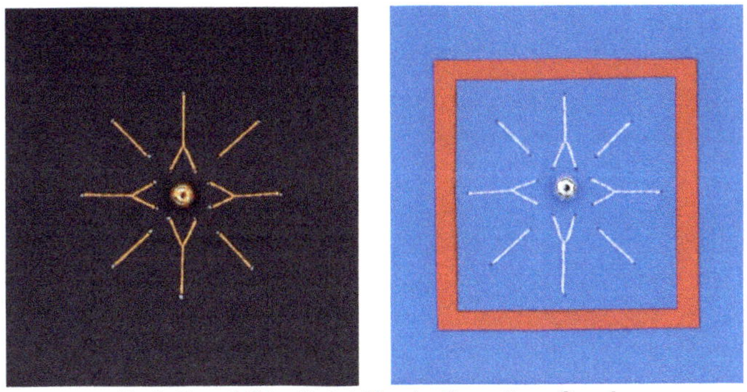

**Details of *Starlight Magic Greeting Cards***

***Silver and black card***

A large orange and gold star and five background stars are stitched through holes pierced in the black square of card. No fabric is used.

The size of this greeting card is 15cm (6") square.

## Shopping list

- Stranded rayon thread: (A) orange
- 1 medium size round bead: (B) gold metallic
- 5 small beads: (D) faceted clear glass
- Tracing paper and other items for transferring the pattern onto the card
- Black card: one piece 11cm (4 3/8") square
- Silver card: one piece 15cm x 30cm wide (6" x 12")
- White paper: 14cm x 29cm wide (5 1/2" x 11 1/2")
- Archival single-sided and double-sided sticky tapes

## Let's begin

See the page opposite for the pattern.

Enlarge the pattern for **Star 1** plus the nearby five background stars to 200% of their original size. Trace the enlarged pattern onto tracing paper. Place a pad of folded fabric under the square of black card. Position the tracing onto the card. Using a fine needle, pierce holes through the tracing and the card at the ends and junctions of all the lines for the rays, and at the dot at the centre of the star. Pierce a hole above and below each dot for the background stars.

## Stitch!

Using the alternative thread and beads, and following the holes in the card, work the stars following the stitch instructions for **Star 1** and the **Background stars** on the previous page, securing the thread ends on the wrong side with the single-sided sticky tape. No beginning or ending off required!

## Let's finish

Fold the rectangle of silver card in half. Using double-sided tape, attach the stitched black square to the front of the silver greeting card. Fold the white paper in half, making the pages. Secure the pages to the inside of the front of the card with double-sided tape.

***Blue and red card***

A large white and silver star is stitched through holes pierced in the small blue square of card. No fabric is used. The size of this greeting card is 15cm (6") square.

## Shopping list

- Stranded rayon thread: (A) white
- 1 medium size round bead: (B) silver metallic
- Tracing paper and other items for transferring the pattern onto the card
- Blue card: one piece 35mm (1 3/8") square, and one piece 15cm x 30cm wide (6" x 12")
- Red card: 42mm (1 5/8") square
- White paper: 14cm x 29cm wide (5 1/2" x 11 1/2")
- Archival single-sided and double-sided sticky tapes

## Let's begin

See the page opposite for the pattern. Enlarge the pattern for **Star 1** to 200% of its original size. Trace the enlarged pattern onto tracing paper. Place a pad of folded fabric under the small square of blue card. Position the tracing onto the card. Using a fine needle, pierce holes through the tracing and the card at the ends and junctions of all the lines, and at the dot at the centre.

## Stitch!

Using the alternative thread and bead, and following the holes in the card, work the stars following the stitch instructions for **Star 1** on the previous page, securing the thread ends on the wrong side with the single-sided sticky tape. No beginning or ending off required!

## Let's finish

Fold the rectangle of blue card in half. Using double-sided sticky tape, attach the stitched blue square of card centrally onto the red square of card, then attach this to the front of the blue greeting card. Fold the white paper in half, making the pages. Secure the pages to the inside of the front of the card with double-sided tape.

## Hint

**Another project**

This star would also be perfect on a gift card or a tag!

# Crystal Forest

In this magical forest, all the flowers and leaves are shining and sparkling like crystals!

## The design

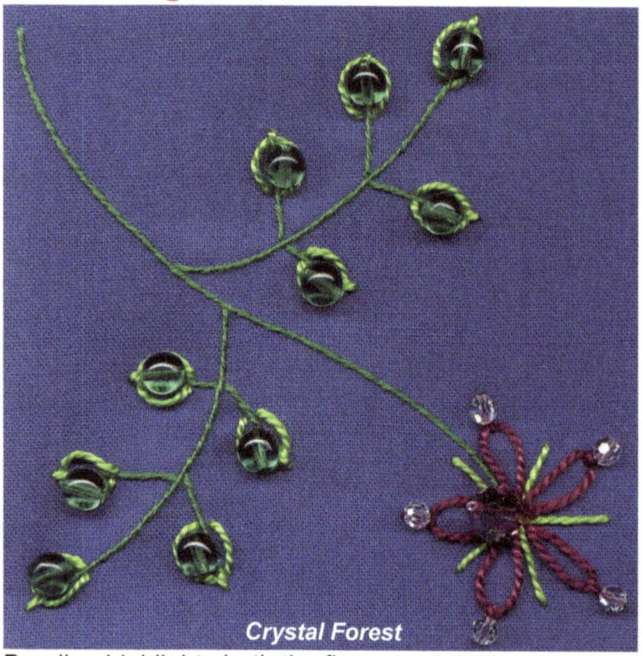


Beading highlights both the flower and the leaves here. Straight stitch, whipped back stitch, and detached chain stitch are also used. Follow the instructions on this page to work the design as above. To feature the flower from the design on a winter scarf, see the next page. As this design uses beads, it is not considered safe for use on projects for babies or very small children.

## The pattern

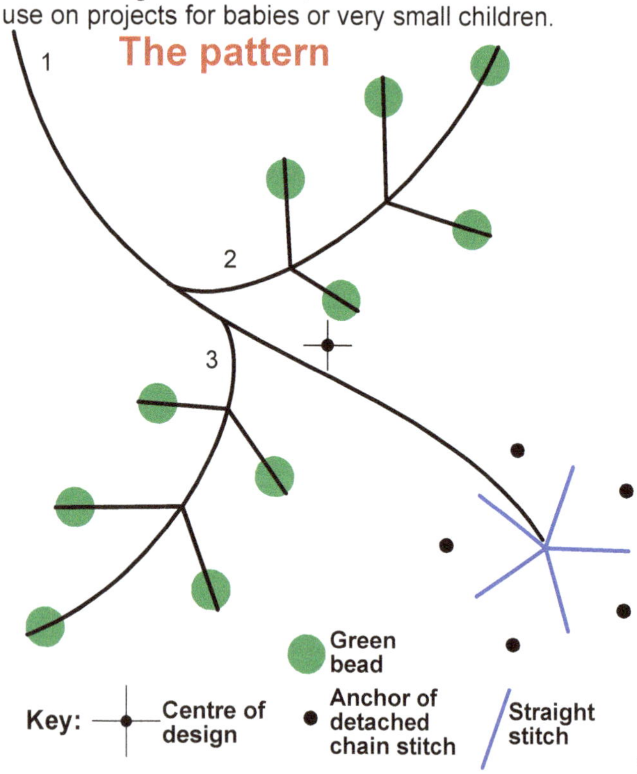


## Shopping list

- Blue cotton fabric for background: 25cm (10") square
- Fabric or interfacing for backing: 25cm (10") square
- Stranded cotton thread:
  (A) medium green (B) dark magenta
- No. 5 perlé cotton thread:
  (C) light green (D) dark magenta
- 1 very large faceted bead: (E) dark magenta glass
- 10 large round beads: (F) medium green
- 5 medium size faceted beads: (G) clear glass
- 1 very small bead: (H) clear glass
- Tracing paper

## Let's begin

Read page 15 for backing the fabric, and pages 22-25 for transferring the pattern onto the fabric, then select and use suitable methods for your fabric. For the blue fabric shown here, the pattern was transferred centrally onto the fabric by tracing with a chalk-based pencil and then the backing fabric was tacked to the wrong side.

## Stitch!

For help, see pages 40-43 for straight stitch, 76-79 for back stitch and whipped back stitch, 166-169 for detached chain stitch, and pages 238-241 for beading.

1 Work **Branch 1** in back stitch (2 strands A), then using a tapestry needle and the same thread, whip the back stitches. Stitch the main stem of **Branch 2** in back stitch (2 strands A), adding a bead onto the last back stitch, forming a leaf (F, attached with 2 strands A). Secure the bead by working a small stitch on the reverse side of the fabric behind the bead. Bring the thread through to the right side and whip the back stitches with the same thread (Diagram 1). Repeat for the small side stems and leaves. Work **Branch 3** in the same way.

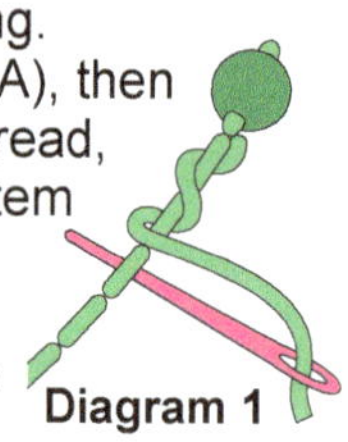

Diagram 1

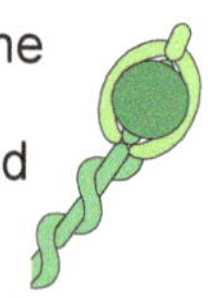

Diagram 2

2 Complete the leaves with a loose detached chain stitch worked around each bead (1 strand C), stitching each with a medium anchor (Diagram 2).

3 Begin the flower with five straight stitches (1 strand C). For the petals, add a detached chain stitch between the straight stitches (1 strand D). Add a bead (G, attached with 2 strands B) at each petal tip with a small straight stitch worked beyond the detached chain stitch anchor (Diagram 3). At the centre, attach the magenta bead (Diagram 4) with a clear bead above it (E and H, attached with 2 strands B).

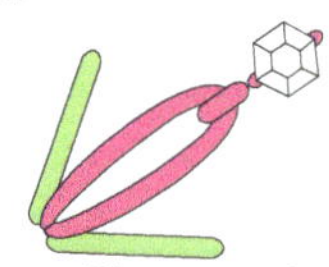

Diagram 3

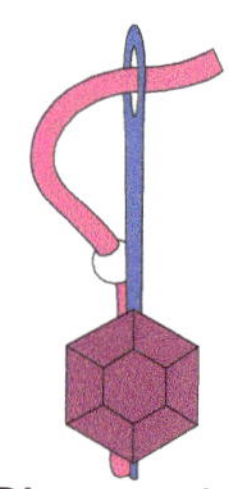

Diagram 4

## Let's finish

Take out tacking. Press or pin out the work. See page 36 for pressing and for pinning out.

# Crystal Forest Winter Scarf

Add the charm of beaded flowers to a special winter scarf.

## The project

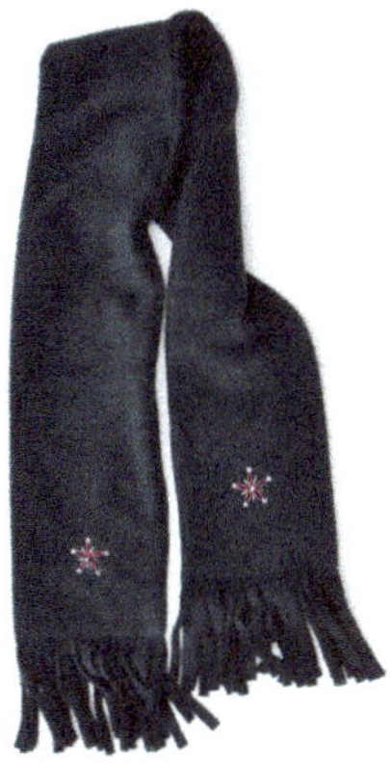

***Crystal Forest Winter Scarf***

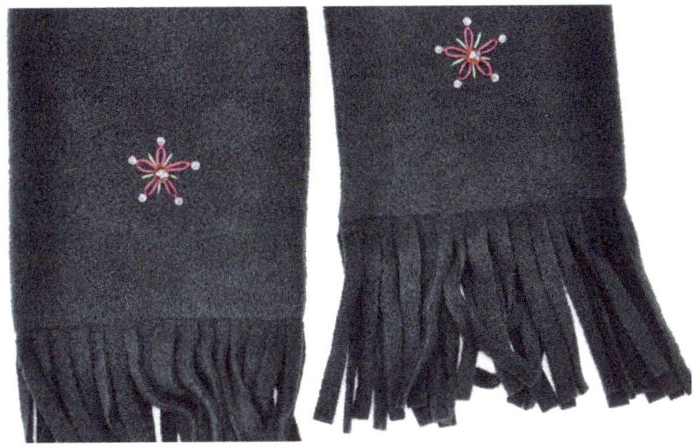

**Detail of *Crystal Forest Winter Scarf***

The beaded flower from *Crystal Forest* is worked at each end of a piece of polar fleece fabric that is then made up into a double-layered scarf. The finished size of this scarf is 17cm x 135cm (7" x 53").

The flower could be worked on a purchased scarf, but note that the back of the stitching may be seen if the scarf is only a single layer of fabric.

## Shopping list

- Dark green polar fleece fabric: 36cm x 135cm wide (14 1/4" x 53")
- Threads (B), (C), and (D) as listed for the original design on the page opposite
- 2 very large faceted beads: (E) dark magenta
- 10 medium size faceted beads: (G) clear
- 2 very small beads: (H) clear
- Machine sewing thread: dark green
- Tracing paper and other items for transferring the pattern onto the fabric

## Let's begin

Trace the flower pattern onto the tracing paper. Place the tracing paper over a pad of folded fabric and pierce holes through the tracing at the flower centre, the ends of the lines, and at each dot, using a large needle. Place the polar fleece fabric right side facing up. Find the placement for the flower by measuring 18cm (7") up from one short end and 9.5cm (3 3/4") in from one long side. Mark the junction with pins. Repeat at the other end, again measuring in from the same long side (Diagram 1). At each position marked by the pins, transfer the pattern for the flower to the right side of the polar fleece using the pierce and dot method with a chalk-based pencil. See page 25 for transferring the pattern using the pierce and dot method.

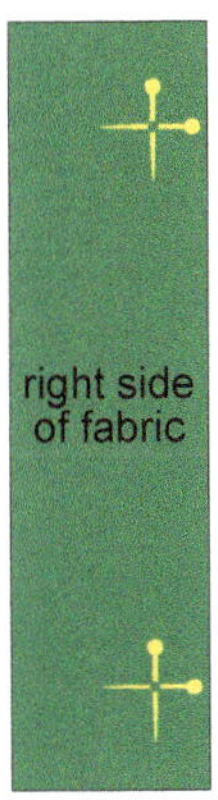


**Diagram 1**

## Stitch!

Work the two flowers following step 3 of the stitch instructions on the page opposite.

## Let's finish

On the wrong side of each end, rule a line 10cm (4") up from the edge using a chalk-based pencil. Beginning at the raw edge and finishing at the ruled line, rule lines 1cm (3/8") apart across the width of the fabric. Cut along these lines to make a fringe.

On each end of the scarf, cut away the first and last strip of the fringe (Diagram 2).

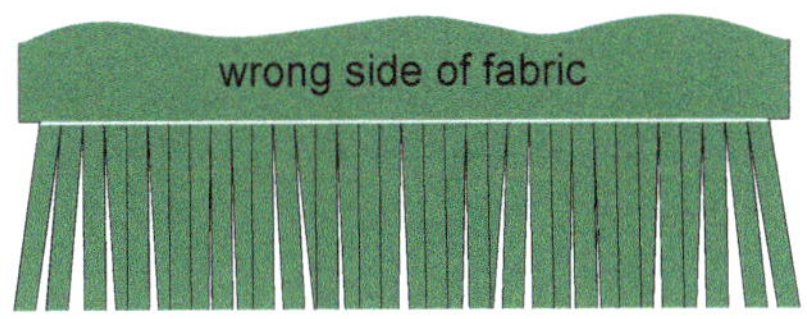


**Diagram 2**

With right sides together, fold the fabric in half along the length. Using a 1cm (3/8") seam allowance, machine stitch the layers together down the long side (Diagram 3).

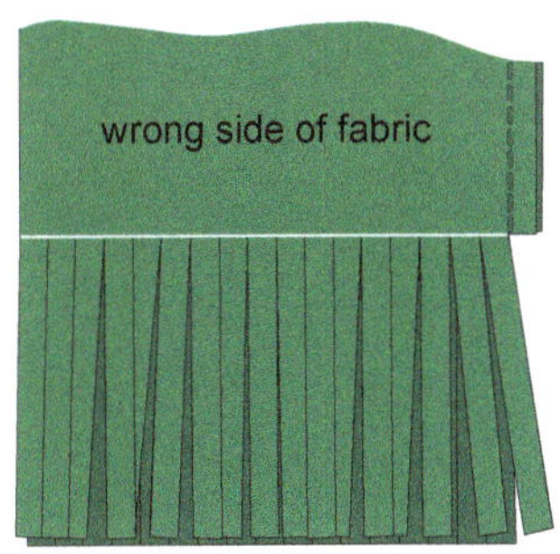


**Diagram 3**

Turn the scarf through to the right side and position the seam so that it lies along one long edge. At each end, pin the layers together and machine stitch across the scarf, just above the beginning of the fringe. Tie the machine thread ends and weave them in so that they are not visible.

# From the authors

## Coral Moss

For me, the journey towards what has become *Stitching Magic* had many beginnings.

I was born in Melbourne, Victoria where I lived, studied, and worked until my marriage and subsequent move to Adelaide, South Australia. Living in the foothills of this beautiful city was a wonderful place to raise our family. I now live in the subtropical paradise of the Whitsundays in North Queensland, where artistic stimulation abounds.

In looking back, I realise most of my working life centred around fashion, design, decoration, and art practices. Early working years spent in the fashion industry placed me in what was once considered 'the heart of the rag trade' – Flinders Lane in Melbourne. The hustle and bustle of this exciting atmosphere was artistically stimulating and it was there that I developed my love for making things. Design and decoration became important.

On moving to South Australia, my desire to impart knowledge was utilised when I joined the Department of Further Education as a technical teacher. Later, I established my own design and patternmaking business, creating for my own label and for several leading Adelaide manufacturers.

A return to art studies highlighted the fact that textile related art forms are my passion. While initially having aspirations to master the fine arts, my patternmaking disciplines and my need to feel fabric between my fingers could not be erased, and I was drawn to more tactile techniques, emerging as a printmaker and textile designer.

Perhaps the most influential aspect that drew me to producing this publication is attributed to the several years spent in the embroidery magazine and book publishing arena, working as a pattern designer, illustrator, editor, and finally, as editor-in-chief. The handling, analysing, recording, and finally seeing the myriad of delightful embroidered works immortalised in print reawakened my senses to all things visual, graphic, romantic, and the fantasy world of staged photography. And so, the journey to hopefully pass on my love for being creative began.

It is a pleasure to see this publication come to fruition. Thank you to my family and friends who have encouraged and supported me along the way. Most importantly, I thank my co-author Wendy for joining me on this journey, and for her dedication in bringing *Stitching Magic* to completion.

It truly has been a labour of love.

Coral

## Designs and project ideas by Coral Moss:

## Wendy Sysouphat

I am an Australian artist, scientist, and author, currently living and working in Adelaide, South Australia. During my early years I spent a great deal of time being creative and learning about nature. I studied and worked for many years in various fields of both art and science. Insights gained through these experiences have added distinctive elements and character to my artworks.

As an artist I focus on numerous textile art techniques, including embroidery, counted thread embroidery, beading, ribbon embroidery, layered fabrics, machine embroidery, garment design and construction, weaving, and natural fibre cordage, plus also various watercolour techniques, oil painting on canvas, drawing with ink, graphite, and conté pencil, as well as computer graphics. My artworks are inspired and informed by the experiences of life, by the natural world and the place of humanity in the universe, and by the mysteries of our existence. My stitched works in this book, *Stitching Magic*, range from depictions of flowers, leaves, and feathers, to love hearts and the epic drama of stars and planets, the sea, a thunderstorm, and a rainbow.

As a scientist, I have particular expertise in general science, botany, zoology, human biology, ecology, and palaeontology.

I have been or currently am a member of numerous embroidery, textile art, other art, and science societies. I am the author of a children's book entitled *The Alphabet Book*, which of course includes some stitching and other art!

In addition to living most of my life in Australia, mainly in Tasmania and South Australia, I have spent time in some other parts of the world, including Asia, the United Kingdom, South America, New Zealand, the Middle East, Europe, and a number of Pacific Islands, including Rapa Nui (Easter Island).

For many years, I have had an extensive collection of cacti and succulents. In addition, I make soft toys, play the guitar, and am an appreciator of music and writing. I am inspired by creativity, wisdom, and kindness.

I would like to thank the many gifted educators, mentors, and others who have taught, assisted, and inspired me in numerous diverse fields of endeavour, including many in the creative field of embroidery.

It is with extreme gratitude that I say thank you to my exceptional husband, children, and other family members, as well as to my truly wonderful friends. I am most grateful to my co-author Coral for sharing this fabulous creative and intellectual adventure with me. I very much appreciate all the enthusiasm, interest, and encouragement that everyone has shown us and given to us throughout this entire process.

Thank you very much also to the many highly skilled people who worked so meticulously and consistently on the production of this book. Their professional advice, technical expertise, and attention to detail has been outstanding.

I hope very much that you find *Stitching Magic* inspiring, useful, and enjoyable.

Wendy

### Designs and project ideas by Wendy Sysouphat:

# Index

## T



## U



## V



## W



## X



## Y



## Z

www.ingramcontent.com/pod-product-compliance
Ingram Content Group UK Ltd.
Pitfield, Milton Keynes, MK11 3LW, UK
UKHW061955290726
14090UKWH00021B/1234

9 780648 726517